THE top10★

OF EVERYTHING

2000

THE
top10*
OF EVERYTHING
2000

RUSSELL ASH

DORLING KINDERSLEY
London · New York · Sydney · Moscow
www.dk.com

CONTENTS

A DORLING KINDERSLEY BOOK
www.dk.com

Senior Editor Adèle Hayward
Senior Designer Tassy King
Project Editor David Tombesi-Walton

DTP Designer Jason Little
Production Controller Silvia La Greca

Managing Editors Stephanie Jackson,
Jonathan Metcalf
Managing Art Editor Nigel Duffield

Produced for Dorling Kindersley by
Cooling Brown, 9–11 High Street,
Hampton, Middlesex TW12 2SA

Editor Alison Bolus
Designers Tish Mills, Elaine Hewson,
Pauline Clarke
Creative Director Arthur Brown

Published in Great Britain in 1999 by
Dorling Kindersley Limited,
9 Henrietta Street,
London WC2E 8PS

2 4 6 8 10 9 7 5 3 1

Copyright © 1999
Dorling Kindersley Limited, London
Text copyright © 1999 Russell Ash

A CIP catalogue record of this book is
available from the British Library.

ISBN 0 7513 0789 0

Reproduction by Colourpath, London
Printed and bound by Printer Industria Grafica, Barcelona

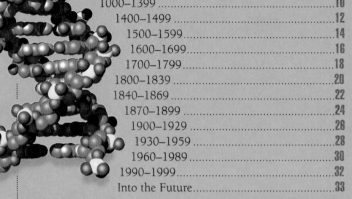

INTRODUCTION

INTO THE NEW MILLENNIUM

Now in its 11th year, *The Top 10 of Everything* celebrates the end of the 20th century and the start of the 21st by presenting more lists than ever! The book's radical re-design has enabled us to expand the content and to introduce a millennium section, in which a timeline and 50 historical lists survey the past 1,000 years. In total there are more than 1,000 Top 10 lists, which encompass many categories. These lists are supplemented by quiz questions, SnapShot features, and "Did You Know?" entries.

WHY LISTS?

Many of us make what might be called "lists for life", the sort of lists you compile to organize yourself, such as shopping lists. Lists of all types are becoming an increasingly prominent feature of the "Information Age": as we are bombarded with information – from newspapers and magazines, radio, television, and the Internet – lists provide a shorthand way of presenting what might otherwise be an impenetrable mass of data. Lists have become a way of simplifying our awareness of the world about us in a form that we can easily absorb.

ENTRY RULES

When I started compiling *The Top 10 of Everything*, I set myself the rule that all the lists should be of things that can be quantified. The book focuses on superlatives in numerous categories but also contains a variety of "firsts" or "latests", which recognize the pioneers and the most recent achievers in various fields of endeavour. Top 10 lists of films are based on worldwide box-office income, and those on topics such as recorded music, videos, and books are based on sales, unless otherwise stated.

INFORMATION RETRIEVAL

Of all the questions I am asked about *The Top 10 of Everything*, the most common is, "Where do you get all the information?" There is no simple answer, as my sources are diverse. I delve into obscure and specialized books, and I use government and other official statistics. Individuals, especially enthusiasts in specialist fields, provide me with information, and I would like to pay tribute not only to them but also to those readers who have taken the trouble to write to me with helpful suggestions and corrections.

FACTS ARE FUN

Even after over a decade's involvement with *The Top 10 of Everything*, I remain enthusiastic and excited by it. Working on the book has led me into innumerable discoveries that I would not otherwise have made. Through countless broadcast interviews, talks, and bookshop presentations, I have met many interesting people. The book has also inspired a successful children's television series that, like the book, conveys to its audience the message that facts are fun.

DATES AND DEADLINES

I endeavour to ensure that all the information in *The Top 10 of Everything* is as up to date as possible. However, some organizations compile statistics slowly: by the time I use them they may be as much as two years old. Conversely, many lists, such as those based on sporting records or film box-office takings, rely on information that changes frequently. This makes updating the lists an ongoing pursuit, but one that continues to fascinate me, and will, I hope, inform and entertain you, too.

GET IN CONTACT

If you have any list ideas or comments, please write to me c/o the publishers or e-mail me direct at ash@pavilion.co.uk.

Other Dorling Kindersley books by Russell Ash:
The Factastic Book of Comparisons
The Factastic Book of 1,001 Lists
Factastic Millennium Facts

SPECIAL FEATURES

- A Millennium Milestones section features a timeline and 50 historical lists that chart 1,000 years of world history, and takes a tentative look into the next century.

- More than 1,000 lists give you the most comprehensive *Top 10 of Everything* ever.

- Illustrated SnapShot features provide entertaining supplementary information.

- Challenging quiz questions with multi-choice answers are scattered throughout the book.

- "Did You Know?" entries offer surprising and unusual facts on many of the subjects explored.

- 121 thematic spreads in 10 categories bring together lists on related topics.

- Sources for many Top 10 lists are displayed at the foot of the lists.

- Explanatory text enlarges on the data provided in many of the lists.

MILLENNIUM MILESTONES

IT IS HARD TO IMAGINE what the world was like a thousand years ago. In this age of space travel, instant global communication, virtual reality, and genetic engineering, it is sometimes impossible to believe that this is the same planet our ancestors inhabited. Things that seemed miraculous even a hundred years ago are now commonplace. Exclusive to this special edition of *The Top 10 of Everything*, the Millennium Milestones section puts the past into perspective, looking at the events that shaped the world over the last thousand years.

MILLENNIUM MILESTONES

BATTLES OF THE FIRST CRUSADE

	LOCATION	TYPE	OUTCOME	YEAR
1	Nicaea	City siege	Crusader victory	1097
2	Dorylaeum	Battle	Crusader victory	1097
3	Tarsus	City siege	Crusader victory	1097
4	Antioch	City siege	Crusader victory	1098
5	Jerusalem	City siege	Crusader victory	1099
6	Ashkelon	Battle	Crusader victory	1099
7	Melitene	Battle	Crusader defeat	1100
8	Mersivan	Battle	Crusader defeat	1101
9	Eregli	Ambush/battle	Crusader defeat	1101
10	Ramleh	Battle	Crusader defeat	1102

1066
BATTLE OF HASTINGS
The events that led to the Battle of Hastings, England, in 1066, culminating in King Harold's death, are depicted in the Bayeux Tapestry, completed in 1080.

1097
SIEGE OF NICAEA
The first victory for the Crusaders occurred in 1097 when they laid siege to the city of Nicaea in Asia Minor.

1148 Arrival of sugar
Sugar, previously almost unknown in Europe, was brought back by the Crusaders returning from the Middle East.

1000

1050

1199

1000 First journey to North America
Leif Ericsson set sail from his Viking settlement in Greenland, and sighted North America.

1088
BOLOGNA UNIVERSITY FOUNDED
This was the first teaching institution in Europe to act independently of the Church. It became famous for its modern approach to teaching jurisdiction.

1192 Yoritomo named Shogun
Minamoto Yoritomo became Shogun (great general). This title was given to him by the Emperor of Japan for restoring peace after a long civil war.

BOLOGNA UNIVERSITY

OLDEST UNIVERSITIES IN THE WORLD

	UNIVERSITY/COUNTRY	YEAR FOUNDED
1	**Quaraouyine**, Fez, Morocco	859
2	**Al-Azhar**, Cairo, Egypt	970
3	**Parma**, Italy	1064
4	**Bologna**, Italy	1088
5	**Modena**, Italy	1175
6	=**Paris**, France	1200
	=**Perugia**, Italy	1200
8	**Padua**, Italy	1222
9	**Naples**, Italy	1224
10	**Siena**, Italy	1240

THE CAPTURE OF CONSTANTINOPLE, 4TH CRUSADE, 1203–4

OLDEST NATIONAL LIBRARIES

	LIBRARY/LOCATION	YEAR FOUNDED
1	**National Library of the Czech Republic**, Prague	1366
2	**National Library of Austria**, Vienna	1368
3	**Biblioteca Nazionale Marciana**, Venice	1468
4	**National Library of France**, Paris	1480
5	**National Library of Malta**, Valetta	1555
6	**Bayericsche Staatsbibliothek**, Munich	1558
7	**National Library of Belgium**, Brussels	1559
8	**National Library of Croatia**, Zagreb	1606
9	**National Library of Finland**, Helsinki	1640
10	**National Library of Denmark**, Copenhagen	1653

1206 Birth of the Mongol Empire
After being elected as supreme leader, Genghis Khan increased the size of the Mongol Empire to include parts of Europe and most of Central Asia.

1271 Marco Polo left Venice
Marco Polo was only a teenager when he set out for China. He spent 17 years there, and was offered the position of governor by the Mongol Emperor.

1366
PRAGUE LIBRARY FOUNDED
The oldest library in the world was founded when Charles IV donated a set of codices to Prague University.

1368 The Ming Dynasty
After defeating the Mongols and driving them out of China, Hong Wu became the new leader of the country and the founder of the Ming Dynasty.

| 1250 | 1300 | 1350 | **1399** |

1202
MEDITERRANEAN EARTHQUAKE

Violent earthquakes can cause devastation through the collapse of structures and can generate catastrophic tidal waves. The worst ever earthquake occurred in 1202 and killed over 1 million people.

1300 Invention of the clock
When first introduced to Europe, mechanical clocks were not fully accurate. They had to be reset every day with the help of a sundial.

1347 The Black Death
The worst ever plague, spread by rats' fleas, started in India at the end of the 1200s. It spread through Asia and reached Europe in the mid-14th century.

1378
ALHAMBRA BUILT
The Alhambra palace built in Grenada was the stronghold of the last Moorish rulers of Spain.

WORST EARTHQUAKES

	LOCATION	DATE	APPROX. NO. OF DEATHS
1	**Near East/Mediterranean**	20 May 1202	1,100,000
2	**Shenshi**, China	2 Feb 1556	820,000
3	**Calcutta**, India	11 Oct 1737	300,000
4	**Antioch**, Syria	20 May 526	250,000
5	**Tang-shan**, China	28 Jul 1976	242,419
6	**Nan-Shan**, China	22 May 1927	200,000
7	**Yeddo**, Japan	(date unknown) 1703	190,000
8	**Kansu**, China	16 Dec 1920	180,000
9	**Messina**, Italy	28 Dec 1908	160,000
10	**Tokyo/Yokohama**, Japan	1 Sep 1923	142,807

Did You Know? The earliest known illustration of a pair of spectacles appeared in a fresco painted in Treviso, Italy, in 1352.

MILLENNIUM MILESTONES

THE 10 ★
LONGEST WARS OF ALL TIME

	WAR/COMBATANTS	DATES	DURATION (YEARS)
1	**Hundred Years War**, France v England	1338–1453	115
2 =	**Wars of the Roses**, Lancaster v York	1455–85	30
=	**Thirty Years War**, Catholic v Protestant	1618–48	30
4	**Peloponnesian War**, Peloponnesian League (Sparta, Corinth, etc.) v Delian League (Athens, etc.)	431–404BC	27
5 =	**First Punic War**, Rome v Carthage	264–241BC	23
=	**Napoleonic Wars**, France v other European countries	1792–1815	23
7 =	**Greco-Persian Wars**, Greece v Persia	499–478BC	21
=	**Second Great Northern War**, Russia v Sweden and War Baltic states	1700–21	21
9	**Vietnam War**, South Vietnam (with US support) v North Vietnam	1957–75	18
10	**Second Punic War**, Rome v Carthage	218–201BC	17

EARLY PRINTING PRESS

1431 Execution of Joan of Arc
Joan of Arc, leader of the rebel forces fighting for French independence, was burnt at the stake by the English.

| 1400 | 1410 | 1420 | 1430 | 1440 |

1418 First exploration of Africa
Portuguese Prince Henry the Navigator encouraged explorations of the African coast by creating a navigation school and sponsoring maritime enterprises. By the time of Henry's death, the Portuguese had explored the whole of the west coast of Africa.

1439 COMPLETION OF NOTRE DAME
Although construction of the Notre Dame Cathedral in Strasbourg started in 1015, it was not until 1439 that the spire was completed.

TOP 10 ★
TALLEST BUILDINGS IN THE MEDIEVAL WORLD

	BUILDING/LOCATION	YEAR	M	FT
1	**Lincoln Cathedral**, England	c.1307	160	525
2	**Rouen Cathedral**, France	1530	156	512
3	**St. Pierre Church**, Beauvais, France	1568	153	502
4	**St. Peter's Church**, Louvain, Flanders (Belgium)	1497	152	500
5	**St. Paul's Cathedral**, London, England	1315	149	489
6	**Great Pyramid**, Giza, Egypt	c.2580BC	146	481
7	**Notre Dame Cathedral**, Strasbourg, France	1439	142	466
8	**St. Stephen's Cathedral**, Vienna, Austria	1433	136	440
9	**Amiens Cathedral**, France	1260	134	440
10	**Chartres Cathedral**, France	1513?	130	427

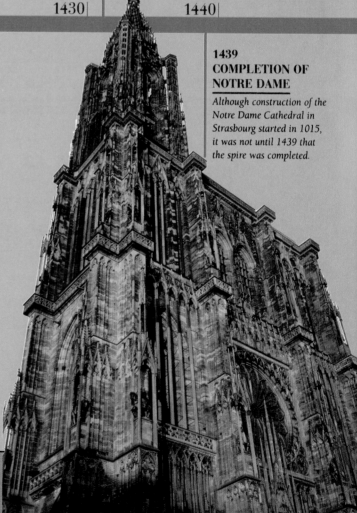

THE 10 ★
FIRST CITIES TO HAVE PRINTING PRESSES

CITY/COUNTRY	YEAR
1 **Mainz**, Germany	1450
2 **Rome**, Italy	1467
3 **Pilsen**, Bohemia	1468
4 **Venice**, Italy	1469
5 =**Paris**, France	1470
=**Nuremberg**, Germany	1470
=**Utrecht**, Netherlands	1470
8 =**Milan**, Italy	1471
=**Naples**, Italy	1471
=**Florence**, Italy	1471

THE 10 ★
FIRST KNOWN EXPLORERS TO LAND IN THE AMERICAS

EXPLORER/NATIONALITY	DISCOVERY/EXPLORATION	YEAR
1 **Christopher Columbus**, Italian	West Indies	1492
2 **John Cabot**, Italian/English	Nova Scotia/Newfoundland	1497
3 **Alonso de Hojeda**, Spanish	Brazil	1499
4 **Vicente Yañez Pinzón**, Spanish	Amazon	1500
5 **Pedro Alvarez Cabral**, Portuguese	Brazil	1500
6 **Gaspar Corte Real**, Portuguese	Labrador	1500
7 **Rodrigo de Bastidas**, Spanish	Central America	1501
8 **Vasco Nuñez de Balboa**, Spanish	Panama	1513
9 **Juan Ponce de León**, Spanish	Florida	1513
10 **Juan Díaz de Solís**, Spanish	Río de la Plata	1515

1450 FIRST PRINTING PRESS
After developing a movable type, Johannes Gutenberg printed the first large book in Europe – a Bible.

1462 Ivan III became Prince of Russia
The reign of Ivan III was the first step towards turning Russia into one of the greatest powers in Europe. He declared himself "Tsar of all the Russias" in 1480.

1478 Start of the Renaissance
After becoming Lord of Florence in 1469, Lorenzo de' Medici started a programme of renewal of the city that marked the beginning of the Renaissance. Under his rule, Florence became the centre of artistic and intellectual excellence.

1450 | 1470 | 1480 | 1490 | 1499

1453 END OF HUNDRED YEARS WAR
The longest war began with England's claims over France. It ended in 1453 after the French recaptured most of their territories.

1478 Spanish Inquisition began
On the orders of Pope Sixtus IV (1471–84), heretics in Spain (initially Jews) were hunted down and punished. Many people were burnt to death.

1492 DISCOVERY OF AMERICA
Searching for a more direct route to Asia, Christopher Columbus reached the Americas on the Santa Maria.

TOP 10 ★
MOST EXPENSIVE RENAISSANCE PAINTINGS EVER SOLD AT AUCTION

PAINTING/ARTIST/SALE	PRICE (£)
1 *Portrait of Duke Cosimo I de Medici*, Jacopo da Carucci (Pontormo), Christie's, New York, 31 May 1989	20,253,164*
2 *Adoration of the Magi*, Andrea Mantegna, Christie's, London, 18 Apr 1985	7,500,000
3 *Venus and Adonis*, Titian, Christie's, London, 13 Dec 1991	16,800,000*
4 *Study for Head and Hand of an Apostle*, Raphael, Christie's, London, 13 Dec 1996	4,800,000
5 *Argonauts in Colchis*, Bartolomeo di Giovanni, Sotheby's, London, 6 Dec 1989	4,600,000
6 *Departure of the Argonauts*, Master of 1487, Sotheby's, London, 6 Dec 1989	4,200,000
7 *Christ and Woman of Samaria*, Michelangelo, Sotheby's, New York, 28 Jan 1998	4,171,779*
8 *Meeting of Infant St. John with Holy Family*, Michelangelo, Christie's, London, 6 Jul 1993	3,800,000
9 *Etude de Draperie*, Leonardo da Vinci, Sotheby's, Monaco, 1 Dec 1989	3,364,879*
10 *Study of Man's Head and Hand*, Raphael, Christie's, London, 3 Jul 1984	3,300,000

* Converted at rate then prevailing

SANTA MARIA

Did You Know? Golf was banned in England in 1457 because it was considered a distraction from the serious pursuit of archery.

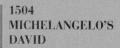

1504
MICHELANGELO'S DAVID

The colossal marble statue of David (4.34m/14ft 3in) was Michelangelo's first public commission. It became the symbol of Florence and was placed outside the Palazzo Signoria. In the 19th century the statue was moved to the Accademia.

THE 10 ★
FIRST PEOPLE TO DISCOVER ELEMENTS*

	DISCOVERER/COUNTRY	ELEMENT	YEAR
1	Julius Caesar Scaliger (1484–1558), Italy	Platinum	1557
2	Hennig Brand (?–c.1692), Germany	Phosphorus	1669
3	Georg Brandt (1694–1768), Sweden	Cobalt	1735/39
4	Andreas Marggraf (1709–82), Germany	Zinc	1746
5	Axel Cronstedt (1722–65), Sweden	Nickel	1751
6	Henry Cavendish (1731–1810), England	Hydrogen	1766
7	Daniel Rutherford (1749–1819), Scotland	Nitrogen	1772
8 =	Carl Wilhelm Scheele (1742–86), Sweden	Chlorine	1774
=	Johan Gahn (1745–1818), Sweden	Manganese	1774
=	Joseph Priestley (1733–1809), England; Carl Wilhelm Scheele (1742–86), Sweden	Oxygen	1774

* Named discoverers, 16th century onwards

1519–21 End of the Aztec Empire
Conquistador Hernán Cortés, welcomed by Emperor Montezuma of Mexico as a reincarnated Aztec god, later killed the emperor and declared himself governor.

1536 Dissolution of the Monasteries
Henry VIII – who assumed full control of the English Church in 1534 – began the dissolution of the monasteries in 1536. This decree led to severe hardship for the nation's poor.

1500 | 1510 | 1520 | 1530 | 1540 |

1506 Work on St. Peter's Basilica began
Construction of St. Peter's Basilica in Rome took over a century, reaching completion in 1612. It remains one of the largest Christian churches in the world.

1522 First circumnavigation of the world
Sebastian del Cano completed the round-the-world voyage begun by Ferdinand Magellan, who was killed in the Philippines.

1545
FIRST BOTANIC GARDENS

The first botanic gardens were founded in Padua, Italy. Such gardens provide an environment where plants can be grown, studied, and displayed.

BOTANIC GARDENS AT PADUA

THE 10 ★
FIRST BOTANIC GARDENS

	CITY/COUNTRY	YEAR
1	**Padua**, Italy	1545
2	**Montpelier**, France	1558
3	**Leyden**, Netherlands	1577
4	**Leipzig**, Germany	1580
5	**Oxford**, England	1621
6	**Paris**, France	1624
7	**Jena**, Germany	1629
8	**Uppsala**, Sweden	1657
9	**Edinburgh**, Scotland	1670
10	**Chelsea**, London, England	1673

THE 10 ★
FIRST BRITISH AMERICAN COLONIES

	COLONY	MODERN STATE	FOUNDER	DATE
1	Roanoke	North Carolina	Sir Walter Raleigh	July 1585
2	Jamestown	Virginia	John Smith	May 1607
3	Plymouth	Massachusetts	William Bradford	Dec 1620
4	New Amsterdam	New York	Peter Minuit*	May 1626
5	New Hampshire	–	John Mason	Nov 1629
6	Massachusetts Bay	Massachusetts	John Winthrop	June 1630
7	Maryland	–	George Calvert	Feb 1634
8	Connecticut	–	Thomas Hooker	May 1636
9	Rhode Island	–	Roger Williams	June 1636
10	Delaware	–	Peter Minuit*	Mar 1638

* Founded by Holland (No. 4) and Sweden (No. 10), but later ceded to Britain

THE 10 ★
FIRST SHAKESPEARE PLAYS

	PLAY	APPROX. YEAR WRITTEN
1	Titus Andronicus	1588–90
2	Love's Labour's Lost	1590
3	Henry VI, Parts I–III	1590–91
4=	The Comedy of Errors	1591
=	Richard III	1591
=	Romeo and Juliet	1591
7	The Two Gentlemen of Verona	1592–93
8	A Midsummer Night's Dream	1593–94
9	Richard II	1594
10	King John	1595

1557
PLATINUM DISCOVERED

Platinum is renowned as the world's noblest metal: it resists tarnishing and is highly durable.

PLATINUM

1585
FIRST US COLONY

Roanoke, founded by Sir Walter Raleigh in 1585, was not revisited until 1590, when, mysteriously, no trace was found of the settlers.

1588
SHAKESPEARE'S FIRST PLAY

William Shakespeare, universally regarded as the greatest playwright that ever lived, began work on Titus Andronicus in 1588.

| 1550 | 1560 | 1570 | 1580 | 1590 | 1599 |

1558 Elizabeth I crowned
Elizabeth I, daughter of Henry VIII, was Queen of England until her death in 1603. She turned England into one of the world's most powerful nations.

1572 St. Bartholomew's Day massacre
The Catholic French king Charles IX instigated the murder of thousands of Protestants who had come to Paris for the wedding of Henry of Navarre.

1588
SPANISH ARMADA

Phillip II of Spain's "Invincible Armada" was scattered by the English fleet, led by Francis Drake. After fleeing to the North Sea, many ships were wrecked by storms.

THE 10 ★
WORST PRE-20TH-CENTURY MARINE DISASTERS

	DATE/INCIDENT	NO. KILLED
1	Aug–Oct 1588, Spanish Armada destroyed off the British coast	c.4,000
2=	22 Aug 1711, Eight British ships sank in storms off Labrador	over 2,000
=	4 Dec 1811, British warships *St. George*, *Defence*, and *Hero* stranded off the Jutland coast	over 2,000
4	27 Apr 1865, *Sultana*, a Mississippi River steamboat, destroyed by a boiler explosion near Memphis, USA	1,547
5	31 Jul 1715, Two Spanish treasure vessels sank in a hurricane at Capitanas, off the Florida coast	over 1,000
6	29 Aug 1782, British warship *Royal George* wrecked off the British coast	over 900
7	3 Sep 1878, Pleasure steamer *Princess Alice* collided with the *Bywell Castle* on the River Thames near Woolwich	786
8	17 Mar 1800, British warship *Queen Charlotte* caught fire in Livorno Harbour, Italy	over 700
9	19 Sep 1890, Turkish frigate wrecked at Ertogrul, off the Japanese coast	587
10	17 Mar 1891, British steamer *Utopia* collided with British warship *Amson* off Gibraltar	576

THE 10 ★ FIRST PLANETARY MOONS TO BE DISCOVERED

	MOON	PLANET	DISCOVERER/COUNTRY	YEAR
1	Moon	Earth	–	Ancient
2 =	Io	Jupiter	Galileo Galilei, Italy	1610
=	Europa	Jupiter	Galileo Galilei	1610
=	Ganymede	Jupiter	Galileo Galilei	1610
=	Callisto	Jupiter	Galileo Galilei	1610
6	Titan	Saturn	Christian Huygens, Holland	1655
7	Iapetus	Saturn	Giovanni Cassini, Italy/France	1671
8	Rhea	Saturn	Giovanni Cassini	1672
9 =	Tethys	Saturn	Giovanni Cassini	1684
=	Dione	Saturn	Giovanni Cassini	1684

1610
GALILEO'S DISCOVERIES

Galileo's discovery of the four satellites of Jupiter proved for the first time that there were celestial bodies rotating around a body other than the Earth.

1612 Tobacco introduced to America
Tobacco was planted in Virginia by Englishman John Rolfe. This led to a successful export trade, affluence for Virginia, and eventually slavery.

1633 Galileo sentenced by the Inquisition
Galileo's theory that the Earth moves round the Sun enraged the Catholic Church, which forced him to deny his beliefs.

1642 Discovery of New Zealand
Dutch sailor Abel Tasman discovered Tasmania and also New Zealand.

1600 |1620 |1630 |1640

1605
LEO XI'S PAPACY

During Pope Leo XI's coronation on 17 April, 1605, he caught the cold that was to cost him his life after just 26 days in office.

1620 Mayflower set sail
The Pilgrims – English religious refugees – set sail for America aboard the *Mayflower*. They landed at what is today Plymouth, Massachusetts.

1636
HARVARD UNIVERSITY

Harvard University was named in 1638 after a John Harvard who left his library and half his estate to the institution.

TOP 10 ★ SHORTEST-SERVING POPES

	POPE	YEAR IN OFFICE	DURATION (DAYS)
1	Urban VII	1590	12
2	Valentine	827	c.14
3	Boniface VI	896	15
4	Celestine IV	1241	16
5	Sisinnius	708	20
6	Sylvester III	1045	21
7	Theodore II	897	c.21
8	Marcellus II	1555	22
9	Damasus II	1048	23
10 =	Pius III	1503	26
=	Leo XI	1605	26

TOP 10 ★ OLDEST UNIVERSITIES AND COLLEGES IN THE US

	UNIVERSITY/LOCATION	YEAR CHARTERED
1	Harvard University, Massachusetts	1636
2	College of William & Mary, Virginia	1692
3	Yale University, Connecticut	1701
4	University of Pennsylvania, Pennsylvania	1740
5	Moravian College, Pennsylvania	1742
6	Princeton University, New Jersey	1746
7	Washington & Lee University, Virginia	1749
8	Columbia University, New York	1754
9	Brown University, Rhode Island	1764
10	Rutgers, the State University of New Jersey	1766

Source: *National Center For Educational Statistics*

Did You Know? Popcorn was first eaten by Europeans in 1621, when settlers in America received a deerskin bag of "popped corn" from Native American Quadequina.

1669
REMBRANDT'S DEATH

Although Rembrandt had been Holland's foremost artist, with a constant flow of important commissions, by the early 1660s he had to auction his house and his goods to pay some of his debts.

TOP 10 ★
MOST EXPENSIVE REMBRANDT PAINTINGS EVER SOLD AT AUCTION

PAINTING/SALE	PRICE (£)
1 *Portrait of a Girl Wearing a Gold-trimmed Cloak*, Sotheby's, London, 10 Dec 1986	6,600,000
2 *Portrait of Bearded Man in Red Coat*, Sotheby's, New York, 30 Jan 1998	5,061,350*
3 *Portrait of Johannes Uyittenbogaert*, Sotheby's, London, 8 Jul 1992	3,800,000
4 *Cupid Blowing a Soap Bubble*, Sotheby's, London, 6 Dec 1995	3,500,000
5 *Bust-length Portrait of Old Man with Beard*, Sotheby's, London, 30 Jan 1997	1,687,500
6 *The Ramparts near the Bulwark beside the St. Anthonlespoort*, Christie's, London, 6 Jul 1987	1,250,000
7 *Aristotle Contemplating the Bust of Homer*, Parke-Bernet Galleries, New York, 15 Nov 1961	821,429*
8 *Portrait of the Artist's Son Titus*, Christie's, London, 19 Mar 1965	798,000
9 *View of Houtewaal near the St. Anthonlespoort*, Sotheby's, New York, 17 Nov 1986	608,392*
10 *View of the Amstel with Castle of Kostverloren*, Christie's, London, 3 Jul 1984	600,000

* Converted from $ at rate then prevailing

1652 Cape Town founded
Jan Van Riebeeck founded this trading post for ships travelling between Europe and Asia.

1679 First European man to see the Niagara Falls in North America
Father Hennepin, a Jesuit missionary, witnessed the beauty of the Falls.

| 1660 | | 1670 | | 1680 | | 1690 | | **1699** |

1653
TAJ MAHAL COMPLETED

The Taj Mahal was commissioned in 1630 by Shah Jehan in honour of his beloved wife Mumtaz, who had died in childbirth.

1687
GRAVITY EXPLAINED

Isaac Newton published his theory on gravity, according to which all bodies gravitate towards the centre of a celestial body, such as the Earth and the Moon.

MILLENNIUM MILESTONES

1711
ST. PAUL'S COMPLETED

Although the first service in St. Paul's Cathedral, London, was held in 1697, work on the building's construction went on until 1711. It took a total of 35 years to build the Cathedral, which was designed by Sir Christopher Wren.

1703 Birth of St. Petersburg
Peter the Great celebrated the new wealth and political stability of Russia by creating a new capital on the Baltic coast, St. Petersburg.

ST. PAUL'S CATHEDRAL, LONDON

1716 Yoshimune made great general of Japan
Yoshimune was one of Japan's most enlightened and capable administrators. As Shogun, he lifted the ban on travel abroad and contact with foreign states, and brought European influences into the country.

MOZART

1700 | 1710 | 1720 | 1730 | 1740 | 1749

1709 Invention of the piano
Florentine harpsichord maker Bartolomeo Cristofori invented the piano. It proved immediately popular and soon supplanted all its predecessors.

1715
LOUIS XIV DIED

Louis XIV, also known as the Sun King, was an enthusiastic patron of the arts, and also encouraged scientific and technological research.

1747 Cure for scurvy discovered
James Lind, an English naval surgeon, discovered that a high consumption of citrus fruit was instrumental in preventing scurvy, the disease that killed sailors on long voyages.

A PORTRAIT OF LOUIS XIV

TOP 10 ★
LONGEST-REIGNING MONARCHS

	MONARCH/COUNTRY	REIGN	YEARS
1	**Louis XIV**, France	1643–1715	72
2	**John II**, Liechtenstein	1858–1929	71
3	**Franz-Josef**, Austria–Hungary	1848–1916	67
4	**Victoria**, Great Britain	1837–1901	63
5	**Hirohito**, Japan	1926–89	62
6	**Kangxi**, China	1662–1722	61
7	**Qianlong**, China	1736–96	60
8	**George III**, Great Britain	1760–1820	59
9	**Louis XV**, France	1715–74	59
10	**Pedro II**, Brazil	1831–89	58

Some authorities claim a 73-year reign for Alfonso I of Portugal, but he ruled as Count before becoming king in 1139, and so reigned for just 46 years.

18

Did You Know? Louis XV was the first person to use an elevator: in 1743 his "flying chair" carried him between the floors of Versailles palace.

THE 10 ★
FIRST MOZART WORKS*

	TITLE/KOCHEL NO.	KEY
1	Minuet for Harpsichord, 1	G Major
2	Andante for Harpsichord, 1	C Major
3	Allegro for Harpsichord, 1b	C Major
4	Allegro for Harpsichord, 1c	F Major
5	Minuet for Harpsichord, 1d	F Major
6	Minuet for Harpsichord, 1e	G Major
7	Minuet for Harpsichord, 1f	C Major
8	Minuet for Harpsichord, 2	F Major
9	Allegro for Harpsichord, 3	B Flat Major
10	Minuet for Harpsichord, 4	F Major

* Based on order of Kochel catalogue numbers

1783
FIRST MANNED BALLOON FLIGHT

Joseph and Etienne Montgolfier's balloon was launched in Paris on 21 September 1783. It was not flown by the brothers themselves, but by Pilâtre de Rozier and François Laurent.

EXECUTION OF LOUIS XVI IN 1793

1756
MOZART'S BIRTH

Wolfgang Amadeus Mozart was born in Salzburg. A child prodigy, he completed his first compositions at the age of four.

1789
FRENCH REVOLUTION

On 14 July 1789 an angry mob stormed the Bastille prison in Paris, symbol of the monarchic tyranny.

| 1750 | 1760 | 1770 | 1780 | 1790 | **1799** |

1776
US INDEPENDENCE

On 4 July 1776, the Declaration of Independence was signed by all 13 US states. It pronounced the 13 rebellious colonies to be "free and independent states".

1799 Rosetta Stone found
This Egyptian stone, which had different languages carved on it, enabled linguists to decipher two ancient scripts written in hieroglyphics.

THE 10 ★
YOUNGEST TO SIGN THE DECLARATION OF INDEPENDENCE

	SIGNER/BIRTHDATE	AGE AT SIGNING
1	Edward Rutledge, 23 Nov 1749	26
2	Thomas Lynch Jr., 5 Aug 1749	26
3	Thomas Heyward Jr., 28 Jul 1746	29
4	Benjamin Rush, 24 Dec 1745	30
5	Elbridge Gerry, 17 Jul 1744	31
6	Thomas Jefferson, 13 Apr 1743	33
7	Thomas Stone*, 1743	33
8	James Wilson, 14 Sep 1742	33
9	William Hooper, 28 Jun 1742	34
10	Arthur Middleton, 26 Jun 1742	34

* Precise birthdate unknown

MILLENNIUM MILESTONES

MOST HIGHLY POPULATED COUNTRIES, 1800

COUNTRY	POPULATION
1 China	295,753,000
2 India	131,000,000
3 Russia	33,000,000
4 France	27,349,000
5 Germany	24,833,000
6 Turkey	20,912,000
7 Vietnam	17,000,000
8 Japan	15,000,000
9 Italy	14,134,000
10 Indonesia	13,476,000

FIRST DINOSAURS TO BE NAMED

NAME	MEANING	NAMED BY	YEAR
1 Megalosaurus	Great lizard	William Buckland	1824
2 Iguanodon	Iguana tooth	Gideon Mantell	1825
3 Hylaeosaurus	Woodland lizard	Gideon Mantell	1832
4 Macrodontophion	Large tooth snake	A. Zborzewski	1834
5 =Thecodontosaurus	Socket-toothed lizard	Samuel Stutchbury and H. Riley	1836
=Palaeosaurus	Ancient lizard	Samuel Stutchbury and H. Riley	1836
7 Plateosaurus	Flat lizard	Hermann von Meyer	1837
8 =Cladeiodon	Branch tooth	Richard Owen	1841
=Cetiosaurus	Whale lizard	Richard Owen	1841
10 Pelorosaurus	Monstrous lizard	Gideon Mantell	1850

1800 POPULATION GROWTH

The vast populations of both China and India dwarfed those of all the other countries in the world.

1812 *Grimms' Fairy Tales*
Jakob and Wilhelm Grimm, German brothers, started writing some of the world's best-known fairy tales, such as *Hansel and Gretel* and *Snow White*.

1800   1805 | 1810 | 1815 | 1819 |

1804 FIRST AUSTRALIAN CITIES

Although Sydney was founded in 1788, extensive civic developments did not start in Australia until the 1800s.

1804 Napoleon declared himself Emperor of France
Napoleon Bonaparte expanded France's empire as far as the Russian border and introduced the Napoleonic code of law.

1815 BATTLE OF WATERLOO

Napoleon's imperialistic invasions came to an end near Waterloo, in Belgium, where the French army was defeated by British and German forces.

FIRST CITIES IN AUSTRALIA

CITY/STATE	FOUNDED
1 Sydney, New South Wales	26 Jan 1788
2 Hobart, Tasmania	26 Feb 1804
3 Newcastle, New South Wales	19 Apr 1804
4 Brisbane, Queensland	28 Sep 1824
5 Canberra, Australian Capital Territory	3 May 1825
6 Perth, Western Australia	12 Aug 1829
7 Bathurst, New South Wales	23 Jan 1833
8 Wollongong, New South Wales	28 Nov 1834
9 Adelaide, South Australia	21 Aug 1836
10 Geelong, Victoria	8 Mar 1837

Did You Know?   The Flat Earth Society was founded in 1800. Today, despite 200 years of evidence to the contrary, members continue to believe that the Earth is flat.

1825
IGUANODON DISCOVERED

The second dinosaur to be named, the Iguanodon, lived about 130 million years ago. It was 9.3 m/ 30 ft long, 5m/16 ft tall and weighed up to 5 tonnes. The name, meaning "iguana tooth", reflects the similarity between its tooth and that of the modern iguana.

1827
DEATH OF BEETHOVEN

Ludwig van Beethoven, who died at the age of 53, is widely acknowledged as the greatest composer of his time.

1828 Birth of the chocolate bar
Dutch manufacturer Conrad J. van Houten used cacao beans from South America to prepare a new confectionery.

THE 10 ★
FIRST BEETHOVEN WORKS*

	WORK	KEY	OPUS/NO
1	Piano Trio No. 1	E flat major	1/1
2	Piano Trio No. 2	G major	1/2
3	Piano Trio No. 3	C minor	1/3
4	Piano Sonata No. 1	F minor	2/1
5	Piano Sonata No. 2	A major	2/2
6	Piano Sonata No. 3	C major	2/3
7	String Trio No. 1	E flat major	3
8	String Quintet	E flat major	4
9	Sonata for Piano and Violincello No. 1	F major	5/1
10	Sonata for Piano and Violincello No. 2	G minor	5/2

* Based on order of Opus numbers

1833 Abolition of slavery in the British Empire
Although Britain had abolished the slave trade in 1807, the actual use of slaves in the colonies did not stop until 1833.

1820	1825	1835	**1839**

1822 Potato famine
This year witnessed the first potato crop failure in Ireland. As a result of this shortage, the country had to withstand disastrous famines.

1829
STEPHENSON'S *ROCKET*

Shortly after the inauguration of the world's first steam railway service by the Stockton and Darlington Railway, UK, Robert Stephenson built The Rocket, the first locomotive to be used for transporting passengers and freight.

1821 Independence for Gran Colombia
Simón Bolívar fought for independence from Spain for the whole of South America. He managed to achieve this objective for the state of Gran Colombia (now Colombia, Ecuador, Panama, and Venezuela).

1839 First Opium War
The First Opium War broke out after the Chinese government, concerned about the effects of the addiction on its people, set fire to a large British shipment of the drug.

THE 10 ★
FIRST COUNTRIES WITH RAILWAYS

	COUNTRY	FIRST RAILWAY ESTABLISHED
1	UK	27 Sep 1825
2	France	7 Nov 1829
3	USA	24 May 1830
4	Ireland	17 Dec 1834
5	Belgium	5 May 1835
6	Germany	7 Dec 1835
7	Canada	21 Jul 1836
8	Russia	30 Oct 1837
9	Austria	6 Jan 1838
10	Netherlands	24 Sep 1839

Although there were earlier horse-drawn railways, the Stockton & Darlington Railway inaugurated the world's first steam service.

THE 10 ★

FIRST COUNTRIES TO ISSUE POSTAGE STAMPS

	COUNTRY	STAMPS FIRST ISSUED
1	Great Britain	1840
2	USA (New York City)	1842
3	Switzerland (Zurich)	1843
4	Brazil	1843
5	Mauritius	1847
6	Bermuda	1848
7	France	1849
8	Belgium	1849
9	Germany (Bavaria)	1849
10	Spain	1850

ROME

1840
WORLD'S FIRST STAMP

The first postage stamp ever printed, the Penny Black, portrayed Queen Victoria; it was placed on sale on 1 May 1840.

1848 *The Communist Manifesto*
Karl Marx and Friedrich Engels published this book, in which they advocated the rebellion of the working class against capitalists and the birth of a classless society based on sharing.

1850
POPULATION EXPANSION

Rome passed the 1 million population mark in ancient times. In the 1850s–70s, many more cities grew to reach this size.

1840   1845 | 1850   1854 |

1840
BIRTH OF MONET

Claude Monet's painting Impression, Sunrise *is regarded as the major influence on the development of the artistic movement known as Impressionism.*

1849 California Gold Rush
Gold was found at Sutter's Mill, California, in 1848. The following year, thousands of prospectors moved to the area hoping to make their fortune.

1853
CRIMEAN WAR

The Crimean War broke out between Turkey and Russia over the protection of the holy places in Palestine. Medical developments, such as the use of anaesthesia, were features of this war, and Florence Nightingale remains famous for her nursing work during this period.

TOP 10 ★

MOST EXPENSIVE MONET PAINTINGS EVER SOLD AT AUCTION

	PAINTING/SALE	PRICE (£)		PAINTING/SALE	PRICE (£)
1	*Bassin aux nymphéas et sentier au bord de l'eau*, Sotheby's, London, 30 Jun 1998	18,000,000	=	*Le jardin de l'artist à Vétheuil*, Christie's, New York, 13 Nov 1996	7,228,916*
2	*Dans la prairie*, Sotheby's, London, 30 Jun 1998	13,000,000	7	*La Cathédrale de Rouen, effet d'après-midi, plein soleil*, Christie's, London, 26 Jun 1995	6,900,000
3	*Le Parlement, coucher de soleil*, Christie's, New York, 10 May 1989	7,975,460*	8	*La Grand Canal*, Sotheby's, New York, 13 May 1998	6,790,000*
4	*Le bassin aux nymphéas*, Christie's, New York, 11 Nov 1992	7,284,770*	9 =	*Nymphéas*, Christie's, New York, 14 Nov 1989	6,774,194*
5 =	*Nymphéas*, Christie's, New York, 13 Nov 1996	7,228,916*	=	*La Grand Canal*, Sotheby's, New York, 15 Nov 1989	6,774,194*

* Converted from $ at rate then prevailing

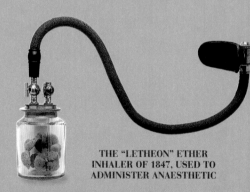

THE "LETHEON" ETHER
INHALER OF 1847, USED TO
ADMINISTER ANAESTHETIC

Did You Know? The first jeans were made in 1849 by Bavarian immigrant Levi Strauss as hard-wearing attire for Californian gold-miners.

FIRST CITIES IN THE WORLD WITH POPULATIONS OF MORE THAN ONE MILLION

	CITY	COUNTRY	APPROX. DATE
1	Rome	Italy	133BC
2	Alexandria	Egypt	30BC
3	Angkor	Cambodia	900
4	Hangchow	China	1200
5	London	UK	1810
6	Paris	France	1850
7	Peking	China	1855
8	Canton	China	1860
9	Berlin	Prussia	1870
10	New York	USA	1874

1862 Pasteurization
French chemist Louis Pasteur's discovery of the micro-organisms that sour wine and milk resulted in the pasteurization process.

1865 Antiseptic surgery
Joseph Lister adopted the antiseptic principles being used in other areas of medicine and applied them to surgery.

| 1860 | 1865 | 1869 |

1856
NEANDERTHAL MAN
The Neander Valley in Germany yielded the fossilized remains of a man from prehistoric times.

1861
START OF US CIVIL WAR
The war started when southern states separated from the Union in protest at Abraham Lincoln's election.

1864 Red Cross established
Jean Henri Dunant, concerned for the lack of healthcare and assistance for war victims, established an international volunteer aid organization, the Red Cross.

WORST US CIVIL WAR BATTLES

	BATTLE	DATE	CASUALTIES*
1	Gettysburg	1–3 July 1863	51,116
2	Seven Days Battles	25 June–1 July 1862	36,463
3	Chickamauga	19–20 Sept 1863	34,624
4	Chancellorsville	1–4 May 1863	29,609
5	The Wilderness#	5–7 May 1862	25,416
6	2nd Bull Run (2nd Manassas)	27 Aug–2 Sept 1862	25,340
7	Murfreesboro (Stone's River)	31 Dec 1862–1 Jan 1863	24,645
8	Shiloh (Pittsburg Landing)	6–7 Apr 1862	23,741
9	Antietam	17 Sept 1862	22,726
10	Fredericksburg	13 Dec 1862	17,962

* Killed, missing, and wounded
# Confederate totals estimated

THE BATTLE OF GETTYSBURG

1874
FIRST IMPRESSIONIST EXHIBITION

Rejected by the Salon des Artistes, a group of French artists, including Monet, Pissarro, and Renoir, organized their own exhibition. Some critics saw the potential of the paintings on show, and encouraged the "Impressionists" to hold further exhibitions.

1870

1870 Discovery of Troy
After analyzing Homer's *Iliad*, German archaeologist Heinrich Schliemann financed an expedition to find the remains of the ancient city of Troy. He finally located it in Turkey.

FIRST "FASTEST MEN ON EARTH"*

	ATHLETE	COUNTRY	DATE	TIME SECS
1	Luther Cary	USA	4 Jul 1891	10.8
2	Emil Ketterer*	Germany	9 Jul 1911	10.5
3	Charles Paddock*	USA	18 Jun 1921	10.2
4	Armin Harry	East Germany	21 Jun 1960	10.0
5	Jim Hines	USA	14 Oct 1968	9.95
6	Carl Lewis	USA	24 Sep 1988	9.92
7	Leroy Burrell	USA	14 Jun 1991	9.90
8	Carl Lewis	USA	25 Aug 1991	9.86
9	Leroy Burrell	USA	6 Jul 1994	9.85
10	Donovan Bailey#	Canada	27 Jul 1996	9.74

* To run 100 metres

\# Unofficial record   + Current record-holder

1877 Diaz became Mexican President
A leader who brought stability and prosperity to Mexico, Porfirio Diaz also put a stop to banditry.

1880

CHARLES PADDOCK

1879
ELECTRIC LIGHT

American Thomas Edison developed the first commercially practical incandescent lamp.

FIRST DAIMLER/BENZ CARS

	CAR	TOP SPEED KM/H	MPH	DATE
1	Benz Patent Motor Car	16	10	1886
2	Daimler Motor Carriage	18	11	1886
3	Daimler Wire Wheel Car	18	11	1889
4	Benz Viktoria	18	11	1893
5	Benz Velo	20	12.5	1894
6	Daimler Belt-Driven Car	18	11	1894
7	Daimler Phoenix	not known		1897
8	Benz Dos-à-Dos	35	21.5	1899
9	Benz Elegant	40	25	1900
10	Daimler Mercedes	70	43.5	1901

BENZ PATENT MOTOR CAR

STILL IMAGE FROM THE LUMIÈRE BROTHERS' FIRST FILM

STEAM-POWER COUNTRIES, 1896

	COUNTRY	FIXED*	RAILWAYS	STEAMSHIPS#	HORSEPOWER TOTAL
1	USA	3,940,000	11,760,000	2,360,000	18,060,000
2	UK	2,300,000	5,100,000	6,300,000	13,700,000
3	Germany	2,400,000	4,800,000	880,000	8,080,000
4	France	1,130,000	4,200,000	590,000	5,920,000
5	Russia	430,000	2,440,000	230,000	3,100,000
6	Austria	480,000	1,890,000	150,000	2,520,000
7	Italy	180,000	1,100,000	240,000	1,520,000
8	Canada	320,000	820,000	250,000	1,390,000
9=	Belgium	390,000	700,000	90,000	1,180,000
=	Spain	50,000	600,000	530,000	1,180,000

* Factories, mines, water pumping stations, etc.   # Excluding warships

1891
FIRST FASTEST MAN

Luther Cary became the first person to be officially recognized as "the fastest man on Earth".

1896
STEAM POWER

By this time steam power was playing a major role in manufacturing and transport.

|1885 |1890 |1895 |**1899**

1889 Eiffel Tower built
The Eiffel Tower was constructed by French engineer Gustave Eiffel for the Paris Exposition.

1895
INVENTION OF CINEMA

French brothers Louis and Auguste Lumière developed the world's first film camera and used it to record a train approaching a station.

1896
FIRST MODERN OLYMPICS

It was Pierre de Coubertin, a young French nobleman, who revived the Olympic Games. At the first Games, 13 countries competed against one other in 9 different disciplines including cycling, fencing, swimming, and wrestling.

1886
FIRST MOTOR CAR

The world's first petrol-powered motor car was invented by German engineer Karl Benz. It was a three-wheeler and received its first public testing in Mannheim on 3 July 1886.

FIRST OLYMPIC GAMES

	SITE/LOCATION	NUMBER	YEAR
1	**Athens**, Greece	I	1896
2	**Paris**, France	II	1900
3	**St. Louis**, USA	III	1904
4	**Athens**, Greece	–	1906
5	**London**, UK	IV	1908
6	**Stockholm**, Sweden	V	1912
7	**Antwerp**, Belgium	VII	1920
8	**Paris**, France	VIII	1924
9	**Amsterdam**, Netherlands	IX	1928
10	**Los Angeles**, USA	X	1932

The so-called Intermediate or Intercalated Games of 1906 were the only ones not to be numbered.

MARATHON DAY AT THE 1896 ATHENS OLYMPICS

Did You Know? Britain's shortest-ever war broke out in 1896: it was declared against Zanzibar, and ended 38 minutes later.

MILLENNIUM MILESTONES

MOST HIGHLY POPULATED COUNTRIES, 1900

	COUNTRY	POPULATION
1	China	303,241,969
2	India	289,187,316
3	Russia	129,211,113
4	USA	62,981,000
5	Germany	52,244,503
6	Austria	41,345,329
7	Japan	40,072,020
8	UK	39,824,563
9	Turkey	39,500,000
10	France	38,517,975

1900
POPULATION GROWTH
China topped the 300 million mark, with India close behind.

1904 Work started on the Panama Canal
The canal created a shortcut between the Pacific and the Caribbean.

1911
MELBOURNE
Established in 1835, Melbourne became Australia's second largest city thanks to the discovery of gold there in 1851.

1914
START OF WORLD WAR I
Trench warfare dominated this war, in which millions of soldiers died.

1900

1905|

1910|

1900
PARK ROW BUILDING
At the dawn of the 20th century, the Park Row Building in New York was the world's tallest building.

1911 China became a republic
The Chinese population rebelled against the Manchu dynasty that had been in power since 1644, and declared the country a republic.

THE 10 ★

FIRST "WORLD'S TALLEST BUILDINGS" IN THE PAST 100 YEARS

	BUILDING/LOCATION	YEAR	STOREYS	M	FT
1	**Park Row Building**, New York	1899	29	118	386
2	**City Hall**, Philadelphia	1901	7	155	511
3	**Singer Building***, New York	1908	34	200	656
4	**Metropolitan Life**, New York	1909	50	212	700
5	**Woolworth Building**, New York	1913	59	241	792
6	**40 Wall Street** (with spire), New York	1929	71	282	927
7	**Chrysler Building** (with spire), New York	1930	77	319	1,046
8	**Empire State Building** (with spire), New York	1931	102	449	1,472
9	**World Trade Center** (with spire), New York	1973	110	521	1,710
10	**Sears Tower** (with spire), Chicago	1974	110	520	1,707

* Demolished 1970

TOP 10 ★

MOST HIGHLY POPULATED TOWNS IN AUSTRALIA, 1911

	TOWN/STATE	POPULATION
1	**Sydney**, New South Wales	637,102
2	**Melbourne**, Victoria	591,830
3	**Adelaide**, South Australia	192,294
4	**Brisbane**, Queensland	141,342
5	**Perth**, Western Australia	84,580
6	**Newcastle**, New South Wales	65,500
7	**Ballarat**, Victoria	44,000
8	**Bendigo**, Victoria	42,000
9	**Hobart**, Tasmania	38,055
10	**Broken Hill**, New South Wales	31,000

BATTLE OF CAMBRAI, WORLD WAR I

THE 10 ★
LARGEST ARMED FORCES
OF WORLD WAR I

	COUNTRY	PERSONNEL*
1	Russia	12,000,000
2	Germany	11,000,000
3	British Empire	8,904,467
4	France	8,410,000
5	Austria-Hungary	7,800,000
6	Italy	5,615,000
7	USA	4,355,000
8	Turkey	2,850,000
9	Bulgaria	1,200,000
10	Japan	800,000

* Total at peak strength

1917 Russian Revolution
A simple protest for better working conditions ended with Lenin's Bolshevik party seizing power and, ultimately, the brutal killings of the tsar and his family.

1920 Gandhi's passive protest
Mahatma Gandhi took control of the Indian National Congress Party, preaching a peaceful approach to independence.

1926 Invention of TV
John Logie Baird invented the first television, which led the way for the electronic models developed in the 1930s.

1929 The Great Depression
A dramatic fall in stock prices led to the New York Stock Exchange collapsing, leaving millions bankrupt.

1915

1920

1925

1929

1915
SUCCESSFUL SILENT FILM

In spite of its controversial portrayal of blacks, director D.W. Griffith's The Birth of a Nation was one of the biggest box-office money-makers in film history.

1928
DISCOVERY OF PENICILLIN

Bacteriologist Alexander Fleming discovered an antibacterial mould that he named penicillin. Fleming was awarded a Nobel Prize in 1945 for his work.

TOP 10 ★
FILMS OF THE
SILENT ERA

	FILM	YEAR
1	The Birth of a Nation	1915
2	The Big Parade	1925
3	Ben Hur	1926
4	The Ten Commandments	1923
5 =	The Covered Wagon	1923
=	What Price Glory?	1926
7 =	Hearts of the World	1918
=	Way Down East	1921
9 =	The Four Horsemen of the Apocalypse	1921
=	Wings	1927

Did You Know? In 1916, to revolutionize trench warfare, Jones Wister of Philadelphia invented a rifle for shooting around corners. It had a curved barrel and periscopic sights.

MILLENNIUM MILESTONES

FIRST HOSTS OF THE FOOTBALL WORLD CUP

	HOST COUNTRY	FINAL (WINNER FIRST)	SCORE	YEAR
1	Uruguay	Uruguay v Argentina	4-2	1930
2	Italy	Italy v Czechoslovakia	2-1	1934
3	France	Italy v Hungary	4-2	1938
4	Brazil	Uruguay v Brazil	1-2	1950
5	Switzerland	West Germany v Hungary	3-2	1954
6	Sweden	Brazil v Sweden	5-2	1958
7	Chile	Brazil v Czechoslovakia	3-1	1962
8	England	England v West Germany	4-2	1966
9	Mexico	Brazil v Italy	4-1	1970
10	West Germany	West Germany v Netherlands	2-1	1974

1930
FIRST FOOTBALL WORLD CUP

Following the success of the football matches at the 1924 Paris Olympics, the first World Cup was held in Uruguay in 1930 and attracted 13 competing nations.

FIRST ELVIS PRESLEY SINGLES RELEASED IN THE US

	TITLE	CAT. NO.	RELEASED
1	*That's All Right (Mama)/Blue Moon of Kentucky*	Sun 209	Jul 1954
2	*Good Rockin' Tonight/ I Don't Care if the Sun Don't Shine*	Sun 210	Sep 1954
3	*You're a Heartbreaker/Milkcow Blues Boogie*	Sun 215	Jan 1955
4	*Baby Let's Play House/ I'm Left, You're Right, She's Gone*	Sun 217	Apr 1955
5	*I Forgot to Remember to Forget/Mystery Train*	Sun 223	Aug 1955
6	=*I Forgot to Remember to Forget/Mystery Train*	RCA 6357	Dec 1955
	=*That's All Right (Mama)/ Blue Moon of Kentucky*	RCA 6380	Dec 1955
	=*You're a Heartbreaker/Milkcow Blues Boogie*	RCA 6382	Dec 1955
	=*Baby Let's Play House/I'm Left, You're Right, She's Gone*	RCA 6383	Dec 1955
10	*Heartbreak Hotel/I Was the One*	RCA 6420	Jan 1956

1930

1935

1940

1933 Nazi Germany
Adolf Hitler became Chancellor and then *Führer* (leader) of Germany. He soon turned the country into a dictatorship, banning other political parties and persecuting minorities.

1936 Spanish Civil War
Franco led a revolt against the republican government. By 1939, he had seized complete power over Spain.

1939
WORLD WAR II

World War II started with Hitler's invasion of Poland in 1939. France and Britain reacted against Germany's military policy and declared war. In the following year, Germany occupied Denmark, Norway, Belgium, Holland, and France. Two years later, Japan came in on Germany's side, and the US on the side of the Allies.

COUNTRIES SUFFERING THE GREATEST MILITARY LOSSES IN WORLD WAR II

	COUNTRY	NO. KILLED
1	USSR	13,600,000*
2	Germany	3,300,000
3	China	1,324,516
4	Japan	1,140,429
5	British Empire# (UK 264,000)	357,116
6	Romania	350,000
7	Poland	320,000
8	Yugoslavia	305,000
9	USA	292,131
10	Italy	279,800

* *Total, of which 7,800,000 battlefield deaths*

\# *Including Australia, Canada, India, New Zealand, etc.*

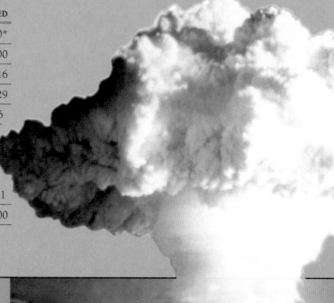

ELVIS PRESLEY

	SATELLITE	COUNTRY OF ORIGIN	LAUNCH DATE
1	*Sputnik 1*	USSR	4 Oct 1957
2	*Sputnik 2*	USSR	3 Nov 1957
3	*Explorer 1*	USA	1 Feb 1958
4	*Vanguard 1*	USA	17 Mar 1958
5	*Explorer 3*	USA	26 Mar 1958
6	*Sputnik 3*	USSR	15 May 1958
7	*Explorer 4*	USA	26 Jul 1958
8	*SCORE*	USA	18 Dec 1958
9	*Vanguard 2*	USA	17 Feb 1959
10	*Discoverer 1*	USA	28 Feb 1959

1953
ELVIS CUTS HIS FIRST RECORD

Arguably the most influential figure of modern popular music, Elvis Presley first entered a recording studio on 18 July to record the song My Happiness. Pictured above is the cover of Elvis' eponymous debut album, released on RCA three years after that momentous date.

1948 South African apartheid
South Africa's National Party came to power and immediately established apartheid, a policy of racial segregation and white supremacy. Apartheid was finally abolished in 1991.

1957 Laika in space
Russia became the first country to send a living creature into space in the shape of a dog called Laika.

1957
FIRST SPACE LAUNCH

Sputnik 1, the first Russian satellite, made about 1,400 orbits before burning up.

| 1945 | 1950 | 1955 | # 1959 |

1945
FIRST ATOMIC BOMB

On 6 August, the US dropped the world's first atomic bomb on the Japanese city of Hiroshima. About 150,000 people were killed outright, but many more died in subsequent years because of radiation exposure. The total number of victims is estimated to be 200,000.

1953 Everest conquered
On 29 May, New Zealander Edmund Hillary and Nepalese Sherpa Tenzing Norgay became the first to climb Mount Everest, the highest mountain in the world at 8,846 m/29,022 ft high.

1959
AUSTRALIAN IMMIGRANTS

After World War II, Australia started an immigration programme to increase the population and boost economic strength.

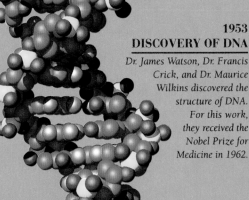

1953
DISCOVERY OF DNA

Dr. James Watson, Dr. Francis Crick, and Dr. Maurice Wilkins discovered the structure of DNA. For this work, they received the Nobel Prize for Medicine in 1962.

	COUNTRY	IMMIGRANTS
1	UK and Ireland	37,851
2	Italy	16,126
3	West Germany	9,406
4	Netherlands	9,328
5	Yugoslavia	6,319
6	Greece	6,214
7	Austria	2,025
8	Finland	1,935
9	Poland	1,836
10	Malta	1,818

Did You Know? In 1959 – after its 1957 success with the Frisbee – the Wham-O company introduced the Hula Hoop and sold 25 million hoops in four months.

MILLENNIUM MILESTONES

FIRST MOONWALKERS

NAME/SPACECRAFT	MISSION DATES
1 Neil Armstrong, *Apollo 11*	16–24 Jul 1969
2 Edwin E. Aldrin, *Apollo 11*	16–24 Jul 1969
3 Charles Conrad Jr., *Apollo 12*	14–24 Nov 1969
4 Alan L. Bean, *Apollo 12*	14–24 Nov 1969
5 Alan B. Shepard, *Apollo 14*	31 Jan–9 Feb 1971
6 Edgar Mitchell, *Apollo 14*	31 Jan–9 Feb 1971
7 David R. Scott, *Apollo 15*	26 Jul–7 Aug 1971
8 James B. Irwin, *Apollo 15*	26 Jul–7 Aug 1971
9 John W. Young, *Apollo 16*	16–27 Apr 1972
10 Charles M. Duke, *Apollo 16*	16–27 Apr 1972

1969
MAN ON THE MOON

The world held its breath as Apollo 11 neared the Moon's surface. With the words "The Eagle has landed", Neil Armstrong announced to the world that he and "Buzz" Aldrin had arrived safely on the Moon.

1960   1965   1970

1963 JFK assassinated
US President John Fitzgerald Kennedy was shot dead during a motorcade through the city of Dallas. Lee Harvey Oswald was accused of being the assassin.

1966 Chinese Cultural Revolution
Mao Zedong's Cultural Revolution was based on a rejection of old ideas, old culture, old customs, and old habits. Those who did not agree with these principles were publicly humiliated and punished by Mao's Red Guards.

1973 End of the Vietnam War
American troops withdrew from Vietnam, conceding defeat in a war that lasted eight years and cost the lives of about 2.5 million people.

1961
BERLIN WALL RAISED

In order to prevent the people of East Germany from fleeing to the West, communist authorities built a wall across Berlin. It divided the city until 1989.

THE 10 ★
FIRST APPLE COMPUTERS

	COMPUTER	LAUNCHED
1	Apple I	Mar 1976
2	Apple II	Apr 1977
3	Apple II+	Jun 1979
4	Apple III	Sep 1980
5	Apple IIe	Jan 1983
6	Apple Lisa	Jan 1983
7	Apple III+	Dec 1983
8	Apple Macintosh	Jan 1984
9	Apple Macintosh 128K	Jan 1984
10	Apple IIc	Apr 1984

1976
BIRTH OF APPLE I
The brainchild of high-school friends Steven Wozniak and Steven Jobs, the first Apple computer, Apple I, was created in 1976.

1985
GORBACHEV ELECTED
Mikhail Gorbachev provided a new policy of openness and freedom of information (glasnost) in the Soviet Union.

1978 First test-tube baby
The first baby conceived by in vitro fertilization (IVF) was born in Britain.

1989 Tiananmen Square
Hundreds of thousands of students gathered in the main square of Beijing, China, to demand democratic reforms. The peaceful protest was crushed by government soldiers, and a massacre followed.

| 1975 | 1980 | 1985 | 1989 |

1979 Khomeini in power
Ayatollah Khomeini organized a coup to depose the Shah of Iran, who had ruled since 1941. Khomeini reintroduced strict Islamic laws and turned Iran into an Islamic republic.

1980
OLDEST PRESIDENT
Ronald Reagan, pictured here with Margaret Thatcher, was the fortieth and oldest US President. He was elected in 1980 and remained in power for two terms, until 1989.

1984 Ethiopian famine
After 10 years of civil war, Ethiopia was struck by a drought that led to extensive crop damage. Thousands of people died of starvation in the ensuing famine.

1989 Nintendo Gameboy
The Japanese company Nintendo introduced a hand-held video game. Today one-third of all American and Japanese homes have one.

1976 CONCORDE
The first civilian Concorde flight took place in January. The aircraft, equipped with four Rolls Royce engines, could reach a speed of 2,155 km/h/ 1,338 mph.

TOP 10 ★
OLDEST US PRESIDENTS

	PRESIDENT	AGE ON TAKING OFFICE	
		YEARS	DAYS
1	Ronald W. Reagan	69	349
2	William H. Harrison	68	23
3	James Buchanan	65	315
4	George H.W. Bush	64	223
5	Zachary Taylor	64	100
6	Dwight D. Eisenhower	62	98
7	Andrew Jackson	61	354
8	John Adams	61	125
9	Gerald R. Ford	61	26
10	Harry Truman	60	339

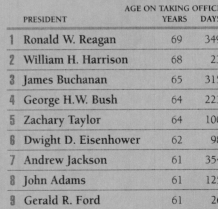

MILLENNIUM MILESTONES

1999 War in Kosovo
On 24 March, in order to put an end to Serbian violence against the Albanian population of Kosovo, NATO started a programme of military action against Serbia.

1990
RELEASE OF MANDELA

After 28 years in prison, Nelson Mandela became a free man. An inspirational figure to all, Mandela was awarded the 1993 Nobel Peace Prize.

1994
MOST RECENT STATE

Palau, an archipelago in the west Pacific, became the world's most recent independent state in 1994.

1997 Hong Kong returned
On 1 July, Britain honoured an agreement signed in 1898 and handed the colony of Hong Kong back to China.

1990

1995

1999

1991 Gulf War
The United Nations reacted to the invasion of Kuwait by Iraqi military forces by authorizing war on Saddam Hussein, leader of Iraq.

1993 Peace in the Middle East
US President Bill Clinton brought together two historical enemies, Israel and Palestine, when he acted as mediator for a peace agreement between them.

1995 End of war in Bosnia
After three and a half years of war between several Balkan states, an agreement was finally reached at Dayton, Ohio, in the US.

1997
DEATH OF DIANA

A sea of flowers commemorated the death of Diana, Princess of Wales, in a car accident.

INTO THE FUTURE

As we enter the third millennium, we find the future full of amazing possibilities. We can only speculate on where human innovation will take us next.

TOP 10 ★
MOST POPULATED COUNTRIES IN 2050

	COUNTRY	1998	2050*
1	India	982,223,000	1,528,853,000
2	China	1,255,698,000	1,477,730,000
3	USA	274,028,000	349,318,000
4	Pakistan	148,166,000	345,484,000
5	Indonesia	206,338,000	311,857,000
6	Nigeria	106,409,000	244,311,000
7	Brazil	165,851,000	244,230,000
8	Bangladesh	124,774,000	212,495,000
9	Ethiopia	59,649,000	169,446,000
10	Dem. Rep. of Congo	49,139,000	160,360,000
	World total	5,901,054,000	8,909,095,000

* *Estimated population*   Source: *United Nations*

2005 Mars visit?
The first Martian soil samples may be brought to Earth by the *Mars Surveyor*.

2022 Extinct animals cloned?
Scientists hope to unveil the first "revived" animal species, brought back from extinction through the cloning of genetic material.

2035 Brain stimulation?
Electrical stimulation of the brain, presently used by the medical profession, may become a widespread training technique.

2050
INDIA OVERTAKES CHINA?

By the year 2050, it is estimated that India will have a larger population than China.

2000 | **2010** | **2020** | **2030** | **2040** | **2050**

2000
GENETIC REPLICAS

Since the arrival of Dolly the sheep, cloning technology has progressed rapidly. It seems that the new millennium marks the beginning of a clone-filled future.

2000
GOING SOLAR?

At the dawn of an era of clean transport, scientists and engineers are increasing their efforts to create a reliable, zero-emission, solar-powered car.

2019
MAN ON MARS?

NASA plans to launch a manned mission to Mars, scheduled to land in 2019, beginning a new era of human presence on the red planet.

2045 Human clone?
Despite current legislation in some nations banning experimentation in the area of genetic modification, by 2045 scientists may be able to create the first human clone.

TOP 10 ★

THE UNIVERSE & THE EARTH

STAR GAZING

The core of the Sun reaches a temperature of 15,400,000°C/ 27,720,000°F. Columns of gas, each the size of France, flare away from the fiery surface at five-minute intervals.

TOP 10 ★
LARGEST BODIES IN THE SOLAR SYSTEM

	BODY	MAXIMUM DIAMETER KM	MILES
1	Sun	1,392,140	865,036
2	Jupiter	142,984	88,846
3	Saturn	120,536	74,898
4	Uranus	51,118	31,763
5	Neptune	49,532	30,778
6	Earth	12,756	7,926
7	Venus	12,103	7,520
8	Mars	6,794	4,222
9	Ganymede	5,269	3,274
10	Titan	5,150	3,200

Most of the planets are visible with the naked eye and have been observed since ancient times. The exceptions are Uranus, discovered on 13 March 1781 by the British astronomer Sir William Herschel; Neptune, found by German astronomer Johann Galle on 23 September 1846; and, outside the Top 10, Pluto, located using photographic techniques by American astronomer Clyde Tombaugh. Its discovery was announced on 13 March 1930; its diameter is uncertain, but is thought to be approximately 2,302 km/ 1,430 miles. Mercury, also outside the Top 10, has a diameter of 4,880 km/3,032 miles.

TOP 10 ★
LONGEST DAYS IN THE SOLAR SYSTEM

	BODY	LENGTH OF DAY* DAYS	HOURS	MINS
1	Venus	244	0	0
2	Mercury	58	14	0
3	Sun	25#	0	0
4	Pluto	6	9	0
5	Mars		24	37
6	Earth		23	56
7	Uranus		17	14
8	Neptune		16	7
9	Saturn		10	39
10	Jupiter		9	55

* *Period of rotation, based on 23'56 Sidereal day*
# *Variable*

TOP 10 ★
BODIES FURTHEST FROM THE SUN*

	BODY	AVERAGE DISTANCE FROM THE SUN KM	MILES
1	Pluto	5,914,000,000	3,675,000,000
2	Neptune	4,497,000,000	2,794,000,000
3	Uranus	2,871,000,000	1,784,000,000
4	Chiron	2,800,000,000	1,740,000,000
5	Saturn	1,427,000,000	887,000,000
6	Jupiter	778,300,000	483,600,000
7	Mars	227,900,000	141,600,000
8	Earth	149,600,000	92,900,000
9	Venus	108,200,000	67,200,000
10	Mercury	57,900,000	36,000,000

* *In the Solar System, excluding satellites and asteroids*

Chiron, a "mystery object" which may be either a comet or an asteroid, was discovered on 1 November 1977 by American astronomer Charles Kowal. It measures 200–300 km/ 124–186 miles in diameter.

TOP 10 STARS NEAREST TO THE EARTH*

	STAR	LIGHT YEARS	KM (MILLIONS)	MILES (MILLIONS)
1	Proxima Centauri	4.22	39,923,310	24,792,500
2	Alpha Centauri	4.35	41,153,175	25,556,250
3	Barnard's Star	5.98	56,573,790	35,132,500
4	Wolf 359	7.75	73,318,875	45,531,250
5	Lalande 21185	8.22	77,765,310	48,292,500
6	Luyten 726-8	8.43	79,752,015	49,526,250
7	Sirius	8.65	81,833,325	50,818,750
8	Ross 154	9.45	89,401,725	55,518,750
9	Ross 248	10.40	98,389,200	61,100,000
10	Epsilon Eridani	10.80	102,173,400	63,450,000

* *Excluding the Sun*

A spaceship travelling at 40,237 km/h/25,000 mph – which is faster than any human has yet reached in space – would take more than 113,200 years to reach the Earth's closest star, Proxima Centauri. While the nearest stars in this list lie just over four light years away from the Earth, others within the Milky Way lie at a distance of 2,500 light years.

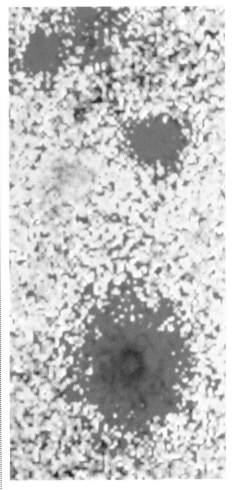

GALAXIES NEAREST TO THE EARTH

	GALAXY	DISTANCE (LIGHT YEARS)
1	Large Cloud of Magellan	169,000
2	Small Cloud of Magellan	190,000
3	Ursa Minor dwarf	250,000
4	Draco dwarf	260,000
5	Sculptor dwarf	280,000
6	Fornax dwarf	420,000
7 =	Leo I dwarf	750,000
=	Leo II dwarf	750,000
9	Barnard's Galaxy	1,700,000
10	Andromeda Spiral	2,200,000

These, and other galaxies, are members of the so-called "Local Group", although with vast distances such as these, "local" is a relative term.

BLACK HOLE

The largest blue spot on this "false colour" X ray image of the Large Cloud of Magellan is LMC X-1, a binary system thought to consist of a black hole gulping material from its ordinary stellar companion.

MOST MASSIVE BODIES IN THE SOLAR SYSTEM*

	BODY	MASS#
1	Sun	332,800.000
2	Jupiter	317.828
3	Saturn	95.161
4	Neptune	17.148
5	Uranus	14.536
6	Earth	1.000
7	Venus	0.815
8	Mars	0.10745
9	Mercury	0.05527
10	Pluto	0.0022

* *Excluding satellites*

\# *Compared with the Earth = 1; the mass of Earth is approximately 73,500,000,000,000 tonnes*

LONGEST YEARS IN THE SOLAR SYSTEM

	BODY	LENGTH OF YEAR* YEARS	DAYS
1	Pluto	247	256
2	Neptune	164	298
3	Uranus	84	4
4	Saturn	29	168
5	Jupiter	11	314
6	Mars		687
7	Earth		365
8	Venus		225
9	Mercury		88
10	Sun		0

* *Period of orbit round the Sun, in Earth years/days*

TOP 10 BRIGHTEST STARS*

(Star/constellation/apparent magnitude)

1 **Sirius**, Canis Major, -1.46 **2** **Canopus**, Carina, -0.73 **3** **Alpha Centauri**, Centaurus, -0.27 **4** **Arcturus**, Boötes, -0.04 **5** **Vega**, Lyra, +0.03 **6** **Capella**, Auriga, +0.08 **7** **Rigel**, Orion, +0.12 **8** **Procyon**, Canis Minor, +0.38 **9** **Achernar**, Eridanus, +0.46 **10** **Beta Centauri**, Centaurus, +0.61

* *Excluding the Sun*

Based on apparent visual magnitude as viewed from the Earth – the lower the number, the brighter the star. At its brightest, the star Betelgeuse is brighter than some of these, but as it is variable its average brightness disqualifies it from the Top 10. The absolute magnitude of Cygnus OB2 No. 12, discovered in 1992, may make it the brightest star in the galaxy, but it is 5,900 light years away.

GIANT PLANET

Jupiter is bigger than all the other planets in the Solar System put together, and has 16 moons of its own.

Who was the oldest man or woman in space?
see p.40 for the answer

A Janice Voss
B Valeri V. Polyakov
C John H. Glenn

ASTEROIDS, METEORITES & COMETS

TOP 10 ★
COMETS COMING CLOSEST TO THE EARTH

	COMET	DATE*	DISTANCE AU#
1	Lexell	1 Jul 1770	2.3
2	Tempel-Tuttle	26 Oct 1366	3.4
3	Halley	10 Apr 837	5.0
4	Biela	9 Dec 1805	5.5
5	Grischow	8 Feb 1743	5.8
6	Pons-Winnecke	26 Jun 1927	5.9
7	La Hire	20 Apr 1702	6.6
8	Schwassmann-Wachmann	31 May 1930	9.3
9	Cassini	8 Jan 1760	10.2
10	Schweizer	29 Apr 1853	12.6

* Of closest approach to the Earth

Astronomical Units: 1 AU = mean distance from the Earth to the Sun (149,598,200 km/92,955,900 miles)

HEAVENLY OBSERVATIONS

The most famous recorded sighting of Halley's comet occurred in 1066, when William the Conqueror regarded it as a sign of his imminent victory over King Harold at the Battle of Hastings.

TOP 10 ★
MOST RECENT OBSERVATIONS OF HALLEY'S COMET

1 1986

The Japanese Suisei probe passed within 151,000 km/93,827 miles of its 15-km/9-mile nucleus on 8 March 1986, revealing a whirling nucleus within a hydrogen cloud emitting 20–50 tons of water per second. The Soviet probes Vega 1 and Vega 2 passed at within 8,890 km/5,524 miles and 8,030 km/4,990 miles respectively. The European Space Agency's Giotto passed as close as 596 km/370 miles on 14 March. All were heavily battered by dust particles, and it was concluded that Halley's comet is composed of dust bonded by water and carbon dioxide ice.

2 1910

Predictions of disaster were widely published, with many people convinced that the world would come to an end. Mark Twain, who had been born at the time of the 1835 appearance and believed that his fate was linked to that of the comet, died when it reappeared in this year.

3 1835

Widely observed, but noticeably dimmer than in 1759.

4 1759

The comet's first return, as predicted by Halley, and thus proving his calculations correct.

5 1682

Observed in Africa and China and extensively in Europe, where it was observed on 5–19 September by Edmund Halley, who predicted its return.

6 1607

Seen extensively in China, Japan, Korea, and Europe, described by German astronomer Johannes Kepler and its position accurately measured by amateur Welsh astronomer Thomas Harriot.

7 1531

Observed in China, Japan, and Korea and in Europe on 13–23 August by Peter Appian, German geographer and astronomer who noted that comets' tails point away from the Sun.

8 1456

Observed in China, Japan, and Korea and by the Turkish army that was threatening to invade Europe. When the Turks were defeated by Papal forces, it was seen as a portent of their victory.

9 1378

Observed in China, Japan, Korea, and Europe.

10 1301

Seen in Iceland, parts of Europe, China, Japan, and Korea.

Before Edmund Halley (1656–1742) studied and predicted the return of the famous comet that now bears his name, no one had succeeded in proving that comets travel in predictable orbits. The dramatic return in 1759, precisely as Astronomer Royal Halley had calculated, of the comet he had observed in 1682, established the science of cometary observation.

TOP 10 MOST FREQUENTLY SEEN COMETS

(Comet/years between appearances)

1 Encke, 3.302 **2** Grigg-Skjellerup, 4.908
3 Honda-Mrkós-Pajdusáková, 5.210
4 Tempel 2, 5.259 **5** Neujmin 2, 5.437
6 Brorsen, 5.463 **7** Tuttle-Giacobini-Kresák, 5.489 **8** Tempel-L. Swift, 5.681
9 Tempel 1, 5.982 **10** Pons-Winnecke, 6.125

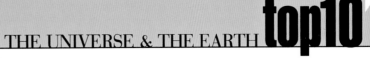

MASSIVE METEORITE

At 2.73 x 2.43 m/9 x 8 ft, the Hoba West meteorite was found on a South African farm in 1920. It consists of 82 per cent iron and 16 per cent nickel.

TOP 10 ★
LARGEST METEORITES EVER FOUND

LOCATION	ESTIMATED WEIGHT TONNES
1 Hoba West, Grootfontein, South Africa	54.4
2 Ahnighito ("The Tent"), Cape York, West Greenland	30.9
3 Bacuberito, Mexico	27.0
4 Mbosi, Tanganyika	26.0
5 Agpalik, Cape York, West Greenland	20.1
6 Armanti, Western Mongolia	20.0
7 Mundrabilla*, Western Australia	17.6
8 = Willamette, Oregon, USA	14.0
= Chupaderos, Mexico	14.0
10 Campo del Cielo, Argentina	13.0

* In two parts – 11.5 and 6.1 tonnes

Meteorites have been known since early times: fragments have been found mounted in a necklace in an Egyptian pyramid and in ancient American Indian burial sites. The number of meteorites falling has been calculated to amount to some 500 a year across the whole globe, although many fall in the sea and in unpopulated areas where their descent goes unnoticed. Apart from occasional unfounded legends, there is no record of anyone being killed by a meteorite, although animals are occasional victims.

TOP 10 ★
LARGEST METEORITES EVER FOUND IN THE UK

LOCATION	DATE FOUND	WEIGHT KG	LB
1 Barwell, Leicestershire	24 Dec 1965	44.0	97.0
2 Wold Cottage, Yorkshire	13 Dec 1795	25.4	56.0
3 Appley Bridge, Lancashire	13 Oct 1914	15.0	33.0
4 Strathmore, Tayside	3 Dec 1917	13.0	28.7
5 Bovedy, Londonderry, N. Ireland	25 Apr 1969	5.4	11.9
6 High Possil, Strathclyde	5 Apr 1804	4.5	9.9
7 Crumlin, Antrim, N. Ireland	13 Sep 1902	4.3	9.5
8 Rowton, Shropshire	20 Apr 1876	3.5	7.7
9 Middlesborough, Cleveland	14 Mar 1881	1.6	3.5
10 Ashdon, Essex	9 Mar 1923	1.3	2.9

DAMAGED ASTEROID

This colour-coded elevation map of Vesta shows a giant crater, suggesting that the asteroid has suffered a large impact.

THE 10 ★
FIRST ASTEROIDS TO BE DISCOVERED

ASTEROID/DISCOVERER	DISCOVERED
1 **Ceres**, Giuseppe Piazzi	1 Jan 1801
2 **Pallas**, Heinrich Olbers	28 Mar 1802
3 **Juno**, Karl Ludwig Harding	1 Sep 1804
4 **Vesta**, Heinrich Olbers	29 Mar 1807
5 **Astraea**, Karl Ludwig Hencke	8 Dec 1845
6 **Hebe**, Karl Ludwig Hencke	1 Jul 1847
7 **Iris**, John Russell Hind	13 Aug 1847
8 **Flora**, John Russell Hind	18 Oct 1847
9 **Metis**, A. Graham	25 Apr 1848
10 **Hygeia**, Annibale de Gasparis	12 Apr 1849

Asteroids, sometimes known as "minor planets", are fragments of rock orbiting between Mars and Jupiter. There are perhaps 45,000 of them, but fewer than 10 per cent have been named.

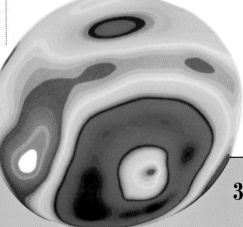

Did You Know? An asteroid that collided with the Earth 65 million years ago may have caused the extinction of the dinosaurs.

SPACE EXPLORATION

PENSIONER IN SPACE

At 77, Glenn became the oldest astronaut by a considerable margin, when he re-entered space aboard the Space Shuttle STS-95 Discovery in 1998.

TOP 10 ★ OLDEST US ASTRONAUTS*

	ASTRONAUT	LAST FLIGHT	AGE#
1	John H. Glenn	6 Nov 1998	77
2	F. Story Musgrave	7 Dec 1996	61
3	Vance D. Brand	11 Dec 1990	59
4	Karl G. Henize	6 Aug 1985	58
5	Roger K. Crouch	17 Jul 1997	56
6	William E. Thornton	6 May 1985	56
7	Don L. Lind	6 May 1985	54
8	Henry W. Hartsfield	6 Nov 1988	54
9	John E. Blaha	7 Dec 1996	54
10	William G. Gregory	18 Mar 1995	54

* *Including payload specialists, etc; to 1 January 1999*

\# *Those of apparently identical age have been ranked according to their precise age in days at the time of their last flight*

At 53, Shannon W. Lucid (born 14 January 1943, last flight 31 March 1996) holds the record as the oldest woman in space.

TOP 10 ★ YOUNGEST US ASTRONAUTS*

	ASTRONAUT	FIRST FLIGHT	AGE#
1	Janice E. Voss	21 Jun 1993	27
2	Kenneth D. Bowersox	25 Jun 1984	28
3	Sally K. Ride	18 Jun 1983	32
4	Tamara E. Jernigan	5 Jun 1991	32
5	Eugene A. Cernan	3 Jun 1966	32
6	Eoichi Wakata	11 Jan 1996	32
7	Steven A. Hawley	30 Aug 1984	32
8	Mary E. Weber	13 Jul 1995	32
9	Kathryn D. Sullivan	5 Oct 1984	33
10	Ronald E. McNair +	3 Feb 1984	33

* *To 1 January 1999*

\# *Those of apparently identical age have been ranked according to their precise age in days at the time of their first flight*

\+ *Killed in Challenger disaster, 28 January 1986*

TOP 10 ★ COUNTRIES WITH MOST SPACEFLIGHT EXPERIENCE*

	COUNTRY	ASTRONAUTS	DAY	HR	MIN	SEC
			TOTAL DURATION OF MISSIONS			
1	USSR/Russia#	88	13,723	19	28	19
2	USA	244	6,331	18	09	49
3	Kazakhstan	2	341	09	55	23
4	Germany	9	298	11	30	13
5	France	8	158	12	44	05
6	Canada	7	89	00	50	33
7	Japan	5	64	02	39	16
8	Italy	3	39	10	35	47
9	Switzerland	1	34	12	53	58
10	Ukraine	1	15	16	34	4

* *To 1 January 1999*

\# *Russia became a separate independent state on 25 December 1991*

The USSR, and now Russia, has clocked up its considerable lead on the rest of the world (with 65 per cent of the total time spent by humans in space) largely through the long-duration stays of its cosmonauts on board the *Mir* space station, which has been occupied since 1986.

TOP 10 ★ MOST EXPERIENCED SPACEMEN*

	SPACEMAN	MISSIONS	DAY	HR	MIN	SEC
			TOTAL DURATION OF MISSIONS			
1	Valeri V. Polyakov	2	678	16	33	18
2	Anatoli Y. Solovyov	5	651	00	11	25
3	Musa K. Manarov	2	541	00	29	38
4	Alexander S. Viktorenko	4	489	01	35	17
5	Sergei K. Krikalyov	4#	483	09	37	26
6	Yuri V. Romanenko	3	430	18	21	30
7	Alexander A. Volkov	3	391	11	52	14
8	Vladimir G. Titov	5#	387	00	51	03
9	Vasily V. Tsibliev	2	381	15	53	02
10	Yuri V. Usachyov	2	375	19	34	36

* *To 1 January 1999*

\# *Including flights aboard US Space Shuttles*

All the missions listed were undertaken by the USSR (and, latterly, Russia). The record-holder, Polyakov, gained 241 days' experience as a USSR *Mir* space station astronaut in 1988, and spent his second mission – and the longest-ever residence in space – aboard *Mir* from 8 January 1994 until 26 March 1995. In recent years, a number of US astronauts have added to their space logs by spending time on board the rapidly ageing *Mir*.

Background image: **MIR SPACE STATION**

40

THE 10 ★
FIRST PLANETARY PROBES

PROBE/COUNTRY	PLANET	ARRIVAL*
1 *Venera 4*, USSR	Venus	18 Oct 1967
2 *Venera 5*, USSR	Venus	16 May 1969
3 *Venera 6*, USSR	Venus	17 May 1969
4 *Venera 7*, USSR	Venus	15 Dec 1970
5 *Mariner 9*, USA	Mars	13 Nov 1971
6 *Mars 2*, USSR	Mars	27 Nov 1971
7 *Mars 3*, USSR	Mars	2 Dec 1971
8 *Venera 8*, USSR	Venus	22 Jul 1972
9 *Venera 9*, USSR	Venus	22 Oct 1975
10 *Venera 10*, USSR	Venus	25 Oct 1975

* Successfully entered orbit or landed

This list excludes "fly-bys" – probes that passed by but did not land on the surface of another planet, such as the USA's *Pioneer 10*, which flew past Jupiter on 4 December 1973. *Venera 4* was the first unmanned probe to land on a planet, and *Venera 9* the first to transmit pictures from a planet's surface. *Mariner 9* was the first to orbit another planet; earlier and later *Mariners* are now either in orbit around the Sun or have travelled beyond the Solar System.

THE 10 FIRST PEOPLE TO ORBIT THE EARTH

NAME/SPACECRAFT	COUNTRY OF ORIGIN	DATE
1 **Yuri A. Gagarin**, *Vostok I*	USSR	12 Apr 1961
2 **Gherman S. Titov**, *Vostok II*	USSR	6–7 Aug 1961
3 **John H. Glenn**, *Friendship 7*	USA	20 Feb 1962
4 **M. Scott Carpenter**, *Aurora 7*	USA	24 May 1962
5 **Andrian G. Nikolayev**, *Vostok III*	USSR	11–15 Aug 1962
6 **Pavel R. Popovich**, *Vostok IV*	USSR	12–15 Aug 1962
7 **Walter M. Schirra**, *Sigma 7*	USA	3 Oct 1962
8 **L. Gordon Cooper**, *Faith 7*	USA	15–16 May 1963
9 **Valeri F. Bykovsky**, *Vostok V*	USSR	14–19 Jun 1963
10 **Valentina V. Tereshkova**, *Vostok VI*	USSR	16–19 Jun 1963

Yuri Gagarin, at the age of 27, orbited the Earth once, taking 1 hour 48 minutes. Titov, the youngest-ever astronaut at 25 years 329 days, performed 17 orbits during 25 hours. The first American to orbit the Earth, John Glenn, is the oldest on this list at 40; he has since gone on to become the oldest astronaut of all time. Bykovsky spent the longest time in space – 119 hours – and Tereshkova was the first woman in space. Among early pioneering flights, neither Alan Shepard (5 May 1961, *Freedom 7*) nor Gus Grissom (21 July 1961, *Liberty Bell 7*) actually orbited, achieving altitudes of only 185 km/115 miles and 190 km/118 miles respectively, neither flight lasted longer than 15 minutes.

THE 10 ★
FIRST SPACEMEN AND WOMEN TO CELEBRATE BIRTHDAYS IN SPACE

SPACEMAN/WOMAN	AGE	BIRTHDAY
1 Viktor I. Patsayev	38	19 Jun 1971
2 Charles Conrad	43	2 Jun 1973
3 William R. Pogue	44	23 Jan 1974
4 Vitali I. Sevastyanov	40	8 Jul 1975
5 Pyotr I. Klimuk	33	10 Jul 1975
6 Alexandr S. Ivanchenkov	38	28 Sep 1978
7 Vladimir A. Lyakhov	38	20 Jul 1979
8 Valeri V. Ryumin	40	16 Aug 1979
9 Valeri V. Ryumin	41	16 Aug 1980
10 Leonid I. Popov	35	31 Aug 1980

THE 10 FIRST ANIMALS IN SPACE
(Name/animal/ country/date)

SPACE DOGS
On 19 August 1960, these four-legged cosmonauts from the USSR, Belka and Strelka, were the first animals to return safely after orbiting the Earth.

❶ **Laika**, dog, USSR, 3 Nov 1957
❷ = **Laska** and **Benjy**, mice, USA, 13 Dec 1958
❹ = **Able**, female rhesus monkey, and **Baker**, female squirrel monkey, USA, 28 May 1959
❻ = **Otvazhnaya**, female Samoyed husky, and an unnamed rabbit, USSR, 2 Jul 1959
❽ **Sam**, male rhesus monkey, USA, 4 Dec 1959 ❾ **Miss Sam**, female rhesus monkey, USA, 21 Jan 1960 ❿ = **Belka** and **Strelka**, female Samoyed huskies, USSR, 19 Aug 1960

Which planet has the longest years in the Solar System?
see p.37 for the answer
A Pluto
B Uranus
C Mars

WATERWORLD

HIGHEST WATERFALLS

	WATERFALL	LOCATION	TOTAL DROP M	FT
1	Angel	Venezuela	979	3,212*
2	Tugela	South Africa	947	3,107
3	Utigård	Norway	800	2,625
4	Mongefossen	Norway	774	2,540
5	Yosemite	California	739	2,425
6	Østre Mardøla Foss	Norway	656	2,152
7	Tyssestrengane	Norway	646	2,120
8	Cuquenán	Venezuela	610	2,000
9	Sutherland	New Zealand	580	1,904
10	Kjellfossen	Norway	561	1,841

* Longest single drop 807 m/2,648 ft

MIGHTY FALLS

The cascades of the Yosemite Falls can be viewed from all over Yosemite Valley. They are best seen in late spring, when the creek that forms them is at its fullest. By September they have often dried up.

COUNTRIES WITH THE GREATEST AREAS OF INLAND WATER

	COUNTRY	PERCENTAGE OF TOTAL AREA	WATER AREA SQ KM	SQ MILES
1	Canada	7.60	755,170	291,573
2	India	9.56	314,400	121,391
3	China	2.82	270,550	104,460
4	USA	2.20	206,010	79,541
5	Ethiopia	9.89	120,900	46,680
6	Colombia	8.80	100,210	38,691
7	Indonesia	4.88	93,000	35,908
8	Russia	0.47	79,400	30,657
9	Australia	0.90	68,920	26,610
10	Tanzania	6.25	59,050	22,799

Large areas of some countries are occupied by major rivers and lakes. Lake Victoria, for example, raises the water area of Uganda to 15.39 per cent of its total. In Europe, three Scandinavian countries have considerable percentages of water: Sweden 8.68 per cent, Finland 9.36 per cent, and Norway 5.05 per cent.

DEEPEST OCEANS AND SEAS

	OCEAN OR SEA	GREATEST DEPTH M	FT	AVERAGE DEPTH M	FT
1	Pacific Ocean	10,924	35,837	4,028	13,215
2	Indian Ocean	7,455	24,460	3,963	13,002
3	Atlantic Ocean	9,219	30,246	3,926	12,880
4	Caribbean Sea	6,946	22,788	2,647	8,685
5	South China Sea	5,016	16,456	1,652	5,419
6	Bering Sea	4,773	15,659	1,547	5,075
7	Gulf of Mexico	3,787	12,425	1,486	4,874
8	Mediterranean Sea	4,632	15,197	1,429	4,688
9	Japan Sea	3,742	12,276	1,350	4,429
10	Arctic Ocean	5,625	18,456	1,205	3,953

The deepest point in the deepest ocean is the Marianas Trench in the Pacific at a depth of 10,924 m/35,837 ft, according to a recent survey, although the slightly lesser depth of 10,916 m/35,814 ft was recorded on 23 January 1960 by Jacques Piccard and Donald Walsh in their 17.7-m/58-ft long bathyscaphe *Trieste 2* during the deepest ever ocean descent. The Pacific is so vast that it contains more water than all the world's other seas put together.

LONGEST RIVERS

	RIVER	LOCATION	LENGTH KM	MILES
1	Nile	Tanzania/Uganda/Sudan/Egypt	6,670	4,145
2	Amazon	Peru/Brazil	6,448	4,007
3	Yangtze–Kiang	China	6,300	3,915
4	Mississippi–Missouri–Red Rock	USA	5,971	3,710
5	Yenisey–Angara–Selenga	Mongolia/Russia	5,540	3,442
6	Huang Ho (Yellow River)	China	5,464	3,395
7	Ob'–Irtysh	Mongolia/Kazakhstan/Russia	5,410	3,362
8	Congo	Angola/Dem. Rep. of Congo	4,700	2,920
9	Lena–Kirenga	Russia	4,400	2,734
10	Mekong	Tibet/China/Myanmar (Burma)/Laos/Cambodia/Vietnam	4,350	2,703

FROZEN NORTH

The island of Novaya Zemlya in the Russian Arctic is almost entirely covered by ice. The main Novaya Zemlya Glacier subdivides into smaller ones, including the Brounov Glacier at Mack's Bay, shown here.

Did You Know? The eight deepest ocean trenches would be deep enough to submerge Mount Everest, which is 8,846 m/29,022 ft above sea level.

TOP 10 ★
LARGEST LAKES IN THE UK

LAKE	LOCATION	APPROX. AREA SQ KM	SQ MILES
1 Lough Neagh	N. Ireland	381.74	147.39
2 Lower Lough Erne	N. Ireland	105.08	40.57
3 Loch Lomond	Scotland	71.22	27.50
4 Loch Ness	Scotland	56.64	21.87
5 Loch Awe	Scotland	38.72	14.95
6 Upper Loch Erne	N. Ireland	31.73	12.25
7 Loch Maree	Scotland	28.49	11.00
8 Loch Morar	Scotland	26.68	10.30
9 Loch Tay	Scotland	26.39	10.19
10 Loch Shin	Scotland	22.53	8.70

TOP 10 ★
LARGEST FRESHWATER LAKES IN THE US*

LAKE	LOCATION	APPROX. AREA SQ KM	SQ MILES
1 Michigan	Illinois/Indiana/ Michigan/Wisconsin	58,016	22,400
2 Iliamna	Alaska	2,590	1,000
3 Okeechobee	Florida	1,813	700
4 Becharof	Alaska	1,186	458
5 Red	Minnesota	1,168	451
6 Teshepuk	Alaska	816	315
7 Naknek	Alaska	627	242
8 Winnebago	Wisconsin	557	215
9 Mille Lacs	Minnesota	536	207
10 Flathead	Montana	510	197

* Excluding those partly in Canada

TOP 10 ★
DEEPEST FRESHWATER LAKES

LAKE	LOCATION	GREATEST DEPTH M	FT
1 Baikal	Russia	1,637	5,371
2 Tanganyika	Burundi/ Tanzania/Dem. Rep. of Congo/Zambia	1,471	4,825
3 Malawi	Malawi/ Mozambique/Tanzania	706	2,316
4 Great Slave	Canada	614	2,015
5 Matana	Celebes, Indonesia	590	1,936
6 Crater	Oregon, USA	589	1,932
7 Toba	Sumatra, Indonesia	529	1,736
8 Hornindals	Norway	514	1,686
9 Sarez	Tajikistan	505	1,657
10 Tahoe	California/ Nevada, USA	501	1,645

TOP 10 ★
DEEPEST DEEP-SEA TRENCHES

TRENCH/OCEAN	DEEPEST POINT M	FT
1 Marianas, Pacific	10,924	35,837
2 Tonga*, Pacific	10,800	35,430
3 Philippine, Pacific	10,497	34,436
4 Kermadec*, Pacific	10,047	32,960
5 Bonin, Pacific	9,994	32,786
6 New Britain, Pacific	9,940	32,609
7 Kuril, Pacific	9,750	31,985
8 Izu, Pacific	9,695	31,805
9 Puerto Rico, Atlantic	8,605	28,229
10 Yap, Pacific	8,527	27,973

*Some authorities consider these parts of one feature

TOP 10 ★
LARGEST LAKES

LAKE	LOCATION	APPROX. AREA SQ KM	SQ MILES
1 Caspian Sea	Azerbaijan/ Iran/Kazakhstan/ Russia/Turkmenistan	371,000	143,205
2 Superior	Canada/USA	82,413	31,820
3 Victoria	Kenya/ Tanzania/Uganda	68,800	26,570
4 Huron	Canada/USA	59,596	23,010
5 Michigan	USA	58,016	22,400
6 Aral Sea	Kazakhstan/ Uzbekistan	40,000	15,444
7 Tanganyika	Burundi/ Tanzania/Dem. Rep. of Congo/Zambia	32,900	13,860
8 Great Bear	Canada	31,150	12,030
9 Baikal	Russia	30,500	11,775
10 Great Slave	Canada	28,570	11,03ß0

TOP 10 ★
LONGEST GLACIERS

GLACIER	LOCATION	LENGTH KM	MILES
1 Lambert-Fisher	Antarctica	515	320
2 Novaya Zemlya	Russia	418	260
3 Arctic Institute	Antarctica	362	225
4 Nimrod-Lennox-King	Antarctica	290	180
5 Denman	Antarctica	241	150
6 =Beardmore	Antarctica	225	140
=Recovery	Antarctica	225	140
8 Petermanns	Greenland	200	124
9 Unnamed	Antarctica	193	120
10 Slessor	Antarctica	185	115

ISLANDS OF THE WORLD

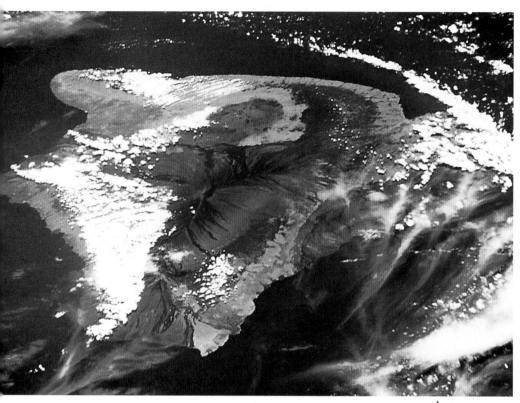

HAWAII

This infrared image from Space Shuttle Columbia shows Hawaii's forested areas (dark red), cultivated land (lighter red and pink), vegetated volcanic summits (green-grey), and recent lava flows (black).

LARGEST ISLANDS IN THE US

ISLAND/LOCATION	AREA SQ KM	AREA SQ MILES
1 **Hawaii**	10,456	4,037
2 **Kodiak**, Alaska	9,510	3,672
3 **Puerto Rico**	8,959	3,459
4 **Prince of Wales**, Alaska	6,700	2,587
5 **Chicagof**, Alaska	5,400	2,085
6 **Saint Lawrence**, Alaska	4,430	1,710
7 **Admiralty**, Alaska	4,270	1,649
8 **Nunivak**, Alaska	4,210	1,625
9 **Unimak**, Alaska	4,160	1,606
10 **Baranof**, Alaska	4,140	1,598

Long Island, New York (3,630 sq km/1,396 sq miles) falls just outside the Top 10.

LARGEST ISLANDS

ISLAND/LOCATION	APPROX. AREA* SQ KM	SQ MILES
1 **Greenland**	2,175,600	840,070
2 **New Guinea**, Papua New Guinea/Indonesia	789,900	312,190
3 **Borneo**, Indonesia/ Malaysia/Brunei	751,000	289,961
4 **Madagascar**	587,041	226,674
5 **Baffin Island**, Canada	507,451	195,926
6 **Sumatra**, Indonesia	422,200	163,011
7 **Honshu**, Japan	230,092	88,839
8 **Great Britain**	218,041	84,186
9 **Victoria Island**, Canada	217,290	83,896
10 **Ellesmere Island**, Canada	196,236	75,767

* Mainlands, including areas of inland water, but excluding offshore islands

Australia is regarded as a continental land mass rather than an island; otherwise it would rank first, at 7,618,493 sq km/2,941,517 sq miles, or 35 times the size of Great Britain.

LARGEST ISLANDS IN EUROPE

ISLAND/LOCATION	AREA SQ KM	SQ MILES
1 **Great Britain**, North Atlantic	218,041	84,186
2 **Iceland**, North Atlantic	103,000	39,769
3 **Ireland**, North Atlantic	83,766	32,342
4 **West Spitsbergen**, Arctic Ocean	39,368	15,200
5 **Sicily**, Mediterranean Sea	25,400	9,807
6 **Sardinia**, Mediterranean Sea	23,800	9,189
7 **North East Land**, Barents Sea	15,000	5,792
8 **Cyprus**, Mediterranean Sea	9,251	3,572
9 **Corsica**, Mediterranean Sea	8,720	3,367
10 **Crete**, Mediterranean Sea	8,260	3,189

LARGEST ISLANDS IN THE UK

ISLAND/LOCATION	POPULATION	AREA SQ KM	SQ MILES
1 **Lewis and Harris**, Outer Hebrides	23,390	2,225.30	859.19
2 **Skye**, Inner Hebrides	8,139	1,666.08	643.27
3 **Mainland**, Shetland	22,184	967.00	373.36
4 **Mull**, Inner Hebrides	2,605	899.25	347.20
5 **Ynys Môn** (Anglesey), Wales	69,800	713.80	275.60
6 **Islay**, Inner Hebrides	3,997	638.79	246.64
7 **Isle of Man**, England	69,788	571.66	220.72
8 **Mainland**, Orkney	14,299	536.10	206.99
9 **Arran**, Inner Hebrides	4,726	435.32	168.08
10 **Isle of Wight**, England	126,600	380.99	147.10

Did You Know? The smallest island with country status is Pitcairn in Polynesia, at just 4,53 sq km/1.75 sq miles.

TOP 10 ★
MOST DENSELY POPULATED ISLANDS*

	ISLAND/LOCATION	AREA SQ KM	AREA SQ MILES	POPULATION#	POPULATION PER SQ KM	POPULATION PER SQ MILE
1	**Manhattan**, New York	57	22	1,487,536	26,316	67,615
2	**Salsette**, India	637	246	13,000,000	20,408	52,846
3	**Hong Kong**, China	75	29	1,330,000	17,733	45,862
4	**Singapore**	543	210	3,476,000	6,317	16,552
5	**Montreal Island**, Canada	521	201	1,800,000	3,455	8,955
6	**Long Island**, New York, USA	3,630	1,402	6,840,000	1,884	4,879
7	**Dakhin Shahbazbur**, Bangladesh	1,590	614	1,700,000	1,069	2,769
8	**Okinawa**, Japan	1,220	471	1,200,000	984	2,548
9	**Java**, Indonesia	129,000	49,807	109,000,000	845	2,188
10	**Sardinia**, Italy	2,380	919	1,640,000	689	1,785

* Includes only islands with populations of more than 1 million
 # Latest available year
Source: *United Nations*

TOP 10 ★
MOST DENSELY POPULATED ISLAND COUNTRIES

	ISLAND	AREA SQ KM	AREA SQ MILES	POPULATION*	POPULATION PER SQ KM	POPULATION PER SQ MILES
1	**Malta**	316	122	382,000	1,209	3,131
2	**Bermuda**	53	21	63,000	1,189	3,000
3	**Maldives**	298	115	310,000	1,040	2,695
4	**Bahrain**	694	268	642,000	925	2,395
5	**Mauritius**	1,865	720	1,194,000	640	1,658
6	**Taiwan**	35,742	13,800	22,214,000	622	1,609
7	**Barbados**	430	166	260,000	605	1,566
8	**Tuvalu**	25	10	11,000	440	1,100
9	**Marshall Islands**	181	70	68,000	376	971
10	**Japan**	372,801	143,939	126,582,000	340	879

* Estimated for the year 2000
Source: *United Nations*

TOP 10 HIGHEST ISLANDS
(Island/location/highest elevation in m/ft)

1 **New Guinea**, Papua New Guinea/Indonesia, 5,030/16,503
2 **Akutan**, Alaska, USA, 4,275/14,026 **3** **Borneo**, Indonesia/Malaysia/Brunei, 4,175/13,698 **4** **Hawaii**, USA, 4,205/13,796 **5** **Formosa**, China, 3,997/13,114 **6** **Sumatra**, Indonesia, 3,804/12,480 **7** **Ross**, Antarctica, 3,794/12,448 **8** **Honshu**, Japan, 3,776/12,388 **9** **South Island**, New Zealand, 3,764/12,349 **10** **Lombok**, Lesser Sunda Islands, Indonesia, 3,726/12,224

Source: *United Nations*

TOP 10 ★
LARGEST VOLCANIC ISLANDS

	ISLAND/LOCATION	TYPE	AREA SQ KM	AREA SQ MILES
1	**Sumatra**, Indonesia	Active volcanic	443,065.8	171,068.7
2	**Honshu**, Japan	Volcanic	225,800.3	87,182.0
3	**Java**, Indonesia	Volcanic	138,793.6	53,588.5
4	**North Island**, New Zealand	Volcanic	111,582.8	43,082.4
5	**Luzon**, Philippines	Active volcanic	109,964.9	42,457.7
6	**Iceland**	Active volcanic	101,826.0	39,315.2
7	**Mindanao**, Philippines	Active volcanic	97,530.0	37,656.5
8	**Hokkaido**, Japan	Active volcanic	78,719.4	30,394.7
9	**New Britain**, Papua New Guinea	High volcanic	35,144.6	13,569.4
10	**Halmahera**, Indonesia	Active volcanic	18,039.6	6,965.1

Source: *United Nations*

BAY OF ISLANDS
The North Island of New Zealand has several active volcanoes. One of New Zealand's biggest lakes, Lake Taupo, lies in a volcanic crater.

Background image: **THE ISLANDS OF JAPAN**

THE FACE OF THE EARTH

TOP 10 ★

HIGHEST MOUNTAINS

MOUNTAIN/LOCATION	HEIGHT* M	FT
1 Everest, Nepal/Tibet	8,846	29,022
2 K2, Kashmir/China	8,611	28,250
3 Kangchenjunga, Nepal/Sikkim	8,598	28,208
4 Lhotse, Nepal/Tibet	8,501	27,890
5 Makalu I, Nepal/Tibet	8,470	27,790
6 Dhaulagiri I, Nepal	8,172	26,810
7 Manaslu I, Nepal	8,156	26,760
8 Cho Oyu, Nepal	8,153	26,750
9 Nanga Parbat, Kashmir	8,126	26,660
10 Annapurna I, Nepal	8,078	26,504

* Height of principal peak; lower peaks of the same mountain are excluded

Dhaulagiri was once believed to be the tallest mountain until Kangchenjunga was surveyed and declared to be even higher. Everest later topped them all when its height was computed.

THE HIGHEST HEIGHTS

Mount Everest was named in 1865 as a tribute to Sir George Everest, the Surveyor General of India who led the 19th-century Great Trigonometrical Survey of India that was to accord Everest its No. 1 position.

TOP 10 ★

DEEPEST DEPRESSIONS

DEPRESSION/LOCATION	MAXIMUM DEPTH BELOW SEA LEVEL M	FT
1 Dead Sea, Israel/Jordan	400	1,312
2 Turfan Depression, China	154	505
3 Qattâra Depression, Egypt	133	436
4 Poluostrov Mangyshlak, Kazakhstan	132	433
5 Danakil Depression, Ethiopia	117	383
6 Death Valley, USA	86	282
7 Salton Sink, USA	72	235
8 Zapadny Chink Ustyurta, Kazakhstan	70	230
9 Prikaspiyskaya Nizmennost', Kazakhstan/Russia	67	220
10 Ozera Sarykamysh, Turkmenistan/Uzbekistan	45	148

The shore of the Dead Sea is the lowest exposed ground below sea level, but the bed of the sea actually reaches 728 m/2,388 ft below sea level. Much of Antarctica is also below sea level.

TOP 10 ★

LONGEST CAVES

CAVE/LOCATION	TOTAL KNOWN LENGTH KM	MILES
1 Mammoth cave system, Kentucky, USA	567	352
2 Optimisticeskaja, Ukraine	201	125
3 Jewel Cave, South Dakota, USA	174	108
4 Hölloch, Switzerland	166	103
5 Lechuguilla Cave, New Mexico, USA	161	100
6 Siebenhengsteholen-system, Switzerland	140	87
7= Fisher Ridge cave system, Kentucky, USA	126	78
= Wind Cave, South Dakota, USA	126	78
9 Ozernay, Ukraine	111	69
10 Gua Air Jernih, Malaysia	109	68

Source: Tony Waltham, BCRA, 1999

TOP 10 ★

DEEPEST CAVES

CAVE SYSTEM/ LOCATION	DEPTH M	FT
1 Lampreschtsofen, Austria	1,632	5,354
2 Gouffre Mirolda, France	1,610	5,282
3 Réseau Jean Bernard, France	1,602	5,256
4 Shakta Pantjukhina, Georgia	1,508	4,948
5 Sistema Huautla, Mexico	1,475	4,839
6 Sistema del Trave, Spain	1,444	4,737
7 Boj Bulok, Uzbekistan	1,415	4,642
8 Puerto di Illamina, Spain	1,408	4,619
9 Lukina Jama, Croatia	1,392	4,567
10 Sistema Cheve, Mexico	1,386	4,547

Which is the highest island in the world?
see p.45 for the answer
A New Guinea
B Hawaii
C Sumatra

TOP 10 ★
HIGHEST ACTIVE VOLCANOES

	VOLCANO	LOCATION	LATEST ACTIVITY	HEIGHT M	FT
1	Guallatiri	Chile	1987	6,060	19,882
2	Lááscar	Chile	1991	5,990	19,652
3	Cotopaxi	Ecuador	1975	5,897	19,347
4	Tupungatito	Chile	1986	5,640	18,504
5	Popocatépetl	Mexico	1995	5,452	17,887
6	Ruiz	Colombia	1992	5,400	17,716
7	Sangay	Ecuador	1988	5,230	17,159
8	Guagua Pichincha	Ecuador	1988	4,784	15,696
9	Purace	Colombia	1977	4,755	15,601
10	Kliuchevskoi	Russia	1995	4,750	15,584

This list includes all volcanoes that have been active at some time during the 20th century. The tallest currently active volcano in Europe is Mt. Etna, Sicily (3,311 m/10,855 ft), which was responsible for numerous deaths in earlier times. Although still active, Etna's last major eruption took place on 11 March 1669 when the lava flow engulfed the town of Catania.

TOP 10 ★
EUROPEAN COUNTRIES WITH THE HIGHEST ELEVATIONS*

	COUNTRY	PEAK	HEIGHT M	FT
1 =	France	Mont Blanc#	4,807	15,771
=	Italy	Monte Bianco#	4,807	15,771
3 =	Switzerland	Dufour#	4,630	15,200
=	Italy	Monte Rosa#	4,630	15,200
5	Austria	Grossglockner	3,797	12,457
6	Spain	Pico del Tiede+	3,716	12,192
7	Germany	Zugspitze	2,962	9,718
8	Andorra	Coma Pedrosa	2.949	9,675
9	Bulgaria	Musala	2,925	9,596
10	Greece	Mount Olympus	2,917	9,568

* Excuding the Caucasus Mountains which border Europe and Asia

Mont Blanc/Monte Bianco and Dufour/Monte Rosa are two peaks on country borders with different national names

+ Highest peak in Canaries; highest on mainland is Mulhacén, 3,478 m/11,411 ft

SAHARAN WILDERNESS

Contrary to its popular image of endless stretches of sand, 80 per cent of the Sahara is in fact composed of smooth rock and rubble. The average annual rainfall here is a mere 15–18 cm/6–7 in.

Background image: **A NASA COMPUTER-GENERATED TOPOGRAPHIC IMAGE OF THE CONTINENTS OF THE EARTH, WITH THE VEGETATION OF THE EARTH SUPERIMPOSED ON IT**

TOP 10 ★
COUNTRIES WITH THE HIGHEST ELEVATIONS*

	COUNTRY	PEAK	HEIGHT M	FT
1	Nepal#	Everest	8,846	29,022
2	Pakistan	K2	8,611	28,250
3	India	Kangchenjunga	8,598	28,208
4	Bhutan	Khula Kangri	7,554	24,784
5	Tajikistan	Mt Garmo (formerly Kommunizma)	7,495	24,590
6	Afghanistan	Noshaq	7,499	24,581
7	Kyrgystan	Pik Pobedy	7,439	24,406
8	Kazakhstan	Khan Tengri	6,995	22,949
9	Argentina	Cerro Aconcagua	6,960	22,834
10	Chile	Ojos del Salado	6,885	22,588

* Based on the tallest peak in each country

Everest straddles Nepal and Tibet, which, now known as Xizang, is a province of China

TOP 10 ★
LARGEST DESERTS

	DESERT	LOCATION	APPROX. AREA SQ KM	SQ MILES
1	Sahara	North Africa	9,000,000	3,500,000
2	Australian	Australia	3,800,000	1,470,000
3	Arabian	Southwest Asia	1,300,000	502,000
4	Gobi	Central Asia	1,036,000	400,000
5	Kalahari	Southern Africa	520,000	201,000
6	Turkestan	Central Asia	450,000	174,000
7	Takla Makan	China	327,000	125,000
8 =	Namib	Southwest Africa	310,000	120,000
=	Sonoran	USA/Mexico	310,000	120,000
10 =	Somali	Somalia	260,000	100,000
=	Thar	Northwest India/Pakistan	260,000	100,000

TOP 10 DEGREES OF HARDNESS*
(Mohs Scale no./substance)

1 Talc **2** Gypsum **3** Calcite **4** Fluorite **5** Apatite **6** Orthoclase

7 Quartz **8** Topaz **9** Corundum **10** Diamond

* According to the Mohs Scale in which No. 1 is the softest mineral and No. 10 is the hardest

TOP 10 ★
MOST VALUABLE TRADED METALLIC ELEMENTS

ELEMENT*	PRICE PER KG ($)
1 Rhodium	28,300
2 Osmium	12,860
3 Iridium	12,541
4 Platinum	11,673
5 Palladium	11,271
6 Gold	9,170
7 Rhenium	1,400
8 Ruthenium	1,254
9 Germanium	1,100
10 Gallium	450

* Based on 10–100 kg quantities of minimum 99.9 per cent purity; excluding radioactive elements, isotopes, and rare earth elements traded in minute quantities

Source: *London Metal Bulletin/Lippman Walton & Co.*

The price of traded metals varies enormously according to their rarity, changes in industrial uses, fashion, and popularity as investments. The price of market-leader rhodium has increased by some 66 per cent in a year. Rhenium, which is used in aero engines, has also risen in price.

RUSSIAN WEALTH
Today platinum is used in oil refining and in reducing car exhaust pollution, but in times past it was used for coinage in several countries, including Russia.

TOP 10 ★
PRINCIPAL COMPONENTS OF AIR

COMPONENT	VOLUME PER CENT
1 Nitrogen	78.110
2 Oxygen	20.953
3 Argon	0.934
4 Carbon dioxide	0.01–0.10
5 Neon	0.001818
6 Helium	0.000524
7 Methane	0.0002
8 Krypton	0.000114
9 = Hydrogen	0.00005
= Nitrous oxide	0.00005

TOP 10 ★
MOST COMMON ELEMENTS IN THE UNIVERSE

ELEMENT	PARTS PER 1,000,000
1 Hydrogen	739,000
2 Helium	240,000
3 Oxygen	10,700
4 Carbon	4,600
5 Neon	1,340
6 Iron	1,090
7 Nitrogen	970
8 Silicon	650
9 Magnesium	580
10 Sulphur	440

TOP 10 ★
MOST EXTRACTED NON-METALLIC ELEMENTS

ELEMENT	ESTIMATED ANNUAL EXTRACTION (TONNES)
1 Hydrogen	350,000,000,000
2 Carbon*	16,200,000,000
3 Phosphorus	5,700,000,000
4 Chlorine	168,000,000
5 Sulphur	54,000,000
6 Nitrogen	44,000,000
7 Oxygen	10,000,000
8 Silicon#	3,885,000
9 Boron	1,000,000
10 Argon	700,000

* Carbon, natural gas, oil, and coal
 # Various forms

TOP 10 ★
METALLIC ELEMENTS WITH THE GREATEST RESERVES

ELEMENT	ESTIMATED GLOBAL RESERVES (TONNES)
1 Iron	110,000,000,000
2 Magnesium	20,000,000,000
3 Potassium	10,000,000,000
4 Aluminium	6,000,000,000
5 Manganese	3,600,000,000
6 Zirconium	>1,000,000,000
7 Chromium	1,000,000,000
8 Barium	450,000,000
9 Titanium	440,000,000
10 Copper	310,000,000

This list includes accessible reserves of commercially mined metallic elements, but excludes two, calcium and sodium, that exist in such vast quantities that their reserves are considered "unlimited" and unquantifiable. In contrast, there are relatively small amounts of certain precious metals: the world's silver reserves are put at 1,000,000 tonnes, mercury at 590,000 tonnes, and gold at 15,000 tonnes.

Did You Know? The metallic element gallium is used in LEDs (light-emitting diodes), its compounds creating the colours seen on computer screens.

TOP 10 ★

MOST EXTRACTED METALLIC ELEMENTS

	ELEMENT	ESTIMATED ANNUAL EXTRACTION (TONNES)
1	Iron	716,000,000
2	Aluminium	15,000,000
3	Copper	6,540,000
4	Manganese	6,220,000
5	Zinc	5,020,000
6	Lead	2,800,000
7	Nickel	510,000
8	Magnesium	325,000
9	Sodium	200,000
10	Tin	165,000

Certain metallic minerals are extracted in relatively small quantities, whereas compounds containing these elements are major industries: contrasting with 200,000 tonnes of metallic sodium, 168 million tonnes of salt are extracted annually; metallic calcium is represented by about 2,000 tonnes, contrasting with some 112 million tonnes of lime (calcium carbonate), and 200 tonnes of the metal potassium contrast with 51 million tonnes of potassium salts.

IRON MINING

Iron (right) has been mined in Britain since c.750BC and is still present in vast reserves. A tough metal that is easy to work, it can be cast, forged, machined, rolled, and alloyed.

TOP 10 ★

LIGHTEST ELEMENTS*

	ELEMENT	DISCOVERER/COUNTRY	YEAR DISCOVERED	DENSITY#
1	Lithium	J.A. Arfvedson, Sweden	1817	0.533
2	Potassium	Sir Humphry Davy, UK	1807	0.859
3	Sodium	Sir Humphry Davy	1807	0.969
4	Calcium	Sir Humphry Davy	1808	1.526
5	Rubidium	R.W. Bunsen/G. Kirchoff, Germany	1861	1.534
6	Magnesium	Sir Humphry Davy	1808[+]	1.737
7	Phosphorus	Hennig Brandt, Germany	1669	1.825
8	Beryllium	F. Wöhler, Germany/ A.A.B. Bussy, France	1828[★]	1.846
9	Caesium	R.W. Bunsen/G. Kirchoff	1860	1.896
10	Sulphur	–	Prehistoric	2.070

* Solids only   # Grams per cu cm at 20°C   + Recognized by Joseph Black, 1755, but not isolated   ★ Recognized by Nicholas Vauquelin, 1797, but not isolated

TOP 10 ★

HEAVIEST ELEMENTS

	ELEMENT	DISCOVERER/COUNTRY	YEAR DISCOVERED	DENSITY*
1	Osmium	S. Tennant, UK	1804	22.59
2	Iridium	S. Tennant	1804	22.56
3	Platinum	J.C. Scaliger#, Italy/France	1557	21.45
4	Rhenium	W. Noddack et al., Germany	1925	21.01
5	Neptunium	Edwin M. McMillan/ Philip H. Abelson, USA	1940	20.47
6	Plutonium	G.T. Seaborg et al., USA	1940	20.26
7	Gold	– Prehistoric		19.29
8	Tungsten	J.J. and F. Elhuijar, Spain	1783	19.26
9	Uranium	M.J. Klaproth, Germany	1789	19.05
10	Tantalum	A.G. Ekeberg, Sweden	1802	16.67

* Grams per cu cm at 20°C
 # Earliest reference to this element

WORLD WEATHER

TWIN TEMPERATURES

A hygrometer is used to measure the moisture content of a gas. The type most often used to gauge air humidity is the dry- and wet-bulb psychrometer.

TOP 10 ★
HOTTEST INHABITED PLACES

WEATHER STATION/LOCATION	AVERAGE TEMPERATURE °C	°F
1 Djibouti, Djibouti	30.0	86.0
2 =Timbuktu, Mali	29.3	84.7
=Tirunelevi, India	29.3	84.7
=Tuticorin, India	29.3	84.7
5 =Nellore, India	29.2	84.6
=Santa Marta, Colombia	29.2	84.6
7 =Aden, South Yemen	28.9	84.0
=Madurai, India	28.9	84.0
=Niamey, Niger	28.9	84.0
10 =Hudaydah, North Yemen	28.8	83.8
=Ouagadougou, Burkina Faso	28.8	83.8
=Thanjavur, India	28.8	83.8
=Tiruchirapalli, India	28.8	83.8

TOP 10 ★
COLDEST INHABITED PLACES

WEATHER STATION/LOCATION	AVERAGE TEMPERATURE °C	°F
1 Norilsk, Russia	−10.9	12.4
2 Yakutsk, Russia	−10.1	13.8
3 Yellowknife, Canada	−5.4	22.3
4 Ulan-Bator, Mongolia	−4.5	23.9
5 Fairbanks, Alaska, USA	−3.4	25.9
6 Surgut, Russia	−3.1	26.4
7 Chita, Russia	−2.7	27.1
8 Nizhnevartovsk, Russia	−2.6	27.3
9 Hailar, Mongolia	−2.4	27.7
10 Bratsk, Russia	−2.2	28.0

TOP 10 ★
WARMEST PLACES IN GREAT BRITAIN

WEATHER STATION/LOCATION	AVERAGE ANNUAL TEMPERATURE* °C	°F
1 St. Mary's, Isles of Scilly	11.5	52.7
2 Penzance, Cornwall	11.1	52.0
3 Ilfracombe, Devon	11.0	51.8
4 =Central London	10.9	51.6
=Southampton, Hampshire	10.9	51.6
=Southsea (Portsmouth), Hampshire	10.9	51.6
=Torbay and Teignmouth, Devon	10.9	51.6
8 =Herne Bay, Kent	10.8	51.4
=Lizard, Cornwall	10.8	51.4
=Ryde and Sandown, Isle of Wight	10.8	51.4

* Based on The Meteorological Office's 30-year averages for the period 1961–90

TOP 10 ★
HOTTEST YEARS IN THE UK

YEAR	AVERAGE TEMPERATURE* °C	°F
1 1990	10.63	51.13
2 1949	10.62	51.12
3 =1995	10.55	50.99
=1997	10.55	50.99
5 1989	10.50	50.90
6 1959	10.48	50.86
7 =1733	10.47	50.85
=1834	10.47	50.85
=1921	10.47	50.85
10 1779	10.40	50.72

* Since 1659, based on Central England averages

TOP 10 ★
COLDEST PLACES IN GREAT BRITAIN

WEATHER STATION/LOCATION	AVERAGE ANNUAL TEMPERATURE* °C	°F
1 Dalwhinnie, Highland	6.0	42.8
2 =Leadhills, Highland	6.3	43.3
=Braemar, Aberdeenshire	6.3	43.3
=Balmoral, Aberdeenshire	6.3	43.3
5 Tomatin, Highland	6.4	43.5
6 Grantown-on-Spey, Highland	6.5	43.7
7 Lagganlia, nr. Kingraig, Highland	6.6	43.9
8 Crawfordjohn, Lanarkshire	6.7	44.1
9 Eskdalemuir, Dumfries and Galloway	6.8	44.2
10 Lerwick, Shetland	6.9	44.4

* Based on The Meteorological Office's 30-year averages for the period 1961–90

TOP 10 ★
COLDEST YEARS IN THE UK

YEAR	AVERAGE TEMPERATURE* °C	°F
1 1740	6.86	44.35
2 1695	7.29	45.12
3 1879	7.44	45.39
4 =1694	7.67	45.81
=1698	7.67	45.81
6 1692	7.73	45.91
7 1814	7.78	46.00
8 1784	7.85	46.13
9 1688	7.86	46.15
10 1675	7.88	46.18

* Since 1659, based on Central England averages

Which is the longest river in the world?
see p.42 for the answer
A Nile
B Mississippi
C Amazon

TOP 10 ★
DRIEST INHABITED PLACES

WEATHER STATION/LOCATION	AVERAGE ANNUAL RAINFALL MM	IN
1 **Aswan**, Egypt	0.5	0.02
2 **Luxor**, Egypt	0.7	0.03
3 **Arica**, Chile	1.1	0.04
4 **Ica**, Peru	2.3	0.09
5 **Antofagasta**, Chile	4.9	0.19
6 **Minya**, Egypt	5.1	0.20
7 **Asyut**, Egypt	5.2	0.21
8 **Callao**, Peru	12.0	0.47
9 **Trujilo**, Peru	14.0	0.54
10 **Fayyum**, Egypt	19.0	0.75

The total annual rainfall of the Top 10 inhabited places, as recorded over extensive periods, is just 64.8 mm/2½ in – the average length of an adult little finger.

TOP 10 ★
WETTEST INHABITED PLACES

WEATHER STATION/LOCATION	AVERAGE ANNUAL RAINFALL MM	IN
1 **Buenaventura**, Colombia	6,743	265.47
2 **Monrovia**, Liberia	5,131	202.01
3 **Pago Pago**, American Samoa	4,990	196.46
4 **Moulmein**, Myanmar	4,852	191.02
5 **Lae**, Papua New Guinea	4,645	182.87
6 **Baguio**, Luzon Island, Philippines	4,573	180.04
7 **Sylhet**, Bangladesh	4,457	175.47
8 **Conakry**, Guinea	4,341	170.91
9 = **Padang**, Sumatra Island, Indonesia	4,225	166.34
= **Bogor**, Java, Indonesia	4,225	166.34

The total annual rainfall of the Top 10 locations is equivalent to more than 26 adults, each measuring 1.83 m/6 ft, standing on top of each other.

TOP 10 ★
WETTEST PLACES IN GREAT BRITAIN

WEATHER STATION/LOCATION	AVERAGE ANNUAL RAINFALL* MM	IN
1 **Dalness**, Glen Etive, Highland	3,306	130.16
2 **Seathwaite**, nr. Borrowdale, Cumbria	3,150	124.02
3 **Glenfinnan**, Loch Shiel, Highland	3,022	118.98
4 **Inverarnan**, Loch Lomond, Stirling	2,701	106.34
5 **Inveruglas**, Loch Lomond, Argyll and Bute	2,662	104.80
6 **Capel Curig**, Gwynedd	2,555	100.59
7 **Wythburn**, Lake Thirlmere, Cumbria	2,535	99.80
8 = **Tyndrum and Crianlarich**, Stirling	2,500	98.43
= **Chapel Stile**, Cumbria	2,500	98.43
10 **Lochgoilhead**, Argyll and Bute	2,464	97.01

* Based on the Meteorological Office's 30-year averages for the period 1961–90

These figures are for the wettest inhabited places (villages and towns) in Great Britain. It should be noted, however, that some uninhabited places in the mountainous parts of Scotland, North Wales, and Cumbria are wetter than those in the Top 10, with annual average rainfall in excess of 3,500 mm/137.8 in.

TOP 10 ★
DRIEST PLACES IN GREAT BRITAIN

WEATHER STATION/LOCATION	AVERAGE ANNUAL RAINFALL* MM	IN
1 **St. Osyth**, Essex	507	19.96
2 **Shoeburyness and Southend-on-Sea**, Essex	509	20.04
3 **Burnham-on-Crouch**, Essex	518	20.39
4 = **Languard Point**, Suffolk	524	20.63
= **Peterborough**, Cambridgeshire	524	20.63
6 **Ely**, Cambridgeshire	526	20.71
7 = **Tilbury and Grays area**, Essex	530	20.87
= **Thamesmead**, East London	530	20.87
9 **Huntingdon**, Cambridgeshire	531	20.91
10 **Walton-on-the-Naze**, Essex	534	21.02

* Based on the Meteorological Office's 30-year averages for the period 1961–90

PREPARING FOR STORMY WEATHER

A monsoon is a strong seasonal wind that occurs mostly in South Asia, the tropics, and sub-tropics, bringing with it heavy rain. This picture shows a young child in the Philippines taking cover under a huge leaf.

NATURAL DISASTERS

WORST EPIDEMICS OF ALL TIME

	EPIDEMIC	LOCATION	DATE	ESTIMATED NO. KILLED
1	Black Death	Europe/Asia	1347–51	75,000,000
2	Influenza	Worldwide	1918–20	21,640,000
3	Plague	India	1896–1948	12,000,000
4	AIDS	Worldwide	1981–	6,400,000
5	Typhus	Eastern Europe	1914–15	3,000,000
6 =	"Plague of Justinian"	Europe/Asia	541–90	millions*
=	Cholera	Worldwide	1846–60	millions*
=	Cholera	Europe	1826–37	millions*
=	Cholera	Worldwide	1893–94	millions*
10	Smallpox	Mexico	1530–45	>1,000,000

* No precise figures available

WORST AVALANCHES AND LANDSLIDES OF THE 20TH CENTURY*

	LOCATION	INCIDENT	DATE	ESTIMATED NO. KILLED
1	Yungay, Peru	Landslide	31 May 1970	17,500
2	Italian Alps	Avalanche	13 Dec 1916	10,000
3	Huarás, Peru	Avalanche	13 Dec 1941	5,000
4	Nevada Huascaran, Peru	Avalanche	10 Jan 1962	3,500
5	Medellin, Colombia	Landslide	27 Sep 1987	683
6	Chungar, Peru	Avalanche	19 Mar 1971	600
7	Rio de Janeiro, Brazil	Landslide	11 Jan 1966	550
8 =	Northern Assam, India	Landslide	15 Feb 1949	500
=	Grand Riviere du Nord, Haiti	Landslide	13/14 Nov 1963	500
10	Blons, Austria	Avalanche	11 Jan 1954	411

* Excluding those where most deaths resulted from flooding, earthquakes, etc., associated with landslides

WORST FLOODS AND STORMS OF THE 20TH CENTURY

	LOCATION	DATE	ESTIMATED NO. KILLED
1	Huang He River, China	Aug 1931	3,700,000
2	Bangladesh	13 Nov 1970	300–500,000
3	Henan, China	Sep 1939	over 200,000
4	Chang Jiang River, China	Sep 1911	100,000
5	Bengal, India	15–16 Nov 1942	40,000
6	Bangladesh	1–2 Jun 1965	30,000
7	Bangladesh	28–29 May 1963	22,000
8	Bangladesh	11–12 May 1965	17,000
9	Morvi, India	11 Aug 1979	5–15,000
10 =	Hong Kong	18 Sep 1906	10,000
=	Bangladesh	25 May 1985	10,000

BANGLADESHI FLOODS

The summer monsoon rains vital for watering the crops can so easily bring disaster, causing devastating floods that wash away people and buildings alike.

Background image: A T-LYMPHOCYTE BLOOD CELL (GREEN) INFECTED WITH THE HIV VIRUS (RED), WHICH CAUSES AIDS

WORST EARTHQUAKES OF THE 20TH CENTURY

	LOCATION	DATE	ESTIMATED NO. KILLED
1	Tang-shan, China	28 Jul 1976	242,419
2	Nan-Shan, China	22 May 1927	200,000
3	Kansu, China	16 Dec 1920	180,000
4	Messina, Italy	28 Dec 1908	160,000
5	Tokyo/Yokohama, Japan	1 Sep 1923	142,807
6	Kansu, China	25 Dec 1932	70,000
7	Yungay, Peru	31 May 1970	66,800
8	Quetta, India*	30 May 1935	50–60,000
9	Armenia	7 Dec 1988	over 55,000
10	Iran	21 Jun 1990	over 40,000

* Now Pakistan

DEVASTATED YOKOHAMA

The worst earthquake ever to hit Japan levelled towns and cities for hundreds of miles around the epicentre of Tokyo, leaving millions homeless.

WORST TSUNAMIS OF THE 20TH CENTURY

	LOCATIONS AFFECTED	DATE	ESTIMATED NO. KILLED
1	Agadir, Morocco*	29 Feb 1960	12,000
2	Papua New Guinea	18 Jul 1998	8,000
3=	Philippines	17 Aug 1976	5,000
=	Chile/Pacific islands/Japan	22 May 1960	5,000
5	Japan/Hawaii	2 Mar 1933	3,000
6	Japan*	21 Dec 1946	1,088
7	Kii, Japan	4 Dec 1944	998
8	Lomblem Island, Indonesia	18 Jul 1979	539
9	Hawaii/Aleutians/California	1 Apr 1946	173
10	Colombia/Ecuador*	12 Dec 1979	133

* Combined effect of earthquake and tsunamis

Tsunamis are powerful waves caused by undersea earthquakes or volcanic eruptions.

WORST VOLCANIC ERUPTIONS OF ALL TIME

LOCATION/DATE/INCIDENT	EST. NO. KILLED
1 Tambora, Indonesia, 5–12 Apr 1815	92,000

The eruption on the island of Sumbawa killed about 10,000 islanders immediately, with a further 82,000 dying subsequently from disease and famine.

2 Miyi-Yama, Java, 1793	53,000

The volcano dominating the island of Kiousiou erupted, engulfing all the local villages in mudslides and killing most of the rural population.

3 Mont Pelée, Martinique, 8 May 1902	40,000

After lying dormant for centuries, Mont Pelée began to erupt in April 1902.

4 Krakatoa, Sumatra/Java, 26–27 Aug 1883	36,380

Krakatoa exploded with what may have been the biggest bang ever heard by humans, audible up to 4,800 km/3,000 miles away.

5 Nevado del Ruiz, Colombia, 13 Nov 1985	22,940

The hot steam, rocks, and ash ejected from Nevado del Ruiz melted its icecap, resulting in a mudslide that completely engulfed the town of Armero.

LOCATION/DATE/INCIDENT	EST. NO. KILLED
6 Mt. Etna, Sicily, 11 Mar 1669	over 20,000

Europe's largest volcano has erupted frequently, but the worst instance occurred in 1669, when the lava flow engulfed the town of Catania.

7 Laki, Iceland, Jan–Jun 1783	20,000

Many villages were engulfed in a river of lava up to 80 km/50 miles long and 30 m/100 ft deep, releasing poisonous gases that killed those who escaped. This was the largest ever recorded lava flow.

8 Vesuvius, Italy, 24 Aug 79	16–20,000

The Roman city of Herculaneum was engulfed by a mud flow while Pompeii was buried under a vast and preserving layer of pumice and volcanic ash.

9 Vesuvius, Italy, 16–17 Dec 1631	up to 18,000

Lava and mudflows gushed down onto the surrounding towns, including Naples.

10 Mt. Etna, Sicily, 1169	over 15,000

Large numbers died in Catania cathedral where they believed they would be safe, and more were killed when a tidal wave caused by the eruption hit the port of Messina.

Did You Know? The eruption of Tambora in 1815 sent 1,700,000 tons of ash into the atmosphere, blocking out the sunlight and affecting the weather. The resulting brilliantly coloured sunsets are captured in J.M.W. Turner's paintings of the period.

LIFE ON EARTH

EXTINCT & ENDANGERED

MOST ENDANGERED BIG CATS*

1 Amur leopard
2 Anatolian leopard
3 Asiatic cheetah
4 Eastern puma
5 Florida cougar
6 North African leopard
7 Siberian tiger
8 South Arabian leopard
9 South China tiger
10 Sumatran tiger

In alphabetical order

Source: *International Union for the Conservation of Nature*

All 10 of these big cats are classed by the International Union for Conservation of Nature as being "critically endangered", that is, facing an extremely high risk of extinction in the wild in the immediate future.

MOST ENDANGERED MAMMALS

MAMMAL	ESTIMATED NO.
1 =Tasmanian wolf	?
=Halcon fruit bat	?
=Ghana fat mouse	?
4 Javan rhinoceros	50
5 Iriomote cat	60
6 Black lion tamarin	130
7 Pygmy hog	150
8 Kouprey	100–200
9 Tamaraw	200
10 Indus dolphin	400

The first three mammals on the list have not been seen for many years and may well be extinct.

RAREST MARINE MAMMALS

MAMMAL	ESTIMATED NO.
1 Caribbean monk seal	200
2 Mediterranean monk seal	400
3 Juan Fernandez fur seal	750
4 West Indian manatee	1,000
5 Guadeloupe fur seal	1,600
6 New Zealand fur seal	2,000
7 =Hooker's sea lion	4,000
=Right whale	4,000
9 Fraser's dolphin	7,800
10 Amazon manatee	8,000

The hunting of seals for their fur and of whales for oil and other products has resulted in a sharp fall in the population of many marine mammals.

TIGER IN DANGER

Of all the endangered big cats listed here, tigers are particularly under threat: there may be as few as 500 Siberian tigers, 400 Sumatran tigers, and only 20 to 30 South China tigers left in the world.

MOST ENDANGERED SPIDERS

SPIDER	COUNTRY
1 Kauai cave wolf spider	USA
2 Doloff cave spider	USA
3 Empire cave pseudoscorpion	USA
4 Glacier Bay wolf spider	USA
5 Great raft spider	Europe
6 Kocevje subterranean spider (*Troglohyphantes gracilis*)	Slovenia
7 Kocevje subterranean spider (*Troglohyphantes similis*)	Slovenia
8 Kocevje subterranean spider (*Troglohyphantes spinipes*)	Slovenia
9 Lake Placid funnel wolf spider	USA
10 Melones cave harvestman	USA

Source: *International Union for the Conservation of Nature*

The first spider on this list is considered by the IUCN as "endangered" (facing a very high risk of extinction in the wild in the near future), and the others as "vulnerable" (facing a high risk of extinction in the wild in the medium-term future).

COUNTRIES WITH THE MOST ELEPHANTS

COUNTRY	ESTIMATED NO.*
1 Tanzania	73,459
2 Dem. Rep. of Congo	65,974
3 Botswana	62,998
4 Gabon	61,794
5 Zimbabwe	56,297
6 Rep. of the Congo	32,563
7 India	20,000
8 Zambia	19,701
9 Kenya	13,834
10 South Africa	9,990

* *The difficulty of surveying animals in the wild means that the data are not always precise.*

The elephant has been associated with humans for thousands of years, used for hunting, in warfare, for transport, and in the logging industry.

Background image: A 26-M/85-FT **SKELETON OF A DIPLODOCUS**

TOP 10 ★
LARGEST DINOSAURS EVER DISCOVERED

DINOSAUR/DESCRIPTION	LENGTH/EST. WEIGHT

1 Seismosaurus — 30–36 m/98–119 ft/ 50–80 tonnes

A skeleton of this colossal plant-eater was excavated in 1985 near Albuquerque, New Mexico, by US palaeontologist David Gillette and given a name that means "earth-shaking lizard". It is currently being studied by the New Mexico Museum of Natural History, which may confirm its position as the largest dinosaur yet discovered, with some claiming a length of up to 52 m/170 ft.

2 Supersaurus — 24–30 m/80–98 ft/50 tonnes

The remains of Supersaurus were found in Colorado in 1972. Some scientists have suggested a length of up to 42 m/138 ft and a weight of 75–100 tonnes for this massive dinosaur.

3 Antarctosaurus — 18–30 m/60–98 ft/ 40–50 tonnes

Named Antarctosaurus ("southern lizard") by German palaeontologist Friedrich von Huene in 1929, this creature's thigh bone alone measures 2.3 m/ 7 ft 6 in. Some authorities have put its weight as high as 80 tonnes.

4 Barosaurus — 23–27.5 m/75–90 ft/uncertain

Barosaurus (meaning "heavy lizard", so named by US palaeontologist Othniel C. Marsh in 1890) has been found in both North America and Africa, thus proving the existence of a land link in Jurassic times (205–140 million years ago).

5 Mamenchisaurus — 27 m/89 ft/uncertain

An almost complete skeleton discovered in 1972 showed that Mamenchisaurus had the longest neck of any known animal, comprising more than half its total body length – perhaps up to 15 m/49 ft. It was named by Chinese palaeontologist Yang Zhong-Jian (known in palaeontological circles as "C.C. Young") after the place in China where it was found.

6 Diplodocus — 23–27 m/75–89 ft/12 tonnes

As it was long and thin, Diplodocus was a relative lightweight in the dinosaur world. It was also probably one of the most stupid dinosaurs, having the smallest brain in relation to its body size. Diplodocus was given its name (which means "double beam") in 1878 by Othniel C. Marsh.

7 Ultrasauros — Over 25 m/82 ft/50 tonnes

Ultrasauros was discovered by US palaeontologist James A. Jensen in Colorado in 1979 but has not yet been fully studied. Some authorities have claimed its weight as an unlikely 100–140 tonnes. It was originally called Ultrasaurus ("ultra lizard"), which was a name also given to another, smaller dinosaur; to avoid confusion its spelling has been altered.

8 Brachiosaurus — 25 m/82 ft/50 tonnes

Its name (given to it in 1903 by US palaeontologist Elmer S. Riggs) means "arm lizard". Some palaeontologists have put the weight of Brachiosaurus as high as 190 tonnes, but this seems improbable (if not impossible), in the light of theories of the maximum possible weight of terrestrial animals.

9 Pelorosaurus — 24 m/80 ft/uncertain

The first fragments of Pelorosaurus (meaning "monstrous lizard") were found in Sussex and named by British doctor and geologist Gideon Algernon Mantell as early as 1850.

10 Apatosaurus — 20–21 m/66–70 ft/ 20–30 tonnes

Apatosaurus (its name, coined by Othniel C. Marsh, means "deceptive lizard") is better known by its former name of Brontosaurus ("thunder lizard"). The bones of the first one ever found, in Colorado in 1879, caused great confusion for many years because its discoverer attached a head from a different species to the rest of the skeleton.

This Top 10 is based on the most reliable recent evidence of their lengths and indicates the probable ranges; as more and more information is assembled, these are undergoing constant revision. Lengths have often been estimated from only a few surviving fossilized bones, and there is much dispute even among experts about these and even more about the weights of most dinosaurs. Some, such as Diplodocus, had squat bodies but extended necks, which made them extremely long but not necessarily very heavy.

Everyone's favourite dinosaur, Tyrannosaurus rex ("tyrant lizard"), does not appear in the Top 10 list because although it was one of the fiercest flesh-eating dinosaurs, it was not as large as many of the herbivorous ones. However, measuring a probable 12 m/39 ft and weighing more than 6 tonnes, it certainly ranks as one of the largest flesh-eating animals yet discovered. Bones of an earlier dinosaur called Epanterias were found in Colorado in 1877 and 1934, but incorrectly identified until recently, when studies suggested that this creature was possibly larger than Tyrannosaurus.

To compare these sizes with living animals, note that the largest recorded crocodile measured 6.2 m/ 20 ft 4 in and the largest elephant 10.7 m/35 ft.

WAITING FOR A MATE

This captive-bred female Spix's macaw, Cyanopsitta spixxi, awaits release into the wild, where it will meet the last surviving male Spix's macaw.

TOP 10 COUNTRIES WITH THE MOST THREATENED SPECIES

(Country/species)

1 USA, 854 **2** Australia, 483 **3** Indonesia, 340 **4** Mexico, 247 **5** Brazil, 240 **6** China, 213 **7** South Africa, 205 **8** India, 193 **9** Philippines, 188 **10** = Japan, 132; = Tanzania, 132

Source: *International Union for the Conservation of Nature*

TOP 10 ★
RAREST BIRDS

BIRD/COUNTRY	ESTIMATED NO.*
1 =Spix's macaw, Brazil	1
=Cebu flower pecker, Philippines	1
3 Hawaiian crow, Hawaii	5
4 Black stilt, New Zealand	12
5 Echo parakeet, Mauritius	13
6 Imperial Amazon parrot, Dominica	15
7 Magpie robin, Seychelles	20
8 Kakapo, New Zealand	24
9 Pink pigeon, Mauritius	70
10 Mauritius kestrel, Mauritius	100

* *Of breeding pairs reported since 1986*

Several rare bird species are known from old records or from only one specimen, but must be assumed to be extinct in absence of recent sightings or records of breeding pairs. Rare birds come under most pressure on islands like Mauritius, where the dodo met its fate.

DEADLIEST SNAKES

SNAKE	MAXIMUM DEATHS PER BITE	MORTALITY RATE RANGE (PER CENT)
1 Black Mamba	200	75–100
2 Forest cobra	50	70–95
3 Russell's viper	150	40–92
4 Taipan	26	10–90
5 Common krait	60	70–80

SNAKE	MAXIMUM DEATHS PER BITE	MORTALITY RATE RANGE (PER CENT)
6 Jararacussa	100	60–80
7 Terciopelo	40	Not known
8 Egyptian cobra	35	50
9 Indian cobra	40	30–35
10 Jararaca	30	25–35

HEAVIEST CARNIVORES

CARNIVORE	LENGTH M	FT	WEIGHT KG	LB
1 Southern elephant seal	6.5	21	3,500	7,716
2 Walrus	3.8	12	1,200	2,646
3 Steller sea lion	3	9	1,100	2,425
4 Grizzly bear	3	9	780	1,720
5 Polar bear	2.6	8	600	1,323
6 Tiger	2.8	9	300	661
7 Lion	1.9	6	250	551
8 American black bear	1.8	6	227	500
9 Giant panda	1.5	5	160	353
10 Spectacled bear	1.8	6	140	309

Of the 273 mammal species in the order *Carnivora* or meat-eaters, many (including its largest representatives on land, the bears) are in fact omnivorous and around 40 specialize in eating fish or insects. All, however, share a common ancestry indicated by the butcher's-knife form of their canine teeth. As the Top 10 would otherwise consist exclusively of seals and related marine carnivores, only three have been included in order to enable the terrestrial heavyweight division to make an appearance. The polar bear is probably the largest land carnivore if shoulder height (when the animal is on all fours) is taken into account: it tops an awesome 1.6 m/5.3 ft, compared with the 1.2 m/4 ft of its nearest rival, the grizzly. The common weasel is probably the smallest carnivore at less than 17 cm/7 in long, not counting the tail.

KING OF THE JUNGLE

Second in size to the tiger in the cat family, the lion weighs in at an impressive 250 kg/551 lb. Lions sleep for 12 hours a day, and can run at 80 km/h/50 mph.

TOP 10 MAMMALS WITH THE SHORTEST GESTATION PERIODS

(Mammal/average gestation in days)

1 Short-nosed bandicoot, 12
2 Opossum, 13   3 Shrew, 14
4 Golden hamster, 16   5 Lemming, 20
6 Mouse, 21   7 Rat, 22   8 Gerbil, 24
9 Rabbit, 30   10 Mole, 38

TOP 10 MAMMALS WITH THE LONGEST GESTATION PERIODS

(Mammal/average gestation in days)

1 African elephant, 660   2 Asiatic elephant, 600   3 Baird's beaked whale, 520   4 White rhinoceros, 490
5 Walrus, 480   6 Giraffe, 460   7 Tapir, 400   8 Arabian camel (dromedary), 390
9 Fin whale, 370   10 Llama, 360

MOST VENOMOUS CREATURES

CREATURE*	TOXIN	FATAL AMOUNT MG#
1 Indian cobra	Peak V	0.009
2 Mamba	Toxin 1	0.02
3 Brown snake	Texilotoxin	0.05
4 =Inland taipan	Paradotoxin	0.10
=Mamba	Dendrotoxin	0.10
6 Taipan	Taipoxin	0.11
7 =Indian cobra	Peak X	0.12
=Poison arrow frog	Batrachotoxin	0.12
9 Indian cobra	Peak 1X	0.17
10 Krait	Bungarotoxin	0.50

* Excluding bacteria
\# Quantity required to kill one average-sized human adult

The venom of these creatures is almost unbelievably powerful: 1 milligram of Mamba Toxin 1 would be sufficient to kill 50 people. Such creatures as scorpions (0.5 mg) and black widow spiders (1.0 mg) fall just outside the Top 10.

Did You Know? Howler monkeys are the noisiest land animals. Their call can be heard over 3 km (2 miles) away.

TOP 10 MOST INTELLIGENT MAMMALS

1 Man **2** Chimpanzee **3** Gorilla **4** Orang-utan **5** Baboon **6** Gibbon
7 Monkey **8** Smaller toothed whale **9** Dolphin **10** Elephant

TOP 10 ★
HEAVIEST TERRESTRIAL MAMMALS

MAMMAL	LENGTH		WEIGHT	
	M	FT	KG	LB
1 African elephant	7.3	24	7,000	14,432
2 White rhinoceros	4.2	14	3,600	7,937
3 Hippopotamus	4.0	13	2,500	5,512
4 Giraffe	5.8	19	1,600	3,527
5 American bison	3.9	13	1,000	2,205
6 Arabian camel (dromedary)	3.5	12	690	1,521
7 Polar bear	2.6	8	600	1,323
8 Moose	3.0	10	550	1,213
9 Siberian tiger	3.3	11	300	661
10 Gorilla	2.0	7	220	485

The list excludes domesticated cattle and horses. It also avoids comparing close kin such as the African and Indian elephants, highlighting instead the sumo stars within distinctive large mammal groups such as the bears, deer, big cats, primates, and bovines (ox-like mammals). Sizes are not necessarily the top of the known range.

AFRICAN GIANTS

At a length of 7.3 m/24 ft and weighing 7,000 kg/ 14, 432 lb, the African elephant is by far the largest and heaviest of all the terrestrial mammals.

TOP 10 ★
MOST COMMON MAMMALS IN THE UK

MAMMAL	ESTIMATED NO.
1 Common rat	76,790,000
2 House mouse	75,192,000
3 Field vole	75,000,000
4 Common shrew	41,700,000
5 Wood mouse	38,000,000
6 Rabbit	37,500,000
7 Mole	31,000,000
8 Bank vole	23,000,000
9 Pygmy shrew	8,600,000
10 Grey squirrel	2,520,000

The populations of only the first three mammals listed exceed the human population of the UK, so purists may argue that Man should be at No. 4.

TOP 10 SLEEPIEST ANIMALS*

(Animal/average hours of sleep per day)

1 Koala, 22 **2** Sloth, 20
3 = Armadillo, 19; = Opossum, 19
5 Lemur, 16 **6** = Hamster, 14;
= Squirrel, 14 **8** = Cat, 13; = Pig, 13
10 Spiny anteater, 12

* Excluding periods of hibernation

CLEVER CHIMP

Based on research conducted by Edward O. Wilson, Professor of Zoology at Harvard University, to assess speed and extent of learning performance over a wide range of tasks, the chimp ranks second in the world.

TOP 10 ★
HEAVIEST PRIMATES

PRIMATE	LENGTH*		WEIGHT	
	CM	IN	KG	LB
1 Gorilla	200	79	220	485
2 Man	177	70	77	170
3 Orang-utan	137	54	75	165
4 Chimpanzee	92	36	50	110
5 =Baboon	100	39	45	99
=Mandrill	95	37	45	99
7 Gelada baboon	75	30	25	55
8 Proboscis monkey	76	30	24	53
9 Hanuman langur	107	42	20	44
10 Siamung gibbon	90	35	13	29

* Excluding tail

The longer, skinnier, and lighter forms of the langurs, gibbons, and monkeys, designed for serious monkeying around in trees, compare sharply with their heavier great ape cousins.

MARINE ANIMALS

HEAVIEST MARINE MAMMALS

MAMMAL	LENGTH M	FT	WEIGHT TONNES
1 Blue whale	33.5	110.0	130.0
2 Fin whale	25.0	82.0	45.0
3 Right whale	17.5	57.4	40.0
4 Sperm whale	18.0	59.0	36.0
5 Grey whale	14.0	46.0	32.7
6 Humpback whale	15.0	49.2	26.5
7 Baird's whale	5.5	18.0	11.0
8 Southern elephant seal	6.5	21.3	3.6
9 Northern elephant seal	5.8	19.0	3.4
10 Pilot whale	6.4	21.0	2.9

Probably the largest animal that ever lived, the blue whale dwarfs even the other whales listed here, all but one of which far outweigh the biggest land animal, the elephant. Among the mammals that frequent inland waters, the dugong, a type of sea cow, is largest at 907 kg/2,000 lb and 4.1 m/13.5 ft.

TOP 10 FISHING COUNTRIES

(Country/annual catch in tonnes)

- 1 China, 33,166,640
- 2 Peru, 9,521,960
- 3 Chile, 7,590,947
- 4 Japan, 6,758,829
- 5 USA, 5,614,534
- 6 India, 5,260,420
- 7 Indonesia, 4,401,940
- 8 Russia, 4,373,827
- 9 Thailand, 3,647,900
- 10 Norway, 2,807,551

SPECIES OF FISH MOST CAUGHT

SPECIES	TONNES CAUGHT PER ANNUM
1 Anchoveta	11,896,808
2 Alaska pollock	4,298,619
3 Chilean jack mackerel	4,254,629
4 Silver carp	2,333,669
5 Atlantic herring	1,886,105
6 Grass carp	1,821,606
7 South American pilchard	1,793,425
8 Common carp	1,627,198
9 Chubb mackerel	1,507,497
10 Skipjack tuna	1,462,637

Among broader groupings of fish, some 3 million tonnes of shrimps and prawns, and a similar tonnage of squids, cuttlefish, and octopuses, is caught annually.

HEAVIEST SHARKS

SHARK	WEIGHT KG	LB
1 Whale shark	21,000	46,297
2 Basking shark	14,515	32,000
3 Great white shark	3,314	7,300
4 Greenland shark	1,020	2,250
5 Tiger shark	939	2,070
6 Great hammerhead shark	844	1,860
7 Six-gill shark	590	1,300
8 Grey nurse shark	556	1,225
9 Mako shark	544	1,200
10 Thresher shark	500	1,100

As well as specimens that have been caught, estimates have been made of beached examples, but such is the notoriety of sharks that many accounts of their size are exaggerated, and this list should be taken as an approximate ranking based on the best available evidence.

SWIMMERS BEWARE!

The great white shark is not only large, but is also very fast, notching up speeds of 48 km/h/30 mph with ease. Its teeth are a fearsome 12 cm/5 in long.

TOP 10 ★
FASTEST FISH

FISH	RECORDED SPEED KM/H	MPH
1 Sailfish	110	68
2 Marlin	80	50
3 Bluefin tuna	74	46
4 Yellowfin tuna	70	44
5 Blue shark	69	43
6 Wahoo	66	41
7 =Bonefish	64	40
=Swordfish	64	40
9 Tarpon	56	35
10 Tiger shark	53	33

Flying fish have a top speed in the water of only 37 km/h/23 mph, but airborne they can reach 56 km/h/35 mph. Many sharks qualify for the list: only two are listed here to prevent the list becoming overly shark-infested.

TOP 10 ★
HEAVIEST TURTLES

TURTLE	WEIGHT KG	LB
1 Pacific leatherback turtle	865	1,908
2 Atlantic leatherback turtle	454	1,000
3 Green sea turtle	408	900
4 Loggerhead turtle	386	850
5 Alligator snapping turtle	183	403
6 Black sea turtle	126	278
7 Flatback turtle	84	185
8 Hawksbill turtle	68	150
9 = Kemps ridley turtle	50	110
=Olive ridley turtle	50	110

Both the sizes and longevity of turtles remain hotly debated by zoologists, and although the weights on which this Top 10 are ranked are from corroborated sources, there are many claims of even larger specimens of *Chelonia*.

STUPENDOUS TURTLE

This green sea turtle would be dwarfed in size by prehistoric monster turtles such as Stupendemys geographicus, which measured up to 3 m/10 ft in length and weighed over 2,040 kg/4,497 lb.

TOP 10 ★
HEAVIEST SPECIES OF FRESHWATER FISH CAUGHT

SPECIES	ANGLER/LOCATION/DATE	WEIGHT KG	LB	OZ
1 White sturgeon	Joey Pallotta III, Benicia, California, USA, 9 Jul 1983	212.28	468	0
2 Alligator gar	Bill Valverde, Rio Grande, Texas, USA, 2 Dec 1951	126.55	279	0
3 Beluga sturgeon	Merete Lehne, Guryev, Kazakhstan, 3 May 1993	101.97	224	13
4 Nile perch	Adrian Brayshaw, Lake Nasser, Egypt,18 Dec 1997	96.62	213	0
5 Flathead catfish	Ken Paulie, Withlacoochee River, Florida, USA, 14 May 1998	56.05	123	9
6 Blue catfish	William P. McKinley, Wheeler Reservoir, Tennessee, USA, 5 Jul 1996	50.35	111	0
7 Chinook salmon	Les Anderson, Kenai River, Alaska, USA, 17 May 1985	44.11	97	4
8 Giant tigerfish	Raymond Houtmans, Zaire River, Zaire, 9 Jul 1988	44.00	97	0
9 Smallmouth buffalo	Randy Collins, Athens Lake, Arkansas,USA, 6 Jun 1993	37.28	82	3
10 Atlantic salmon	Henrik Henrikson, Tana River, Norway (date unknown) 1928	35.89	79	2

Source: *International Game Fish Association*

TOP 10 ★
HEAVIEST SPECIES OF SALTWATER FISH CAUGHT

SPECIES	ANGLER/LOCATION/DATE	WEIGHT KG	LB	OZ
1 Great white shark	Alfred Dean, Ceduna, South Australia, 21 Apr 1959	1,208.39	2,664	0
2 Tiger shark	Walter Maxwell, Cherry Grove, California, USA, 14 Jun 1964	807.41	1,780	0
3 Greenland shark	Terje Nordtvedt, Trondheimsfjord, Norway, 18 Oct 1987	775.0	1,708	9
4 Black marlin	A.C. Glassell, Jr., Cabo Blanco, Peru, 4 Aug 1953	707.62	1,560	0
5 Bluefin tuna	Ken Fraser, Aulds Cove, Nova Scotia, Canada, 26 Oct 1979	678.59	1,496	0
6 Atlantic blue marlin	Paulo Amorim, Vitoria, Brazil, 29 Feb 1992	635.99	1,402	2
7 Pacific blue marlin	Jay W. de Beaubien, Kaaiwi Point, Kona, 31 May 1982	624.15	1,376	0
8 Swordfish	L. Marron, Iquique, Chile, 7 May 1953	536.16	1,182	0
9 Mako shark	Patrick Guillanton, Black River, Mauritius, 16 Nov 1988	505.76	1,115	0
10 Hammerhead shark	Allen Ogle, Sarasota, Florida, USA, 20 May 1982	449.52	991	0

Source: *International Game Fish Association*

Which country produces most rubber?
see p.70 for the answer
A Malaysia
B Thailand
C Sri Lanka

FLYING ANIMALS

BAT BOMBS

During World War II, the US airforce captured millions of bats. They planned to make them carry tiny bombs, fly into buildings, and explode. Fortunately for the bats, the war ended before the plan could be put into action.

TOP 10 ★
SMALLEST BATS

BAT/HABITAT	WEIGHT		LENGTH	
	G	OZ	CM	IN
1 Kitti's hognosed bat (*Craseonycteris thonglongyai*), Thailand	2.0	0.07	2.9	1.10
2 Proboscis bat (*Rhynchonycteris naso*), Central and South America	2.5	0.09	3.8	1.50
3 =Banana bat (*Pipistrellus nanus*), Africa	3.0	0.11	3.8	1.50
=Smoky bat (*Furiptera horrens*), Central and South America	3.0	0.11	3.8	1.50
5 =Little yellow bat (*Rhogeessa mira*), Central America	3.5	0.12	4.0	1.57
=Lesser bamboo bat (*Tylonycteris pachypus*), Southeast Asia	3.5	0.12	4.0	1.57
7 Disc-winged bat (*Thyroptera tricolor*), Central and South America	4.0	0.14	3.6	1.42
8 Lesser horseshoe bat (*Rhynolophus hipposideros*), Europe and Western Asia	5.0	0.18	3.7	1.46
9 California myotis (*Myotis californienses*), North America	5.0	0.18	4.3	1.69
10 Northern blossom bat (*Macroglossus minimus*), Southeast Asia to Australia	15.0	0.53	6.4	2.52

This list focuses on the smallest example of 10 different bat families. The weights shown are typical, rather than extreme – and as a bat can eat more than half its own weight, the weights of individual examples may vary considerably. The smallest of all weighs less than a table-tennis ball, and even the heaviest listed here weighs less than an empty aluminium drink can. Length is of head and body only, since tail lengths vary from zero (as in Kitti's hognosed bat and the Northern blossom bat) to long (as in the Proboscis bat and Lesser horseshoe bat).

TOP 10 ★
HEAVIEST FLIGHTED BIRDS

BIRD	WINGSPAN		WEIGHT		
	M	FT	KG	LB	OZ
1 Great bustard	2.7	9	20.9	46	1
2 Trumpeter swan	3.4	11	16.8	37	1
3 Mute swan	3.1	10	16.3	35	15
4 =Albatross	3.7	12	15.8	34	13
=Whooper swan	3.1	10	15.8	34	13
6 Manchurian crane	2.1	7	14.9	32	14
7 Kori bustard	2.7	9	13.6	30	0
8 Grey pelican	3.1	10	13.0	28	11
9 Black vulture	3.1	10	12.5	27	8
10 Griffon vulture	2.1	7	12.0	26	7

Wing size does not necessarily correspond to weight in flighted birds. The 4-m/13-ft wingspan of the marabou stork beats all the birds listed here, even the mighty albatross, yet its body weight is normally no heavier than any of these. When laden with a meal of carrion, however, the marabou can double its weight and needs all the lift it can get to take off. It often fails altogether and has to put up with flightlessness until digestion takes its course.

TOP 10 ISLANDS WITH THE MOST ENDEMIC BIRD SPECIES*

(Island/species)

1 New Guinea, 195 **2** Jamaica, 26
3 Cuba, 23 **4** New Caledonia, 20
5 Rennell, Solomon Islands, 15 **6** São Tomé, 14 **7** = Aldabra, Seychelles, 13;
= Grand Cayman, Cayman Islands, 13
9 Puerto Rico, 12 **10** New Britain, Papua New Guinea, 11

* Birds that are found uniquely on these islands.
Source: *United Nations*

LOOKING FOR A MEAL

A native of the southern US states and the American tropics, the Black vulture lives on a diet of carrion.

TOP 10 ★
LARGEST BIRDS IN THE UK

BIRD	BEAK-TO-TAIL LENGTH	
	CM	IN
1= Mute swan	145–160	57–63
=Whooper swan	145–160	57–63
3 Bewick's swan	116–128	46–50
4 Canada goose	up to 110	up to 43
5 Grey heron	90–100	35–39
6 Cormorant	84–98	33–39
7 Gannet	86–96	34–38
8 Golden eagle	76–91	30–36
9 White-tailed sea eagle	69–91	27–36
10 Capercaillie (male)	82–90	32–35

Because of its size, the mute swan (which weighs up to 12 kg/26 lb) needs very strong and long feathers to power its flight: its outer wing feathers can be up to 45 cm/18 in long, but even so each feather weighs only 15 g/0.5 oz. Pheasants sometimes measure 91 cm/36 in, but are not included in this list because more than half their total length is tail.

PURPOSE-BUILT BIRD
The marabou stork's long legs are perfect for wading in water when hunting fish, while its huge wingspan enables effortless long-distance soaring.

TOP 10 ★
BIRDS WITH THE LARGEST WINGSPANS

BIRD	WINGSPAN M	FT
1 Marabou stork	4.0	13
2 Albatross	3.7	12
3 Trumpeter swan	3.4	11
4 =Mute swan	3.1	10
=Whooper swan	3.1	10
=Grey pelican	3.1	10
=Californian condor	3.1	10
=Black vulture	3.1	10
9 =Great bustard	2.7	9
=Kori bustard	2.7	9

TOP 10 ★
FASTEST BIRDS

BIRD	RECORDED SPEED KM/H	MPH
1 Spine-tailed swift	171	106
2 Frigate bird	153	95
3 Spur-winged goose	142	88
4 Red-breasted merganser	129	80
5 White-rumped swift	124	77
6 Canvasback duck	116	72
7 Eider duck	113	70
8 Teal	109	68
9 =Mallard	105	65
=Pintail	105	65

Until early aeroplane pilots cracked 306 km/h/ 190 mph in 1919, birds were the fastest animals on the Earth: stooping (diving) peregrine falcons clock up speeds approaching 298 km/h/185 mph.

TOP 10 ★
MOST COMMON NORTH AMERICAN GARDEN BIRDS

BIRD	PERCENTAGE OF FEEDERS VISITED
1 Dark-eyed junco	83
2 House finch	70
3 =American goldfinch	69
=Downy woodpecker	69
5 Blue jay	67
6 Mourning dove	65
7 Black-capped chickadee	60
8 House sparrow	59
9 Northern cardinal	56
10 European starling	52

Source: *Project FeederWatch/Cornell Lab of Ornithology*

These are the birds that watchers are most likely to see at their feeders in North America.

TOP 10 ★
MOST COMMON BREEDING BIRDS IN THE US

1 Red-winged blackbird
2 House sparrow
3 Mourning dove
4 European starling
5 American robin
6 Horned lark
7 Common grackle
8 American crow
9 Western meadowlark
10 Brown-headed cowbird

Source: *US Fish and Wildlife Service*

This list, based on research carried out by the Breeding Bird Survey of the US Fish and Wildlife Service, ranks birds breeding in the US.

TOP 10 ★
MOST COMMON BIRDS IN THE UK

BIRD	ESTIMATED PAIRS
1 Wren	7,600,000
2 Chaffinch	5,800,000
3 Blackbird	4,700,000
4 Robin	4,500,000
5 House sparrow	3,850,000
6 Blue tit	3,500,000
7 Willow warbler	2,500,000
8 Woodpigeon	2,450,000
9 =Dunnock	2,100,000
=Skylark	2,100,000

Source: *Royal Society for the Protection of Birds*

Which country has more horses than people? *see p.69 for the answer*
A Mongolia
B Ethiopia
C Brazil

DOMESTIC PETS

TOP 10 ★ DOG NAMES IN THE UK

FEMALE		MALE
Trixie	1	Sam
Polly	2	Spot
Jessie	3	Pip
Lucy	4	Duke
Bonnie	5	Piper
Cassie	6	Max
Daisy	7	Charlie
Heidi	8	Rocky
Susie	9	Zak
Holly	10	Tiny

As we have observed in previous editions of this book, a move away from traditional dogs' names occurred during the 1980s, with the demise of perennial (and specifically canine) names such as Shep, Rex, Lassie, and, of course, Rover, and an increasing tendency toward human first names.

TOP 10 ★ MOST INTELLIGENT DOG BREEDS

1	Border collie
2	Poodle
3	German shepherd (Alsatian)
4	Golden retriever
5	Doberman pinscher
6	Shetland sheepdog
7	Labrador retriever
8	Papillon
9	Rottweiler
10	Australian cattle dog

Source: *Stanley Coren, The Intelligence of Dogs (Scribner, 1994)*

American psychology professor and pet trainer Stanley Coren devised a ranking of 133 breeds of dogs after studying their responses to a range of IQ tests, as well as the opinions of judges in dog obedience tests. Dog owners who have criticized the results point out that dogs are bred for specialized abilities, such as speed or ferocity, and obedience to their human masters is only one feature of their "intelligence".

TOP 10 BUDGERIGAR NAMES IN THE UK*

1 Joey 2 Billy 3 Bluey 4 Bobby
5 Snowy 6 Peter 7 Charlie
8 Magic 9 George 10 Tweety

* Based on an RSPCA survey conducted during National Pet Week

SPOT ON

Although not a Top 10 dog for either intelligence or popularity, the Dalmatian, with its distinctive coat and powerful build, is the star of the two highest-rated films starring dogs.

TOP 10 ★ FILMS STARRING DOGS

	FILM	YEAR
1	101 Dalmatians	1996
2	One Hundred and One Dalmatians*	1961
3	Lady and the Tramp*	1955
4	Oliver & Company*	1988
5	Turner & Hooch	1989
6	The Fox and the Hound*	1981
7	Beethoven	1992
8	Homeward Bound II: Lost in San Francisco	1996
9	Beethoven's 2nd	1993
10	K-9	1991

* Animated

Man's best friend has been stealing scenes since the earliest years of film-making, with the 1905 low-budget *Rescued by Rover* outstanding as one of the most successful productions of the pioneer period. The numerous silent era films starring Rin Tin Tin, an ex-German army dog who emigrated to the USA, and his successor Lassie, whose long series of feature and TV films date from the 1940s onwards, are among the most enduring in cinematic history.

TOP 10 ★ DOG BREEDS IN THE UK

	BREED	NO. REGISTERED BY KENNEL CLUB
1	Labrador retriever	35,978
2	German shepherd (Alsatian)	20,953
3	West Highland white terrier	15,131
4	Golden retriever	14,803
5	Cocker spaniel	14,117
6	English springer spaniel	12,741
7	Cavalier King Charles spaniel	12,702
8	Boxer	9,612
9	Yorkshire terrier	8,818
10	Staffordshire bull terrier	8,563

The 10 principal breeds of dogs registered by the Kennel Club in 1998 were identical to those of previous years, and in the same order, with boxers staying as popular (they overtook Yorkshire terriers for the first time in 1997). Independent surveys of dog ownership present a similar picture, though with certain other popular breeds making a stronger showing than in this list.

TOP 10 ★
TYPES OF PET IN THE UK

PET	PERCENTAGE OF HOUSEHOLDS OWNING
1 Dog	23.4
2 Cat	21.4
3 Goldfish	9.3
4 Rabbit	3.9
5 Budgerigar	3.6
6 Hamster	3.2
7 Other bird	2.6
8 Tropical fish	2.4
9 Guinea pig	1.6
10 Canary	0.8

Source: *Pet Food Manufacturers' Association*

Half of the households in the UK own a pet, ranging from dogs, cats, and rabbits to the more exotic snakes and spiders.

TOP 10 ★
PEDIGREE CAT BREEDS IN THE UK

BREED	NO. REGISTERED BY CAT FANCY (1998)
1 Persian long hair	7,815
2 Siamese	4,596
3 British short hair	4,563
4 Burmese	3,190
5 Birman	2,207
6 Bengal	1,503
7 Maine coon	1,390
8 Oriental short hair	1,321
9 Ragdoll	933
10 Exotic short hair	744

This Top 10 is based on a total of 32,327 cats registered with the Governing Council of the Cat Fancy in 1998.

TOP 10 CAT NAMES IN THE UK*

1 Sooty 2 Tigger 3 Tiger 4 Smokey 5 Ginger 6 Tom 7 Fluffy 8 Lucy 9 Sam 10 Lucky

* Based on an RSPCA survey conducted during National Pet Week

TOP 10 STICK INSECT NAMES IN THE UK*

1 Sticky 2 Fred 3 Twiggy 4 Tom 5 George 6 Stick 7 Sam 8 Billy 9 Freddie 10 Charlie

* Based on an RSPCA survey conducted during National Pet Week

TOP 10 GOLDFISH NAMES IN THE UK*

1 Jaws 2 Goldie 3 Fred 4 Tom 5 Bubbles 6 George 7 Flipper 8 Ben 9 Jerry 10 Sam

* Based on an RSPCA survey conducted during National Pet Week

INSECTS & CREEPY-CRAWLIES

DEADLIEST SPIDERS

SPIDER/LOCATION

1 **Banana spider** (*Phonenutria nigriventer*), Central and South America

2 **Sydney funnel web** (*Atrax robusteus*), Australia

3 **Wolf spider** (*Lycosa raptoria/erythrognatha*), Central and South America

4 **Black widow** (*Latrodectus species*), Worldwide

5 **Violin spider/Recluse spider**, Worldwide

6 **Sac spider**, Southern Europe

7 **Tarantula** (*Eurypelma rubropilosum*), Neotropics

8 **Tarantula** (*Acanthoscurria atrox*), Neotropics

9 **Tarantula** (*Lasiodora klugi*), Neotropics

10 **Tarantula** (*Pamphobeteus species*), Neotropics

This list ranks spiders according to their "lethal potential" – their venom yield divided by their venom potency. The Banana spider, for example, yields 6 mg of venom, with 1 mg the estimated lethal dose in man. However, few spiders are capable of killing humans – there were just 14 recorded deaths caused by Black widows in the US in the whole of the 19th century.

LARGEST BUTTERFLIES

BUTTERFLY	WINGSPAN MM	IN
1 Queen Alexandra's birdwing	280	11.0
2 African giant swallowtail	230	9.1
3 Goliath birdwing	210	8.3
4 =*Trogonoptera trojana*	200	7.9
=*Buru opalescent birdwing*	200	7.9
=*Troides hypolitus*	200	7.9
7 =*Ornithoptera lydius*	190	7.5
=*Chimaera birdwing*	190	7.5
=*Troides magellanus*	190	7.5
=*Troides miranda*	190	7.5

KING-SIZED BUTTERFLY

Queen Alexandra's birdwing, the largest butterfly in the world, is a protected species found in southeast Papua New Guinea. The male (shown here) is smaller and more colourful than the female.

LARGEST SNAILS

SNAIL	LENGTH MM	IN
1 Californian sea hare (*Aplysia californica*)	750	30
2 Trumpet or baler conch (*Syrinx aruanus*)	700	28
3 Apple (*Pomacea scalaris*)	500	20
4 =*Dolabella dolabella*	400	15
=Trumpet shell (*Charonia tritorus*)	400	15
6 =African land (*Achatina achatina*)	300	10
=*Aplysia fasciata*	300	10
=*Carinaria mediterranea*	300	10
9 =Green turban (*Turbo marmoratus*)	200	5
=*Tetus niloticus*	200	5

This list includes both marine and land gastropods. Of these, the African land snail (*Achatina achatina*) is the largest land snail. The longest snail in the world is *Parenteroxenos doglieli*, which measures 1,300 mm (50 in) in length but is only 50 mm/2 in in diameter. It lives as a parasite in the body cavity of a sea cucumber.

MOST POPULAR US STATE INSECTS

INSECT/STATES	NO.
1 **Honey bee**, Arkansas, Georgia, Kansas, Louisiana, Maine, Mississippi, Missouri, Nebraska, New Jersey, North Carolina, South Dakota, Utah, Wisconsin	13
2 **Swallowtail butterfly**, Florida (giant), Georgia (tiger), Mississippi (spicebush), Ohio (tiger), Oklahoma (black), Oregon (Oregon), Virginia (tiger), Wyoming (western)	8
3 **Ladybird beetle/ladybug**, Delaware (convergent), Iowa, Massachusetts, New York (nine-spotted), New Hampshire, Ohio, Tennessee (ladybug)	7
4 **Monarch butterfly**, Alabama, Illinois, Texas, Vermont	4
5 **Firefly**, Pennsylvania, Tennessee	2
6 =**Baltimore checkerspot butterfly**, Maryland	1
=**California dogface butterfly**, California	1
=**Carolina mantis**, South Carolina	1
=**Colorado hairstreak butterfly**, Colorado	1
=**European praying mantis**, Connecticut	1
=**Four-spotted skimmer**, Alaska	1
=**Tarantula hawk wasp**, New Mexico	1
=**Viceroy butterfly**, Kentucky	1

Along with birds, trees, flowers, and other state symbols, most US states have officially adopted an insect or butterfly. These are nominated by members of the public.

TOP 10 COUNTRIES WITH THE MOST THREATENED INVERTEBRATES

(Country/threatened invertebrate species)

❶ USA, 594 ❷ Australia, 281 ❸ South Africa, 101 ❹ Portugal, 67 ❺ France, 61 ❻ Spain, 57 ❼ Tanzania, 46 ❽ = Japan, 45; = Dem. Rep. of Congo, 45 ❿ = Austria, 41; = Italy, 41

Source: *International Union for the Conservation of Nature*

Background image: **SPIDER'S WEB COVERED IN DEW**

BIG MOTH STRIKES AGAIN

The unusual shape and colours of the Atlas moth's wings make it quite unique. The largest moth in the world, it is found from Indonesia and Sri Lanka to China and Malaysia.

TOP 10 ★
LARGEST MOTHS

MOTH	WINGSPAN MM	IN
1 **Atlas moth** (*Attacus atlas*)	300	11.8
2 **Owlet moth** (*Thysania agrippina*)*	290	11.4
3 *Haematopis grataria*	260	10.2
4 **Hercules emperor moth** (*Coscinocera hercules*)	210	8.3
5 **Malagasy silk moth** (*Argema mitraei*)	180	7.1
6 *Eacles imperialis*	175	6.9
7= **Common emperor moth** (*Bunaea alcinoe*)	160	6.3
= **Giant peacock moth** (*Saturnia pyri*)	160	6.3
9 **Gray moth** (*Brahmaea wallichii*)	155	6.1
10= **Black witch** (*Ascalapha odorata*)	150	5.9
= **Regal moth** (*Citheronia regalis*)	150	5.9
= **Polyphemus moth** (*Antheraea polyphemus*)	150	5.9

* Exceptional specimen measured at 308 mm/12.2 in

DISTINCT SPHINX

The Verdant sphinx moth takes its name from its incredible green forewings. It is found south of the Sahara desert in Africa.

TOP 10 ★
FASTEST FLYING INSECTS

SPECIES	KM/H	MPH
1 **Hawkmoth** (*Sphingidaei*)	53.6	33.3
2= **West Indian butterfly** (*Nymphalidae prepona*)	48.0	30.0
= **Deer bot fly** (*Cephenemyia pratti*)	48.0	30.0
4 **Deer bot fly** (*Chrysops*)	40.0	25.0
5 **West Indian butterfly** (*Hesperiidae* sp.)	30.0	18.6
6 **Dragonfly** (*Anax parthenope*)	28.6	17.8
7 **Hornet** (*Vespa crabro*)	21.4	13.3
8 **Bumble bee** (*Bombus lapidarius*)	17.9	11.1
9 **Horsefly** (*Tabanus bovinus*)	14.3	8.9
10 **Honey bee** (*Apis millefera*)	11.6	7.2

Few accurate assessments of these speeds have been attempted, and this list reflects only the results of those scientific studies recognized by entomologists.

TOP 10 ★
MOST COMMON INSECTS*

SPECIES	APPROXIMATE NO. OF KNOWN SPECIES
1 **Beetles** (*Coleoptera*)	400,000
2 **Butterflies and moths** (*Lepidoptera*)	165,000
3 **Ants, bees, and wasps** (*Hymenoptera*)	140,000
4 **True flies** (*Diptera*)	120,000
5 **Bugs** (*Hemiptera*)	90,000
6 **Crickets, grasshoppers, and locusts** (*Orthoptera*)	20,000
7 **Caddisflies** (*Trichoptera*)	10,000
8 **Lice** (*Phthiraptera/Psocoptera*)	7,000
9 **Dragonflies and damselflies** (*Odonata*)	5,500
10 **Lacewings** (*Neuroptera*)	4,700

* By number of known species

This list includes only species that have been discovered and named: it is surmised that many thousands of species still await discovery.

TOP 10 CREATURES WITH THE MOST LEGS
(Creature/average. no of legs)

1 *Millipede Illacme plenipes*, 750 **2** *Centipede Himantarum gabrielis*, 354 **3** *Centipede Haplophilus subterraneus*, 86 **4** Millipedes*, 30 **5** Symphylans, 24 **6** Caterpillars*, 16 **7** Woodlice, 14 **8** Crabs, shrimps, 10 **9** Spiders, 8 **10** Insects, 6

* Most species

"Centipede" means "100 feet" and "millipede" "1,000 feet", however, despite their names, centipedes, depending on their species, have anything from 28 to 354 legs, and millipedes up to 400, with the record standing at around 700. The other principal difference between them is that each body segment of a centipede has two legs, whereas that of a millipede has four.

PASSIONATE POSTMAN

This intimidating beast is the caterpillar of a butterfly known as the Postman. It is common from Central America to southern Brazil, and its food of choice is the passion flower.

LIVESTOCK & FOOD CROPS

TOP 10 ★
MILK-PRODUCING COUNTRIES

	COUNTRY	1998 PRODUCTION TONNES*
1	USA	71,260,000
2	India	34,500,000
3	Russia	32,000,000
4	Germany	28,500,000
5	France	24,500,000
6	Brazil	20,213,000
7	UK	14,650,000
8	Ukraine	12,500,000
9	Poland	11,800,000
10	Netherlands	11,400,000
	World total	469,715,952

* Fresh cow's milk

TOP 10 ★
COFFEE-PRODUCING COUNTRIES

	COUNTRY	1998 PRODUCTION TONNES
1	Brazil	1,653,020
2	Colombia	720,000
3	Indonesia	455,119
4	Vietnam	378,000
5	Côte d'Ivoire	332,355
6	Mexico	288,000
7	India	228,000
8	Ethiopia	204,000
9 =	Guatemala	180,000
=	Uganda	180,000
	World total	6,301,923

Source: *Food and Agriculture Organization of the United Nations*

In recent years, there has been a decline in coffee production, from its former world peak of over 6 million tonnes. Kenya, perhaps surprisingly, does not appear in this list as its annual total of 57,000 tonnes places it at No. 21.

TOP 10 ★
RICE-PRODUCING COUNTRIES

	COUNTRY	1998 PRODUCTION TONNES
1	China	192,971,300
2	India	122,244,000
3	Indonesia	46,290,460
4	Bangladesh	28,292,900
5	Vietnam	27,645,800
6	Thailand	21,000,000
7	Myanmar	16,600,000
8	Japan	12,531,000
9	Philippines	10,004,200
10	USA	8,183,000
	World total	571,741,700

Source: *Food and Agriculture Organization of the United Nations*

World production of rice rose dramatically during the twentieth century. It remains the staple diet for a huge proportion of the global population, especially in Asian countries. Relatively small quantities are grown in the US and also in Europe, where Italy is the leading producer with 1,394,500 tonnes.

TOP 10 ★
ORANGE-PRODUCING COUNTRIES

	COUNTRY	1998 PRODUCTION TONNES
1	Brazil	23,020,900
2	USA	12,571,000
3	Mexico	4,005,265
4	China	2,804,222
5	Spain	2,500,000
6	India	2,080,000
7	Italy	1,874,967
8	Iran	1,800,000
9	Egypt	1,570,000
10	Pakistan	1,410,000
	World total	66,332,379

Source: *Food and Agriculture Organization of the United Nations*

TOP 10 ★
WHEAT-PRODUCING COUNTRIES

	COUNTRY	1998 PRODUCTION TONNES
1	China	110,000,200
2	USA	69,604,000
3	India	66,000,000
4	France	39,862,000
5	Russia	24,800,000
6	Canada	23,158,000
7	Australia	21,855,000
8	Turkey	21,000,000
9	Germany	20,073,300
10	Pakistan	19,000,000
	UK	16,300,000
	World total	589,116,126

Source: *Food and Agriculture Organization of the United Nations*

TOP 10 ★
VEGETABLE-PRODUCING COUNTRIES*

	COUNTRY	1998 PRODUCTION TONNES
1	China	237,136,300
2	India	54,967,000
3	USA	34,964,670
4	Turkey	21,196,020
5	Japan	13,613,500
6	Italy	13,580,690
7	Egypt	12,245,480
8	Russia	12,097,500
9	South Korea	10,943,440
10	Spain	10,889,900
	UK	3,277,723
	World total	597,770,256

* Including watermelons; only vegetables grown for human consumption, excluding any crops grown in private gardens

Source: *Food and Agriculture Organization of the United Nations*

Did You Know? There are more pigs than humans in Denmark. A total of 11,081,000 pigs outnumber the 5,215,718 humans by more than two to one!

TOP 10 ★
PIG COUNTRIES

	COUNTRY	PIGS (1998)
1	China	485,698,400
2	USA	60,250,000
3	Brazil	35,900,000
4	Germany	24,782,200
5	Poland	19,240,000
6	Spain	18,155,000
7	Vietnam	18,060,000
8	Russia	16,579,000
9	India	16,005,000
10	Mexico	15,500,000
	UK	7,959,000
	World total	938,944,200

The distribution of the world's pig population is determined by cultural, religious, and dietary factors – few pigs are found in African and Islamic countries, for example – with the result that there is a disproportionate concentration of pigs in those countries that do not have such prohibitions: 74 per cent of the world total is found in the Top 10 countries. Historically, pigs have been considered "unclean" by many because they do not chew the cud, and because they have less-than-fastidious habits such as wallowing in mud and eating almost anything.

TOP TEN WOOL-PRODUCING COUNTRIES*

(Country/tonnes)

1 Australia, 687,000 **2** China, 287,000 **3** New Zealand, 254,000 **4** Uruguay, 81,847 **5** Russia, 70,000 **6** South Africa, 67,000 **7** UK, 65,000 **8** Argentina, 64,000 **9** Iran, 62,700 **10** Pakistan, 57,163

* 1998 production

TOP 10 ★
HORSE COUNTRIES

	COUNTRY	HORSES (1998)
1	China	8,854,800
2	Brazil	6,394,140
3	Mexico	6,250,000
4	USA	6,150,000
5	Argentina	3,300,000
6	Mongolia	2,900,000
7	Ethiopia	2,750,000
8	Colombia	2,450,000
9	Russia	2,200,000
10	Kazakhstan	1,082,700
	UK	172,600
	World total	60,774,795

Mongolia makes an appearance in few Top 10 lists – but here it scores doubly as it is not only the sixth-largest rearer of horses in the world, but also the only country in the world where the horse population is greater than its human population (2,363,000). Throughout the world, and especially in the US where there were once more than 10 million horses, the equine population has steadily declined as they have been replaced by motor vehicles. Horses are still used extensively in agriculture in many developing countries, while in the West they tend to be kept for sport and other recreational purposes.

TOP 10 ★
CATTLE COUNTRIES

	COUNTRY	CATTLE (1998)
1	India	209,084,000
2	Brazil	161,000,000
3	USA	99,501,000
4	China	96,192,530
5	Argentina	50,277,000
6	Russia	31,700,000
7	Ethiopia	29,900,000
8	Colombia	28,261,000
9	Australia	26,330,000
10	Mexico	25,580,000
	UK	11,347,000
	World total	1,303,927,390

Source: *Food and Agriculture Organization of the United Nations*

TOP 10 CAMEL COUNTRIES

(Country/camels, 1998)

1 Somalia, 6,100,000 **2** Sudan, 2,950,000 **3** India, 1,520,000 **4** = Mauritania, 1,100,000; = Pakistan, 1,100,000 **6** Ethiopia, 1,030,000 **7** Kenya, 810,000 **8** Chad, 650,000 **9** Saudi Arabia, 422,000 **10** Niger, 392,000

Source: *Food and Agriculture Organization of the United Nations*

TREES & NON-FOOD CROPS

TOP 10 ★
LARGEST NATIONAL FORESTS IN THE US

	FOREST	LOCATION	AREA SQ KM	SQ MILES
1	Tongass National Forest	Sitka, Alaska	67,177	25,937
2	Chugach National Forest	Anchorage, Alaska	21,448	8,281
3	Toiyabe National Forest	Sparks, Nevada	12,950	5,000
4	Tonto National Forest	Phoenix, Arizona	11,735	4,531
5=	Boise National Forest	Boise, Idaho	10,925	4,218
=	Gila National Forest	Silver City, New Mexico	10,925	4,218
7=	Humboldt National Forest	Elko, Nevada	10,116	3,906
=	Challis National Forest	Challis, Idaho	10,116	3,906
9=	Shoshone National Forest	Cody, Wyoming	9,712	3,750
=	Flathead National Forest	Kalispell, Montana	9,712	3,750

The list's No. 1 is actually larger than all 10 of the smallest states in the United States and the District of Columbia. Even the much smaller No. 2 is larger than Connecticut, while the two at the bottom of the list cover an area similar to that of Delaware and Rhode Island combined.

TOP 10 ★
NON-FOOD CROPS

	CROP	1998 PRODUCTION TONNES
1	Cotton	18,169,714
2	Tobacco	6,937,024
3	Rubber	6,780,089
4	Jute	2,850,535
5	Castor beans	1,190,122
6	Coir	649,890
7	Flax	641,155
8	Sisal	332,454
9	Kapok	123,215
10	Hops	116,818

Source: *Food and Agriculture Organization of the United Nations*

COTTON PICKING

In a "snowy" field in Queensland, Australia, cotton is being harvested. As the No. 1 non-food crop in the world, cotton is used mainly for clothing; world production reaches a massive 19,560,000 tonnes.

TOP 10 ★
RUBBER-PRODUCING COUNTRIES

	COUNTRY	1998 PRODUCTION TONNES
1	Thailand	2,162,411
2	Indonesia	1,564,324
3	Malaysia	1,082,400
4	India	542,000
5	China	450,000
6	Philippines	200,000
7	Vietnam	180,700
8	Côte d'Ivoire	115,668
9	Sri Lanka	105,783
10	Nigeria	90,000
	World total	6,780,089

Source: *Food and Agriculture Organization of the United Nations*

TOP 10 ★
COTTON-PRODUCING COUNTRIES

	COUNTRY	1998 PRODUCTION TONNES
1	China	4,000,000
2	USA	2,881,000
3	India	2,720,000
4	Pakistan	1,562,000
5	Uzbekistan	975,000
6	Turkey	750,000
7	Australia	666,000
8=	Brazil	418,791
=	Greece	418,791
10	Egypt	342,030
	World total	18,169,714

Source: *Food and Agriculture Organization of the United Nations*

Did You Know? The planet's total area of forests and woodland has barely fluctuated in the past quarter-century. In 1972 the forested proportion stood at just over 32 per cent, and today it is just under 32 per cent.

TOP 10 ★
MOST COMMON TREES IN THE UK

	TREE	PERCENTAGE OF TOTAL FOREST AREA
1	Sitka spruce	28
2	Scots pine	13
3	Oak	9
4	Lodgepole pine	7
5=	Larch	6
=	Norway spruce	6
7=	Ash	4
=	Beech	4
=	Birch	4
10	Sycamore	3

REACH FOR THE SKY

This giant sequoia is the General Grant tree in King's Canyon National Park, California. Another Californian example, the General Sherman, at 83.8 m/ 275 ft high is the tallest living thing on the Earth.

TOP 10 ★
TIMBER-PRODUCING COUNTRIES

	COUNTRY	1998 PRODUCTION CU M	CU FT
1	USA	495,305,000	17,491,532,624
2	China	312,957,000	11,051,973,179
3	India	304,339,000	10,747,631,353
4	Brazil	220,363,000	7,782,046,625
5	Indonesia	200,784,500	7,090,638,359
6	Canada	188,432,000	6,654,413,897
7	Nigeria	114,311,000	4,036,855,242
8	Russia	96,250,000	3,399,036,988
9	Sweden	56,424,000	1,992,594,940
10	Ethiopia	49,354,700	1,742,944,943
	World total	3,354,292,510	118,455,733,074

Source: Food and Agriculture Organization of the United Nations

TOP 10 ★
MOST FORESTED COUNTRIES

	COUNTRY	PERCENTAGE FOREST COVER
1	Surinam	92
2	Papua New Guinea	91
3	Solomon Islands	85
4	French Guiana	81
5	Guyana	77
6	Gabon	74
7	Finland	69
8=	Bhutan	66
=	Japan	66
10	North Korea	65

Source: Food and Agriculture Organization of the United Nations

These countries have the greatest area of forest and woodland as a percentage of their total land area. With increasing deforestation, the world average has fallen to about 31 per cent. The UK stands at less than 10 per cent, with Ireland at under 5 per cent. The least forested countries are the desert lands of the Middle East and North Africa, such as Libya with under 0.5 per cent.

TOP 10 ★
TALLEST TREES IN THE UK*

	TREE	LOCATION	HEIGHT M	FT
1=	Douglas fir	The Hermitage, Dunkeld, Tayside	64.5	212
=	Douglas fir	Dunans, Strathclyde	64.5	212
3	Sitka spruce	Private estate, Strathearn, Tayside	61.5	202
4	Grand fir	Ardkinglass Arboretum, Strathclyde	60.0	197
5	Giant sequoia	Castle Leod, Strathpeffer, Highland	53.0	174
6=	Noble fir	Ardkinglass House, Strathclyde	52.0	171
=	Norway spruce	Moniac Glen, Highland	52.0	171
=	Japanese larch	Diana's Grove, Blair Castle, Tayside	52.0	171
9	Western hemlock	Benmore Younger Botanic Gardens, Argyll, Strathclyde	51.0	167
10=	European silver fir	Thirlmere, Cumbria	50.0	164
=	Caucasian fir	Cragside, Northumberland	50.0	164

* The tallest known example of each of the 10 tallest species
Source: The Tree Register of the British Isles

THE HUMAN WORLD

THE HUMAN BODY & HEALTH

COUNTRIES THAT SPEND THE MOST ON HEALTH CARE

COUNTRY	TOTAL SPENDING AS A PERCENTAGE OF GDP*
1 USA	14.2
2 Argentina	10.6
3 Germany	10.4
4 Croatia	10.1
5 Switzerland	10.0
6 France	9.9
7 =Canada	9.6
=Czech Republic	9.6
9 =Australia	8.9
=Austria	8.9
UK	6.9

* Gross Domestic Product

Source: World Bank, World Development Indicators 1998

The figures are for total health care spending, public and private. In some countries, private spending on health is greater than public spending (in the US, for example, public spending is 6.3 per cent of GDP, private spending is 7.9 per cent). In other countries, government accounts for a much greater share (in Croatia, public spending is 8.5 per cent of GDP while private spending is 1.6 per cent). The UK spends under half the proportion spent by the top spender, the US, and private health spending is still a relatively small proportion of total spending (public spending is 5.8 per cent of GDP while private spending is 1.1 per cent).

THE 10 MOST COMMON HOSPITAL CASUALTY COMPLAINTS

1. Cuts 2. Bruises 3. Dog bites
4. Sprained ankles 5. Eye injuries
6. Head injuries 7. Minor burns
8. Fractures 9. Upper respiratory tract infections 10. Gastroenteritis

COUNTRIES WITH THE MOST PATIENTS PER DOCTOR

COUNTRY	PATIENTS PER DOCTOR
1 Niger	53,986
2 Malawi	44,205
3 Mozambique	36,225
4 Burkina Faso	34,804
5 Ethiopia	32,499
6 Chad	30,030
7 Central African Republic	25,920
8 Rwanda	24,967
9 Lesotho	24,095
10 Angola	23,725
England	1,885

Source: World Bank, World Development Indicators 1997

Comparing countries' ratios of people to doctors is fraught with problems, but on the basis of available data, the 10 countries on this list, all of which are in Africa, are the worst served in terms of access to doctors, and contrast markedly with countries in North America and Western Europe.

MOST COMMON REASONS FOR VISITS TO THE DOCTOR

COMPLAINT	RATE*
1 Acute upper respiratory infections	772
2 Acute bronchitis and bronchitis	719
3 Asthma	425
4 Disorders of conjunctiva (eye)	415
5 Hypertension (high blood pressure)	412
6 =Disorders of external ear	409
=Acute pharyngitis (sore throat)	409
8 Acute tonsillitis	407
9 Ill-defined intestinal infections	394
10 Various unspecified disorders of back	372

* Per 10,000 patients per annum

LONGEST BONES IN THE HUMAN BODY

BONE	AVERAGE LENGTH CM	IN
1 Femur (thighbone – upper leg)	50.50	19.88
2 Tibia (shinbone – inner lower leg)	43.03	16.94
3 Fibula (outer lower leg)	40.50	15.94
4 Humerus (upper arm)	36.46	14.35
5 Ulna (inner lower arm)	28.20	11.10
6 Radius (outer lower arm)	26.42	10.40
7 7th rib	24.00	9.45
8 8th rib	23.00	9.06
9 Innominate bone (hipbone – half pelvis)	18.50	7.28
10 Sternum (breastbone)	17.00	6.69

These are average dimensions of the bones of an adult male measured from their extremities (ribs are curved, and the pelvis is measured diagonally). The same bones in the female skeleton are usually 6 to 13 per cent smaller, with the exception of the sternum which is virtually identical.

MOST COMMON ELEMENTS IN THE HUMAN BODY

ELEMENT	AVERAGE WEIGHT G	OZ*
1 Oxygen	45,500	1,608
2 Carbon	12,600	445
3 Hydrogen	7,000	247
4 Nitrogen	2,100	74
5 Calcium	1,050	37
6 Phosphorus	700	25
7 Sulphur	175	6
8 Potassium	140	5
9 =Chlorine	105	4
=Sodium	105	4

* Average in 70 kg/154 lb person

The remaining 1 per cent comprises minute quantities of metallic elements.

Did You Know? Keraunothnetophobia is a fear of satellites falling to Earth. Other strange phobias include geniophobia (a fear of chins), linonophobia (a fear of string), and chrometophobia (a fear of money).

TOP 10 ★
LARGEST HUMAN ORGANS

ORGAN		AVERAGE WEIGHT G	OZ
1 Skin		10,886	384.0
2 Liver		1,560	55.0
3 Brain	male	1,408	49.7
	female	1,263	44.6
4 Lungs	right	580	20.5
	left	510	18.0
	total	1,090	38.5
5 Heart	male	315	11.1
	female	265	9.3
6 Kidneys	right	140	4.9
	left	150	5.3
	total	290	10.2
7 Spleen		170	6.0
8 Pancreas		98	3.5
9 Thyroid		35	1.2
10 Prostate (male only)		20	0.7

This list is based on average immediate postmortem weights, as recorded by St. Bartholemew's Hospital, London, and other sources during a 10-year period. Various instances of organs far in excess of the average have been recorded, including male brains of over 2,000 g/70.6 oz. The Victorians believed that the heavier the brain, the greater the intelligence, and were impressed by recorded weights of 1,658 g/58 oz and 1,907 g/67 oz for William Makepeace Thackeray and Otto von Bismarck, respectively.

SKIN DEEP
Considered the largest human organ, the human skin (seen here in close-up, with a hair follicle) accounts for an area of 2 sq m/21 sq ft. It averages 1–2 mm (0.04–0.08 in) thick, but may measure up to 6 mm (0.2 in) thick on the soles of the feet, while the eyelids may be as little as 0.5 mm (0.02 in) thick. Skin is constantly replaced: it takes 50 days for new tissue completely to replace the old, which sheds at a rate of some 50,000 microscopic flakes per minute. In a lifetime, a person loses a total of 18 kg/40 lb. The skin contains about 3 million sweat glands overall, which release on average 0.3 litres (0.5 pints) of sweat per day – up to 3.5 litres (6 pints) in hot climates.

SNAP SHOTS ★

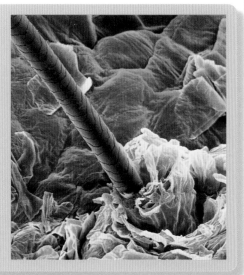

TOP 10 ★
MOST COMMON PHOBIAS

OBJECT OF PHOBIA	MEDICAL TERM
1 Spiders	Arachnephobia or arachnophobia
2 People and social situations	Anthropophobia or sociophobia
3 Flying	Aerophobia or aviatophobia
4 Open spaces	Agoraphobia, cenophobia or kenophobia
5 Confined spaces	Claustrophobia, cleisiophobia, cleithrophobia, or clithrophobia
6 =Vomiting	Emetophobia or emitophobia
=Heights	Acrophobia, altophobia, hypsophobia, or hypsiphobia
8 Cancer	Carcinomaphobia, carcinophobia, carcinomatophobia, cancerphobia, or cancerophobia
9 Thunderstorms	Brontophobia or keraunophobia
10 =Death	Necrophobia or thanatophobia
=Heart disease	Cardiophobia

A phobia is a morbid fear that is out of all proportion to the object of the fear. Many people would admit to being uncomfortable about these principal phobias, as well as others, such as snakes (ophiophobia) or ghosts (phasmophobia), but most do not become obsessive about them and allow such fears to rule their lives. Technophobia, the fear of modern technology such as computers, is increasingly reported.

HAIRY SCARY

A fear of spiders is not necessarily groundless: many spiders, such as black widows, hobo spiders, and tarantulas, have a painful, or even fatal, bite.

THE 10 ★
MOST COMMON CAUSES OF ILLNESS

CAUSE	NEW CASES ANNUALLY
1 Diarrhoea (including dysentery)	4,002,000,000
2 Malaria	up to 500,000,000
3 Acute lower respiratory infections	395,000,000
4 Occupational injuries	350,000,000
5 Occupational diseases	217,000,000
6 Trichomoniasis	170,000,000
7 Mood (affective) disorders	122,865,000
8 Chlamydial infections	89,000,000
9 Alcohol dependence syndrome	75,000,000
10 Gonococcal (bacterial) infections	62,000,000

Source: *World Health Organization*

BIRTHS, MARRIAGES & DEATHS

THE 10 MOST SUICIDAL COUNTRIES

(Country/suicides per 100,000 population)

1. Lithuania, 45.8
2. Russia, 41.8
3. Estonia, 41.0
4. Latvia, 40.7
5. Hungary, 32.9
6. Slovenia, 28.4
7. Belarus, 27.9
8. Finland, 27.3
9. Kazakstan, 23.8
10. Croatia, 22.8

Source: *United Nations*
The lowest suicide rate recorded is in Egypt – fewer than one suicide per 1 million people.

THE 10 COUNTRIES WITH THE HIGHEST DIVORCE RATE

(Country/divorce rate per 1,000)

1. Maldives, 10.75
2. Cuba, 5.95
3. China, 4.63
4. Russia, 4.60
5. USA, 4.57
6. Belarus, 4.26
7. Surinam, 4.15
8. Ukraine, 4.00
9. Estonia, 3.74
10. Latvia, 3.20

Source: *United Nations*
The UK has the highest divorce rate in Europe (excluding republics of the former Soviet Union). According to UN statistics, the Isle of Man, if it were an independent country, would appear in seventh place in this list, with a divorce rate of 4.2 per 1,000 population.

TOP 10 ★ COUNTRIES WITH THE HIGHEST FEMALE LIFE EXPECTANCY

	COUNTRY	LIFE EXPECTANCY AT BIRTH (YEARS)
1	Japan	82.5
2	Switzerland	81.2
3	Sweden	81.1
4=	France	80.8
=	Iceland	80.8
6	Canada	80.7
7=	Australia	80.6
=	Italy	80.6
9	Spain	80.5
10	Netherlands	80.4

Source: *United Nations*

TOP 10 ★ COUNTRIES WITH THE HIGHEST MALE LIFE EXPECTANCY

	COUNTRY	LIFE EXPECTANCY AT BIRTH (YEARS)
1	Japan	76.4
2	Iceland	75.8
3	Sweden	75.4
4	Greece	75.0
5	Cyprus	74.8
6=	Australia	74.7
=	Switzerland	74.7
8=	Israel	74.6
=	Spain	74.6
10	Netherlands	74.4

Source: *United Nations*

TOP 10 COUNTRIES WITH THE HIGHEST MARRIAGE RATE

(Country/marriage rate per 1,000, per annum)

1. Maldives, 19.7
2. Cuba, 17.7
3. Bermuda, 14.2
4. Liechtenstein, 12.9
5. Seychelles, 11.9
6. Barbados, 11.2
7. Bangladesh, 10.9
8. Tajikistan, 9.6
9. Mauritius, 9.5
10. Bahamas, 9.3

Source: *United Nations*

TOP 10 ★ PROFESSIONS OF COMPUTER-DATING MEMBERS IN THE UK

WOMEN'S PROFESSIONS	PERCENTAGE OF THOSE REGISTERED		PERCENTAGE OF THOSE REGISTERED	MEN'S PROFESSIONS
Teachers	7.8	1	6.1	Engineers
Solicitors	5.1	2	5.0	Company directors
Nurses	4.9	3	4.7	Computer programmers
Accountants	4.5	4	4.6	Architects/Designers
Civil servants	3.9	5	4.4	Accountants
Secretaries	3.8	6	4.2	Teachers
Women at home	3.5	7	4.0	Doctors
Doctors	3.1	8	3.7	Managers
Social workers	2.8	9	2.5	Civil servants
Students	1.3	10	1.4	Farmers

Source: *Based on figures supplied by Dateline, Britain's largest and oldest-established computer dating agency*

THE 10 ★ COUNTRIES WITH THE HIGHEST DEATH RATE

	COUNTRY	DEATH RATE PER 1,000
1	Sierra Leone	25.1
2	Afghanistan	21.8
3	Guinea Bissau	21.3
4	Guinea	20.3
5=	Angola	19.2
=	Uganda	19.2
7	Niger	18.9
8	The Gambia	18.8
9=	Mozambique	18.5
=	Somalia	18.5
	UK	10.7

Source: *United Nations*

Background image: **WEDDING IN THE COOK ISLANDS**

What is the most popular boy's name in the US?
see p.79 for the answer

A Jacob
B Michael
C Christopher

THE 10 ★
MOST COMMON CAUSES OF DEATH

CAUSE	APPROXIMATE DEATHS PER ANNUM
1 Ischaemic heart disease	7,200,000
2 Cancers	6,346,000
3 Cerebrovascular disease	4,600,000
4 Acute lower respiratory infection	3,905,000
5 Tuberculosis	3,000,000
6 Chronic obstructive pulmonary disease	2,888,000
7 Diarrhoea (including dysentery)	2,473,000
8 Malaria	1,500,000–2,700,000
9 HIV/AIDS	1,500,000
10 Hepatitis B	1,156,000

Source: *World Health Organization*

SMOKERS' DISEASE

This magnification of the epithelium – the mucous membrane that lines the lung airways – shows the chaotic cell growth caused by lung cancer. Blood cells (in red) have also leaked out due to haemorrhage.

THE 10 ★
COUNTRIES WITH THE MOST DEATHS FROM HEART DISEASE

COUNTRY	DEATH RATE PER 100,000
1 Czech Republic	314.4
2 Scotland	258.3
3 New Zealand	248.6
4 Finland	243.2
5 Hungary	240.0
6 Bulgaria	230.1
7 Denmark	211.1
8 England and Wales	210.0
9 Sweden	209.3
10 Australia	200.5

TOP 10 ★
YEARS WITH MOST BIRTHS IN THE UK

YEAR	BIRTHS
1 1920	1,194,068
2 1903	1,183,627
3 1904	1,181,770
4 1902	1,174,639
5 1908	1,173,759
6 1906	1,170,622
7 1905	1,163,535
8 1899	1,163,279
9 1901	1,162,975
10 1900	1,159,922

The total number of births in the UK more than doubled in the 19th century. High figures were also experienced in the early years of the 20th century, with an all-time peak in 1920.

THE 10 COUNTRIES WITH THE HIGHEST BIRTH RATE

(Country/live births per 1,000 per annum)

1 Niger, 52.5 2 Uganda, 51.8
3 Angola, 51.3 4 Guinea, 50.6
5 = Afghanistan, 50.2; = Somalia, 50.2
7 Côte d'Ivoire, 49.8 8 Yemen, 49.4
9 Sierra Leone, 49.1 10 = Benin, 48.7; = Mali, 48.7

THE 10 COUNTRIES WITH THE LOWEST BIRTH RATE

(Country/live births per 1,000 per annum)

1 Bulgaria, 8.1 2 Latvia, 8.5
3 Estonia, 8.8 4 Spain, 9.1 5 Italy, 9.2
6 = Czech Republic, 9.3; = Germany, 9.3; = Russia, 9.3 9 Slovenia, 9.6
10 = Greece, 9.8; = San Marino, 9.8

Source: *United Nations*
If counted as an independent country, the Vatican City, with a birth rate of zero, would head this list.

BABY BOOM

The population is expanding fast, with more people being born and living longer than ever before. The human boom is set to continue until 2080, when it will reach just over 10 billion.

WHAT'S IN A NAME?

TOP 10 MOST COMMON SURNAMES IN THE UK

1 Smith **2** Jones **3** Williams **4** Brown **5** Taylor **6** Davies/Davis **7** Evans **8** Thomas **9** Roberts **10** Johnson

The list of top surnames in the UK has a number of entries in common with its US counterpart, reflecting the British ancestry of a high proportion of American citizens. Smith heads the list in both countries.

MASTER...?

One hundred years ago, this little boy would quite possibly have been called William, John, or George. None of the boys' names popular in the US then are still favoured today, but in the UK Thomas and James remain perennial favourites.

TOP 10 ★ BOYS' NAMES IN ENGLAND AND WALES

1988		1998
Daniel	1	Jack
Christopher	2	Thomas
Michael	3	James
James	4	Daniel
Matthew	5	Joshua
Andrew	6	Matthew
Adam	7	Samuel
Thomas	8	Callum
David	9	Joseph
Richard	10	Jordan

TOP 10 MOST COMMON SURNAMES IN THE US

(Name/per cent of all US surnames)

1 Smith, 1.006 **2** Johnson, 0.810 **3** Williams, 0.699 **4** = Jones, 0.621; = Brown, 0.621 **6** Davis, 0.480 **7** Miller, 0.424 **8** Wilson, 0.339 **9** Moore, 0.312 **10** = Anderson, 0.311; = Taylor, 0.311; = Thomas, 0.311

The Top 10 (or, in view of those in equal 10th place, 12) US surnames together make up over 6 per cent of the entire US population – in other words, one American in every 16 bears one of these names.

TOP 10 ★ GIRLS' AND BOYS' NAMES IN THE US 100 YEARS AGO

GIRLS		BOYS
Mary	1	John
Helen	2	William
Anna	3	James
Margaret	4	George
Ruth	5	Charles
Elizabeth	6	Joseph
Marie	7	Frank
Rose	8	Henry
Florence	9	Robert
Bertha	10	Harry

TOP 10 ★ GIRLS' AND BOYS' NAMES IN THE UK 100 YEARS AGO

GIRLS		BOYS
Florence	1	William
Mary	2	John
Alice	3	George
Annie	4	Thomas
Elsie	5	Charles
Edith	6	Frederick
Elizabeth	7	Arthur
Doris	8	James
Dorothy	9	Albert
Ethel	10	Ernest

TOP 10 ★ SURNAMES IN THE LONDON TELEPHONE DIRECTORY

1	Smith
2	Brown/Browne
3	Jones
4	Williams/Williamson
5	Clark/Clarke
6	Harris/Harrison
7	Taylor
8	Roberts/Robertson
9	Patel
10	James

IT'S A GIRL!
Emily and Hannah are popular choices today on both sides of the Atlantic. Ten years' ago, Sarah and Samantha were shared favourites.

TOP 10 ⭐
GIRLS' NAMES IN THE US

1988		1998
Ashley	1	Kaitlyn
Jessica	2	Emily
Amanda	3	Sarah
Jennifer	4	Hannah
Brittany	5	Ashley
Sarah	6	Brianna
Stephanie	7	Alexis
Samantha	8	Samantha
Heather	9	Taylor
Elizabeth	10	Madison

TOP 10 TERMS OF ENDEARMENT USED IN THE US

❶ Honey ❷ Baby ❸ Sweetheart
❹ Dear ❺ Lover ❻ Darling
❼ Sugar ❽ = Angel; = Pumpkin
❿ = Beautiful; = Precious

A survey of romance conducted by a US champagne company concluded that 26 per cent of American adults favoured "honey" as their most frequently used term of endearment. Curiously, identical numbers were undecided whether to call their loved one an angel or a pumpkin ....

TOP 10 ⭐
BOYS' NAMES IN THE US

1988		1998
Michael	1	Michael
Christopher	2	Jacob
Matthew	3	Matthew
Joshua	4	Nicholas
David	5	Joshua
Daniel	6	Christopher
Andrew	7	Brandon
Justin	8	Austin
Robert	9	Tyler
Joseph	10	Zachary

TOP 10 ⭐
GIRLS' NAMES IN ENGLAND AND WALES

1988		1998
Rebecca	1	Chloe
Sarah	2	Emily
Emma	3	Megan
Laura	4	Jessica
Rachel	5	Sophie
Samantha	6	Charlotte
Charlotte	7	Hannah
Kirsty	8	Lauren
Nicola	9	Rebecca
Amy	10	Lucy

Did You Know? At least 800,000 people in England and Wales have Smith for their surname, which means that one person in every 61 is called Smith.

THE POLITICAL WORLD

TOP 10 LONGEST-SERVING PRESIDENTS TODAY

	PRESIDENT	COUNTRY	TOOK OFFICE
1	General Gnassingbé Eyadéma	Togo	14 Apr 1967
2	El Hadj Omar Bongo	Gabon	2 Dec 1967
3	Colonel Mu'ammar Gadhafi	Libya	1 Sep 1969
4	Lt.-General Hafiz al-Asad	Syria	22 Feb 1971
5	Zayid ibn Sultan al-Nuhayyan	United Arab Emirates	2 Dec 1971
6	Fidel Castro	Cuba	2 Dec 1976
7	France-Albert René	Seychelles	5 Jun 1977
8	Hassan Gouled Aptidon	Djibouti	30 Sep 1977
9	Daniel Teroitich arap Moi	Kenya	14 Oct 1978
10	Saddam Hussein	Iraq	16 Jul 1979

All the presidents in this list have been in power for more than 20 – some for over 30 – years. Among those no longer in office, Félix Houhouët-Boigny, President of the Côte d'Ivoire, died on 7 December 1993; he was, at 88, the oldest president in the world.

TOP 10 ★ BRITISH PRIME MINISTERS WITH THE MOST CHILDREN

	PRIME MINISTER/PARTY/OFFICE	CHILDREN
1	Earl Grey, W, 1830–34	17
2	Duke of Grafton, W, 1768–70	16
3	Spencer Perceval, T, 1809–12	12
4	Earl of Bute, T, 1762–63	11
5	George Grenville, W, 1763–65	9
6 =	Henry Pelham, W, 1743–54	8
=	Henry Addington, T, 1801–04	8
=	Earl of Aberdeen, P, 1852–55	8
=	William E. Gladstone, Lib, 1868–74, 1880–85, 1886	8
=	Marquess of Salisbury, Con, 1885–86, 1886–92, 1895–1902	8

Con = Conservative; Lib = Liberal; P = Peelite; T = Tory; W = Whig

THE 10 ★ FIRST COUNTRIES TO RATIFY THE UN CHARTER

	COUNTRY	DATE
1	Nicaragua	6 Jul 1945
2	USA	8 Aug 1945
3	France	31 Aug 1945
4	Dominican Republic	4 Sep 1945
5	New Zealand	19 Sep 1945
6	Brazil	21 Sep 1945
7	Argentina	24 Sep 1945
8	China	28 Sep 1945
9	Denmark	9 Oct 1945
10	Chile	11 Oct 1945

In New York on 26 June 1945, barely weeks after the end of World War II in Europe (the Japanese did not surrender until 3 September), 50 nations signed the World Security Charter, thereby establishing the United Nations as an international peacekeeping organization. The UN came into effect on 24 October, which has since been celebrated as United Nations Day.

INTERNATIONAL RELIEF

The UN's Operation Lifeline Sudan brought food and medical supplies to thousands of starving Sudanese in 1994. One of the UN's most high-profile activities is its supply of relief aid.

TOP 10 ★
PARLIAMENTS WITH THE MOST WOMEN MEMBERS*

	PARLIAMENT/ ELECTION	WOMEN MEMBERS	TOTAL MEMBERS	% WOMEN
1	**Sweden**, 1998	149	349	42.7
2	**Denmark**, 1998	67	179	37.4
3	**Norway**, 1997	60	165	36.4
4	**Netherlands**, 1998	54	150	36.0
5	**Finland**, 1995	67	200	33.5
6	**Germany**, 1998	207	669	30.9
7	**South Africa**, 1994	118	400	29.6
8	**New Zealand**, 1996	35	120	29.2
9	=**Argentina**, 1997	71	257	27.6
	=**Cuba**, 1998	166	601	27.6
	UK, *1997*	*120*	*659*	*18.0*

* As at 1 January 1999

Source: *Inter-Parliamentary Union*

THE 10 ★
FIRST FEMALE PRIME MINISTERS AND PRESIDENTS

	PRIME MINISTER OR PRESIDENT	COUNTRY/ PERIOD IN OFFICE
1	**Sirimavo Bandaranaike** (PM)	Sri Lanka, 1960–64/1970–77
2	**Indira Gandhi** (PM)	India, 1966–84
3	**Golda Meir** (PM)	Israel, 1969–74
4	**Maria Estela Perón** (P)	Argentina, 1974–75
5	**Elisabeth Domitien** (PM)	Central African Republic, 1975–present
6	**Margaret Thatcher** (PM)	UK, May 1979–Nov 1990
7	**Dr. Maria Lurdes Pintasilgo** (PM)	Portugal, Aug–Nov 1979
8	**Vigdís Finnbogadóttir** (P)	Iceland, Jun 1980–present
9	**Mary Eugenia Charles** (PM)	Dominica, Jul 1980–present
10	**Gro Harlem Brundtland** (PM)	Norway, Feb–Oct 1981/ May 1986–Oct 1989

VOTES FOR WOMEN

Campaigners such as Sylvia Pankhurst, the daughter of British Suffragette leader Emmeline Pankhurst, were often jailed for their public demonstrations in support of the Women's Suffrage movement. The movement gained momentum on both sides of the Atlantic, and women were gradually allowed to vote in most Western countries, including Great Britain and Ireland in 1918, and in 1920 in the US. A number of European countries, such as France and Italy, did not permit women to vote until 1945. Liechtenstein was one of the last countries to relent, as recently as 1984.

THE 10 FIRST COUNTRIES TO GIVE WOMEN THE VOTE
(Country/year)

1 **New Zealand**, 1893 **2** **Australia**, 1902 (South Australia, 1894; Western Australia, 1898; Australia united, 1901) **3** **Finland** (a Grand Duchy under the Russian Crown), 1906 **4** **Norway**, 1907 (restricted franchise; all women over 25 in 1913) **5** **Denmark and Iceland** (a Danish dependency until 1918), 1915 **6** = **Netherlands**, 1917; = **USSR**, 1917 **8** = **Austria**, 1918; = **Canada**, 1918; = **Germany**, 1918; = **Great Britain and Ireland**, 1918 (Ireland part of the United Kingdom until 1921; women over 30 – lowered to 21 in 1928); = **Poland**, 1918

TOP 10 ★
YOUNGEST BRITISH PRIME MINISTERS

	PRIME MINISTER	LIFESPAN	YEAR ELECTED	AGE ON TAKING OFFICE* YEARS	DAYS
1	**William Pitt**	1759–1806	1783	24	205
2	**Duke of Grafton**	1735–1811	1768	33	16
3	**Marquess of Rockingham**	1730–82	1765	35	61
4	**Duke of Devonshire**	1720–64	1756	c.36	–
5	**Lord North**	1732–92	1770	37	290
6	**Earl of Liverpool**	1770–1828	1812	42	1
7	**Henry Addington**	1757–1844	1801	43	291
8	**Tony Blair**	b. 6 May 1953	1997	43	360
9	**Sir Robert Walpole**	1676–1745	1721	44	107
10	**Viscount Goderich**	1782–1859	1827	44	305

* Where a prime minister served in more than one ministry, only the first is listed

At 24 years 205 days, William Pitt was by a wide margin the youngest prime minister ever. He had entered Cambridge University at 14 and Parliament at 22, becoming Chancellor of the Exchequer at 23. The title "prime minister" was not officially used until 1878, so all those on this list except Tony Blair technically held the office as "First Lord of the Treasury".

Did You Know? The United Nations has grown from its 50 founding nations to a total of 184 nations.

81

HUMAN ACHIEVEMENTS

FIRST PEOPLE TO REACH THE SOUTH POLE

NAME/NATIONALITY	DATE
1 =Roald Amundsen*, Norwegian	14 Dec 1911
=Olav Olavsen Bjaaland, Norwegian	14 Dec 1911
=Helmer Julius Hanssen, Norwegian	14 Dec 1911
=Helge Sverre Hassel, Norwegian	14 Dec 1911
=Oscar Wisting, Norwegian	14 Dec 1911
6 =Robert Falcon Scott*, British	17 Jan 1912
=Henry Robertson Bowers, British	17 Jan 1912
=Edgar Evans, British	17 Jan 1912
=Lawrence Edward Oates, British	17 Jan 1912
=Edward Adrian Wilson, British	17 Jan 1912

* Expedition leader

AMUNDSEN AT THE POLE

Just 33 days separated the first two expeditions to reach the South Pole. While Scott's team struggled towards its goal, the Norwegians arrived first. The exhausted British team died on the return journey.

FIRST PEOPLE TO GO OVER NIAGARA FALLS AND SURVIVE

NAME/METHOD	DATE
1 Annie Edson Taylor, Wooden barrel	24 Oct 1901
2 Bobby Leach, Steel barrel	25 Jul 1911
3 Jean Lussier, Steel and rubber ball fitted with oxygen cylinders	4 Jul 1928
4 William Fitzgerald (aka Nathan Boya), Steel and rubber ball fitted with oxygen cylinders	15 Jul 1961
5 Karel Soucek, Barrel	3 Jul 1984
6 Steven Trotter, Barrel	18 Aug 1985
7 Dave Mundy, Barrel	5 Oct 1985
8 =Peter deBernardi, Metal container	28 Sep 1989
=Jeffrey Petkovich, Metal container	28 Sep 1989
10 Dave Mundy, Diving bell	26 Sep 1993

Source: *Niagara Falls Museum*

FIRST *TIME* MAGAZINE "MEN OF THE YEAR"

YEAR	RECIPIENT/DATES	DESCRIPTION
1927	**Charles Lindbergh** (1902–74)	US aviator
1928	**Walter P. Chrysler** (1875–1940)	US businessman
1929	**Owen D. Young** (1874–1962)	US lawyer
1930	**Mahatma Gandhi** (1869–1948)	Indian politician
1931	**Pierre Laval** (1883–1945)	French President
1932	**Franklin D. Roosevelt** (1882–1945)	US President
1933	**Hugh S. Johnson** (1882–1942)	US soldier
1934	**Franklin D. Roosevelt** (1882–1945)	US President
1935	**Haile Salassie** (1891–1975)	Emperor of Ethiopia
1936	**Wallis Simpson** (1896–1986)	Duchess of Windsor

The most newsworthy "Man of the Year", nominated annually by the editors of *Time* magazine, may be one man, a group of men, a couple, a woman (as in the case of No. 10 in this list), a group of women, a machine, or even, as in 1988, "Endangered Earth". The lives of two of the First 10 ended violently: Gandhi was assassinated, while Laval was executed by firing squad after being found guilty of treason.

CIRCUMNAVIGATION FIRSTS

CIRCUMNAVIGATION/CRAFT	CAPTAIN(S)	RETURN DATE
1 First, *Vittoria*	Juan Sebastian de Elcano*	6 Sep 1522
2 First in less than 80 days, Various	"Nellie Bly"#	25 Jan 1890
3 First solo, *Spray*	Capt. Joshua Slocum	3 Jul 1898
4 First by air, *Chicago* / *New Orleans*	Lt. Lowell Smith / Lt. Leslie P. Arnold	28 Sep 1924
5 First non-stop by air, *Lucky Lady II*	Capt. James Gallagher	2 Mar 1949
6 First underwater, *Triton*	Capt. Edward Latimer Beach	25 Apr 1960
7 First non-stop solo, *Suhali*	Robin Knox-Johnston	22 Apr 1969
8 First helicopter, *Spirit of Texas*	H. Ross Perot Jr. and Jay Coburn	30 Sep 1982
9 First air without refuelling, *Voyager*	Richard Ruttan and Jeana Yaeger	23 Dec 1986
10 First by balloon, *Breitling Orbiter 3*	Brian Jones and Bertrand Piccard	21 Mar 1999

* *The expedition was led by Ferdinand Magellan, but he did not survive the voyage.*

Real name Elizabeth Cochrane. This US journalist set out to beat the fictitious "record" established in Jules Verne's novel, Around the World in 80 Days.

Did You Know? The youngest person to swim the English Channel was just 11 years old: Thomas Gregory, a British boy, took 11 hours 54 minutes to complete the crossing in 1988.

FIRST TO THE TOP

Edmund Hillary and Tenzing Norgay climbed the south col of Mount Everest, reaching the pinnacle at 11.30 a.m. on 29 May 1953. They planted the flags of Britain, Nepal, India, and the United Nations.

TOP 10 ★
FASTEST CROSS-CHANNEL SWIMMERS

SWIMMER/NATIONALITY	YEAR	TIME HRS:MINS
1 **Chad Hundeby**, American	1994	7:17
2 **Penny Lee Dean**, American	1978	7:40
3 **Tamara Bruce**, Australian	1994	7:53
4 **Philip Rush**, New Zealander	1987	7:55
5 **Hans van Goor**, Dutch	1995	8:02
6 **Richard Davey**, British	1988	8:05
7 **Irene van der Laan**, Dutch	1982	8:06
8 **Paul Asmuth**, American	1985	8:12
9 **Anita Sood**, Indian	1987	8:15
10 **John van Wisse**, Australian	1994	8:17

THE 10 ★
FIRST MOUNTAINEERS TO CLIMB EVEREST

MOUNTAINEER/NATIONALITY	DATE
1 **Edmund Hillary**, New Zealander	29 May 1953
2 **Tenzing Norgay**, Nepalese	29 May 1953
3 **Jürg Marmet**, Swiss	23 May 1956
4 **Ernst Schmied**, Swiss	23 May 1956
5 **Hans-Rudolf von Gunten**, Swiss	24 May 1956
6 **Adolf Reist**, Swiss	24 May 1956
7 **Wang Fu-chou**, Chinese	25 May 1960
8 **Chu Ying-hua**, Chinese	25 May 1960
9 **Konbu**, Tibetan	25 May 1960
10= **Nawang Gombu**, Indian	1 May 1963
= **James Whittaker**, American	1 May 1963

Nawang Gombu and James Whittaker are 10th equal because they ascended the last feet to the summit side by side.

THE 10 ★
NORTH POLE FIRSTS

1 First to reach the Pole?
American adventurer Frederick Albert Cook claimed that he had reached the Pole, accompanied by two Inuits, on 21 April 1908, but his claim is disputed. It is more likely that Robert Edwin Peary, Matthew Alexander Henson (both Americans), and four Inuits were first at the Pole on 6 April 1909.

2 First to fly over the Pole in an aeroplane
Two Americans, Lt.-Cdr. (later Admiral) Richard Evelyn Byrd (team-leader and navigator) and Floyd Bennett (pilot) traversed the Pole on 9 May 1926 in a three-engined Fokker F.VIII-3m named Josephine Ford *after Henry Ford's granddaughter.*

3 First to fly over the Pole in an airship
A team of 16 led by Roald Amundsen, the Norwegian explorer who first reached the South Pole in 1911, flew across the North Pole on 12 May 1926 in the Italian-built airship Norge.

4 First to land at the Pole in an aircraft
Soviets Pavel Afanaseyevich Geordiyenko, Mikhail Yemel'yenovich Ostrekin, Pavel Kononovich Sen'ko, and Mikhail Mikhaylovich Somov arrived at and departed from the Pole by air on 23 April 1948.

5 First solo flight over the Pole in a single-engined aircraft
Capt. Charles Francis Blair Jr. of the US flew a single-engined Mustang fighter, Excalibur III, *on 29 May 1951, crossing from Bardufoss, Norway, to Fairbanks, Alaska .*

6 First confirmed overland journey to the Pole
American explorer Ralph S. Plaisted, with companions Walter Pederson, Gerald Pitzel, and Jean Luc Bombardier, reached the Pole on 18 April 1968.

7 First woman at the Pole
Fran Phipps, a Canadian, arrived at the Pole by aeroplane on 5 April 1971.

8 First solo overland journey to the Pole
Japanese explorer Naomi Uemura reached the Pole on 1 May 1978, travelling by dog sled, and was then picked up by an aeroplane.

9 First crossing on a Pole-to-Pole expedition
Sir Ranulph Fiennes and Charles Burton walked over the North Pole on 10 April 1982, having crossed the South Pole on 15 December 1980.

10 First to reach the Pole on a motorcycle
Fukashi Kazami of Japan arrived at the Pole on 20 April 1987 on a specially adapted 250cc motorcycle, after which he was picked up by an aeroplane.

TOUCHDOWN

The first non-stop round-the-world balloon trip was completed by Bertrand Piccard (Switzerland) and Brian Jones (UK) on board the *Breitling Orbiter 3*. Launched from Château d'Oex, in the Swiss Alps, on 1 March 1999, the balloon flew around the globe for 19 days, 21 hours, and 55 minutes, breaking all previous records of distance and duration. During the journey, the crew endured dramatic changes in weather. After travelling 42,810 km (26,585 miles), they landed safely in south-east Egypt.

TOP 10 NOBEL PRIZE-WINNING COUNTRIES*

	COUNTRY	PHY	CHE	PH/MED	LIT	PCE	ECO	TOTAL
1	USA	67	43	78	10	18	25	241
2	UK	21	25	24	8	13	7	98
3	Germany	20	27	15	6	4	1	73
4	France	12	7	7	12	9	1	48
5	Sweden	4	4	7	7	5	2	29
6	Switzerland	2	5	6	2	3	–	18
7	USSR	7	1	2	3	2	1	16
8	Italy	3	1	3	6	1	–	14
9	Netherlands	6	3	2	–	1	1	13
10	Denmark	3	–	5	3	1	–	12

Phy – Physics; Che – Chemistry; Ph/Med – Physiology or Medicine; Lit – Literature; Pce – Peace; Eco – Economic Sciences. Germany includes the united country before 1948, West Germany to 1990 and the united country since 1990.

* In addition, institutions including the Red Cross have been awarded 16 Nobel Peace Prizes

TOP 10 ★ NOBEL PHYSICS PRIZE-WINNING COUNTRIES

	COUNTRY	PRIZES
1	USA	67
2	UK	21
3	Germany	20
4	France	12
5	USSR	7
6	Netherlands	6
7	Sweden	4
8 =	Austria	3
=	Denmark	3
=	Italy	3
=	Japan	3

TOP 10 ★ NOBEL PEACE PRIZE-WINNING COUNTRIES

	COUNTRY	PRIZES
1	USA	18
2	International institutions	16
3	UK	13
4	France	9
5	Sweden	5
6 =	Germany	4
=	South Africa	4
8 =	Belgium	3
=	Israel	3
=	Switzerland	3

TOP 10 ★ NOBEL PHYSIOLOGY OR MEDICINE PRIZE-WINNING COUNTRIES

	COUNTRY	PRIZES
1	USA	78
2	UK	24
3	Germany	15
4 =	France	7
=	Sweden	7
6	Switzerland	6
7	Denmark	5
8 =	Austria	4
=	Belgium	4
10 =	Italy	3
=	Australia	3

TOP 10 ★ NOBEL LITERATURE PRIZE-WINNING COUNTRIES

	COUNTRY	PRIZES
1	France	12
2	USA	10
3	UK	8
4	Sweden	7
5 =	Germany	6
=	Italy	6
7	Spain	5
8 =	Denmark	3
=	Ireland	3
=	Norway	3
=	Poland	3
=	USSR	3

TOP 10 NOBEL CHEMISTRY PRIZE-WINNING COUNTRIES

(Country/prizes)

1 USA, 43 **2** Germany, 27 **3** UK, 25 **4** France, 17 **5** Switzerland, 5 **6** Sweden, 4 **7** = Canada, 3; = Netherlands, 3 **9** = Argentina, 1; = Austria, 1; = Belgium, 1; = Czechoslovakia, 1; = Finland, 1; = Hungary, 1; = Italy, 1; = Japan, 1; = Mexico, 1; = Norway, 1; = USSR, 1

Background image: **THE TWO SIDES OF THE NOBEL PRIZE MEDAL**

THE 10 ★
LATEST WINNERS OF THE NOBEL PRIZE FOR LITERATURE

	WINNER	COUNTRY	YEAR
1	José Saramago	Portugal	1998
2	Dario Fo	Italy	1997
3	Wislawa Szymborska	Poland	1996
4	Seamus Heaney	Ireland	1995
5	Kenzaburo Oe	Japan	1994
6	Toni Morrison	USA	1993
7	Derek Walcott	Saint Lucia	1992
8	Nadine Gordimer	South Africa	1991
9	Octavio Paz	Mexico	1990
10	Camilo José Cela	Spain	1989

THE 10 ★
LATEST WINNERS OF THE NOBEL PRIZE FOR PHYSICS

	WINNER	COUNTRY	YEAR
1=	Robert B. Laughlin	USA	1998
=	Horst L. Störmer	Germany	1998
=	Daniel C. Tsui	USA	1998
4=	Steven Chu	USA	1997
=	William D. Phillips	USA	1997
=	Professor Claude Cohen-Tannoudji	France	1997
7=	David M. Lee	USA	1996
=	Douglas D. Osheroff	USA	1996
=	Robert C. Richardson	USA	1996
10=	Martin L. Perl	USA	1995
=	Frederick Reines	USA	1995

THE 10 ★
LATEST WINNERS OF THE NOBEL PRIZE FOR PHYSIOLOGY OR MEDICINE

	WINNER	COUNTRY	YEAR
1=	Robert F. Furchgott	USA	1998
=	Louis J. Ignarro	USA	1998
=	Ferid Murad	USA	1998
4	Stanley B. Prusiner	USA	1997
5=	Peter C. Doherty	Australia	1996
=	Rolf M. Zinkernagel	Switzerland	1996
7=	Christiane Nüsslein-Volhard	Germany	1995
=	Eric F. Wieschaus	USA	1995
=	Edward B. Lewis	USA	1995
10=	Alfred G. Gilman	USA	1994
=	Martin Rodbell	USA	1994

THE 10 LATEST WINNERS OF THE NOBEL PRIZE FOR CHEMISTRY
(Winner/country/year)

1=Walter Kohn, USA, 1998; = John A. Pople, UK, 1998 **3**= Paul D. Boyer, USA, 1997; = John E. Walker, UK, 1997; = Jens C. Skou, Denmark, 1997 **6**= Sir Harold W. Kroto, UK, 1996; = Richard E. Smalley, USA, 1996 **8**= Paul Crutzen, Netherlands, 1995; = Mario Molina Mexico, 1995; = Frank Sherwood Rowland, USA, 1995

THE 10 ★
LATEST WINNERS OF THE NOBEL PEACE PRIZE

	WINNER	COUNTRY	YEAR
1=	John Hume	UK	1998
=	David Trimble	UK	1998
3=	International Campaign to Ban Landmines	–	1997
=	Jody Williams	USA	1997
5=	Carlos Filipe Ximenes Belo	East Timor	1996
=	José Ramos-Horta	East Timor	1996
7	Joseph Rotblat	UK	1995
8=	Yasir Arafat	Palestine	1994
=	Shimon Peres	Israel	1994
=	Itzhak Rabin	Israel	1994

PEACE AT LAST?

John Hume and David Trimble celebrate the signing of the Good Friday Agreement in 1998. All the parties at Stormont Castle agreed to work towards peace in Northern Ireland.

Who was the youngest UK prime minister? *see p.81 for the answer*

A William Pitt
B Duke of Grafton
C Duke of Devonshire

CRIMINAL RECORDS

LARGEST PRISONS IN THE UK

PRISON/LOCATION	INMATES
1 **Walton**, Liverpool	1,467
2 **Wormwood Scrubs**, London	1,360
3 **Barlinnie**, Glasgow	1,150
4 **Armley**, Leeds	1,148
5 **Doncaster**	1,042
6 **Winson Green**, Birmingham	1,023
7 **Strangeways**, Manchester	999
8 **Holme House**, Cleveland	945
9 **Pentonville**, London	920
10 **Durham**	916

COUNTRIES WITH THE MOST PRISONERS

COUNTRY	PRISONERS*
1 **USA**	1,630,940
2 **Russia**	1,051,515
3 **Germany**	71,047
4 **Poland**	57,320
5 **England and Wales**	55,537
6 **France**	54,014
7 **Italy**	48,747
8 **Spain**	42,105
9 **Japan**	40,389
10 **Canada**	33,785

* In latest year for which figures are available

FINGER OF SUSPICION

In 1892 the first murder was solved by an incriminating fingerprint. Today, dusting a crime scene for prints is commonplace.

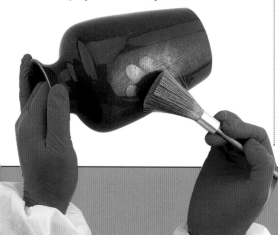

COUNTRIES WITH THE HIGHEST CRIME RATES

COUNTRY	RATE*
1 **Gibraltar**	18,316
2 **Surinam**	17,819
3 **St. Kitts and Nevis**	15,468
4 **Finland**	14,799
5 **Rwanda**	14,550
6 **New Zealand**	13,854
7 **Sweden**	12,982
8 **Denmark**	10,525
9 **Canada**	10,451
10 **US Virgin Islands**	10,441
England and Wales	9,980

* Reported crime per 100,000 population

An appearance in this list does not necessarily confirm these as the most crime-ridden countries, since the rate of reporting relates closely to such factors as confidence in local law enforcement.

MOST COMMON OFFENCES IN ENGLAND AND WALES

OFFENCE	OFFENDERS FOUND GUILTY (1996)
1 **Motoring offences**	658,900
2 **Summary offences** (other than motoring)	488,400
3 **Theft and handling stolen goods**	114,500
4 **Other offences**	43,500
5 **Drug offences**	34,100
6 **Burglary**	32,200
7 **Violence against the person**	30,000
8 **Fraud and forgery**	16,300
9 **Criminal damage**	9,800
10 **Robbery**	5,900
Total (indictable 300,600/ summary 1,137,400)	1,438,000

PHOTOFIT

Introduced in 1969, the police's Photofit method of depicting suspects is a more realistic development of the original Identikit system devised ten years earlier.

COUNTRIES WITH THE FEWEST POLICE OFFICERS

COUNTRY	POPULATION PER POLICE OFFICER
1 **Maldives**	35,710
2 **Canada**	8,640
3 **Rwanda**	4,650
4 **Côte d'Ivoire**	4,640
5 **The Gambia**	3,310
6 **Benin**	3,250
7 **Madagascar**	2,900
8 **Central African Republic**	2,740
9 **Bangladesh**	2,560
10 **Niger**	2,350*

* Including paramilitary forces

The saying "there's never a policeman when you need one" is nowhere truer than in these countries, where the police are very thin on the ground. There are various possible and contradictory explanations for these ratios: countries may be so law-abiding that there is simply no need for large numbers of police officers, or the force may be so underfunded and inefficient as to be irrelevant.

THE 10 ★
LAST PEOPLE EXECUTED AT THE TOWER OF LONDON

PERSON/CRIME	DATE

1 Wilhelm Johannes Roos — 30 Jul 1915
A Dutchman who had posed as a cigar salesman, whilst sending coded messages to a firm in Holland detailing warship movements in British ports. Roos was the third spy of World War I to be shot at the Tower of London.

2 Haike Marinus Petrus Janssen — 30 Jul 1915
An accomplice of Roos who used the same methods to send his messages to Holland. They were tried together, with Janssen shot just 10 minutes after Roos, at 6.10 am.

3 Ernst Waldemar Melin — 10 Sep 1915
A German spy, shot after being tried at a General Court Martial.

4 Agusto Alfredo Roggen — 17 Sep 1915
A German who attempted to escape the death penalty by claiming to be Uruguayan, he was found guilty of spying on tests of a new torpedo at Loch Lomond, sending his information in invisible ink.

5 Fernando Buschman — 19 Oct 1915
Posing as a Dutch violinist, he spied while offering entertainment at Royal Navy bases.

6 Georg T. Breeckow — 26 Oct 1915
Posing as an American, Reginald Rowland, with a forged passport, he was caught when he sent a parcel containing secret messages, but addressed in the German style, with country and town name preceding that of the street.

7 Irving Guy Ries — 27 Oct 1915
A German commercial traveller sentenced to death on spying charges.

8 Albert Meyer — 2 Dec 1915
Like Ries, Meyer was a German spy posing as a commercial traveller.

9 Y.L. Zender-Hurwitz — 11 Apr 1916
A spy of Peruvian descent charged with sending information to Germany about British troop movements, for which he received a handsome salary of £30 a month.

10 Josef Jakobs — 15 Aug 1941
A German army sergeant caught when he parachuted into England wearing civilian clothes and with an identity card in the name of James Rymer. Following General Court Martial, he was shot at 7.15 am – the only spy executed at the Tower in World War II.

THE 10 ★
FIRST COUNTRIES TO ABOLISH CAPITAL PUNISHMENT

COUNTRY	ABOLISHED
1 Russia	1826
2 Venezuela	1863
3 Portugal	1867
4 = Brazil	1882
= Costa Rica	1882
6 Ecuador	1897
7 Panama	1903
8 Norway	1905
9 Uruguay	1907
10 Colombia	1910
UK	1965

Some countries abolished capital punishment in peacetime only, or for all crimes except treason, generally extending it totally at a more recent date, although several later reinstated it. Some countries retained capital punishment on their statute books, but effectively abolished it: the last execution in Liechtenstein, for example, took place in 1795, in Mexico in 1946, and in Belgium in 1950. Finland abolished the death penalty at the same time as Russia (under whose rule it was at the time), but reintroduced it in 1882 – although no criminal has been executed in that country since 1824. One US state, Michigan, abolished capital punishment for every offence except treason in 1846.

THE 10 STATES WITH THE MOST PRISONERS ON DEATH ROW
(State/prisoners under death sentence)*

1 California, 519 **2** Texas, 441
3 Florida, 390 **4** Pennsylvania, 226
5 North Carolina, 209 **6** Ohio, 191
7 Alabama, 173 **8** Illinois, 162
9 Oklahoma, 151 **10** Georgia, 123

* As at 1 January 1999
Source: *Department of Justice*

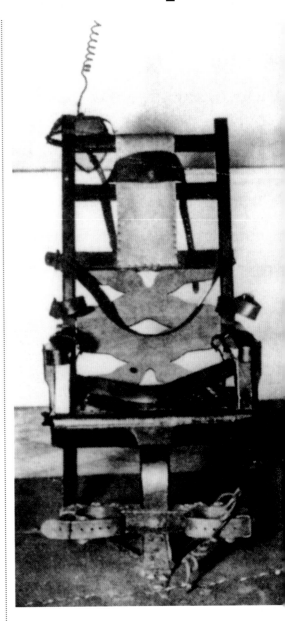

HOT SEAT
"An awful spectacle, far worse than hanging" was how the New York Times *described the electric chair, first used at Auburn Prison, New York, in 1890. A year later, the electric chair was installed in Sing Sing Prison, Ossining, New York. By 1963, when the chair was used for the last time, a total of 614 victims had been electrocuted at Sing Sing.*

Which country has the most submarines?
see p.90 for the answer
A USA
B China
C Russia

87

MURDER FILE

COUNTRIES WITH THE HIGHEST MURDER RATES

COUNTRY	MURDERS P.A. PER 100,000 POPULATION
1 Swaziland	87.8
2 Bahamas	52.6
3 Monaco	36.0
4 Philippines	30.1
5 Guatemala	27.4
6 Jamaica	20.9
7 Russia	19.9*
8 Botswana	19.5
9 Zimbabwe	17.9
10 Netherlands	14.8
England and Wales	1.2

* Includes attempted murder

COUNTRIES WITH THE LOWEST MURDER RATES

COUNTRY	MURDERS P.A. PER 100,000 POPULATION
1 =Argentina	0.1
=Brunei	0.1
3 =Burkina Faso	0.2
=Niger	0.2
5 =Guinea	0.5
=Guinea-Bissau	0.5
=Iran	0.5
8 =Finland	0.6
=Saudi Arabia	0.6
10 =Cameroon	0.7
=Ireland	0.7
=Mongolia	0.7

RELATIONSHIPS OF MURDER VICTIMS TO PRINCIPAL SUSPECTS IN THE US

RELATIONSHIP	VICTIMS (1996)
1 Acquaintance	4,797
2 Stranger	2,321
3 Wife	679
4 Friend	478
5 Girlfriend	424
6 Son	261
7 Daughter	207
8 Husband	206
9 Boyfriend	163
10 Neighbour	162

These offences – which remain in similar order from year to year – accounted for 9,698, or over 60 per cent, of the 15,848 murders committed in the US in 1996. FBI statistics also recorded 5,498 murders where the victim's relationship to the suspect was unknown, 283 "other family members" (those not specified elsewhere), 125 fathers, 107 mothers, 98 brothers, and 19 sisters.

THE 10 WORST YEARS FOR GUN MURDERS IN THE US

(Year/victims)

1 1993, 16,136 **2** 1994, 15,546 **3** 1992, 15,489 **4** 1991, 14,373 **5** 1980, 13,650
6 1990, 13,035 **7** 1981, 12,523 **8** 1974, 12,474 **9** 1975, 12,061 **10** 1989, 11,832

DNA FINGERPRINTING

DNA – deoxyribonucleic acid – which is found in all animal tissue, contains genetic information that is unique to the individual that produced it. In 1985 British scientist Professor Alec J. Jeffreys, head of the genetic laboratory at the University of Leicester, used this characteristic to develop the process of DNA fingerprinting in which cells taken from almost any sample of human tissue, including skin, blood, saliva, and hair, however small, can be analysed for sequences of DNA. This "genetic identity card" has since been successfully used worldwide to identify both criminals and the victims of murders, and has added a new and extremely accurate weapon to the law enforcement arsenal. The scientists who, in 1953, discovered the structure of DNA, Dr. James Watson, Dr. Francis Crick, and Dr. Maurice Wilkins, won the Nobel Prize for Physiology or Medicine.

SNAP ★ SHOTS

Which country has the largest Buddhist population?
see p.92 for the answer

A Thailand
B Japan
C China

TOP 10 ★
RELATIONSHIPS OF MURDER VICTIMS TO PRINCIPAL SUSPECTS IN ENGLAND AND WALES

	RELATIONSHIP	VICTIMS (1997)
1	Male friend or acquaintance	134
2	Male stranger	115
3	Current or former wife, female cohabitant, or lover	105
4	Son	36
5	Current or former husband, male cohabitant, or lover	34
6	Female friend or acquaintance	25
7	Female stranger	22
8	Mother	21
9	Daughter	17
10	Father	6

In addition to these offences, Home Office statistics record that in 1997, 12 murder victims were unspecified male and eight female family members, while seven men and five women are described as "other person in course of employment", such as security guards killed during hold-ups.

THE 10 ★
WORST STATES FOR MURDER IN THE US

	STATE	FIREARMS USED	TOTAL MURDERS
1	California	2,061	2,916
2	Texas	962	1,476
3	Illinois*	585	765
4	Louisiana	547	704
5	Michigan	480	695
6	Pennsylvania	493	665
7	North Carolina	397	615
8	Georgia	445	610
9	Maryland	424	578
10	Virginia	322	490

* Provisional figures, 1996

THE 10 ★
MOST COMMON MURDER WEAPONS AND METHODS IN ENGLAND AND WALES

	WEAPON/METHOD	VICTIMS (1997)
1	Sharp instrument	203
2	Hitting and kicking	109
3	Blunt instrument	74
4	Strangulation and asphyxiation	70
5	Shooting	58
6	Burning	30
7	Poison or drugs	24
8	Motor vehicle	15
9	Drowning	7
10	Explosion	1

THE 10 ★
WORST CITIES FOR MURDER IN THE US

	CITY	MURDERS*
1	Chicago	335
2	New York	299
3	Los Angeles	193
4	Detroit	192
5	Baltimore	156
6	New Orleans	139
7	Dallas	133
8	Washington, DC	122
9	Houston	114
10	Atlanta	75

* Provisional figures, January–June 1998; figure for Philadelphia not published

The identity of America's 10 murder capitals remains fairly consistent from year to year, with only some slight adjustment to the order.

THE 10 ★
MOST COMMON MURDER WEAPONS AND METHODS IN THE US

	WEAPON/METHOD	VICTIMS (1996)
1	Handguns	8,594
2	Knives or cutting instruments	2,142
3	"Personal weapons" (hands, feet, fists, etc.)	939
4	Firearms (type not stated)	911
5	Blunt objects (hammers, clubs, etc.)	733
6	Shotguns	673
7	Rifles	546
8	Strangulation	243
9	Fire	151
10	Asphyxiation	92

TOP 10 ★
REASONS FOR MURDER IN THE US

	REASON	MURDERS
1	Arguments	335
2	Robbery	299
3	Juvenile gang killings	193
4	Narcotic drug laws	192
5	Arguments over money or property	156
6	Brawl due to influence of alcohol	139
7	Romantic triangle	133
8	Brawl due to influence of narcotics	122
9	Burglary	114
10	Arson	75

Source: FBI Uniform Crime Reports

A total of 15,848 murders were reported in 1996, including 2,208 without a specified reason and 4,582 which were unknown.

MILITARY MATTERS

THE 10 20TH-CENTURY WARS WITH THE MOST MILITARY FATALITIES

	WAR	YEARS	MILITARY FATALITIES
1	World War II	1939–45	15,843,000
2	World War I	1914–18	8,545,800
3	Korean War	1950–53	1,893,100
4 =	Sino-Japanese War	1937–41	1,000,000
=	Biafra–Nigeria Civil War	1967–70	1,000,000
6	Spanish Civil War	1936–39	611,000
7	Vietnam War	1961–73	546,000
8 =	India–Pakistan War	1947	200,000
=	USSR invasion of Afghanistan	1979–89	200,000
=	Iran–Iraq War	1980–88	200,000

The statistics of warfare have always been an imperfect science. Not only are battle deaths seldom recorded accurately, but figures are often deliberately inflated by both sides in a conflict. For political reasons and to maintain morale, each is anxious to enhance reports of its military success and low casualty figures, so that often quite contradictory reports of the same battle may be issued. These figures thus represent military historians' "best guesses" – and fail to take into account the enormous toll of deaths among civilian populations during the many wars that have beset the 20th century.

TOP 10 ★ SMALLEST ARMED FORCES*

	COUNTRY	ESTIMATED TOTAL ACTIVE FORCES
1	Antigua and Barbuda	150
2	Seychelles	400
3	Barbados	610
4	The Gambia	800
5	Luxembourg	811
6	Bahamas	860
7	Belize	1,050
8	Cape Verde	1,100
9	Equatorial Guinea	1,320
10	Guyana	1,600

Excluding countries not declaring a defence budget

TOP 10 ★ COUNTRIES WITH THE LARGEST DEFENCE BUDGETS

	COUNTRY	BUDGET ($)
1	USA	270,500,000,000
2	UK	37,200,000,000
3	Japan	35,200,000,000
4	Russia	34,000,000,000
5	France	30,400,000,000
6	Germany	26,400,000,000
7	Saudi Arabia	18,400,000,000
8	Italy	17,800,000,000
9	China	11,000,000,000
10	South Korea	10,200,000,000
	Canada	7,100,000,000
	Australia	6,900,000,000

The so-called "peace dividend" – the savings made as a consequence of the end of the Cold War between the West and the former Soviet Union – means that both the numbers of personnel and the defence budgets of many countries have been cut. That of the USA has gone down from its 1989 peak of $303.6 billion.

TOP 10 COUNTRIES WITH THE MOST SUBMARINES

(Country/submarines)

❶ Russia (and assoc. states), 98 ❷ USA, 84 ❸ China, 63 ❹ North Korea, 26 ❺ India, 19 ❻ = Japan, 16; = Turkey, 16 ❽ UK, 15 ❾ = France, 14; = Germany, 14; = South Korea, 14

TOP 10 COUNTRIES WITH THE LARGEST NAVIES

(Country/manpower)*

❶ USA, 380,600 ❷ China, 260,000 ❸ Russia, 180,000 ❹ Taiwan, 68,000 ❺ France, 63,300 ❻ South Korea, 60,000 ❼ India, 55,000 ❽ Turkey, 51,000 ❾ North Korea, 46,000 ❿ UK, 44,500

* Including naval air forces and marines

TOP 10 ★ COUNTRIES WITH THE MOST CONSCRIPTED PERSONNEL

	COUNTRY	CONSCRIPTS
1	China	1,275,000
2	Turkey	528,000
3	Russia	381,000
4	Egypt	320,000
5	Iran	250,000
6	South Korea	159,000
7	Poland	141,600
8	Israel	138,500
9	Germany	137,500
10	Italy	134,100

Most countries have abolished peacetime conscription (the UK did so in 1960 and the US in 1973), and now recruit their forces on an entirely voluntary basis.

Did You Know? Boomerang bullets were patented in the US in 1870. Designed to fire in a curved line, their obvious drawback lay in the danger of the bullet travelling in a complete circle...!

TOP 10 ★

LARGEST ARMED FORCES

	COUNTRY	ARMY	ESTIMATED ACTIVE FORCES		TOTAL
			NAVY	AIR	
1	China	2,090,000	260,000	470,000	2,820,000
2	USA	479,000	380,600	370,300	1,401,600*
3	India	980,000	55,000	140,000	1,175,000
4	Russia	420,000	180,000	210,000	1,159,000#
5	North Korea	923,000	46,000	85,000	1,054,000
6	South Korea	560,000	60,000	52,000	672,000
7	Turkey	525,000	51,000	63,000	639,000
8	Pakistan	520,000	22,000	45,000	587,000
9	Iran	350,000	20,600	45–50,000	540–545,600+
10	Vietnam	420,000	42,000	30,000	484,000
	UK	113,900	44,500	52,540	210,940

* Includes 174,900 Marine Corps

 # Includes Strategic Deterrent Forces, Paramilitary, National Guard, etc.

+ Includes 125,000 Revolutionary Guards

In addition to the active forces listed here, many of the world's foremost countries have substantial reserves on standby: South Korea's has been estimated at some 4,500,000, Vietnam's at 3 million – 4 million, and China's at 1,200,000. Russia's former total of 3 million has steadily dwindled as a result of both the end of the Cold War and the economic problems faced by the post-Soviet military establishment. China is also notable for having a massive arsenal of military equipment at its disposal, including some 8,000 tanks, 4,600 fighter aircraft, and 1,225 bombers and ground-attack aircraft.

TOP 10 ★

COUNTRIES WITH THE HIGHEST MILITARY/ CIVILIAN RATIO

	COUNTRY	RATIO* (1998)
1	North Korea	421
2	Israel	296
3	United Arab Emirates	250
4	Singapore	236
5	Jordan	214
6	Qatar	205
7	Syria	202
8	Iraq	185
9	Bahrain	180
10	Taiwan	174
	UK	36

* Military personnel per 10,000 population

WAR OF FUTILITY

America's involvement in the Vietnam War was deeply unpopular with the people, who held large anti-war demonstrations in protest against the massive casualties.

WORLD RELIGIONS

TOP 10 ★ CHRISTIAN DENOMINATIONS

	DENOMINATION	MEMBERS
1	Roman Catholic	912,636,000
2	Orthodox	139,544,000
3	Pentecostal	105,756,000
4	Lutheran	84,521,000
5	Baptist	67,146,000
6	Anglican	53,217,000
7	Presbyterian	47,972,000
8	Methodist	25,599,000
9	Seventh Day Adventist	10,650,000
10	Churches of Christ	6,400,000

Source: *Christian Research*

TOP 10 ★ LARGEST CHRISTIAN POPULATIONS

	COUNTRY	TOTAL CHRISTIAN POPULATION
1	USA	182,674,000
2	Brazil	157,973,000
3	Mexico	88,380,000
4	China	73,300,000
5	Philippines	65,217,000
6	Germany	63,332,000
7	Italy	47,403,000
8	France	45,624,000
9	Nigeria	38,969,000
10	Dem. Rep. of Congo	37,922,000
	World total	1,965,993,000

Source: *Christian Research*

Of the total Christian population of the UK, only about one-sixth regularly attends church services.

TOP 10 ★ LARGEST BUDDHIST POPULATIONS

	COUNTRY	TOTAL BUDDHIST POPULATION
1	China	104,000,000
2	Japan	90,510,000
3	Thailand	57,450,000
4	Vietnam	50,080,000
5	Myanmar	41,880,000
6	Sri Lanka	12,540,000
7	South Korea	11,110,000
8	Cambodia	9,870,000
9	India	7,000,000
10	Malaysia	3,770,000
	World total	356,875,000

TOP 10 RELIGIOUS BELIEFS

	RELIGION	MEMBERS*
1	Christianity	1,965,993,000
2	Islam	1,179,326,000
3	Hinduism	865,000,000
4	No religion	766,672,000
5	Buddhism	356,875,000
6	Tribal religions	244,164,000
7	Atheism	146,406,000
8	New religions	99,191,000
9	Sikhism	22,874,000
10	Judaism	15,050,000

* Estimated total projections to mid-1998

HIS HOLINESS

Elected in 1978, John Paul II (born in Poland as Karol Wojtyia) became the first non-Italian Pope since the Dutch-born Hadrian VI in 1522.

BLUE MOSQUE

Istanbul's 17th-century mosque is one of Turkey's most magnificent centres of Muslim worship.

TOP 10 ⭐
LARGEST HINDU POPULATIONS

	COUNTRY	TOTAL HINDU POPULATION
1	India	814,632,942
2	Nepal	21,136,118
3	Bangladesh	14,802,899
4	Indonesia	3,974,895
5	Sri Lanka	2,713,900
6	Pakistan	2,112,071
7	Malaysia	1,043,500
8	USA	798,582
9	South Africa	649,980
10	Mauritius	587,884
	World total	865,000,000

More than 99 per cent of the world's Hindu population lives in Asia, with 94 per cent in India.

TOP 10 ⭐
LARGEST MUSLIM POPULATIONS

	COUNTRY	TOTAL MUSLIM POPULATION
1	Pakistan	157,349,290
2	Indonesia	156,213,374
3	Bangladesh	133,873,621
4	India	130,316,250
5	Iran	74,087,700
6	Turkey	66,462,107
7	Russia	64,624,770
8	Egypt	57,624,098
9	Nigeria	46,384,120
10	Morocco	33,542,780
	World total	1,179,326,000

Historically, Islam spread as a result of missionary activity and through contacts with Muslim traders. In such countries as Indonesia, its appeal lay in part in its opposition to Western colonial influences, which, along with the concept of Islamic community and other tenets, has attracted followers worldwide.

TOP 10 ⭐
LARGEST JEWISH POPULATIONS

	COUNTRY	TOTAL JEWISH POPULATION
1	USA	6,122,462
2	Israel	4,354,900
3	France	640,156
4	Russia	460,266
5	Ukraine	424,136
6	UK	345,054
7	Canada	342,096
8	Argentina	253,666
9	Brazil	107,692
10	Belarus	107,350
	World total	15,050,000

The Diaspora or scattering of Jewish people has been in progress for nearly 2,000 years, and Jewish communities are found in virtually every country in the world. In 1939 the total world Jewish population was around 17,000,000. Some 6,000,000 fell victim to Nazi persecution, but numbers have since grown to 15,050,000.

Did You Know? One-fifth of the world's population is Muslim.

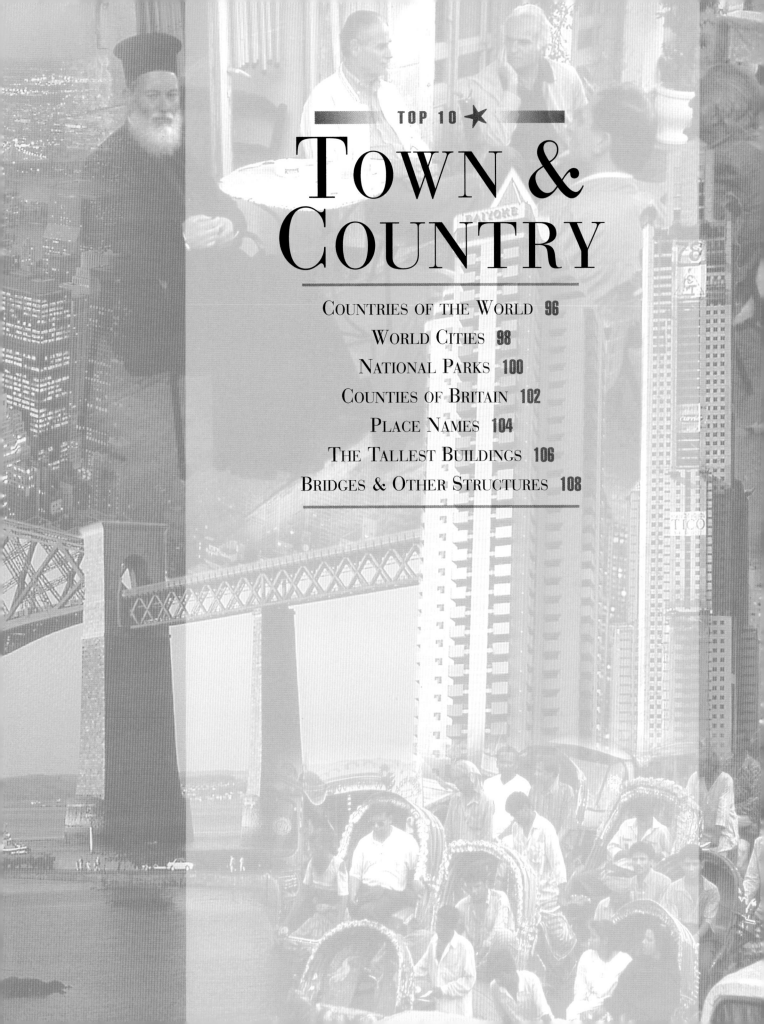

TOWN & COUNTRY

COUNTRIES OF THE WORLD

TOP 10 ★

COUNTRIES IN WHICH WOMEN MOST OUTNUMBER MEN

	COUNTRY	WOMEN PER 100 MEN
1	Latvia	116.7
2	Ukraine	115.2
3	Russia	113.3
4	Belarus	112.9
5=	Estonia	112.5
=	Lithuania	112.5
7	Georgia	109.6
8	Moldova	109.4
9	Hungary	108.8
10	Swaziland	108.7

TOP 10 ★

COUNTRIES IN WHICH MEN MOST OUTNUMBER WOMEN

	COUNTRY	MEN PER 100 WOMEN
1	Qatar	197.1
2	United Arab Emirates	176.6
3	Bahrain	134.4
4	Saudi Arabia	125.8
5	Oman	110.4
6	Brunei	109.6
7	Libya	108.7
8	Pakistan	107.2
9	India	106.9
10	Papua New Guinea	106.6

TOP 10 ★

LONGEST BORDERS

	COUNTRY	BORDERS KM	MILES
1	China	22,143	13,759
2	Russia	20,139	12,514
3	Brazil	14,691	9,129
4	India	14,103	8,763
5	USA	12,248	7,611
6	Dem. Rep. of Congo	10,271	6,382
7	Argentina	9,665	6,006
8	Canada	8,893	5,526
9	Mongolia	8,114	5,042
10	Sudan	7,697	4,783

This list represents the total length of borders, compiled by adding together the lengths of individual land borders.

TOP 10 ★

MOST DENSELY POPULATED COUNTRIES

	COUNTRY	AREA (SQ KM)	ESTIMATED POPULATION	POPULATION PER SQ KM
1	Monaco	1*	27,000	14,917.0
2	Singapore	618	3,439,000	5,564.7
3	Malta	316	371,000	1,174.1
4	Maldives	298	273,000	916.1
5	Bangladesh	143,998	122,013,000	847.3
6	Bahrain	694	582,000	838.6
7	Mauritius	1,865	1,141,000	611.8
8	Barbados	430	262,000	609.3
9	South Korea	99,274	45,717,000	460.5
10	San Marino	61	25,000	409.8
	UK	244,101	58,201,000	238.4
	World	135,807,000	5,847,465,000	43.1

* Rounded; precise area used for calculation of population density
Source: United Nations

RUSH HOUR IN THE SUBCONTINENT

Traffic congestion in Old Dacca, Bangladesh, illustrates the massive overcrowding experienced in some parts of this country. The population is unevenly spread, so some rural areas will be relatively empty while the cities teem with life.

Background image: **POLITICAL MAP OF THE WORLD**

SOCIALIZING AT A GREEK STREET CAFÉ

All of the Top 10 countries with the oldest populations are in Western Europe, implying that this region has lower death rates and a higher life expectancy than the rest of the world.

TOP 10 ★
LARGEST COUNTRIES IN EUROPE

| COUNTRY | AREA | |
	SQ KM	SQ MILES
1 Russia (in Europe)	4,710,227	1,818,629
2 Ukraine	603,700	233,090
3 France	547,026	211,208
4 Spain*	504,781	194,897
5 Sweden	449,964	173,732
6 Germany	356,999	137,838
7 Finland	337,007	130,119
8 Norway	324,220	125,182
9 Poland	312,676	120,725
10 Italy	301,226	116,304

* Including offshore islands

The UK falls just outside the Top 10 at 244,101 sq km/94,247 sq miles. Geographically, the total area of the British Isles (including the whole island of Ireland) is 314,384 sq km/121,383 sq miles.

TOP 10 ★
COUNTRIES WITH THE OLDEST POPULATIONS

COUNTRY	PERCENTAGE OVER 60
1 Sweden	17.3
2 Italy	16.0
3 = Greece	15.9
= Norway	15.9
5 Belgium	15.8
6 UK	15.5
7 = Denmark	15.2
= Germany	15.2
9 = Austria	14.9
= France	14.9
= Spain	14.9

Source: *World Health Organization*

On average, one in every eight people in Europe is over the age of 54 (12.5 per cent). By contrast, the lowest percentages of old people are found in Africa, where the average is only 3 per cent (one in every 33 people).

TOP 10 ★
COUNTRIES WITH THE YOUNGEST POPULATIONS

COUNTRY	PERCENTAGE UNDER 15
1 Côte d'Ivoire	49.1
2 Uganda	48.8
3 Comoros	48.7
4 Niger	48.4
5 Dem. Rep. of Congo	48.0
6 Kenya	47.7
7 = Oman	47.5
= Somalia	47.5
9 = Benin	47.4
= Mali	47.4
= Zambia	47.4
UK	19.6

Source: *World Health Organization*

Countries with high proportions of their people under the age of 15 are usually characterized by high birth rates and high death rates.

THE 10 ★
LARGEST COUNTRIES

| COUNTRY | AREA | |
	SQ KM	SQ MILES
1 Russia	17,070,289	6,590,876
2 Canada	9,970,599	3,849,670
3 China	9,596,961	3,705,408
4 USA	9,169,389	3,540,321
5 Brazil	8,511,965	3,286,488
6 Australia	7,686,848	2,967,909
7 India	3,287,590	1,269,346
8 Argentina	2,780,400	1,073,512
9 Kazakhstan	2,717,300	1,049,156
10 Sudan	2,505,813	967,500
UK	244,101	94,247
World total	136,597,770	52,740,700

The list of the world's largest countries, the Top 10 of which comprise more than 53 per cent of the total Earth's surface, has undergone great revision of late. The break-up of the former Soviet Union has introduced two new countries, with Russia taking pre-eminent position, occupying a massive 12.5 per cent of the total. At the other end of the list, Sudan accounts for a more modest, but still sizeable, 1.8 per cent.

THE 10 ★
SMALLEST COUNTRIES

| COUNTRY | AREA | |
	SQ KM	SQ MILES
1 Vatican City	0.44	0.17
2 Monaco	1.81	0.7
3 Gibraltar	6.47	2.5
4 Macao	16.06	6.2
5 Nauru	21.23	8.2
6 Tuvalu	25.90	10.0
7 Bermuda	53.35	20.6
8 San Marino	59.57	23.0
9 Liechtenstein	157.99	61.0
10 Antigua	279.72	108.0

The "country" status of several of these micro-states is questionable, since their government, defence, currency, and other features are often intricately linked with those of larger countries, such as the Vatican City with Italy.

Which country has the largest area of protected land?
see p.101 for the answer
A Brazil
B Greenland
C USA

WORLD CITIES

HIGHEST CITIES

	CITY/COUNTRY	HEIGHT M	HEIGHT FT
1	**Wenchuan**, China	5,099	16,730
2	**Potosí**, Bolivia	3,976	13,045
3	**Oruro**, Bolivia	3,702	12,146
4	**Lhasa**, Tibet	3,684	12,087
5	**La Paz**, Bolivia	3,632	11,916
6	**Cuzco**, Peru	3,399	11,152
7	**Huancayo**, Peru	3,249	10,660
8	**Sucre**, Bolivia	2,835	9,301
9	**Tunja**, Colombia	2,820	9,252
10	**Quito**, Ecuador	2,819	9,249

Lhasa was formerly the highest capital city in the world, a role now occupied by La Paz, capital of Bolivia. Wenchuan is situated at more than half the elevation of Everest, and even the cities at the foot of this list are more than one-third as high.

THE 10 ★
FIRST UK CITIES TO BE GRANTED CHARTERS

	CITY	ORIGINAL CHARTER GRANTED
1	Ripon	886
2	London	1066
3	Edinburgh	1124
4	Chichester	1135
5 =	Derby	1154
=	Lincoln	1154
=	Oxford	1154
8 =	Nottingham	1155
=	Winchester	1155
10	Exeter	1156

There are 48 cities in England, four in Scotland and Wales, and three in Northern Ireland. Although most of them were settled in earlier times, their status as cities is dated from when their charters, issued by the Crown and establishing certain privileges, such as the power to enact local laws or collect taxes, were granted. Some dates are disputed: Norwich, for example, claims to have received its original charter in 996, but 1194 is the more accepted date.

TOP 10 ★
LARGEST NON-CAPITAL CITIES

	CITY/COUNTRY/CAPITAL CITY	POPULATION
1	**Shanghai**, China	13,400,000
	Beijing	*10,940,000*
2	**Bombay**, India	12,596,243
	New Delhi	*8,419,000*
3	**Calcutta***, India	11,021,918
	New Delhi	*8,419,000*
4	**Sâo Paulo**, Brazil	9,394,000
	Brasília	*1,601,094*
5	**Tianjin**, China	9,090,000
	Beijing	*10,940,000*
6	**Istanbul***, Turkey	7,774,169
	Ankara,	*2,782,200*
7	**New York**, USA	7,380,906
	Washington, DC	*567,094*
8	**Karachi***, Pakistan	7,183,000
	Islamabad	*320,000*
9	**Rio de Janeiro***, Brazil	5,547,033
	Brasília	*1,601,094*
10	**St. Petersburg***, Russia	4,273,001
	Moscow	*8,436,447*

* *Former capital*

ON TOP OF THE WORLD

Potosí in Bolivia is the highest city in the Americas, established in the 16th century after the discovery of silver and other minerals in the mountain of the same name.

TOP 10 ★
MOST DENSELY POPULATED CITIES*

	CITY/COUNTRY	POPULATION PER SQ KM	SQ MILE
1	**Hong Kong**, China	98, 053	253,957
2	**Lagos**, Nigeria	67,561	174,982
3	**Dhaka**, Bangladesh	63,900	165,500
4	**Jakarta**, Indonesia	56,650	146,724
5	**Bombay**, India	54,997	142,442
6	**Ahmadabad**, India	50,676	131,250
7	**Ho Chi Minh**, Vietnam	50,617	131,097
8	**Shenyang**, China	44,125	114,282
9	**Bangalore**, India	43,583	112,880
10	**Cairo**, Egypt	41,413	107,260

* *Includes only cities with populations of over 2 million*

Source: *US Bureau of the Census*

Did You Know? Hong Kong has a density equivalent to a cramped 10.5 sq m/113 sq ft per person. By comparison, London appears positively spacious with 248 sq m/2,673 sq ft per person.

TOP 10 ★

MOST POPULATED FORMER CAPITAL CITIES

	CITY/COUNTRY	CEASED TO BE CAPITAL	POPULATION*
1	**Calcutta**, India	1912	11,021,918
2	**Istanbul**, Turkey	1923	7,774,169
3	**Karachi**, Pakistan	1968	7,183,000
4	**Rio de Janeiro**, Brazil	1960	5,547,033
5	**St. Petersburg**, Russia	1980	4,273,001
6	**Berlin**, Germany	1949	3,472,009
7	**Alexandria**, Egypt	c.641	3,380,000
8	**Melbourne**, Australia	1927	3,189,200
9	**Nanjiang**, China	1949	2,610,594
10	**Philadelphia**, USA	1800	1,524,249

* Within administrative boundaries

TOP 10 ★

LARGEST CITIES IN THE US*

	CITY/STATE	POPULATION
1	**New York**, New York	7,380,906
2	**Los Angeles**, California	3,553,638
3	**Chicago**, Illinois	2,721,547
4	**Houston**, Texas	1,744,058
5	**Philadelphia**, Pennsylvania	1,478,002
6	**San Diego**, California	1,171,121
7	**Phoenix**, Arizona	1,159,014
8	**San Antonio**, Texas	1,067,816
9	**Dallas**, Texas	1,053,292
10	**Detroit**, Michigan	1,000,272

* Estimated figures up to 1 July 1996
Source: *US Bureau of the Census*

These are estimates for central city areas only, not for the total metropolitan areas that surround them, which may be several times as large.

THE BIG APPLE

New York's vibrant character is largely due to the vast numbers of immigrants that have come to this city. Irish, Greeks, Italians, Russians, Canadians, English, Dutch, and Puerto Ricans have all made it their home.

LIFE IN THE CITY

Mahatma Ghandi Road in Calcutta, which teems with trams, cars, lorries, rickshaws, and people, epitomizes the colourful – and noisy – hustle and bustle of daily life in India's former capital city.

TOP 10 ★

LARGEST CITIES IN NORTH AMERICA

	CITY/COUNTRY	POPULATION*
1	**New York**, USA	16,329,000
2	**Mexico City**, Mexico	15,643,000
3	**Los Angeles**, USA	12,410,000
4	**Chicago**, USA	6,846,000
5	**Toronto**, Canada	4,483,000
6	**Philadelphia**, USA	4,304,000
7	**Washington DC**, USA	4,111,000
8	**San Fransisco**, USA	3,866,000
9	**Detroit**, USA	3,725,000
10	**Dallas**, USA	3,612,000

* Of urban agglomeration
Source: *United Nations*

TOP 10 LARGEST CITIES IN EUROPE

(City/country/population*)

1 **Paris**, France, 9,469,000
2 **Moscow**, Russia, 9,233,000 **3** **London**, UK, 7,335,000 **4** **Essen**, Germany, 6,481,000 **5** **St. Petersburg**, Russia, 5,111,000 **6** **Milan**, Italy, 4,251,000 **7** **Madrid**, Spain, 4,072,000 **8** **Athens**, Greece, 3,693,000 **9** **Frankfurt**, Germany, 3,606,000 **10** **Katowice**, Poland, 3,552,000

* Of urban agglomeration
Source: *United Nations*

TOP 10 ★

FASTEST-GROWING CITIES

	CITY/COUNTRY	RATE*
1	**Tanjung Karang**, Indonesia	6.52
2	**Maputo**, Mozambique	6.07
3	**Esfahan**, Iran	5.66
4	**Kabul**, Afghanistan	5.56
5	**Conakry**, Guinea	5.17
6	**Nairobi**, Kenya	5.16
7	**Lagos**, Nigeria	5.05
8	**Dacca**, Bangladesh	5.03
9	**Luanda**, Angola	4.99
10	**Yaounde**, Cameroon	4.94

* Population growth rate, per cent per annum
Source: *United Nations*

NATIONAL PARKS

TOP 10 ★
LARGEST NATIONAL PARKS IN ENGLAND AND WALES

	NATIONAL PARK	ESTABLISHED	AREA SQ KM	SQ MILES
1	Lake District	9 May 1951	2,292	885
2	Snowdonia	18 Oct 1951	2,142	827
3	Yorkshire Dales	13 Oct 1954	1,769	683
4	Peak District	17 Apr 1951	1,438	555
5	North York Moors	28 Nov 1952	1,436	554
6	Brecon Beacons	17 Apr 1957	1,351	522
7	Northumberland	6 Apr 1956	1,049	405
8	Dartmoor	30 Oct 1951	954	368
9	Exmoor	19 Oct 1954	693	268
10	Pembrokeshire Coast	29 Feb 1952	584	225

Following the National Parks and Access to the Countryside Act of 1949, the National Parks were established in the 1950s to conserve and protect some of the most picturesque landscapes of England and Wales from unsuitable development, at the same time allowing the public free access to them. The total area is 14,011 sq km/5,410 sq miles (about 9 per cent of the total area of the two countries), of which 9,934 sq km/3,836 sq miles is in England and 4,077 sq km/1,574 sq miles in Wales.

TOP 10 ★
LONGEST NATIONAL TRAILS IN ENGLAND AND WALES

	NATIONAL TRAIL	OPENED	LENGTH KM	MILES
1	South West Coast Path	May 1973/ Sep 1974/ May 1978	962	598
2	Pennine Way	Apr 1965	412	256
3	Thames Path	Jul 1996	344	214
4	Pembrokeshire Coast Path	May 1970	292	181
5	Offa's Dyke Path	Jul 1971	285	177
6	North Downs Way	Sep 1978	246	153
7	Cleveland Way	May 1969	176	109
8	South Downs Way	Jul 1972	171	106
9	Peddars Way and Norfolk Coast Path	Jul 1986	150	93
10	Ridgeway	Sep 1973	137	85

The trails are managed by the Countryside Commission, which is responsible for repairing the erosion caused by walkers.

TOP 10 ★
LARGEST NATURE RESERVES IN SCOTLAND

	NATURE RESERVE/ LOCATION	AREA HECTARES	ACRES
1	Cairngorms, Grampian and Highland Regions	25,949	64,121
2	Inverpolly, Highland Region	10,857	26,828
3	Rum, Highland Region	10,684	26,401
4	Caerlaverock, Dumfries and Galloway Region	7,706	19,042
5	Ben Wyvis, Highland Region	5,673	14,026
6	Beinn Eighe, Highland Region	4,758	11,757
7	Glen Tanar, Grampian Region	4,185	10,341
8	Ben Lawers, Tayside and Central Regions	4,060	10,032
9	Creag Meagaidh, Highland Region	3,948	9,756
10	Gualin, Sutherland	2,522	6,232

TOP 10 LARGEST NATURE RESERVES IN WALES

(Nature reserve/location/area in hectares/acres)

1 **Berwyn**, Powys, 3,238/8,001 **2** **Dyfi**, Dyfed, 2,268/5,604 **3** **Y Wyddfa-Snowdon**, Gwynedd, 1,677/4,144 **4** **Morfa Harlech**, Gwynedd, 884/2,184 **5** **Cors Caron**, Dyfed, 816/2,016 **6** **Claerwen**, Powys, 789/1,950 **7** **Whiteford**, West Glamorgan, 782/1,932 **8** **Rhinog**, Gwynedd, 598/1,478 **9** **Kenfig Pool and Dunes**, Mid Glamorgan, 518/1,280 **10** **Cader Idris**, Gwynedd, 430/1,063

Source: *Cyngor Cefn Gwlad Cymru/Countryside Council for Wales*

TOP 10 ★
LARGEST NATURE RESERVES IN ENGLAND

	NATURE RESERVE/ LOCATION	AREA HECTARES	ACRES
1	The Wash, Lincolnshire	9,899	24,461
2	Ribble Marshes, Lancashire/Merseyside	4,520	11,169
3	Moor House, Cumbria	3,894	9,622
4	Holkham, Norfolk	3,851	9,516
5	Lindisfarne, Northumberland	3,541	8,750
6	Upper Teesdale, North Yorkshire	3,509	8,671
7	Bridgewater Bay, Somerset	2,559	6,323
8	Dengie, Essex	2,544	6,286
9	Lizard, Cornwall	1,662	4,107
10	Blackwater Estuary, Essex	1,031	2,548

Nature Reserves are sites designated under the National Parks and Access to the Countryside Act of 1949 for the study and preservation of flora and fauna or geological or physiological features. They are either owned or controlled by English Nature or approved bodies such as Wildlife Trusts. In 1999 there were 199 such sites in England, a total of 80,827 hectares/199,728 acres. In addition, there are 705 Local Nature Reserves in the UK.

TOP 10 ★
LARGEST AREAS OF OUTSTANDING NATURAL BEAUTY IN ENGLAND AND WALES

	AREA	ESTABLISHED	AREA SQ KM	SQ MILES
1	Cotswolds	Aug 1966/Dec 1990	2,038	787
2	North Pennines	Jun 1988	1,983	766
3	North Wessex Downs	Dec 1972	1,730	668
4	High Weald	Oct 1983	1,460	564
5	Dorset	Jul 1959	1,129	436
6=	Sussex Downs	Apr 1966	983	380
=	Cranborne Chase and West Wiltshire Downs	Oct 1983	983	380
8	Cornwall	Nov 1959/Oct 1983	958	370
9	Kent Downs	Jul 1968	878	339
10	Chilterns	Dec 1965/Mar 1990	833	322

Between them, England and Wales have 42 "Areas of Outstanding Natural Beauty". There are also nine such areas in Northern Ireland.

TOP 10 ★
LONGEST HERITAGE COASTS IN THE UK

	HERITAGE COAST	DEFINED	KM	LENGTH MILES
1	Pembrokeshire	Jul 1974	232	145
2	North Northumberland	Apr 1992	110	68
3	Lleyn	Mar 1974	90	56
4	South Devon	Dec 1986	75	47
5=	Isles of Scilly	Dec 1974	64	40
=	North Norfolk	Apr 1975	64	40
7	Gower	Jun 1973	59	37
8=	Suffolk	Sep 1979	57	35
=	North Yorkshire and Cleveland	May 1981	57	35
10	Penwith	Apr 1986	54	34

The total length of Heritage Coasts in England and Wales is 1,539 km/956 miles. No new areas of coast have been so defined since 1991.

ULURU
Once known as Ayers Rock, this giant block of red sandstone is the world's largest free-standing rock, and lies in one of Australia's protected areas. Its name means "giant pebble" in Aborigine.

TOP 10 COUNTRIES WITH THE LARGEST PROTECTED AREAS

	COUNTRY	PER CENT OF TOTAL AREA	DESIGNATED AREA SQ KM	SQ MILES
1	Brazil	16.8	1,430,167	552,191
2	USA	10.6	993,547	383,611
3	Greenland	45.2	982,500	379,345
4	Australia	10.9	837,843	323,493
5	Colombia	71.9	818,346	316,158
6	Canada	5.6	554,369	214,092
7	Venezuela	60.7	553,496	213,706
8	Tanzania	38.9	365,115	140,972
9	Indonesia	17.2	330,059	127,437
10	China	3.2	308,970	119,294

Which world city has the most skyscrapers? *see p.106 for the answer* A Hong Kong B New York C Chicago

COUNTIES OF BRITAIN

LARGEST ENGLISH COUNTIES

COUNTY	AREA SQ KM	SQ MILES
1 North Yorkshire	8,038	3,208
2 Cumbria	6,824	2,635
3 Devon	6,703	2,588
4 Lincolnshire	5,921	2,286
5 Norfolk	5,372	2,074
6 Northumberland	5,026	1,941
7 Hereford and Worcester	3,923	1,515
8 Suffolk	3,798	1,466
9 Hampshire	3,689	1,459
10 Kent	3,735	1,442

SMALLEST ENGLISH COUNTIES

COUNTY	AREA SQ KM	SQ MILES
1 Isle of Wight	380	147
2 Tyne and Wear	540	208
3 Cleveland	597	231
4 Merseyside	655	253
5 West Midlands	899	347
6 Bedfordshire	1,236	477
7 Berkshire	1,259	486
8 Greater Manchester	1,286	497
9 Avon	1,332	514
10 South Yorkshire	1,559	602

LEAST DENSELY POPULATED COUNTIES IN ENGLAND

COUNTY	POPULATION PER SQ KM	SQ MILE
1 Northumberland	61	158
2 Cumbria	72	186
3 North Yorkshire	88	228
4 Lincolnshire	103	267
5 Shropshire	120	311
6 Cornwall	136	352
7 Somerset	139	360
8 Norfolk	144	373
9 Devon	158	409
10 Wiltshire	170	440

SMALLEST COUNTIES IN THE UK

COUNTY/LOCATION	AREA SQ KM	SQ MILES
1 Dundee City, Scotland	65	25
2 = Carrickfergus, Northern Ireland	81	31
= North Down, Northern Ireland	81	31
4 Castlereagh, Northern Ireland	85	33
5 Blaenau Gwent, Wales	109	42
6 Belfast, Northern Ireland	110	42
7 Merthyr Tydfil, Wales	111	43
8 Torfaen, Wales	126	49
9 Cardiff, Wales	140	54
10 Newtonabbey, Northern Ireland	151	58

Following local government reorganization in 1996, counties have been replaced by council areas in Scotland, of which there are 32, and by unitary authorities in Wales, of which there are 22 and Northern Ireland (26). These sub-regions are considerably smaller than the old counties, which means that the list of smallest British counties is now comprised entirely of areas in Scotland, Wales, and Northern Ireland.

MOST HIGHLY POPULATED COUNTIES IN THE UK

COUNTY*	POPULATION
1 Greater London	7,074,000
2 West Midlands	2,642,000
3 Greater Manchester	2,576,000
4 West Yorkshire	2,109,000
5 Essex	1,586,000
6 Kent	1,557,000
7 Lancashire	1,425,000
8 Merseyside	1,420,000
9 South Yorkshire	1,305,000
10 Hampshire	1,222,000

*All in England

The 149 counties, unitary authorities (which are sometimes synonymous with counties), and metropolitan boroughs of England created in 1974 are now among the most populated in Britain. Even a century ago, Lancashire had the second largest population in the country, a total (according to the 1901 census) of 4,437,518, but under the revised county structure, it was divided into the metropolitan counties of Greater Manchester and Merseyside, with Lancashire comprising the remainder.

LEAST DENSELY POPULATED COUNTIES IN THE UK

COUNTY/LOCATION	POPULATION PER SQ KM	SQ MILE
1 Highland, Scotland	8	21
2 Eilean Siar (Western Isles), Scotland	9	23
3 Argyll and Bute, Scotland	13	34
4 Shetland Islands, Scotland	16	41
5 Orkney Islands, Scotland	20	52
6 The Scottish Borders, Scotland	22	57
7 Dumfries and Galloway, Scotland	23	60
8 Powys, Wales	24	62
9 Perth and Kinross, Scotland	25	65
10 Moyle, Northern Ireland	30	78

TOP 10 ★
LEAST-POPULATED COUNTIES OF ENGLAND

	COUNTY	POPULATION
1	Isle of Wight	125,500
2	Shropshire	277,100
3	Northumberland	307,400
4	Bedfordshire	367,300
5	Wiltshire	418,700
6	Somerset	482,700
7	Cornwall and the Isles of Scilly	483,300
8	Cumbria	490,600
9	Warwickshire	500,600
10	Gloucestershire	556,300

TOP 10 ★
MOST DENSELY POPULATED COUNTIES IN ENGLAND

	COUNTY	POPULATION PER SQ KM	SQ MILE
1	Greater London	4,482	11,608
2	West Midlands	2,940	7,615
3	Merseyside	2,168	5,615
4	Tyne and Wear	2,086	5,503
5	Greater Manchester	2,003	5,188
6	West Yorkshire	1,035	2,681
7	South Yorkshire	836	2,165
8	Berkshire	628	1,627
9	Surrey	624	1,616
10	Hertfordshire	620	1,606

TOP 10 ★
MOST DENSELY POPULATED COUNTIES IN THE UK

	COUNTY/LOCATION	POPULATION PER SQ KM	SQ MILE
1	Greater London, England	4,482	11,608
2	Glasgow City, Scotland	3,522	9,122
3	West Midlands, England	2,940	7,615
4	Belfast, Northern Ireland	2,712	7,024
5	Dundee City, Scotland	2,306	5,973
6	Cardiff, Wales	2,250	5,827
7	Merseyside, England	2,168	5,615
8	Tyne and Wear, England	2,086	5,403
9	Greater Manchester, England	2,003	5,188
10	Edinburgh City, Scotland	1,711	4,431

TOP 10 ★
LEAST POPULATED COUNTIES OF THE UK

	COUNTY/LOCATION	POPULATION
1	Moyle, Northern Ireland	14,900
2	Orkney, Scotland	20,000
3	Shetland Islands, Scotland	22,522
4	Ballymoney, Northern Ireland	24,800
5	Eilean Siar (Western Isles), Scotland	28,240
6	Larne, Northern Ireland	30,200
7	Limavady, Northern Ireland	30,500
8	Cookstown, Northern Ireland	31,700
9	Strabane, Northern Ireland	36,500
10	Banbridge, Northern Ireland	37,400

The traditional counties of Northern Ireland have been replaced by unitary authorities which are considerably smaller than most counties in the rest of Britain, and hence dominate this list.

TOP 10 LARGEST COUNTIES AND REGIONS IN THE UK

	COUNTY/LOCATION	AREA SQ KM	SQ MILES
1	Highland, Scotland	25,784	9,952
2	North Yorkshire, England	8,038	3,208
3	Argyll and Bute, Scotland	6,930	2,676
4	Cumbria, England	6,824	2,635
5	Devon, England	6,703	2,588
6	Dumfries and Galloway, Scotland	6,439	2,486
7	Aberdeenshire, Scotland	6,318	2,439
8	Lincolnshire, England	5,921	2,286
9	Norfolk, England	5,372	2,074
10	Perth and Kinross, Scotland	5,311	2,051

Which is the most densely populated country in the world? *see p.96 for the answer*   A Bangladesh   B Monaco   C Singapore

103

PLACE NAMES

TOP 10 ★
COUNTRIES WITH THE LONGEST OFFICIAL NAMES

	OFFICIAL NAME*	COMMON ENGLISH NAME	LETTERS
1	al-Jamāhīrīyah al-ʿArabīya al-Lībīyah ash-Shaʿbīyah al-Ishtirākīyah	Libya	56
2	al-Jumhūrīyah al-Jazāʾirīyah ad-Dīmuqrāṭīyah ash-Shaʿbīyah	Algeria	49
3	United Kingdom of Great Britain and Northern Ireland	United Kingdom	45
4	Sri Lankā Prajathanthrika Samajavadi Janarajaya	Sri Lanka	43
5	ʿJumhurīyat al-Qumur al-Ittihādīyah al-Islāmīyah	Comoros	41
6=	al-Jumhūrīyah al-Islāmīyah al-Mūrītānīyah	Mauritania	36
=	The Federation of St. Christopher and Nevis	St. Kitts and Nevis	36
8	Jamhuuriyadda Dimuqraadiga Soomaaliya	Somalia	35
9	al-Mamlakah al-Urdunnīyah al-Hāshimīyah	Jordan	34
10	Repoblika Demokratika n'i Madagaskar	Madagascar	32

* Some official names have been transliterated from languages that do not use the Roman alphabet; their length may vary according to the method used.

TOP 10 MOST COMMON HOUSE NAMES IN THE UK

1 The Cottage 2 The Bungalow 3 Rose Cottage 4 The Lodge 5 The Coach House 6 The School House 7 The White House 8 Woodlands 9 Hill Crest 10 The Gables

When they purchase a house, most people retain its existing name, rather than change it. During the past decade The Cottage overtook The Bungalow to take first place.

TOP 10 ★
MOST COMMON STREET NAMES IN THE US

1 Second Street
2 Park Street
3 Third Street
4 Fourth Street
5 Fifth Street
6 First Street
7 Sixth Street
8 Seventh Street
9 Washington Street
10 Maple Street

CITY OF ANGELS
Bangkok, the city with the world's longest name, lies on the banks of the River Chao Phraya.

TOP 10 MOST COMMON PLACE NAMES IN GREAT BRITAIN

(Name/occurrences)

1 Newton, 150 2 Blackhill/Black Hill, 141 3 Mountpleasant/Mount Pleasant, 130 4 Castlehill/Castle Hill, 127 5 Woodside/Wood Side, 116 6 Newtown/New Town, 111 7 Greenhill/ Green Hill, 108 8 Woodend/Wood End, 106 9 Burnside, 105 10 Beacon Hill, 94

These entries include the names of towns and villages, as well as woods, hills, and other named locations.

TOP 10 ★
LONGEST PLACE NAMES*

NAME	LETTERS
1 Krung thep mahanakhon bovorn ratanakosin mahintharayutthaya mahadilok pop noparatratchathani burirom udomratchanivetmahasathan amornpiman avatarnsathit sakkathattiyavisnukarmprasit	167

When the poetic name of Bangkok, capital of Thailand, is used, it is usually abbreviated to "Krung Thep" (city of angels).

2 Taumatawhakatangihangakoauauotamateaturipukakapikimaungahoronukupokaiw-henuakitanatahu	85

This is the longer version (the other has a mere 83 letters) of the Maori name of a hill in New Zealand. It translates as "The place where Tamatea, the man with the big knees, who slid, climbed and swallowed mountains, known as land-eater, played on the flute to his loved one".

3 Gorsafawddacha'idraigodanheddogleddollônpenrhynareurdraethceredigion	67

A name contrived by the Fairbourne Steam Railway, Gwynedd, North Wales, for publicity purposes and in order to outdo its rival, No. 4. It means "The Mawddach station and its dragon teeth at the Northern Penrhyn Road on the golden beach of Cardigan Bay".

4 Llanfairpwllgwyngyllgogerychwyrndrobwllllantysiliogogogoch	58

This is the place in Gwynedd famed especially for the length of its railway tickets. It means "St Mary's Church in the hollow of the white hazel near to the rapid whirlpool of Llantysilio of the Red Cave". Questions have been raised about its authenticity, since its official name comprises only the first 20 letters, and the full name appears to have been invented as a hoax in the 19th century by a local poet, John Evans, known as Y Bardd Cocos. It also has Britain's longest Internet site name: http://www.llanfairpwllgwyngyllgogerychwyrndrobwllllantysilio-gogogoch.-wales.com/llanfair

5 El Pueblo de Nuestra Señora la Reina de los Angeles de la Porciuncula	57

The site of a Franciscan mission and the full Spanish name of Los Angeles; it means "the town of Our Lady the Queen of the Angels of the Little Portion". Nowadays it is customarily known by its initial letters, "LA", making it also one of the shortest-named cities in the world.

6 Chargoggagoggmanchauggagoggchaubunagungamaugg	45

America's second longest place name, a lake near Webster, Massachusetts. Its Indian name, loosely translated, means "You fish on your side, I'll fish on mine, and no one fishes in the middle". It is said to be pronounced "Char-gogg-a-gogg (pause) man-chaugg-a-gogg (pause) chau-bun-a-gung-amaugg". It is, however, an invented extension of its real name (Chagungungamaug Pond, or "boundary fishing place"), devised in the 1920s by Larry Daly, the editor of the Webster Times.

7 = Lower North Branch Little Southwest Miramichi	40

Canada's longest place name – a short river in New Brunswick.

= Villa Real de la Santa Fe de San Francisco de Asis	40

The full Spanish name of Santa Fe, New Mexico, translates as, "Royal city of the holy faith of St Francis of Assisi".

9 Te Whakatakanga-o-te-ngarehu-o-te-ahi-a-Tamatea	38

The Maori name of Hammer Springs, New Zealand; like the second name in this list, it refers to a legend of Tamatea, explaining how the springs were warmed by "the falling of the cinders of the fire of Tamatea". Its name is variously written either hyphenated or as a single word.

10 Meallan Liath Coire Mhic Dhubhghaill	32

The longest multiple name in Scotland, a place near Aultanrynie, Highland, this is alternatively spelled Meallan Liath Coire Mhic Dhughaill (30 letters).

* Including single-word, hyphenated, and multiple-word names

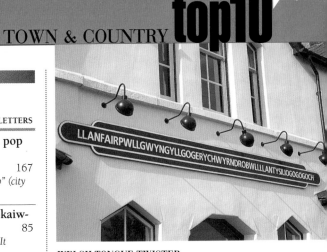

WELSH TONGUE TWISTER

This small village with a very long name on the island of Anglesey, in North Wales, is known to its residents as simply Llanfair.

TOP 10 ★
LONGEST PLACE NAMES IN THE UK*

NAME/LOCATION	LETTERS
1 Gorsafawddachaidraigddanhed-dogleddollônpenrhyn-areurdraethceredigion (see Top 10 Longest Place Names)	67
2 Llanfairpwllgwyngyllgogery-chwyrndrobwllllantysiliogo-gogoch (see Top 10 Longest Place Names)	58
3 Sutton-under-Whitestonecliffe, North Yorkshire	27
4 Llanfihangel-yng-Ngwynfa, Powys	22
5 = Llanfihangel-y-Creuddyn, Dyfed	21
= Llanfihangel-y-traethau, Gwynedd	21
7 Cottonshopeburnfoot, Northumberland	19
8 = Blakehopeburnhaugh, Northumberland	18
= Coignafeuinternich, Inverness-shire	18
10 = Claddach-baleshare, North Uist, Outer Hebrides	17
= Claddach-knockline, North Uist, Outer Hebrides	17

*Single and hyphenated only

STREETS AHEAD

Towards the end of the 1900s in America, civic authorities demanded that street names be made uniform, following a system that avoided duplication.

TOP 10 MOST COMMON STREET NAMES IN THE UK

1 High Street **2** Station Road **3** Church Road **4** Park Road **5** The Drive
6 Station Approach **7** Green Lane **8** The Avenue **9** London Road **10** Church Lane

Did You Know? The shortest place name in the UK is Ae in Dumfries and Galloway, Scotland.

THE TALLEST BUILDINGS

TALLEST HABITABLE BUILDINGS

BUILDING/YEAR/LOCATION	STOREYS	HEIGHT M	FT
1 Petronas Towers, 1996, Kuala Lumpur, Malaysia	96	452	1,482
2 Sears Tower, 1974, Chicago, USA	110	443	1,454
with spires		520	1,707
3 World Trade Center*, 1973, New York, USA	110	417	1,368
4 Jin Mao Building, 1997, Shanghai, China	93	382	1,255
with spire		420	1,378
5 Empire State Building, 1931, New York, USA	102	381	1,250
with spire		449	1,472
6 T & C Tower, 1997, Kao-hsiung, Taiwan	85	348	1,142
7 Amoco Building, 1973, Chicago, USA	80	346	1,136
8 John Hancock Center, 1968, Chicago, USA	100	343	1,127
with spires		450	1,476
9 Shun Hing Square, 1996, Shenzen, China	80	330	1,082
with spires		384	1,263
10 Sky Central Plaza, 1996, Guangzhou, China	80	323	1,060
with spires		391	1,283

* Twin towers; the second tower is slightly smaller

TOP 10 TALLEST MASTS

(Mast/location/height in m/ft)

1 KTHI-TV Mast, Fargo, North Dakota, 629/2,063 **2** KSLA-TV Mast, Shreveport, Louisiana, 579/1,898 **3** = WBIR-TV Mast, Knoxville, Tennessee, 533/1,749; = WTVM & WRBL TV Mast, Columbus, Georgia, 533/1,749 **5** KFVS TV Mast, Cape Girardeau, Missouri, 511/1,676 **6** WPSD-TV Mast, Paducah, Kentucky, 499/1,638 **7** WGAN TV Mast, Portland, Maine, 493/ 1,619 **8** KWTV TV Mast, Oklahoma City, Oklahoma, 479/1,572 **9** BREN Tower, Area 25, Nevada Test Site, Nevada, 464/1,521 **10** Omega Base Navigational Mast, Gippsland, Victoria, Australia, 426/1,400

TALLEST REINFORCED CONCRETE BUILDINGS

BUILDING/YEAR/LOCATION	STOREYS	HEIGHT M	FT
1 Baiyoke II Tower, 1997, Bangkok, Thailand	89	319	1,046
2 Central Plaza, 1992, Hong Kong, China	78	309	1,015
with spire		374	1,228
3 311 South Wacker Drive, 1990, Chicago, USA	65	296	970
4 2 Prudential Plaza, 1990, Chicago, USA	64	275	901
with spire		298	978
5 NCNB, 1992, Charlotte, USA	60	265	871
6 Water Tower Place, 1975, Chicago, USA	74	262	859
7 Messeturm, 1990, Frankfurt, Germany	70	256	841
8 Citispire, 1989, New York, USA	72	245	802
9 Rialto Tower, 1985, Melbourne, Australia	60	242	794
10 Tun Abdul Rasak Building, 1985, Penang, Malaysia	61	232	761

Reinforced concrete was patented in France on 16 March 1867 by Joseph Monier (1823–1906) and developed by another Frenchman, François Hennebique (1842–1921). The first American buildings constructed from it date from a century ago, since when it has become one of the most important of all building materials. Steel bars set within concrete slabs expand and contract at the same rate as the concrete, providing great tensile strength and fire resistance. These qualities make it the ideal material for huge structures such as bridge spans and skyscrapers.

TOP HOTEL

At 319 m/1,046 ft, the Baiyoke II Tower is also the tallest hotel in the world. The second-tallest hotel – the Yu Kyong in North Korea – has a greater number of storeys, however: 105 to the Baiyoke's 89.

TOP 10 CITIES WITH THE MOST SKYSCRAPERS*

(City/location/skyscrapers)

1 New York City, USA, 140 **2** Chicago, USA, 68 **3** = Hong Kong, China, 36; = Houston, USA, 36 **5** Kuala Lumpur, Malaysia, 25 **6** Los Angeles, USA, 24 **7** Dallas, USA, 22 **8** = San Francisco, USA, 20; = Shanghai, China, 20 **10** = Singapore, 18; = Sydney, Australia, 18

* Habitable buildings of more than 152 m/500 ft

TALLEST CYLINDRICAL BUILDINGS

BUILDING/YEAR/LOCATION	STOREYS	HEIGHT M	FT
1 Treasury Building, 1986, Singapore	52	235	770
2 Tun Abdul Prazak Building, 1985, Penang, Malaysia	61	232	760
3 Westin Peachtree Plaza, 1973, Atlanta, USA	71	220	721
4 Renaissance Centre, 1977, Detroit, USA	73	219	718
5 Hopewell Centre, 1980, Hong Kong, China	64	215	705
6 Marina City Apartments (twin towers), 1969, Chicago, USA	61	179	588
7 Australia Square Tower, 1968, Sydney, Australia	46	170	560
8 Amartapura Condominium 1, 1996, Tangerang, Indonesia	54	163	535
9 Shenzen City Plaza, 1996, Shenzen, China	37	150	490
10 Amartapura Condominium 2, 1997, Tangerang, Indonesia	36	136	445

When completed in 1968, the misleadingly named Australia Square Tower in Sydney became the world's tallest cylindrical building as well as the tallest concrete building. It also claims the world's largest revolving restaurant, measuring 41 m/135 ft in diameter and situated at a dizzy 153 m/502 ft above street level.

TWIN TOWERS

The World Trade Center in New York has a staggering 3,140 stairs. In 1977, instead of taking this indoor route to the top, George Willig climbed up the outside of the center – without using any ropes.

TOP 10 ★
TALLEST APARTMENT BUILDINGS

BUILDING/YEAR/LOCATION	STOREYS	HEIGHT M	FT
1 **Lake Point Tower**, 1968, Chicago, USA	70	197	645
2 **Central Park Place**, 1988, New York City, USA	56	191	628
3 **Olympic Tower**, 1976, New York City, USA	51	189	620
4 **May Road Apartments**, 1993, Hong Kong, China	58	180	590
5 **Marina City Apartments**, 1968, Chicago, USA	61	179	588
6 **North Pier Apartments**, 1990, Chicago, USA	61	177	581
7 **Onterie Center**, 1985, Chicago, USA	58	174	570
8= **Triple Towers**, U/C, Mang Tzeng, China	57	172	564
= **Newton Tower**, U/C, Hong Kong, China	43	172	564
10 **30 Broad Street**, 1980, New York City, USA	48	171	562

U/C = under construction

TOP 10 ★
HIGHEST PUBLIC OBSERVATORIES

BUILDING/LOCATION	OBSERVATORY	YEAR	HEIGHT M	FT
1 **CN Tower,** Toronto, Canada	Space deck	1975	447	1,465
2 **World Trade Center**, New York City, USA	Rooftop Tower B	1973	415	1,360
3 **Sears Tower**, Chicago, USA	103rd floor	1974	412	1,353
4 **Empire State Building**, New York, USA	102nd floor Outdoor observatory	1931	381 320	1,250 1,050
5 **Ostankino Tower**, Moscow, Russia	5th floor turret	1967	360	1,181
6 **Oriental Pearl Broadcasting Tower**, Shanghai, China	VIP observation level Public observation level	1995	350 263	1,148 863
7 **Jin Mao Building**, Shanghai, China	88th floor	1997	340	1,115
8 **John Hancock Center**, Chicago, USA	94th floor	1968	314	1,030
9 **Sky Central Plaza**, Guanghshou, China	90th floor	1996	310	1,016
10 **KL Tower**, Kuala Lumpur, Malaysia	Revolving restaurant Public observation level	1995	282 276	925 907

TOP 10 ★
TALLEST TELECOMMUNICATIONS TOWERS

TOWER/YEAR/LOCATION	HEIGHT M	FT
1 **CN Tower**, 1975, Toronto, Canada	555	1,821
2 **Ostankino Tower**, 1967, Moscow, Russia	537	1,762
3 **Oriental Pearl Broadcasting Tower**, 1995, Shanghai, China	468	1,535
4 **Menara Telecom Tower**, 1996, Kuala Lumpur, Malaysia	421	1,381
5 **Tianjin TV and Radio Tower**, 1991, Tianjin, China	415	1,362
6 **Central Radio and TV Tower**, 1994, Beijing, China	405	1,328
7 **TV Tower**, 1983, Tashkent, Uzbekistan	375	1,230
8 **Liberation Tower**, 1998, Kuwait City, Kuwait	372	1,220
9 **Alma-Ata Tower**, 1983, Kazakhstan	370	1,214
10 **TV Tower**, 1969, Berlin, Germany	365	1,198

All the towers listed are self-supporting, rather than masts braced with guy wires, and all have observation facilities, the highest being that in the CN Tower, Toronto, at 447 m/1,467 ft. The completion of the Telecom Tower, Kuala Lumpur, means that the Eiffel Tower dropped out of the Top 10.

PEARL OF THE ORIENT

Shanghai's Oriental Pearl, the highest tower in Asia, was designed by Chinese architect Jia Huan Cheng to represent a string of pearls.

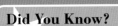

Did You Know? The Menara Jakarta, a tower under construction in Jakarta, Indonesia, is intended to be 558 m/1,831 ft tall. If it is completed, it will be the tallest structure of any kind in the southern hemisphere.

BRIDGES & OTHER STRUCTURES

LONGEST CANTILEVER BRIDGES

BRIDGE/YEAR/LOCATION	LONGEST SPAN	
	M	FT
1 Pont de Québec, 1917, Canada	549	1,800
2 Firth of Forth, 1890, Scotland	521	1,710
3 Minato, Osaka, 1974, Japan	510	1,673
4 Commodore John Barry, 1974, New Jersey/Pennsylvania, USA	494	1,622
5 =Greater New Orleans 1, 1958, Louisiana, USA	480	1,575
=Greater New Orleans 2, 1988, Louisiana, USA	480	1,575
7 Howrah, 1943, Calcutta, India	457	1,500
8 Gramercy, 1995, Louisiana, USA	445	1,460
9 Transbay, 1936, San Francisco, USA	427	1,400
10 Baton Rouge, 1969, Louisiana, USA	376	1,235

LONGEST UNDERWATER TUNNELS*

TUNNEL/YEAR/LOCATION	LENGTH	
	KM	MILES
1 Seikan, 1988, Japan	53.90	33.49
2 Channel Tunnel, 1994, France/England	49.94	31.03
3 Dai–Shimizu, 1982, Japan	22.17	13.78
4 Shin–Kanmon, 1975, Japan	18.68	11.61
5 Great Belt Fixed Link, 1997, Eastern Tunnel, Denmark	8.00	4.97
6 Severn, 1886, UK	7.01	4.36
7 Haneda, 1971, Japan	5.98	3.72
8 BART, 1970, San Francisco, USA	5.83	3.62
9 Kammon, 1942, Japan	3.60	2.24
10 Kammon, 1958, Japan	3.46	2.15

* All are rail tunnels, except No. 10 which is road

The need to connect the Japanese islands of Honshu, Kyushu, and Hokkaido has resulted in a wave of undersea tunnel building in recent years, with the Seikan the most ambitious project of all. Connecting Honshu and Hokkaido, 23.3 km/ 14.4 miles of the tunnel is 100 m/328 ft below the sea bed. It took 24 years to complete.

HIGHEST DAMS

DAM/YEAR/RIVER/LOCATION	HEIGHT	
	M	FT
1 Rogun, U/C, Vakhsh, Tajikistan	335	1,099
2 Nurek, 1980, Vakhsh, Tajikistan	300	984
3 Grand Dixence, 1961, Dixence, Switzerland	285	935
4 Inguri, 1980, Inguri, Georgia	272	892
5 =Chicoasén, U/C, Grijalva, Mexico	261	856
=Tehri, U/C, Bhagirathi, India	261	856
7 Kishau, U/C, Tons, India	253	830
8 =Ertan, U/C, Yangtse-kiang, China	245	804
=Sayano–Shushensk, U/C, Yeniesei, Russia	245	804
10 Guavio, U/C, Guavio, Colombia	243	797

U/C = under construction

LONGEST CABLE-STAYED BRIDGES

BRIDGE/YEAR/LOCATION	LENGTH OF MAIN SPAN	
	M	FT
1 Tatara, 1999, Onomichi–Imabari, Japan	890	2,920
2 Pont de Normandie, 1994, Le Havre, France	856	2,808
3 Qunghzhou Minjiang, 1996, Fozhou, China	605	1,985
4 Yangpu, 1993, Shanghai, China	602	1,975
5 =Meiko–Chuo, 1997, Nagoya, Japan	590	1,936
=Xupu, 1997, Shanghai, China	590	1,936
7 Skarnsundet, 1991, Trondheim Fjord, Norway	530	1,739
8 =Ikuchi, 1994, Onomichi–Imabari, Japan	490	1,608
=Öresund, 2000, Copenhagen–Malmö, Denmark/Sweden)	490	1,608
10 Higashi–Kobe, 1992, Kobe, Japan	485	1,591

BRIDGE OF SIZE

Crossing the Seine estuary, the Pont de Normandie links Le Havre with the route westward.

Background image: FORTH RAIL BRIDGE, UK

TOP 10 ★
LONGEST SUSPENSION BRIDGES

BRIDGE/YEAR/LOCATION	LENGTH OF MAIN SPAN	
	M	FT
1 Akashi–Kaiko, 1998, Kobe–Naruto, Japan	1,990	6,529
2 = Great Belt, 1997, Denmark	1,624	5,328
= Jiangyin, 1998, China	1,624	5,328
4 Humber Estuary, 1980, UK	1,410	4,626
5 Tsing Ma, 1997, Hong Kong, China	1,377	4,518
6 Verrazano Narrows, 1964, New York, USA	1,298	4,260
7 Golden Gate, 1937, San Francisco, USA	1,280	4,200
8 Höga Kusten, 1997, Veda, Sweden	1,210	3,970
9 Mackinac Straits, 1957, Michigan, USA	1,158	3,800
10 Minami Bisan-seto, 1988, Kojima–Sakaide, Japan	1,100	3,609

The Messina Strait Bridge between Sicily and Calabria, Italy, remains a speculative project, but if constructed according to plan it will have by far the longest centre span of any bridge at 3,320 m/10,892 ft, although at 3,910 m/12,828 ft Japan's Akashi–Kaiko bridge, completed in 1998, and with a main span of 1,990 m/6,528 ft, is the world's longest overall.

TOP 10 ★
LARGEST SPORTS STADIUMS

STADIUM/LOCATION	CAPACITY
1 Strahov Stadium, Prague, Czech Republic	240,000
2 Maracaña Municipal Stadium, Rio de Janeiro, Brazil	220,000
3 Rungnado Stadium, Pyongyang, South Korea	150,000
4 Estadio Maghalaes Pinto, Belo Horizonte, Brazil	125,000
5 = Estadio Morumbi, São Paulo, Brazil	120,000
= Estadio da Luz, Lisbon, Portugal	120,000
= Senayan Main Stadium, Jakarta, Indonesia	120,000
= Yuba Bharati Krirangan, Nr Calcutta, India	120,000
9 Estadio Castelão, Fortaleza, Brazil	119,000
10 = Estadio Arrudâo, Recife, Brazil	115,000
= Estadio Azteca, Mexico City, Mexico	115,000
= Nou Camp, Barcelona, Spain	115,000

The Aztec Stadium, Mexico City, holds 107,000, with most of the seats under cover. The New Orleans Superdome is the largest indoor stadium, with a capacity of 97,365. The largest stadium in the United Kingdom is Wembley Stadium, with a capacity of 80,000.

SUPER STADIUM

Brazil's giant Maracaña Municipal Stadium, named after the nearby river, holds up to 178,000 seated and 42,000 standing. It was begun in 1945, and completed in 1965.

TOP 10 ★
LONGEST ROAD TUNNELS

TUNNEL/YEAR	LOCATION	LENGTH	
		KM	MILES
1 St. Gotthard, 1980	Switzerland	16.32	10.14
2 Arlberg, 1978	Austria	13.98	8.69
3 = Fréjus, 1980	France/Italy	12.90	8.02
= Pinglin Highway, U/C	Taiwan	12.90	8.02
5 Mont-Blanc, 1965	France/Italy	11.60	7.21
6 Gudvangen, 1992	Norway	11.40	7.08
7 Leirfjord, U/C	Norway	11.11	6.90
8 Kan-Etsu, 1991	Japan	11.01	6.84
9 Kan-Etsu, 1985	Japan	10.93	6.79
10 Gran Sasso, 1984	Italy	10.17	6.32

U/C = under construction

TOP 10 ★
LONGEST STEEL ARCH BRIDGES

BRIDGE/YEAR/LOCATION	LONGEST SPAN	
	M	FT
1 New River Gorge, 1977, Fayetteville, West Virginia, USA	518	1,700
2 Kill Van Kull, 1931, Bayonne, New Jersey/ Staten Island, New York, USA	504	1,654
3 Sydney Harbour, 1932, Australia	503	1,650
4 Fremont, 1973, Portland, Oregon, USA	383	1,257
5 Port Mann, 1964, Vancouver, Canada	366	1,200
6 Thatcher Ferry, 1962, Panama Canal	344	1,128
7 Laviolette, 1967, Quebec, Canada	335	1,100
8 = Runcorn–Widnes, 1961, UK	330	1,082
= Zdákov, 1967, Lake Orlik, Czech Republic	330	1,082
10 = Birchenough, 1935, Fort Victoria, Zimbabwe	329	1,080
= Roosevelt Lake, 1990, Arizona, USA	329	1,080

Which is the highest city in the world?
see p.98 for the answer

A Wenchuan
B Sucre
C Potosí

CULTURE & LEARNING

WORD POWER

TOP 10 ★
LONGEST WORDS IN THE ENGLISH LANGUAGE

WORD/MEANING	LETTERS

1 MethionylglutaminylarginyltyrosylglutamylserylleucylphenylalanylalanylglutaminylleucyllysylglutamylarginyllysylglutamylglycylalanylphenylalanylvalylprolylphenylalanylyalylthreonylleucylglycylaspartylprolylglycylisoleucylglutamylglutaminylserylleucyllysylisoleucylaspartylthreonylleucylisoleucylglutamylalanylglycylalanylaspartylalanylleucylglutamylleucylglycylisoleucylprolylphenylalanylserylaspartylprolylleucelalanylaspartylglycylprolylthreonylisoleucylglutaminylasparaginylalanylthreonylleucylarginylalanylphenylalanylalanylalanylglycylvalylthreonylprolylalanylglutaminylcysteinylphenylalanylglutamylmethionylleucyalanylleucylisoleucylarginylglutaminyllysylhistidylprolylthreonylisoleucylproIylisoleucylglycylleucylleucylmethionyltyrosylalanylasparaginylleucyvalylphenylalanylasparaginyllysylglycylisoleucylaspartylglutamylphenylalanyltyrosylalanylglutaminylcysteinylglutamyllysylvalylglycylvalylaspartylserylvalylleucylvalylalanylaspartylvalylprolylvalylglutaminylglutamylserylalanylprolylphenylalanylarginylglutaminylalanylalanylleucylarginylhistidylasparaginylvalylalanylprolylisoleucylphenylalanylisoleucylcysteinylprolylprolylaspartylalanylaspartylaspartylaspartylleucylleucylarginylglutaminylisoleucylalanylseryltyrosylglycylarginylglycyltyrosylthreonyltyrosylleucylleucylserylarginylalanylglycylvalylthreonylglycylalanylglutamylasparaginylarginylalanylalanylleucylprolylleucylaspaaginylhistidylleucylvalylalanyllysylleucyllysylglutamyltyrosylasparaginylalanylalanylprolylprolylleucylglutaminylglycylphenylalanylglycylisoleucylserylalanylprolylaspartylglutaminylvalyllysylalanylalanylisoleucylaspartylalanylglycylalanylalanylglycylalanylisoleucylserylglycylserylalanylisoleucylbalyllysylisoleucylisoleucylglutamylglutaminylhistidylasparaginylisoleucylglutamylprolylglutamyllysylmethionylleucylalanylalanylleucyllysylvalylphenylalanylvalylglutaminylprolylmethionyllysylalanylalanylthreonylarginylserine **1,909**

Tryptophan synthetase A protein, an enzyme consisting of 267 amino acids, stretches to a record 1,909 letters. It has actually appeared in print in various publications.

2 Acetylseryltyrosylserylisoleucylthreonylserylprolylserylglutaminylphenylalanylvalylphenylalanylleucylserylserylvalyltryptophylalanylaspartylprolylisoleucylglutamylleucylleucyllaspasaraginylvalylcysteinylthreonylserylserylleucylglyclaspasaraginylglutaminylphenylalanylglutaminylthreonylglutaminylglutaminylalanylarginylthreonylthreonylglutaminylvalylglutaminylglutaminylphenylalanylserylglutaminylvalyltryptophyllysylprolylphenylalanylprolylglutaminylserylthreonylvalylarginylphenylalanylprolylglycylaspartylvalyltyrosyllsylvalyltyrosylarginyltyrosylasparaginylalanylvalylleucylaspartylprolylleucylisoleucylthreonylalanylleucylleucylglycylthreonylphenylalanylaspartylthreonylarginylasparaginylarginylisoleucylisoleucylglutamylvalylglutamylasparaginylglutaminylglutaminylserylprolylthreonylthreonylalanylglutamylthreonylleucylaspartylalanylthreonylarginylarginylvalylaspartylaspartylalanylthreonylvalylalanylisoleucylarginylserylalanylasparaginylisoleucylasparaginylleucylvallasparaginylglutamylleucylvalylarginylglycylthreonylglycylleucyltyrosylasparaginylglutaminylasparaginylthreonylphenylalanylglutamylserylmethionylserylglycylleucylvalyltryptophylthreonylserylalanylprolylalanylserine **1,185**

The word for the Tobacco Mosaic Virus, Dahlemense Strain, qualifies as the second longest word in English because it has actually been used in print (in the American Chemical Society's Chemical Abstracts).

3 Ornicopytheobibliopsychocrystarroscioaerogenethliometeoroaustrohieroanthropoichthyopyrosiderochpnomyoalectryoophiobotanopegohydrorhabdocrithoaleuroalphitohalomolybdoclerobeloaxinocoscinodactyliogeolithopessopsephocatoptrotephraoneirochiroonychodactyloarithstichooxogeloscogastrogyroceurobletonooenoscapulinaniac **310**

Medieval scribes used this word (and variations of it) when writing about superstition, to refer to a deluded human who indulges in superstitious practices.

4 Lopadotemachoselachogaleokranioleipsanodrimhypotrimmatosilphioparaomelitokatakechymenokichlepikossyphophattoperisteralektryonoptekephalliokigklopeleiolagoiosiraiobaphetraganopterygon **182**

The English transliteration of a 170-letter Greek word that appears in The Ecclesiazusae by the Greek playwright Aristophanes (c.448–380BC). It is used as a description of a 17-ingredient dish.

5 Aequeosalinocalcalinosetaceoaluminosocupreovitriolic **52**

Invented by a medical writer, Dr. Edward Strother (1675–1737), to describe the spa waters at Bath.

6 Osseocarnisanguineoviscericartilaginonervomedullary **51**

Coined by writer and East India Company official Thomas Love Peacock (1785–1866), and used in his satire Headlong Hall (1816) as a description of the structure of the human body.

7 Pneumonoultramicroscopicsilicovolcanoconiosis **45**

It first appeared in print (though ending in "koniosis") in F. Scully's Bedside Manna [sic] (1936). It is said to mean a lung disease caused by breathing fine dust.

8 Hepaticocholecystostcholecystenterostomies **42**

Surgical operations to create channels of communication between gall bladders and hepatic ducts or intestines.

9 Praetertranssubstantiationalistically **37**

The adverb describing surpassing the act of transubstantiation; the word is found in Mark McShane's novel Untimely Ripped (1963).

10 = Pseudoantidisestablishmentarianism **34**

A word meaning "false opposition to the withdrawal of state support from a Church", derived from that perennial favourite long word, antidisestablishmentarianism (a mere 28 letters). Another composite made from it (though usually hyphenated) is ultra-antidisestablishmentarianism (33 letters)

= Supercalifragilisticexpialidocious **34**

An invented word, but perhaps now eligible since it has appeared in the Oxford English Dictionary. It was popularized by the song of this title in the film Mary Poppins (1964), where it is used to mean "wonderful", but it was originally written in 1949 in an unpublished song by Parker and Young who spelt it "supercalafajalistickespialadojus" (32 letters). In 1965–66, Parker and Young unsuccessfully sued the makers of Mary Poppins, claiming infringement of copyright. In summarizing the case, the US Court decided against repeating this mouthful, stating that "All variants of this tongue-twister will hereinafter be referred to collectively as 'the word'."

What is the most expensive painting by Andy Warhol?
see p.130 for the answer

A Shot Red Marilyn
B Orange Marilyn
C Marilyn Monroe, twenty times

TOP 10 ★
MOST WIDELY SPOKEN LANGUAGES

	LANGUAGE	APPROXIMATE NO. OF SPEAKERS
1	Chinese (Mandarin)	1,070,000,000
2	English	508,000,000
3	Hindustani	497,000,000
4	Spanish	392,000,000
5	Russian	277,000,000
6	Arabic	246,000,000
7	Bengali	211,000,000
8	Portuguese	191,000,000
9	Malay-Indonesian	159,000,000
10	French	129,000,000

According to 1998 estimates by Sidney S. Culbert of the University of Washington, in addition to those languages appearing in the Top 10, there are three further languages that are spoken by more than 100 million individuals: German (128 million), Japanese (126 million), and Urdu (105 million). A further 13 languages are spoken by 50–100 million: Punjabi (94 million), Korean (77 million), Telugu (76 million), Tamil (74 million), Marathi (71 million), Cantonese (71 million), Wu (70 million), Vietnamese (67 million), Javanese (64 million), Italian (63 million), Turkish (61 million), Tagalog (58 million), and Thai (52 million).

ANCIENT SCRIPT

As early as 1390BC writing made an appearance in China: the Shang people made inscriptions on oracle bones and bronze ritual vessels.

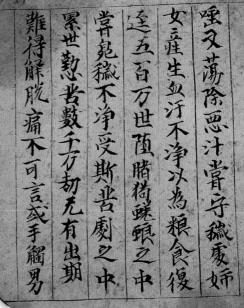

TOP 10 ★
LANGUAGES OFFICIALLY SPOKEN IN THE MOST COUNTRIES

	LANGUAGE	COUNTRIES
1	English	54
2	French	33
3	Arabic	24
4	Spanish	21
5	Portuguese	8
6	German	5
7 =	Malay	4
=	Dutch	4
9	Chinese (Mandarin)	3
10 =	Italian	2
=	Russian	2
=	Tamil	2

There are many countries in the world with more than one official language – both English and French are recognized officially in Canada, for example. English is also used in numerous countries as the lingua franca.

TOP 10 ★
COUNTRIES WITH THE MOST ENGLISH-LANGUAGE SPEAKERS

	COUNTRY	APPROXIMATE NO. OF SPEAKERS
1	USA	230,8300,000
2	UK	57,320,000
3	Canada	18,448,000
4	Australia	15,027,000
5	South Africa	3,860,000
6	Irish Republic	3,580,000
7	New Zealand	3,321,000
8	Jamaica	2,380,000
9	Trinidad and Tobago	1,193,000
10	Guyana	746,000

This Top 10 represents the countries with the greatest numbers of inhabitants who speak English as their mother-tongue. After the 10th entry, the figures dive to under 260,000 in the case of the Bahamas, Barbados, and Zimbabwe.

UNITED NATIONS

Members from around the world come together at the United Nations. Many different languages are represented here, and translators are kept busy relaying the necessary information to participants.

TOP 10 MOST STUDIED FOREIGN LANGUAGES IN THE UK

1 French **2** Spanish **3** Arabic **4** Chinese (Mandarin) **5** German **6** Italian **7** Russian **8** Japanese **9** Dutch **10** Portuguese

This ranking is based on language courses studied at the School of Languages at the University of Westminster (formerly the Polytechnic of Central London), the largest source of language teaching in the state sector in the whole of Europe, which offers courses in 28 different languages.

A REVOLUTION IN PRINTING

The Gutenberg Bible was printed by Johann Gutenberg, a 15th-century goldsmith who invented moveable type.

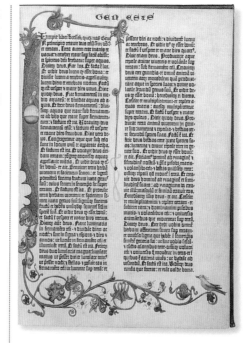

THE 10 ★
FIRST PENGUIN PAPERBACKS
AUTHOR/BOOK

1 André Maurois, *Ariel*
2 Ernest Hemingway, *A Farewell to Arms*
3 Eric Linklater, *Poet's Pub*
4 Susan Ertz, *Madame Claire*
5 Dorothy L. Sayers, *The Unpleasantness at the Bellona Club*
6 Agatha Christie, *The Mysterious Affair at Styles*
7 Beverley Nichols, *Twenty-five*
8 E.H. Young, *William*
9 Mary Webb, *Gone to Earth*
10 Compton Mackenzie, *Carnival*

The British publisher Allen Lane (1902–70; knighted 1952) who, remarking "I would be the first to admit that there is no fortune in this series for anyone concerned", launched his first "Penguin" titles in Great Britain on 30 July 1935. Originally Penguins were quality, low-priced paperback reprints of books that had been previously published as hardbacks.

PICK UP A PENGUIN

The first Penguin paperback was published in 1935, the brainchild of Allen Lane. Legend has it that Lane was inspired to create a paperback collection after a weekend at Agatha Christie's house. On his way back to London, he was disappointed by the books available at Exeter station, and realized that the market was in need of affordable versions of contemporary titles. In 1961, Penguin published the first unabridged version of D.H. Lawrence's *Lady Chatterley's Lover*. Charged under the Obscene Publications Act, Penguin had to go to court to defend their rights to publish the infamous novel.

SNAP ★ SHOTS

TOP 10 TYPES OF BOOK PUBLISHED IN THE UK

(Subject/new titles published in 1997)

1 Fiction 8,965
2 Children's 8,208
3 Economics 4,305
4 Social sciences 4,254
5 History 4,168
6 Religion 4,109
7 Medicine 4,052
8 Biography 3,164
9 Management 3,086
10 School textbooks 3,049

TOP 10 ★
MOST EXPENSIVE BOOKS AND MANUSCRIPTS EVER SOLD AT AUCTION

BOOK/MANUSCRIPT/SALE — PRICE (£)*

1 **The Codex Hammer**, Christie's, New York, 11 Nov 1994 ($30,800,000) 19,230,000
This Leonardo da Vinci notebook was bought by Bill Gates, the billionaire founder of Microsoft.

2 **The Gospels of Henry the Lion**, c.1173–75, Sotheby's, London, 6 Dec 1983 7,400,000
At the time of its sale, this became the most expensive manuscript or book ever sold.

3 **The Canterbury Tales**, Geoffrey Chaucer, c.1476–77, Christie's, London, 8 Jul 1998 4,600,000
This is the world's most expensive book.

4 **The Gutenberg Bible**, 1455, Christie's, New York, 22 Oct 1987 ($5,390,000) 2,934,131
This is one of the first books ever printed, by Johann Gutenberg and Johann Fust in 1455.

5 **The Northumberland Bestiary**, c.1250–60, Sotheby's, London, 29 Nov 1990 2,700,000
This holds the record for an English manuscript.

6 **Autograph manuscript of nine symphonies by Wolfgang Amadeus Mozart**, c.1773–74, Sotheby's, London, 22 May 1987 2,350,000
This holds the record for any music manuscript.

7 **The Birds of America**, John James Audubon, 1827–38, Sotheby's, New York, 6 Jun 1989 ($3,600,000) 2,292,993
This holds the record for any natural history book.

8 **The Bible** in Hebrew, Sotheby's, London, 5 Dec 1989 1,850,000
This holds the record for any Hebrew manuscript.

9 **The Monypenny Breviary**, illuminated manuscript, c.1490–95, Sotheby's, London, 19 Jun 1989 1,700,000
This holds the record for any French manuscript.

10 **The Hours and Psalter of Elizabeth de Bohun**, Countess of Northampton, c.1340–45, Sotheby's, London, 21 Jun 1988 1,400,000

* Excluding premiums

TOP 10 BESTSELLING BOOKS

	BOOK	APPROXIMATE SALES
1	*The Bible*	6,000,000,000
2	*Quotations from the Works of Mao Tse-tung*	800,000,000
3	*American Spelling Book* by Noah Webster	100,000,000
4	*The Guinness Book of Records*	81,000,000*
5	*The McGuffey Readers* by William Holmes McGuffey	60,000,000
6	*A Message to Garcia* by Elbert Hubbard	40–50,000,000
7	*World Almanac*	over 40,000,000*
8	*The Common Sense Book of Baby and Child Care* by Benjamin Spock	over 39,200,000
9	*Valley of the Dolls* by Jacqueline Susann	30,000,000
10	*In His Steps: "What Would Jesus Do?"* by Rev. Charles Monroe Sheldon	28,500,000

* Aggregate sales of annual publication

It is extremely difficult to establish precise sales even of contemporary books, and virtually impossible to do so with books published long ago. How can one calculate how many copies of *The Complete Works of Shakespeare* have been sold in countless editions?

THE 10 ★
FIRST BOOKS PUBLISHED BY AVON BOOKS

AUTHOR/BOOK

1. Sinclair Lewis, *Elmer Gantry*
2. Edward Fitzgerald, *The Rubáiyát of Omar Khayyam*
3. Agatha Christie, *The Big Four*
4. James Hilton, *Ill Wind*
5. John Rhode, *Dr. Priestly Investigates*
6. Wilkie Collins, *The Haunted Hotel and 25 Other Ghost Stories*
7. John Dickson Carr, *The Plague Court Murders*
8. R.A.J. Walling, *The Corpse in the Green Pajamas*
9. Freeman Wills Crofts, *Willful and Premeditated*
10. R. Austin Freeman, *Dr. Thorndyke's Discovery*

The first 13 numbered Avon paperbacks were issued in the US in November 1941.

THE 10 ★
FIRST BOOKS PUBLISHED BY BANTAM BOOKS

AUTHOR/BOOK

1. Mark Twain, *Life on the Mississippi*
2. Frank Gruber, *The Gift Horse*
3. Zane Grey, *Nevada*
4. Elizabeth Daly, *Evidence of Things Seen*
5. Rafael Sabatini, *Scaramouche*
6. Robert George Dean, *A Murder by Marriage*
7. John Steinbeck, *The Grapes of Wrath*
8. F. Scott Fitzgerald, *The Great Gatsby*
9. Geoffrey Household, *Rogue Male*
10. Marjorie Kinnan Rawlings, *South Moon Under*

The first 20 numbered titles published as Bantam paperbacks went on sale in the US on 3 January 1946, priced at 25 cents each.

THE 10 ★
FIRST PUBLICATIONS PRINTED IN ENGLAND

AUTHOR/BOOK

1. *Propositio ad Carolum ducem Burgundiae**
2. Cato, *Disticha de Morbidus*
3. Geoffrey Chaucer, *The Canterbury Tales*
4. *Ordinale seu Pica ad usem Sarum* ("Sarum Pie")
5. John Lydgate, *The Temple of Glass*
6. John Lydgate, *Stans puer mensam*
7. John Lydgate, *The Horse, the Sheep and the Goose*
8. John Lydgate, *The Churl and the Bird*
9. *Infanta Salvatoris*
10. William Caxton, advertisement for "Sarum Pie"

* This work was printed before September 1476; all the others were printed in either 1476 or 1477.

THE 10 ★
FIRST POCKET BOOKS

AUTHOR/BOOK

1. James Hilton, *Lost Horizon*
2. Dorothea Brande, *Wake Up and Live!*
3. William Shakespeare, *Five Great Tragedies*
4. Thorne Smith, *Topper*
5. Agatha Christie, *The Murder of Roger Ackroyd*
6. Dorothy Parker, *Enough Rope*
7. Emily Brontë, *Wuthering Heights*
8. Samuel Butler, *The Way of All Flesh*
9. Thornton Wilder, *The Bridge of San Luis Rey*
10. Felix Salten, *Bambi*

All 10 Pocket Books were published in the US in 1939 (a single title, Pearl S. Buck's Nobel Prize-winning *The Good Earth*, had been test-marketed the previous year, but only in New York). Unlike Penguins, Pocket Books all had pictorial covers.

Which country has the most public libraries?
see p.116 for the answer

A Ukraine
B UK
C Russia

THE BARD

Almost 400 years after his death, William Shakespeare (1564–1616) remains one of the most translated, most written-about, and most widely read authors in the world. His plays are also among the most frequently performed, and, through a recent wave of enthusiasm for converting them into films, or basing films on them, such as the Oscar-winning *Shakespeare in Love*, are attracting growing audiences around the world. Shakespeare's own life remains tantalizingly enigmatic, his early career and development as a playwright an almost complete mystery. This has led to a range of theories about his true identity, and the authorship of his works has been ascribed to various contemporaries, from Francis Bacon to Queen Elizabeth I. It is even questioned if his remains occupy his tomb at his birthplace, Stratford-upon-Avon.

SNAP SHOTS ★

TOP 10 ★
LARGEST PUBLIC LIBRARIES IN THE UK

	LIBRARY	FOUNDED	BOOKS
1	Hampshire	1974	3,500,000
2	Kent	1921	3,300,000
3	Lancashire	1924	3,189,800
4	Essex	1926	3,006,349
5	Glasgow	1877	2,557,554
6	Manchester	1852	2,430,000
7 =	Devon	1974	2,000,000
=	Leeds	1870	2,000,000
=	Liverpool	1852	2,000,000
10	Hertfordshire	1925	1,932,393

These figures are for the number of books held by each county in its public libraries. No figures are available for the number of books held by individual public libraries in the UK.

THE 10 ★
FIRST PUBLIC LIBRARIES IN THE UK

	LIBRARY	FOUNDED
1	Canterbury	1847
2	Warrington	1848
3	Salford	1850
4	Winchester	1851
5 =	Manchester Free	1852
=	Liverpool	1852
7 =	Bolton	1853
=	Ipswich	1853
9	Oxford	1854
10 =	Cambridge	1855
=	Kidderminster	1855

Various specialist institutions, such as theological libraries, existed in Britain as early as the 17th century, and were joined in the 18th and 19th by others that charged a small fee to borrowers. The Museums Act of 1845 enabled several local authorities to fund libraries attached to museums, with a maximum admission charge of one penny. Following the 1850 Public Libraries Act, the Manchester Free Library, which opened on 6 September 1852, was the first free municipally supported lending library open to the public.

TOP 10 ★
COUNTRIES WITH THE MOST PUBLIC LIBRARIES

	COUNTRY	LIBRARIES
1	Russia	96,177
2	UK	24,869
3	Ukraine	21,857
4	USA	15,900
5	Kazakhstan	15,055
6	Germany	13,032
7	Poland	9,505
8	Belarus	9,121
9	Czech Republic	7,986
10	Mexico	5,630

Source: *UNESCO*

The very high figure given for the former Soviet Union was probably due to the propaganda value attached to cultural status. Recent changes in these countries make such a high level of expenditure unlikely to continue. National literary traditions play a major role in determining the ratio of libraries to population. The Japanese do not customarily borrow books, and consequently the country has only 1,950 public libraries.

TOP 10 MOST BORROWED CHILDREN'S AUTHORS IN THE UK, 1997–98

1 R.L. Stine **2** Janet and Allan Ahlberg **3** Ann M. Martin **4** Roald Dahl **5** Enid Blyton **6** Dick King-Smith **7** John Cunliffe **8** Goscinny **9** Mick Inkpen **10** Eric Hill

Source: *Public Lending Right*

TOP 10 MOST BORROWED CLASSIC AUTHORS IN THE UK, 1997–98

1 Beatrix Potter **2** Daphne Du Maurier **3** A.A. Milne **4** Jane Austen **5** William Shakespeare **6** J.R.R. Tolkien **7** Charles Dickens **8** Thomas Hardy **9** Anthony Trollope **10** E.M. Forster

Source: *Public Lending Right*

Public Lending Right figures show that books by the authors featured here were borrowed 200,000–500,000 times, though some, being out of copyright, do not benefit from PLR payments.

Which country boasts the three bestselling newspapers in the world?
see p.120 for the answer

A Japan
B China
C UK

TOP 10 MOST BORROWED ADULTS' AUTHORS IN THE UK, 1997–98

1 Catherine Cookson **2** Danielle Steel **3** Dick Francis **4** Josephine Cox
5 Ruth Rendell **6** Jack Higgins **7** Agatha Christie **8** Emma Blair
9 Terry Pratchett **10** Barbara Taylor Bradford

Source: *Public Lending Right*

TOP 10 ★
LARGEST LIBRARIES

	LIBRARY	LOCATION	FOUNDED	BOOKS
1	Library of Congress	Washington DC, USA	1800	23,041,334
2	National Library of China	Beijing, China	1909	15,980,636
3	National Library of Canada	Ottawa, Canada	1953	14,500,000
4	Deutsche Bibliothek*	Frankfurt, Germany	1990	14,350,000
5	British Library#	London, UK	1753	13,000,000
6	Harvard University Library	Cambridge, Massachusetts, USA	1638	12,877,360
7	Russian State Library+	Moscow, Russia	1862	11,750,000
8	New York Public Library	New York, USA	1895★	11,445,971
9	National Diet Library	Tokyo, Japan	1948	11,304,139
10	Yale University Library	New Haven, Connecticut, USA	1701	9,485,823

* Formed in 1990 through the unification of the Deutsche Bibliothek, Frankfurt (founded 1947) and the Deutsche Bücherei, Leipzig

\# Founded as part of the British Museum, 1753; became an independent body in 1973

\+ Founded 1862 as Rumyantsev Library, formerly State V.I. Lenin Library

★ Astor Library founded 1848, consolidated with Lenox Library and Tilden Trust to form New York Public Library in 1895

THE MASTER STORYTELLER

Dickens first came to public attention with his sketches of London life signed "Boz". His novels were published in monthly or weekly parts, and his readers waited with eager anticipation for each instalment.

TOP 10 ★
MOST CITED AUTHORS OF ALL TIME

	AUTHOR/COUNTRY	DATES
1	**William Shakespeare**, UK	1564–1616
2	**Charles Dickens**, UK	1812–70
3	**Sir Walter Scott**, UK	1771–1832
4	**Johann Goethe**, Germany	1749–1832
5	**Aristotle**, Greece	384–322BC
6	**Alexandre Dumas (père)**, France	1802–70
7	**Robert Louis Stevenson**, UK	1850–94
8	**Mark Twain**, USA	1835–1910
9	**Marcus Tullius Cicero**, Italy	106–43BC
10	**Honoré de Balzac**, France	1799–1850

This Top 10 is based on a search of a major US library computer database, Citations, which includes books both by and about the author, with a total of more than 15,000 for Shakespeare.

READING ROOM

The Library of Congress contains more than 100 million catalogued items, has 856 km/532 miles of shelving, and approximately 4,600 employees. In 1897 it moved to its present building, which cost $7 million (£4.4 million).

THE 10 ★
LATEST BOOKER PRIZE WINNERS

YEAR	AUTHOR/TITLE
1998	Ian McEwan, *Amsterdam*
1997	Arundhati Roy, *The God of Small Things*
1996	Graham Swift, *Last Orders*
1995	Pat Barker, *The Ghost Road*
1994	James Kelman, *How Late It Was, How Late*
1993	Roddy Doyle, *Paddy Clarke Ha Ha Ha*
1992 =	Michael Ondaatje, *The English Patient*
=	Barry Unsworth, *Sacred Hunger*
1991	Ben Okri, *Famished Road*
1990	A.S. Byatt, *Possession: A Romance*

THE 10 ★
LATEST WINNERS OF THE PULITZER PRIZE FOR FICTION

YEAR	AUTHOR/TITLE
1999	Michael Cunningham, *The Hours*
1998	Philip Roth, *American Pastoral*
1997	Steven Millhauser, *Martin Dressler: The Tale of an American Dreamer*
1996	Richard Ford, *Independence Day*
1995	Carol Shields, *The Stone Diaries*
1994	E. Annie Proulx, *The Shipping News*
1993	Robert Olen Butler, *A Good Scent from a Strange Mountain: Stories*
1992	Jane Smiley, *A Thousand Acres*
1991	John Updike, *Rabbit at Rest*
1990	Oscar Hijuelos, *The Mambo Kings Play*

LITERARY FIRST
Richard Ford's sixth novel, Independence Day, *set during the 4th of July weekend, is the first novel to win both the Pulitzer Prize and the PEN/Faulkner Award for fiction.*

TOP 10 ★
ANNUAL FICTION PRIZES AND AWARDS IN THE UK*

	PRIZE/AWARD	CATEGORY	TOTAL VALUE (£)
1	International IMPAC Award	A work of fiction	86,637 (IR£100,000)
2=	David Cohen British Literature Prize	Awarded for body of work in English (biennial)	30,000#
=	Orange Prize for Fiction	Best fiction title by a woman	30,000
4	Irish Times Literature Prizes	Fiction or poetry in English or Irish	23,880 (IR£27,500)
5	Whitbread Book of the Year	Books by residents of the UK or Ireland	21,000
6	Booker Prize	Best novel in English	20,000
7=	Commonwealth Writers Prize	A work of fiction by a Commonwealth citizen	10,000
=	Hawthornden Prize	Work of imaginative literature	10,000
=	Heywood Hill Literary Prize	Distinguished literary career	10,000
=	Stakis Prize for Scottish Writer of the Year	Writers born or resident in Scotland, or whose work is influenced by Scotland	10,000
=	W.H. Smith Literary Award	Outstanding work of fiction	10,000

* Including Irish awards for which UK writers are eligible

Plus £10,000 provided by the Arts Council, to enable the winner to encourage writing and readers

While the Booker Prize attracts the most publicity, there are numerous other valuable literary prizes awarded in the UK. The relatively newly established David Cohen British Literature Prize was first awarded in 1993 (to V.S. Naipaul), but is not annual. In addition, there are many other awards that total more than some of those in the Top 10, but are divided between several recipients, and many others worth less than £10,000 – some for as little as £100 or just a certificate or gift.

THE 10 ★
LATEST WINNERS OF HUGO AWARDS FOR BEST SCIENCE FICTION NOVEL

YEAR	AUTHOR/TITLE
1998	Joe Haldeman, *Forever Peace*
1997	Kim Stanley Robinson, *Blue Mars*
1996	Neal Stephenson, *The Diamond Age*
1995	Lois McMaster Bujold, *Mirror Dance*
1994	Kim Stanley Robinson, *Green Mars*
1993	Vernor Vinge, *A Fire Upon the Deep*
1992	Connie Willis, *Doomsday Book*
1991	Lois McMaster Bujold, *Barrayar*
1990	Lois McMaster Bujold, *The Vor Game*
1989	Dan Simmons, *Hyperion*

Hugo Awards for science fiction novels, short stories, and other fiction and non-fiction works are presented by the World Science Fiction Society. They were established in 1953 as "Science Fiction Achievement Awards for the best science fiction writing".

Background image: **THE PULITZER PRIZE GOLD MEDAL**

TOP 10 GENERAL NON-FICTION TITLES OF 1998 IN THE UK

(Title/author/sales)

1 *The Little Book of Calm*, Paul Wilson, 483,535 **2** *Delia's How to Cook*, Delia Smith, 460,320 **3** *Angela's Ashes*, Frank McCourt, 332,920 **4** *Men Are from Mars, Women Are from Venus*, John Gray, 308,168 **5** *Notes from a Small Island*, Bill Bryson, 286,703 **6** *Longitude*, Dava Sobel, 214,223 **7** *A Walk in the Woods*, Bill Bryson, 192,789 **8** *Falling Leaves*, Adeline Yen Mah, 180,015 **9** *Notes from a Big Country*, Bill Bryson, 146,036 **10** *Complete Theory Test: Cars and Motorcycles*, DSA, 143,491

Source: *Bookwatch*

THE 10 ★ LATEST WINNERS OF THE NATIONAL BOOK AWARD FOR FICTION

YEAR	AUTHOR/TITLE
1998	Alice McDermott, *Charming Billy*
1997	Charles Frazier, *Cold Mountain*
1996	Andrea Barrett, *Ship Fever and Other Stories*
1995	Philip Roth, *Sabbath's Theater*
1994	William Gaddis, *A Frolic of His Own*
1993	E. Annie Proulx, *The Shipping News*
1992	Cormac McCarthy, *All the Pretty Horses*
1991	Norman Rush, *Mating*
1990	Charles Johnson, *Middle Passage*
1989	John Casey, *Spartina*

The National Book Award is presented by the National Book Foundation as part of its programme to foster reading in the United States through such activities as author events and fund raising for literacy campaigns. Award winners are announced each November, and receive $10,000. Past recipients include many books that are now regarded as modern classics, some of which have since been filmed, among them William Styron's *Sophie's Choice* and John Irving's *The World According to Garp*.

TOP 10 ★ FICTION TITLES OF 1998 IN THE UK

TITLE/AUTHOR	SALES
1 *Captain Corelli's Mandolin*, Louis de Bernières	560,781
2 *Bridget Jones's Diary*, Helen Fielding	488,247
3 *The God of Small Things*, Arundhati Roy	391,423
4 = *The Partner*, John Grisham	252,121
= *Enduring Love*, Ian McEwan	252,121
6 *Cold Mountain*, Charles Frazier	195,502
7 *Memoirs of a Geisha*, Arthur Golden	182,800
8 *Bondage of Love*, Catherine Cookson	182,097
9 *Unnatural Exposure*, Patricia D. Cornwell	170,190
10 *Hornet's Nest*, Patricia D. Cornwell	153,604

Source: *Bookwatch*

TRIPLE WINNER
National Book Award (1993) and Pulitzer Prize (1994) winner, Canadian writer E. Annie Proulx has also won the 1993 Irish Times *International Prize* for The Shipping News.

THE 10 ★ LATEST KATE GREENAWAY MEDAL WINNERS*

YEAR	ILLUSTRATOR/TITLE
1997	P.J. Lynch (text Amy Hest), *When Jessie Came Across the Sea*
1996	Helen Cooper, *The Baby Who Wouldn't Go to Bed*
1995	P.J. Lynch (text Susan Wojciechowski), *The Christmas Miracle of Jonathan Toomey*
1994	Gregory Rogers (text Libby Hathorn), *The Way Home*
1993	Alan Lee (text Rosemary Sutcliff), *Black Ships Before Troy*
1992	Anthony Browne, *Zoo*
1991	Janet Ahlberg (text Allan Ahlberg), *The Jolly Christmas Postman*
1990	Gary Blythe (text Dyan Sheldon), *The Whales' Song*
1989	Michael Foreman, *War Boy*
1988	Barbara Firth (text Martin Waddell), *Can't you Sleep, Little Bear?*

* Awarded for the most distinguished work in the illustration of children's books published in the UK

TOP 10 ★ CHILDREN'S TITLES OF 1998 IN THE UK

TITLE/AUTHOR	SALES
1 *Children's Book of Books*	515,030
2 *The Beano Book 1999*	145,574
3 *Harry Potter and the Philospher's Stone*, J.K. Rowling	124,704
4 *The Lottie Project*, Jacqueline Wilson	63,329
5 *Bad Girls*, Jacqueline Wilson	50,750
6 *Harry Potter and the Chamber of Secrets*, J.K. Rowling	39,028
7 *The Dandy Annual 1999*	37,312
8 *Matilda*, Roald Dahl	35,651
9 *Double Act*, Jacqueline Wilson	35,559
10 *Northern Lights*, Philip Pulman	35,317

Source: *Bookwatch*

THE PRESS

TOP 10 ★
LONGEST-RUNNING CHILDREN'S COMICS AND MAGAZINES IN THE UK

PUBLICATION	FIRST ISSUE
1 *Dandy*	4 Dec 1937
2 *Beano*	30 Jul 1938
3 *Bunty*	14 Jan 1958
4 *Buster* (incorporating *Whizzer & Chips**)	28 May 1960
5 *The Brownie* (monthly)	Jan 1962
6 *Plus* (monthly)	Jan 1966
7 *Twinkle*	27 Jan 1968
8 *Quiz Kid*	Aug 1983
9 *Playdays*	Jul 1990
10 *Disney & Me*	17 Apr 1991

* First published 18 Oct 1969; amalgamated 3 Nov 1990

TOP 10 ★
BESTSELLING BRITISH COMICS OF ALL TIME*

PUBLICATION	YEARS
1 *Beano*	1938–
2 *Comic Cuts*	1890–1953
3 *Dandy*	1937–
4 *Eagle*	1950–69; revived 1982
5 *Film Fun*	1920–62
6 *Illustrated Chips*	1890–1953
7 *Mickey Mouse Weekly*	1936–57
8 *Radio Fun*	1938–61
9 *Rainbow*	1914–56
10 *School Friend*	1950–65

* In alphabetical order

Accurate circulation figures are hard to come by, but information from the Association of Comics Enthusiasts indicates that all 10 comics achieved very high circulation figures, with *Eagle*, *Film Fun*, *Rainbow*, and *School Friend* peaking at 1 million.

STOP PRESS!

Since 59BC, when the Acta Diurna *(Daily News) was posted daily in the Forum of Rome, news of political events, wars, and social affairs have been enjoyed by an ever-increasing readership.*

TOP 10 ★
COUNTRIES WITH THE MOST DAILY NEWSPAPERS PER CAPITA

COUNTRY	SALES PER 1,000 INHABITANTS
1 Norway	596
2 Japan	576
3 Iceland	510
4 Finland	468
5 Sweden	460
6 South Korea	394
7 Kuwait	387
8 Switzerland	371
9 UK	344
10 Luxembourg	332

Source: *UNESCO*

The Vatican City's sole newspaper, *l'Osservatore Romano*, sells around 70,000, which implies a daily sale of 95 copies per head. In fact, of course, most of them are sent outside the Holy See.

YESTERDAY'S NEWS

Discarded newspapers provide a massive amount of waste: 28,000 tonnes of newsprint is dumped every day in the US, of which only 13,000 tonnes is recycled.

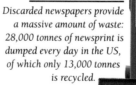

TOP 10 ★
DAILY NEWSPAPERS

NEWSPAPER	COUNTRY	AVERAGE DAILY CIRCULATION
1 *Yomiuri Shimbun*	Japan	14,485,453
2 *Asahi Shimbun*	Japan	12,660,066
3 *Mainichi Shimbun*	Japan	5,867,224
4 *MZ Guangbo Dianshi*	China	5,348,000
5 *Xinmin Wanbao*	China	5,227,000
6 *Bild-Zeitung*	Germany	4,644,000
7 *Nihon Keizai Shimbun*	Japan	4,550,311
8 *Chunichi Shimbun*	Japan	4,394,849
9 *The Sun*	UK	3,767,941
10 *BJ Guangbo Dianshi*	China	3,372,000

Source: *World Association of Newspapers*

TOP 10 ★
ENGLISH-LANGUAGE DAILY NEWSPAPERS

NEWSPAPER	COUNTRY	AVERAGE DAILY CIRCULATION
1 *The Sun*	UK	3,698,300
2 *The Mirror*	UK	2,351,815
3 *Daily Mail*	UK	2,343,494
4 *Wall Street Journal*	USA	1,774,880
5 *USA Today*	USA	1,629,665
6 *The Express*	UK	1,134,719
7 *The New York Times*	USA	1,074,741
8 *The Daily Telegraph*	UK	1,062,853
9 *Los Angeles Times*	USA	1,050,176
10 *Washington Post*	USA	775,894

TOP 10 ★
OLDEST NATIONAL NEWSPAPERS PUBLISHED IN THE UK

NEWSPAPER	FIRST PUBLISHED

1 London Gazette — 16 Nov 1665
Originally published in Oxford as the Oxford Gazette, while the royal court resided there during an outbreak of the plague. After 23 issues, it moved to London with the court and changed its name.

2 Lloyd's List — 1726
Providing shipping news, first on a weekly basis (as Lloyd's News), but since 1734 as Britain's oldest daily.

3 The Times — 1 Jan 1785
First published as the Daily Universal Register, it changed its name to The Times on 1 March 1788.

4 The Observer — 4 Dec 1791
The Observer is the longest-running Sunday paper.

5 The Licensee — 8 Feb 1794
Britain's oldest trade newspaper (a daily established by the Licensed Victuallers Association to earn income for its charity), and the first national paper on Fleet Street, the Morning Advertiser changed its name to The Licensee and became a twice-weekly news magazine in 1994, at the time of its 200th anniversary.

6 The Scotsman — 25 Jan 1817
Originally published weekly, the Daily Scotsman was published from July 1855 to December 1859, and retitled The Scotsman in January 1860.

7 The Sunday Times — Feb 1821
Issued as the New Observer until March 1821 and the Independent Observer from April 1821 until 22 October 1822, when it changed its name to The Sunday Times. On 4 February 1962 it became the first British newspaper to issue a colour supplement.

8 The Guardian — 5 May 1821
A weekly until 1855 (and called The Manchester Guardian until 1959).

9 The News of the World — 1 Oct 1843
In April 1951, sales peaked at 8,480,878 copies – the highest-ever circulation of any British newspaper.

10 The Daily Telegraph — 29 Jun 1855
The first issues were published as the Daily Telegraph and Courier, but from 20 Aug 1855, Courier was dropped from the title.

PAPARAZZI
In the desperate search for that ultimate scoop, journalists will go to almost any lengths to take photographs of famous people. Their increasingly intrusive behaviour has resulted in the introduction of new codes of conduct.

TOP 10 ★
CONSUMER MAGAZINES IN THE UK

	MAGAZINE	AVERAGE CIRCULATION PER ISSUE
1	Sky TV Guide	3,403,912
2	Cable Guide	1,860,622
3	What's on TV	1,765,369
4	Reader's Digest	1,493,312
5	Radio Times	1,400,331
6	TV Times	850,282
7	FHM	751,493
8	Woman	711,133
9	Woman's Own	654,473
10	Bella	610,843

In addition to the magazines in this Top 10, among the fastest growing are two devoted to Sony PlayStation, both of which are published by Future Publishing: *Official PlayStation Magazine* (circulation 380,186, up 85 per cent on the previous year), and *Essential PlayStation* (circulation 173,412, up 300.7 per cent).

TOP 10 WOMEN'S MONTHLY MAGAZINES IN THE UK
(Magazine/average circulation per issue)

1 *Prima*, 510,142
2 *Cosmopolitan*, 476,288 **3** *Candis*, 458,773 **4** *Marie Claire*, 445,289
5 *Good Housekeeping*, 400,063
6 *Woman & Home*, 330,001
7 *Essentials*, 296,904 **8** *Company*, 290,402 **9** *Family Circle*, 280,687
10 *New Woman*, 261,681

TOP 10 TEEN MAGAZINES IN THE UK
(Magazine/average circulation per issue)

1 *Sugar*, 451,696 **2** *Top of the Pops*, 437,090 **3** *It's Bliss*, 337,188 **4** *Smash Hits*, 295,061 **5** *More*, 293,369 **6** *TV Hits*, 269,061 **7** *J17*, 242,516 **8** *B*, 231,612 **9** *19*, 173,244 **10** *Live & Kicking*, 165,248

TOP 10 ★
MOST LANDED-ON SQUARES IN MONOPOLY®*

US GAME		UK GAME
Illinois Avenue	1	Trafalgar Square
Go	2	Go
B. & O. Railroad	3	Fenchurch Street Station
Free Parking	4	Free Parking
Tennessee Avenue	5	Marlborough Street
New York Avenue	6	Vine Street
Reading Railroad	7	King's Cross Station
St. James Place	8	Bow Street
Water Works	9	Water Works
Pennsylvania Railroad	10	Marylebone Station

* Based on a computer analysis of the probability of landing on each square

Monopoly® is a registered trade mark of Parker Brothers division of Tonka Corporation, USA, under licence to Waddington Games Ltd.

TOP 10 ★
LEISURE ACTIVITIES AMONG ADULTS IN THE UK

	ACTIVITY	PER CENT PARTICIPATING*
1	Watching television	99
2	Visiting/entertaining	96
3	Listening to the radio	88
4	Listening to records/tapes/CDs	78
5 =	Reading books	65
=	Visiting a pub	65
7	Meal in a restaurant (not fast food)	62
8	Gardening	49
9	Driving for pleasure	47
10	Walking	45

* Based on percentage over 16 years old participating in each activity in the three months prior to interview for activities away from the home, or in the four weeks prior to interview for activities in the home

TOP 10 BESTSELLING GAMES AT W.H. SMITH

1 Jenga 2 Bart Simpson Chess Set 3 Press the Bomb 4 Wallace and Gromit Game 5 Monopoly 6 Uno Cards 7 Articulate 8 Scrabble 9 Boggle 10 Cluedo

TOP 10 TOYS AND GAMES OF 1998 IN THE UK*

1 Furby 2 Pro-yo III 3 Action Man Polar Mission 4 Action Man Roller Extreme 5 Bounce Around Tigger 6 Monopoly 7 Laa Laa Talking Teletubby 8 Teletubbies' Bean Bags 9 Rebound 6v 4x4 10 Gyrocopter

* Ranked by value of retail sales
Source: NPD Group Worldwide

TALKATIVE PET

A Furby is an interactive toy that can communicate with fellow Furbies in Furbish but can also be taught to converse in English.

TOP 10 ★
HIGHEST-SCORING SCRABBLE WORDS

	WORD/PLAY	SCORE
1	QUARTZY	164/162

(i) Play across a triple-word-score (red) square with the Z on a double-letter-score (light blue) square
(ii) Play across two double-word-score (pink) squares with Q and Y on pink squares

2 =	BEZIQUE	161/158

(i) Play across a red square with either the Z or the Q on a light blue square
(ii) Play across two pink squares with the B and second E on two pink squares

=	CAZIQUE	161/158

(i) Play across a red square with either the Z or the Q on a light blue square
(ii) Play across two pink squares with the C and E on two pink squares

4	ZINKIFY	158

Play across a red square with the Z on a light blue square

5 =	QUETZAL	155

Play across a red square with either the Q or the Z on a light blue square

=	JAZZILY	155

(Using a blank as one of the Zs) Play across a red square with the non-blank Z on a light blue square

=	QUIZZED	155

(Using a blank as one of the Zs) Play across a red square with the non-blank Z or the Q on a light blue square

8 =	ZEPHYRS	152

Play across a red square with the Z on a light blue square

=	ZINCIFY	152

Play across a red square with the Z on a light blue square

=	ZYTHUMS	152

Play across a red square with the Z on a light blue square

All the Top 10 words contain seven letters and therefore earn the premium of 50 for using all the letters in the rack. Being able to play them depends on there already being suitable words on the board to which they can be added. In an actual game, the face values of the perpendicular words to which they are joined would also be counted, but these are discounted here as the total score variations would be infinite. Scrabble was invented in the US during the Depression, by an unemployed architect, Alfred Butts, and developed in the 1940s by James Brunot.

Did You Know? Twelve black "mourning" Steiff teddy bears were made to commemorate the sinking of the *Titanic* in 1912.

TOP 10 ⭐
MOST EXPENSIVE DOLLS SOLD AT AUCTION IN THE UK

DOLL/SALE	PRICE (£)
1 **Kämmer and Reinhardt doll**, Sotheby's, London, 8 February 1994	188,500
2 **Kämmer and Reinhardt bisque character doll**, German, c.1909, Sotheby's, London, 17 October 1996	108,200
(Previously sold at Sotheby's, London, 16 February 1989 for £90,200)	
3 **Kämmer and Reinhardt bisque character doll**, German, c.1909, Sotheby's, London, 17 October 1996	91,700
4 **Albert Marque bisque character doll**, Sotheby's, London, 17 October 1996	71,900
5 = **William and Mary wooden doll**, English, c.1690, Sotheby's, London, 24 March 1987	67,000
= **Wooden doll, Charles II**, 17th century, Christie's, London, 18 May 1989	67,000
7 **Albert Marque bisque character doll**, Sotheby's, London, 17 October 1996	58,700
8 = **Albert Marque bisque character doll**, Christie's, London, 23 May 1997	56,500
= **Mulatto pressed bisque swivel-head Madagascar doll**, Sotheby's, London, 17 October 1996	56,500
10 **Shellacked pressed bisque swivel-head doll**, Sotheby's, London, 17 October 1996	45,500

TOP 10 BESTSELLING COMPUTER GAMES AT W.H. SMITH

1 Metal Gear Solid (PlayStation)
2 South Park (Nintendo 64)
3 A Bug's Life **4** Grand Theft Auto
5 Sim City 3000 (CD-ROM) **6** Alpha Centauri (CD-ROM) **7** Myst Desk Top Pack **8** Premier Manager '99
9 FIFA '99 (PlayStation) **10** Rugrats – Search for Reptar (PlayStation)

TOP 10 ⭐
MOST EXPENSIVE TOYS EVER SOLD AT AUCTION IN THE UK*

TOY/SALE	PRICE (£)
1 **Titania's Palace, a doll's house with 2,000 items of furniture**, Christie's, London, 10 January 1978	135,000
2 **Hornby 00-gauge train set** (the largest ever sold at auction), Christies, London, 27 November 1992	80,178
3 **Russian carousel** (tinplate ferris wheel), c.1904, Sotheby's, London, 10 February 1993	62,500
4 = **Tinplate carousel by Märklin**, c.1910, Sotheby's, London, 23 January 1992	47,300
= **Set of Märklin horse-drawn fire appliances**, c.1902, Sotheby's, London, 23 January 1992	47,300
6 **Tinplate 4-volt electric ocean liner, *Augusta Victoria*, by Märklin**, Christie's, London, 21 May 1992	41,800
7 **Tinplate clockwork battleship, *Maine*, by Märklin**, c.1904, Sotheby's, London, 16 Feb 1989	39,600
8 **Märklin Gauge I locomotive**, Christie's, London, 23 May 1997	35,200
9 **Pierrot serenading the moon, a clockwork musical automaton by G. Vichy**, Christie's, London, 19 Mar 1991	31,900
10 **Tinplate clockwork paddleboat, *Emily*, by Märklin**, c.1902, Sotheby's, London, 19 Sep 1989	28,600

* Excluding dolls and teddy bears

TOP 10 ⭐
MOST EXPENSIVE TEDDY BEARS SOLD AT AUCTION IN THE UK

BEAR/SALE	PRICE (£)*
1 **"Teddy Girl"**, Christie's, London, 5 December 1994	110,000
A 1904 Steiff formerly owned by Lt.-Col. Bob Henderson, precisely doubled the previous world record for a teddy bear when it was acquired by Yoshiro Sekiguchi for display at his teddy bear museum near Tokyo.	
2 **"Happy"**, a dual-plush Steiff teddy bear, 1926, Sotheby's, London, 19 September 1989	55,000
Although estimated at £700–£900, competitive bidding pushed the price up to the then world record, when it was acquired by collector Paul Volpp.	
3 **"Elliot"**, a blue Steiff bear, 1908, Christie's, London, 6 December 1993	49,500
Produced as a sample for Harrods, but never manufactured commercially.	
4 **Teddy Edward**, a golden mohair teddy bear, star of *Watch with Mother*, Christie's, London, 9 December 1996	34,500
5 **Black Steiff teddy bear**, c.1912, Sotheby's, London, 18 May 1990	24,200
6 **Steiff teddy bear**, c.1905, Christie's, London, 8 December 1997	23,000
7 **"Albert"**, a Steiff teddy bear c.1910, Christie's, London, 9 December 1996	18,400
8 **"Theodore"**, a miniature Steiff teddy bear, 9 cm/3½ in tall, c.1948, Christie's, London, 11 December 1995	14,625
9 = **"Black Jack"**, black Steiff teddy bear, Christie's, London, 22 May 1997	13,800
= **Cinnamon Steiff teddy bear**, c.1905, Christie's, London, 23 May 1997	13,800

* Prices include buyer's premium

Margarete Steiff, a German toymaker, began making her first toy bears in 1903, exporting them to the US to meet the demand for "Teddy's Bears" (named after "Teddy" Roosevelt).

SONY'S WINNER

The Sony PlayStation console is the best-selling games console on the market, and in the year 2000 the company will be launching PlayStation 2, an improved version of the product.

TOP 10 ★
MOST EXPENSIVE PAINTINGS BY WOMEN ARTISTS EVER SOLD AT AUCTION

PAINTING/ARTIST/SALE	PRICE (£)
1 *In the Box*, **Mary Cassatt** (American; 1844–1926), Christie's, New York, 23 May 1996	2,450,331 ($3,700,000)
2 *The Conversation*, **Mary Cassatt**, Christie's, New York, 11 May 1988	2,180,850 ($4,100,000)
3 *Mother, Sara and the Baby*, **Mary Cassatt**, Christie's, New York, 10 May 1989	2,147,239 ($3,500,000)
4 *From the Plains*, **Georgia O'Keeffe** (American; 1887–1986), Sotheby's, New York, 3 Dec 1997	2,000,000 ($3,300,000)
5 *Après le déjeuner*, **Berthe Morisot** (French; 1841–95), Christie's, New York, 14 May 1997	1,993,865 ($3,250,000)
6 *Autoretrato con chango y loro*, **Frida Kahlo** (Mexican; 1907–54), Sotheby's, New York, 17 May 1995	1,847,134 ($2,900,000)
7 *Augusta Reading to her Daughter*, **Mary Cassatt**, Sotheby's, New York, 9 May 1989	1,717,790 ($2,800,000)
8 *Children Playing with a Cat*, **Mary Cassatt**, Sotheby's, New York, 3 Dec 1998	1,626,506 ($2,700,000)
9 = *Young Lady in a Loge, Gazing to the Right*, **Mary Cassatt**, Sotheby's, New York, 10 Nov 1992	1,523,179 ($2,300,000)
= *Calla Lily with Red Roses*, **Georgia O'Keeffe**, Sotheby's, New York, 20 May 1998	1,523,179 ($2,400,000)

TOP 10 ARTISTS WITH MOST WORKS SOLD FOR MORE THAN ONE MILLION POUNDS
(Artist/works sold)

❶ Pablo Picasso (Spanish; 1881–1973), 160 **❷ Claude Monet** (French; 1888–1926), 132 **❸ Pierre Auguste Renoir** (French; 1841–1919), 97 **❹ Edgar Degas** (French; 1834–1917), 54 **❺ Paul Cézanne** (French; 1839–1906), 46 **❻ Amedeo Modigliani** (Italian; 1884–1920), 42 **❼** = **Henri Matisse** (French; 1869–1954), 38; = **Vincent van Gogh** (Dutch; 1853–90), 38 **❾ Camille Pissaro** (French; 1830–1903), 30 **❿ Paul Gauguin** (French; 1848–1903), 27

SPANISH GENIUS
Pablo Picasso, one of the 20th century's greatest artists, photographed in April 1971, two years before his death.

IMPRESSIONISM
Pierre-Auguste Renoir's Au Moulin de la Galette, *an animated panorama of the crowd under the trees at the pleasure resort of Montmartre, was first shown in 1876.*

TOP 10 ★
MOST EXPENSIVE PAINTINGS EVER SOLD AT AUCTION

PAINTING/ARTIST/SALE	PRICE (£)
1 *Portrait of Dr. Gachet*, **Vincent van Gogh** (Dutch; 1853–90), Christie's, New York, 15 May 1990	44,378,696 ($75,000,000)
Both this painting and the one in No. 2 position were bought by Ryoei Saito, chairman of the Japanese firm Daishowa Paper Manufacturing.	
2 *Au Moulin de la Galette*, **Pierre-Auguste Renoir** (French; 1841–1919), Sotheby's, New York, 17 May 1990	42,011,832 ($71,000,000)
3 *Portrait de l'artiste sans barbe*, **Vincent van Gogh**, Christie's, New York, 19 Nov 1998	39,393,940 ($65,000,000)
4 *Les noces de Pierrette*, **Pablo Picasso** (Spanish; 1881–1973), Binoche et Godeau, Paris, 30 Nov 1989	33,123,028 (F.Fr315,000,000)
This painting was sold by Swedish financier Fredrik Roos and bought by Tomonori Tsurumaki, a Japanese property developer, bidding from Tokyo by telephone.	
5 *Irises*, **Vincent van Gogh**, Sotheby's, New York, 11 Nov 1987	28,000,000 ($49,000,000)
The Australian businessman Alan Bond was unable to pay for this painting in full, so its former status as the world's most expensive work of art has been disputed.	
6 *Self Portrait: Yo Picasso*, **Pablo Picasso**, Sotheby's, New York, 9 May 1989	26,687,116 ($43,500,000)
The purchaser has remained anonymous but unconfirmed reports have identified him as Stavros Niarchos, the Greek shipping magnate.	
7 *Le rêve*, **Pablo Picasso**, Christie's, New York, 10 Nov 1997	26,035,502 ($44,000,000)
Victor and Sally Ganz had paid $7,000 for this painting in 1941.	
8 *Au Lapin Agile*, **Pablo Picasso**, Sotheby's, New York, 15 Nov 1989	23,870,968 ($37,000,000)
The painting depicts Picasso as a harlequin at the bar of the café Lapin Agile.	
9 *Sunflowers*, **Vincent van Gogh**, Christie's, London, 30 Mar 1987	22,500,000
At the time, this was the most expensive picture ever sold (and is still the most expensive sold in the UK).	
10 *Portrait of Duke Cosimo I de Medici*, **Jacopo da Carucci (Pontormo)** (Italian; 1494–1556/7), Christie's, New York, 31 May 1989	20,253,164 ($32,000,000)
This is the world record price paid for an Old Master – the only one in the Top 10	

One of Claude Monet's water-lily studies is offered for sale at Sotheby's. When the Impressionist painters first exhibited in Paris in 1874 their works attracted ridicule and incomprehension, but their popularity now is unparalleled.

TOP 10 ★
MOST EXPENSIVE PAINTINGS EVER SOLD IN THE UK

PAINTING/ARTIST/SALE	PRICE (£)
1 *Sunflowers*, **Vincent van Gogh**, Christie's, London, 30 Mar 1987	22,500,000
2 *Acrobate et jeune Arlequin*, **Pablo Picasso**, Christie's, London, 28 Nov 1988	19,000,000
3 *Basin aux nymphaeas et sentier au bord de l'eau*, **Claude Monet**, Sotheby's, London, 30 June 1998	18,000,000
4 *Schloss Kammer am Attersee II*, **Gustav Klimt**, Christie's, London, 9 October 1997	13,200,000
5 *Dans la prairie*, **Claude Monet**, Sotheby's, London, 28 June 1988	13,000,000
6 *Les Tuileries*, **Pablo Picasso**, Christie's, London, 25 June 1990	12,500,000
7 *Le Pont de Trinquetaille*, **Vincent van Gogh**, Christie's, London, 29 June 1987	11,500,000
8 *Pommes et serviette*, **Paul Cézanne**, Christie's, London, 27 November 1989	10,000,000
9 *The Lock*, **John Constable**, Sotheby's, London, 14 November 1990	9,800,000
10 *La promenade*, **Pierre Auguste Renoir**, Sotheby's, London, 4 April 1989	9,400,000

TOP 10 ★
MOST EXPENSIVE BRITISH PAINTINGS EVER SOLD AT AUCTION

PAINTING/ARTIST/SALE	PRICE (£)
1 *The Lock*, **John Constable** (1776–1837), Sotheby's, London, 14 Nov 1990	9,800,000
2 *Seascape, Folkestone*, **J.M.W. Turner** (1775–1851), Sotheby's, London, 5 July 1984	6,700,000
3 *Cashmere*, **John Singer Sargent** (1856–1925), Sotheby's, New York, 5 Dec 1996	6,158,537 ($10,100,000)
4 *In the Garden, Corfu*, **John Singer Sargent**, Sotheby's, New York, 3 December 1997	4,606,061 ($7,600,000)
5 *Spanish Dancer*, **John Singer Sargent**, Sotheby's, New York, 25 May 1994	4,600,000 ($6,900,000)
6 *Triptych May–June*, **Francis Bacon** (1909–92), Sotheby's, New York, 2 May 1989	3,433,735 ($6,270,000)
7 *Study for Pope*, **Francis Bacon**, Christie's, New York, 7 November 1989	3,291,139 ($5,200,000)
8 *Large Interior, W11*, **Lucian Freud** (b.1922), Sotheby's, New York, 14 May 1998	3,271,605 ($5,300,000)
9 *Study for Portrait of van Gogh II*, **Francis Bacon**, Sotheby's, New York, 2 May 198	3,192,770 ($5,300,000)
10 *Study for Portrait*, **Francis Bacon**, Sotheby's, New York, 8 May 1990	2,976,190 ($5,000,000)

What is the most widely spoken language in the world? *see p.113 for the answer*

A English
B Chinese (Mandarin)
C Arabic

125

ART ON SHOW

TOP 10 ★ OLDEST OUTDOOR STATUES IN LONDON

	STATUE/LOCATION	DATE
1	**Sekhmet**, over Sotheby's, 34 Bond Street	c.1600 BC
2	**King Alfred** (?), Trinity Church Square	Late 14th century
3	**Queen Elizabeth I**, St. Dunstan in the West, Fleet Street	1586
4	**Charles I**, Trafalgar Square	1633
5	**Guy of Warwick**, corner of Newgate Street and Warwick Lane	1668
6 =	**Robert Devereux, Earl of Essex**, above the Devereux Inn, Devereux Court	1676
=	**Charles II**, Chelsea Hospital	1676
8	**Charles II**, Soho Square	1681
9	**Pannier Boy**, Panyer Alley	1688
10	**Henry VIII**, over the gateway of St. Bartholemew's Hospital	1702

LADY LIBERTY

The Statue of Liberty consists of sheets of copper on an iron frame, which weighs 229 tonnes. It stands on a massive pedestal that more than doubles the overall height to 93 m/305 ft from the base to the torch.

TOP 10 ★ TALLEST FREE-STANDING STATUES

	STATUE/LOCATION	HEIGHT M	FT
1	**Chief Crazy Horse**, Thunderhead Mountain, South Dakota, USA	172	563

Started in 1948 by Polish-American sculptor Korczak Ziolkowski, and continued after his death in 1982 by his widow and eight of his children, this gigantic equestrian statue is even longer than it is high (195 m/641 ft). It is being carved out of the granite mountain by dynamiting and drilling.

2	**Buddha**, Tokyo, Japan	120	394

This Japan–Taiwanese project, unveiled in 1993, took seven years to complete and weighs 1,000 tonnes.

3	**The Indian Rope Trick**, Riddersberg Säteri, Jönköping, Sweden	103	337

Sculptor Calle Ornemark's 144-tonne wooden sculpture depicts a long strand of "rope" held by a fakir, while another figure ascends.

4	**Motherland**, 1967, Volgograd, Russia	82	270

This concrete statue of a woman with a raised sword, designed by Yevgeniy Vuchetich, commemorates the Soviet victory at the Battle of Stalingrad (1942–43).

5	**Buddha**, Bamian, Afghanistan	53	173

This dates from the 3rd–4th centuries AD.

6	**Kannon**, Otsubo-yama, near Tokyo, Japan	52	170

The immense statue of the goddess of mercy was unveiled in 1961 in honour of the dead of World War II.

7	**Statue of Liberty**, New York, USA	46	151

Designed by Auguste Bartholdi and presented to the USA by the people of France, the statue was shipped in sections to Liberty (formerly Bedloes) Island where it was assembled, before being unveiled on 28 October 1886, and restored on 4 July 1986.

8	**Christ**, Rio de Janeiro, Brazil	38	125

The work of sculptor Paul Landowski and engineer Heitor da Silva Costa, the figure of Christ was unveiled in 1931.

9	**Tian Tan (Temple of Heaven) Buddha**, Po Lin Monastery, Lantau Island, Hong Kong	34	112

This was completed after 20 years' work and unveiled on 29 December 1993.

10	**Colossi of Memnon**, Karnak, Egypt	21	70

This statue portrays two seated sandstone figures of Pharaoh Amenhotep III.

TOP 10 ★ LARGEST MUSEUMS IN THE UK

	MUSEUM	FLOOR AREA SQ M	SQ FT
1	**British Museum** (Natural History), London	87,000	936,459
2	**British Museum**, London	80,000	861,112
3	**Science Museum**, London	42,873	461,481
4	**Doncaster Museum and Art Gallery**	36,000	387,500
5	**Harewood House**, Harewood, Leeds	35,000	376,737
6	**Black Country Museum**, Dudley	32,000	344,445
7	**David Livingstone Centre**, Blantyre, Strathclyde	31,972	344,143
8 =	**Ulster Folk and Transport Museum**, Holywood, County Down	25,000	269,098
=	**National Railway Museum**, York	25,000	269,098
10	**Grosvenor Museum**, Chester	18,395	198,002

TOP 10 OLDEST MUSEUMS AND ART GALLERIES IN THE UK

(Museum or art gallery/founded)

1. **Ashmolean Museum**, Oxford, 1683
2. **British Museum**, London, 1753
3. **National Museum of Antiquities**, Edinburgh, 1780
4. **Hunterian Museum**, Glasgow, 1807
5. **Royal College of Surgeons Museum**, London, 1813
6. **Museum of Antiquities**, Newcastle upon Tyne, 1813
7. **Dulwich Picture Gallery**, London, 1814
8. **Fitzwilliam Museum**, Cambridge, 1816
9. **Leeds City Museum**, 1820
10. **Manchester Museum**, 1821

There are some arguments for stating that the Tower Armouries at the Tower of London are the UK's oldest museum. However, although they were established during the reign of Henry VIII (1509–47) and became a showplace for the collection of royal armour, they were not open to the public until much later.

Did You Know? The Angel of the North, Gateshead, UK, with a wingspan of 54 m/177 ft, is the largest sculpture of an angel in the world.

126

THE ARTIST'S GARDEN

This painting of the garden at Giverny, Monet's home, is exhibited at the Musée d'Orsay in Paris, but also appears in touring exhibitions, such as the popular 1999 show at the Royal Academy in London.

TOP 10 ⭐
BEST-ATTENDED EXHIBITIONS AT THE BRITISH MUSEUM, LONDON

	EXHIBITION/YEAR	TOTAL ATTENDANCE
1	Treasures of Tutankhamun*, 1972–73	1,694,117
2	Turner Watercolours, 1975	585,046
3	The Vikings*, 1980	465,000
4	Thracian Treasures from Bulgaria, 1976	424,465
5	From Manet to Toulouse-Lautrec: French Lithographs 1860–1900, 1978	355,354
6	The Ancient Olympic Games, 1980	334,354
7	Treasures for the Nation*, 1988–89	297,837
8	Excavating in Egypt, 1982–83	285,736
9	Heraldry, 1978	262,183
10	Drawings by Michelangelo, 1975	250,000

* Admission charged

WELCOME TO THE LOUVRE

The Louvre Museum in Paris, which contains one of the most important art collections in the world, was given its imposing glass pyramid entrance in 1989.

TOP 10 BEST-ATTENDED EXHIBITIONS, 1998

	EXHIBITION/VENUE	TOTAL ATTENDANCE
1	**Monet in the 20th Century**, Museum of Fine Arts, Boston, USA	586,000
2	**The Collection of Edgar Degas**, Metropolitan Museum, New York, USA	528,000
3	**Van Gogh's van Goghs**, National Gallery, Washington, DC, USA	480,000
4	**Gianni Versace**, Metropolitan Museum, New York, USA	410,000
5	**Delacroix: The Late Works**, Museum of Art, Philadelphia, USA	306,000
6	**René Magritte**, Musées Royaux des Beaux-Arts, Brussels, Belgium	302,000
7	**The Art of the Motorcycle**, Guggenheim Museum, New York, USA	301,000
8	**Alexander Calder, 1898–1976**, Museum of Modern Art, San Francisco, USA	300,000
9	**China: 5,000 Years**, Guggenheim Museum, New York, USA	300,000
10	**Recognizing van Eyck**, Museum of Art, Philadelphia, USA	153,000

TOP 10 ⭐
LARGEST PAINTINGS IN THE LOUVRE MUSEUM, PARIS

	PAINTING/ARTIST	SIZE (HEIGHT X WIDTH) M	FT
1	*Interior of Westminster Abbey*, Jean-Pierre Alaux	19.0 x 40.0	62 x 131
2	*Interior of St. Peter's, Rome*, Jean-Pierre Alaux	17.5 x 40.0	57 x 131
3	*Palace Ceiling*, Francesco Fontebasso	8.0 x 10.0	26 x 33
4	*The Marriage Feast at Cana*, Paolo Veronese	6.7 x 9.9	22 x 32
5	*The Coronation of Napoleon*, Jacques-Louis David	6.2 x 9.8	20 x 32
6	*The Battle of Arbela*, Charles Lebrun	4.7 x 12.7	15 x 42
7	*Alexander and Porus*, Charles Lebrun	4.7 x 12.6	15 x 41
8	*Crossing the Granicus*, Charles Lebrun	4.7 x 12.1	15 x 40
9	*The Battle of Eylau*, Antoine-Jean Gros	5.2 x 7.8	17 x 26
10	*Napoleon Visiting the Plague Victims of Jaffa*, Antoine-Jean Gros	5.2 x 7.2	17 x 24

ART ON SALE

TOP 10 ★
MOST EXPENSIVE SCIENTIFIC INSTRUMENTS EVER SOLD AT AUCTION BY CHRISTIE'S, LONDON

	INSTRUMENT/DATE/SALE	PRICE (£)
1	Pair of globes, terrestrial and celestial, attributed to Gerard Mercator, 1579, 30 Oct 1991	1,023,000
2	Ptolemaic armillary sphere, c.1579, 9 Apr 1997	771,500
3	Astrolabe by Ersamus Habermel, c.1590, 11 Oct 1995	540,000
4	Astrolabe by Walter Arsenius, 1559, 29 Sep 1988	385,000
5	Ptolemaic armillary sphere, 8 Apr 1998	265,000
6	Gilt-brass universal rectilinear dial, c.1590, 8 Apr 1998	221,500
7	The Regiomontanus Astrolabe, 1462, 28 Sep 1989	209,000
8	Astrolabe quadrant by Christopher Schissler, 1576, 28 Sep 1989	187,000
9	Section of Difference Engine No.1 by Charles and Henry Prevost Babbage, 16 Nov 1995	176,750
10	Arithmometre (mechanical calculator) by Thomas de Colmar, 1848, 9 Apr 1997	166,500

Astrolabes are instruments for calculating the altitude of heavenly bodies and were once used by astronomers, astrologers, and travellers. They were originally made by Islamic artisans, but during the Renaissance were manufactured by Western craftsmen, often for wealthy connoisseurs (the Habermel astrolabe at No.3, for example, was made for the Duke of Parma), and many skilfully made and richly decorated examples have survived. They are now so desirable among collectors that they dominate this Top 10. The "Difference Engine" designed by Charles Babbage (1791–1871), a precursor of the computer, was abandoned in 1833 and completed by his son Henry Prevost Babbage in 1879. Just outside the Top 10, high prices have also been paid for other astrolabes, globes, compasses, and calculating devices, and substantial prices have also been achieved for rare examples of microscopes.

CELESTIAL SPHERE

The armillary sphere is a type of sundial used by early astronomers to pinpoint the position of the stars.

RARE PAIR

Carved from porphyry and featuring lions, swags, and serpents, a pair of these Louis XV vases sold for nearly £2 million.

TOP 10 ★
MOST EXPENSIVE ITEMS OF FURNITURE EVER SOLD AT AUCTION

	ITEM/SALE	PRICE (£)
1	18th-century "Badminton Cabinet", Christie's, London, 5 Jul 1990	8,580,000
2	1760s mahogany desk by John Goddard, Christie's, New York, 3 Jun 1989	7,786,358 ($12,100,000)
3	Carved silver-mounted plum-pudding mahogany dome-top secretary bookcase by Nathaniel Appleton, Sotheby's, New York, 17 Jan 1999	5,065,380 ($8,252,500)
4	Porcelain-mounted jewel coffer by Martin Carlin, Ader Picard & Tajan, Paris, 7 Nov 1991	2,581,395 (FrF.25,700,000)
5	Louis XIV bureau plat by A-C Boulle, Christie's, Monaco, 4 Dec 1993	2,144,318 (FFr.18,869,996)
6	Pair of Louis XV porphyry and gilt-bronze two-handled vases, Christie's, London, 8 Dec 1994	1,926,500
7	Louis XVI ormolu and Sèvres porcelain-mounted table, Sotheby's, New York, 5 Nov 1998	1,790,630 ($2,972,500)
8	Porcelain-mounted commode by Martin Carlin, Ader Picard & Tajan, Paris, 7 Nov 1991	1,668,352 (FrF.16,600,000)
9	Le mobilier Crozat, a suite of Regency seat furniture, Christie's, Monaco, 7 Dec 1987	1,665,000 (FFr.16,836,735)
10	Early 17th-century Italian baroque inlaid marble tabletop, Sotheby's, New York, 5 Nov 1998	1,658,110 ($2,752,500)

TOP 10 BESTSELLING POSTCARDS IN THE VICTORIA AND ALBERT MUSEUM, LONDON

1 Photograph of the Museum from Cromwell Road **2** *Roses* watercolour by J.J. Walther (1600–79) **3** **Lion,** detail from "The Forest" tapestry by William Morris and Henry Dearle, 1887 **4** **"Strawberry Thief"**, fabric design by William Morris, *c.*1883 **5** **Teddy Bear dressed as a World War I sailor**, German, 1911 **6** *Salisbury Cathedral* by John Constable, 1823 **7** **"Tippoo's Tiger"**, mechanical organ, *c.*1795 **8** **"Cat and Butterfly"**, wallpaper design by William Morris **9** **Samson Slaying a Philistine**, by Giovanni Bologna, 1562 **10** Court mantua and petticoat, red silk with silver thread, English, *c.*1740–45

TOP 10 ★ BESTSELLING POSTCARDS IN THE TATE GALLERY, LONDON

	ARTIST/PAINTING	DATE
1	John William Waterhouse, *The Lady of Shalott*	1888
2	John Everett Millais, *Ophelia*	1851–52
3	Henri Matisse, *Snail*	1953
4	Salvador Dali, *Lobster Telephone*	1936
5	Salvador Dali, *Metamorphosis of Narcissus*	1937
6	Pablo Picasso, *Weeping Woman*	1937
7	Andy Warhol, *Marilyn Diptych*	1962
8	Mark Rothko, *Light Red over Black*	1957
9	Arthur Hughes, *April Love*	1855–56
10	Salvador Dali, *Autumn Cannibalism*	1936

While the Spanish Surrealist Dali maintains his preeminence in this Top 10, the popularity of the Pre-Raphaelites (Waterhouse, Millais, and Hughes) remains as strong as ever, alongside such modern painters as Warhol and Rothko whose works have recently entered the list.

TOP 10 ★ BESTSELLING POSTCARDS IN THE NATIONAL GALLERY, LONDON

	ARTIST/PAINTING	QUANTITY 1998/99
1	Vincent van Gogh, *Sunflowers*	45,920
2	Claude Monet, *The Water-Lily Pond*	28,940
3	Pierre-Auguste Renoir, *The Umbrellas*	21,380
4	Vincent van Gogh, *A Cornfield with Cypresses*	20,890
5	Georges Pierre Seurat, *Bathers, Asnières*	17,800
6	Claude Monet, *The Thames Below Westminster*	17,090
7	Jan van Eyck, *The Marriage of Giovanni (?) Arnolfini and Giovanna Cenami (?)*	16,775
8	Vincent van Gogh, *Chair and Pipe*	15,800
9	George Stubbs, *Whistle Jacket*	15,400
10	Jean-Auguste-Dominique Ingres, *Mme. Moittessier*	15,300

MONET, MONET, MONET

The Water-Lily Pond, one of Monet's many water-lily studies, has become a bestselling postcard.

TOP 10 ★ BESTSELLING POSTCARDS IN THE BRITISH LIBRARY, LONDON

	IMAGE	DATE
1	Exterior of the new British Library	–
2	Interior of the new British Library	–
3	Exterior of the new British Library showing the Edouardo Paolozzi statue of Isaac Newton	–
4	Interior of the new British Library showing the R.B. Kitaj tapestry	–
5	View of the King's Library	–
6	*Magna Carta*	1215
7	St. Luke's Gospels, from the *Lindisfarne Gospels*	*c.*698
8	Decorated cross from page preceding St. Luke's Gospels, from the *Lindisfarne Gospels*	*c.*698
9	The *Codex Sinaiticus* (Greek Bible)	4th century AD
10	Manuscript of The Beatles' song *I Want to Hold your Hand*	1963

TOP 10 BESTSELLING POSTCARDS IN THE NATIONAL PORTRAIT GALLERY, LONDON

1 Elizabeth I **2** Henry VIII **3** William Shakespeare **4** Virginia Woolf **5** Oscar Wilde **6** A.A. Milne **7** Anne Boleyn **8** Mary I **9** The Brontë Sisters **10** Stan Laurel

Which van Gogh is the most expensive painting ever sold at auction?
see p.124 for the answer
A *Sunflowers*
B *Portrait of Dr. Gachet*
C *Irises*

TOP 10 ★
MOST EXPENSIVE PAINTINGS BY ANDY WARHOL

PAINTING*/SALE	PRICE (£)
1 *Orange Marilyn*, Sotheby's, New York, 14 May 1998	9,722,223 ($15,750,000)
2 *Marilyn X 100*, Sotheby's, New York, 17 Nov 1992	2,251,656 ($3,400,000)
3 *Shot Red Marilyn*, Sotheby's, New York, 3 May 1989	2,228,916 ($3,700,000)
4 *Shot Red Marilyn*, Sotheby's, New York, 2 Nov 1994	2,062,500 ($3,300,000)
5 *Marilyn Monroe, twenty times*, Sotheby's, New York, 10 Nov 1988	2,000,000 ($3,600,000)
6 *Big Torn Campbell's Soup Can*, Christie's, New York, 7 May 1997	1,987,578 ($3,200,000)
7 *Orange Marilyn*, Christie's, New York, 19 Nov 1998	1,515,152 ($2,500,000)
8 *Self Portrait*, Christie's, New York, 12 May 1998	1,358,025 ($2,200,000)
9 *Liz*, Christie's, New York, 7 Nov 1989	1,297,468 ($2,050,000)
10 *Four Marilyns*, Sotheby's, New York, 17 Nov 1998	1,272,727 ($2,100,000)

* Including silkscreen works

HIGH PRIEST OF POP ART
Andy Warhol is famous for turning everyday images into high art through repetitive silkscreen works.

TOP 10 ★
MOST EXPENSIVE PAINTINGS BY 20TH-CENTURY ARTISTS*

PAINTING/ARTIST	SALE	PRICE (£)
1 *Interchange*, Willem de Kooning (American/Dutch; 1904–97)	Sotheby's, New York, 8 Nov 1989	11,898,735 ($18,800,000)
2 *Fugue*, Wassily Kandinsky (Russian; 1866–1944)	Sotheby's, New York, 17 May 1990	11,242,604 ($19,000,000)
3 *Harmonie jaune*, Henri Matisse (French; 1869–1954)	Christie's, New York, 11 Nov 1992	8,741,723 ($13,200,000)
4 *False Start*, Jasper Johns (American; b.1930)	Sotheby's, New York, 10 November 1988	8,611,112 ($15,500,000)
5 *La pose Hindoue*, Henri Matisse	Sotheby's, New York, 8 May 1995	8,598,727 ($13,500,000)
6 *Contrastes de Formes*, Fernand Léger (French; 1881–1955)	Christie's, London, 27 Nov 1989	8,500,000
7 *La Mulatresse Fatma*, Henri Matisse	Sotheby's, New York, 11 May 1993	8,496,733 ($13,000,000)
8 *Woman*, Willem de Kooning	Christie's, New York, 20 Nov 1996	8,452,382 ($14,200,000)
9 *La vis*, Henri Matisse	Sotheby's, New York, 3 Nov 1993	8,445,947 ($14,200,000)
10 *Anniversaire*, Marc Chagall (French/Russian; 1887–1985)	Sotheby's, New York, 17 May 1990	7,988,166 ($13,500,000)

* Excluding Picasso

TOP 10 ★
MOST EXPENSIVE PAINTINGS BY ROY LICHTENSTEIN

PAINTING/SALE	PRICE (£)
1 *Kiss II*, Christie's, New York, 7 May 1990	3,273,810 ($5,500,000)
2 *Torpedo... Los*, Christie's, New York, 7 Nov 1989	3,164,557 ($5,000,000)
3 *Tex!*, Christie's, New York, 20 Nov 1996	2,142,857 ($3,600,000)
4 *Blang*, Christie's, New York, 7 May 1997	1,614,907 ($2,600,000)
5 *Kiss II*, Christie's, New York, 3 May 1995	1,437,500 ($2,300,000)
6 *I... I'm Sorry!*, Sotheby's, New York, 1 Nov 1994	1,406,250 ($2,250,000)
7 *The Ring*, Sotheby's, New York, 19 Nov 1997	1,190,476 ($2,000,000)
8 *Forest Scene*, Sotheby's, New York, 19 Nov 1996	1,130,952 ($1,900,000)
9 *Girl with Piano*, Sotheby's, New York, 17 Nov 1992	1,092,715 ($1,650,000)
10 *I can see the whole room... and there's nobody in it*, Christie's, New York, 9 Nov 1988	1,055,556 ($1,900,000)

Did You Know? Jasper Johns' *False Start* holds the current world record for the most expensive painting by a living artist.

TOP 10 ★
MOST EXPENSIVE PAINTINGS BY JACKSON POLLOCK

PAINTING*/SALE	PRICE (£)
1 *Number 8, 1950*, Sotheby's, New York, 2 May 1989	6,325,302 ($10,500,000)
2 *Frieze*, Christie's, New York, 9 Nov 1988	2,888,889 ($5,200,000)
3 *Search*, Sotheby's, New York, 2 May 1988	2,352,940 ($4,400,000)
4 *Number 19, 1949*, Sotheby's, New York, 2 May 1989	2,168,675 ($3,600,000)
5 *Number 31, 1949*, Christie's, New York, 3 May 1988	1,711,230 ($3,200,000)
6 *Number 26, 1950*, Sotheby's, New York, 4 May 1987	1,506,025 ($2,500,000)
7 *Something of the past*, Christie's, New York, 7 May 1996	1,447,369 ($2,200,000)
8 *Number 19, 1948*, Christie's, New York, 4 May 1993	1,437,909 ($2,200,000)
9 *Number 13*, Christie's, New York, 7 Nov 1990	1,428,570 ($2,800,000)
10 *Number 20*, Sotheby's, New York, 8 May 1990	1,309,524 ($2,200,000)

* Includes mixed media compositions

TOP 10 MOST EXPENSIVE PAINTINGS BY JASPER JOHNS
(Work/sale date/price in £)

1 *False Start*, 10 Nov 1988, 8,611,112
2 *Two Flags*, 8 Nov 1989, 6,962,025
3 *Corpse and Mirror*, 10 Nov 1997, 4,497,042 **4** *White Numbers*, 10 Nov 1987, 4,260,355 **5** *White Flag*, 9 Nov 1988, 3,555,556 **6** *Jubilee*, 13 Nov 1991, 2,513,967
7 *Decoy*, 10 Nov 1997, 2,366,864 **8** *Small False Start*, 7 Nov 1989, 2,341,772 **9** *Out of the Window*, 10 Nov 1986, 2,307,693
10 *Device Circle*, 12 Nov 1991, 2,234,637

SURREAL MEALS

As well as his surreal paintings, Salvador Dali promoted "Futurist" food, including herrings and raspberry jam, and sausage with nougat.

TOP 10 ★
MOST EXPENSIVE PAINTINGS BY SALVADOR DALI

PAINTING/SALE	PRICE (£)
1 *Assumpta corpuscularia lapislazulina*, Christie's, New York, 15 May 1990	2,189,349 ($3,700,000)
2 *Cygnes reflétant des Elephants*, Sotheby's, New York, 9 May 1995	2,038,217 ($3,200,000)
3 *L'ascension de Christ – Pietà*, Christie's, New York, 2 Nov 1993	1,486,487 ($2,200,000)
4 *La bataille de Tetouan*, Christie's, New York, 10 May 1994	1,333,333 ($2,000,000)
5 *The Battle of Tetuan*, Sotheby's, New York, 11 Nov 1987	1,257,143 ($2,200,000)
6 *Printemps nécrophilique*, Christie's, London, 10 Dec 1998	1,240,000
7 *Portrait de Paul Eluard*, Christie's, New York, 14 Nov 1989	1,225,807 ($1,900,000)
8 *Le Christ de Gala*, Christie's, New York, 10 May 1994	633,333 ($950,000)
9 *Surrealist Composition*, Christie's, New York, 12 May 1998	617,284 ($1,000,000)
10 *Bataille autour d'un pissenlit*, Guy Loudmer, Paris, 21 Mar 1988	573,614 (F.Fr6,000,000)

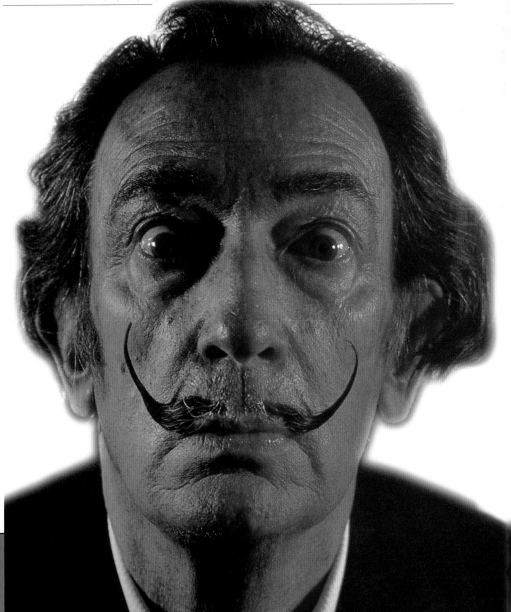

TOP 10 ★
MUSIC

CHART HITS

TOP 10 ALBUMS OF ALL TIME IN THE UK
(Title/artist or group/year)

1. *Sgt. Pepper's Lonely Hearts Club Band*, The Beatles, 1967
2. *(What's the Story) Morning Glory?*, Oasis, 1995
3. *Bad*, Michael Jackson, 1987
4. *Brothers in Arms*, Dire Straits, 1985
5. *Stars*, Simply Red, 1991
6. *Thriller*, Michael Jackson, 1982
7. *Greatest Hits*, Queen, 1981
8. *Spice*, Spice Girls, 1996
9. *The Immaculate Collection*, Madonna, 1990
10. *The Very Best of Elton John*, Elton John, 1990

Source: *BPI*

TOP 10 SINGLES OF ALL TIME IN THE UK

TITLE/ARTIST OR GROUP/YEAR	EST. UK SALES
1. *Candle in the Wind (1997)/ Something About the Way You Look Tonight*, Elton John, 1997	4,800,000
2. *Do They Know It's Christmas?*, Band Aid, 1984	3,510,000
3. *Bohemian Rhapsody*, Queen, 1975/91	2,130,000
4. *Mull of Kintyre*, Wings, 1977	2,050,000
5. *Rivers of Babylon/Brown Girl in the Ring*, Boney M, 1978	1,995,000
6. *Relax*, Frankie Goes to Hollywood, 1984	1,910,000
7. *She Loves You*, The Beatles, 1963	1,890,000
8. *You're the One that I Want*, John Travolta and Olivia Newton-John, 1978	1,870,000
9. *Unchained Melody*, Robson Green and Jerome Flynn, 1995	1,820,000
10. *Mary's Boy Child/Oh My Lord*, Boney M, 1978	1,790,000

Source: *BPI*

More than 50 singles have sold over one million copies apiece in the UK during the last 40 years, and these are the cream of that crop. The Band Aid single had a host of special circumstances surrounding it, and it took the remarkable response to the death of Diana, Princess of Wales, to generate sales capable of overtaking it. The only act to appear twice is Boney M, a group masterminded by German producer Frank Farian.

TOP 10 SINGLES THAT STAYED LONGEST IN THE UK CHARTS

TITLE/ARTIST OR GROUP/ FIRST CHART ENTRY	WEEKS IN CHART
1. *Release Me*, Engelbert Humperdinck, 1967	56
2. *Stranger on the Shore*, Mr. Acker Bilk, 1961	55
3. *Relax*, Frankie Goes to Hollywood, 1984	48
4. *My Way*, Frank Sinatra, 1969	47
5. *Rivers of Babylon*, Boney M, 1978	40
6. =*I Love You Because*, Jim Reeves, 1964	39
=*Tie a Yellow Ribbon Round the Old Oak Tree*, Dawn featuring Tony Orlando, 1973	39
8. =*A Scottish Soldier*, Andy Stewart, 1961	38
=*White Lines (Don't Don't Do It)*, Grandmaster Flash and Melle Mel, 1983	38
10. *Love Is All Around*, Wet Wet Wet, 1994	37

Source: *The Popular Music Database*

TOP 10 SINGLES OF ALL TIME
(Title/artist or group/sales exceed)

1. *Candle in the Wind (1997)/Something About the Way You Look Tonight*, Elton John, 37,000,000
2. *White Christmas*, Bing Crosby, 30,000,000
3. *Rock Around the Clock*, Bill Haley and His Comets, 17,000,000
4. *I Want to Hold Your Hand*, The Beatles, 12,000,000
5. = *Hey Jude*, The Beatles, 10,000,000; = *It's Now or Never*, Elvis Presley, 10,000,000; = *I Will Always Love You*, Whitney Houston, 10,000,000
8. = *Hound Dog/Don't Be Cruel*, Elvis Presley, 9,000,000; = *Diana*, Paul Anka, 9,000,000
10. = *I'm a Believer*, The Monkees, 8,000,000; = *(Everything I Do) I Do It for You*, Bryan Adams, 8,000,000

TOP 10 OLDEST SINGERS TO HAVE A TOP 10 HIT IN THE UK

ARTIST/TITLE	AGE YRS	MTHS
1. Frank Sinatra, *New York, New York*	70	4
2. Louis Armstrong, *What a Wonderful World*	68	0
3. Honor Blackman, *Kinky Boots*	64	0
4. James Brown, *Living in America*	56	10
5. Ted Heath, *Swingin' Shepherd Blues*	56	2
6. Petula Clark, *Downtown '88 Remix*	56	0
7. Bobby Vinton, *Blue Velvet*	55	6
8. Nina Simone, *My Baby Just Cares for Me*	54	10
9. Bing Crosby, *Around the World*	54	2
10. Cher, *Believe*	52	8

Source: *MRIB*

The ages listed are those of the artists at the end of the Top 10 run by their most recent Top 10 hit.

TOP 10 ARTISTS WITH THE MOST WEEKS ON THE UK SINGLES CHART*

ARTIST OR GROUP	TOTAL WEEKS
1. Elvis Presley	1,155
2. Cliff Richard	1,114
3. Elton John	541
4. Michael Jackson	480
5. Rod Stewart	458
6. The Beatles	456
7. Madonna	448
8. Frank Sinatra	439
9. David Bowie	432
10. Diana Ross	430

* Up to 31 December 1997

Source: *The Popular Music Database*

Background image: SGT. PEPPER'S LONELY HEARTS CLUB BAND ALBUM COVER

Did You Know? It took 55 years for a record to overtake Bing Crosby's 1942 *White Christmas* as the top-selling single of all time.

TOP 10 ARTISTS WITH THE MOST CONSECUTIVE UK TOP 10 ALBUMS

(Artist or group/period/albums)

1 **Elvis Presley**, Nov 1958–Jul 1964, 17 **2** **Queen**, Nov 1974–Jun 1989, 14 **3** = **The Rolling Stones**, Apr 1964–May 1971, 13; = **David Bowie**, May 1973–Jan 1981, 13 **5** = **Bob Dylan**, May 1965–Nov 1970, 12; = **Bob Dylan**, Feb 1974–Nov 1983, 12; = **Depeche Mode**, Nov 1981–Oct 1998, 12; = **Madonna**, Feb 1984–Mar 1998, 12 **9** = **Cliff Richard**, Apr 1959–Jul 1964, 11; = **Led Zeppelin**, Apr 1969–Oct 1990, 11; = **Elton John**, Jun 1972–Nov 1978, 11

Source: *The Popular Music Database*

TOP 10 ALBUMS OF ALL TIME

(Title/artist or group)

1 *Thriller*, Michael Jackson
2 *Dark Side of the Moon*, Pink Floyd
3 *Their Greatest Hits 1971–1975*, Eagles
4 *The Bodyguard*, Soundtrack
5 *Rumours*, Fleetwood Mac
6 *Sgt. Pepper's Lonely Hearts Club Band*, The Beatles **7** *Led Zeppelin IV*, Led Zeppelin **8** *Greatest Hits*, Elton John
9 *Jagged Little Pill*, Alanis Morissette
10 *Bat out of Hell*, Meat Loaf

Total worldwide sales of albums have traditionally been notoriously hard to gauge, but even with the huge expansion of the album market during the 1980s, and multiple million sales of many major releases, this Top 10 is still élite territory.

STRUTTING HIS STUFF

Mick Jagger, singer with the Rolling Stones, formed the band with Keith Richards while still a student at the London School of Economics.

TOP 10 ★

ARTISTS WITH THE MOST CONSECUTIVE UK TOP 10 HITS

ARTIST OR GROUP/PERIOD	HITS
1 **Madonna**, Nov 1984–Dec 1994	35
2 **Cliff Richard**, Jun 1960–Mar 1965	21
3 = **The Beatles**, Jul 1964–Mar 1976	18
= **Abba**, Sep 1975–Dec 1981	18
5 **The Rolling Stones**, Feb 1964–Apr 1971	14
6 = **Kylie Minogue**, Jan 1988–Jun 1991	13
= **Boyzone**, Dec 1994–Dec 1998	13
8 = **The Shadows**, Jul 1960–May 1964	12
= **Slade**, Oct 1971–Oct 1974	12
= **Take That**, Oct 1992–Mar 1996	12

Source: *The Popular Music Database*

TOP 10 ★

YOUNGEST SINGERS OF ALL TIME IN THE UK SINGLES CHARTS

ARTIST/TITLE/YEAR	HIGHEST POSITION	AGE* YRS	MTHS
1 **Microbe (Ian Doody)**, *Groovy Baby*, 1969	29	3	0
2 **Natalie Casey**, *Chick Chick Chicken*, 1984	72	3	0
3 **Little Jimmy Osmond**, *Long Haired Lover from Liverpool*, 1974	1	9	7
4 **Lena Zavaroni**, *Ma He's Making Eyes at Me*, 1974	10	10	4
5 **Neil Reid**, *Mother of Mine*, 1972	2	11	0
6 **Michael Jackson**, *Got to Be There*, 1972	5	13	5
7 **Laurie London**, *He's Got the Whole World in His Hands*, 1957	12	13	9
8 **Jimmy Boyd**, *I Saw Mommy Kissing Santa Claus*, 1953	3	13	10
9 **Marie Osmond**, *Paper Roses*, 1973	2	14	1
10 **Helen Shapiro**, *Don't Treat Me Like a Child*, 1961	3	14	5

* *Those of apparently identical age have been ranked according to their age in days during their first-ever week in the UK singles chart*

CHILD STAR

Michael Jackson's career started at the age of five, when – along with four of his elder brothers – he was a member of the pop band Jackson Five.

RECORD FIRSTS

THE 10 FIRST UK CHART SINGLES

(Single/artist)

1 *Here in My Heart*, Al Martino **2** *You Belong to Me*, Jo Stafford **3** *Somewhere Along the Way*, Nat "King" Cole **4** *Isle of Innisfree*, Bing Crosby **5** *Feet Up*, Guy Mitchell **6** *Half as Much*, Rosemary Clooney **7** = *High Noon*, Frankie Laine; = *Forget Me Not*, Vera Lynn **9** = *Sugarbush*, Doris Day and Frankie Laine; = *Blue Tango*, Ray Martin

Source: *New Musical Express (for week ending 15 November 1952)*

THE 10 ★ FIRST AMERICAN GROUPS TO HAVE A NO. 1 SINGLE IN THE UK

GROUP/SINGLE	DATE AT NO. 1
1 **Bill Haley and His Comets**, *Rock Around the Clock*	25 Nov 1955
2 **Dream Weavers**, *It's Almost Tomorrow*	16 Mar 1956
3 **Teenagers featuring Frankie Lymon**, *Why Do Fools Fall in Love?*	20 Jul 1956
4 **The Crickets**, *That'll Be the Day*	1 Nov 1957
5 **Platters**, *Smoke Gets in your Eyes*	20 Mar 1959
6 **Marcels**, *Blue Moon*	4 May 1961
7 **Highwaymen**, *Michael*	12 Oct 1961
8 **B. Bumble and the Stingers**, *Rocker*	17 May 1962
9 **Supremes**, *Baby Love*	19 Nov 1964
10 **Byrds**, *Mr. Tambourine Man*	22 Jul 1965

Source: *The Popular Music Database*

THE 10 ★ FIRST MILLION-SELLING UK SINGLES

SINGLE/ARTIST	YEAR
1 *Rock Around the Clock*, Bill Haley and His Comets	1954
2 *Mary's Boy Child*, Harry Belafonte	1957
3 *Diana*, Paul Anka	1957
4 *It's Now or Never*, Elvis Presley	1960
5 *Stranger on the Shore*, Mr. Acker Bilk	1961
6 *The Young Ones*, Cliff Richard	1962
7 *I Remember You*, Frank Ifield	1962
8 *She Loves You*, The Beatles	1963
9 *I Want to Hold Your Hand*, The Beatles	1963
10 *Can't Buy Me Love*, The Beatles	1964

The Beatles are the all-time platinum singles sales kings: they amassed five

HALEY'S CLOCK

Rock Around the Clock *became a rock 'n' roll anthem after being chosen as the theme song for the film* Blackboard Jungle.

THE 10 ★ FIRST BRITISH GROUPS TO HAVE A NO. 1 SINGLE IN THE US

GROUP/SINGLE	DATE AT NO. 1
1 **Tornados**, *Telstar*	22 Dec 1962
2 **The Beatles**, *I Want to Hold Your Hand*	1 Feb 1964
3 **The Animals**, *House of the Rising Sun*	5 Sep 1964
4 **Manfred Mann**, *Do Wah Diddy Diddy*	17 Oct 1964
5 **Freddie and the Dreamers**, *I'm Telling You Now*	10 Apr 1965
6 **Wayne Fontana and the Mindbenders**, *The Game of Love*	24 Apr 1965
7 **Herman's Hermits**, *Mrs. Brown You've Got a Lovely Daughter*	1 May 1965
8 **The Rolling Stones**, *(I Can't Get No) Satisfaction*	10 Jul 1965
9 **Dave Clark Five**, *Over and Over*	25 Dec 1965
10 **Troggs**, *Wild Thing*	30 Jul 1966

Source: *The Popular Music Database*

ANIMAL APPEAL

Formed in Newcastle in 1962, the Animals had a string of hits including House of the Rising Sun *and* We Gotta Get Out of this Place.

Bill Haley & His Comets
ROCK AROUND THE CLOCK
20 ROCK 'N' ROLL CLASSICS

THE 10 ★
FIRST BRITISH SOLO ARTISTS TO HAVE A NO. 1 SINGLE IN THE US

	ARTIST/SINGLE	DATE AT NO. 1
1	**Mr. Acker Bilk**, *Stranger on the Shore*	26 May 1962
2	**Petula Clark**, *Downtown*	23 Jan 1965
3	**Donovan**, *Sunshine Superman*	3 Sep 1966
4	**Lulu**, *To Sir with Love*	21 Oct 1967
5	**George Harrison**, *My Sweet Lord*	26 Dec 1970
6	**Rod Stewart**, *Maggie May*	2 Oct 1971
7	**Gilbert O'Sullivan**, *Alone Again Naturally*	29 Jul 1972
8	**Elton John**, *Crocodile Rock*	3 Feb 1973
9	**Ringo Starr**, *Photograph*	24 Nov 1973
10	**Eric Clapton**, *I Shot the Sheriff*	14 Sep 1974

Source: *The Popular Music Database*

THE 10 ★
FIRST AMERICAN SOLO ARTISTS TO HAVE A NO. 1 SINGLE IN THE UK

	ARTIST/SINGLE	DATE AT NO. 1
1	**Al Martino**, *Here in My Heart*	14 Nov 1952
2	**Jo Stafford**, *You Belong to Me*	16 Jan 1953
3	**Kay Starr**, *Comes A-Long A-Love*	23 Jan 1953
4	**Eddie Fisher**, *Outside of Heaven*	30 Jan 1953
5	**Perry Como**, *Don't Let the Stars Get in Your Eyes*	6 Feb 1953
6	**Guy Mitchell**, *She Wears Red Feathers*	13 Mar 1953
7	**Frankie Laine**, *I Believe*	24 Apr 1953
8	**Doris Day**, *Secret Love*	16 Apr 1954
9	**Johnnie Ray**, *Such a Night*	30 Apr 1954
10	**Kitty Kallen**, *Little Things Mean a Lot*	10 Sep 1954

Source: *The Popular Music Database*

Clearly, in the 1950s it was much easier for American solo artists to top the UK survey than it was for British artists to compete in the US market.

THE 10 ★
FIRST FEMALE SINGERS TO HAVE A NO. 1 SINGLE IN THE UK

	ARTIST/SINGLE	DATE AT NO. 1
1	**Jo Stafford**, *You Belong to Me*	16 Jan 1953
2	**Kay Starr**, *Comes A-Long A-Love*	23 Jan 1953
3	**Lita Roza**, *(How Much is That) Doggie in the Window?*	17 Apr 1953
4	**Doris Day**, *Secret Love*	16 Apr 1954
5	**Kitty Kallen**, *Little Things Mean a Lot*	10 Sep 1954
6	**Vera Lynn**, *My Son, My Son*	5 Nov 1954
7	**Rosemary Clooney**, *This Ole House*	26 Nov 1954
8	**Ruby Murray**, *Softly Softly*	18 Feb 1955
9	**Alma Cogan**, *Dreamboat*	15 Jul 1955
10	**Anne Shelton**, *Lay Down Your Arms*	21 Sep 1956

Source: *The Popular Music Database*

The UK singles chart was launched in November 1952, and in replacing the inaugural chart-topper (Al Martino's *Here in My Heart*), Jo Stafford's *You Belong to Me* was only the second single to reach No.1 on it.

THE 10 ★
FIRST UK CHART ALBUMS

	ALBUM	ARTIST OR GROUP
1	*South Pacific*	Soundtrack
2	*Come Fly with Me*	Frank Sinatra
3	*Elvis' Golden Records*	Elvis Presley
4	*King Creole*	Elvis Presley
5	*My Fair Lady*	Broadway Cast
6	*Warm*	Johnny Mathis
7	*The King and I*	Soundtrack
8	*Dear Perry*	Perry Como
9	*Oklahoma!*	Soundtrack
10	*Songs by Tom Lehrer*	Tom Lehrer

Source: *Melody Maker*

The first album chart was printed in *Melody Maker* for the week ending 8 November 1958, and represents a time capsule of the popular music of the era, a transitional period when crooners, comedy singers, and musicals rubbed shoulders with up-and-coming rock artists.

PET'S STAYING POWER

Petula Clark was a child star during World War II. More recently she moved into musical theatre, playing Norma Desmond in Sunset Boulevard.

Which is the largest opera house in the world? **A** Cincinnati Opera
see p.163 for the answer **B** Lyric Opera of Chicago
C The Metropolitan Opera, New York

137

CHART TOPPERS

ARTISTS WITH THE MOST NO. 1 SINGLES IN THE UK

ARTIST OR GROUP	NO. 1 SINGLES
1 = The Beatles	17
= Elvis Presley	17
3 Cliff Richard	13
4 Abba	9
5 = The Rolling Stones	8
= Take That	8
= Madonna	8
= Spice Girls	8
9 = George Michael	7
10 = Slade	6
= Rod Stewart	6

Source: *The Popular Music Database*

QUEEN OF THE CHARTS

Madonna burst onto the pop scene in 1984. Her constantly changing image and the gossip surrounding her private life, as well as her chart-topping records, have made her a household name.

SINGLES WITH MOST WEEKS AT NO. 1 IN THE UK

TITLE/ARTIST OR GROUP/YEAR	WEEKS AT NO. 1
1 *I Believe*, Frankie Laine, 1953	18
2 *(Everything I Do) I Do It for You*, Bryan Adams, 1991	16
3 *Love Is All Around*, Wet Wet Wet, 1994	15
4 *Bohemian Rhapsody*, Queen, 1975/1991	14
5 *Rose Marie*, Slim Whitman, 1955	11
6 = *Cara Mia*, David Whitfield, 1954	10
= *I Will Always Love You*, Whitney Houston, 1993	10
8 = *Diana*, Paul Anka, 1957	9
= *Here in My Heart*, Al Martino, 1952	9
= *Mull of Kintyre*, Wings, 1977	9
= *Oh Mein Papa*, Eddie Calvert, 1954	9
= *Secret Love*, Doris Day, 1954	9
= *Two Tribes*, Frankie Goes To Hollywood, 1984	9
= *You're the One that I Want*, John Travolta and Olivia Newton-John, 1978	9

Source: *The Popular Music Database*

YOUNGEST ARTISTS TO HAVE A NO. 1 SINGLE IN THE UK*

ARTIST/TITLE/YEAR	AGE# YRS	MTHS
1 Little Jimmy Osmond, *Long Haired Lover from Liverpool*, 1972	9	8
2 Donny Osmond, *Puppy Love*, 1972	14	6
3 Helen Shapiro, *You Don't Know*, 1961	14	10
4 Billie, *Because We Want To*, 1998	15	9
5 Paul Anka, *Diana*, 1957	16	0
6 Tiffany, *I think We're Alone Now*, 1987	16	3
7 Nicole, *A Little Peace*, 1982	17	0
8 Britney Spears, *...Baby One More Time*, 1999	17	2
9 Sandie Shaw, *There's Always Something There to Remind Me*, 1964	17	7
10 Glenn Medeiros, *Nothing's Gonna Change My Love*, 1988	18	0

* To 1 March 1999

During first week of debut No. 1 UK single

Source: *The Popular Music Database*

LONGEST GAPS BETWEEN NO. 1 HIT SINGLES IN THE UK

ARTIST OR GROUP	PERIOD	GAP YRS	MTHS
1 The Righteous Brothers	11 Feb 1965–28 Oct 1990	25	8
2 The Hollies	15 July 1965–18 Sep 1988	23	2
3 Blondie	22 Nov 1980–13 Feb 1999	18	3
4 Queen	24 Jan 1976–20 Jan 1991	15	0
5 Diana Ross	11 Sep 1971–2 Mar 1986	14	6
6 Frank Sinatra	1 Oct 1954–27 May 1966	11	7
7 Cliff Richard	17 Apr 1968–19 Aug 1979	11	4
8 Bee Gees	4 Sep 1968–23 Apr 1978	9	7
9 Cliff Richard	15 Sep 1979–4 Dec 1988	9	3
10 Bee Gees	10 Mar 1979–11 Oct 1987	8	7

Source: *The Popular Music Database*

TOP 10 ★
ARTISTS WITH THE MOST CONSECUTIVE NO. 1 SINGLES IN THE UK

ARTIST OR GROUP	PERIOD	NO. 1s
1 The Beatles	1963–66	11
2 = The Beatles	1967–69	6
= Spice Girls	1996–97	6
4 = Elvis Presley	1961–62	5
= The Rolling Stones	1964–65	5
6 = Take That	1993–94	4
= Take That	1994–96	4
8 = Frank Ifield	1962–63	3
= Gerry and the Pacemakers	1963	3
= Abba	1975–76	3
= Abba	1977–78	3
= Police	1979–80	3
= Blondie	1980	3
= John Lennon	1980	3
= Frankie Goes to Hollywood	1984	3
= Jive Bunny	1989	3
= Robson and Jerome	1995–96	3
= All Saints	1998	3
= B*Witched	1998	3

Source: *The Popular Music Database*

TOP 10 ALBUMS LONGEST AT NO. 1 IN THE UK
(Title/artist or group/weeks at No. 1)

1 *South Pacific*, Soundtrack, 115 **2** *The Sound of Music*, Soundtrack, 70 **3** *Bridge Over Troubled Water*, Simon and Garfunkel, 41 **4** *Please Please Me*, The Beatles, 30 **5** *Sgt. Pepper's Lonely Hearts Club Band*, The Beatles, 27 **6** *G.I. Blues*, Elvis Presley/Soundtrack, 22 **7** = *With The Beatles*, The Beatles, 21; = *A Hard Day's Night*, The Beatles/Soundtrack, 21 **9** = *Blue Hawaii*, Elvis Presley/Soundtrack, 18; = *Saturday Night Fever*, Soundtrack, 18

Source: *The Popular Music Database*

TOP 10 ★
OLDEST ARTISTS TO HAVE A NO. 1 SINGLE IN THE UK*

ARTIST OR GROUP/TITLE	AGE# YRS	MTHS
1 Louis Armstrong, *What a Wonderful World*	67	10
2 Cher, *Believe*	52	7
3 Elton John, *Candle in the Wind (1997)/Something About the Way You Look Tonight*	51	7
4 Frank Sinatra, *Somethin' Stupid*	51	4
5 Telly Savalas, *If*	51	1
6 Cliff Richard, *Saviour's Day*	50	2
7 The Righteous Brothers, *Unchained Melody*	50	2/
	50	1
8 Charles Aznavour, *She*	50	1
9 Clive Dunn, *Grandad*	49	0
10 Ben E. King, *Stand by Me*	48	5

* To 1 March 1999
# Ranked according to their precise age in days
Source: *The Popular Music Database*

TOP 10 SLOWEST UK ALBUM CHART RISES TO NO. 1
(Title/artist or group/weeks to reach No. 1)

1 Tyrannosaurus Rex, *My People Were Fair and Had Sky in Their Hair... But Now They're Content to Wear Stars on Their Brows*, 199 **2** Elvis Presley, *40 Greatest Hits*, 114 **3** Various artists, *Fame (Original Soundtrack)*, 98 **4** Cranberries, *Everybody Else is Doing it, So Why Can't We?*, 67 **5** Mike Oldfield, *Tubular Bells*, 65 **6** Ace of Base, *Happy Nation*, 54 **7** Fleetwood Mac, *Rumours*, 49 **8** Bob Dylan, *The Freewheelin' Bob Dylan*, 48 **9** Celine Dion, *The Colour of My Love*, 47 **10** = Elton John, *Sleeping with the Past*, 44 = Madonna, *Like a Virgin*, 44

Source: *The Popular Music Database*

THE HILLBILLY CAT

This is the name Elvis Presley used while touring at the start of his singing career. He later became famous for hits such as Love Me Tender and Hound Dog.

TOP 10 ★
ALBUMS WITH THE MOST CONSECUTIVE WEEKS AT NO. 1 IN THE UK

TITLE/ARTIST OR GROUP	WEEKS AT NO. 1
1 *South Pacific*, Soundtrack	70
2 *Please Please Me*, The Beatles	30
3 *Sgt. Pepper's Lonely Hearts Club Band*, The Beatles	23
4 = *With The Beatles*, The Beatles	21
= *A Hard Day's Night*, The Beatles/Soundtrack	21
6 *South Pacific*, Soundtrack	19
7 = *The Sound of Music*, Soundtrack	18
= *Saturday Night Fever*, Soundtrack	18
9 *Blue Hawaii*, Elvis Presley/Soundtrack	17
10 *Summer Holiday*, Cliff Richard and the Shadows/Soundtrack	14

Source: *The Popular Music Database*

Did You Know? The Tyrannosaurus Rex album *My People Were Fair...* holds the distinction of being the album with the longest title ever to chart.

139

HIT SINGLES OF THE DECADES

TOP 10 ★
SINGLES OF THE 1960s IN THE UK

SINGLE/ARTIST OR GROUP	YEAR
1 *She Loves You*, The Beatles	1963
2 *I Want to Hold Your Hand*, The Beatles	1963
3 *Tears*, Ken Dodd	1965
4 *Can't Buy Me Love*, The Beatles	1964
5 *I Feel Fine*, The Beatles	1964
6 *We Can Work It Out/Day Tripper*, The Beatles	1965
7 *The Carnival Is Over*, The Seekers	1965
8 *Release Me*, Engelbert Humperdinck	1967
9 *It's Now or Never*, Elvis Presley	1960
10 *Green, Green Grass of Home*, Tom Jones	1966

The Beatles' domination of the 1960s is clear, with five of the decade's top six singles being by the group. Intriguingly, all the other five in this Top 10 are ballads of varying degrees of what, in those days, would have been termed squareness. This was an era when the great silent majority of occasional record buyers purchased singles, not albums, and Messrs Humperdinck, Dodd, *et al.* were the lucky recipients of their custom.

THE FAB FOUR

The Beatles, together with Elvis Presley, are co-holders of the record for the greatest amount of UK No. 1 hit singles, which currently stands at 17. The majority of these hits were penned by John Lennon (second from right) and Paul McCartney (far left).

TOP 10 ★
SINGLES OF THE 1970s IN THE UK

SINGLE/ARTIST OR GROUP	YEAR
1 *Mull of Kintyre*, Wings	1977
2 *Rivers of Babylon/Brown Girl in The Ring*, Boney M	1978
3 *You're the One That I Want*, John Travolta and Olivia Newton-John	1978
4 *Mary's Boy Child/Oh My Lord*, Boney M	1978
5 *Summer Nights*, John Travolta and Olivia Newton-John	1978
6 *Y.M.C.A.*, Village People	1979
7 *Bohemian Rhapsody*, Queen	1975
8 *Heart of Glass*, Blondie	1979
9 *Merry Xmas Everybody*, Slade	1973
10 *Don't Give up on Us*, David Soul	1977

Most of the biggest sellers of the 1970s occurred in an 18-month period between December 1977 and May 1979. *Mull of Kintyre* was the first-ever record in Britain to top 2 million copies.

TOP 10 ★
SINGLES OF THE 1980s IN THE UK

SINGLE/ARTIST OR GROUP	YEAR
1 *Do They Know It's Christmas?*, Band Aid	1984
2 *Relax*, Frankie Goes to Hollywood	1984
3 *I Just Called to Say I Love You*, Stevie Wonder	1984
4 *Two Tribes*, Frankie Goes to Hollywood	1984
5 *Don't You Want Me*, Human League	1981
6 *Last Christmas*, Wham!	1984
7 *Karma Chameleon*, Culture Club	1983
8 *Careless Whisper*, George Michael	1984
9 *The Power of Love*, Jennifer Rush	1985
10 *Come on Eileen*, Dexy's Midnight Runners	1982

Singles from the boom year of 1984 dominate the UK 1980s Top 10, two of them by newcomers Frankie Goes to Hollywood, and two by Wham!/George Michael (who also sang one of the Band Aid leads – as did Boy George from Culture Club).

TOP 10 ★
SINGLES OF EACH YEAR IN THE 1960s IN THE UK

YEAR	SINGLE/ARTIST OR GROUP
1960	*It's Now or Never*, Elvis Presley
1961	*Are You Lonesome Tonight?*, Elvis Presley
1962	*I Remember You*, Frank Ifield
1963	*She Loves You*, The Beatles
1964	*Can't Buy Me Love*, The Beatles
1965	*Tears*, Ken Dodd
1966	*Green, Green Grass of Home*, Tom Jones
1967	*Release Me*, Engelbert Humperdinck
1968	*Hey Jude*, The Beatles
1969	*Sugar Sugar*, The Archies

While the top-selling singles of several years were identical on both sides of the Atlantic, the UK version contains uniquely British aberrations, such as *Tears* by comedian Ken Dodd – one of the dozen bestselling British singles of all time.

Background image: **JUKEBOX**

TOP 10 ★
SINGLES OF EACH YEAR IN THE 1970s IN THE UK

YEAR	SINGLE/ARTIST OR GROUP
1970	*The Wonder of You*, Elvis Presley
1971	*My Sweet Lord*, George Harrison
1972	*I'd Like to Teach the World to Sing*, The New Seekers
1973	*I Love You Love Me Love*, Gary Glitter
1974	*You Won't Find Another Fool Like Me*, The New Seekers
1975	*Bohemian Rhapsody*, Queen
1976	*Save Your Kisses for Me*, Brotherhood of Man
1977	*Mull of Kintyre*, Wings
1978	*Rivers of Babylon/Brown Girl in the Ring*, Boney M
1979	*Y.M.C.A.*, Village People

TOP 10 ★
SINGLES OF EACH YEAR IN THE 1980s IN THE UK

YEAR	SINGLE/ARTIST OR GROUP
1980	*Don't Stand So Close To Me*, Police
1981	*Don't You Want Me*, Human League
1982	*Come on Eileen*, Dexy's Midnight Runners
1983	*Karma Chameleon*, Culture Club
1984	*Do They Know It's Christmas?*, Band Aid
1985	*The Power of Love*, Jennifer Rush
1986	*Every Loser Wins*, Nick Berry
1987	*Never Gonna Give You up*, Rick Astley
1988	*Mistletoe and Wine*, Cliff Richard
1989	*Ride on Time*, Black Box

Jennifer Rush is the sole US entrant in this Top 10. Together with another American, Stevie Wonder, these two singers were the only Americans to have UK million-sellers during this decade.

TOP 10 ★
SINGLES OF THE 1990s IN THE UK

	SINGLE/ARTIST OR GROUP	YEAR
1	*Candle in the Wind (1997)/Something About the Way You Look Tonight*, Elton John	1997
2	*Believe*, Cher	1998
3	*My Heart Will Go on*, Celine Dion	1998
4	*I Will Always Love You*, Whitney Houston	1992
5	*(Everything I Do) I Do It for You*, Bryan Adams	1991
6	*Love Is All Around*, Wet Wet Wet	1994
7	*Unchained Melody/The White Cliffs of Dover*, Robson and Jerome	1995
8	*Angels*, Robbie Williams	1998
9	*I'll Be Missing You*, Puff Daddy and Faith Evans (featuring 911)	1997
10	*Killing Me Softly*, The Fugees	1996

TOP 10 ★
SINGLES OF THE 1990s IN THE UK (MALE)

	SINGLE/ARTIST	YEAR
1	*Candle in the Wind (1997)/Something About the Way You Look Tonight*, Elton John	1997
2	*(Everything I Do) I Do It for You*, Bryan Adams	1991
3	*Angels*, Robbie Williams	1998
4	*I'd Do Anything for Love (But I Won't Do That)*, Meat Loaf	1991
5	*Earth Song*, Michael Jackson	1996
6	*Ice Ice Baby*, Vanilla Ice	1990
7	*Sacrifice/Healing Hands*, Elton John	1990
8	*Baby Come Back*, Pato Banton	1994
9	*Men in Black*, Will Smith	1997
10	*The One and Only*, Chesney Hawkes	1991

BAD BOY

Puff Daddy, aka Sean "Puffy" Combs, was a highly acclaimed record producer for his own label, Bad Boy Records, before becoming a global superstar with I'll Be Missing You, a duet with Faith Evans.

TOP 10 ★
SINGLES OF THE 1990s IN THE UK (FEMALE)

	SINGLE/ARTIST	YEAR
1	*Believe*, Cher	1998
2	*My Heart Will Go on*, Celine Dion	1998
3	*I Will Always Love You*, Whitney Houston	1992
4	*Baby One More Time*, Britney Spears	1999
5	*How Do I Live*, LeAnn Rimes	1998
6	*Think Twice*, Celine Dion	1995
7	*Saturday Night*, Whigfield	1994
8	*The Shoop Shoop Song (It's in His Kiss)*, Cher	1991
9	*Without You*, Mariah Carey	1994
10	*Vogue*, Madonna	1990

Did You Know? Elton John's phenomenally successful double single *Candle in the Wind (1997)/Something About the Way You Look Tonight* topped the lists of bestselling singles on both sides of the Atlantic.

TOP 10 ALBUMS OF THE 1990s IN THE UK

	ALBUM/ARTIST OR GROUP	YEAR
1	**(What's the Story) Morning Glory?**, Oasis	1995
2	**Stars**, Simply Red	1991
3	**Spice**, Spice Girls	1996
4	**Jagged Little Pill**, Alanis Morissette	1995
5	**Urban Hymns**, The Verve	1997
6	**The Bodyguard**, Soundtrack	1992
7	**The Immaculate Collection**, Madonna	1990
8	**Falling into You**, Celine Dion	1998
9	**Talk on Corners**, The Corrs	1997
10	**Ladies and Gentlemen – The Best of George Michael**, George Michael	1998

Source: BPI

TOP 10 ★ ALBUMS OF EACH YEAR IN THE 1960s IN THE UK

YEAR	ALBUM/ARTIST OR GROUP
1960	*South Pacific*, Soundtrack
1961	*G.I. Blues*, Elvis Presley, Soundtrack
1962	*West Side Story*, Soundtrack
1963	*With the Beatles*, The Beatles
1964	*Beatles for Sale*, The Beatles
1965	*The Sound of Music*, Soundtrack
1966	*The Sound of Music*, Soundtrack
1967	*Sgt. Pepper's Lonely Hearts Club Band*, The Beatles
1968	*The Sound of Music*, Soundtrack
1969	*Abbey Road*, The Beatles

TOP 10 ★ ALBUMS OF EACH YEAR IN THE 1970s IN THE UK

YEAR	ALBUM/ARTIST OR GROUP
1970	*Bridge over Troubled Water*, Simon and Garfunkel
1971	*Bridge over Troubled Water*, Simon and Garfunkel
1972	*20 Dynamic Hits*, Various artists
1973	*Don't Shoot Me, I'm Only the Piano Player*, Elton John
1974	*The Singles, 1969–1973*, The Carpenters
1975	*The Best of the Stylistics*, The Stylistics
1976	*Greatest Hits*, Abba
1977	*Arrival*, Abba
1978	*Saturday Night Fever*, Soundtrack
1979	*Breakfast in America*, Supertramp

EARLY STARTER

Canadian singer/songwriter Alanis Morissette was born in Ottawa in 1974, and released her first single at the age of 11.

TOP 10 ★

ALBUMS OF THE 1960s IN THE UK

ALBUM/ARTIST OR GROUP		YEAR
1	*Sgt. Pepper's Lonely Hearts Club Band*, The Beatles	1967
2	*The Sound of Music*, Soundtrack	1965
3	*With the Beatles*, The Beatles	1963
4	*Abbey Road*, The Beatles	1969
5	*South Pacific*, Soundtrack	1958
6	*Beatles for Sale*, The Beatles	1964
7	*A Hard Day's Night*, The Beatles, Soundtrack	1964
8	*Rubber Soul*, The Beatles	1965
9	*The Beatles ("White Album")*, The Beatles	1968
10	*West Side Story*, Soundtrack	1962

Not only did the Beatles dominate the Top 10, but three further albums by them, *Revolver*, *Please Please Me*, and *Help!*, were the 11th, 12th, and 13th bestselling albums of the decade.

TOP 10 ★

ALBUMS OF EACH YEAR IN THE 1980s IN THE UK

YEAR	ALBUM/ARTIST OR GROUP
1980	*Super Trouper*, Abba
1981	*Kings of the Wild Frontier*, Adam and the Ants
1982	*Love Songs*, Barbra Streisand
1983	*Thriller*, Michael Jackson
1984	*Can't Slow Down*, Lionel Richie
1985	*Brothers in Arms*, Dire Straits
1986	*True Blue*, Madonna
1987	*Bad*, Michael Jackson
1988	*Kylie*, Kylie Minogue
1989	*Ten Good Reasons*, Jason Donovan

TOP 10 ★

ALBUMS OF THE 1970s IN THE UK

ALBUM/ARTIST OR GROUP		YEAR
1	*Bridge over Troubled Water*, Simon and Garfunkel	1970
2	*Simon and Garfunkel's Greatest Hits*, Simon and Garfunkel	1972
3	*Rumours*, Fleetwood Mac	1977
4	*Dark Side of the Moon*, Pink Floyd	1973
5	*Tubular Bells*, Mike Oldfield	1973
6	*Greatest Hits*, Abba	1976
7	*Bat out of Hell*, Meat Loaf	1978
8	*Saturday Night Fever*, Soundtrack	1978
9	*And I Love You So*, Perry Como	1973
10	*The Singles 1969–1973*, The Carpenters	1974

Each of the top five albums of the 1970s clocked up over 250 weeks on the British chart, with Fleetwood Mac's *Rumours* outdistancing them all with an astonishing 443 weeks on the survey.

TOP 10 ★

ALBUMS OF THE 1980s IN THE UK

ALBUM/ARTIST OR GROUP		YEAR
1	*Brothers in Arms*, Dire Straits	1985
2	*Bad*, Michael Jackson	1987
3	*Thriller*, Michael Jackson	1982
4	*Greatest Hits*, Queen	1981
5	*Kylie*, Kylie Minogue	1988
6	*Whitney*, Whitney Houston	1987
7	*Tango in the Night*, Fleetwood Mac	1987
8	*No Jacket Required*, Phil Collins	1985
9	*True Blue*, Madonna	1986
10	*The Joshua Tree*, U2	1987

Brothers in Arms stayed in the chart for nearly four years during the 1980s, becoming the UK's third bestselling album ever. While Michael Jackson's *Thriller* was his bestselling album in most countries around the world, British buyers eventually preferred *Bad*. Fleetwood Mac is the only act to feature on the bestseller lists in two decades, following their achievement with *Rumours* in the 1970s. During the 1990s, classical albums sold in sufficient numbers to enable violinist Nigel Kennedy and tenors José Carreras, Placido Domingo, and Luciano Pavarotti to rub chart shoulders with pop stars.

RECORD BREAKER
The eponymous album by Whitney Houston sold 14 million copies and was the first album by a female artist to enter the US Billboard chart at No. 1.

Did You Know? *Tubular Bells*, recorded by Mike Oldfield for a pittance, proved to be the business building block upon which Virgin label boss Richard Branson would create his Virgin empire.

WOMEN IN THE CHARTS

VOCAL VIRTUOSO

Whitney Houston's first album spawned three No. 1 hit singles and went straight into the record books as the best-selling debut album by a female solo singer.

TOP 10 ★ FEMALE GROUPS OF ALL TIME IN THE UK*

	GROUP	NO. 1	TOP 10	TOP 20
1	The Supremes	1	13	18
2	Bananarama	–	10	15
3	Eternal	–	10	12
4	The Three Degrees	1	5	7
5	Sister Sledge	1	4	7
6	The Nolans	–	3	7
7	Salt-n-Pepa	–	4	5
8	Bangles	1	3	5
9	The Pointer Sisters	–	2	5
10	Spice Girls	4	4	4

* To 31 March 1999; ranked according to total number of Top 20 singles

The Supremes also had three other Top 20 hits, not included here, in partnership with Motown male groups the Four Tops and Temptations. However, Bananarama's charity revival of *Help!* has been included since both co-singers (Dawn French and Jennifer Saunders) are female.

TOP 10 ★ FEMALE SINGERS WITH THE MOST TOP 10 HITS IN THE UK

	SINGER	TOP 10 HITS
1	Madonna	44
2	Diana Ross (including duets with Marvin Gaye and Lionel Richie)	17
3	Kylie Minogue (including a duet with Keith Washington)	16
4	Mariah Carey (including duets with Boyz II Men, Luther Vandross, and Whitney Houston)	15
5 =	Janet Jackson (including duets with Michael Jackson and Luther Vandross)	13
=	Celine Dion (including duets with Peabo Bryson, the Bee Gees, and R. Kelly)	13
7 =	Petula Clark	12
=	Whitney Houston (including a duet with Mariah Carey)	12
9 =	Cher	10
=	Connie Francis	10
=	Olivia Newton-John (including duets with John Travolta and Electric Light Orchestra)	10

The hitmaking careers of many of these artists, most noticeably Diana Ross, Petula Clark, Connie Francis, and Olivia Newton-John, have either slowed down or ceased altogether in recent years. By contrast, those of other singers show remarkable longevity: Madonna's first UK Top 10 single, *Holiday*, reached No. 6 in 1984, while Cher's first solo Top 10 hit, *All I Really Want To Do*, was released in 1965, 33 years before her single *Believe* became the second bestselling single of the 1990s.

TOP 10 ★ YOUNGEST FEMALE SINGERS TO HAVE A NO. 1 SINGLE IN THE UK

	SINGER	YEARS	AGE MONTHS	DAYS
1	Helen Shapiro	14	10	13
2	Billie	15	9	20
3	Tiffany	16	3	28
4	Nicole	17	0	0
5	Britney Spears	17	3	26
6	Sandie Shaw	17	7	26
7	Mary Hopkin	18	4	22
8	Sonia	18	5	9
9	Connie Francis	19	5	4
10	Kate Bush	19	7	12

The ages shown are those of each artist on the publication date of the chart in which she achieved her first No. 1 single.

FAMILY FORTUNES

The youngest of the talented Jackson siblings, Janet Jackson became the highest paid singer in the world, surpassing even her megastar brother Michael, when she signed a $70-million deal with Virgin Records in 1997.

Background image: MADONNA

144

TOP 10 ★
OLDEST FEMALE SINGERS TO HAVE A NO. 1 SINGLE IN THE UK

	SINGER	YEARS	AGE MONTHS	DAYS
1	Cher	52	5	12
2	Barbra Streisand	38	6	1
3	Vera Lynn	35	7	16
4	Tammy Wynette	33	0	12
5	Kitty Kallen	32	3	16
6	Robin Beck	32	2	12
7	Jo Stafford	32	2	4
8	Charlene	32	0	25
9	Doris Day	32	0	13
10	Chaka Khan	31	7	18

The ages shown are those of each artist on the publication date of the chart in which her first No. 1 single reached the top.

TOP 10 ★
ALBUMS BY FEMALE GROUPS IN THE UK

	TITLE/GROUP	YEAR
1	*Spice*, Spice Girls	1996
2	*Spiceworld*, Spice Girls	1997
3	*All Saints*, All Saints	1997
4	*Always and Forever*, Eternal	1993
5	*Greatest Hits*, Eternal	1997
6	*The Greatest Hits Collection*, Bananarama	1988
7	*Power of a Woman*, Eternal	1995
8	*B*Witched*, B*Witched	1998
9	*Different Light*, Bangles	1986
10	*Greatest Hits*, Bangles	1990

All of these albums were released within the last two decades, and the three biggest sellers of all within the last six years. All of these groups are British, except B*Witched, who are Irish, and the Bangles, who are American.

TOP 10 ★
SINGLES BY FEMALE GROUPS IN THE UK

	TITLE/GROUP	YEAR
1	*Wannabe*, Spice Girls	1996
2	*Say You'll Be There*, Spice Girls	1996
3	*2 Become 1*, Spice Girls	1996
4	*Never Ever*, All Saints	1997
5	*C'Est La Vie*, B*Witched	1998
6	*Goodbye*, Spice Girls	1998
7	*Viva Forever*, Spice Girls	1998
8	*Spice up Your Life*, Spice Girls	1997
9	*Too Much*, Spice Girls	1997
10	*Mama/Who Do You Think You Are*, Spice Girls	1997

Such has been the Spice Girls' impact on popular music that they have totally rewritten the record book as far as successful girl-group singles are concerned, snatching the eight all-time biggest sellers in the UK.

TOP 10 SINGLES BY FEMALE GROUPS IN THE US

(Title/group/year)

❶ *Don't Let Go*, En Vogue, 1996 ❷ *Hold on*, En Vogue, 1990 ❸ *Wannabe*, Spice Girls, 1997 ❹ *Whatta Man*, Salt 'n Pepa, 1994 ❺ *Expressions*, Salt 'n Pepa, 1990 ❻ *Push It*, Salt 'n Pepa, 1987 ❼ *Waterfall*, TLC, 1995 ❽ *Creep*, TLC, 1995 ❾ *Weak*, SWV, 1993 ❿ *Baby, Baby, Baby*, TLC, 1992

Source: *The Popular Music Database*

TOP 10 ★
SINGLES BY FEMALE SINGERS IN THE UK

	TITLE/ARTIST	YEAR
1	*Believe*, Cher	1998
2	*I Will Always Love You*, Whitney Houston	1992
3	*The Power of Love*, Jennifer Rush	1985
4	*My Heart Will Go on*, Celine Dion	1998
5	*Think Twice*, Celine Dion	1994
6	*Don't Cry for Me Argentina*, Julie Covington	1977
7	*Fame*, Irene Cara	1982
8	*Anyone Who Had a Heart*, Cilla Black	1964
9	*Feels Like I'm in Love*, Kelly Marie	1980
10	*Woman in Love*, Barbra Streisand	1980

CHART-TOPPER

Since the massive success of her single Think Twice, Celine Dion has become increasingly popular. In 1999 she won 10 prestigious music awards.

Which artist won the latest Grammy record of the year award?

see p.161 for the answer

A Shawn Colvin
B Celine Dion
C Eric Clapton

SUPERGROUPS

ALBUMS OF ALL TIME IN THE UK

ALBUM/GROUP OR ARTIST	YEAR
1 *Sgt. Pepper's Lonely Hearts Club Band*, The Beatles	1967
2 *(What's the Story) Morning Glory?*, Oasis	1995
3 *Bad,* Michael Jackson	1987
4 *Brothers in Arms*, Dire Straits	1985
5 *Stars*, Simply Red	1991
6 *Thriller*, Michael Jackson	1982
7 *Greatest Hits*, Queen	1981
8 *Spice*, Spice Girls	1996
9 *The Immaculate Collection*, Madonna	1990
10 *The Very Best of Elton John*, Elton John	1990

Source: *BPI*

ALBUMS OF ALL TIME BY GROUPS IN THE US

ALBUM/GROUP	YEAR
1 *Their Greatest Hits, 1971–1975*, The Eagles	1976
2 *The Wall,* Pink Floyd	1979
3 *Rumours*, Fleetwood Mac	1977
4 *Led Zeppelin IV*, Led Zeppelin	1971
5 *The Beatles*, The Beatles	1968
6 *Boston*, Boston	1976
7 *Back in Black*, AC/DC	1980
8 *Dark Side of the Moon*, Pink Floyd	1973
9 *Hotel California*, The Eagles	1977
10 *Cracked Rear View*, Hootie and the Blowfish	1995

This list has changed considerably in recent times, with official sales figures being updated in the US on several perennially big-selling albums – most notably those by the recently resurrected Eagles.

SINGLES OF ALL TIME BY GROUPS IN THE UK

SINGLE/GROUP	YEAR
1 *Bohemian Rhapsody*, Queen	1975
2 *Mull of Kintyre*, Wings	1977
3 *Rivers of Babylon/Brown Girl in the Ring*, Boney M	1978
4 *Relax*, Frankie Goes to Hollywood	1984
5 *She Loves You*, The Beatles	1963
6 *Mary's Boy Child/ Oh My Lord*, Boney M	1978
7 *Love Is All Around*, Wet Wet Wet	1994
8 *I Want to Hold Your Hand*, The Beatles	1963
9 *Can't Buy Me Love*, The Beatles	1964
10 *Two Tribes*, Frankie Goes to Hollywood	1984

The Beatles appear three times in this Top 10, with Paul McCartney scoring a bonus entry via the Wings single.

GROUPS OF THE 1990s IN THE US

1	Boyz II Men
2	Guns N' Roses
3	Pearl Jam
4	The Beatles
5	Spice Girls
6	U2
7	Aerosmith
8	Hootie and the Blowfish
9	Wilson Phillips
10	Backstreet Boys

This "biggest so far" listing for the current decade is based on comparative US single and album chart performances of the 1990s.

SLASH N' BURN

Lead guitarist of Guns N' Roses from 1985, Saul "Slash" Hudson (b. 1965) left the band in 1996, citing musical differences with frontman Axl Rose. Although the guitar hero grew up in Los Angeles, he was born in Stoke on Trent, England.

TOP 10 GROUPS OF THE 1960s IN THE UK

❶ The Beatles ❷ The Rolling Stones ❸ The Shadows
❹ The Hollies ❺ The Beach Boys ❻ The Kinks
❼ The Four Tops ❽ Manfred Mann ❾ The Seekers
❿ The Bachelors

Based on comparative UK singles chart performance

TOP 10 GROUPS OF THE 1970s IN THE UK

❶ Abba ❷ Slade ❸ T. Rex ❹ Bay City Rollers
❺ The Sweet ❻ Showaddywaddy ❼ Mud ❽ Wings
❾ The Electric Light Orchestra ❿ The Osmonds

Based on comparative UK singles chart performance

TOP 10 GROUPS OF THE 1980s IN THE UK

❶ Police ❷ Wham! ❸ Dire Straits ❹ U2 ❺ Queen
❻ Simple Minds ❼ Pet Shop Boys ❽ Duran Duran
❾ Adam and the Ants ❿ Madness

Based on comparative UK singles and albums chart performance

It should be noted that apart from U2, who are from Ireland, all 10 of these groups are British. With the exception of Queen, none of them had achieved any success prior to the tail-end of the 1970s.

TOP 10 GROUPS OF THE 1960s IN THE US

❶ The Beatles ❷ The Supremes ❸ The Four Seasons
❹ The Beach Boys ❺ The Rolling Stones ❻ The Miracles
❼ The Temptations ❽ Tommy James and The Shondells
❾ Dave Clark Five ❿ Herman's Hermits

Based on comparative US singles chart performance

TOP 10 GROUPS OF THE 1970s IN THE US

❶ Bee Gees ❷ The Carpenters ❸ Chicago
❹ Jackson 5/Jacksons ❺ Three Dog Night ❻ Gladys Knight and the Pips ❼ Dawn ❽ Earth, Wind and Fire
❾ The Eagles ❿ Fleetwood Mac

Based on comparative US singles chart performance

TOP 10 GROUPS OF THE 1980s IN THE US

❶ Wham! ❷ Kool and the Gang ❸ Huey Lewis and the News ❹ Journey ❺ Duran Duran ❻ U2
❼ The Rolling Stones ❽ Alabama ❾ The Pointer Sisters
❿ Jefferson Starship/Starship

Based on comparative US singles and albums chart performance

TOP 10 ★
GROUPS OF THE 1990s IN THE UK

1	Spice Girls
2	Oasis
3	Manic Street Preachers
4	Take That
5	Blur
6	Simply Red
7	Wet Wet Wet
8	Lighthouse Family
9	Verve
10	Boyzone

... THANK YOU, MA'AM!
Wham! (George Michael and Andrew Ridgeley) had their first hit in 1982; they split in 1986.

Which female singer has had the most hits in the UK?
see p.144 for the answer

A Janet Jackson
B Madonna
C Whitney Houston

STAR SINGLES & ALBUMS

TOP 10 ★
ELTON JOHN SINGLES IN THE UK

	SINGLE	YEAR
1	*Candle in the Wind (1997)/ Something About the Way You Look Tonight*	1997
2	*Don't Go Breaking My Heart (with Kiki Dee)*	1976
3	*Sacrifice*	1990
4	*Rocket Man*	1972
5	*Nikita*	1985
6	*Crocodile Rock*	1972
7	*Daniel*	1973
8	*Song For Guy*	1978
9	*I Guess That's Why They Call It the Blues*	1983
10	*I'm Still Standing*	1983

Source: *MRIB*

TOP 10 ★
FLEETWOOD MAC ALBUMS IN THE UK

	ALBUM	YEAR
1	*Rumours*	1977
2	*Tango in the Night*	1982
3	*Greatest Hits**	1988
4	*Mirage*	1982
5	*Tusk*	1979
6	*Fleetwood Mac#*	1968
7	*Behind the Mask*	1990
8	*Then Play On*	1969
9	Mr. Wonderful	1968
10	Fleetwood Mac	1976

* *Warner Bros. label: not to be confused with the 1972 Greatest Hits compilation (CBS label)*

\# *Blue Horizon label: not to be confused with No. 10 (Reprise label)*

One of the world's bestselling albums of all time, *Rumours* spent 443 weeks on the British chart.

TOP 10 ★
BRUCE SPRINGSTEEN ALBUMS IN THE US

	ALBUM	YEAR
1	*Born in the U.S.A.*	1984
2	*Bruce Springsteen & the E Street Band Live/1975–85*	1986
3	*Born to Run*	1975
4	*The River*	1980
5	*Tunnel of Love*	1987
6	*Greatest Hits*	1995
7	*Darkness on the Edge of Town*	1978
8	*Greetings from Asbury Park, N.J.*	1975
9	*Nebraska*	1982
10	*The Wild, the Innocent & the E Street Shuffle*	1975

Source: *The Popular Music Database*

THE BOSS
After 25 years of recording, Bruce Springsteen became part of the Rock and Roll Hall of Fame in 1999.

TOP 10 ★
ROLLING STONES ALBUMS IN THE UK

	ALBUM	YEAR
1	*The Rolling Stones No. 2*	1965
2	*Aftermath*	1966
3	*Rolled Gold – The Very Best of The Rolling Stones*	1975
4	*Let It Bleed*	1969
5	*Sticky Fingers*	1971
6	*Some Girls*	1978
7	*Emotional Rescue*	1980
8	*Exile on Main Street*	1972
9	*The Rolling Stones*	1964
10	*Tattoo You*	1981

Source: *MRIB*

Most stages of the band's career are represented among their top 10 titles. While they may not still have their 1960's pre-eminence, higher general album sales in the 1980s have boosted several later releases proportionately.

TOP 10 ★
BEATLES SINGLES IN THE UK

	SINGLE	YEAR
1	*She Loves You*	1963
2	*I Want to Hold Your Hand*	1963
3	*Can't Buy Me Love*	1964
4	*I Feel Fine*	1964
5	*We Can Work It Out/Day Tripper*	1965
6	*Help!*	1965
7	*Hey Jude*	1968
8	*A Hard Day's Night*	1964
9	*From Me to You*	1963
10	*Hello Goodbye*	1967

The Beatles' two bestselling UK singles, both from the late 1963 "Beatlemania" period, remain among the UK's all-time Top 15 singles, 30 years on. Their sales in the later 1960s were generally lower, although *Hey Jude* proved a match for the earlier mega-hits. Amazingly, numbers one to five were all million-plus UK sellers – no other act had ever had more than two million-selling UK singles.

Elvis Presley memorabilia are among the most sought-after rock 'n' roll collectibles, and range from mugs and badges to soaps and toilet seat covers.

TOP 10
JOHN LENNON SINGLES IN THE UK

	SINGLE	YEAR
1	Imagine	1975
2	Woman	1981
3	(Just Like) Starting Over	1980
4	Happy Xmas (War is Over)	1972
5	Give Peace a Chance	1969
6	Instant Karma	1970
7	Power to the People	1971
8	Nobody Told Me	1984
9	Cold Turkey	1969
10	Mind Games	1973

Source: MRIB

John Lennon began his extra-curricular recording projects during the year before the Beatles actually split: *Give Peace a Chance* appeared in 1969, credited to the Plastic Ono Band. *Imagine* was a hit twice, the second occasion being immediately after Lennon's death, when its UK sales soared to over 1,000,000 and it reached No. 1. *Nobody Told Me* was a posthumous Top 10 chart entry just over three years after he died.

JOHN LENNON

Born during a Nazi bombardment of Liverpool, John Lennon grew to condemn the insanity of war in pacifist songs such as Give Peace a Chance.

TOP 10
ELVIS PRESLEY SINGLES IN THE UK

	SINGLE	YEAR
1	It's Now or Never	1960
2	Jailhouse Rock	1958
3	Are You Lonesome Tonight?	1961
4	Wooden Heart	1961
5	Return to Sender	1962
6	Can't Help Falling in Love	1962
7	The Wonder of You	1970
8	Surrender	1961
9	Way Down	1977
10	All Shook Up	1957

Source: MRIB

Elvis's sales peak in the UK was not in his 1950's heyday, but shortly after he left the army in the early 1960's. *It's Now or Never* was his only million-seller on UK sales alone, though all the records in this list registered sales in excess of 600,000, and, between them, these 10 singles accounted for a total of 46 weeks at the top of the UK chart.

TOP 10
MADONNA SINGLES IN THE UK

	SINGLE	YEAR
1	Like a Virgin	1984
2	Into the Groove	1985
3	Papa Don't Preach	1986
4	Crazy for You	1985
5	Holiday	1984
6	True Blue	1986
7	Vogue	1990
8	La Isla Bonita	1987
9	Like a Prayer	1989
10	Who's That Girl?	1987

Source: MRIB

The most successful chart artist of the 1980s, Madonna scored 25 UK Top 10 hits by the end of the decade, including seven No. 1s, despite not entering the charts until the beginning of 1984. Her biggest seller, *Like a Virgin*, failed to make No. 1 – being held at No. 3 over Christmas 1984 by the gigantic sales of the Band Aid single and Wham!'s *Last Christmas*.

Did You Know? The top five Fleetwood Mac albums all date from the years 1974–87 and feature Lindsey Buckingham. After he left in 1987, the band never achieved quite the same level of success.

POP STARS OF THE '90S

BLUR SINGLES IN THE UK

	SINGLE	YEAR
1	Country House	1995
2	Beetlebum	1997
3	Tender	1999
4	Song 2	1997
5	The Universal	1995
6	Girls and Boys	1994
7	Charmless Man	1996
8	On Your Own	1997
9	Stereotypes	1996
10	There's No Other Way	1991

PULP SINGLES IN THE UK

	SINGLE	YEAR
1	Common People	1995
2	Mis-Shapes/ Sorted for E's and Wizz	1995
3	Disco 2000	1995
4	Help the Aged	1997
5	Something Changed	1996
6	This Is Hardcore	1998
7	The Sisters (EP)	1994
8	Party Hard	1998
9	A Little Soul	1998
10	Do You Remember the First Time?	1994

TOP 10 PRODIGY SINGLES IN THE UK
(Single/year)

1 *Firestarter*, 1996 **2** *Breathe*, 1996
3 *Everybody in the Place* (EP), 1996
4 *Charly*, 1991 **5** *Out of Space/Ruff in the Jungle*, 1996 **6** *No Good (Start the Dance)*, 1996 **7** *Smack My Bitch up*, 1997
8 *Wind It up (Rewound)*, 1996
9 *Fire/Jericho*, 1992
10 *Voodoo People*, 1996

SUEDE SINGLES IN THE UK

	SINGLE	YEAR
1	Trash	1996
2	Stay Together	1994
3	Beautiful Ones	1996
4	Animal Nitrate	1993
5	Saturday Night	1997
6	Filmstar	1997
7	Lazy	1997
8	The Wild Ones	1994
9	Metal Mickey	1992
10	We Are the Pigs	1994

Although eclipsed by fellow Britpoppers Blur and Oasis, Suede have consistently remained among the top echelon, mainly due to the presence of their androgynous lead singer Brett Anderson, and show no signs of waning.

TOP 10 GEORGE MICHAEL SINGLES OF THE 1990s IN THE UK
(Single/year)

1 *Outside*, 1998 **2** *Fast Love*, 1996 **3** *Jesus to a Child*, 1996
4 *You Have Been Loved/The Strangest Thing '97*, 1997 **5** *Star People '97*, 1997
6 *Spinning the Wheel*, 1996 **7** *Older/I Can't Make You Love Me*, 1997
8 *Too Funky*, 1992 **9** *Praying for Time*, 1990 **10** *Freedom*, 1990

SPICE GIRLS SINGLES IN THE UK

	SINGLE	YEAR
1	Wannabe	1996
2	2 Become 1	1996
3	Too Much	1997
4	Goodbye	1998
5	Say You'll Be There	1996
6	Spice up Your Life	1997
7	Viva Forever	1998
8	Mama/Who Do You Think You Are	1997
9	Stop	1998
10	When You're Gone (Bryan Adams featuring Melanie C)	1998

OASIS SINGLES IN THE UK

	SINGLE	YEAR
1	Don't Look Back in Anger	1996
2	D'You Know What I Mean?	1997
3	Wonderwall	1995
4	Some Might Say	1995
5	Stand by Me	1998
6	All Around the World	1998
7	Roll With It	1995
8	Whatever	1994
9	Cigarettes and Alcohol	1994
10	Live Forever	1994

Of all the Britpop bands, Oasis stands head and shoulders above their rivals in terms of sales success. Led by Noel Gallagher's songs and his brother Liam's perfect pop voice, Oasis have logged a great catalogue of hits in just five years.

BOYZONE SINGLES IN THE UK

	SINGLE	YEAR
1	No Matter What	1998
2	Words	1996
3	All That I Need	1998
4	A Different Beat	1996
5	Father and Son	1995
6	Picture of You	1999
7	I Love the Way You Love Me	1998
8	Isn't It a Wonder	1997
9	Love Me for a Reason	1994
10	Baby Can I Hold You/Shooting Star	1997

Background image: **FENDER STRATOCASTER GUITAR**

TOP 10 ★
MANIC STREET PREACHERS SINGLES IN THE UK

SINGLE	YEAR
1 If You Tolerate This Your Children Will Be Next	1998
2 A Design for Life	1996
3 Everything Must Go	1996
4 Australia	1996
5 You Stole the Sun from My Heart	1999
6 Theme from M*A*S*H (Suicide Is Painless)	1992
7 Kevin Carter	1996
8 The Everlasting	1998
9 Motorcycle Emptiness	1992
10 You Love Us	1992

TOP 10 ★
CHER SINGLES OF THE 1990s IN THE UK

SINGLE	YEAR
1 Believe	1998
2 The Shoop Shoop Song (It's in His Kiss)	1991
3 One by One	1996
4 Love and Understanding	1991
5 Walking in Memphis	1995
6 Just Like Jesse James	1990
7 Oh No Not My Baby	1992
8 Love Hurts	1991
9 Could've Been You	1992
10 The Sun Ain't Gonna Shine Anymore	1996

THANKS FOR CHER-ING

The ability to reinvent herself and change her style to match the times is surely the reason why Cher's musical career has spanned four decades and shows no signs of slowing. She is also an Oscar-winning actress.

TOP 10 ★
TAKE THAT SINGLES IN THE UK

SINGLE	YEAR
1 Relight My Fire	1993
2 Sure	1994
3 Back for Good	1995
4 How Deep is Your Love	1996
5 Babe	1993
6 Everything Changes	1994
7 Pray	1993
8 Never Forget	1995
9 Could It Be Magic	1992
10 Why Can't I Wake Up with You	1993

The successful career of this Manchester-based band seemed doomed when Robbie Williams announced his intention to leave in July 1995. When the remaining foursome declared their intention to split in Feruary 1996, the Childline helpline and the Samaritans were overwhelmed with phone calls from unhappy fans.

Did You Know? The original line-up of the band Pulp formed in 1979 while its leader, Jarvis Cocker, was still at school. Early shows were performed during lunch breaks in the school canteen.

TOP 10 ★
COUNTRY ALBUMS IN THE UK

	ALBUM/ARTIST	YEAR
1	*Johnny Cash at San Quentin*, Johnny Cash	1969
2	*20 Golden Greats*, Glen Campbell	1976
3	*The Best of John Denver*, John Denver	1974
4	*40 Golden Greats*, Jim Reeves	1975
5	*Images*, Don Williams	1978
6	*Greatest Hits*, Glen Campbell	1971
7	*The Very Best of Slim Whitman*, Slim Whitman	1976
8	*The Best of Tammy Wynette*, Tammy Wynette	1975
9	*Live in London*, John Denver	1976
10	*Johnny Cash Live at Folsom Prison*, Johnny Cash	1968

Source: *MRIB*

Of Johnny Cash's two celebrated live albums recorded at two of America's most severe penal institutions, the San Quentin release holds the record for the longest-charting Country album in UK chart history, with 114 weeks notched up between 1969 and 1971. Country music sales in the UK and elsewhere in Europe have never matched those in its native United States.

STARTING YOUNG
Kenny Rogers' first million-seller was Crazy Feeling *in 1957, when he was only 19, but* Lucille *was the hit that made him an international country star.*

TOP 10 ★
JAZZ ALBUMS IN THE UK

	ALBUM/ARTIST OR GROUP	YEAR
1	*We Are in Love*, Harry Connick Jr.	1990
2	*Blue Light, Red Light*, Harry Connick Jr.	1991
3	*Jazz on a Summer's Day*, Various	1992
4	*Morning Dance*, Spyro Gyra	1979
5	*In Flight*, George Benson	1977
6	*Duotones*, Kenny G	1987
7	*Best of Ball, Barber and Bilk*, Kenny Ball, Chris Barber, and Acker Bilk	1962
8	*Sinatra/Basie*, Frank Sinatra and Count Basie	1963
9	*Kenny Ball's Golden Hits*, Kenny Ball	1963
10	*Time Out Featuring Take Five*, Dave Brubeck Quartet	1960

Source: *MRIB*

Despite a solid base of afficionados, jazz has always been a comparatively poor-selling musical genre in the UK, and the jazz albums that have made the Top 10 through the years can be counted on little more than two hands. The only jazz album ever to top the UK chart was the Ball, Barber, and Bilk compilation, long ago in 1962, when the British fad for trad jazz was running at its height.

JAZZ GIANT
Harry Connick Jr's combination of jazz with Big Band, American classics, and New Orleans funk has won nominations for Oscars, Grammys, and Emmys, as well as ensuring a high place in both jazz and pop charts.

TOP 10 ★
COUNTRY SINGLES IN THE UK

	SINGLE/ARTIST	YEAR
1	*I Love You Because*, Jim Reeves	1964
2	*I Won't Forget You*, Jim Reeves	1964
3	*Ruby (Don't Take Your Love to Town)*, Kenny Rogers	1969
4	*King of the Road*, Roger Miller	1965
5	*Lucille*, Kenny Rogers	1977
6	*Stand by Your Man*, Tammy Wynette	1975
7	*Coward of the County*, Kenny Rogers	1980
8	*Distant Drums*, Jim Reeves	1966
9	*Rose Marie*, Slim Whitman	1955
10	*Give Me Your Word*, Tennessee Ernie Ford	1955

Source: *MRIB*

Even though *I Love You Because* made only UK No. 5, it is still the bestselling Country single ever in Britain, selling over 750,000 copies in 1964.

TOP 10 ★
INSTRUMENTAL SINGLES IN THE UK

	SINGLE/ARTIST OR GROUP	YEAR
1	*Stranger on the Shore*, Mr. Acker Bilk	1961
2	*Eye Level*, Simon Park Orchestra	1973
3	*Telstar*, The Tornados	1962
4	*The Harry Lime Theme (The Third Man)*, Anton Karas	1950
5	*Amazing Grace*, Royal Scots Dragoon Guards Band	1972
6	*Chi Mai*, Ennio Morricone	1981
7	*Wonderful Land*, The Shadows	1962
8	*Apache*, The Shadows	1960
9	*Albatross*, Fleetwood Mac	1968
10	*Mouldy Old Dough*, Lieutenant Pigeon	1972

Source: *MRIB*

If this Top 10 reveals anything, it is that non-vocal hits are more likely to be found in the "middle-of-the-road" sector than in Rock 'n' Roll.

What was the bestselling album in the world in 1998?
see p.155 for the answer

A *Titanic* (Soundtrack)
B *Ray of Light* (Madonna)
C *Hello Nasty* (Beastie Boys)

TOP 10 ORIGINAL CAST RECORDING ALBUMS IN THE UK

(Album/year)

1 *The Phantom of the Opera*, 1987
2 *Hair*, 1968 3 *Joseph and the Amazing Technicolor Dreamcoat*, 1991
4 *My Fair Lady*, 1958 5 *The Sound of Music*, 1961 6 *Oliver!*, 1960 7 *Evita*, 1977 8 *Cats*, 1981 9 *Fiddler on the Roof*, 1967 10 *Jesus Christ Superstar*, 1972

Source: *MRIB*

TOP 10 ORIGINAL SOUNDTRACK ALBUMS IN THE UK

(Album/year)

1 *The Sound of Music*, 1965
2 *Saturday Night Fever*, 1978
3 *The Bodyguard*, 1992 4 *Grease*, 1978
5 *Dirty Dancing*, 1987 6 *South Pacific*, 1958 7 *West Side Story*, 1962
8 *Top Gun*, 1986 9 *A Star is Born*, 1977
10 *Fame*, 1980

Source: *MRIB*

TOP 10 ★
HEAVY METAL SINGLES IN THE UK

	SINGLE/ARTIST OR GROUP	YEAR
1	*I'd Do Anything for Love (But I Won't Do That)*, Meat Loaf	1993
2	*Eye of the Tiger*, Survivor	1982
3	*The Final Countdown*, Europe	1986
4	*I Want to Know What Love Is*, Foreigner	1984
5	*All Right Now*, Free	1970
6	*Paranoid*, Black Sabbath	1970
7	*School's Out*, Alice Cooper	1972
8	*Down Down*, Status Quo	1974
9	*Black Night*, Deep Purple	1970
10	*Voodoo Chile*, Jimi Hendrix Experience	1970

Source: *MRIB*

MELODIC METAL

Bon Jovi, fronted by singer-turned-actor Jon Bon Jovi, have moved from tuneful heavy metal to pop and ballads, and achieved multi-platinum sales with Slippery When Wet.

TOP 10 ★
"GREATEST HITS" ALBUMS IN THE UK

	ALBUM	ARTIST OR GROUP	YEAR
1	*Greatest Hits*	Queen	1981
2	*The Immaculate Collection*	Madonna	1990
3	*Simon and Garfunkel's Greatest Hits*	Simon and Garfunkel	1972
4	*The Very Best of Elton John*	Elton John	1990
5	*Legend*	Bob Marley and the Wailers	1984
6	*Greatest Hits II*	Queen	1991
7	*Carry On up the Charts – The Best of*	Beautiful South	1994
8	*The Best of Rod Stewart*	Rod Stewart	1989
9	*Money for Nothing*	Dire Straits	1989
10	*Abba's Greatest Hits*	Abba	1976

Source: *MRIB*

TOP 10 ★
HEAVY METAL ALBUMS IN THE UK

	ALBUM/ARTIST OR GROUP	YEAR
1	*Bat out of Hell*, Meat Loaf	1978
2	*Bat out of Hell II – Back to Hell*, Meat Loaf	1993
3	*Led Zeppelin II*, Led Zeppelin	1969
4	*Hysteria*, Def Leppard	1987
5	*Led Zeppelin IV*, Led Zeppelin	1971
6	*Cross Road – The Best of Bon Jovi*, Bon Jovi	1994
7	*So Far So Good*, Bryan Adams	1993
8	*Eliminator*, ZZ Top	1983
9	*Appetite for Destruction*, Guns N' Roses	1987
10	*Slippery When Wet*, Bon Jovi	1986

Source: *MRIB*

TOP 10 ★

IRISH ALBUMS IN THE UK

	ALBUM/GROUP	YEAR
1	*The Joshua Tree*, U2	1987
2	*Where We Belong*, Boyzone	1998
3	*Watermark*, Enya	1988
4	*Shepherd Moons*, Enya	1991
5	*Rattle and Hum*, U2	1988
6	*Achtung Baby!*, U2	1991
7	*Said and Done*, Boyzone	1995
8	*U2 Live – Under a Blood Red Sky*, U2	1983
9	*No Need to Argue*, Cranberries	1994
10	*A Different Beat*, Boyzone	1996

Source: *The Popular Music Database*

PERFECT POP

U2, the sincere stadium rockers, together since 1977, have had consistently huge record sales since their first album Boy *in the early 1980s, though critical acclaim has been patchy.*

TOP 10 ★

REGGAE ALBUMS IN THE UK

	ALBUM/GROUP	YEAR
1	*Legend*, Bob Marley and the Wailers	1984
2	*The Best of UB40 Vol. 1*, UB40	1987
3	*Labour of Love II*, UB40	1989
4	*Labour of Love*, UB40	1983
5	*Promises and Lies*, UB40	1993
6	*Present Arms*, UB40	1981
7	*Signing Off*, UB40	1980
8	*Tease Me*, Chaka Demus and Pliers	1993
9	*Labour of Love III*, UB40	1998
10	*Exodus*, Bob Marley and the Wailers	1977

Source: *The Popular Music Database*

TOP 10 ★

TROPICAL/SALSA ALBUMS IN THE US, 1998

	ALBUM	ARTIST OR GROUP
1	*Buena Vista Social Club*	Buena Vista Social Club
2	*Contra La Corriente*	Marc Anthony
3	*Dance with Me*	Soundtrack
4	*Suavemente*	Elvis Crespo
5	*Sentimientos*	Charlie Zaa
6	*Un Segundo Sentimiento*	Charlie Zaa
7	*Sobre El Fuego*	India
8	*Ironias*	Victor Manuelle
9	*Alto Honor*	Grupo Mania
10	*A Toda Cuba Le Gusta*	Afro-Cuban All Stars

Source: Billboard

TOP 10 LATIN POP ALBUMS IN THE US, 1998

(Album/artist or group)

❶ *Me Estoy Enamorando*, Alejandro Fernández ❷ *Vuelve*, Ricky Martin ❸ *Suenos Liquidos*, Maná ❹ *Romances*, Luis Miguel ❺ *Mas*, Alejandro Sanz ❻ *Inolvidable*, Jose Luis Rodriguez with Los Panchos ❼ *Cosas Del Amor*, Enrique Iglesias ❽ *Donde Estan Los Ladrones?*, Shakira ❾ *Lo Mejor De Mi*, Cristian ❿ *Compas*, Gipsy Kings

Source: Billboard

TOP 10 ★
ALBUMS IN THE WORLD, 1998*

	ALBUM	ARTIST OR GROUP
1	Ray of Light	Madonna
2	Hello Nasty	Beastie Boys
3	Armageddon	Soundtrack
4	Adore	Smashing Pumpkins
5	Titanic	Soundtrack
6	Let's Talk About Love	Celine Dion
7	Vuelve	Ricky Martin
8	Back for Good	Modern Talking
9	City of Angels	Soundtrack
10	Talk on Corners	The Corrs

* Based on CNN's "Worldbeat" album chart, launched on 6 June 1998

Source: *The Popular Music Database*

TOP 10 ★
REGGAE ALBUMS IN THE US, 1998

	ALBUM	ARTIST OR GROUP
1	Many Moods of Moses	Beenie Man
2	Reggae Gold 1998	Various
3	Pure Reggae	Various
4	Inna Heights	Buju Banton
5	Best of Bob Marley	Bob Marley
6	Strictly the Best 19	Various
7	Reggae Gold 1997	Various
8	Maverick a Strike	Finley Quaye
9	Think Like a Girl	Diana King
10	Midnight Lover	Shaggy

Source: Billboard

BRAT ROCKERS
The ultimate middle-class rebels, the Beastie Boys are known for their loud, brash mixture of rap, punk, and heavy metal.

TOP 10 ★
WORLD MUSIC ALBUMS
IN THE US, 1998

	ALBUM	ARTIST OR GROUP
1	Romanza	Andrea Bocelli
2	The Book of Secrets	Loreena McKennitt
3	Buena Vista Social Club	Buena Vista Social Club
4	Celtic Christmas III	Various
5	Celtic Moods	Various
6	Riverdance	Bill Whelan
7	Michael Flatley's Lord of the Dance	Ronan Hardiman
8	Deep Forest III – Comparasa	Deep Forest
9	Compas	Gipsy Kings
10	Mamaloshen	Mandy Patinkin

Source: Billboard

SIMPLY ADORABLE
Adore has been the Smashing Pumpkins' biggest seller since their 1995 double-CD album Mellon Collie and the Infinite Sadness.

What was the first ever Grammy Record of the Year?
see p.161 for the answer

A *Moon River* (Henry Mancini)
B *Mack the Knife* (Bobby Darin)
C *Nel Blu Dipinto di Blu (Volare)* (Domenico Modugno)

155

GOLD & PLATINUM DISCS

FEMALE ARTISTS WITH THE MOST GOLD ALBUMS IN THE UK

ARTIST	GOLD ALBUMS
1 Diana Ross	17
2 =Barbra Streisand	12
=Madonna	12
4 Donna Summer	9
5 Mariah Carey	8
6 =Kate Bush	7
=Tina Turner	7
8 =Joan Armatrading	6
=Janet Jackson	6
=Cher	6
=Celine Dion	6

Source: *BPI*

MALE ARTISTS WITH THE MOST GOLD ALBUMS IN THE UK

ARTIST	GOLD ALBUMS
1 =Elton John	20
=Cliff Richard	20
3 Rod Stewart	19
4 =Neil Diamond	17
=James Last	17
=Paul McCartney*	17
7 Mike Oldfield	16
8 =David Bowie	15
=Elvis Presley	15
10 Prince	13

* Including gold albums with Wings
Source: *BPI*

SYMBOLISM

Born Prince Rogers Nelson in Minneapolis, one of The Artist's previous incarnations was as Prince. A talented musician, he famously played almost all the instruments on his debut album.

FEMALE ARTISTS WITH THE MOST PLATINUM ALBUMS IN THE UK

ARTIST	PLATINUM ALBUMS
1 Madonna	34
2 Celine Dion	19
3 Whitney Houston	18
4 Tina Turner	17
5 =Enya	12
=Gloria Estefan	12
7 =Kylie Minogue	10
=Mariah Carey	10
=Alanis Morissette	10
10 Kate Bush	9

Source: *BPI*

TOP 10 MALE ARTISTS WITH THE MOST GOLD ALBUMS IN THE US

(Artist/gold albums)

1 Elvis Presley, 62 **2** Neil Diamond, 35 **3** Elton John, 32 **4** Kenny Rogers, 28 **5** Frank Sinatra, 26 **6** Bob Dylan, 24 **7** = George Strait, 23; = Willie Nelson, 23 **9** Hank Williams Jr., **10** = Paul McCartney/Wings; = Rod Stewart, 20

Source: *RIAA*

TOP 10 FEMALE ARTISTS WITH THE MOST GOLD ALBUMS IN THE US

(Artist/gold albums)

1 Barbra Streisand, 40 **2** Reba McEntire, 19 **3** Linda Ronstadt, 17 **4** Olivia Newton-John, 15 **5** = Aretha Franklin, 13; = Madonna, 13; = Dolly Parton, 13 **8** = Gloria Estefan*, 12; = Anne Murray, 12; = Tanya Tucker, 12

* Includes hits with Miami Sound Machine
Source: *RIAA*

TOP 10 ⭐
FEMALE ARTISTS WITH THE MOST PLATINUM ALBUMS IN THE US

ARTIST	PLATINUM ALBUMS
1 Barbra Streisand	49
2 Madonna	47
3= Whitney Houston	45
= Mariah Carey	45
5 Celine Dion	34
6 Reba McEntire	24
7 Linda Ronstadt	23
8= Janet Jackson	19
= Shania Twain	19
10= Sade	18
= Gloria Estefan	18

Source: *RIAA*

TOP 10 ⭐
MALE ARTISTS WITH THE MOST PLATINUM ALBUMS IN THE UK

ARTIST	PLATINUM ALBUMS
1 Michael Jackson	38
2 Phil Collins	30
3 George Michael	20
4 Elton John	19
5 Meat Loaf	17
6= Rod Stewart	14
= Chris Rea	14
8= Cliff Richard	13
= Michael Bolton	13
10 Robbie Williams	12

Platinum albums in the UK are those that have achieved sales of 300,000. Relative to the population of the UK, where it represents approximately one sale per 195 inhabitants, this is a greater attainment than a US platinum award, where the ratio is one per 266.

Source: *BPI*

PRESIDENTIAL CHOICE
Famous for their ever-changing line-up, Fleetwood Mac derive their name from the only two consistent members of the band, drummer Mick Fleetwood and bass player John McVie. The band played at President Bill Clinton's inauguration in early 1993.

TOP 10 ⭐
GROUPS WITH THE MOST PLATINUM ALBUMS IN THE UK

GROUP	PLATINUM ALBUMS
1 Simply Red	36
2 Queen	29
3 Dire Straits	27
4 Oasis	26
5 U2	24
6 Fleetwood Mac	19
7= UB40	17
= Wet Wet Wet	17
9 R.E.M.	16
10= Eurythmics	15
= Spice Girls	15

Source: *BPI*

TOP 10 ⭐
GROUPS WITH THE MOST GOLD ALBUMS IN THE UK

GROUP	GOLD ALBUMS
1 Queen	21
2 Status Quo	19
3 The Rolling Stones	18
4= Abba	14
= Genesis	14
6= The Beatles	13
= Roxy Music	13
8 UB40	12
9 Pink Floyd	11
10 10cc	10

Gold discs have been awarded in the UK since 1 April 1973. They are presented for sales of 400,000 singles or 100,000 albums, cassettes, and CDs (200,000 for budget-priced products). Although neither "groups" nor "solo artists", there are a number of duos who have received multiple gold albums; two with sufficient to qualify them for a place in this list are the Carpenters (14) and Foster and Allen (12).

Source: *BPI*

Which song from a film won the Oscar for "Best Song" in 1989?
see p.159 for the answer
A *Take My Breath Away (Top Gun)*
B *Under the Sea (The Little Mermaid)*
C *Let the River Run (Working Girl)*

FILM MUSIC

THE 10 ★
"BEST SONG" OSCAR WINNERS OF THE 1950s

YEAR	TITLE/FILM
1950	*Mona Lisa*, Captain Carey
1951	*In the Cool, Cool, Cool of the Evening*, Here Comes the Groom
1952	*High Noon (Do Not Forsake Me, Oh My Darling)*, High Noon
1953	*Secret Love*, Calamity Jane
1954	*Three Coins in the Fountain*, Three Coins in the Fountain
1955	*Love is a Many-Splendored Thing*, Love is a Many-Splendored Thing
1956	*Whatever Will Be, Will Be (Que Sera, Sera)*, The Man Who Knew Too Much
1957	*All the Way*, The Joker is Wild
1958	*Gigi*, Gigi
1959	*High Hopes*, A Hole in the Head

Doris Day benefited strongly from these Oscars, scoring million-selling singles with *Secret Love* and *Whatever Will Be, Will Be*, both from films in which she starred.

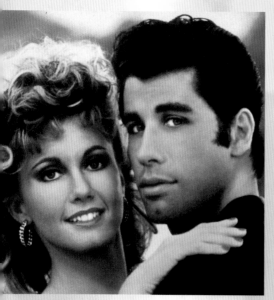

GREASE IS THE WORD
Olivia Newton-John and John Travolta starred in the film Grease, as well as scoring several hit singles from the movie's soundtrack, such as Sandy and Hopelessly Devoted (to You).

THE 10 ★
"BEST SONG" OSCAR WINNERS OF THE 1960s

YEAR	TITLE/FILM
1960	*Never on Sunday*, Never on Sunday
1961	*Moon River*, Breakfast at Tiffany's
1962	*Days of Wine and Roses*, Days of Wine and Roses
1963	*Call Me Irresponsible*, Papa's Delicate Condition
1964	*Chim Chim Cheree*, Mary Poppins
1965	*The Shadow of Your Smile*, The Sandpiper
1966	*Born Free*, Born Free
1967	*Talk to the Animals*, Dr. Dolittle
1968	*The Windmills of Your Mind*, The Thomas Crown Affair
1969	*Raindrops Keep Fallin' on My Head*, Butch Cassidy and the Sundance Kid

Both *The Windmills of Your Mind* and *Raindrops Keep Fallin' on My Head* hit the US Top 10. Sacha Distel's cover version of the 1969 Oscar winner charted five times in the UK in 1970.

TOP 10 ★
MUSICAL FILMS*

	TITLE	YEAR
1	*Grease*	1978
2	*Saturday Night Fever*	1977
3	*The Sound of Music*	1965
4	*Footloose*	1984
5	*American Graffiti*	1973
6	*Mary Poppins*	1964
7	*Flashdance*	1983
8	*The Rocky Horror Picture Show*	1975
9	*Coal Miner's Daughter*	1980
10	*My Fair Lady*	1964

* *Traditional musicals (in which the cast actually sing) and films in which a musical soundtrack is a major component of the film are included*

The era of the blockbuster musical may be over, but in recent years animated films with a strong musical content appear to have taken over, such as *Aladdin*, *The Lion King*, and *Pocahontas*.

THE 10 "BEST SONG" OSCAR WINNERS OF THE 1970s

(Year/title/film)

❶ 1970, *For All We Know*, Lovers and Other Strangers ❷ 1971, *Theme from "Shaft"*, Shaft ❸ 1972, *The Morning After*, The Poseidon Adventure ❹ 1973, *The Way We Were*, The Way We Were ❺ 1974, *We May Never Love Like This Again*, The Towering Inferno ❻ 1975, *I'm Easy*, Nashville ❼ 1976, *Evergreen*, A Star is Born ❽ 1977, *You Light up My Life*, You Light up My Life ❾ 1978, *Last Dance*, Thank God It's Friday ❿ 1979, *It Goes Like It Goes*, Norma Rae

TINA'S TRIUMPH
What's Love Got to Do with It *is based on the life of Tina Turner. In the 1993 film, actress Angela Bassett offered a convincing portrayal of the pop star.*

TOP 10 POP MUSIC FILMS

❶ *The Blues Brothers*, 1980 ❷ *Purple Rain*, 1984 ❸ *La Bamba*, 1987 ❹ *The Doors*, 1991 ❺ *What's Love Got to Do with It*, 1993 ❻ *Xanadu*, 1980 ❼ *The Jazz Singer*, 1980 ❽ *Sgt. Pepper's Lonely Hearts Club Band*, 1978 ❾ *Lady Sings the Blues*, 1972 ❿ *Pink Floyd – The Wall*, 1982

THE 10 ★
"BEST SONG" OSCAR WINNERS OF THE 1980s

YEAR	TITLE/FILM
1980	*Fame*, Fame
1981	*Up Where We Belong*, An Officer and a Gentleman
1982	*Arthur's Theme (Best That You Can Do)*, Arthur
1983	*Flashdance... What a Feeling*, Flashdance
1984	*I Just Called to Say I Love You*, The Woman in Red
1985	*Say You, Say Me*, White Nights
1986	*Take My Breath Away*, Top Gun
1987	*(I've Had) The Time of My Life*, Dirty Dancing
1988	*Let the River Run*, Working Girl
1989	*Under the Sea*, The Little Mermaid

THE 10 ★
LATEST "BEST SONG" OSCAR WINNERS

YEAR	TITLE/FILM
1998	*When You Believe*, Prince of Egypt
1997	*My Heart Will Go On*, Titanic
1996	*You Must Love Me*, Evita
1995	*Colors of the Wind*, Pocahontas
1994	*Can You Feel the Love Tonight*, The Lion King
1993	*Streets of Philadelphia*, Philadelphia
1992	*Whole New World*, Aladdin
1991	*Beauty and the Beast*, Beauty and the Beast
1990	*Sooner or Later (I Always Get My Man)*, Dick Tracy
1989	*Under the Sea*, The Little Mermaid

OSCAR-WINNING SINGER
Pop star and actress Madonna has won Oscars for two songs from films in which she also starred: Evita (pictured here) and Dick Tracy.

TOP 10 ★
ARTISTS WITH THE MOST "BEST SONG" OSCAR NOMINATIONS

	ARTIST/WINS/YEARS	NOMINATIONS
1	Sammy Cahn, 4, 1942–75	26
2	Johnny Mercer, 4, 1938–71	18
3 =	Paul Francis Webster, 3, 1944–76	16
=	Alan and Marilyn Bergman, 2, 1968–95	16
5	James Van Heusen, 4, 1944–68	14
6 =	Henry Warren, 3, 1935–57	11
=	Henry Mancini, 2, 1961–86	11
=	Ned Washington, 1, 1940–61	11
9 =	Alan Menken, 4, 1986–97	10
=	Sammy Fain, 2, 1937–77	10
=	Leo Robin, 1, 1934–53	10
=	Jule Styne, 1, 1940–68	10

It was not until 1934 that the category of "Best Song" was added to the many accolades bestowed on films. The Awards are often multiple, including the writers of the music and the lyrics.

TOP 10 ★
"BEST SONG" OSCAR-WINNING SINGLES IN THE UK

	TITLE/ARTIST OR GROUP	YEAR
1	*I Just Called to Say I Love You*, Stevie Wonder	1984
2	*Fame*, Irene Cara	1980
3	*Take My Breath Away*, Berlin	1986
4	*My Heart Will Go On*, Celine Dion	1997
5	*Flashdance...What a Feeling*, Irene Cara	1983
6	*Evergreen*, Barbra Streisand	1976
7	*Streets of Philadelphia*, Bruce Springsteen	1994
8	*Moon River*, Danny Williams	1961
9	*Whatever Will Be, Will Be (Que Sera, Sera)*, Doris Day	1956
10	*Raindrops Keep Fallin' on My Head*, Sacha Distel	1969

Source: *The Popular Music Database*

TOP 10 ★
JAMES BOND FILM THEMES IN THE UK

	TITLE/ARTIST OR GROUP	YEAR
1	*A View To A Kill*, Duran Duran	1985
2	*We Have All the Time in the World* (from *On Her Majesty's Secret Service*), Louis Armstrong	1994
3	*The Living Daylights*, a-ha	1987
4	*Licence to Kill*, Gladys Knight	1989
5	*Nobody Does it Better* (from *The Spy Who Loved Me*), Carly Simon	1977
6	*For Your Eyes Only*, Sheena Easton	1981
7	*Live and Let Die*, Paul McCartney and Wings	1973
8	*GoldenEye*, Tina Turner	1995
9	*You Only Live Twice*, Nancy Sinatra	1967
10	*Tomorrow Never Dies*, Sheryl Crow	1997

All the songs on this list reached the Top 20 but there has never been a Bond-associated UK No. 1. Themes from two films, *The Man with the Golden Gun* and *Moonraker*, failed to chart at all, even though Lulu and Shirley Bassey were involved.

Did You Know? The film soundtrack of *Titanic* is the bestselling soundtrack album of all time.

MUSIC AWARDS

LATEST WINNERS OF THE BRIT AWARD FOR BEST SINGLE BY A BRITISH ARTIST

YEAR	ARTIST OR GROUP/TITLE
1999	Robbie Williams, *Angels*
1998	All Saints, *Never Ever*
1997	Spice Girls, *Wannabe*
1996	Take That, *Back for Good*
1995	Blur, *Parklife*
1994	Take That, *Pray*
1993	Take That, *Could It Be Magic*
1992	Queen, *These Are The Days of Our Lives*
1991	Depeche Mode, *Enjoy the Silence*
1990	Phil Collins, *Another Day in Paradise*

THE 10 ★

LATEST WINNERS OF THE BRIT AWARD FOR BEST BRITISH VIDEO*

YEAR	ARTIST OR GROUP/TITLE
1999	Robbie Williams, *Millennium*
1998	All Saints, *Never Ever*
1997	Spice Girls, *Say You'll Be There*
1996	Oasis, *Wonderwall*
1995	Blur, *Parklife*
1994	Take That, *Pray*
1993	Shakespears Sister, *Stay*
1992	Seal, *Killer*
1991	The Beautiful South, *A Little Time*
1990	The Cure, *Lullaby*

* *Formerly "Best Video", hence open to international acts*

TOP 10 ★

ARTISTS WITH MOST GRAMMY AWARDS

	ARTIST	AWARDS
1	Sir George Solti	31
2	Quincy Jones	26
3	Vladimir Horowitz	25
4	Pierre Boulez	22
5 =	Henry Mancini	20
=	Stevie Wonder	20
7	John T. Williams	17
8	Leonard Bernstein	16
9 =	Aretha Franklin	15
=	Itzhak Perlman	15

The Grammy Awards ceremony has been held annually in the US since its inauguration on 4 May 1959, and the awards are considered to be the most prestigious award in the music industry. The proliferation of classical artists in this Top 10 (not least conductor Sir George Solti) is largely attributable to the large number of classical award categories at the Grammys.

TOP 10 ★

ARTISTS WITH THE MOST BRIT AWARDS

	ARTIST	AWARDS
1	Annie Lennox	8
2 =	Phil Collins	6*
=	Prince	6#
4 =	Michael Jackson	5
=	George Michael	5+
6	Blur	4
=	Bjork	4
=	Oasis	4
=	Dave Stewart	4
=	Take That	4
=	U2	4

* *Includes award for "Best Film Soundtrack" (1989, for* Buster *Original Soundtrack)*

\# *Includes award for "Best Film Soundtrack" (1990, for* Batman *Original Soundtrack)*

\+ *Includes two awards with Wham! (1985 and 1986)*

THE 10 ★

LATEST WINNERS OF THE BRIT AWARD FOR OUTSTANDING CONTRIBUTION TO THE BRITISH RECORD INDUSTRY

YEAR	ARTIST OR GROUP
1999	Eurythmics
1998	Fleetwood Mac
1997	Bee Gees
1996	David Bowie
1995	Elton John
1994	Van Morrison
1993	Rod Stewart
1992	Freddie Mercury
1991	Status Quo
1990	Queen

WONDERFUL TALENT

Stevie Wonder is regarded by many as a musical genius. His unique style reflects his gospel background, as well as the influence of jazz, rock, and African rhythms.

Which female singer has had the most Top 10 hits?
see p.144 for the answer

A Madonna
B Whitney Houston
C Janet Jackson

STYLISH SINGER

Formerly a backing singer, Sheryl Crow has achieved enormous success and critical acclaim as a singer/songwriter and musician through her creative and soul-baring approach to lyrics and melody.

THE 10 ⭐
LATEST GRAMMY RECORDS OF THE YEAR

YEAR	RECORD/ARTIST
1999	*My Heart Will Go On*, Celine Dion
1998	*Sunny Came Home*, Shawn Colvin
1997	*Change the World*, Eric Clapton
1996	*Kiss from a Rose*, Seal
1995	*All I Wanna Do*, Sheryl Crow
1994	*I Will Always Love You*, Whitney Houston
1993	*Tears in Heaven*, Eric Clapton
1992	*Unforgettable*, Natalie Cole with Nat "King" Cole
1991	*Another Day in Paradise*, Phil Collins
1990	*The Wind Beneath My Wings*, Bette Midler

THE 10 ⭐
FIRST GRAMMY RECORDS OF THE YEAR

YEAR	RECORD/ARTIST OR GROUP
1958	*Nel Blu Dipinto di Blu (Volare)*, Domenico Modugno
1959	*Mack the Knife*, Bobby Darin
1960	*Theme from A Summer Place*, Percy Faith
1961	*Moon River*, Henry Mancini
1962	*I Left My Heart in San Francisco*, Tony Bennett
1963	*The Days of Wine and Roses*, Henry Mancini
1964	*The Girl from Ipanema*, Stan Getz and Astrud Gilberto
1965	*A Taste of Honey*, Herb Alpert and the Tijuana Brass
1966	*Strangers in the Night*, Frank Sinatra
1967	*Up Up and Away*, 5th Dimension

TOP 10 ⭐
COUNTRIES WITH MOST WINS AT THE EUROVISION SONG CONTEST

	COUNTRY/YEARS	WINS
1	**Ireland**, 1970, 1980, 1987, 1992, 1993, 1994, 1996	7
2=	**France**, 1958, 1960, 1962, 1969*, 1977	5
=	**Luxembourg**, 1961, 1965, 1972, 1973, 1983	5
=	**UK**, 1967, 1969*, 1976, 1981, 1997	5
5=	**Netherlands**, 1957, 1959, 1969*, 1975	4
=	**Sweden**, 1974, 1984, 1991, 1999	4
7	**Israel**, 1978, 1979, 1998	3
8=	**Italy**, 1964, 1990	2
=	**Norway**, 1984, 1995	2
=	**Spain**, 1968, 1969*	2
=	**Switzerland**, 1956, 1988	2

* All four countries tied as winners in 1969

The Eurovision Song Contest has been an annual event since its 24 May 1956 debut at Lugarno, Switzerland, which was won by Swiss singer Lys Assia with the song *Refrain*. On that occasion, each of seven countries submitted two songs each, and the jury's votes were not made public. Since then, the number of competing countries has risen – in 1997, 24 countries took part – and the points awarded have become an integral part of the event. Six other countries have each won on a single occasion.

SEAL OF APPROVAL

Kiss from a Rose, *used on the* Batman Forever *soundtrack, sent Seal's album* Seal *multiplatinum, selling 4 million copies in the US alone, and remaining in the charts for 45 weeks.*

CLASSICAL & OPERA

LATEST WINNERS OF THE "BEST CLASSICAL ALBUM" GRAMMY AWARD

YEAR	COMPOSER/TITLE	CONDUCTOR/SOLOIST/ORCHESTRA
1999	Barber, *Prayers of Kierkegaard*/ Vaughan Williams, *Dona Nobis Pacem*/ Bartok, *Cantata Profana*	Robert Shaw, Richard Clement, Nathan Gunn, Atlanta Symphony Orchestra and chorus
1998	Danielpour, Kirchner, Rouse, *Premières – Cello Concertos*	Yo-Yo Ma, David Zinman, Philadelphia Orchestra
1997	Corigliano, *Of Rage and Remembrance*	Leonard Slatkin, National Symphony Orchestra
1996	Claude Debussy, *La Mer*	Pierre Boulez, Cleveland Orchestra
1995	Béla Bartók, *Concerto for Orchestra; Four Orchestral Pieces, Op. 12*	Pierre Boulez, Chicago Symphony Orchestra
1994	Béla Bartók, *The Wooden Prince*	Pierre Boulez, Chicago Symphony Orchestra and Chorus
1993	Gustav Mahler, *Symphony No. 9*	Leonard Bernstein, Berlin Philharmonic Orchestra
1992	Leonard Bernstein, *Candide*	Leonard Bernstein, London Symphony Orchestra
1991	Charles Ives, *Symphony No. 2 (and Three Short Works)*	Leonard Bernstein, New York Philharmonic Orchestra
1990	Béla Bartók, *Six String Quartets*	Emerson String Quartet

Source: *NARAS*

The three consecutive awards to Leonard Bernstein in 1991–93 brought his overall Grammy tally to 16.

THREE OF THE BEST

The Three Tenors – Placido Domingo, José Carreras, and Luciano Pavarotti – have brought excerpts of opera and other popular pieces to an audience of billions worldwide.

LATEST WINNERS OF THE "BEST OPERA RECORDING" GRAMMY AWARD

YEAR	COMPOSER/TITLE	SOLOISTS/ORCHESTRA
1999	Bartok, *Bluebeard's Castle*	Jessye Norman, Laszlo Polgar, Karl-August Naegler, Chicago Symphony Orchestra
1998	Richard Wagner, *Die Meistersinger Von Nürnberg*	Ben Heppner, Herbert Lippert, Karita Mattila, Alan Opie, Rene Pape, Jose van Dam, Iris Vermillion, Chicago Symphony Chorus, Chicago Symphony Orchestra
1997	Benjamin Britten, *Peter Grimes*	Philip Langridge, Alan Opie, Janice Watson, Opera London, London Symphony Chorus, City of London Sinfonia
1996	Hector Berlioz, *Les Troyens*	Charles Dutoit, Orchestra Symphonie de Montreal
1995	Carlisle Floyd, *Susannah*	Jerry Hadley, Samuel Ramey, Cheryl Studer, Kenn Chester
1994	George Handel, *Semele*	Kathleen Battle, Marilyn Horne, Samuel Ramey, Sylvia McNair, Michael Chance
1993	Richard Strauss, *Die Frau Ohne Schatten*	Placido Domingo, Jose Van Dam, Hildegard Behrens
1992	Richard Wagner, *Götterdämmerung*	Hildegard Behrens, Ekkehard Wlashiha
1991	Richard Wagner, *Das Rheingold*	James Morris, Kurt Moll, Christa Ludwig
1990	Richard Wagner, *Die Walküre*	Gary Lakes, Jessye Norman, Kurt Moll

Source: *NARAS*

TOP 10 LONGEST OPERAS PERFORMED AT THE ROYAL OPERA HOUSE, COVENT GARDEN

(Opera/composer/running time* in hrs:mins)

1. *Götterdämmerung*, Richard Wagner, 6:0
2. *Die Meistersinger von Nürnberg*, Richard Wagner, 5:40
3. *Siegfried*, Richard Wagner, 5:25
4. *Tristan und Isolde*, Richard Wagner, 5:19
5. *Die Walküre*, Richard Wagner, 5:15
6. *Parsifal*, Richard Wagner, 5:09
7. *Donnerstag aus Licht*, Karlheinz Stockhausen, 4:42
8. *Lohengrin*, Richard Wagner, 4:26
9. *Der Rosenkavalier*, Richard Strauss, 4:25
10. *Don Carlo*, Giuseppe Verdi, 4:19

* Including intervals

TOP 10 MOST PROLIFIC CLASSICAL COMPOSERS

(Composer/nationality/hours of music)

1 Joseph Haydn (1732–1809), Austrian, 340 **2** George Handel (1685–1759), German–English, 303 **3** Wolfgang Amadeus Mozart (1756–91), Austrian, 202 **4** Johann Sebastian Bach (1685–1750), German, 175 **5** Franz Schubert (1797–1828), German, 134 **6** Ludwig van Beethoven (1770–1827), German, 120 **7** Henry Purcell (1659–95), English, 116 **8** Giuseppe Verdi (1813–1901), Italian, 87 **9** Anton Dvořák (1841–1904), Czech, 79 **10** =Franz Liszt (1811–86), Hungarian, 76; =Peter Tchaikovsky (1840–93), Russian, 76

This list is based on a survey conducted by *Classical Music*, which ranked classical composers by the total number of hours of music each composed.

TOP 10 LARGEST OPERA HOUSES

(Opera house/location/total capacity)*

1 The Metropolitan Opera, New York, USA, 4,065 **2** Cincinnati Opera, Cincinnati, USA, 3,630 **3** Lyric Opera of Chicago, Chicago, USA, 3,563 **4** San Francisco Opera, San Francisco, USA 3,476 **5** The Dallas Opera, Dallas, USA, 3,420 **6** Canadian Opera Company, Toronto, Canada, 3,167 **7** Los Angeles Music Center Opera, Los Angeles, USA, 3,098 **8** San Diego Opera, San Diego, USA, 3,076 **9** Seattle Opera, Seattle, USA, 3,017 **10** L'Opéra de Montréal, Montreal, Canada, 2,874

* Seating plus standing, where applicable.

CLASSICAL SOUNDTRACK
The Philadelphia Orchestra's conductor, Leopold Stokowski, led the recording of the 1939 soundtrack of Fantasia, *digitally remastered for the film's 50th anniversary.*

TOP 10 ⭐ CLASSICAL ALBUMS IN THE UK

TITLE/PERFORMER/ORCHESTRA

1 *The Essential Pavarotti*, Luciano Pavarotti
2 *The Three Tenors in Concert*, Carreras, Domingo, Pavarotti
3 *Vivaldi: The Four Seasons*, Nigel Kennedy/English Chamber Orchestra
4 *The Essential Mozart*, Various
5 *Essential Opera*, Various
6 *The Three Tenors – In Concert 1994*, Pavarotti, Mehta, Carreras, Domingo
7 *Mendelssohn/Bruch Violin Concertos*, Nigel Kennedy/English Chamber Orchestra
8 *Brahms: Violin Concerto*, Nigel Kennedy/New Philharmonia Orchestra
9 *Górecki: Symphony No. 3*, London Sinfonia/David Zinman
10 *The Essential Pavarotti, 2*, Luciano Pavarotti

Source: *MRIB*

TOP 10 ⭐ CLASSICAL ALBUMS IN THE US

TITLE/PERFORMER/ORCHESTRA

1 *The Three Tenors in Concert*, Carreras, Domingo, Pavarotti
2 *Chant*, Benedictine Monks of Santo Domingo De Silos
3 *In Concert*, Carreras, Domingo, Pavarotti
4 *Tchaikovsky: Piano Concerto No. 1*, Van Cliburn
5 *Fantasia (50th Anniversary Edition)*, Soundtrack, Philadelphia Orchestra
6 *Perhaps Love*, Placido Domingo
7 *Amadeus*, Neville Marriner
8 *O Holy Night*, Luciano Pavarotti
9 *Tchaikovsky: 1812 Overture/Capriccio Italien*, Antal Dorati/Minneapolis Symphony Orchestra
10 *Switched-On Bach*, Walter Carlos

The *Fantasia* soundtrack contained short pieces or excerpts by a number of composers, including Bach, Beethoven, and Stravinsky. According to some criteria, the soundtrack album of *Titanic* is regarded as a "classical" album; if accepted as such, it would appear at No. 1 in this Top 10.

Did You Know? The shortest opera – *The Sands of Time* by Rees and Reynolds – lasts just 4 minutes.

TOP 10 ★

STAGE & SCREEN

ALL THE WORLD'S A STAGE

TOP 10 ★
FILMS OF SHAKESPEARE PLAYS

	FILM	YEAR
1	William Shakespeare's Romeo & Juliet	1996
2	Romeo and Juliet	1968
3	Much Ado About Nothing	1993
4	Hamlet	1990
5	Henry V	1989
6	Hamlet	1996
7	Richard III	1995
8	Othello	1995
9	The Taming of the Shrew	1967
10	Hamlet	1948

The romantic appeal of *Romeo and Juliet* has ensured its appearance in first and second places, with, respectively, those directed by Baz Luhrmann and Franco Zeffirelli. If all the films of his plays are considered, William Shakespeare could be regarded as the most prolific film writer of all time, with well over 300 cinematic versions made in a period of almost 100 years.

TOP 10 ★
MOST PRODUCED PLAYS BY SHAKESPEARE

	PLAY	PRODUCTIONS
1	Twelfth Night	75
2	Hamlet	74
3=	As You Like It	72
=	The Taming of the Shrew	72
5=	Much Ado About Nothing	68
=	The Merchant of Venice	68
7	A Midsummer Night's Dream	66
8	Macbeth	60
9	The Merry Wives of Windsor	58
10	Romeo and Juliet	56

This Top 10 list, based on analyses of productions staged during the period from 31 December 1878 to 30 April 1998 at Stratford-upon-Avon, and by the Royal Shakespeare Company in London and on tour, provides a reasonable picture of Shakespeare's most popular plays.

STAR-CROSSED LOVERS
Clare Danes and Leonardo DiCaprio starred as the doomed lovers in the 1996 film version of Romeo and Juliet, *directed by Baz Luhrmann.*

TOP 10
MOST-FILMED PLAYS BY SHAKESPEARE

1. *Hamlet* 2. *Romeo and Juliet* 3. *Macbeth* 4. *A Midsummer Night's Dream* 5. *Julius Caesar* 6. *Othello* 7. *Richard III* 8. *Henry V* 9. *The Merchant of Venice* 10. *Antony and Cleopatra*

Counting modern versions, including those in foreign languages, but discounting made-for-TV films, parodies, and derivative stories, *Hamlet* appears to be the most-filmed of Shakespeare's works (70 releases to date), while *Romeo and Juliet* has been remade on at least 40 occasions.

THE 10 ★
LATEST WINNERS OF THE LAURENCE OLIVIER AWARD FOR BEST PLAY*

YEAR	PLAY	PLAYWRIGHT
1999	The Weir	Conor McPherson
1998	Closer	Patrick Marber
1997	Stanley	Pam Gems
1996	Skylight	David Hare
1995	Broken Glass	Arthur Miller
1994	Arcadia	Tom Stoppard
1993	Six Degrees of Separation	John Guare
1992	Death and the Maiden	Ariel Dorfman
1991	Dancing at Lughnasa	Brian Friel
1990	Racing Demon	David Hare

* *"BBC Award for Best Play" until 1996; "Best New Play" thereafter*

Did You Know? If stories derived from Shakespeare's plays were taken into account, *West Side Story* (1961), based on *Romeo and Juliet*, would be second in the list of Top 10 films made of his plays; *Shakespeare in Love* (1998), which focuses on the same play, would come first.

LONGEST-RUNNING SHOWS IN THE UK

SHOW	PERFORMANCES
1 *The Mousetrap* (1952–)	19,289*
2 *Cats* (1981–)	7,656*
3 *No Sex, Please – We're British* (1971–81; 1982–86; 1986–87)	6,761
4 *Starlight Express* (1984–)	6,261*
5 *Les Misérables* (1985–)	5,523*
6 *The Phantom of the Opera* (1986–)	5,177*
7 *Miss Saigon* (1989–)	4,151*
8 *Oliver!* (1960–69)	4,125
9 *Oh! Calcutta!* (1970–80)	3,918
10 *Jesus Christ, Superstar* (1972–80)	3,357

* Still running; total as at 31 March 1999

All the longest-running shows in the UK have been London productions. *The Mousetrap* opened on 25 November 1952 at the Ambassadors Theatre. After 8,862 performances it transferred to St. Martin's Theatre where it re-opened on 25 March 1974. It is not the only play in the world to have run continuously since the 1950s – Eugène Ionesco's *La Cantatrice Chauve* was first performed in Paris on 11 May 1950 and ran, on a double bill with *La Leçon*, until 31 December 1996. The two plays were seen by over 920,000 people.

FELINE SUCCESS

The now-famous poster for the musical Cats, *based on the* Old Possum's Book of Practical Cats *by T.S. Eliot.*

LONGEST-RUNNING MUSICALS IN THE UK

SHOW	PERFORMANCES
1 *Cats* (1981–)	7,656*
2 *Starlight Express* (1984–)	6,261*
3 *Les Misérables* (1985–)	5,523*
4 *The Phantom of the Opera* (1986–)	5,177*
5 *Miss Saigon* (1989–)	4,151*
6 *Oliver!* (1960–69)	4,125
7 *Jesus Christ, Superstar* (1972–80)	3,357
8 *Evita* (1978–86)	2,900
9 *The Sound of Music* (1961–67)	2,386
10 *Salad Days* (1954–60)	2,283

* Still running; total as at 31 March 1999

On 26 January 1996, with its 6,138th performance, *Cats* became the longest-running musical of all time in either the West End or on Broadway.

LATEST WINNERS OF THE AMERICAN EXPRESS AWARD FOR BEST NEW MUSICAL*

YEAR	MUSICAL
1999	*Kat and the Kings*
1998	*Beauty and the Beast*
1997	*Martin Guerre*
1996	*Jolson*
1995	*Once on this Island*
1994	*City of Angels*
1993	*Crazy for You*
1992	*Carmen Jones*
1991	*Sunday in the Park with George*
1990	*Return to the Forbidden Planet*

* Originally called the Laurence Olivier "Musical of the Year" Award

TM© 1981 RUG LTD

CATS

MUSIC BY ANDREW LLOYD WEBBER
BASED ON 'OLD POSSUM'S BOOK OF PRACTICAL CATS' BY T.S. ELIOT

NOW AND FOREVER

FILM HITS & MISSES

TOP 10 HIGHEST-GROSSING FILMS OF ALL TIME

	FILM	YEAR	GROSS INCOME ($) USA	WORLD TOTAL
1	*Titanic*	1998	600,800,000	1,814,800,000
2	*Jurassic Park*	1993	357,100,000	920,100,000
3	*Independence Day*	1996	306,200,000	811,200,000
4	*Star Wars*	1977/97	461,000,000	783,700,000
5	*The Lion King*	1994	312,900,000	766,900,000
6	*E.T.: the Extra-Terrestrial*	1982	399,800,000	704,800,000
7	*Forrest Gump*	1994	329,700,000	679,700,000
8	*The Lost World: Jurassic Park*	1997	229,100,000	614,100,000
9	*Men in Black*	1997	250,100,000	586,100,000
10	*Return of the Jedi*	1983/97	309,100,000	572,900,000

FILM OPENINGS OF ALL TIME IN THE US

	FILM/RELEASE DATE	OPENING WEEKEND GROSS ($)
1	*The Lost World: Jurassic Park**, 23 May 1997	92,729,064
2	*Mission: Impossible**, 22 May 1996	56,811,602
3	*Godzilla*, 20 May 1998	55,726,951
4	*Batman Forever*, 16 June 1995	52,784,433
5	*Men in Black*, 2 July 1997	51,068,455
6	*Independence Day*, 3 July 1996	50,228,264
7	*Jurassic Park*, 11 June 1993	50,159,460
8	*Batman Returns*, 19 June 1992	45,687,711
9	*Batman & Robin*, 20 June 1997	42,872,606
10	*Batman*, 22 June 1989	42,705,884

* Estimate based on four-day holiday weekend

TOP 10 HIGHEST-GROSSING FILMS OF ALL TIME IN THE UK

(Film/year/UK gross in £)

1 *Titanic*, 1998, 68,532,000 **2** *The Full Monty*, 1997, 51,992,000 **3** *Jurassic Park*, 1993, 47,140,000 **4** *Independence Day*, 1996, 36,800,000 **5** *Men in Black*, 1997, 35,400,000 **6** *Four Weddings and a Funeral*, 1994, 27,800,000 **7** *The Lost World: Jurassic Park*, 1997, 25,300,000 **8** *Ghost*, 1990, 23,300,000 **9** *The Lion King*, 1994, 23,100,000 **10** *A Bug's Life*, 1998, 22,894,000

From the nadir of the late 1960s and 1970s, today's films are both more widely viewed (even excluding video) than those of 15 to 25 years ago, as well as grossing considerably more at the box office.

ADULATION AHOY

The phenomenal success of Titanic *catapulted its two young stars (Kate Winslet and Leonardo DiCaprio) into the stratosphere of movie megastardom, making them the darlings of Tinseltown.*

HIGHEST-GROSSING FILMS OF ALL TIME IN THE US

	FILM	YEAR	US GROSS ($)
1	*Titanic*	1998	600,800,000
2	*Star Wars*	1977/97	461,000,000
3	*E.T.: the Extra-Terrestrial*	1982	399,800,000
4	*Jurassic Park*	1993	357,100,000
5	*Forrest Gump*	1994	329,700,000
6	*The Lion King*	1994	312,900,000
7	*Return of the Jedi*	1983/97	309,100,000
8	*Independence Day*	1996	306,200,000
9	*The Empire Strikes Back*	1980/97	290,200,000
10	*Home Alone*	1990	285,800,000

Inevitably, bearing inflation in mind, the top-grossing films of all time are releases from the 1990s, although it is also true that US cinema admissions have risen sharply in recent years.

TOP 10 ★
FILM SEQUELS THAT EARNED THE GREATEST AMOUNT MORE THAN THE ORIGINAL*

ORIGINAL	OUTEARNED BY
1 The Terminator	Terminator 2: Judgment Day
2 First Blood	Rambo: First Blood Part II / Rambo III
3 Die Hard	Die Hard With a Vengeance
4 Lethal Weapon	Lethal Weapon 2/3/4
5 Ace Ventura: Pet Detective	Ace Ventura: When Nature Calls
6 Raiders of the Lost Ark	Indiana Jones and the Last Crusade
7 Star Trek: The Motion Picture	Star Trek IV/VI/ Star Trek: First Contact
8 Patriot Games	Clear and Present Danger
9 The Karate Kid	The Karate Kid, Part II
10 A Nightmare on Elm Street	A Nightmare on Elm Street 3/4/5

* Ranked by greatest differential between original and highest-earning sequel

THE 10 BIGGEST FILM FLOPS OF ALL TIME

(Film/year/estimated loss in $)

❶ *Cutthroat Island*, 1995, 81,000,000
❷ *The Adventures of Baron Munchausen*, 1988, 48,100,000 ❸ *Ishtar*, 1987, 47,300,000 ❹ *Hudson Hawk*, 1991, 47,000,000 ❺ *Inchon*, 1981, 44,100,000 ❻ *The Cotton Club*, 1984, 38,100,000 ❼ *Santa Claus – The Movie*, 1985, 37,000,000 ❽ *Heaven's Gate*, 1980, 34,200,000 ❾ *Billy Bathgate*, 1991, 33,000,000 ❿ *Pirates*, 1986, 30,300,000

Since the figures shown here are based upon North American earnings balanced against the films' original production cost, some may eventually recoup some of their losses via overseas earnings, video, and TV revenue, while for *Inchon* and *Pirates* time has run out.

TOP 10 ★
FILM SERIES OF ALL TIME

FILM SERIES	DATES
1 Star Wars/The Empire Strikes Back/Return of the Jedi/Episode I: The Phantom Menace	1977–99
2 Jurassic Park/The Lost World: Jurassic Park	1993–97
3 Batman/Batman Returns/Batman Forever/Batman & Robin	1989–97
4 Raiders of the Lost Ark/ Indiana Jones and the Temple of Doom/Indiana Jones and the Last Crusade	1981–89
5 Star Trek: The Motion Picture/ Star Trek II/III/IV/V/VI/ Generations/First Contact	1979–96
6 Home Alone/2	1990–92
7 Back to the Future/II/III	1985–90
8 Die Hard/2/Die Hard with a Vengeance	1988–95
9 Jaws/2/3(-D)/: The Revenge	1975–87
10 Rocky/II/III/IV/V	1976–90

Based on total earnings of the original film and all its sequels up to 1998, the *Star Wars* trilogy just beats *Jurassic Park* and its sequel *The Lost World: Jurassic Park*.

TOP 10 ★
MOST EXPENSIVE FILMS EVER MADE

FILM	YEAR	ESTIMATED COST ($)
1 Titanic	1997	200,000,000
2 Waterworld	1995	175,000,000
3 =Armageddon	1998	140,000,000
=Lethal Weapon 4	1998	140,000,000
5 Godzilla	1998	125,000,000
6 Dante's Peak	1997	116,000,000
7 =Batman & Robin	1997	110,000,000
=Speed 2: Cruise Control	1997	110,000,000
=Tomorrow Never Dies	1997	110,000,000

THE CAPED CRUSADER

In the movies, the colourful, comic book treatment of the original TV series gives way to a darker style in which Batman is portrayed as an avenging vigilante whose life is cursed by his endless fight against crime.

What is the most popular time travel film?
see p.172 for the answer
A *Back to the Future*
B *Back to the Future II*
C *Terminator II: Judgment Day*
169

FILMS OF THE DECADES

ADORABLE ALIEN
Steven Spielberg's touching tale of E.T. – an alien creature stranded on Earth and befriended by a fatherless boy – charmed children and adults alike.

* Winner of "Best Picture" Academy Award

Gone with the Wind and *Snow White and the Seven Dwarfs* have generated more income than any other pre-war film.

BIG GUNS
New York secret agents Tommy Lee Jones and Will Smith were the Men in Black who, with some futuristic weaponry and their own razor-sharp wits, saved the Earth from intergalactic terrorists.

TOP 10 ★
FILMS OF THE 1940s

1	Bambi	1942
2	Pinocchio	1940
3	Fantasia	1940
4	Cinderella	1949
5	Song of the South	1946
6	The Best Years of Our Lives*	1946
7	The Bells of St. Mary's	1945
8	Duel in the Sun	1946
9	Mom and Dad	1948
10	Samson and Delilah	1949

* Winner of "Best Picture" Academy Award

With the top four films of the decade classic Disney cartoons, the 1940s may be regarded as the "golden age" of the animated film.

TOP 10 ★
FILMS OF THE 1950s

1	Lady and the Tramp	1955
2	Peter Pan	1953
3	Ben-Hur*	1959
4	The Ten Commandments	1956
5	Sleeping Beauty	1959
6	Around the World in 80 Days*	1956
7=	The Robe	1953
=	The Greatest Show on Earth*	1952
9	The Bridge on the River Kwai*	1957
10	Peyton Place	1957

* Winner of "Best Picture" Academy Award

While the popularity of animated films continued, the 1950s was outstanding as the decade of the "big" picture (in cast and scale).

TOP 10 FILMS OF THE 1960s

1 One Hundred and One Dalmatians, 1961 **2** The Jungle Book, 1967 **3** The Sound of Music*, 1965 **4** Thunderball, 1965 **5** Goldfinger, 1964 **6** Doctor Zhivago, 1965 **7** You Only Live Twice, 1967 **8** The Graduate, 1968 **9** Mary Poppins, 1964 **10** Butch Cassidy and the Sundance Kid, 1969

* Winner of "Best Picture" Academy Award

FILMS OF THE 1970s

1	Star Wars	1977/97
2	Jaws	1975
3	Close Encounters of the Third Kind	1977/80
4	Moonraker	1979
5	The Spy Who Loved Me	1977
6	The Exorcist	1973
7	The Sting*	1973
8	Grease	1978
9	The Godfather*	1972
10	Saturday Night Fever	1977

* Winner of "Best Picture" Academy Award

In the 1970s the arrival of Steven Spielberg and George Lucas set the scene for the high-adventure blockbusters whose domination has continued ever since. Lucas wrote and directed Star Wars, formerly the highest-earning film of all time. Spielberg directed Jaws and wrote and directed Close Encounters of the Third Kind.

FILMS OF THE 1980s

1	E.T.: the Extra-Terrestrial	1982
2	Indiana Jones and the Last Crusade	1989
3	Batman	1989
4	Rain Man	1988
5	Return of the Jedi	1983
6	Raiders of the Lost Ark	1981
7	The Empire Strikes Back	1980
8	Who Framed Roger Rabbit	1988
9	Back to the Future	1985
10	Top Gun	1986

The 1980s was clearly the decade of the adventure film, with George Lucas and Steven Spielberg continuing to assert their control of Hollywood, carving up the Top 10 between them, with Lucas as producer of 5 and 7 and Spielberg director of 1, 2, 6, 8, and 9. The 10 highest-earning films scooped in more than $4 billion between them at the global box office.

WHEN DINOSAURS ROAMED THE EARTH...

A monster movie in more ways than one, The Lost World: Jurassic Park, with its breathtaking dinosaur creations, grossed $611 million.

FILMS OF THE 1990s

1	Titanic*	1997
2	Jurassic Park	1993
3	Independence Day	1996
4	The Lion King	1994
5	Forrest Gump*	1994
6	The Lost World: Jurassic Park	1997
7	Men in Black	1997
8	Home Alone	1990
9	Ghost	1990
10	Terminator 2: Judgment Day	1991

* Winner of "Best Picture" Academy Award

Each of the Top 10 films of the present decade has earned more than $500 million around the world, a total of almost $8 billion between them.

Did You Know? If the income of *Gone with the Wind* was adjusted to allow for inflation in the period since its release, it could be regarded as the most successful film ever.

171

FILM GENRES

TIME TRAVEL FILMS

1	Terminator II: Judgment Day	1991
2	Back to the Future	1985
3	Back to the Future III	1990
4	Back to the Future II	1989
5	Timecop	1994
6	The Terminator	1984
7	Time Bandits	1981
8	Bill and Ted's Excellent Adventure	1989
9	Highlander III: The Sorcerer	1994
10	Highlander	1986

VAMPIRE FILMS

1	Interview with the Vampire	1994
2	Bram Stoker's Dracula	1992
3	Love at First Bite	1979
4	The Lost Boys	1987
5	Dracula	1979
6	Fright Night	1985
7	Vampire in Brooklyn	1995
8	Buffy the Vampire Slayer	1992
9	Dracula: Dead and Loving It	1995
10	Transylvania 6-5000	1985

HORROR FILMS

1	Jurassic Park	1993
2	The Lost World: Jurassic Park	1997
3	Jaws	1975
4	Godzilla	1998
5	The Exorcist	1973/98
6	Interview with the Vampire	1994
7	Jaws II	1978
8	Bram Stoker's Dracula	1992
9	Scream	1996
10	Scream 2	1997

COMEDY FILMS

1	Forrest Gump	1994
2	Home Alone	1990
3	Ghost	1990
4	Pretty Woman	1990
5	Mrs. Doubtfire	1993
6	The Flintstones	1994
7	Who Framed Roger Rabbit	1988
8	There's Something About Mary	1998
9	The Mask	1994
10	Beverly Hills Cop	1984

GHOST FILMS

1	Ghost	1990
2	Ghostbusters	1984
3	Casper	1995
4	Ghostbusters II	1989
5	Beetlejuice	1988
6	Scrooged	1988
7	The Frighteners	1996
8	Ghost Dad	1990
9	Hamlet	1990
10	The Sixth Man	1997

SCIENCE-FICTION FILMS

1	Jurassic Park	1993
2	Independence Day	1996
3	Star Wars	1977/97
4	E.T.: the Extra-Terrestrial	1982
5	The Lost World: Jurassic Park	1997
6	Men in Black	1997
7	The Empire Strikes Back	1980/97
8	Terminator 2: Judgment Day	1991
9	Return of the Jedi	1983/97
10	Batman	1989

DOUBLE-ACT WITH A DIFFERENCE

The adventures of C-3P0, the pessimistic robot diplomat, and his sidekick, R2-D2, were a central element of the Star Wars films. Their endearing personalities made them as popular as their human co-stars.

TOP 10 ★
WAR FILMS

1	Saving Private Ryan	1998
2	Platoon	1986
3	Good Morning, Vietnam	1987
4	Apocalypse Now	1979
5	M*A*S*H	1970
6	Patton	1970
7	The Deer Hunter	1978
8	Full Metal Jacket	1987
9	Midway	1976
10	The Dirty Dozen	1967

Until the hugely successful and Oscar-winning *Saving Private Ryan*, surprisingly few war films appeared in the high-earning bracket in the late 1990s, which led some to consider that the days of big-budget films in this genre were over. The release of *The Thin Red Line* in 1998 to critical acclaim, however, put this genre firmly back on the map. This list excludes successful films that are not technically "war" films but which have military themes.

TOP 10 ★
COP FILMS

1	Die Hard with a Vengeance	1995
2	The Fugitive	1993
3	Basic Instinct	1992
4	Se7en	1995
5	Lethal Weapon 3	1993
6	Beverly Hills Cop	1984
7	Beverly Hills Cop II	1987
8	Lethal Weapon 4	1998
9	Speed	1994
10	Lethal Weapon 2	1989

Although films in which one of the central characters is a policeman have never been among the most successful films of all time, many have earned respectable amounts at the box office. They are divided between those with a comic slant, such as all three *Beverly Hills Cop* films, and darker police thrillers, such as *Basic Instinct*. Films featuring FBI and CIA agents have been excluded here, thus eliminating blockbusters such as *Mission: Impossible* and *The Silence of the Lambs*.

EXPLOSIVE ACTION
Die Hard with a Vengeance, *the third in the series, outgrossed its two predecessors in terms of both box office takings and graphically portrayed violence.*

TOP 10 ★
DISASTER FILMS

1	Titanic	1997
2	Twister	1996
3	Die Hard with a Vengeance	1995
4	Apollo 13	1995
5	Outbreak	1995
6	Dante's Peak	1997
7	Daylight	1996
8	Die Hard	1988
9	Volcano	1997
10	Die Hard 2	1990

Disasters involving blazing buildings, natural disasters such as volcanoes, earthquakes, and tidal waves, train and air crashes, sinking ships, and terrorist attacks, have long been a high-earning staple of Hollywood films.

Which was the most successful Tom Cruise film?
see p.180 for the answer

A *Top Gun*
B *Mission: Impossible*
C *Jerry Maguire*

OSCAR-WINNING FILMS

HIGHEST-EARNING "BEST PICTURE" OSCAR WINNERS

	FILM	YEAR
1	Titanic	1997
2	Forrest Gump	1994
3	Dances with Wolves	1990
4	Rain Man	1988
5	Schindler's List	1993
6	The English Patient	1996
7	Braveheart	1995
8	Gone with the Wind	1939
9	The Sound of Music	1965
10	The Sting	1973

Winning the Academy Award for "Best Picture" is no guarantee of box-office success: the award is given for a picture released the previous year, and by the time the Oscar ceremony takes place, the film-going public has already effectively decided on the winning picture's fate. Receiving the Oscar may enhance a successful picture's continuing earnings, but it is generally too late to revive a film that may already have been judged mediocre.

TOP 10 FILMS TO WIN THE MOST OSCARS*

	FILM	YEAR	NOMINATIONS	AWARDS
1 =	Ben-Hur	1959	12	11
=	Titanic	1997	14	11
3	West Side Story	1961	11	10
4 =	Gigi	1958	9	9
=	The Last Emperor	1987	9	9
=	The English Patient	1996	12	9
7 =	Gone with the Wind	1939	13	8#
=	From Here to Eternity	1953	13	8
=	On the Waterfront	1954	12	8
=	My Fair Lady	1964	12	8
=	Cabaret	1972	10	8
=	Gandhi	1982	11	8
=	Amadeus	1984	11	8

* Oscar® is a Registered Trade Mark

\# Plus two special awards

VOYAGE OF DOOM

The enormous global success of Titanic ensured it a place in cinematic history. Despite the enormous cost of making the film, the profits were huge.

TOP 10 FILMS NOMINATED FOR THE MOST OSCARS

(Film/year/awards/nominations)

1 = *All About Eve*, 1950, 6, 14; = *Titanic*, 1997, 11, 14 **3** *Gone with the Wind*, 1939 ,8*, 13; = *From Here to Eternity*, 1953, 8, 13; = *Mary Poppins*, 1964, 5, 13; = *Who's Afraid of Virginia Woolf?*, 1966, 5, 13; = *Forrest Gump*, 1994, 6, 13; = *Shakespeare in Love*, 1998, 7, 13 **9** = *Mrs. Miniver*, 1942, 6, 12; = *The Song of Bernadette*, 1943, 4, 12; = *Johnny Belinda*, 1948, 1, 12; = *A Streetcar Named Desire*, 1951, 4, 12; = *On the Waterfront*, 1954, 8, 12; = *Ben-Hur*, 1959, 11, 12; = *Becket*, 1964, 1, 12; = *My Fair Lady*, 1964, 8, 12; = *Reds*, 1981, 3, 12; = *Dances with Wolves*, 1990, 7, 12; = *Schindler's List*, 1993, 7, 12; = *The English Patient*, 1996 , 9, 12

* Plus two special awards

SOME REGAL ADVICE
Dame Judi Dench as Queen Elizabeth in Shakespeare in Love warns Colin Firth about his future wife's attraction to the playhouse.

THE 10 "BEST PICTURE" OSCAR WINNERS OF THE 1950s

(Year/film)

1950 *All About Eve* **1951** *An American in Paris* **1952** *The Greatest Show on Earth* **1953** *From Here to Eternity* **1954** *On the Waterfront* **1955** *Marty* **1956** *Around the World in 80 Days* **1957** *The Bridge on the River Kwai* **1958** *Gigi* **1959** *Ben-Hur*

THE 10 "BEST PICTURE" OSCAR WINNERS OF THE 1960s

(Year/film)

1960 *The Apartment* **1961** *West Side Story* **1962** *Lawrence of Arabia* **1963** *Tom Jones* **1964** *My Fair Lady* **1965** *The Sound of Music* **1966** *A Man for All Seasons* **1967** *In the Heat of the Night* **1968** *Oliver!* **1969** *Midnight Cowboy*

THE 10 ★ "BEST PICTURE" OSCAR WINNERS OF THE 1970s

YEAR	FILM
1970	Patton
1971	The French Connection
1972	The Godfather
1973	The Sting
1974	The Godfather Part II
1975	One Flew Over the Cuckoo's Nest*
1976	Rocky
1977	Annie Hall
1978	The Deer Hunter
1979	Kramer vs. Kramer

* *Winner of Oscars for "Best Director", "Best Actor", "Best Actress", and "Best Screenplay"*

THE 10 ★ "BEST PICTURE" OSCAR WINNERS OF THE 1980s

YEAR	FILM
1980	Ordinary People
1981	Chariots of Fire
1982	Gandhi
1983	Terms of Endearment
1984	Amadeus
1985	Out of Africa
1986	Platoon
1987	The Last Emperor
1988	Rain Man
1989	Driving Miss Daisy

THE 10 ★ LATEST "BEST PICTURE" OSCAR WINNERS

YEAR	FILM
1998	Shakespeare in Love
1997	Titanic
1996	The English Patient
1995	Braveheart
1994	Forrest Gump
1993	Schindler's List
1992	Unforgiven
1991	The Silence of the Lambs
1990	Dances with Wolves
1989	Driving Miss Daisy

TOP 10 STUDIOS WITH THE MOST "BEST PICTURE" OSCARS

(Studio/awards)

1 United Artists, 13 **2** Columbia, 12 **3** Paramount, 11 **4** MGM, 9 **5** Twentieth Century Fox, 7 **6** Warner Bros, 6 **7** Universal, 5 **8** Orion, 4 **9** RKO, 2 **10** Miramax, 1

Did You Know? Both *The Turning Point* (1977) and *The Color Purple* (1985) suffered the ignominy of receiving 11 Oscar nominations without a single win.

OSCAR-WINNING STARS

THE 10 ★
"BEST ACTOR" OSCAR WINNERS OF THE 1970s

YEAR	ACTOR/FILM
1970	George C. Scott, *Patton**
1971	Gene Hackman, *The French Connection**
1972	Marlon Brando, *The Godfather**
1973	Jack Lemmon, *Save the Tiger*
1974	Art Carney, *Harry and Tonto*
1975	Jack Nicholson, *One Flew Over the Cuckoo's Nest***#*
1976	Peter Finch, *Network*
1977	Richard Dreyfuss, *The Goodbye Girl*
1978	John Voight, *Coming Home*
1979	Dustin Hoffman, *Kramer vs. Kramer**

* Winner of "Best Picture" Oscar

\# Winner of "Best Director", "Best Actress", and "Best Screenplay" Oscars

THE 10 ★
"BEST ACTRESS" OSCAR WINNERS OF THE 1970s

YEAR	ACTRESS/FILM
1970	Glenda Jackson, *Women in Love*
1971	Jane Fonda, *Klute*
1972	Liza Minelli, *Cabaret*
1973	Glenda Jackson, *A Touch of Class*
1974	Ellen Burstyn, *Alice Doesn't Live Here Any More*
1975	Louise Fletcher, *One Flew Over the Cuckoo's Nest***#*
1976	Faye Dunaway, *Network*
1977	Diane Keaton, *Annie Hall**
1978	Jane Fonda, *Coming Home*
1979	Sally Field, *Norma Rae*

* Winner of "Best Picture" Oscar

\# Winner of "Best Director", "Best Actor", and "Best Screenplay" Oscars

FIGHTING FOR SUCCESS

Robert De Niro won the 1980 Best Actor award for his role in Raging Bull. The film marked his fourth collaboration with director Martin Scorsese.

THE 10 ★
OLDEST OSCAR-WINNING ACTORS AND ACTRESSES

	ACTOR OR ACTRESS	AWARD/FILM (WHERE SPECIFIED)	YEAR	AGE*
1	Jessica Tandy	"Best Actress" (*Driving Miss Daisy*)	1989	80
2	George Burns	"Best Supporting Actor" (*The Sunshine Boys*)	1975	80
3	Melvyn Douglas	"Best Supporting Actor" (*Being There*)	1979	79
4	John Gielgud	"Best Supporting Actor" (*Arthur*)	1981	77
5	Don Ameche	"Best Supporting Actor" (*Cocoon*)	1985	77
6	Peggy Ashcroft	"Best Supporting Actress" (*A Passage to India*)	1984	77
7	Henry Fonda	"Best Actor" (*On Golden Pond*)	1981	76
8	Katharine Hepburn	"Best Actress" (*On Golden Pond*)	1981	74
9	Edmund Gwenn	"Best Supporting Actor" (*Miracle on 34th Street*)	1947	72
10	Ruth Gordon	"Best Supporting Actress" (*Rosemary's Baby*)	1968	72

* At the time of the Award ceremony; those of apparently identical age have been ranked according to their precise age in days at the time of the ceremony

THE 10 ★
YOUNGEST OSCAR-WINNING ACTORS AND ACTRESSES

	ACTOR OR ACTRESS	AWARD/FILM (WHERE SPECIFIED)	YEAR	AGE*
1	Shirley Temple	Special Award – outstanding contribution during 1934	1934	6
2	Margaret O' Brien	Special Award (*Meet Me in St Louis*)	1944	8
3	Vincent Winter	Special Award (*The Little Kidnappers*)	1954	8
4	Ivan Jandl	Special Award (*The Search*)	1948	9
5	Jon Whiteley	Special Award (*The Little Kidnappers*)	1954	10
6	Tatum O'Neal	"Best Supporting Actress" (*Paper Moon*)	1973	10
7	Anna Paquin	"Best Supporting Actress" (*The Piano*)	1993	11
8	Claude Jarman Jr.	Special Award (*The Yearling*)	1946	12
9	Bobby Driscoll	Special Award (*The Window*)	1949	13
10	Hayley Mills	Special Award (*Pollyanna*)	1960	13

* At the time of the Award ceremony; those of apparently identical age have been ranked according to their precise age in days at the time of the ceremony

The Academy Awards ceremony usually takes place at the end of March in the year following that in which the film was released in the US, so the winners are generally at least a year older when they receive their Oscars than when they acted in their award-winning films.

Did You Know? Peter Finch was the first "Best Actor" to be honoured posthumously: he died on 14 January 1977, and the award was announced on 28 March 1977.

THE 10 ⭐
"BEST ACTOR" OSCAR WINNERS OF THE 1980s

YEAR	ACTOR/FILM
1980	Robert De Niro, *Raging Bull*
1981	Henry Fonda, *On Golden Pond**
1982	Ben Kingsley, *Gandhi*#
1983	Robert Duvall, *Tender Mercies*
1984	F. Murray Abraham, *Amadeus*#
1985	William Hurt, *Kiss of the Spider Woman*
1986	Paul Newman, *The Color of Money*
1987	Michael Douglas, *Wall Street*
1988	Dustin Hoffman, *Rain Man*#
1989	Daniel Day-Lewis, *My Left Foot*

* *Winner of "Best Actress" Oscar*

Winner of "Best Picture" Oscar

THE 10 ⭐
"BEST ACTRESS" OSCAR WINNERS OF THE 1980s

YEAR	ACTRESS/FILM
1980	Sissy Spacek, *Coal Miner's Daughter*
1981	Katharine Hepburn, *On Golden Pond**
1982	Meryl Streep, *Sophie's Choice*
1983	Shirley MacLaine, *Terms of Endearment*#
1984	Sally Field, *Places in the Heart*
1985	Geraldine Page, *The Trip to Bountiful*
1986	Marlee Matlin, *Children of a Lesser God*
1987	Cher, *Moonstruck*
1988	Jodie Foster, *The Accused*
1989	Jessica Tandy, *Driving Miss Daisy*#

* *Winner of "Best Actor" Oscar*

Winner of "Best Picture" Oscar

THE 10 ⭐
LATEST "BEST ACTOR" OSCAR WINNERS

YEAR	ACTOR/FILM
1998	Roberto Benigni, *La vita è bella (Life Is Beautiful)*
1997	Jack Nicholson, *As Good As It Gets*#
1996	Geoffrey Rush, *Shine*
1995	Nicolas Cage, *Leaving Las Vegas*
1994	Tom Hanks, *Forrest Gump**
1993	Tom Hanks, *Philadelphia*
1992	Al Pacino, *Scent of a Woman*
1991	Anthony Hopkins, *The Silence of the Lambs**#
1990	Jeremy Irons, *Reversal of Fortune*
1989	Daniel Day-Lewis, *My Left Foot*

* *Winner of "Best Picture" Oscar*

Winner of "Best Actress" Oscar

Tom Hanks shares the honour of consecutive wins with Spencer Tracy, who was awarded an Oscar in 1937 and 1938. Only three other actors have won twice: Marlon Brando (1954; 1972), Gary Cooper (1941; 1952), and Dustin Hoffman (1977; 1988).

THE 10 LATEST "BEST ACTRESS" OSCAR WINNERS

(Year/actress/film)

1998 Gwyneth Paltrow, *Shakespeare in Love* **1997** Helen Hunt, *As Good As It Gets** **1996** Frances McDormand, *Fargo* **1995** Susan Sarandon, *Dead Man Walking* **1994** Jessica Lange, *Blue Sky* **1993** Holly Hunter, *The Piano* **1992** Emma Thompson, *Howards End* **1991** Jodie Foster, *The Silence of the Lambs**# **1990** Kathy Bates, *Misery* **1989** Jessica Tandy, *Driving Miss Daisy*#

* *Winner of "Best Actor" Oscar*

Winner of "Best Picture" Oscar

OSCAR CEREMONY

Some of the winners for 1998 films: Roberto Benigni, Dame Judi Dench, Gwyneth Paltrow, and James Coburn.

AND THE WINNER IS...

FIRST WINNERS OF THE BAFTA "BEST ACTOR" AWARD

YEAR	ACTOR/FILM/COUNTRY
1968	Spencer Tracy, *Guess Who's Coming to Dinner* (USA)
1969	Dustin Hoffman, *Midnight Cowboy* (USA) and *John and Mary* (USA)
1970	Robert Redford, *Butch Cassidy and the Sundance Kid* (USA), *Tell Them Willie Boy is Here* (USA), and *Downhill Racer* (USA)
1971	Peter Finch, *Sunday, Bloody Sunday* (UK)
1972	Gene Hackman, *The French Connection* (USA) and *The Poseidon Adventure* (USA)
1973	Walter Matthau, *Pete 'n Tillie* (USA) and *Charley Varrick* (USA)
1974	Jack Nicholson, *The Last Detail* (USA) and *Chinatown* (USA)
1975	Al Pacino, *The Godfather Part II* (USA) and *Dog Day Afternoon* (USA)
1976	Jack Nicholson, *One Flew Over the Cuckoo's Nest* (USA)
1977	Peter Finch, *Network* (USA)

Other than Peter Finch's double, British actors made a poor showing in the early years of the BAFTA "Best Actor" award. However, the balance was redressed in the early 1980s with wins for John Hurt in *The Elephant Man* (1980), Ben Kingsley in *Gandhi* (1982), and Michael Caine in *Educating Rita*.

THE 10 LATEST WINNERS OF THE BAFTA "BEST ACTOR" AWARD
(Year/actor/film/country)

1998 Roberto Benigni, *La vita bella (Life is Beautiful)* (Italy) **1997** Robert Carlyle, *The Full Monty* (UK) **1996** Geoffrey Rush, *Shine* (Australia) **1995** Nigel Hawthorne, *The Madness of King George* (UK) **1994** Hugh Grant, *Four Weddings and a Funeral* (UK) **1993** Anthony Hopkins, *The Remains of the Day* (UK) **1992** Robert Downey Jr., *Chaplin* (UK) **1991** Anthony Hopkins, *The Silence of the Lambs* (USA) **1990** Philippe Noiret, *Cinema Paradiso* (Italy/France) **1989** Daniel Day Lewis, *My Left Foot* (UK)

FIRST CANNES FESTIVAL GRAND PRIZE/PALME D'OR AWARDS

YEAR	DIRECTOR/FILM/COUNTRY
1949	Carol Reed, *The Third Man* (UK)
1950	No festival
1951	Vittorio De Sica, *Miracle in Milan* (Italy) and Alf Sjöberg, *Miss Julie* (Sweden)*
1952	Orson Welles, *Othello* (Morocco) and Renato Castellani, *Two Cents Worth of Hope* (Italy)*
1953	Henri-Georges Clouzot, *Wages of Fear* (France)
1954	Teinosuke Kinugasa, *Gates of Hell* (Japan)
1955	Delbart Mann, *Marty* (USA)
1956	Louis Malle and Jacques-Yves Cousteau, *World of Silence* (France)
1957	William Wyler, *Friendly Persuasion* (USA)
1958	Mikhail Kalatozov, *The Cranes Are Flying* (USSR)
1959	Marcel Camus, *Black Orpheus* (France)

* Prize shared

THE FIRST WINNERS OF THE BAFTA "BEST ACTRESS" AWARD
(Year/actress/film/country)

1968 Katharine Hepburn, *Guess Who's Coming to Dinner* (USA) and *The Lion in Winter* (UK) **1969** Maggie Smith, *The Pride of Miss Jean Brodie* (UK) **1970** Katharine Ross, *Tell Them Willie Boy is Here* (USA) and *Butch Cassidy and the Sundance Kid* (USA) **1971** Glenda Jackson, *Sunday, Bloody Sunday* (UK) **1972** Liza Minnelli, *Cabaret* (USA) **1973** Stephane Audrane, *The Discreet Charm of the Bourgeoisie* (France/Spain/Italy) and *Just Before Nightfall* (France) **1974** Joanne Woodward, *Summer Wishes, Winter Dreams* (USA) **1975** Ellen Burstyn, *Alice Doesn't Live Here Anymore* (USA) **1976** Louise Fletcher, *One Flew Over the Cuckoo's Nest* (USA) **1977** Diane Keaton, *Annie Hall* (USA)

OFF TO CHURCH
Four Weddings and a Funeral was a low-budget film that shot to success and made Hugh Grant a household name.

THE 10 ★
LATEST WINNERS OF THE CANNES PALME D'OR FOR "BEST FILM"

YEAR	FILM/COUNTRY
1998	*Eternity and a Day* (Greece)
1997	*The Eel* (Japan)/ *The Taste of Cherries* (Iran)
1996	*Secrets and Lies* (UK)
1995	*Underground* (Yugoslavia)
1994	*Pulp Fiction* (USA)
1993	*Farewell My Concubine* (China)/ *The Piano* (Australia)
1992	*Best Intentions* (Denmark)
1991	*Barton Fink* (USA)
1990	*Wild at Heart* (USA)
1989	*sex, lies, and videotape* (USA)

In the early years of the Cannes Film Festival there was no single "Best Film" award. Several films were honoured jointly, including such unlikely bedfellows as David Lean's *Brief Encounter* and Walt Disney's *Dumbo*. Since 1955, the "Grand Prize" has been known as the "Palme d'Or".

THE 10 ★
FIRST WINNERS OF THE BAFTA "BEST DIRECTOR" AWARD

YEAR	DIRECTOR/FILM/COUNTRY
1968	Mike Nichols, *The Graduate* (USA)
1969	John Schlesinger, *Midnight Cowboy* (USA)
1970	George Roy Hill, *Butch Cassidy and the Sundance Kid* (USA)
1971	John Schlesinger, *Sunday, Bloody Sunday* (UK)
1972	Bob Fosse, *Cabaret* (USA)
1973	François Truffault, *Day For Night* (France)
1974	Roman Polanski, *Chinatown* (USA)
1975	Stanley Kubrick, *Barry Lyndon* (UK)
1976	Milos Forman, *One Flew Over the Cuckoo's Nest* (USA)
1977	Woody Allen, *Annie Hall* (USA)

FEMME FATALE
Uma Thurman plays an enigmatic temptress in Quentin Tarantino's Pulp Fiction. The film won the Palme d'Or at Cannes in 1994.

THE 10 ★
LATEST WINNERS OF THE BAFTA "BEST FILM" AWARD

YEAR	FILM/COUNTRY
1998	*Shakespeare in Love* (USA)
1997	*The Full Monty* (UK)
1996	*The English Patient* (UK)
1995	*Sense and Sensibility* (UK)
1994	*Four Weddings and a Funeral* (UK)
1993	*Schindler's List* (USA)
1992	*Howards End* (UK)
1991	*The Commitments* (USA/UK)
1990	*GoodFellas* (USA)
1989	*Dead Poets Society* (USA)

THE 10 LATEST WINNERS OF THE BAFTA "BEST ACTRESS" AWARD

(Year/actress/film/country)

1998 Cate Blanchett in *Elizabeth* (UK), **1997** Judi Dench in *Mrs. Brown* (UK) **1996** Brenda Blethyn in *Secrets and Lies* (UK) **1995** Emma Thompson in *Sense and Sensibility* (UK) **1994** Susan Sarandon in *The Client* (USA) **1993** Holly Hunter in *The Piano* (Australia) **1992** Emma Thompson in *Howards End* (UK) **1991** Jodie Foster in *The Silence of the Lambs* (USA) **1990** Jessica Tandy in *Driving Miss Daisy* (USA) **1989** Pauline Collins in *Shirley Valentine* (USA/UK)

THE 10 ★
LATEST WINNERS OF THE BAFTA "BEST DIRECTOR" AWARD

YEAR	DIRECTOR/FILM/COUNTRY
1998	Peter Weir, *The Truman Show* (USA)
1997	Baz Luhrmann, *William Shakespeare's Romeo & Juliet* (USA)
1996	Joel Cohen, *Fargo* (USA)
1995	Michael Radford, *Il Postino* (Italy)
1994	Mike Newell, *Four Weddings and a Funeral* (UK)
1993	Steven Spielberg, *Schindler's List* (USA)
1992	Robert Altman, *The Player* (USA)
1991	Alan Parker, *The Commitments* (USA/UK)
1990	Martin Scorsese, *GoodFellas* (USA)
1989	Kenneth Branagh, *Henry V* (UK)

THE 10 FIRST WINNERS OF THE BAFTA "BEST FILM" AWARD

(Year/film/country)

1947 *The Best Years of Our Lives* (USA) **1948** *Hamlet* (UK) **1949** *Bicycle Thieves* (Italy) **1950** *All About Eve* (USA) **1951** *La Ronde* (France) **1952** *The Sound Barrier* (UK) **1953** *Jeux Interdits* (France) **1954** *Le Salaire de la Peur* (France) **1955** *Richard III* (UK) **1956** *Gervaise* (France)

Did You Know? Although the Cannes Film Festival was established in 1939, World War II delayed its inaugural ceremony until 1946.

179

FILM ACTORS

TOP 10 ★
BRAD PITT FILMS

1	Se7en	1995
2	Interview with the Vampire	1994
3	Sleepers	1996
4	Legends of the Fall	1994
5	Twelve Monkeys	1995
6	The Devil's Own	1997
7	Seven Years in Tibet	1997
8	Meet Joe Black	1998
9	Thelma & Louise	1991
10	A River Runs Through It	1992

TOP 10 ★
TOM CRUISE FILMS

1	Mission: Impossible	1996
2	Rain Man	1988
3	Top Gun	1986
4	Jerry Maguire	1996
5	The Firm	1993
6	A Few Good Men	1992
7	Interview with the Vampire	1994
8	Days of Thunder	1990
9	Cocktail	1988
10	Born on the Fourth of July*	1989

Nominated for Academy Award for "Best Actor"

TOP 10 ★
ARNOLD SCHWARZENEGGER FILMS

1	Terminator 2: Judgment Day	1991
2	True Lies	1994
3	Total Recall	1990
4	Eraser	1996
5	Twins	1988
6	Kindergarten Cop	1990
7	Jingle All the Way	1996
8	Last Action Hero	1993
9	Junior	1994
10	The Terminator	1984

TOP 10 JACK NICHOLSON FILMS

❶ *Batman*, 1989 ❷ *A Few Good Men*, 1992 ❸ *As Good As It Gets**, 1997 ❹ *Terms of Endearment*#, 1983 ❺ *Wolf*, 1994 ❻ *One Flew Over the Cuckoo's Nest**, 1975 ❼ *Mars Attacks!*, 1996 ❽ *The Witches of Eastwick*, 1987 ❾ *The Shining*, 1980 ❿ *Broadcast News*, 1987

* Academy Award for "Best Actor"
 # Academy Award for "Best Supporting Actor"

TOP 10 TOM HANKS FILMS

❶ *Forrest Gump**, 1994 ❷ *Saving Private Ryan*, 1998 ❸ *Apollo 13*, 1995 ❹ *Sleepless in Seattle*, 1993 ❺ *Philadelphia**, 1993 ❻ *Big*, 1998 ❼ *You've Got Mail*, 1998 ❽ *A League of Their Own*, 1992 ❾ *Turner & Hooch*, 1989 ❿ *Splash!*, 1984

*Academy Award for "Best Actor"

TOP 10 ⭐
SAMUEL L. JACKSON FILMS

1	*Jurassic Park*	1993
2	*Die Hard with a Vengeance*	1995
3	*Coming to America*	1988
4	*Pulp Fiction*	1994
5	*Patriot Games*	1992
6	*A Time to Kill*	1996
7	*Sea of Love*	1989
8	*Jackie Brown*	1997
9	*The Long Kiss Goodnight*	1996
10	*Sphere*	1998

TOP 10 ⭐
MEL GIBSON FILMS

1	*Lethal Weapon 4*	1998
2	*Lethal Weapon 2*	1989
3	*Lethal Weapon 3*	1992
4	*Braveheart**	1995
5	*Ransom*	1996
6	*Forever Young*	1992
7	*Maverick*	1994
8	*Bird on a Wire*	1990
9	*Lethal Weapon*	1987
10	*Tequila Sunrise*	1988

* Academy Award for "Best Director"

TOP 10 NICOLAS CAGE FILMS

1 *The Rock*, 1996 **2** *Face/Off*, 1997 **3** *Con Air*, 1997 **4** *City of Angels*, 1998 **5** *Snake Eyes*, 1998 **6** *Moonstruck*, 1987 **7** *Leaving Las Vegas*, 1995 **8** *Peggy Sue Got Married*, 1986 **9** *It Could Happen to You*, 1994 **10** *Honeymoon in Vegas*, 1992

DISCO MANIA

John Travolta in Saturday Night Fever wowed 1970s cinema goers with his energetic dance routines and that famous white suit.

TOP 10 ⭐
JOHN TRAVOLTA FILMS

1	*Face/Off*	1997
2	*Grease*	1978
3	*Look Who's Talking*	1989
4	*Saturday Night Fever**	1977
5	*Pulp Fiction*	1994
6	*Phenomenon*	1996
7	*Broken Arrow*	1996
8	*Staying Alive*	1983
9	*Get Shorty*	1995
10	*Michael*	1996

* Nominated for Academy Award for "Best Actor"

GRIM REALISM

Despite the overwhelming critical acclaim for Saving Private Ryan, *and for Tom Hanks' profoundly moving performance, neither "Best Picture" nor "Best Actor" were among the five Academy Awards won by this film.*

TOP 10 JOHNNY DEPP FILMS

1 *Platoon*, 1986 **2** *Donnie Brasco*, 1997 **3** *Edward Scissorhands*, 1990 **4** *Don Juan DeMarco*, 1995 **5** *Freddy's Dead: The Final Nightmare**, 1991 **6** *A Nightmare on Elm Street*, 1984 **7** *Fear and Loathing in Las Vegas*, 1998 **8** *What's Eating Gilbert Grape*, 1993 **9** *Cry-Baby*, 1990 **10** *Nick of Time*, 1995

* Uncredited appearance

HOLLYWOOD HEART-THROB

Despite his pin-up image, Johnny Depp tends to be associated with films with artistic integrity such as the poignant What's Eating Gilbert Grape.

Which Jim Carrey film has been the most successful?
see p.185 for the answer

A *The Mask*
B *Liar Liar*
C *Batman Forever*

FILM ACTRESSES

TOP 10 ★
JODIE FOSTER FILMS

1	*The Silence of the Lambs**	1990
2	*Maverick*	1994
3	*Contact*	1997
4	*Sommersby*	1993
5	*Nell*#	1994
6	*The Accused**	1988
7	*Taxi Driver*#	1976
8	*Freaky Friday*	1976
9	*Little Man Tate*+	1991
10	*Home for the Holidays**	1995

* *Academy Award for "Best Actress"*

\# *Academy Award nomination*

+ *Acted and directed*

★ *Directed only*

After a career as a child TV star, Jodie Foster (born 19 November 1962, Los Angeles, California) moved into films at the age of 10, oscillating roles between childish innocence and street-wise "bad girl". She won Best Actress Oscars for *The Accused* and *The Silence of the Lambs*, since when she has launched into directing with *Little Man Tate*.

TOP 10 ★
WINONA RYDER FILMS

1	*Bram Stoker's Dracula*	1992
2	*Alien: Resurrection*	1997
3	*Edward Scissorhands*	1990
4	*Beetlejuice*	1988
5	*Little Women*	1994
6	*Mermaids*	1990
7	*The Age of Innocence*	1993
8	*How to Make an American Quilt*	1995
9	*Reality Bites*	1994
10	*The Crucible*	1996

TOP 10 ★
UMA THURMAN FILMS

1	*Batman & Robin*	1997
2	*Pulp Fiction*	1994
3	*The Truth About Cats & Dogs*	1996
4	*The Avengers*	1998
5	*Dangerous Liaisons*	1988
6	*Final Analysis*	1992
7	*Beautiful Girls*	1996
8	*Johnny Be Good*	1988
9	*Gattaca*	1997
10	*Les Misérables*	1998

TOP 10 DEMI MOORE FILMS

1 *Ghost*, 1990 **2** *Indecent Proposal*, 1993 **3** *A Few Good Men*, 1992 **4** *Disclosure*, 1995 **5** *Striptease*, 1996 **6** *G.I. Jane*, 1997 **7** *The Juror*, 1996 **8** *About Last Night*, 1986 **9** *St. Elmo's Fire*, 1985 **10** *Young Doctors in Love*, 1982

Demi Moore has progressed from working as a teenaged model through the TV soap *General Hospital* to Hollywood movies. She provided the voice of Esmeralda in the animated film *The Hunchback of Notre Dame* (1996). If included in her Top 10, it would be in second place. Although uncredited, her voice appears in *Beavis and Butt-head Do America* (1996), which would also merit a place in her Top 10.

TOP 10 ★
GWYNETH PALTROW FILMS

1	*Se7en*	1995
2	*Hook*	1991
3	*Shakespeare in Love**	1998
4	*A Perfect Murder*	1998
5	*Great Expectations*	1998
6	*Malice*	1993
7	*Emma*	1996
8	*Sliding Doors*	1998
9	*Hush*	1998
10	*Flesh and Bone*	1993

* *Academy Award for "Best Actress"*

HONOURARY ENGLISHWOMAN

Gwyneth Paltrow's impeccable accent convinces many that she is the quintessential English rose.

TOP 10 ★
MICHELLE PFEIFFER FILMS

1	*Batman Returns*	1992
2	*Dangerous Minds*	1995
3	*Wolf*	1994
4	*Up Close & Personal*	1996
5	*One Fine Day*	1996
6	*The Witches of Eastwick*	1987
7	*Tequila Sunrise*	1988
8	*Scarface*	1983
9	*Dangerous Liaisons*	1988
10	*The Age of Innocence*	1993

Michelle Pfeiffer provided the voice of Tzipporah in the animated film *Prince of Egypt* (1998). If included in her Top 10, it would feature in second place.

TOP 10 ★
NICOLE KIDMAN FILMS

1	Batman Forever	1995
2	Days of Thunder	1990
3	The Peacemaker	1997
4	Practical Magic	1998
5	Far and Away	1992
6	Malice	1993
7	My Life	1993
8	To Die For	1995
9	Billy Bathgate	1991
10	Dead Calm	1989

NICOLE'S SENSATIONAL ROLE

With her husband Tom Cruise, Nicole Kidman stars in Stanley Kubrick's controversial film Eyes Wide Shut, *which was completed shortly before the director's death in 1999.*

TOP 10
JULIA ROBERTS FILMS

❶ *Pretty Woman**, 1990 ❷ *My Best Friend's Wedding*, 1997 ❸ *The Pelican Brief*, 1993 ❹ *Six Days, Seven Nights*, 1998 ❺ *Sleeping with the Enemy*, 1991 ❻ *Conspiracy Theory*, 1997 ❼ *Hook*, 1991 ❽ *Steel Magnolias#*, 1989 ❾ *Stepmom*, 1998 ❿ *Flatliners*, 1990

* Academy Award nomination for "Best Actress"
 # Academy Award nomination for
"Best Supporting Actress"

TOP 10 ★
MEG RYAN FILMS

1	Top Gun	1986
2	Sleepless in Seattle	1993
3	City of Angels	1998
4	You've Got Mail	1998
5	French Kiss	1995
6	Courage under Fire	1996
7	When Harry Met Sally	1989
8	Addicted to Love	1997
9	When a Man Loves a Woman	1994
10	Joe Versus the Volcano	1990

Meg Ryan provided the voice of Anastasia in the 1997 film of that title. If included, it would appear in seventh place.

TOP 10 ★
SHARON STONE FILMS

1	Basic Instinct	1992
2	Total Recall	1990
3	The Specialist	1995
4	Last Action Hero	1993
5	Sliver	1993
6	Sphere	1998
7	Casino*	1995
8	Diabolique	1996
9	Police Academy 4: Citizens on Patrol	1987
10	Intersection	1994

 # Academy Award nomination

Sharon Stone's part in *Last Action Hero* amounted to no more than a brief cameo. If discounted, *Action Jackson* (1988) would occupy 10th place. She provided the voice of Bala in *Antz* (1998).

TOP 10 ★
DREW BARRYMORE FILMS

1	E.T.: the Extra-Terrestrial	1982
2	Batman Forever	1995
3	Scream	1996
4	The Wedding Singer	1998
5	Ever After	1998
6	Wayne's World 2	1993
7	Everyone Says I Love You	1996
8	Boys on the Side	1995
9	Mad Love	1995
10	Bad Girls	1994

TROUBLESOME TEENAGER

Drew Barrymore has cast aside her notorious wild-child image to become a sophisticated and successful film star.

What was the most successful animated film?
see p.190 for the answer

A *Bambi*
B *Toy Story*
C *The Lion King*

THE FUNNIES

TOP 10 ★
WHOOPI GOLDBERG FILMS

1	Ghost	1990
2	Sister Act	1992
3	The Color Purple*	1985
4	Star Trek: Generations	1994
5	Made in America	1993
6	In & Out	1997
7	Sister Act 2: Back in the Habit	1993
8	The Little Rascals	1994
9	Eddie	1996
10	How Stella Got Her Groove Back	1998

* Academy Award nomination for "Best Actress"

Whoopi Goldberg provided the voice of Shenzi in *The Lion King* (1994). If that were taken into the reckoning, it would appear in No. 1 position in her Top 10. Her voice was also that of Ranger Margaret in *The Rugrats Movie* (1998), which would appear in 6th position.

DIVINE COMEDY

From intergalactic agony aunt to the singing "nun" on the run in Sister Act, Whoopi Goldberg, real name Caryn Johnson, is one of America's most well-loved and highly paid actresses.

TOP 10 BILL MURRAY FILMS

1 *Ghostbusters*, 1984 **2** *Tootsie*, 1982 **3** *Ghostbusters II*, 1989 **4** *Stripes*, 1981 **5** *Groundhog Day*, 1993 **6** *What About Bob?*, 1991 **7** *Scrooged*, 1988 **8** *Meatballs*, 1979 **9** *Caddyshack*, 1980 **10** *Little Shop of Horrors*, 1986

TOP 10 ★
STEVE MARTIN FILMS

1	Parenthood	1989
2	The Jerk*	1979
3	Father of the Bride	1991
4	Father of the Bride Part II	1995
5	Housesitter	1992
6	Planes, Trains and Automobiles	1987
7	Dirty Rotten Scoundrels	1988
8	Roxanne	1987
9	¡Three Amigos!*	1986
10	Little Shop of Horrors	1986

*Also co-writer

Steve Martin provided the voice of Hotep in *Prince of Egypt*, which would head his Top 10. He was one of the many guest stars in *The Muppet Movie*.

TOP 10 ★
DAN AYKROYD FILMS

1	Indiana Jones and the Temple of Doom	1984
2	Ghostbusters	1984
3	Casper	1995
4	Ghostbusters II	1989
5	Driving Miss Daisy	1989
6	Trading Places	1983
7	Spies Like Us	1985
8	My Girl	1991
9	Dragnet	1987
10	The Blues Brothers	1980

Aykroyd's directorial debut with *Nothing but Trouble* (1991), in which he also starred, was one of his least commercially successful films.

TOP 10 ★
EDDIE MURPHY FILMS

1	Beverly Hills Cop	1984
2	Beverly Hills Cop II	1987
3	Coming to America	1988
4	The Nutty Professor	1996
5	Doctor Dolittle	1998
6	Boomerang	1992
7	Harlem Nights*	1989
8	Trading Places	1983
9	Another 48 Hrs.	1990
10	The Golden Child	1986

* Also director

Eddie Murphy also provided the voice of Mushu in the animated film *Mulan* (1998), which would rank third in his Top 10.

Did You Know? The most successful comedy film of all time is *Forrest Gump* starring Tom Hanks.

TOP 10 ★
BETTE MIDLER FILMS

1	The First Wives Club	1996
2	Get Shorty	1995
3	Ruthless People	1986
4	Down and Out in Beverly Hills	1986
5	Beaches*	1988
6	Outrageous Fortune	1987
7	The Rose	1979
8	Big Business	1988
9	Hocus Pocus	1993
10	Hawaii	1966

* Also producer

Bette Midler's role in *Get Shorty* is no more than a cameo, and that in *Hawaii*, her first film part, is as an extra. If these were excluded, *Stella* (1990) and *For the Boys* (1991), which she also produced, would join the list. Her voice appears as that of the character Georgette in the animated film *Oliver & Company* (1988).

TOP 10 ★
ROBIN WILLIAMS FILMS

1	Mrs. Doubtfire	1993
2	Hook	1991
3	Jumanji	1995
4	Dead Poets Society	1989
5	The birdcage	1996
6	Good Will Hunting*	1997
7	Nine Months	1995
8	Good Morning, Vietnam	1987
9	Jack	1996
10	Patch Adams	1998

* Academy Award for "Best Supporting Actor"

Robin Williams (born 21 July 1952, Chicago, Illinois) first came to public attention on TV through his appearances in *Rowan and Martin's Laugh-In* and as the alien Mork in *Mork and Mindy*, since when he has made 15 films, typically playing crazed individuals – such as the DJ in *Good Morning, Vietnam*, and the certifiable down-and-out in *The Fisher King*. Williams has also played some impressive dramatic roles, as in *Dead Poets Society* and *Awakenings*.

TOP 10 ★
CHEVY CHASE FILMS

1	National Lampoon's Christmas Vacation	1989
2	National Lampoon's Vacation	1983
3	Spies Like Us	1985
4	Foul Play	1978
5	National Lampoon's European Vacation	1985
6	Fletch	1985
7	Seems Like Old Times	1980
8	Caddyshack	1980
9	Man of the House	1995
10	¡Three Amigos!	1986

Chevy Chase (real name Cornelius Crane) was born on 8 October 1943. He made his name as a comedian on the anarchic US TV show *Saturday Night Live* before starring in comedy films such as the hugely successful *National Lampoon* series.

TOP 10 ★
JIM CARREY FILMS

1	Batman Forever	1995
2	The Mask	1994
3	Liar Liar	1997
4	The Truman Show	1998
5	Dumb & Dumber	1994
6	Ace Ventura: When Nature Calls	1995
7	The Cable Guy	1996
8	Ace Ventura: Pet Detective	1994
9	Peggy Sue Got Married	1986
10	The Dead Pool	1988

RUBBER FEATURES

Jim Carrey's extraordinary repertoire of facial expressions, with or without the help of special effects, combined with his split-second comic timing, have helped to make him one of the '90s most successful comedy actors.

TOP 10 ★
DANNY DEVITO FILMS

1	Batman Returns	1992
2	Get Shorty	1995
3	Romancing the Stone	1984
4	One Flew Over the Cuckoo's Nest	1975
5	Twins	1988
6	Terms of Endearment	1983
7	Mars Attacks!	1996
8	Junior	1994
9	The War of the Roses*	1989
10	Ruthless People	1986

* Also director

Danny DeVito had a relatively minor role in *One Flew Over the Cuckoo's Nest*. If this is discounted from the reckoning, his 10th most successful film becomes *L.A. Confidential* (1997). He provided the voices of Whiskers in *Last Action Hero* (1993), Rocks in *Look Who's Talking Now* (1993), and Swackhammer in *Space Jam* (1996), and directed, appeared in, and narrated *Matilda* (1996), which just fails to make his own Top 10.

THE DIRECTORS

RETURN TO *CAPE FEAR*

Scorsese directed Cape Fear 30 years after the original film by J. Lee-Thompson. His cast included two of the original actors: Gregory Peck and Robert Mitchum.

TOP 10 ★
FILMS DIRECTED BY ACTORS

	FILM/YEAR	DIRECTOR
1	*Pretty Woman*, 1990	Garry Marshall
2	*Dances with Wolves*, 1990	Kevin Costner
3	*3 Men and a Baby*, 1987	Leonard Nimoy
4	*Rocky IV*, 1985	Sylvester Stallone
5	*A Few Good Men*, 1992	Rob Reiner
6	*Rocky III*, 1982	Sylvester Stallone
7	*On Golden Pond*, 1981	Mark Rydell
8	*Dick Tracy*, 1990	Warren Beatty
9	*Stir Crazy*, 1980	Sidney Poitier
10	*Star Trek IV: The Voyage Home*, 1986	Leonard Nimoy

The role of actor-director has a long cinema tradition, numbering such luminaries as Orson Welles and John Huston among its ranks. Heading this list, Pretty Woman director Garry Marshall is the brother of actress-director Penny Marshall, who only just misses a place in this Top 10 herself.

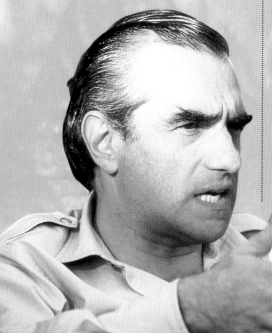

TOP 10 ★
FILMS DIRECTED BY MARTIN SCORSESE

1	*Cape Fear*	1991
2	*The Color of Money*	1986
3	*GoodFellas*	1990
4	*Casino*	1995
5	*The Age of Innocence*	1993
6	*Taxi Driver*	1976
7	*Raging Bull*	1980
8	*Alice Doesn't Live Here Anymore*	1975
9	*New York New York*	1977
10	*New York Stories**	1989

* Part only; other segments directed by Francis Ford Coppola and Woody Allen

TOP 10 ★
FILMS DIRECTED BY JOHN CARPENTER

1	*Halloween*	1978
2	*Escape from L.A.*	1996
3	*Starman*	1984
4	*Escape from New York*	1981
5	*The Fog*	1980
6	*Christine*	1983
7	*Vampires*	1998
8	*Memoirs of an Invisible Man*	1992
9	*Prince of Darkness*	1987
10	*They Live*	1988

THE ITALIAN CONNECTION

Martin Scorsese was born into an Italian-American family in New York, the city that provides the backdrop for most of his films.

What is Nicole Kidman's most successful film?
see p.183 for the answer

A *Days of Thunder*
B *Batman Forever*
C *The Peacemaker*

TOP 10 ⭐
FILMS DIRECTED BY STEVEN SPIELBERG

1	Jurassic Park	1993
2	E.T.: the Extra-Terrestrial	1982
3	Indiana Jones and the Last Crusade	1989
4	Jaws	1975
5	Saving Private Ryan	1998
6	Raiders of the Lost Ark	1981
7	Schindler's List	1993
8	Close Encounters of the Third Kind	1977/80*
9	Indiana Jones and the Temple of Doom	1984
10	The Lost World: Jurassic Park	1997

* Re-edited and re-released as "Special Edition"

Steven Spielberg has directed some of the most successful films of all time: the top five in this list appear among the top 22 films of all time, while the cumulative world box-office gross of his Top 10 amounts to almost $4.5 billion.

TOP 10 FILMS DIRECTED BY STANLEY KUBRICK

1 *The Shining*, 1980 **2** *2001: A Space Odyssey*, 1968 **3** *Full Metal Jacket*, 1987 **4** *A Clockwork Orange*, 1971 **5** *Spartacus*, 1960; = *Barry Lyndon*, 1975 **7** *Dr. Strangelove or: How I Learned to Stop Worrying and Love the Bomb*, 1964 **8** *Lolita*, 1962 **9** *Paths of Glory*, 1957 **10** *The Killing*, 1956

TOP 10 FILMS DIRECTED BY ROBERT ZEMECKIS

1 *Forrest Gump*, 1994 **2** *Who Framed Roger Rabbit*, 1988 **3** *Back to the Future*, 1985 **4** *Back to the Future III*, 1990 **5** *Back to the Future II*, 1989 **6** *Contact*, 1997 **7** *Death Becomes Her*, 1992 **8** *Romancing the Stone*, 1984 **9** *Used Cars*, 1980 **10** *I Wanna Hold Your Hand*, 1978

TOP 10 ⭐
FILMS DIRECTED BY WOMEN

	FILM/YEAR	DIRECTOR
1	Look Who's Talking, 1989	Amy Heckerling
2	Sleepless in Seattle, 1993	Nora Ephron
3	Wayne's World, 1992	Penelope Spheeris
4	Big, 1988	Penny Marshall
5	A League of Their Own, 1992	Penny Marshall
6	The Prince of Tides, 1991	Barbra Streisand
7	Pet Sematary, 1989	Mary Lambert
8	Clueless, 1995	Amy Heckerling
9	Michael, 1996	Nora Ephron
10	National Lampoon's European Vacation, 1985	Amy Heckerling

TOP 10 FILMS DIRECTED BY FRANCIS FORD COPPOLA

1 *Bram Stoker's Dracula*, 1992 **2** *The Godfather*, 1972 **3** *Jack*, 1996 **4** *The Godfather Part III*, 1990 **5** *Apocalypse Now*, 1979 **6** *The Godfather Part II*, 1974 **7** *The Rainmaker*, 1997 **8** *Peggy Sue Got Married*, 1986 **9** *The Cotton Club*, 1984 **10** *The Outsiders*, 1983

TOP 10 ⭐
FILMS DIRECTED OR PRODUCED BY GEORGE LUCAS

1	Star Wars*	1977/97
2	The Empire Strikes Back#	1980/97
3	Indiana Jones and the Last Crusade#	1989
4	Return of the Jedi#	1983
5	Raiders of the Lost Ark#	1981
6	Indiana Jones and the Temple of Doom#	1984
7	American Graffiti*	1973
8	Willow#	1988
9	The Land Before Time#	1988
10	Tucker: The Man and His Dream#	1988

* Director

Producer

STANLEY KUBRICK

Born in New York in 1928, Stanley Kubrick moved to England in the early 1960s. He never shied away from tackling controversial issues in his films, from the dangers of a nuclear war (*Dr Stangelove or: How I Learned to Stop Worrying and Love the Bomb*), to the portrayal of a society where violence is the prerogative of both the government and the individual (*A Clockwork Orange*). He died in March 1999, just after completing his last film, *Eyes Wide Shut*.

SNAP ⭐ SHOTS

BOLLYWOOD

Bombay is the centre of the huge Hindi cinema industry, producing hundreds of action- and music-packed films every year.

FILMS WITH THE MOST EXTRAS

	FILM/COUNTRY/YEAR	EXTRAS
1	*Gandhi*, UK, 1982	300,000
2	*Kolberg*, Germany, 1945	187,000
3	*Monster Wang-magwi*, South Korea, 1967	157,000
4	*War and Peace*, USSR, 1967	120,000
5	*Ilya Muromets*, USSR, 1956	106,000
6	*Tonko*, Japan, 1988	100,000
7	*The War of Independence*, Romania, 1912	80,000
8	*Around the World in 80 Days*, USA, 1956	68,894
9=	*Intolerance*, USA, 1916	60,000
=	*Dny Zrady*, Czechoslovakia, 1972	60,000

TOP 10 MOST PROLIFIC FILM-PRODUCING COUNTRIES

(Country/average no. of films produced per annum in 1991–96)

1 India, 851　**2** USA, 569　**3** Japan, 252　**4** Russia, 192　**5** France, 143
6 China, 137　**7** Italy, 107　**8** South Korea, 80　**9** Turkey, 71　**10** UK, 65

Source: Screen Digest

TOP 10 CINEMA-GOING COUNTRIES

(Country/total annual attendance)

1 China, 14,428,400,000　**2** India, 4,297,500,000　**3** USA, 981,900,000　**4** Russia, 140,100,000　**5** Japan, 130,700,000　**6** France, 130,100,000　**7** Germany, 124,500,000　**8** UK, 114,600,000　**9** Australia, 69,000,000　**10** Lebanon, 99,200,000

Source: *UNESCO*

COUNTRIES WITH THE MOST CINEMAS

	COUNTRY	CINEMAS
1	USA	23,662
2	Ukraine	14,960
3	India	8,975
4	China	4,639
5	France	4,365
6	Italy	3,816
7	Germany	3,814
8	Belarus	3,780
9	Uzbekistan	2,365
10	Spain	2,090
	UK	2,019

Source: Screen Digest

Did You Know? The longest-ever film was the 85-hour *The Cure for Insomnia*, which was not released commercially.

TOP 10 CINEMA ATTENDERS

(Country/annual attendance per inhabitant)

1 Lebanon, 35.3 **2** China, 12.3 **3** Georgia, 5.6 **4** India, 5.0
5 Iceland, 4.5 **6** = Australia, 3.9; = New Zealand, 3.9; = USA,
3.9 **9** Monaco, 3.7 **10** Canada, 2.8
UK, 2.0   Source: UNESCO

TOP 10 ★
YEARS WITH MOST CINEMA VISITS IN THE US, 1946–98

	YEAR	NO. OF FILMS RELEASED	BOX OFFICE GROSS ($)	ADMISSIONS
1	1946	400	1,692,000,000	4,067,300,000
2	1947	426	1,594,000,000	3,664,400,000
3	1948	444	1,506,000,000	3,422,700,000
4	1949	490	1,448,000,000	3,168,500,000
5	1950	483	1,379,000,000	3,017,500,000
6	1951	433	1,332,000,000	2,840,100,000
7	1952	389	1,325,000,000	2,777,700,000
8	1953	404	1,339,000,000	2,630,600,000
9	1954	369	1,251,000,000	2,270,400,000
10	1955	319	1,204,000,000	2,072,300,000

Source: *Motion Picture Association of America, Inc.*

From 1956, admissions continued to decline, reaching an all-time low in 1971 of 820,300,000. Since 1991, admissions have increased each year.

TOP 10 ★
LONGEST FILMS EVER SCREENED

	FILM	COUNTRY/YEAR	HRS	MINS
1	*The Longest and Most Meaningless Movie in the World*	UK, 1970	48	0
2	*The Burning of the Red Lotus Temple*	China, 1928–31	27	0
3	****	USA, 1967	25	0
4	*Heimat*	West Germany, 1984	15	40
5	*Berlin Alexanderplatz*	West Germany/Italy, 1980	15	21
6	*The Journey*	Sweden, 1987	14	33
7	*The Old Testament*	Italy, 1922	13	0
8	*Comment Yukong déplace les montagnes*	France, 1976	12	43
9	*Out 1: Noli me Tangere*	France, 1971	12	40
10	*Ningen No Joken* (The Human Condition)	Japan, 1958–60	9	29

The list includes commercially screened films, but not "stunt" films created solely to break endurance records (particularly those of their audiences).

TOP 10 ★
MOST EXPENSIVE ITEMS OF FILM MEMORABILIA EVER SOLD AT AUCTION

	ITEM/SALE	PRICE (£)*
1	Vivien Leigh's Oscar for *Gone with the Wind*, Sotheby's, New York, 15 Dec 1993	380,743
2	Clark Gable's Oscar for *It Happened One Night*, Christie's, Los Angeles, 15 Dec 1996	364,500
3	Poster for *The Mummy, 1932*, Sotheby's, New York, 1 Mar 1997	252,109
4	James Bond's Aston Martin DB5 from *Goldfinger*, Sotheby's, New York, 28 Jun 1986	179,793
5	Clark Gable's personal script for *Gone with the Wind*, Christie's, Los Angeles, 15 Dec 1996	146,700
6	"Rosebud" sled from *Citizen Kane*, Christie's, Los Angeles, 15 Dec 1996	140,000
7	Herman J. Mankiewicz's scripts for *Citizen Kane* and *The American*, Christie's, New York, 21 Jun 1989	139,157
8	Judy Garland's ruby slippers from *The Wizard of Oz*, Christie's, New York, 21 Jun 1988	104,430
9	Piano from the Paris scene in *Casablanca*, Sotheby's, New York, 16 Dec 1988	97,469
10	Charlie Chaplin's hat and cane, Christie's, London, 11 Dec 1987 (resold at Christie's, London, 17 Dec 1993, for £55,000)	82,500

* $/£ conversion at rate then prevailing

This list excludes animated film celluloids or "cels" – the individually painted scenes that are shot in sequence to make up cartoon films – which are now attaining colossal prices: just one of the 150,000 colour cels from *Snow White and the Seven Dwarfs* (1937) was sold in 1991 for $209,000/£115,000, and in 1989 $286,000/£171,250 was reached for a black-and-white cel depicting Donald Duck in *Orphan's Benefit* (1934).

SILENT STAR

Chaplin's trademark hat, and the stick that he twirled on screen, made him the most instantly recognizable of the silent film stars.

ANIMATION

TOP 10 ANIMATED FILMS

1	*The Lion King*	1994
2	*Aladdin*	1992
3	*A Bug's Life*	1998
4	*Toy Story*	1995
5	*Beauty and the Beast*	1991
6	*Who Framed Roger Rabbit**	1988
7	*Pocahontas*	1995
8	*The Hunchback of Notre Dame*	1996
9	*Mulan*	1998
10	*Casper**	1995

* Part animated, part live action

The 1990s have already provided nine of the 10 most successful animated films of all time, which have ejected a number of their high-earning predecessors – such as *Bambi*, *Fantasia*, and *Snow White and the Seven Dwarfs* – from this Top 10. Animated films stand out among the leading money-makers of each decade.

THE 10 ★
FIRST FULL-LENGTH SIMPSONS EPISODES

	EPISODE	FIRST SCREENED
1	Simpsons Roasting on an Open Fire	17 Dec 1989
2	Bart the Genius	14 Jan 1990
3	Homer's Odyssey	21 Jan 1990
4	There's No Disgrace Like Homer	28 Jan 1990
5	Bart the General	4 Feb 1990
6	Moaning Lisa	11 Feb 1990
7	The Call of the Simpsons	18 Feb 1990
8	The Telltale Head	25 Feb 1990
9	Life in the Fast Lane	18 Mar 1990
10	Homer's Night Out	25 Mar 1990

THE 10 ★
FIRST OSCAR-WINNING ANIMATED FILMS*

YEAR	FILM	DIRECTOR#
1933	Flowers and Trees	Walt Disney
1934	The Three Little Pigs	Walt Disney
1935	The Tortoise and the Hare	Walt Disney
1936	Three Orphan Kittens	Walt Disney
1937	The Country Cousin	Walt Disney
1938	The Old Mill	Walt Disney
1939	Ferdinand the Bull	Walt Disney
1940	The Ugly Duckling	Walt Disney
1941	The Milky Way	Rudolf Ising
1942	Lend a Paw	Walt Disney

* In the category "Short Films (Cartoons)"
 # All US

THE 10 ★
LATEST OSCAR-WINNING ANIMATED FILMS*

YEAR	FILM	DIRECTOR/COUNTRY
1998	Bunny	Chris Wedge, USA
1997	Geri's Game	Jan Pinkava, USA
1996	Quest	Tyron Montgomery, UK
1995	A Close Shave	Nick Park, UK
1994	Bob's Birthday	David Fine and Alison Snowden, UK
1993	The Wrong Trousers	Nick Park, UK
1992	Mona Lisa Descending a Staircase	Joan C. Gratz, USA
1991	Manipulation	Daniel Greaves, UK
1990	Creature Comforts	Nick Park, UK
1989	Balance	Christoph and Wolfgang Lauenstein, West Germany

* In the category "Short Films (Animated)"

TOP 10 PART ANIMATION/PART LIVE ACTION FILMS

❶ *Who Framed Roger Rabbit*, 1988 ❷ *Casper*, 1995 ❸ *Space Jam*, 1996 ❹ *9 to 5*, 1980 ❺ *Mary Poppins*, 1964 ❻ *Song of the South*, 1946 ❼ *Pete's Dragon*, 1977 ❽ *Fletch Lives*, 1989 ❾ *Bedknobs and Broomsticks*, 1971 ❿ *Xanadu*, 1980

© DISNEY

TOP 10 WALT DISNEY ANIMATED FILMS

1 *The Lion King*, 1994 **2** *Aladdin*, 1992
3 *A Bug's Life*, 1998 **4** *Toy Story*, 1995
5 *Beauty and the Beast*, 1991
6 *Who Framed Roger Rabbit*, 1988
7 *Pocahontas*, 1995 **8** *The Hunchback of Notre Dame*, 1996 **9** *Mulan*, 1998
10 *Bambi*, 1942

In 1923, having started his business in Kansas City, Walt Disney moved to California where he experienced modest success with his animated films, until the advent of sound made a notable commercial success of *Steamboat Willie* (1928).

"YOU'RE NOT REAL!"
Woody tries unsuccessfully to convince Buzz that he is only a toy, not a real spaceman, in Toy Story, *the first ever completely computer-generated animated film.*

TOP 10 ★ NON-DISNEY ANIMATED FEATURE FILMS

1	*Prince of Egypt*	1998
2	*Antz*	1998
3	*The Rugrats Movie*	1998
4	*The Land Before Time*	1988
5	*An American Tail*	1986
6	*The Lord of the Rings*	1978
7	*All Dogs Go to Heaven*	1989
8	*Heavy Metal*	1981
9	*FernGully: The Last Rainforest*	1992
10	*Jetsons: The Movie*	1990

THE 10 ★ FIRST DISNEY ANIMATED FEATURES

1	*Snow White and the Seven Dwarfs*	1937
2	*Pinocchio*	1940
3	*Fantasia*	1940
4	*Dumbo*	1941
5	*Bambi*	1942
6	*Victory Through Air Power*	1943
7	*The Three Caballeros*	1945
8	*Make Mine Music*	1946
9	*Fun and Fancy Free*	1947
10	*Melody Time*	1948

Excluding part-animated fims such as *Song of the South* and *Mary Poppins*, and films made specially for television serialization, Disney has made a total of 37 full-length animated feature films up to its 1998 release, *Mulan*.

THE 10 ★ FIRST TOM AND JERRY CARTOONS

	CARTOON	RELEASE DATE
1	*Puss Gets the Boot**	20 Feb 1940
2	*The Midnight Snack*	19 Jul 1941
3	*The Night Before Christmas**	6 Dec 1941
4	*Fraidy Cat*	17 Jan 1942
5	*Dog Trouble*	18 Apr 1942
6	*Puss 'N' Toots*	30 May 1942
7	*The Bowling Alley-Cat*	18 Jul 1942
8	*Fine Feathered Friend*	10 Oct 1942
9	*Sufferin' Cats!*	16 Jan 1943
10	*The Lonesome Mouse*	22 May 1943

* *Academy Award nomination*

The duo were created by William Hanna and Joseph Barbera. and have been perennially popular during six decades.

What was the most successful Martin Scorsese film?
see p.186 for the answer
A *Cape Fear*
B *GoodFellas*
C *The Color of Money*

ON THE RADIO

BESTSELLING RADIO COLLECTION COMEDY TITLES

1 *Hancock's Half Hour* Vol. 10
2 *I'm Sorry I Haven't a Clue* Vol. 4
3 *Dad's Army* Vol. 8: *My British Buddy*
4 *Only Fools and Horses*
5 *The Goons at Christmas, Vol. 15*
6 *The Blackadder Collection*
7 *Round the Horne* Vol. 10
8 *Hancock's Half Hour* Vol. 9
9 *I'm Sorry I Haven't a Clue* Vol. 1
10 *The Navy Lark: "HMS Troutbridge Goes Dutch"*

Source: *BBC Worldwide*

TOP 10 ★

RADIO STATIONS IN THE UK

STATION	LISTENER HOURS*
1 BBC Radio 2	108,479,000
2 BBC Radio 1	88,179,000
3 BBC Radio 4	87,140,000
4 EMAP#	67,026,000
5 Capital Radio#	62,538,000
6 GWR Group#	48,615,000
7 Classic FM	30,898,000
8 BBC Radio 5 Live	29,619,000
9 Virgin Radio#	28,394,000
10 Chrysalis#	25,391,000

* *Total number of hours spent by all adults (over 15) listening to the station in an average week, Sep–Dec 1998*

\# *Split frequency stations; listener hours are totals for all frequencies*

Source: *RAJAR*

TOP 10 ★

BESTSELLING RADIO COLLECTION FICTION AND DRAMA TITLES*

1 *Talking Heads* Vol. 2
2 *Lord of the Rings* (CD)
3 *Lord of the Rings*
4 *The HitchHiker's Guide to the Galaxy* (boxed set)
5 *Talking Heads* Vol. 1
6 *The Clothes They Stood up in*
7 *Bombed*
8 *Captain Corelli's Mandolin*
9 *The Hobbit*
10 *The Murder of Roger Ackroyd/Murder on the Links*

* *Tapes, unless otherwise stated*

Source: *BBC Worldwide*

TOP 10 ★

BBC RADIO 1 PROGRAMMES

1 *The Radio 1 Breakfast Show*
2 *Dave Pearce – Drivetime*
3 *Simon Mayo*
4 *Mark Radcliffe*
5 *Jo Whiley*
6 *The Top 40*
7 *The Evening Session with Steve Lamacq*
8 *Mark Goodier* (Saturday)
9 *Mark Goodier* (Sunday)
10 *Pete Tong – Essential Selection*

HER FATHER'S DAUGHTER
Zoe Ball presents the Breakfast Show on BBC Radio 1 every weekday. Until recently one of the hosts of children's TV show Live and Kicking, she followed the career path of her father, TV presenter Johnny Ball.

Background Image: PORTABLE RADIO

TOP 10 ★
LONGEST-RUNNING PROGRAMMES ON BBC RADIO

	PROGRAMME	FIRST BROADCAST
1	*The Week's Good Cause*	24 Jan 1926
2	*The Shipping Forecast*	26 Jan 1926
3	*Choral Evensong*	7 Oct 1926
4	*Daily Service*	2 Jan 1928*
5	*The Week in Westminster*	6 Nov 1929
6	*Sunday Half Hour*	14 Jul 1940
7	*Desert Island Discs*	29 Jan 1942
8	*Saturday Night Theatre*	3 Apr 1943
9	*Composer of the Week*#	2 Aug 1943
10	*Letter from America*+	24 Mar 1946

* *Experimental broadcast; national transmission began December 1929*

Formerly This Week's Composer

+ *Formerly* American Letter

In addition to these long-running programmes, a further seven that started in the 1940s are still on the air, including *From Our Own Correspondent* (first broadcast 4 October 1946), *Woman's Hour* (7 October 1946 – although the BBC's London station 2LO had previously first broadcast a programme with this name on 2 May 1923), and *Down Your Way* (29 December 1946).

THE 10 ★
BESTSELLING RADIO COLLECTION CHILDREN'S TITLES

1	*The Hobbit* (children's version)
2	*The Lion, the Witch and the Wardrobe*
3	*The Alan Bennett Children's Library*
4	*Wallace and Gromit*
5	*Winnie the Pooh/House at Pooh Corner*
6	*The Wind in the Willows*
7	*Treasure Island*
8	*The Voyages of Doctor Dolittle*
9	*Peter Pan and Wendy*
10	*Hodgeheg/Martin's Mice*

Source: *BBC Worldwide*

TOP 10 ★
RADIO-OWNING COUNTRIES

	COUNTRY	RADIO SETS PER 1,000 POPULATION
1	USA	2,093
2	UK	1,433
3	Australia	1,304
4	Canada	1,053
5	Denmark	1,034
6	South Korea	1,024
7	Monaco	1,019
8	Finland	1,008
9	New Zealand	997
10	Germany	944

The top eight countries in this list have at least one radio per person. In addition, many small island communities in the world have very high numbers of radios for their small populations to enable them to maintain regular contact with the outside world. In Bermuda there are 1,285 per 1,000 population (or 1.3 per person), in Gibraltar 1,300 per 1,000 population, and in Guam there are 1,407 radios per 1,000 population. The world record, however, is still held by the US, with over two radio sets per inhabitant.

Source: *UNESCO*

THE 10 ★
LATEST SONY RADIO AWARDS

YEAR	GOLD AWARD	PERSONALITY/ BROADCASTER OF THE YEAR
1998	Chris Evans	Anna Raeburn
1997	Jimmy Young	John Inverdale
1996	Richard Baker	Chris Evans
1995	Alistair Cooke	Neil Fox
1994	Kenny Everett	Henry Kelly
1993	Humphrey Lyttelton	John Peel
1992	Sir James Savile	Danny Baker
1991	Charlie Gillett	James Naughtie
1990	Roy Hudd	Chris Tarrant
1989	Tony Blackburn	Sue Lawley

THE 10 ★
FIRST YEARS OF SONY RADIO AWARDS

YEAR	GOLD AWARD	PERSONALITY/ BROADCASTER OF THE YEAR
1983	Frank Muir	Brian Johnston
	Denis Norden	Sue MacGregor
1984	David Jacobs	Brian Matthew
		Margaret Howard
1985	British Forces Broadcasting Service	Jimmy Young
1986	John Timpson	Douglas Cameron
1987	*The Archers*	Derek Jameson
1988	Gerald Mansell	Alan Freeman
1989	Tony Blackburn	Sue Lawley
1990	Roy Hudd	Chris Tarrant
1991	Charlie Gillett	James Naughtie
1992	Sir James Savile	Danny Baker

The electronics company Sony have sponsored the British radio awards that bear their name since 1983. They are presented to "celebrate the quality, creativity, and excellence of those whose work brings enjoyment to millions of listeners".

TOP 10 ★
RADIO FORMATS IN THE US

	FORMAT	SHARE (PER CENT)*
1	**AOR/Classic Rock/New Rock**	14.72
2	**Black/Urban**	11.23
3	**Country**	10.63
4	**News/Talk**	10.13
5	**CHR (Top 40)**	10.00
6	**Adult Contemporary**	9.43
7	**Oldies/Classic Hits**	6.96
8	**Hispanic**	6.04
9	**Soft AC**	4.72
10	**Standards/EZ Listening**	3.83

* *Of all radio listening during an average week, 6 am to midnight, 1998, for listeners aged 12+*

Source: *Duncan's Radio*

Did You Know? The very first radio broadcast in the US was sent on 24 December 1906 from Brant Rock, MA, by Professor Reginald Aubrey Fessenden.

TOP TV

TOP 10 ★
CHANNEL 4 AUDIENCES, 1998

	PROGRAMME*	DATE	AUDIENCE
1	Brookside	15 Apr	7,600,000
2	Father Ted	1 May	7,100,000
3	Dispatches (on the crash that killed Diana, Princess of Wales)	4 Jun	6,800,000
4	Friends	11 Dec	6,500,000
5	Muriel's Wedding (film)	3 May	5,500,000
6	Brassed Off (film)	24 May	4,900,000
7	Countdown	16 Jan	4,800,000
8	Drop the Dead Donkey	4 Nov	4,700,000
9 =	Jack & Sarah (film)	8 Feb	4,400,000
=	Tourist Trap	12 May	4,400,000

* The highest-rated episode only of series shown

JUST GOOD FRIENDS
The coffee-loving stars of the internationally top-rated TV show Friends *have all gone on to launch successful film careers in their own right.*

THE 10 ★
FIRST PROGRAMMES BROADCAST ON BBC 2

	PROGRAMME	TIME*
1	Play School	11.00
2	Zero Minus Five (introductory programme)	19.15
3	Line-Up (arts programme)	19.20
4	The Alberts' Channel Too (variety show)	19.30
5	Kiss Me Kate (musical starring Howard Keel and Millicent Martin)	20.00
6	Arkady Raikin (Soviet comedian)	21.35
7	Off with a Bang (fireworks from Southend pier)	22.20
8	Newsroom	22.35
9	Jazz 625 (Duke Ellington in concert)	23.02
10	Play School	11.00

* Nos. 1 to 9 were broadcast on 21 April 1964; No. 10 was on 22 April

The programmes for the official opening night on Monday 20 April 1964 were postponed after much of central London was blacked out by a power cut, and only a handful of announcements and news items were actually transmitted.

TOP 10 ★
LONGEST-RUNNING PROGRAMMES ON BRITISH TELEVISION

	PROGRAMME	FIRST SHOWN
1	Panorama	11 Nov 1953
2	What the Papers Say	5 Nov 1956
3	The Sky at Night	24 Apr 1957
4	Grandstand	11 Oct 1958
5	Blue Peter	16 Oct 1958
6	Coronation Street	9 Dec 1960
7	Songs of Praise	1 Oct 1961
8	Top of the Pops	1 Jan 1964
9	Horizon	2 May 1964
10	Match of the Day	22 Aug 1964

Only programmes appearing every year since their first screenings are listed in this Top 10, and all are BBC programmes except *Coronation Street* (ITV). Several other BBC programmes, such as *The Good Old Days* (1953–83), ran for many years but are now defunct. *The Sky at Night* has the additional distinction of having had the same presenter, Patrick Moore, since its first programme over 40 years ago.

THE 10 ★
FIRST PROGRAMMES BROADCAST ON CHANNEL 5

	PROGRAMME	TIME*
1	This Is 5! (introduction)	18.00
2	Family Affairs (soap opera)	18.30
3	Two Little Boys (documentary on the childhoods of Tony Blair and John Major)	19.00
4	Hospital! (comedy)	20.00
5	Beyond Fear (drama)	21.00
6	The Jack Docherty Show (comedy)	22.30
7	The Comedy Store Special	23.10
8	Turnstile (sport review)	23.40
9	Live and Dangerous	00.10
10	This Is 5!	05.30

* No. 1 to 8 were broadcast on 30 March 1997; Nos. 9 and 10 were on 31 March

Background image: **1940s BAKELITE ELECTRONIC TELEVISION**

TOP 10 ⭐
ITV AUDIENCES, 1998

	PROGRAMME*	DATE	AUDIENCE
1	*World Cup – Argentina v England*	30 Jun	23,782,000
2	*World Cup – Romania v England*	22 Jun	19,480,000
3	*Coronation Street*	16 Nov	18,620,000
4	*Heartbeat*	22 Feb	16,451,000
5	*Celebrity Stars in Their Eyes*	2 Dec	16,337,000
6	*World Cup – Brazil v Holland*	7 Jul	14,095,000
7	*You've Been Framed*	13 Sep	13,859,000
8	*Goodnight Mr. Tom*	25 Oct	13,811,000
9	*Emmerdale*	10 Feb	13,276,000
10	*London's Burning*	11 Jan	12,823,000

* The highest-rated episode only of series shown

TOP 10 TELEVISION-WATCHING COUNTRIES

(Country/average daily viewing time in hrs:mins)

1 USA, 3:59 **2** = Italy, 3:36; = Turkey, 3:36 **4** UK, 3:35
5 Spain, 3:34 **6** Hungary, 3:33 **7** Japan, 3:25
8 Greece, 3:22 **9** Canada, 3:12 **10** Argentina, 3:11

Source: Screen Digest/Eurodate TV

TOP 10 ⭐
BBC 1 AUDIENCES, 1998

	PROGRAMME*	DATE	AUDIENCE
1	*Eastenders*#	25/27 Dec	22,140,000
2	*World Cup: Colombia v England*	26 Jun	19,130,000
3	*Casualty*	28 Feb	15,740,000
4	*World Cup: Brazil v France*	12 Jul	15,650,000
5	*Men Behaving Badly*	28 Dec	15,190,000
6	*Forrest Gump* (film)	1 Jan	15,080,000
7	*World Cup: France v Croatia*	8 Jul	14,620,000
8	*Birds of a Feather*	19 Jan	13,330,000
9	*The National Lottery Live*	28 Feb	13,200,000
10	*The Cruise*	13 Jan	12,860,000

* The highest-rated episode only of series shown

Aggregate audience

TOP 10 CABLE TELEVISION COUNTRIES

(Country/subscribers)

1 USA, 67,011,180 **2** Germany, 18,740,260
3 Netherlands, 6,227,472 **4** Russia, 5,784,432
5 Belgium, 3,945,342 **6** Poland, 3,830,788 **7** Romania,
3,000,000 **8** UK, 2,666,783 **9** France, 2,478,630
10 Switzerland, 2,156,120

Source: *The Phillips Group*

Although the USA is the world's most cabled country, its services are fragmented between numerous operators, with TCI the foremost company, followed by Time Warner Cable. In Europe, a smaller number of large companies dominate the market, with Germany's Deutsche Telekom providing service to more homes than any single US operator.

THE 10 FIRST COUNTRIES TO HAVE TELEVISION*

(Country/year#)

1 UK, 1936 **2** USA, 1939 **3** USSR, 1939 **4** France, 1948
5 Brazil, 1950 **6** Cuba, 1950 **7** Mexico, 1950 **8** Argentina,
1951 **9** Denmark, 1951 **10** Netherlands, 1951

* High-definition regular public broadcasting service
# Countries sharing the same year are ranked by month

TOP 10 ⭐
TELEVISION AUDIENCES OF ALL TIME IN THE UK

	PROGRAMME	DATE	AUDIENCE
1	*Royal Wedding of HRH Prince Charles to Lady Diana Spencer*	29 Jul 1981	39,000,000
2	*Brazil v England 1970 World Cup*	10 Jun 1970	32,500,000
3 =	*England v West Germany 1966 World Cup Final*	30 Jul 1966	32,000,000
=	*Chelsea v Leeds Cup Final Replay*	28 Apr 1970	32,000,000
5	*Funeral of Diana, Princess of Wales*	6 Sep 1997	31,000,000
6	*EastEnders Christmas episode*	26 Dec 1987	30,000,000
7	*Morecambe and Wise Christmas Show*	25 Dec 1977	28,000,000
8 =	*World Heavyweight Boxing Championship: Joe Frazier v Muhammad Ali*	8 Mar 1971	27,000,000
=	*Dallas*	22 Nov 1980	27,000,000
10	*Only Fools and Horses*	29 Dec 1996	24,350,000

The 22 November 1980 screening of *Dallas* was the most-watched because it was the episode that revealed who shot J.R. Ewing. The most-watched film of all time on British television is *Live and Let Die*. Although already seven years old when it was first broadcast on 20 January 1980, it attracted an audience of 23,500,000.

Background image: 1970s SPACE-AGE TELEVISION

Did You Know? The first demonstration of television was given by John Logie Baird in 1926, but his mechanical "Televisor" could not transmit both pictures and sound at the same time.

TV OF THE DECADES

TOP 10

TV PROGRAMMES OF THE 1990s IN THE UK

	PROGRAMME	CHANNEL	BROADCAST	AUDIENCE
1	*Only Fools and Horses*	BBC 1	29 Dec 1996	24,350,000
2	*Panorama* (Diana, Princess of Wales interview)	BBC 1	20 Nov 1995	22,750,000
3	*Only Fools and Horses*	BBC 1	27 Dec 1996	21,350,000
4	*Only Fools and Horses*	BBC 1	25 Dec 1996	21,300,000
5	*Coronation Street*	Granada	22 Mar 1993	20,750,000
6	*Olympic Ice Dancing* (Torvill and Dean)	BBC 1	21 Feb 1994	20,650,000
7	*Coronation Street*	Granada	6 Jan 1993	20,500,000
8=	*Coronation Street*	Granada	25 Nov 1991	20,450,000
=	*Coronation Street*	Granada	22 Jan 1992	20,450,000
10	*Coronation Street*	Granada	11 Jan 1993	20,400,000

Source: *Royal Television Society*

TV PROGRAMMES OF THE 1980s IN THE UK

	PROGRAMME	CHANNEL	BROADCAST	AUDIENCE
1	*Live and Let Die*	ITV	20 Jan 1980	23,500,000
2	*Jaws*	ITV	8 Oct 1981	23,250,000
3	*The Spy Who Loved Me*	ITV	28 Mar 1982	22,900,000
4	*Diamonds Are Forever*	ITV	15 Mar 1981	22,150,000
5	*Crocodile Dundee*	BBC 1	25 Dec 1989	21,750,000
6	*Dallas*	BBC 1	22 Nov 1980	21,600,000
7	*To the Manor Born*	BBC 1	9 Nov 1980	21,550,000
8	*Coronation Street*	Granada	2 Jan 1985	21,400,000
9	*Bread*	BBC 1	11 Dec 1988	20,950,000
10	*Coronation Street*	Granada	18 Feb 1981	20,800,000

Source: *Royal Television Society*

TV PROGRAMMES OF THE 1970s IN THE UK

	PROGRAMME	CHANNEL	BROADCAST	AUDIENCE
1	*To the Manor Born*	BBC 1	11 Nov 1979	23,950,000
2	*Mike Yarwood Christmas Show*	BBC 1	25 Dec 1977	21,400,000
3	*Morecambe and Wise Show*	BBC 1	25 Dec 1977	21,300,000
4	*Silver Jubilee Royal Variety*	ATV	4 Dec 1977	21,200,000
5	*Benny Hill Show*	Thames	14 Mar 1979	20,850,000
6	*You Only Live Twice*	ITV	20 Nov 1977	20,800,000
7	*Sale of the Century*	Anglia	19 Nov 1977	20,600,000
8	*This Is Your Life*	Thames	18 Jan 1978	20,450,000
9	*Coronation Street*	Granada	18 Jan 1978	20,400,000
10	*Miss World Beauty Contest*	BBC 1	20 Nov 1970	20,250,000

Source: *Royal Television Society*

THE 10 FIRST SUBJECTS FEATURED ON *THIS IS YOUR LIFE*

	NAME	PROFESSION	PROGRAMME
1	Eamonn Andrews	TV presenter	20 Jul 1955
2	Yvonne Bailey	French Resistance heroine	25 Sep 1955
3	Ted Ray	Entertainer	23 Oct 1955
4	Rev. James Butterworth	Children's social worker	20 Nov 1955
5	C.B. Fry	Cricketer and writer	18 Dec 1955
6	Johanna Harris	British Red Cross worker	1 Jan 1956
7	Donald Campbell	Speed record-breaker	15 Jan 1956
8	Joe Brannelly	Music publisher	29 Jan 1956
9	Stanley Matthews	Footballer	12 Feb 1956
10	Henry Starling	Billingsgate Market porter	26 Feb 1956

Eamonn Andrews, himself the subject of the pilot *This Is Your Life* programme, went on to present it, first on BBC and, after 1969, on ITV, until his death in 1987, when it was taken over by Michael Aspel.

THE 10 FIRST PRODUCTS ADVERTISED ON ITV

1 Gibbs' SR toothpaste 2 Guinness 3 Batchelor's peas 4 Brillo pads 5 Cadbury's 6 Crosse & Blackwell 7 Dunlop rubber 8 Esso 9 Ford 10 Remington Rand

Britain's first TV advertisements were broadcast on 22 September 1955, the first day of Independent Television. All were screened in black and white, the first British TV commercial in colour (for Birds Eye peas) not appearing until 15 November 1969.

Background image: **SCENE FROM** *DALLAS*

THE 10 ★
LATEST WINNERS OF THE BAFTA COMEDY SERIES AWARD

YEAR	PROGRAMME
1998	*Father Ted*
1997	*I'm Alan Partridge*
1996	*Only Fools and Horses*
1995	*Father Ted*
1994	*Three Fights, Two Weddings and a Funeral*
1993	*Drop the Dead Donkey*
1992	*Absolutely Fabulous*
1991	*One Foot in the Grave*
1990	*The New Statesman*
1989	*Blackadder Goes Forth*

THE 10 ★
LATEST WINNERS OF THE BAFTA TV DRAMA SERIES/SERIAL AWARD*

YEAR	PROGRAMME
1998	Series: *The Cops* Serial: *Our Mutual Friend*
1997	Series: *Jonathan Creek* Serial: *London, Holding On*
1996	Series: *EastEnders* Serial: *Our Friends in the North*
1995	Series: *Cracker* Serial: *The Politician's Wife*
1994	Series: *Cracker* Serial: *Takin' over the Asylum*
1993	Series: no award Serial: *Prime Suspect 3*
1992	Series: *Inspector Morse* Serial: *Anglo-Saxon Attitudes*
1991	Series: *Inspector Morse* Serial: *Prime Suspect*
1990	*Oranges Are Not the Only Fruit*
1989	*Traffik*

* Since 1991, separate awards have been presented for series and serials.

THE 10 ★
LATEST WINNERS OF THE BAFTA TV LIGHT ENTERTAINMENT AWARD

YEAR	PROGRAMME
1998	*Who Wants to Be a Millionaire?*
1997	*The Fast Show*
1996	*Shooting Stars*
1995	*The Mrs. Merton Show*
1994	*Don't Forget Your Toothbrush*
1993	*Rory Bremner – Who Else?*
1992	*Noel's House Party*
1991	*Have I Got News For You?*
1990	*Whose Line Is It Anyway?*
1989	*Clive James on the 80s*

THE 10 1980s WINNERS OF THE BAFTA COMEDY SERIES AWARD
(Year/programme)

1 1980, *Yes Minister* **2** 1981, *Yes Minister*
3 1982, *Yes Minister* **4** 1983, *Hi-De-Hi*
5 1984, *The Young Ones* **6** 1985, *Only Fools and Horses* **7** 1986, *Just Good Friends*
8 1987, *Blackadder the Third* **9** 1988, *Only Fools and Horses* **10** 1989, *The New Statesman*

THE 10 ★
FIRST GOLDEN ROSE OF MONTREUX AWARDS WON BY BRITISH TV

YEAR	PROGRAMME
1961	*The Black and White Minstrel Show* (BBC)
1967	*Frost over England* (BBC)
1972	*Marty: The Best of the Comedy Machine* (ATV)
1977	*The Muppet Show* (ATV)
1982	*Dizzy Feet* (Central Television)
1985	*The Paul Daniels Magic Easter Show* (BBC)
1988	*The Comic Strip Presents* (Channel 4)
1989	*Hale and Pace* (London Weekend)
1990	*Mr. Bean* (Thames)
1995	*Don't Forget Your Toothbrush* (Channel 4)

GEORGE CLOONEY

After years as a struggling actor in failed TV pilots and low-budget films, George Clooney finally made the big time playing heartthrob paediatrician Doug Ross in Michael Crichton's medical drama *ER*. He has gone on to star in a series of major movies, including *One Fine Day*, *Out of Sight*, and Robert Rodriguez' *From Dusk Till Dawn*; he also took the title role in Tim Burton's *Batman*. *ER* is one of the top-rated shows in the US, pulling in audiences of 18 million households. In the UK, although popular, it enjoys more of a cult status. His army of fans mourned his departure from *ER* in May 1999.

SNAP SHOTS

Which was the first country to have television?
see p.195 for the answer

A USA
B UK
C USSR

CHILDREN'S TV & VIDEO

FILMS ON UK TELEVISION WATCHED BY MOST CHILDREN, 1998–99*

FILM	CHANNEL	AUDIENCE[#]
1 Ace Ventura – When Nature Calls	ITV	2,328,000
2 Willy Wonka and the Chocolate Factory	BBC 2	2,199,000
3 Home Alone 2	ITV	2,154,000
4 The Santa Clause	BBC 1	2,087,000
5 Addams Family Values	BBC 1	2,079,000
6 Home Alone	ITV	1,945,000
7 Indiana Jones and the Last Crusade	BBC 1	1,626,000
8 Hocus Pocus	ITV	1,594,000
9 Beethoven's 2nd	BBC 1	1,552,000
10 GoldenEye	ITV	1,492,000

* From 20 April 1998 to 18 April 1999 (52 consecutive weeks) # Children only

CARTOONS ON UK TELEVISION WATCHED BY MOST CHILDREN, 1998–99*

CARTOON	CHANNEL	AUDIENCE[#]
1 Cartoon Critters	BBC 1	1,528,000
2 Casper	BBC 1	1,482,000
3 The Wizard of Oz	BBC 1	1,132,000
4 Rugrats	BBC 1	1,109,000
5 Hey Arnold	ITV	1,016,000
6 Inch High Private Eye	BBC 1	942,000
7 Taz-Mania[+]	BBC 2	938,000
8 Alvin and the Chipmunks	BBC 1	928,000
9 Taz-Mania[+]	BBC 2	912,000
10 House of Toons	ITV	911,000

* From 20 April 1998 to 18 April 1999 (52 consecutive weeks)

 # Children only   + Two separate screenings

CHILDREN'S PROGRAMMES ON BRITISH TELEVISION, 1998

PROGRAMME	DATE	AUDIENCE
1 Children of the New Forest	15 Nov	5,799,000
2 Children's BBC	14 Dec	5,704,000
3 Blue Peter	23 Dec	4,567,000
4 Tom and Jerry	19 Apr	4,413,000
5 Bananaman	15 Jun	4,348,000
6 It'll Never Work	22 Dec	3,914,000
7 Newsround	23 Dec	3,845,000
8 The Queen's Nose	23 Dec	3,410,000
9 The Demon Headmaster	6 Jan	3,245,000
10 Goosebumps	21 Dec	3,213,000

GLUED TO THE TV

When ranking their favourite activities, children tend to put watching TV a long way down the list. However, research shows that they spend, on average, between 4 and 6 hours a day in front of the TV.

198

TOP 10 ★
TELEVISION PROGRAMMES WATCHED BY MOST CHILDREN IN THE UK, 1998–99*

PROGRAMME	CHANNEL	AUDIENCE[#]
1 World Cup: Argentina v England	ITV	2,922,000
2 Ace Ventura – When Nature Calls	ITV	2,328,000
3 Coronation Street	ITV	2,327,000
4 The Simpsons	BBC 2	2,292,000
5 EastEnders	BBC 1	2,258,000
6 Celebrity Stars in Their Eyes	ITV	2,252,000
7 Willy Wonka and the Chocolate Factory	BBC 2	2,199,000
8 Home Alone 2	ITV	2,154,000
9 Who Wants to Be a Millionaire?	ITV	2,114,000
10 The Santa Clause	BBC 1	2,087,000

* From 20 April 1998 to 18 April 1999 (52 consecutive weeks)

[#] Children only

TOP 10 ★
BESTSELLING CHILDREN'S VIDEOS IN THE UK*

1 The Jungle Book
2 The Lion King
3 Snow White and the Seven Dwarfs
4 Toy Story
5 Fantasia
6 One Hundred and One Dalmatians
7 Lady and the Tramp
8 Beauty and the Beast
9 Aladdin
10 Cinderella

* To 30 April 1999

TOP 10 ★
CHILDREN'S VIDEOS IN THE US, 1998

VIDEO	LABEL
1 The Lion King II – Simba's Pride	Buena Vista
2 Pocahontas – Journey to a New World	Disney
3 The Land Before Time VI: The Secret of Saurus Rock	Universal
4 Dr. Seuss: How the Grinch Stole Christmas	MGM
5 The Land Before Time V: The Mysterious Island	Universal
6 Billboard Dad	Warner
7 Blues Clues Storytime	Paramount
8 Scooby Doo on Zombie Island	Turner
9 Dance with the Teletubbies	PBS
10 Elmopalooza	Sony Wonder

Source: *Videoscan, Inc.*

TOP 10 ★
CHILDREN'S VIDEOS IN THE UK, 1998

1 Lady and the Tramp
2 Hercules
3 Peter Pan
4 Anastasia
5 The Little Mermaid
6 Rudolph the Red-Nosed Reindeer
7 Beauty and the Beast: Enchanted Christmas
8 Cinderella
9 Teletubbies – Nursery Rhymes
10 Teletubbies – Happy Xmas

Source: *British Video Association*

VIRTUAL VIDEO
The story of Woody the cowboy and his rival, Buzz Lightyear the space ranger, was the first entirely computer-generated full-length feature film. Its stunningly realistic animation won its creator John Lasseter an Oscar.

© DISNEY

What is the bestselling non-Disney animated feature film?
see p.191 for the answer

A *Antz*
B *The Land Before Time*
C *Prince of Egypt*

TOP 10 ★

VIDEO CONSUMERS IN EUROPE

COUNTRY	SPENDING PER VIDEO HOUSEHOLD (US $)		
	RENTAL	PURCHASE	TOTAL
1 Iceland	241.4	37.9	279.3
2 Ireland	116.3	36.8	153.1
3 Denmark	51.3	64.6	115.9
4 UK	40.7	66.6	107.3
5 Norway	65.1	41.9	107.0
6 France	14.0	82.3	96.3
7 Belgium	23.9	49.1	73.0
8 Sweden	40.0	31.3	71.2
9 Luxembourg	22.3	45.3	67.6
10 Switzerland	21.7	45.3	67.0
EU average	23.1	44.4	67.5
Western Europe average	23.6	44.3	68.0

Source: Screen Digest

TOP 10 ★

COUNTRIES WITH THE MOST VIDEO RENTAL OUTLETS

COUNTRY	EST. NO. OF RENTAL OUTLETS
1 USA	27,944
2 Pakistan	25,000
3 China	20,000
4 South Korea	19,000
5 Romania	15,000
6 =Bulgaria	10,000
=India	10,000
=Japan	10,000
=Poland	10,000
10 Brazil	9,710
UK	4,860

Source: Screen Digest

TAPE LEISURE

The advent of the video age has revolutionized our television viewing habits. No longer constrained by the programme schedules, people can now watch what they want, when it suits them.

TOP 10 ★

MOST-PURCHASED VIDEO CATEGORIES IN THE UK

CATEGORY	PER CENT OF TOTAL SALES
1 Feature films	40.5
2 Children's entertainment	26.5
3 TV shows	12.0
4 Music	8.5
5 Live comedy	6.5
6 Sport (excluding football)	1.8
7 Fitness	1.5
8 =Football	1.2
=Miscellaneous	1.2
10 Reality video	0.3

Based upon an analysis of UK high-street video sales, it is clear that by far the biggest proportion of people who buy tapes do so in order to own copies of feature films and, to a lesser extent, favourite TV programmes. The "miscellaneous" category includes history, nature, and transport documentaries, and instructional and hobby tapes.

TOP 10 ★

COUNTRIES WITH THE MOST VIDEO RENTAL OUTLETS PER 1,000,000 POPULATION

COUNTRY	OUTLETS PER 1,000,000 POPULATION
1 Bulgaria	1,186.5
2 Iceland	697.1
3 Romania	663.5
4 South Korea	415.6
5 Denmark	323.9
6 Ireland	311.0
7 Canada	267.2
8 Poland	258.8
9 Sri Lanka	231.6
10 Hungary	200.2
UK	83.5

Source: Screen Digest

What has been Whoopi Goldberg's most successful film?
see p.184 for the answer

A *The Color Purple*
B *Sister Act*
C *Ghost*

VIDEOS THAT SPENT LONGEST AT NO. 1 IN THE RENTAL CHART

TITLE/YEAR	WEEKS AT NO.1
1 *Raiders of the Lost Ark*, 1983	14
2 *Police Academy*, 1985	13
3 *First Blood*, 1983	11
4 =*An Officer and a Gentleman*, 1984	9
=*Tightrope*, 1985*	9
=*Se7en*, 1996	9
7 =*Trading Places*, 1984–85	8
=*The Goonies*, 1986	8
=*Aliens*, 1987	8
=*Big Trouble in Little China*, 1987	8

* Tightrope's *tenure at the top was split into two runs of six weeks and three weeks*

Source: *MRIB*

A film that can hold No.1 for a full month now is special indeed, such is the urgency with which recent box office successes transfer to video.

COUNTRIES WITH THE MOST VCRs

COUNTRY/PER CENT OF HOMES	VCRs
1 USA, 89.6	86,825,000
2 China, 13.3	40,000,000
3 Japan, 80.4	34,309,000
4 Germany, 71.8	26,328,000
5 UK, 81.7	18,848,000
6 Brazil, 37.2	15,488,000
7 France, 70.4	15,483,000
8 Italy, 60.2	13,161,000
9 Russia, 20.6	10,315,000
10 Mexico, 56.7	8,540,000

Source: Screen Digest

TOP 10 MOST RENTED VIDEOS IN THE UK, 1998

TITLE	RENTALS
1 *Men in Black*	3,391,894
2 *Face/Off*	2,862,585
3 *Air Force One*	2,269,835
4 *Starship Troopers*	2,262,552
5 *The Fifth Element*	2,108,525
6 *The Full Monty*	2,000,084
7 *The Lost World: Jurassic Park*	1,928,168
8 *The Devil's Advocate*	1,906,479
9 *Austin Powers: International Man of Mystery*	1,885,738
10 *The Jackal*	1,873,391

Source: *MRIB*

TOP 10 MOST RENTED VIDEOS OF ALL TIME IN THE UK*

1. *Four Weddings and a Funeral*
2. *Dirty Dancing* 3. *Basic Instinct*
4. *Crocodile Dundee* 5. *Sister Act*
6. *Forrest Gump* 7. *Home Alone*
8. *Ghost* 9. *Pretty Woman*
10. *Speed*

* To 31 December 1998
Source: *MRIB*

SPECIAL DELIVERY
Will Smith, one of the Men in Black, takes a break from blasting extraterrestrials into oblivion to assist at the birth of an alien baby.

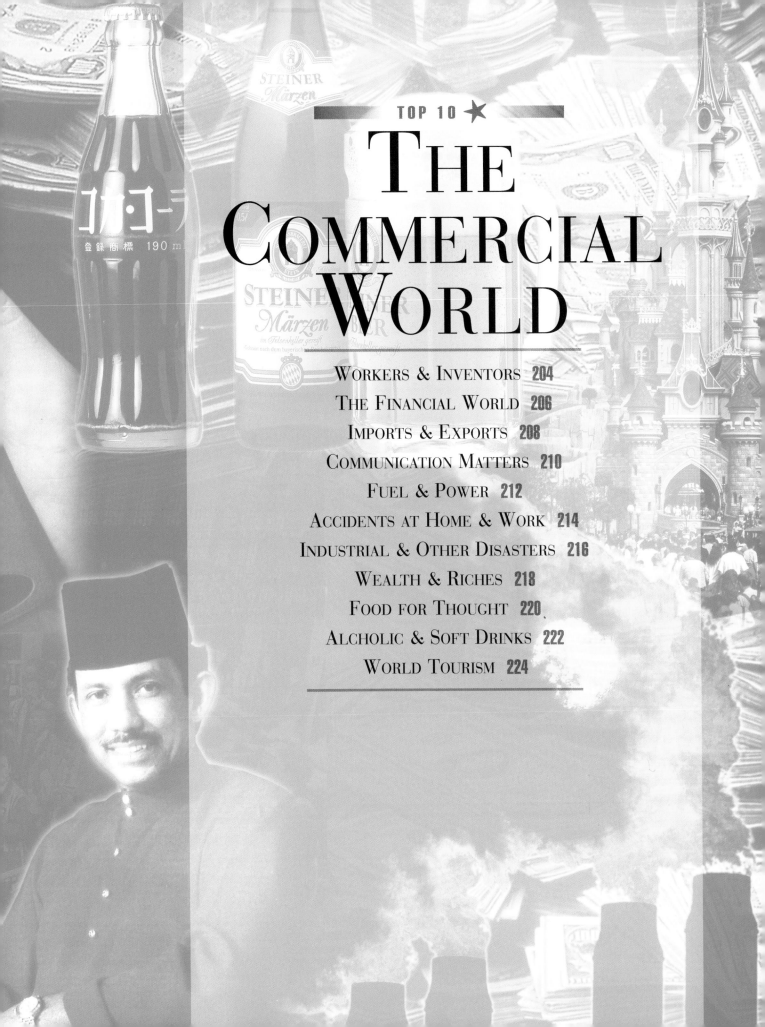

WORKERS & INVENTORS

WORKERS OF THE WORLD
Migrant workers at this clothes factory in
Guangdong province account for just some of
China's massive work force.

TOP 10 ★

COUNTRIES WITH THE MOST WORKERS

	COUNTRY	WORKERS*
1	China	709,000,000
2	India	398,000,000
3	USA	133,000,000
4	Indonesia	89,000,000
5	Russia	77,000,000
6	Brazil	71,000,000
7	Japan	66,000,000
8	Bangladesh	60,000,000
9	Pakistan	46,000,000
10	Nigeria	44,000,000
	UK	29,000,000

* Based on people aged 15–64 who are currently
employed; unpaid groups are not included.

Source: World Bank

THE 10 ★

FIRST PATENTS IN THE UK

	PATENTEE	PATENT*	DATE
1	Nicholas Hillyard	Engraving and printing the king's head on documents	5 May 1617
2	John Gason	Locks, mills, and other river and canal improvements	1 Jul 1617
3	John Miller and John Jasper Wolfen	Oil for suits of armour	3 Nov 1617
4	Robert Crumpe	Tunnels and pumps	9 Jan 1618
5	Aaron Rathburne and Roger Burges	Making maps of English cities	11 Mar 1618
6	John Gilbert	River dredger	16 Jul 1618
7	Clement Dawbeney	Water-powered engine for making nails	11 Dec 1618
8	Thomas Murray	Sword blades	11 Jan 1619
9	Thomas Wildgoose and David Ramsey	Ploughs, pumps, and ships' engines	17 Jan 1619
10	Abram Baker	Smalt (glass) manufacture	16 Feb 1619

* Patents issued prior to 1617 were not codified, and are excluded from this list.

The world's first patent, by which the architect Filippo Brunelleschi was granted the exclusive licence to make a barge crane to transport marble, was issued in Florence in 1421.

Did You Know? In 1596, Queen Elizabeth I issued a patent to Sir John Harington for a water closet.

THE 10 ★
FIRST TRADEMARKS ISSUED IN THE US

	ISSUED TO	PRODUCT
1	Averill Chemical-Paint Company	Liquid paint
2	J.B. Baldy & Co.	Mustard
3	Ellis Branson	Retail coal
4	Tracy Coit	Fish
5	William Lanfair Ellis & Co.	Oyster packing
6	Evans, Clow, Dalzell & Co.	Wrought-iron pipe
7	W.E. Garrett & Sons	Snuff
8	William G. Hamilton	Cartwheel
9	John K. Hogg	Soap
10	Abraham P. Olzendam	Woollen hose

All of these trademarks were registered on the same day, 25 October 1870, and are ranked only by the trademark numbers assigned to them.

TOP 10 ★
OCCUPATIONS IN THE UK

	JOB SECTOR	EMPLOYEES
1	Manufacturing	4,076,000
2	Wholesale and retail (including motor)	4,037,000
3	Real estate, renting, and business activities	3,007,000
4	Health and social work	2,582,000
5	Education	1,896,000
6	Transport, storage, and communication	1,389,000
7	Public administration and defence	1,350,000
8	Hotels and restaurants	1,316,000
9	Financial intermediation	1,064,000
10	Other community, social, and personal service activities	1,024,000

PRODUCTION LINE

A Ford worker at the Halewood factory near Liverpool, UK. Motor manufacturing is still big business, but some plants have had to close due to falling sales.

THE 10 ★
FIRST WOMEN PATENTEES IN THE US

	PATENTEE	PATENT	DATE
1	Mary Kies	Straw weaving with silk or thread	5 May 1809
2	Mary Brush	Corset	21 Jul 1815
3	Sophia Usher	Carbonated liquid	11 Sep 1819
4	Julia Planton	Foot stove	4 Nov 1822
5	Lucy Burnap	Weaving grass hats	16 Feb 1823
6	Diana H. Tuttle	Accelerating spinning-wheel heads	17 May 1824
7	Catharine Elliot	Manufacturing moccasins	26 Jan 1825
8	Phoebe Collier	Sawing wheel-fellies (rims)	20 May 1826
9	Elizabeth H. Buckley	Sheet-iron shovel	28 Feb 1828
10	Henrietta Cooper	Whitening leghorn straw	12 Nov 1828

TOP 10 BRITISH COMPANIES WITH THE MOST EMPLOYEES

(Company/employees)

1 British Telecom, 129,600 **2** BTR, 115,805 **3** HSBC Holdings, 109,298 **4** Compass Group, 107,843 **5** Rentokil Initial, 107,765 **6** J. Sainsbury, 102,544 **7** Tesco, 98,440 **8** Lonrho, 93,597 **9** Lloyds TSB Group, 90,383 **10** Barclays, 87,400

This list includes only publicly quoted companies (companies whose shares are on the Stock Exchange). As well as these, there are government and other organizations that are major employers – the National Health Service, for example, employs about a million people, and the Post Office almost 200,000.

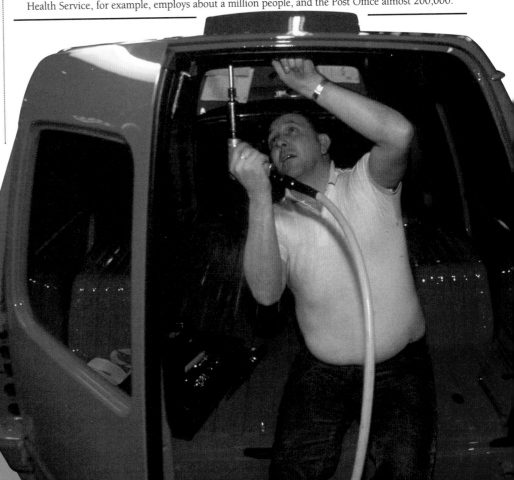

TOP 10 ★
LARGEST PRIVATIZED BRITISH COMPANIES

COMPANY/SALE	PROCEEDS (£)
1 British Telecom, 1984–93	17,604,000,000
2 Regional electricity companies, 1990	7,997,000,000
3 British Gas, 1986–90	7,793,000,000
4 British Petroleum, 1979–90	5,273,000,000
5 Regional water authorities, 1989–92	3,468,000,000
6 Electricity generating companies, 1991	2,486,000,000
7 British Steel, 1988	2,425,000,000
8 Enterprise Oil, 1984	2,106,900,000
9 British Airports Authority, 1987–89	1,332,000,000
10 Rolls-Royce, 1987	1,031,000,000

The Top 10 privatized companies alone generated income for the Treasury totalling more than £50,000,000,000, equivalent to over £1,000 for every British adult, or £10 for every person in the world.

TOP 10 OLDEST ESTABLISHED BUSINESSES IN THE UK
(Business/location/founded)

❶ **The Royal Mint**, Cardiff (formerly London), 886 ❷ **Kirkstall Forge** (axles, etc), Kirkstall, Leeds, 1200 ❸ **The Shore Porters Society of Aberdeen**, Aberdeen, 1498 ❹ **Cambridge University Press**, Cambridge, 1534 ❺ **John Brooke and Sons** (property management), Huddersfield, 1541 ❻ **Child's Bank** (now part of Royal Bank of Scotland), London, 1559 ❼ **Whitechapel Bell Foundry**, London, 1570 ❽ **Oxford University Press**, Oxford, 1585 ❾ **Richard Durtnell and Sons** (builders), Brasted, nr. Westerham, Kent, 1591 ❿ **Hays at Guildford** (office services), Guildford (formerly London), 1651

SHARE DEALING

Trading is brisk at the Petroleum Exchange in London. The traders' different coloured jackets denote the company to which they belong.

TOP 10 ★
SUPERMARKET GROUPS* IN THE UK

GROUP	SALES 1997/98 (£)#
1 Tesco	14,621,000,000
2 J. Sainsbury+	10,836,000,000
3 Asda	7,600,800,000
4 Safeway★	6,978,700,000
5 Somerfield♦	6,055,900,000
6 William Morrison	2,297,000,000
7 Waitrose (John Lewis Partnership)	1,584,900,000
8 Iceland	1,566,400,000
9 Aldi	678,300,000
10 Budgens	362,600,000

* *Excluding Co-ops and "mixed goods" retailers, such as Marks & Spencer*
# *Excluding VAT*
+ *Including Savacentre*
★ *Including Presto*
♦ *Merged with Kwik Save in 1998*

Source: The Retail Rankings (1999) published by Corporate Intelligence on Retailing

THE 10 ★
COUNTRIES MOST IN DEBT

COUNTRY	TOTAL EXTERNAL DEBT ($)
1 Mexico	165,743,000,000
2 Brazil	159,139,000,000
3 Russia	120,461,000,000
4 China	118,090,000,000
5 Indonesia	107,831,000,000
6 India	93,766,000,000
7 Argentina	89,747,000,000
8 Turkey	73,592,000,000
9 Thailand	56,789,000,000
10 Poland	42,291,000,000

Source: World Bank

The World Bank's annual debt calculations estimate the total indebtedness of low and middle income countries at $2,177,000,000,000 in 1996.

TOP 10 ★
US COMPANIES MAKING THE GREATEST PROFIT PER SECOND

COMPANY	PROFIT PER SEC ($)
1 Ford Motor Co.	699
2 General Electric	294
3 AT&T	202
4 Exxon Corporation	201
5 IBM	200
6 Intel Corp.	192
7 Citigroup	184
8 Philip Morris Companies, Inc.	170
9 Merck	166
10 BankAmerica Corporation	163

TOP 10 ★
INTERNATIONAL INDUSTRIAL COMPANIES

COMPANY/ LOCATION/SECTOR	ANNUAL SALES ($)
1 General Motors Corp., US, Transport	178,174,000,000
2 Ford Motor Co., US, Transport	153,627,000,000
3 Mitsui and Co. Ltd., Japan, Trading	142,688,000,000
4 Mitsubishi Corp., Japan, Trading	128,922,000,000
5 Royal Dutch/Shell Group, UK/Netherlands, Oil, gas, fuel	128,142,000,000
6 Itochu Corp., Japan, Trading	126,632,000,000
7 Exxon Corp., US, Oil, gas, fuel	122,379,000,000
8 Wal-Mart Stores, Inc., US, Retailing	119,299,000,000
9 Marubeni Corp., Japan Trading	111,121,000,000
10 Sumitomo Corp., Japan Trading	102,395,000,000

Source: Fortune Global 500

TOP 10 ★
RICHEST COUNTRIES

COUNTRY	GDP PER CAPITA ($)
1 Liechtenstein	42,416
= Switzerland	42,416
3 Japan	41,718
4 Luxembourg	35,109
5 Norway	33,734
6 Denmark	33,191
7 Germany	29,632
8 Austria	29,006
9 Belgium	26,582
10 Monaco	26,470
UK	18,913

Source: United Nations

GDP (Gross Domestic Product) is the total value of all the goods and services produced annually within a country (Gross National Product, GNP, also includes income from overseas). Dividing GDP by the country's population produces GDP per capita, which is often used as a measure of how "rich" a country is.

THE 10 ★
POOREST COUNTRIES

COUNTRY	GDP PER CAPITA ($)
1 Sudan	36
2 São Tomé and Principe	49
3 Mozambique	77
4 = Eritrea	96
= Ethiopia	96
6 Dem. Rep. of Congo	117
7 Somalia	119
8 Tajikistan	122
9 Cambodia	130
10 Guinea-Bissau	131

Source: United Nations

It is hard to imagine living on as little as $36 per year (about £24), but $1 in Sudan, for example, purchases far more than in the US and UK.

Who is the youngest $ billionaire in the US? *see p.219 for the answer*
A Daniel Morton Ziff
B Michael Dell
C Robert David Ziff

IMPORTS & EXPORTS

TOP 10 ⭐
DUTY-FREE COUNTRIES

COUNTRY	ANNUAL SALES ($)
1 UK	2,452,000,000
2 USA	1,652,000,000
3 Finland	962,000,000
4 South Korea	908,000,000
5 Germany	864,000,000
6 France	683,000,000
7 Denmark	646,000,000
8 US Virgin Islands	611,000,000
9 Australia	570,000,000
10 Japan	568,000,000

In 1997 the UK led the world in duty- and tax-free shopping, accounting for 11.7 per cent of total sales. Europe as a whole took almost half (46.6 per cent) of global sales.

TOP 10 ⭐
DUTY-FREE AIRPORTS

AIRPORT/LOCATION	ANNUAL SALES ($)
1 London Heathrow, UK	*
2 Honolulu, Hawaii, USA	360,000,000
3 Amsterdam Schiphol, Netherlands	353,300,000
4 Singapore Changi	310,000,000
5 Paris Charles De Gaulle, France	309,800,000
6 Frankfurt, Germany	260,300,000
7 Hong Kong, China	250,000,000
8 Manila N. Aquino, Philippines	242,800,000
9 Tokyo Narita, Japan	220,000,000
10 São Paulo, Brazil	*

Precise figure confidential

TOP 10 ⭐
DUTY-FREE SHOPS

SHOP/LOCATION
1 London Heathrow Airport, UK
2 Silja Ferries, Finland
3 Honolulu Airport, Hawaii, USA
4 Amsterdam Schiphol Airport, Netherlands
5 Singapore Changi Airport, Singapore
6 Paris Charles De Gaulle Airport, France
7 Viking Line Ferries, Finland
8 Frankfurt Airport, Germany
9 London Gatwick Airport, UK
10 Stena Line UK, UK

In 1997 total global duty- and tax-free sales were worth $21 billion. Sales of several of those outlets featured in the Top 10 are confidential, but industry insiders have ranked them and place them in the range of over $270 million at the bottom of the list to over $500 million at the top. Although London Heathrow Airport achieves the greatest total sales, Honolulu Airport has the highest average sales, amounting in 1996 to $95.41 per passenger.

TOP 10 DUTY-FREE PRODUCTS
(Product/sales in $)

❶ **Women's fragrances**, 2,250,000,000 ❷ **Cigarettes**, 2,235,000,000 ❸ **Women's cosmetics**, 1,767,000,000 ❹ **Scotch whisky**, 1,663,000,000 ❺ **Cognac**, 1,235,000,000 ❻ **Men's fragrances and toiletries**, 1,109,000,000 ❼ **Accessories**, 1,050,000,000 ❽ **Confectionery**, 1,049,000,000 ❾ **Leather goods** (handbags, belts, etc.), 902,000,000 ❿ **Watches**, 703,000,000

TOP 10 ⭐
DUTY-FREE FERRY OPERATORS

FERRY OPERATOR/LOCATION	ANNUAL SALES ($)
1 Silja Ferries, Finland	245,000,000
2 Eurotunnel, UK/France	225,000,000
3 P&O European Ferries, UK	220,000,000
4 Stena Line, UK	190,900,000
5 Viking Line Ferries, Finland	190,000,000
6 Stena Line, Sweden	168,100,000
7 Scandlines, Denmark	*
8 Color Line, Norway	119,900,000
9 Hoverspeed, UK	80,900,000
10 Brittany Ferries, France	*

Precise figure confidential

END OF AN ERA

Under new EC laws, duty-free sales in member countries were axed in July 1999, much to the disappointment of millions of travellers.

208

PRODUCTS IMPORTED TO THE UK

PRODUCT	TOTAL VALUE OF 1997 IMPORTS (£)
1 Electrical machinery	37,272,000,000
2 Road vehicles	22,222,000,000
3 Chemicals	18,017,000,000
4 Mechanical machinery	17,612,000,000
5 Food and live animals	13,997,000,000
6 Clothing and footwear	8,814,000,000
7 Fuels (petrol, coal, gas, electricity)	6,526,000,000
8 Scientific and photographic equipment	6,304,000,000
9 Crude minerals	6,186,000,000
10 Transport equipment	5,654,000,000
Total (including goods not in Top 10)	189,079,000,000

EXPORT MARKETS FOR PRODUCTS FROM THE UK

MARKET	TOTAL VALUE OF 1997 EXPORTS (£)
1 USA	20,993,000,000
2 Germany	20,659,000,000
3 France	16,583,000,000
4 Netherlands	13,909,000,000
5 Ireland	9,348,000,000
6 Belgium/Luxembourg	8,446,000,000
7 Italy	8,205,000,000
8 Spain	6,739,000,000
9 Sweden	4,448,000,000
10 Japan	4,182,000,000

In 1997, the USA regained its former place as Britain's pre-eminent export market – a position that since 1990 had been usurped by Germany.

ATLANTIC TRADE

Cargo from the UK is unloaded at Baltimore, USA. Trade between the two countries has been important for well over 100 years.

Which country has the most Internet users?
see p.211 for the answer
A Japan
B USA
C UK

COMMUNICATION MATTERS

COUNTRIES WITH THE HIGHEST RATIO OF CELLULAR MOBILE PHONE USERS

	COUNTRY	SUBSCRIBERS	SUBSCRIBERS PER 1,000 INHABITANTS
1	Finland	2.148,000	418.7
2	Norway	1,685,000	383.0
3	Sweden	3,187,000	358.1
4	Australia	4,400,000	291.9
5	Denmark	1,489,000	282.0
6	Singapore	710,000	229.0
7	Japan	28,800,000	228.5
8	USA	55,000,000	205.5
9	Italy	11,500,000	200.4
10	New Zealand	600,000	165.7
	UK	8,344,000	141.7
	World total	205,000,000	35.0

Source: *Siemens AG*

COUNTRIES MAKING THE MOST INTERNATIONAL PHONE CALLS*

	COUNTRY	CALLS PER HEAD PER ANNUM	TOTAL CALLS PER ANNUM
1	USA	9.0	2,847,633,000
2	Germany	17.0	1,420,300,000
3	UK	9.1	528,000,000#
4	Italy	8.7	503,990,000
5	China	0.3	497,000,000
6	Switzerland	60.0	488,764,000
7	Netherlands	26.5	462,000,000
8	Canada	11.9	332,750,000#
9	Austria	38.9	314,571,000
10	Spain	7.5	295,450,000

* For latest year for which figures are available
# Estimated

Source: *Siemens AG*

COUNTRIES WITH THE MOST TELEPHONES

	COUNTRY	TELEPHONES PER 100 INHABITANTS
1	Sweden	68.54
2	Switzerland	66.20
3	Denmark	62.88
4	USA	62.56
5	Luxembourg	61.02
6	Norway	60.91
7	Iceland	60.00
8	France	58.36
9	Canada	57.88
10	Germany	56.16
	UK	53.65

The world average "teledensity" is 13.47 phones per 100 inhabitants. On a continental basis, Oceania (Australia, New Zealand, and their neighbours) has the highest ratio of telephones per 100 people – an average of 40.33 – followed by Europe with 35.64. The Americas as a whole has an average of 30.35 because even the high US figure fails to compensate for the much lower numbers in Central and South American countries. Asia's average is 6.70 and Africa's the lowest at 2.05, with many countries falling well below even this level: Tanzania has just 0.3.

MOBILE PHONES

The first mobile phone system was a simple walkie-talkie device developed in 1921 by the Detroit Police Department. Originally used only by emergency services and utility companies, mobile telephony finally became a commercial enterprise in 1946. Just over 50 years later, in 1998, the European Global System for Mobile Communications (GSM) boasted 100 million subscribers and 5 million new users every month. Portable phones have gone through many changes in technology and design. Today's phones are fashionable accessories which, it is believed, will one day cause the disappearance of fixed-point phones.

SNAP ★ SHOTS

ITEMS BOUGHT ON THE INTERNET

	ITEM	PERCENTAGE OF INTERNET USERS WHO HAVE PURCHASED
1	Computer software	43
2	Computer hardware	37
3	Books	23
4	Music CDs	17
5 =	Consumer electronics	14
=	Travel	14
7	Games	11
8	Clothing	8
9	Flowers	7
10	Information	6

Source: *NOP survey*

In terms of value of sales, travel has emerged as the No. 1 online commodity, followed by computer hardware and books. Sectors of the online marketplace that are currently relatively small, but for which phenomenal growth has been predicted by industry forecasters, include grocery, entertainment tickets, and toys.

TOP 10 ★
COUNTRIES WITH THE MOST COMPUTERS

	COUNTRY	NO. OF COMPUTERS
1	USA	129,000,000
2	Japan	32,800,000
3	Germany	21,100,000
4	UK	18,250,000
5=	France	15,350,000
6=	Canada	11,750,000
7	Italy	10,550,000
8	China	8,260,000
9	Australia	7,680,000
10	South Korea	6,650,000

Source: *Computer Industry Almanac, Inc.*

Computer industry estimates put the number of computers in the world at 98 million in 1990, and 364,400,000 at the end of 1998. By the year 2000, the total is predicted to rise to 579 million.

TOP 10 ★
COUNTRIES WITH THE MOST INTERNET USERS

	COUNTRY	PERCENTAGE OF POPULATION	INTERNET USERS*
1	USA	29	76,500,000
2	Japan	8	9,750,000
3	UK	14	8,100,000
4	Germany	9	7,140,000
5	Canada	22	6,490,000
6	Australia	24	4,360,000
7	France	5	2,790,000
8	Sweden	29	2,580,000
9	Italy	4	2,140,000
10	Spain	5	1,980,000
	World total	2.5	147,800,000

* Estimates for weekly usage as at end of 1998

Source: *Computer Industry Almanac, Inc.*

One of the principal aims of the Internet is the dissemination of information. It is therefore ironic that information about its own users should be so patchy and erratic.

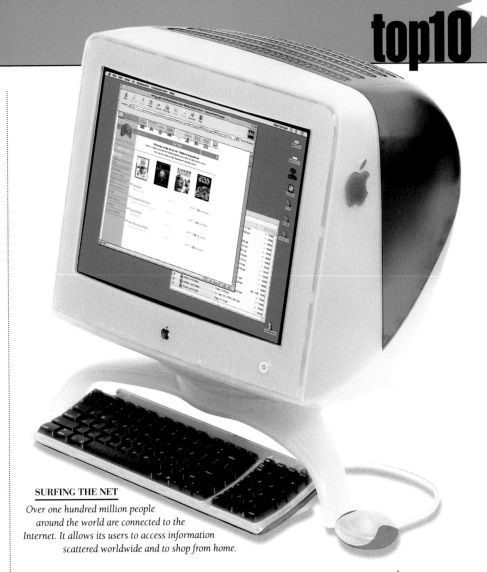

SURFING THE NET
Over one hundred million people around the world are connected to the Internet. It allows its users to access information scattered worldwide and to shop from home.

TOP 10 ★
BESTSELLING BRITISH COMMEMORATIVE STAMPS

	ISSUE	DATE
1	Nature conservation	May 1986
2	British butterflies	May 1981
3	RSPCA	Jan 1990
4	Flowers	Mar 1979
5	Shire horses	Jul 1978
6	Birds	Jan 1980
7	Dogs	Feb 1979
8	Birds/RSPB centenary	Jan 1989
9	Queen Mother's 80th birthday	Aug 1980
10	Wedding of Prince Charles and Lady Diana Spencer	Jul 1981

TOP 10 ★
COUNTRIES WITH THE MOST POST OFFICES

	COUNTRY	POST OFFICES*
1	India	153,021
2	China	129,455
3	USA	44,619
4	Russia	43,900
5	Japan	24,680
6	Germany	20,567
7	Turkey	19,063
8	UK	18,993
9	France	17,148
10	Ukraine	15,786

* 1997 or latest year available

Which country has the most workers?
see p.204 for the answer
A India
B China
C Russia

FUEL & POWER

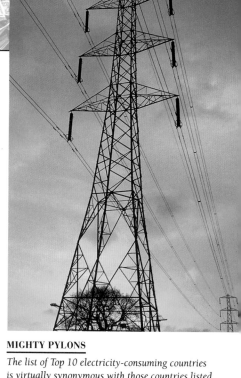

TOP 10 ★
NATURAL GAS-CONSUMING COUNTRIES

	COUNTRY	1997 CONSUMPTION BILLION CU M	BILLION CU FT
1	USA	632.5	22,336.5
2	Russia	331.1	11,692.7
3	UK	85.8	3,030.0
4	Germany	79.0	2,789.9
5	Canada	74.9	2,645.1
6	Ukraine	72.2	2,549.7
7	Japan	65.1	2,299.0
8	Italy	53.9	1,903.5
9	Saudi Arabia	43.9	1,550.3
10	Iran	42.9	1,515.0
	World total	2,196.7	77,575.7

Source: *BP Statistical Review of World Energy 1998*

TOP 10 ★
OIL-CONSUMING COUNTRIES

	COUNTRY	1997 CONSUMPTION (TONNES)
1	USA	846,500,000
2	Japan	266,400,000
3	China	185,600,000
4	Germany	136,500,000
5	Russia	128,000,000
6	South Korea	105,900,000
7	Italy	94,600,000
8	France	91,900,000
9	Brazil	82,800,000
10	Canada	82,100,000
	UK	81,200,000

Source: *BP Statistical Review of World Energy 1998*

MIGHTY PYLONS

The list of Top 10 electricity-consuming countries is virtually synonymous with those countries listed below, since relatively little electricity is transmitted across national boundaries.

TOP 10 COUNTRIES WITH THE MOST NUCLEAR REACTORS
(Country/reactors*)

1 USA, 110 **2** France, 57 **3** Japan, 53
4 UK, 35 **5** Russia, 29 **6** Canada, 21
7 Germany, 20 **8** Ukraine, 16
9 Sweden, 12 **10** South Korea, 11

* Civilian nuclear power reactors only, excluding those devoted to military purposes

Source: *International Atomic Energy Agency*

TOP 10 COAL-CONSUMING COUNTRIES
(Country/consumption in tonnes of oil equivalent)

1 China, 681,800,000 **2** USA, 527,900,000 **3** India, 146,400,000
4 Russia, 113,000,000 **5** Japan, 89,800,000
6 Germany, 86,800,000 **7** South Africa, 83,100,000 **8** Poland, 71,200,000
9 Australia, 46,700,000 **10** UK, 40,400,000

Source: *BP Statistical Review of World Energy 1998*

TOP 10 ★
ELECTRICITY-PRODUCING COUNTRIES

	COUNTRY	PRODUCTION KW/HR
1	USA	3,145,892,000,000
2	Russia	956,587,000,000
3	Japan	906,705,000,000
4	China	839,453,000,000
5	Canada	527,316,000,000
6	Germany	525,721,000,000
7	France	471,448,000,000
8	India	356,519,000,000
9	UK	323,029,000,000
10	Brazil	251,484,000,000

TIMBER!

Logging mahogany trees in Brazil. In the years 1990–95, some 47,740 sq km/18,568 sq miles of tropical forest were lost in South America each year.

TOP 10 DEFORESTING COUNTRIES
(Country/average annual forest loss 1990–95 in sq km)

1 Brazil, 25,540 **2** Indonesia, 10,840 **3** Dem. Rep. of the Congo, 7,400 **4** Bolivia, 5,810 **5** Mexico, 5,080 **6** Venezuela, 5,030 **7** Malaysia, 4,000 **8** Myanmar, 3,870 **9** Sudan, 3,530 **10** Thailand, 3,290

Source: *Food and Agriculture Organization of the United Nations*

Did You Know? The world produces 9.5 million tonnes of oil every day.

ENERGY-CONSUMING COUNTRIES

COUNTRY	OIL	GAS	1997 ENERGY CONSUMPTION* COAL	NUCLEAR	HYDRO	TOTAL
1 USA	846.5	569.3	527.9	170.9	29.6	2,144.2
2 China	185.6	17.4	681.8	3.7	16.2	904.7
3 Russia	128.0	298.0	113.0	27.9	13.5	580.4
4 Japan	266.4	58.6	89.8	83.4	8.1	506.3
5 Germany	136.5	71.1	86.8	43.9	1.8	340.1
6 India	83.1	22.0	146.4	2.5	6.2	260.2
7 France	91.9	31.2	13.2	102.1	5.8	244.2
8 Canada	82.1	67.4	26.5	21.3	30.0	227.3
9 UK	81.2	77.2	40.4	25.5	0.5	224.8
10 South Korea	105.9	14.8	34.0	19.9	0.5	175.1
World	3,395.5	1,977.3	2,293.4	617.4	225.9	8,509.5

* Millions of tonnes of oil equivalent

Source: *BP Statistical Review of World Energy 1998*

ENVIRONMENTAL CONCERNS IN THE UK

CONCERN	PERCENTAGE OF PEOPLE CONCERNED
1 Traffic (congestion, fumes, noise)	37
2 Global warming/climate change	32
3 Air pollution	30
4 Pollution of lakes, rivers, and seas	23
5 Depletion of the ozone layer	22
6 Loss of tropical rainforest	15
7 Population growth	14
8 Consumption of natural resources	12
9 = Radioactive wastes	10
= Toxic waste	10
= Loss of countryside to urban development	10

Source: *Department of the Environment, Transport and the Regions*

When considering the environment, people tend to think about issues close to home rather than global ones.

AIR POLLUTION

Carbon dioxide emissions have increased drastically since World War II, as a result of industrialization. Most countries are actively trying to reverse this trend.

SULPHUR DIOXIDE-EMITTING COUNTRIES

COUNTRY	ANNUAL SO₂ EMISSIONS PER HEAD KG	LB	OZ
1 Czech Republic	149.4	329	6
2 Former Yugoslavia	138.2	304	11
3 Bulgaria	116.8	257	8
4 Canada	104.0	229	4
5 Hungary	81.4	179	7
6 = Romania	79.2	174	10
= USA	79.2	174	10
8 Poland	71.1	156	12
9 Slovakia	70.0	154	5
10 Belarus	57.5	126	12

Source: *World Resources Institute*

CARBON DIOXIDE-EMITTING COUNTRIES

COUNTRY	ANNUAL CO₂ EMISSIONS PER HEAD (TONNES)
1 Qatar	52.18
2 United Arab Emirates	36.20
3 Kuwait	25.24
4 Luxembourg	20.12
5 USA	19.68
6 Singapore	19.45
7 Bahrain	18.53
8 Trinidad and Tobago	17.14
9 Australia	16.96
10 Brunei	16.89
UK	9.48

Source: *Carbon Dioxide Information Analysis Center*

ACCIDENTS AT HOME & WORK

THE 10 ★ MOST COMMON SOURCES OF DOMESTIC FIRES IN THE UK

	SOURCE OF IGNITION	FIRES PER ANNUM
1	Electric cooker	18,855
2	Gas cooker	7,839
3	Smokers' materials	4,881
4	Washing machine	2,262
5	Wire and cable	1,678
6	Candle	1,375
7	Electric space heater	1,040
8	Matches	1,024
9	Gas space heater	861
10	Blanket, bed warmer	817
	UK total	53,267

THE 10 ★ MOST COMMON ACCIDENTS IN UK HOMES

	ACCIDENT	NO. PER ANNUM
1	Unspecified falls	413,000
2	Struck by static object	293,000
3	Fall on same level	284,000
4	Cut/tear by sharp object	280,000
5	Fall on/from stairs	230,000
6	Struck by moving object	140,000
7	Foreign body	121,000
8	Struck (unspecified)	100,000
9	Thermal effect	89,000
10	Pinched/crushed by blunt object	80,000

Falls are the leading cause of accidents in the home. Official statistics also list 196,000 accidents of unknown or other causes. Figures cover only non-fatal accidents within homes and gardens (and hence exclude traffic accidents, accidents at work, etc.), and do not include self-inflicted injury, suspected suicide attempts or attack by other people.

TAKE CARE...

Most house fires result from the negligence of householders. In the words of Benjamin Franklin: "An ounce of prevention is worth a pound of cure."

THE 10 ★ MOST COMMON ANIMALS INVOLVED IN ACCIDENTS IN THE UK

	ANIMAL/INSECT	INJURIES CAUSED PER ANNUM
1	Dog	3,271
2	Bee, wasp	1,057
3	Cat	721
4	Unspecified insect	431
5	Rabbit, hamster, etc.	176
6	Horse, pony, donkey	164
7	"Other insect"	118
8	Wild animal	37
9	Chicken, swan, duck	32
10	"Other domestic animal"	30

THE 10 ★ MOST COMMON CAUSES OF DOMESTIC FIRES IN THE UK

	CAUSE	APPROX. NO. OF FIRES PER ANNUM
1	Misuse of equipment or appliances	17,100
2	Malicious (or suspected malicious)	15,500
3	Chip/fat pan fires	12,300
4	Faulty appliances and leads	9,000
5	Careless handling of fire or hot substances	5,400
6	Placing articles too close to heat	4,800
7	Other accidental	4,100
8	Faulty fuel supplies	1,900
9	Playing with fire	1,100
10	Unspecified	900
	UK total	72,200

THE 10 ★
MOST COMMON ACCIDENTAL CAUSES OF DEATH AT WORK IN THE UK

ACCIDENT	FATALITIES (1996/97)
1 Falls from a height	56
2 Struck by a moving object (including flying/falling)	43
3 Struck by a moving vehicle	32
4 = Contact with electricity	15
= Contact with moving machinery	15
6 Trapped by something collapsing/overturning	10
7 Drowning or asphyxiation	7
8 Exposure to an explosion	6
9 Exposure or contact with a harmful substance	4
10 = Slip, trip, or fall on same level	3
= Struck against something fixed or stationary	3
Total (all causes)	210

THE 10 ★
ARTICLES MOST FREQUENTLY INVOLVED IN ACCIDENTS IN THE HOME IN THE UK

ARTICLE	ACCIDENTS PER ANNUM*
1 Construction feature	775,000
2 Furniture	329,000
3 Person	230,000
4 Outdoor surface	194,000
5 Clothing/footwear	191,000
6 Building/raw materials	159,000
7 Furnishings	145,000
8 Cooking/kitchen equipment	134,000
9 Animal/insect	113,000
10 Food/drink	109,000
Total	2,502,000

* *National estimates based on actual Home Accident Surveillance System figures for sample population*

THE 10 MOST DANGEROUS JOBS IN THE UK

1. Formula One driver
2. Bomb disposal officer   3. Test pilot
4. SAS employee   5. Circus performer
6. Film stuntman   7. Commercial diver
8. Oil rig worker   9. Scaffolder
10. = Fisherman; = Miner; = Dockworker
= Sailor in Merchant Navy; = Linesman
(electrical industry)

Life assurance companies carefully base their premiums on actuarial statistics that take into account the likelihood of people in each job being involved in an accident that injures or kills them at work, or as a result of their contact with dangerous substances. This does not mean that assurance companies will not provide cover for such professions, but the riskier the job, the higher the premium. All the jobs mentioned above would incur an extra penalty per £1,000 insured.

THE 10 ★
MOST DANGEROUS INDUSTRIES IN THE UK

INDUSTRY	INJURIES* PER 100,000 EMPLOYEES
1 Mining and quarrying	655.0
2 Manufacturing wood and wood products	468.2
3 Construction	402.8
4 Manufacturing food products, beverages, and tobacco products	332.0
5 Manufacturing other non-metallic mineral products	319.5
6 Manufacturing basic metals and fabricated metal products	277.4
7 Agriculture, hunting, forestry, and fishing	271.8
8 Manufacturing rubber and plastic products	268.3
9 Manufacturing chemicals, chemical products, and man-made fibres	224.0
10 Electricity, gas, and water supply	222.6
Average for all industries	126.8

* *Fatal and major injuries only*

THE 10 MOST ACCIDENT-PRONE COUNTRIES

(Country/accidental death rate per 100,000 population)

1. Estonia 153.5   2. Lithuania 120.7
3. South Africa 99.4   4. Hungary 74.3
5. Moldova 72.1   6. Latvia 71.7
7. Czech Republic 60.7
8. South Korea 59.9   9. Romania 57.1
10. Slovenia 55.2

UK 21.5
Source: *United Nations*

THE 10 ★
MOST COMMON CAUSES OF INJURY AT WORK IN THE UK

CAUSE	FATALITIES	INJURIES*
1 Handling, lifting, or carrying	–	47,889
2 Slip, trip, or fall on same level	3	32,343
3 Struck by moving (including flying or falling) object	43	22,335
4 Fall from height	56	13,220
5 Struck against something fixed or stationary	3	8,713
6 Contact with moving machinery	15	7,266
7 Exposure to or contact with a harmful substance	4	4,641
8 Acts of violence	2	4,374
9 Struck by moving vehicle	32	3,647
10 Animal	1	901
Total (including causes not in Top 10)	210	151,741

* *Resulting in work absence of more than three days, employees only (excluding self-employed), 1996/97 provisional figures*

"Acts of violence" is a new category included for the first time in the 1996/97 statistics, and appears as the eighth most common cause of injury at work.

Which country is visited by most tourists?
see p.224 for the answer

A Italy
B USA
C France

INDUSTRIAL & OTHER DISASTERS

MISERY IN BHOPAL

Lethal gas escaping from an underground storage tank at the Union Carbide factory brought death and sickness to thousands of local residents. Many awoke with burning eyes, vomiting, and dizziness; others simply died in their sleep.

THE 10 ★ WORST EXPLOSIONS*

	LOCATION/DATE	TYPE	NO. KILLED
1	**Rhodes**, Greece, 1856#	Lightning strike of gunpowder store	4,000
2	**Breschia**, Italy, 1769#	Arsenal	over 3,000
3	**Lanchow**, China, 26 Oct 1935	Arsenal	2,000
4	**Halifax**, Nova Scotia, 6 Dec 1917	Ammunition ship *Mont Blanc*	1,963
5	**Memphis**, USA, 27 Apr 1865	*Sultana* boiler explosion	1,547
6	**Bombay**, India, 14 Apr 1944	Ammunition ship *Fort Stikine*	1,376
7	**Cali**, Colombia, 7 Aug 1956	Ammunition trucks	up to 1,200
8	**Salang Tunnel**, Afghanistan, 2 Nov 1982	Petrol tanker collision	over 1,100
9	**Chelyabinsk**, USSR, 3 Jun 1989	Liquid gas beside railway	up to 800
10	**Texas City**, Texas, USA, 16 Apr 1947	Ammonium nitrate on cargo ships	576

* Excluding mining disasters, terrorist and military bombs and natural explosions, such as volcanoes

 # Precise date unknown

THE 10 ★ WORST FIRES*

	LOCATION/DATE	TYPE	NO. KILLED
1	**Kwanto**, Japan, 1 Sep 1923	Following earthquake	60,000
2	**London**, UK, 11 Jul 1212	London Bridge	3,000#
3	**Peshtigo**, Wisconsin, USA, 8 Oct 1871	Forest	2,682
4	**Santiago**, Chile, 8 Dec 1863	Church of La Compañía	2,500
5	**Chungking**, China, 2 Sep 1949	Docks	1,700
6	**Hakodate**, Japan, 22 Mar 1934	City	1,500
7	**Constantinople**, Turkey, 5 Jun 1870	City	900
8	**San Francisco**, USA, 18 Apr 1906	Following earthquake	600–700
9	**Cloquet**, Minnesota, USA, 12 Oct 1918	Forest	559
10=	**Lagunillas**, Venezuela, 14 Nov 1939	Oil refinery and city	over 500
=	**Mandi Dabwali**, India, 23 Dec 1995	School tent	over 500

* Excluding sports and entertainment venues, mining disasters, and the results of military action

 # Burned, crushed, and drowned in ensuing panic

THE 10 ★ WORST FIRES OF THE 20TH CENTURY*

	LOCATION/DATE	TYPE	NO. KILLED
1	**Kwanto**, Japan, 1 Sep 1923	Following earthquake	60,000
2	**Chungking**, China, 2 Sep 1949	Docks	1,700
3	**Hakodate**, Japan, 22 Mar 1934	City	1,500
4	**San Francisco**, 18 April 1906	Following earthquake	600–700
5	**Cloquet**, Minnesota, USA, 12 Oct 1918	Forest	559
6=	**Lagunillas**, Venezuela, 14 Nov 1939	Oil refinery and city	over 500
=	**Mandi Dabwali**, India, 23 Dec 1995	School tent	over 500
8	**Hoboken**, New Jersey, USA, 30 Jun 1900	Docks	326
9	**Brussels**, Belgium, 22 May 1967	Department store	322
10	**Columbus**, Ohio, USA, 21 April 1930	State Penitentiary	320

* Excluding sports and entertainment venues, mining disasters, and the results of military action

THE 10 WORST MINING DISASTERS

(Location/date/no.killed)

1 **Hinkeiko**, China, 26 Apr 1942, 1,549 **2** **Courrières**, France, 10 Mar 1906, 1,060 **3** **Omuta**, Japan, 9 Nov 1963, 447 **4** **Senghenydd**, UK, 14 Oct 1913, 439 **5** **Coalbrook**, South Africa, 21 Jan 1960, 437 **6** **Wankie**, Rhodesia, 6 Jun 1972, 427 **7** **Dhanbad**, India, 28 May 1965, 375 **8** **Chasnala**, India, 27 Dec 1975, 372 **9** **Monongah**, USA, 6 Dec 1907, 362 **10** **Barnsley**, UK, 12 Dec 1866, 361*

* Including 27 killed the following day while searching for survivors

Which country has the most nuclear reactors? *see p.212 for the answer* A France B Japan C USA

THE 10 ★
WORST COMMERCIAL AND INDUSTRIAL DISASTERS*

LOCATION/DATE/TYPE	NO. KILLED
1 Bhopal, India, 3 Dec 1984, Methyl isocyante gas escape at Union Carbide plant	up to 3,000
2 Seoul, Korea, 29 Jun 1995, Collapse of Sampoong Department Store	640
3 Oppau, Germany, 21 Sep 1921, Chemical plant explosion	561
4 Mexico City, Mexico, 20 Nov 1984, Explosion at a PEMEX liquified petroleum gas plant	540
5 Brussels, Belgium, 22 May 1967, Fire in L'Innovation department store	322
6 Novosibirsk, USSR, April 1979#, Anthrax infection following accident at biological and chemical warfare plant	up to 300
7 Guadalajara, Mexico, 22 Apr 1992, Explosions caused by gas leak into sewers	230
8 São Paulo, Brazil, 1 Feb 1974, Fire in Joelma bank and office building	227
9 Oakdale, USA, 18 May 1918, Chemical plant explosion	193
10 Bangkok, Thailand, 10 May 1993, Fire engulfed a four-storey doll factory	187

* Including industrial sites, factories, offices, and stores; excluding military, mining, marine, and other transport disasters

Precise date unknown

THE 10 ★
WORST DISASTERS AT SPORTS VENUES IN THE 20TH CENTURY

LOCATION/DATE/TYPE	NO. KILLED
1 Hong Kong Jockey Club, 26 Feb 1918, Stand collapse and fire	604
2 Lenin Stadium, Moscow, 20 Oct 1982, Crush in football stadium	340
3 Lima, Peru, 24 May 1964, Riot in football stadium	320
4 Sinceljo, Colombia, 20 Jan 1980, Bullring stand collapse	222
5 Hillsborough, Sheffield, UK, 15 Apr 1989, Crush in football stadium	96
6 Guatemala City, Guatemala, 16 Oct 1996, Stampede in Mateo Flores National Stadium	83
7 Le Mans, France, 11 Jun 1955, Racing car crash	82
8 Katmandu, Nepal, 12 Mar 1988, Stampede in football stadium	80
9 Buenos Aires, Argentina, 23 May 1968, Riot in football stadium	74
10 Ibrox Park, Glasgow, Scotland, 2 Jan 1971, Barrier collapse in football stadium	66

THE 10 ★
WORST FIRES AT THEATRE AND ENTERTAINMENT VENUES*

LOCATION/DATE/TYPE	NO. KILLED
1 Canton, China, 25 May 1845, Theatre	1,670
2 Shanghai, China, Jun 1871, Theatre	900
3 Vienna, Austria, 8 Dec 1881, Ring Theatre	640–850
4 St. Petersburg, Russia, 14 Feb 1836, Lehmann Circus	800
5 Antoung, China, 13 Feb 1937, Cinema	658
6 Chicago, USA, 30 Dec 1903, Iroquois Theater	591
7 Boston, USA, 28 Nov 1942, Cocoanut Grove Night Club	491
8 Abadan, Iran, 20 Aug 1978, Theatre	422
9 Niteroi, Brazil, 17 Dec 1961, Circus	323
10 Brooklyn Theater, New York 5 Dec 1876	295

* 19th and 20th centuries, excluding sports stadiums and race tracks

The figure given for the first entry is a conservative estimate; some sources put the figure as high as 2,500.

MELTDOWN

On 30 April 1986 the Soviet Union admitted that a major accident had occurred at the Chernobyl nuclear generating plant in the Ukraine. The immediate death toll was said to be 31 people, but it has been suggested that by 1992 some 6,000–8,000 people had died as a result of radioactive contamination, a toll that will continue for many years. Since the accident, Soviet scientists have been monitoring the effects on plant life in the area. The radioactive particles still in the soil will contaminate future crops and, therefore, the animals and people that eat them.

SNAP ★ SHOTS

WEALTH & RICHES

TOP 10 ★
RICHEST RULERS

RULER/COUNTRY/IN POWER SINCE	ESTIMATED WEALTH ($)
1 **Sultan Haji Hassanal Bolkiah**, Brunei, 1967	36,000,000,000
2 **King Fahd bin Abdul Aziz Al Saud**, Saudi Arabia, 1982	25,000,000,000
3= **Presdient Sheikh Zayed bin Sultan al-Nahyan**, United Arab Emirates, 1971	15,000,000,000
= **Sheikh Jaber al-Ahmed al Jaber Al-Sabah**, Kuwait, 1977	15,000,000,000
5= **Amir Hamad bin Khalifa Al-Thani**, Qatar, 1995	5,000,000,000
= **President Saddam Hussein**, Iraq, 1979	5,000,000,000
7 **Queen Beatrix***, Netherlands, 1980	4,700,000,000
8 **Prime Minister Rafic Al-Hariri#**, Lebanon, 1992	3,600,000,000
9 **President Hafez Al-Assad**, Syria, 1971	2,000,000,000
10 **President Fidel Castro**, Cuba, 1959	100,000,000

Jointly with her mother, Princess Juliana

 # Officially deputy to President, but de facto ruler

Source: Forbes *magazine*

TOP 10 RICHEST PEOPLE IN THE US
(Name/source of wealth/assets in $)

❶ **Bill Gates**, Computer software, 58,400,000,000 ❷ **Warren Edward Buffett**, Textiles, etc., 29,400,000,000 ❸ **Paul Gardner Allen**, Computer software, 21,000,000,000 ❹ **Michael Dell**, Computers, 13,000,000,000 ❺ **Steven Ballmer**, Computer software, 12,000,000,000 ❻ = **Helen R. Walton**, Retailing, 11,000,000,000; = **John T. Walton**, Retailing, 11,000,000,000; = **Alice L. Walton**, Retailing, 11,000,000,000; = **S. Robson Walton**, Retailing, 11,000,000,000; = **Jim C. Walton**, Retailing, 11,000,000,000

Source: Forbes *magazine*

TOP 10 ★
COUNTRIES WITH THE MOST DOLLAR BILLIONAIRES*

COUNTRY	BILLIONAIRES
1 USA	70
2 Germany	18
3 Japan	12
4 China (Hong Kong)	8
5= France	7
= Mexico	7
= Saudi Arabia	7
8= Switzerland	6
= UK	6
10= Philippines	5
= Taiwan	5

Individuals and families with a net worth of $1,000,000,000 or more

Source: Forbes *magazine*

RICHEST RULER

Ruler of the small state of Brunei since 1967, the Sultan's colossal wealth derives from his country's oil and natural gas resources.

PERFECT GEM

The world's most expensive diamond was bought at auction in 1995 by Sheikh Ahmed Fitahi, the owner of a chain of Saudi Arabian jewellery shops.

TOP 10 ★
MOST EXPENSIVE SINGLE DIAMONDS SOLD AT AUCTION

DIAMOND/SALE	PRICE ($)
1 **Pear-shaped 100.10-carat "D" Flawless diamond**, Sotheby's, Geneva, 17 May 1995	16,548,750 (SF19,958,500)
2 **The Mouawad Splendor pear-shaped 11-sided 101.84-carat diamond**, Sotheby's, Geneva, 14 Nov 1990	12,760,000 (SF15,950,000)
3 **Rectangular-cut 100.36-carat diamond**, Sotheby's, Geneva, 17 Nov 1993	11,882,333 (SF17,823,500)
4 **Fancy blue emerald-cut 20.17-carat diamond ring**, Sotheby's, New York, 18 Oct 1994	9,902,500
5 **Unnamed pear-shaped 85.91-carat pendant**, Sotheby's, New York, 19 Apr 1988	9,130,000
6 **Rectangular-cut fancy deep blue 13.49-carat diamond ring**, Christie's, New York, 13 Apr 1995	7,482,500
7 **Rectangular-cut 52.59-carat diamond ring**, Christie's, New York, 20 Apr 1988	7,480,000
8 **Fancy pink rectangular-cut 19.66-carat diamond**, Christie's, Geneva, 17 Nov 1994	7,421,318 (SF9,573,500)
9 **The Jeddah Bride rectangular-cut 80.02-carat diamond**, Sotheby's, New York, 24 Oct 1991	7,150,000
10 **The Agra Diamond Fancy light pink cushion-shaped 32.24-carat diamond**, Christie's, London, 20 June 1990	6,959,700 (£4,070,000)

Background image: **ONE MILLION US DOLLARS**

TOP 10 ⭐ LARGEST ROUGH DIAMONDS

DIAMOND/DESCRIPTION	CARATS
1 Cullinan	3,106.00

Measuring roughly 10 x 6.5 x 5 cm/4 x 2½ x 2 in, and weighing 621 g/1 lb 6 oz, the Cullinan was unearthed in 1905, and bought by the Transvaal Government for £150,000. It was presented to King Edward VII, who had it cut; the most important of the separate gems are among the British Crown Jewels.

2 Excelsior	995.20

Found at the Jagersfontein Mine on 30 June 1893, it was cut by the celebrated Amsterdam firm of Asscher in 1903, producing 21 superb stones.

3 Star of Sierra Leone	968.80

Found in Sierra Leone on St. Valentine's Day, 1972, the rough diamond weighed 225 g/8 oz and measured 63.5 x 38.1 mm/2½ x 1½ in.

4 Incomparable	890.00

Discovered in 1980 at Mbuji-Mayi, Dem. Rep. of Congo (then Zaïre).

5 Great Mogul	787.50

When found in 1650 in the Gani Mine, India, it was presented to Shah Jehan, the builder of the Taj Mahal.

6 Woyie River	770.00

Found in 1945 beside the Woyie River in Sierra Leone, it was cut into 30 stones. The largest of these, known as Victory and weighing 31.35 carats, was auctioned at Christie's, New York in 1984 for $880,000.

7 Golden Jubilee	755.50

Found in 1986 in the Premier Mine (the home of the Cullinan), the polished diamond cut from it is, at 545.67 carats, the largest in the world.

8 Presidente Vargas	726.60

Discovered in the Antonio River, Brazil, in 1938, it was named after the then President, Getulio Vargas.

9 Jonker	726.00

In 1934 Jacobus Jonker found this massive diamond after it had been exposed by a heavy storm. Acquired by Harry Winston, it was exhibited in the American Museum of Natural History to enormous crowds.

10 Jubilee	650.80

Like the Excelsior, it was found in the Jagersfontein Mine in South Africa in 1895. The largest polished stone cut from it is called the Reitz.

The weight of diamonds is measured in carats (the word derives from the carob bean, which was once used as a measure). There are approximately 142 carats to the ounce. Fewer than 1,000 rough diamonds weighing more than 100 carats have ever been recorded.

TOP 10 GOLD-PRODUCING COUNTRIES

(Country/1997 production in tonnes)

1 South Africa, 489.2		**2** USA, 351.4	
3 Australia, 311.4		**4** Canada, 168.5	
5 China, 156.8		**6** Russia, 137.0	
7 Indonesia, 101.4		**8** Uzbekistan, 81.7	
9 Peru, 74.8		**10** Brazil, 59.1	

As reported by Gold Fields Mineral Services Ltd, world-dominating gold producer South Africa saw its output fall again for the fifth consecutive year. Australia's output has increased dramatically over recent years: the country's record annual production had stood at 119 tonnes since 1903, but in 1988 it rocketed to 152 tonnes, and in 1992 for the first time overtook that of Russia.

TOP 10 ⭐ YOUNGEST BILLIONAIRES IN THE US

NAME/SOURCE OF WEALTH	ASSETS ($)	AGE
1 Daniel Morton Ziff, Ziff Brothers Investments	1,200,000,000	26
2 Robert David Ziff, Ziff Brothers Investments	1,200,000,000	32
3 Michael Dell, Dell Computer Corp.	13,000,000,000	33
4 =Jeffrey P. Bezos, Amazon.com	1,600,000,000	34
= Dirk Edward Ziff, Ziff Brothers Investments	1,200,000,000	34
6 Theodore W. Waitt, Gateway 2000 Computers	3,200,000,000	35
7 Abigail Johnson, Fidelity Investments	4,200,000,000	36
8 =Steven Anthony Ballmer, Microsoft Corp.	12,000,000,000	42
=Lee Marshall Bass, Oil, investments	3,300,000,000	42
=Bill Gates, Microsoft Corp.	58,400,000,000	42

Source: Forbes *magazine*

WINFREY'S WEALTH

Through international syndication of her TV shows, as well as bestselling books and acting roles, Oprah Winfrey has become one of the world's richest entertainers.

TOP 10 ⭐ HIGHEST-EARNING ENTERTAINERS*

ENTERTAINER/PROFESSION	1998 INCOME ($)
1 Jerry Seinfeld, TV performer	225,000,000
2 Larry David, Co-creator of *Seinfeld* TV show	200,000,000
3 Steven Spielberg, Film producer/director	175,000,000
4 Oprah Winfrey, TV host/producer	125,000,000
5 James Cameron, Film director	115,000,000
6 Michael Crichton, Novelist/screenwriter	65,000,000
7 =Mike Judge	53,000,000
= Greg Daniels, Co-creators of *Beavis & Butt-head* cartoon	53,000,000
9 Chris Carter, TV writer (*X-Files*)	52,000,000
10 David Copperfield, Illusionist	49,500,000

* *Other than actors and pop stars*

Source: Forbes *magazine*

Did You Know? The song *Diamonds Are a Girl's Best Friend* celebrates the famous New York diamond dealer Harry Winston, who acquired the Star of Sierra Leone.

FOOD FOR THOUGHT

CALORIE-CONSUMING COUNTRIES

COUNTRY	AVERAGE DAILY PER CAPITA CONSUMPTION
1 Denmark	3,808
2 Portugal	3,658
3 USA	3,642
4 Ireland	3,636
5 Greece	3,575
6 Turkey	3,568
7 France	3,551
8 Belgium/Luxembourg	3,543
9 Italy	3,504
10 Malta	3,417
UK	3,237
World average	2,745

Source: *Food and Agriculture Organization of the United Nations*

While people in most countries in Western Europe consume more than 3,000 calories per head, the consumption in some of the poorest African nations falls below 2,000: in Somalia it is 1,532 – less than half that of the countries in the Top 10.

TOP 10 CHOCOLATE BRANDS IN THE UK

1 Cadbury's Dairy Milk 2 Kit Kat
3 Mars 4 Galaxy 5 Cadbury's Roses
6 Twix 7 Maltesers 8 Snickers
9 Quality Street 10 Aero

TOP 10 SWEET BRANDS IN THE UK*

1 Wrigley's Extra 2 Rowntree Polo
3 Trebor Extra Strong Mints
4 Wrigley's Orbit 5 Trebor Softmints
6 Maynards Wine Gums 7 Rowntree Fruit Pastilles 8 Mars Opal Fruits
9 Werthers Original 10 Leaf Chewits

* Excluding chocolate

TOP 10 ★

OLDEST-ESTABLISHED BRITISH CHOCOLATE PRODUCTS

PRODUCT	YEAR INTRODUCED
1 Fry's Chocolate Cream	1853
2 Fry's Easter Egg	1873
3 Cadbury's Easter Egg	1875
4 Cadbury's Chocolate Drops*	1904
5 Cadbury's Dairy Milk	1905
6 Cadbury's Bournville	1908
7 Fry's Turkish Delight	1915
8 =Cadbury's Milk Tray	1920
=Cadbury's Milk Chocolate Flake	1920
10 Cadbury's Creme Egg#	1923

* Now Chocolate Buttons

 # Original version

THE 10 ★

FIRST MARS PRODUCTS

PRODUCT	YEAR INTRODUCED
1 =Milky Way bar	1923
=Snickers bar (non-chocolate)	1923
3 Snickers bar (chocolate)	1930
4 3 Musketeers bar	1932
5 Maltesers	1937
6 Kitekat (catfood; now a Whiskas product)	1939
7 Mars almond bar	1940
8 M&M's plain chocolate candies	1941
9 Uncle Ben's Converted brand rice	1942
10 =M&M's peanut chocolate candies	1954
=Pal (dogfood)	1954

American candy manufacturer Franklin C. Mars established his first business in Tacoma, Washington, in 1911, and formed the Mar-O-Bar company in Minneapolis (later moving it to Chicago) in 1922, with the first of its products, the Milky Way bar. The founder's son Forrest E. Mars set up in the UK in 1932, merging the firm with its American counterpart in 1964.

TOP 10 ★

SUGAR-CONSUMING COUNTRIES

COUNTRY	ANNUAL CONSUMPTION PER CAPITA KG	LB	OZ
1 Israel	98	216	1
2 =Belize	71	156	8
=USA	71	156	8
4 Iceland	63	138	14
5 Barbados	61	134	8
=Cuba	61	134	8
=New Zealand	61	134	8
8 =Costa Rica	60	132	4
=Malaysia	60	132	4
10 =Swaziland	59	130	1
=Trinidad and Tobago	59	130	1
UK	39	86	0

Source: *Food and Agriculture Organization of the United Nations*

TOP 10 COUNTRIES WITH THE MOST McDONALD'S RESTAURANTS

(Country/no. of restaurants)

1 USA, 12,094 **2** Japan, 2,004
3 Canada, 992 **4** Germany, 743
5 UK, 650 **6** Australia, 608 **7** France, 541 **8** Brazil, 337 **9** Taiwan, 163
10 Netherlands, 151

TOP 10 ★
FISH-CONSUMING COUNTRIES

COUNTRY	ANNUAL CONSUMPTION PER CAPITA		
	KG	LB	OZ
1 Japan	66.9	147	8
2 Norway	45.0	99	3
3 Portugal	43.0	94	13
4 =Spain	30.0	66	2
=Sweden	30.0	66	2
6 Belgium	19.0	41	14
7 =Germany	14.0	30	14
=Italy	14.0	30	14
=Netherlands	14.0	30	14
=Poland	14.0	30	14

Source: *Food and Agriculture Organization of the United Nations*

TOP 10 CONSUMERS OF KELLOGG'S CORNFLAKES*

1 Ireland **2** UK **3** Australia
4 Denmark **5** Sweden **6** Norway
7 Canada **8** USA **9** Mexico
10 Venezuela

* Based on per capita consumption

In 1894 the brothers Will Keith Kellogg and Dr John Harvey Kellogg discovered, by accident, that boiled and rolled wheat dough turned into flakes if left overnight; once baked, they turned into a tasty cereal. In 1898 they replaced wheat with corn, thereby creating the Cornflakes we know today. Will Keith Kellogg went into business manufacturing Cornflakes, with his distinctive signature on the packet. Today, Cornflakes remain Kellogg's bestselling product.

THE 10 ★
FIRST HEINZ'S "57 VARIETIES"

PRODUCT	YEAR PRODUCTS INTRODUCED
1 Horseradish	1869
2 =Sour gherkins	1870
=Sour mixed pickles	1870
=Chow chow pickle	1870
=Sour onions	1870
=Prepared mustard	1870
=Sauerkraut in crocks	1870
8 =Heinz and Noble catsup	1873
=Vinegar	1873
10 =Green pepper sauce	1879
=Red pepper sauce	1879
=Worcestershire sauce	1879

The company that Henry John Heinz launched in 1869 with horseradish rapidly expanded. In 1896, inspired by a sign he saw on the New York Third Avenue railway advertising "21 Styles" of shoe, he counted his products and then relaunched them as his famous "57 Varieties".

TOP 10 ★
MEAT-EATING COUNTRIES

COUNTRY	ANNUAL CONSUMPTION PER CAPITA		
	KG	LB	OZ
1 USA	118.4	261	0
2 New Zealand	117.6	259	4
3 Australia	108.5	239	4
4 Cyprus	107.0	235	14
5 Uruguay	104.5	230	6
6 Austria	104.0	229	4
7 Saint Lucia	100.9	222	7
8 Denmark	99.5	219	5
9 Spain	95.8	211	3
10 Canada	95.7	210	15
UK	45.1	108	4

Figures from the Meat and Livestock Commission show a huge range of consumption around the world, ranging from the USA at No. 1, to very poor countries such as India, where consumption may be as little as 3.4 kg/7 lb 8 oz per person per year.

TOP 10 ★
HOTTEST CHILLIES

EXAMPLES OF CHILLIES	SCOVILLE UNITS
1 Datil, Habanero, Scotch Bonnet	100,000–350,000
2 Chiltepin, Santaka, Thai	50,000–100,000
3 Aji, Cayenne, Piquin, Tabasco	30,000–50,000
4 de Arbol	15,000–30,000
5 Serrano, Yellow Wax	5,000–15,000
6 Chipolte, Jalapeno, Mirasol	2,500–5,000
7 Cascabel, Sandia, Rocotillo	1,500–2,500
8 Ancho, Espanola, Pasilla, Poblano	1,000–1,500
9 Anaheim, New Mexico	500–1,000
10 Cherry, Peperoncini	100–500

Hot peppers contain substances called capsaicinoids, which determins how "hot" they are. In 1912 pharmacist Wilbur Scoville pioneered a test, based on which chillies are ranked by Scoville Units. According to this scale, one part of capsaicin (the principal capsaicinoid) per million equals 15,000 Scoville Units. Pure capsaicin registers 16 million on the Scoville scale – one drop diluted with 100,000 drops of water will still blister the tongue – while at the other end of the scale, bell peppers and pimento register zero.

ALCOHOLIC & SOFT DRINKS

FIRST COCA-COLA PRODUCTS

	PRODUCT	YEAR INTRODUCED
1	Coca-Cola	May 1886
2	Fanta	Jun 1960
3	Sprite	Feb 1961
4	TAB	May 1963
5	Fresca	Feb 1966
6	Mr. PiBB*	Jun 1972
7	Hi-C Soft Drinks	Aug 1977
8	Mello Yello	Mar 1979
9	Ramblin' Root Beer	Jun 1979
10	Diet Coke	Jul 1982

* Mr. PiBB without Sugar launched Sep 1974; changed name to Sugar-free Mr. PiBB, 1975

TOP 10 MOST COMMON PUB NAMES IN THE UK

1 The Red Lion 2 The Crown
3 The Royal Oak 4 The White
Hart 5 The King's Head
6 The Bull 7 The Coach
and Horses 8 The George
9 The Plough 10 The Swan

ALCOHOL-CONSUMING COUNTRIES

	COUNTRY	ANNUAL CONSUMPTION PER CAPITA (100 PER CENT ALCOHOL)	
		LITRES	PINTS
1	Portugal	11.3	19.9
2	Luxembourg	11.2	19.7
3	France	10.9	19.2
4 =	Hungary	10.1	17.8
=	Spain	10.1	17.8
6	Czech Republic	10.0	17.6
7	Denmark	9.9	17.4
8 =	Germany	9.5	16.7
=	Austria	9.5	16.7
10	Switzerland	9.2	16.2
	UK	7.7	13.6

After heading this list for many years – and with an annual consumption that peaked at 17.7 litres/ 31.1 pints per head in 1961 – France was first overtaken by Luxembourg and then by Portugal.

BEER-DRINKING COUNTRIES

	COUNTRY	ANNUAL CONSUMPTION PER CAPITA	
		LITRES	PINTS
1	Czech Republic	158.8	279.5
2	Ireland	140.0	246.4
3	Germany	131.1	230.7
4	Denmark	113.7	200.1
5	Austria	113.2	199.2
6	Luxembourg	110.8	195.0
7	UK	103.6	182.3
8	Belgium	102.0	179.5
9	Slovak Republic	94.8	166.8
10	Australia	94.7	166.7

Though it is the world's leading producer of beer, the USA is not in the Top 10 list – it is ranked in 14th place.

MONKS' BREW

Beer used to be brewed in households and monasteries for private consumption until the late Middle Ages, when it became a commercial product.

CHAMPAGNE-IMPORTING COUNTRIES

	COUNTRY	BOTTLES IMPORTED (1998)
1	UK	24,247,123
2	Germany	19,312,910
3	USA	16,949,417
4	Belgium	9,474,456
5	Switzerland	8,387,721
6	Italy	8,157,053
7	Japan	2,975,680
8	Netherlands	2,370,322
9	Spain	1,425,927
10	Canada	1,360,935

In 1998 France consumed 179,004,405 bottles of Champagne and exported 113,453,686. In that year Canada increased its imports by a record 45 per cent, entering the global Top 10 list for the first time.

THE ART OF FERMENTATION

Champagne first became available in 1698, when Dom Pierre Perignon perfected the art of fermenting wine in the bottle at the abbey of Hautvillers in Champagne. Cork stoppers replaced the previously used rag seals, and strong English glass was used to withstand the pressure of fermentation.

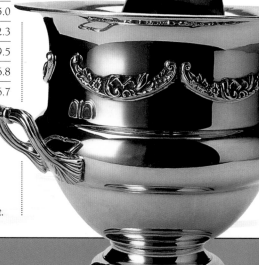

CHEERS!

The French produce 15,000 tonnes of wine every day – that's 20 million bottles a day.

TOP 10 ★
WINE-DRINKING COUNTRIES

	COUNTRY	ANNUAL CONSUMPTION PER CAPITA	
		LITRES	PINTS
1	Portugal	61.0	107.3
2	France	60.0	105.6
3	Italy	53.5	94.2
4	Luxembourg	52.0	91.5
5	Switzerland	43.5	76.6
6	Argentina	40.0	70.4
7	Greece	34.9	61.4
8	Spain	34.8	61.2
9	Uruguay	34.0	59.8
10	Austria	30.0	52.8
	UK	14.3	25.2

The UK still does not make it into the Top 10 or even Top 20 wine-drinking countries in the world, but consumption of wine has become more and more popular over the last 25 years. Between 1970 and 1997, wine consumption increased by over 350 per cent. By contrast, in France, people have been drinking less.

TOP 10 ★
SOFT DRINK-CONSUMING COUNTRIES*

	COUNTRY	ANNUAL CONSUMPTION PER CAPITA	
		LITRES	PINTS
1	USA	207	364
2	Bahrain	147	259
3	Iceland	135	238
4	Norway	132	232
5	Mexico	130	229
6	=Australia	110	194
	=Canada	110	194
	=Israel	110	1944
9	Ireland	105	174
10	Chile	99	174

* Carbonated only

Source: Zenith International

As one might expect, affluent Western countries feature prominently in this list and, despite the spread of so-called "Coca-Cola culture", former Eastern Bloc and Third World countries rank very low – some African nations recording extremely low consumption figures of less than 1 litre/1.76 pints per annum.

TOP 10 ★
SOFT DRINKS IN THE UK

	DRINK	ADVERTISING SPEND (£)	ANNUAL SALES (£)*
1	Coca-Cola	26,169,500	over 542,000,000
2	Pepsi	8,558,200	180–185,000,000
3	Robinsons	3,300,900	160–165,000,000
4	Ribena	909,100	130–135,000,000
5	Lucozade	7,021,100	105–110,000,000
6	Tango	6,584,300	100–105,000,000
7	Irn-Bru	367,300	55–60,000,000
8	=Del Monte	519,900	50–55,000,000
	=Lilt	3,034,200	50–55,000,000
	=Schweppes Mixers	17,800	50–55,000,000

* Estimated range

Source: Marketing

TOP 10 ★
TEA-DRINKING COUNTRIES

	COUNTRY	ANNUAL CONSUMPTION PER CAPITA			
		KG	LB	OZ	CUPS*
1	Irish Republic	3.17	7	0	1,395
2	Kuwait	2.66	5	14	1,170
3	UK	2.46	5	7	1,082
4	Qatar	2.00	4	7	880
5	Turkey	1.93	4	4	849
6	Syria	1.44	3	3	634
7	Bahrain	1.37	3	0	603
8	Sri Lanka	1.29	2	14	568
9	=New Zealand	1.23	2	11	541
	=Morocco	1.23	2	11	541

* Based on 440 cups per kg/2 lb 3 oz

Source: International Tea Committee

TOP 10 MILK-DRINKING COUNTRIES

(Country*/annual consumption per capita in litres/pints)

❶ Ireland, 155.6/273.9 ❷ Finland, 153.4/ 270.0 ❸ Iceland, 152.2/267.9 ❹ Norway, 150.1/264.2 ❺ Ukraine, 134.3/ 236.4 ❻ Luxembourg, 130.1/229.0 ❼ UK, 127.1/223.7 ❽ Sweden, 125.5/220.9 ❾ Australia, 111.4/196.1 ❿ Spain, 104.8/ 184.4

* Only those reporting to the International Dairy Federation

Source: National Dairy Council

MEDICINE MAN

Coca-Cola was created by John Styth Pemberton, a pharmacist from Atlanta, Georgia, in 1886.

Which country is the most accident prone?
see p.215 for the answer

A South Africa
B Lithuania
C Estonia

WORLD TOURISM

TOP 10 ★ SPENDING TOURISTS

	COUNTRY OF ORIGIN	PERCENTAGE OF WORLD TOTAL	TOTAL EXPENDITURE $ (1997)
1	USA	13.6	51,220,000,000
2	Germany	12.2	46,200,000,000
3	Japan	8.7	33,041,000,000
4	UK	7.3	27,710,000,000
5	Italy	4.4	16,631,000,000
6	France	4.4	16,576,000,000
7	Canada	3.0	11,304,000,000
8	Austria	2.9	10,992,000,000
9	Netherlands	2.7	10,232,000,000
10	China	2.7	10,166,000,000

Source: *World Tourism Organization*

In 1997, the world spent $377,776 million on tourism.

TOP 10 ★ TOURIST COUNTRIES

	COUNTRY	PERCENTAGE OF WORLD TOTAL	VISITS 1997*
1	France	10.9	66,800,000
2	USA	8.0	49,038,000
3	Spain	7.1	43,403,000
4	Italy	5.6	34,087,000
5	UK	4.2	25,960,000
6	China	3.9	23,770,000
7	Poland	3.2	19,514,000
8	Mexico	3.2	19,351,000
9	Canada	2.9	17,610,000
10	Czech Republic	2.8	17,400,000

* *International tourist arrivals, excluding same-day visitors*

Source: *World Tourism Organization*

In 1997, it was reckoned that 613,488,000 people – almost one in 10 of the world's population – travelled as tourists to another country. Of these, more than half (51.8 per cent) visited these Top 10 destinations.

GOTHIC CASTLE

The Gothic spires of the Château de la Belle au Bois Dormant, Sleeping Beauty's castle, in Disneyland® Paris, provide an impressive centrepiece for the park.

TOP 10 ★ AMUSEMENT AND THEME PARKS*

	PARK/LOCATION	VISITS (1998)
1	**Tokyo Disneyland®**, Tokyo, Japan	16,686,000
2	**Disneyland® Paris**, Marne-La-Vallée, France	12,500,000#
3	**Everland**, Kyonggi-Do, South Korea	7,326,000
4	**Blackpool Pleasure Beach**, Blackpool, UK	6,600,000#
5	**Lotte World**, Seoul, South Korea	5,800,000
6	**Yokohama Hakkeijima Sea Paradise**, Yokohama, Japan	5,737,000
7	**Huis Ten Bosch**, Sasebo, Japan	4,130,300
8	**Suzuka Circuit**, Suzuka, Japan	3,238,000
9	**Nagashima Spa Land**, Kuwana, Japan	3,200,000
10	**Paramount Canada's Wonderland**, Maple, Canada	3,025,000#

* *Excluding USA*

Estimated attendance

Source: *Amusement Business*

TOP 10 TOURIST ATTRACTIONS CHARGING ADMISSION IN THE UK

(Attraction/location/visits 1998)

1 **Alton Towers**, Staffordshire, 2,782,000 **2** **Madame Tussaud's**, London, 2,772,500 **3** **Tower of London**, 2,551,459 **4** **Natural History Museum**, London, 1,904,539 **5** **Chessington World of Adventures**, 1,650,000 **6** **Legoland**, Windsor, 1,645,296 **7** **Science Museum**, London, 1,599,817 **8** **Canterbury Cathedral**, 1,500,000 **9** **Windsor Castle**, 1,495,465 **10** **Edinburgh Castle**, 1,219,055

Source: *English Tourist Board*

TOP 10 ★
OLDEST ROLLER COASTERS*

ROLLER COASTER/LOCATION	YEAR FOUNDED
1 **Scenic Railway**, Luna Park, Melbourne, Australia	1912
2 **Rutschbanen**, Tivoli, Copenhagen, Denmark	1914
3 **Jack Rabbit**, Clementon Amusement Park, Clementon, NJ, USA	1919
4= **Jack Rabbit**, Sea Breeze Park, Rochester, NY, USA	1920
= **Scenic Railway**, Dreamland, Margate, UK	1920
6= **Jack Rabbit**, Kennywood, West Mifflin, PA, USA	1921
= **Roller Coaster**, Lagoon, Farmington, UT, USA	1921
8= **Zippin Pippin**, Libertyland, Memphis, TN, USA	1923
= **Big Dipper**, Blackpool Pleasure Beach, Blackpool, UK	1923
10 **Giant Dipper**, Santa Cruz Beach Boardwalk, Santa Cruz, CA, USA	1924

* In operation at same location since founded

TOP 10 ★
MUSEUMS AND GALLERIES IN THE UK

MUSEUM OR GALLERY/LOCATION	VISITS (1998)
1 **British Museum**, London	5,620,081*
2 **National Gallery**, London	4,770,330*
3 **Tate Gallery**, London	2,180,665*
4 **Natural History Museum**, London	1,904,539
5 **Science Museum**, London	1,599,817
6 **Glasgow Art Gallery and Museum**	1,128,455*
7 **Victoria and Albert Museum**, London	1,110,000
8 **National Portrait Gallery**, London	1,017,265*
9 **Royal Academy**, London	912,714
10 **Birmingham Museum and Art Gallery**	828,250*

* Free admission

Source: English Tourist Board

KEEP ON TURNING
Vienna's amusement park, the Prater, is symbolized by the Giant Ferris Wheel which is 65 m/213 ft high. It was built in 1896–97.

TOP 10 ★
HISTORIC HOUSES AND MONUMENTS IN THE UK

PROPERTY/LOCATION	VISITS (1998)
1 **Tower of London**	2,551,459
2 **Windsor Castle**	1,495,465
3 **Edinburgh Castle**	1,219,055
4 **Roman Baths and Pump Room**, Bath	905,426
5 **Stonehenge**, Wiltshire	817,493
6 **Warwick Castle**	777,500
7 **Hampton Court Palace**	605,230
8 **Leeds Castle**, Kent	551,377
9 **Shakespeare's birthplace**, Stratford-upon-Avon	520,108
10 **Chatsworth House**, Derbyshire	475,000

Source: English Tourist Board

TOP 10 ★
LEISURE PARKS AND PIERS IN THE UK

LEISURE PARK OR PIER/LOCATION	VISITS (1998)
1 **Blackpool Pleasure Beach**	7,100,000*#
2 **Palace Pier**, Brighton	3,500,000*#
3 **Eastbourne Pier**	2,800,000
4 **Alton Towers**, Staffordshire	2,782,000*#
5 **Pleasureland**, Southport	2,100,000*
6 **Chessington World of Adventures**	1,650,000
7 **Legoland**, Windsor	1,646,296*
8 **Peter Pan's Adventure Island**, Southend	1,500,000*
9 **Pleasure Beach**, Great Yarmouth	1,400,000
10 **Flamingo Land Theme**, North Yorkshire	1,105,000

* Estimated   # Free admission

Source: English Tourist Board

TOP 10 ★
OLDEST AMUSEMENT PARKS

PARK/LOCATION	YEAR FOUNDED
1 **Bakken**, Klampenborg, Denmark	1583
2 **The Prater**, Vienna, Austria	1766
3 **Blackgang Chine Cliff Top Theme Park**, Ventnor, Isle of Wight, UK	1842
4 **Tivoli**, Copenhagen, Denmark	1843
5 **Lake Compounce Amusement Park**, Bristol, CT, USA	1846
6 **Hanayashiki**, Tokyo, Japan	1853
7 **Grand Pier**, Teignmouth, UK	1865
8 **Blackpool Central Pier**, Blackpool, UK	1868
9 **Cedar Point**, Sandusky, OH, USA	1870
10 **Clacton Pier**, Clacton, UK	1871

Who is the biggest consumer of Kellogg's cornflakes?
see p.221 for the answer

A Australia
B UK
C Ireland

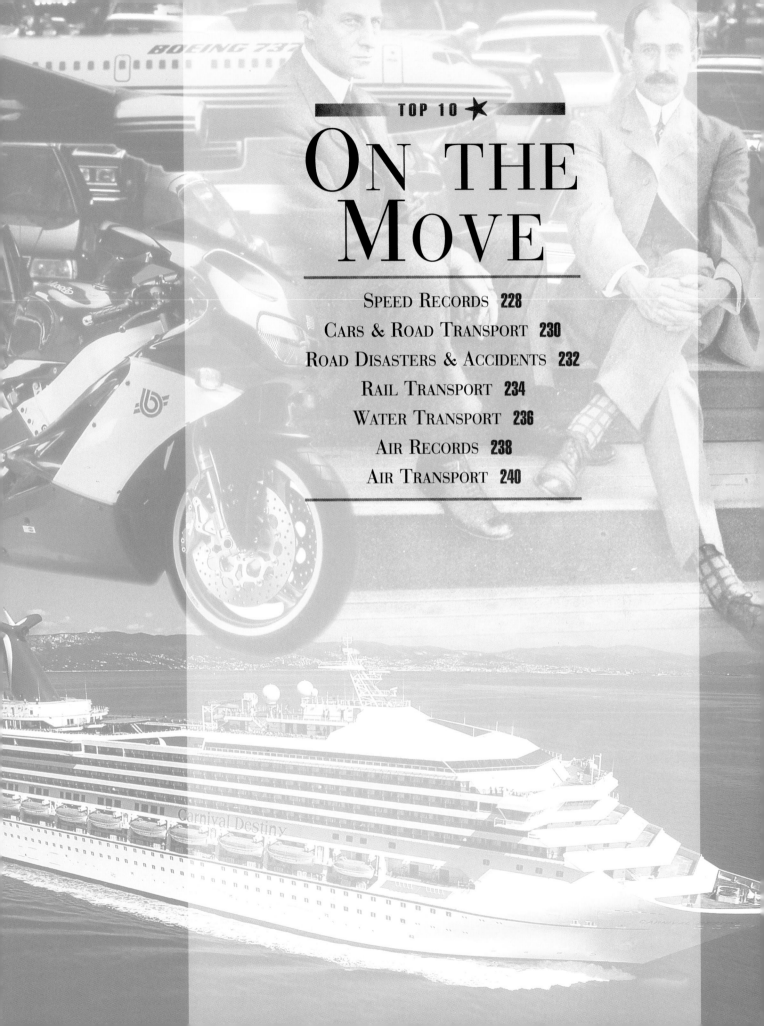

SPEED RECORDS

FIRST AMERICAN HOLDERS OF THE LAND SPEED RECORD

	DRIVER*/CAR/LOCATION	DATE	KM/H	MPH
1	**William Vanderbilt**, *Mors*, Albis, France	5 Aug 1902	121.72	76.08
2	**Henry Ford**, *Ford Arrow*, Lake St. Clair, USA	12 Jan 1904	146.19	91.37
3	**Fred Marriott**, *Stanley Rocket*, Daytona Beach, USA	23 Jan 1906	194.51	121.57
4	**Barney Oldfield**, *Benz*, Daytona Beach, USA	16 Mar 1910	210.03	131.27
5	**Bob Burman**, *Benz*, Daytona Beach, USA	23 Apr 1911	226.19	141.37
6	**Ralph de Palma**, *Packard*, Daytona Beach, USA	17 Feb 1919	239.79	149.87
7	**Tommy Milton**, *Duesenberg*, Daytona Beach, USA	27 Apr 1920	249.64	156.03
8	**Ray Keech**, *White Triplex*, Daytona Beach, USA	22 Apr 1928	332.08	207.55
9	**Craig Breedlove**, *Spirit of America*, Bonneville Salt Flats, USA	5 Aug 1963	651.92	407.45
10	**Tom Green**, *Wingfoot Express*, Bonneville Salt Flats, USA	2 Oct 1964	661.12	413.20

* Excluding those who subsequently broke their own records

FIRST HOLDERS OF THE LAND SPEED RECORD

	DRIVER/CAR/LOCATION	DATE	KM/H	MPH
1	**Gaston de Chasseloup-Laubat**, *Jeantaud*, Achères, France	18 Dec 1898	62.78	39.24
2	**Camile Jenatzy**, *Jenatzy*, Achères, France	17 Jan 1899	66.27	41.42
3	**Gaston de Chasseloup-Laubat**, *Jeantaud*, Achères, France	17 Jan 1899	69.90	43.69
4	**Camile Jenatzy**, *Jenatzy*, Achères, France	27 Jan 1899	79.37	49.92
5	**Gaston de Chasseloup-Laubat**, *Jeantaud*, Achères, France	4 Mar 1899	92.16	57.60
6	**Camile Jenatzy**, *Jenatzy*, Achères, France	29 Apr 1899	105.26	65.79
7	**Leon Serpollet**, *Serpollet*, Nice, France	13 Apr 1902	120.09	75.06
8	**William Vanderbilt**, *Mors*, Albis, France	5 Aug 1902	121.72	76.08
9	**Henri Fournier**, *Mors*, Dourdan, France	5 Nov 1902	122.56	76.60
10	**M. Augières**, *Mors*, Dourdan, France	17 Nov 1902	123.40	77.13

The first official land speed records were all broken within three years, the first six of them by rival French racers Comte Gaston de Chasseloup-Laubat and Camile Jenatzy. Both the *Jeantaud* and the *Jenatzy* were electrically powered.

LATEST HOLDERS OF THE LAND SPEED RECORD

	DRIVER/CAR/LOCATION	DATE	KM/H	MPH
1	**Andy Green**, UK, *Thrust SSC*, Black Rock Desert, USA	15 Oct 1997	1,227.99	763.04
2	**Richard Noble**, UK, *Thrust 2*, Black Rock Desert, USA	4 Oct 1983	1,013.47	633.47
3	**Gary Gabelich**, USA, *The Blue Flame*, Bonneville Salt Flats, USA	23 Oct 1970	995.85	622.41
4	**Craig Breedlove**, USA, *Spirit of America – Sonic 1*, Bonneville Salt Flats, USA	15 Nov 1965	960.96	600.60
5	**Art Arfons**, USA, *Green Monster*, Bonneville Salt Flats, USA	7 Nov 1965	922.48	576.55
6	**Craig Breedlove**, USA, *Spirit of America – Sonic 1*, Bonneville Salt Flats, USA	2 Nov 1965	888.76	555.48
7	**Art Arfons**, USA, *Green Monster*, Bonneville Salt Flats, USA	27 Oct 1964	858.73	536.71
8	**Craig Breedlove**, USA, *Spirit of America*, Bonneville Salt Flats, USA	15 Oct 1964	842.04	526.28
9	**Craig Breedlove**, USA, *Spirit of America*, Bonneville Salt Flats, USA	13 Oct 1964	749.95	468.72
10	**Art Arfons**, USA, *Green Monster*, Bonneville Salt Flats, USA	5 Oct 1964	694.43	434.02

FASTER THAN THE SPEED OF SOUND
Fifty years after the sound barrier was broken by an aircraft, Thrust SSC became the first vehicle to do so on land.

Background image: **THRUST SSC BREAKING THE LAND SPEED RECORD IN BLACK ROCK DESERT, USA**

TOP 10 ★
WORLD LAND SPEED RECORDS HELD BY MALCOLM AND DONALD CAMPBELL

	DRIVER	DATE	KM/H	MPH
1	Malcolm Campbell	25 Sep 1924	233.85	146.16
2	Malcolm Campbell	21 Jul 1925	241.21	150.76
3	Malcolm Campbell	4 Feb 1927	279.80	174.88
4	Malcolm Campbell	19 Feb 1928	331.12	206.95
5	Malcolm Campbell	5 Feb 1931	393.74	246.09
6	Sir Malcolm Campbell*	24 Feb 1932	406.35	253.97
7	Sir Malcolm Campbell	22 Feb 1933	435.93	272.46
8	Sir Malcolm Campbell	7 Mar 1935	442.91	276.82
9	Sir Malcolm Campbell	3 Sep 1935	480.20	301.13
10	Donald Campbell	17 Jul 1964	644.96	403.10

* Knighted 1931

Sir Malcolm Campbell (1885–1949) and his son Donald (1921–67) are unique in land speed record history, as the only father and son to hold the record.

THE 10 ★
LATEST HOLDERS OF THE MOTORCYCLE SPEED RECORD

	RIDER/MOTORCYCLE	YEAR	KM/H	MPH
1	**Dave Campos**, Twin 1,491 cc/91 cu in Ruxton Harley-Davidson Easyriders	1990	518.45	322.15
2	**Donald A. Vesco**, Twin 1,016 cc Kawasaki LightningBolt	1978	512.73	318.60
3	**Donald A. Vesco**, 1,496 cc Yamaha Silver Bird	1975	487.50	302.93
4	**Calvin Rayborn**, 1,480 cc Harley-Davidson	1970	426.40	264.96
5	**Calvin Rayborn** 1,480 cc Harley-Davidson	1970	410.37	254.99
6	**Donald A. Vesco**, 700 cc Yamaha	1970	405.25	251.82
7	**Robert Leppan**, 1,298 cc Triumph	1966	395.27	245.62
8	**William A. Johnson**, 667 cc Triumph	1962	361.40	224.57
9	**Wilhelm Herz**, 499 cc NSU	1956	338.08	210.08
10	**Russell Wright**, 998 cc Vincent HRD	1955	297.64	184.95

All the records listed here were achieved at the Bonneville Salt Flats, USA, with the exception of No. 10, which was attained at Christchurch, New Zealand. To break a Fédération Internationale Motorcycliste record, the motorcycle has to cover a measured distance, making two runs within one hour, and taking the average of the two. American Motorcycling Association records require a turnround within two hours. Although all those listed were specially adapted for their record attempts, the two most recent had two engines and were stretched to 6.4 m/21 ft and 7 m/23 ft respectively.

TOP 10 ★
FASTEST PRODUCTION CARS

	MODEL*	KM/H#	MPH#
1	Lamborghini Diablo 5.7	325	202
2	Ferrari 550M	320	199
3	Aston Martin V8 Vantage	299	186
4	Chrysler Viper	298	185
5	Venturi Atlantique Twin-turbo	283	176
6	Lotus Esprit 3.5	282	175
7	Porsche 911	280	174
8 =	Bentley Continental T	274	170
=	Honda NSX 3.2	274	170
=	Marcos Mantis	274	170
=	Shelby Series 1	274	170
=	TVR Cerbera 4.5	274	170

* Fastest of each manufacturer

\# May vary according to specification modifications to meet national legal requirements

ITALIAN SPEED

This Bimota SB6R and its fellow YB11, both Italian-made 1,000 cc-plus superbikes, appear among the world's 10 fastest.

TOP 10 FASTEST PRODUCTION MOTORCYCLES
(Model/km/h/mph)

1 Suzuki GSX1300R Hayabusa, 299/186 **2** Honda CBR1100XX Blackbird, 291/181 **3** Bimota SBR, 290/180 **4** Bimota YB11, 282/175 **5** Kawasaki ZZ-R1100, 280/174 **6** Yamaha YZF-R1, 278/173 **7** MV Agusta M4, 275/171 **8** Kawasaki Ninja ZX-9R, 274/170 **9** = Kawasaki Ninja ZX-7RR, 272/169; = Kawasaki Ninja ZX-6R, 272/169

Did You Know? The reason why Malcolm and Donald Campbell called both of their cars *Bluebird* was because of a play of the same name by Maurice Maeterlink in which the bird symbolized the unattainable.

CARS & ROAD TRANSPORT

MOTOR VEHICLE-OWNING COUNTRIES

	COUNTRY	CARS	COMMERCIAL VEHICLES	TOTAL
1	USA	134,981,000	65,465,000	200,446,000
2	Japan	44,680,000	22,173,463	66,853,463
3	Germany	40,499,442	3,061,874	43,561,316
4	Italy	30,000,000	2,806,500	32,806,500
5	France	25,100,000	5,195,000	30,295,000
6	UK	24,306,781	3,635,176	27,941,957
7	Russia	13,638,600	9,856,000	23,494,600
8	Spain	14,212,259	3,071,621	17,283,880
9	Canada	13,182,996	3,484,616	16,667,612
10	Brazil	12,000,000	3,160,689	15,160,689
	World total	477,010,289	169,748,819	646,759,108

COUNTRIES PRODUCING THE MOST MOTOR VEHICLES

	COUNTRY	CARS	COMMERCIAL VEHICLES	TOTAL
1	USA	6,083,227	5,715,678	11,798,905
2	Japan	7,863,763	2,482,023	10,345,786
3	Germany	4,539,583	303,326	4,842,909
4	France	3,147,622	442,965	3,590,587
5	South Korea	2,264,709	548,005	2,812,714
6	Spain	2,213,102	199,207	2,412,309
7	Canada	1,279,312	1,117,731	2,397,043
8	UK	1,686,134	238,263	1,924,397
9	Brazil	1,466,900	345,700	1,812,600
10	Italy	1,317,995	227,370	1,545,365
	World total	37,318,281	14,194,882	51,513,163

Source: *American Automobile Manufacturers Association*

AF-FORD-ABLE

Launched in 1908, the Model T Ford became immediately popular, thanks to its affordable price and easy use. It remained on the market until 1927.

TOP 10 BESTSELLING CARS IN THE UK

(Model/1998 sales)

1 **Ford Fiesta**, 116,110
2 **Ford Escort**, 113,560 3 **Ford Mondeo**, 99,729 4 **Vauxhall Vectra**, 92,719 5 **Renault Mégane**, 82,998 6 **Vauxhall Astra**, 81,494 7 **Vauxhall Corsa**, 75,613 8 **Peugeot 306**, 70,169 9 **Rover 200**, 64,928 10 **Rover 400**, 57,318

Source: *The Society of Motor Manufacturers and Traders Ltd.*

BESTSELLING CARS OF ALL TIME

	MANUFACTURER/MODEL	FIRST YEAR PRODUCED	ESTIMATED NO. MADE
1	Toyota Corolla	1966	23,000,000
2	Volkswagen Beetle	1937*	21,376,331
3	Lada Riva	1972	19,000,000
4	Volkswagen Golf	1974	18,453,646
5	Ford Model T	1908	16,536,075
6	Nissan Sunny/Pulsar	1966	13,571,100
7=	Ford Escort/Orion	1967	12,000,000
=	Honda Civic	1972	12,000,000
9	Mazda 323	1977	9,500,000
10	Renault 4	1961	8,100,000

* Original model still produced in Mexico and Brazil

Estimates of manufacturers' output of their bestselling models vary from the vague to the unusually precise: 16,536,075 of the Model T Ford, with 15,007,033 produced in the US and the rest in Canada and the UK in 1908–27.

Which port is the busiest in the world?
see p.237 for the answer

A Singapore
B Hong Kong
C Rotterdam

TOP 10 ★
MOST COMMON TYPES OF PROPERTY LOST ON LONDON TRANSPORT, 1997–98

	TYPE	ITEMS FOUND
1	Books, cheque books, and credit cards	22,430
2	"Value items" (handbags, purses, wallets, etc.)	19,421
3	Clothing	18,307
4	Cases and bags	12,001
5	Umbrellas	10,080
6	Cameras, electronic articles, mobile telephones, and jewellery	9,621
7	Keys	8,187
8	Spectacles	6,328
9	Gloves (pairs)	3,798
10	Gloves (odd)	665
	Total items in Top 10	109,838

Among the stranger items that have been lost in recent years are a skeleton, a box of glass eyes, breast implants, artificial legs and hands, a Yamaha outboard motor, a complete double bed, a theatrical coffin, a wedding dress, a stuffed gorilla, and an urn containing human ashes. (The latter was never claimed, and the ashes were eventually scattered reverently in a flowerbed in Regent's Park.)

THE BIRTH OF THE BEETLE

The Volkswagen – literally "people's car" – was the brainchild of Ferdinand Porsche. In Germany in 1934, only one person in 49 owned a car: Porsche recognized the need for a small car that the masses could afford. Construction of the first Volkswagen factory started in 1938 at Fahensleben. It was opened officially by Adolf Hitler, then switched from producing cars to armaments and military vehicles when World War II broke out. It was not until 1941 that the production of the first series Beetle was completed. Since then the car has come to be regarded as a design icon.

SNAP SHOTS

TOP 10 MOST COMMON CAUSES OF CAR BREAKDOWN IN THE UK*
(Cause/breakdowns)

1 Battery (flat or faulty), 685,845 **2** Tyres, 211,615 **3** Keys (key/locks/immobilizers), 192,837 **4** Alternator, 100,980 **5** Starter motor, 96,987 **6** Engine, 87,321 **7** Distributor, 81,894 **8** Spark plugs, 78,019 **9** Clutch cable, 75,692 **10** Fuel, 65,131

* Based on calls to the Automobile Association

ON THE ROAD
The network of roads in the US is so vast that you could drive around the country at top speed night and day for four years and still not cover it all.

THE 10 ★
FIRST COUNTRIES TO MAKE SEAT BELTS COMPULSORY

	COUNTRY	INTRODUCED
1	Czechoslovakia	Jan 1969
2	Ivory Coast	Jan 1970
3	Japan	Dec 1971
4	Australia	Jan 1972
5 =	Brazil	Jun 1972
=	New Zealand	Jun 1972
7	Puerto Rico	Jan 1974
8	Spain	Oct 1974
9	Sweden	Jan 1975
10 =	Netherlands	Jun 1975
=	Belgium	Jun 1975
=	Luxembourg	Jun 1975

Seat belts, long in use in aeroplanes, were not designed for use in private cars until the 1950s. Ford was the first manufacturer in Europe to fit anchorage-points, and belts were first fitted as standard equipment in Swedish Volvos from 1959.

ROAD DISASTERS & ACCIDENTS

THE 10 ★
WORST MOTOR VEHICLE AND ROAD DISASTERS

LOCATION/DATE/INCIDENT	NO. KILLED

1 Afghanistan, 3 Nov 1982 — over 2,000
Following a collision with a Soviet army truck, a petrol tanker exploded in the 2.7-km/1.7-mile Salang Tunnel. Some authorities have put the death toll from the explosion, fire, and fumes as high as 3,000.

2 Colombia, 7 Aug 1956 — 1,200
Seven army ammunition trucks exploded at night in the centre of Cali, destroying eight city blocks, including a barracks where 500 soldiers were sleeping.

3 Thailand, 15 Feb 1990 — over 150
A dynamite truck exploded.

4 Nepal, 23 Nov 1974 — 148
Hindu pilgrims were killed when a suspension bridge over the River Mahahali collapsed.

5 Egypt, 9 Aug 1973 — 127
A bus drove into an irrigation canal.

6 Togo, 6 Dec 1965 — over 125
Two lorries collided with dancers during a festival at Sotouboua.

7 Spain, 11 Jul 1978 — over 120
A liquid gas tanker exploded in a camping site at San Carlos de la Rapita.

8 South Korea, 28 Apr 1995 — 110
An undergound explosion destroyed vehicles and caused about 100 cars and buses to plunge into the pit it created.

9 =The Gambia, 12 Nov 1992 — c.100
After brake failure, a bus ferrying passengers to a dock plunged into a river.

=Kenya, early Dec 1992 — c.100
A bus carrying 112 people skidded, hit a bridge, and plunged into a river.

The worst-ever motor racing accident occurred on 13 June 1955, at Le Mans, France, when, in attempting to avoid other cars, French driver Pierre Levegh's Mercedes-Benz 300 SLR went out of control, hit a wall, and exploded in mid-air, showering wreckage into the crowd and killing 82. It is believed that the worst-ever accident involving a single car occurred on 17 Dec 1956, when eight adults and four children were killed when their car was hit by a train near Phoenix, Arizona.

CARNAGE ON THE ROADS
Although fatal crashes are common, road accidents resulting in very large numbers of deaths are, thankfully, comparatively rare.

THE 10 MOST ACCIDENT-PRONE CAR COLOURS

(Colour/accidents per 10,000 cars of each colour)

1 Black, 179 **2** White, 160 **3** Red, 157 **4** Blue, 149 **5** Grey, 147 **6** Gold, 145
7 Silver, 142 **8** Beige, 137 **9** Green, 134 **10** = Brown, 133; = Yellow, 133

THE 10 ★ COUNTRIES WITH THE MOST DEATHS BY MOTOR ACCIDENTS

COUNTRY	DEATH RATE PER 100,000 POPULATION
1 South Africa	99.4
2 Latvia	35.3
3 South Korea	33.1
4 Estonia	26.7
5 Russia	23.6
6 Portugal	22.8
7 Lithuania	22.1
8 Greece	21.3
9 Venezuala	20.7
10=El Salvador	20.3
=Kuwait	20.3

Source: *United Nations*

THE 10 ★ COUNTRIES WITH THE HIGHEST NUMBER OF ROAD DEATHS

COUNTRY	TOTAL DEATHS*
1 USA	41,907
2 Thailand	15,176
3 Japan	11,674
4 South Korea	10,087
5 Germany	8,758
6 France	8,541
7 Brazil	6,759
8 Poland	6,744
9 Italy	6,688
10 Turkey	6,108

* In latest year for which figures are available

BEWARE!

Skidding and collisions with other objects or vehicles account for most road accidents; those people aged 20–24 are most at risk of being killed or injured.

THE 10 ★ AGE GROUPS MOST VULNERABLE TO MOTOR ACCIDENTS IN GREAT BRITAIN

AGE GROUP	NO. KILLED OR INJURED (1997)
1 20–24	42,506
2 15–19	41,677
3 25–29	41,308
4 30–34	35,535
5 35–39	26,190
6 10–14	19,773
7 40–44	19,647
8 45–49	17,135
9 5–9	14,759
10 50–54	14,178

The high proportion of accidents among teenagers and people in their early twenties is accounted for partly by inexperience and recklessness in controlling motor cycles and cars. The most vulnerable single age is 18, with 11,368 accidents and fatalities.

THE 10 ★ MOST COMMON OBJECTS INVOLVED IN MOTOR ACCIDENTS IN THE UK

OBJECT	ACCIDENTS (1997)
1 No object	54,753
2 Various permanent objects	7,764
3 Tree	3,095
4 Lamp post	2,525
5 Ditch	2,148
6 Crash barrier	1,929
7 Road sign/traffic signal	1,388
8 Telegraph/electricity pole	830
9 Bus stop/shelter	157
10 Submerged	32

THE 10 ★ MOST COMMON MANOEUVRES CAUSING MOTOR ACCIDENTS IN THE UK*

MANOEUVRE	ACCIDENTS (1997)
1 Going ahead (various)	188,636
2 Turning right, or waiting to do so	50,020
3 Going ahead on a bend	33,857
4 Held up while waiting to go ahead	32,398
5 Stopping	18,925
6 Parked	15,954
7 Overtaking	14,722
8 Turning left, or waiting to do so	14,254
9 Changing lane	6,124
10 Starting	5,621

* By manoeuvre; vehicles other than 2-wheel

THE 10 WORST YEARS FOR ROAD FATALITIES IN GREAT BRITAIN

(Year/no. killed)

1 1941, 9,169 **2** 1940, 8,609 **3** 1939, 8,272 **4** 1966, 7,985 **5** 1965, 7,952 **6** 1964, 7,820 **5** 1972, 7,763 **8** 1971, 7,699 **9** 1970, 7,499 **10** 1973, 7,406

What was the biggest airship ever built?
see p.39 for the answer
A *Graf Zeppelin II*
B *Hindenburg*
C *Graf Zeppelin*

THE 10 ★ WORST RAIL DISASTERS

LOCATION/DATE/INCIDENT   **NO. KILLED**

1 Bagmati River, India, 6 Jun 1981   *c.*800
The carriages of a train travelling from Samastipur to Banmukhi in Bihar plunged off a bridge over the River Bagmati near Mansi – when the driver braked, apparently to avoid hitting a sacred cow. Although the official death toll was said to have been 268, many authorities have claimed that the train was so massively overcrowded that the actual figure was in excess of 800, making it probably the worst rail disaster of all time.

2 Chelyabinsk, Russia, 3 Jun 1989   up to 800
Two passenger trains, laden with holidaymakers heading to and from Black Sea resorts, were destroyed when liquid gas from a nearby pipeline exploded.

3 Guadalajara, Mexico, 18 Jan 1915   over 600
A train derailed on a steep incline, but political strife in the country meant that full details of the disaster were suppressed.

4 Modane, France, 12 Dec 1917   573
A troop-carrying train ran out of control and was derailed. It has been claimed that the train was overloaded and that as many as 1,000 may have died.

5 Balvano, Italy, 2 Mar 1944   521
A heavily-laden train stalled in the Armi Tunnel, and many passengers were asphyxiated. Like the disaster at Torre (No. 6), wartime secrecy prevented full details from being published.

6 Torre, Spain, 3 Jan 1944   over 500
A double collision and fire in a tunnel resulted in many deaths – some have put the total as high as 800.

7 Awash, Ethiopia, 13 Jan 1985   428
A derailment hurled a train laden with some 1,000 passengers into a ravine.

8 Cireau, Romania, 7 Jan 1917   374
An overcrowded passenger train crashed into a military train and was derailed.

9 Quipungo, Angola, 31 May 1993   355
A trail was derailed by UNITA guerrilla action.

10 Sangi, Pakistan, 4 Jan 1990   306
A train was diverted onto the wrong line, resulting in a fatal collision.

RAIL WRECKAGE
The sparks from two trains travelling through the Ural mountains ignited gas leaking from the nearby Trans-Siberian pipeline.

THE 10 ★ WORST RAIL DISASTERS IN THE UK

LOCATION/DATE/INCIDENT   **NO. KILLED**

1 Quintinshill, nr. Gretna Green, Scotland, 22 May 1915   227
A troop train carrying 500 soldiers from Larbert to Liverpool collided head-on with a local passenger train. Barely a minute later, the Scottish express, drawn by two engines and weighing a total of 600 tons, ploughed into the wreckage. The 15 coaches of the troop train, 195 m/640 feet long, were crushed down to just 61 m/200 feet long. The gas-lit troop train then caught fire. In addition to the deaths, 246 people were injured, many very seriously.

2 Harrow and Wealdstone Station, Middlesex, 8 Oct 1952   122
In patchy fog, Robert Jones, the relief driver of the Perth to Euston sleeping-car express, pulled by the City of Glasgow, failed to see a series of signal lights warning him of danger and at 8.19 a.m. collided with the waiting Watford to Euston train. Seconds later, the Euston to Liverpool and Manchester express hit the wreckage of the two trains.

3 Lewisham, South London, 4 Dec 1957   90
A steam and an electric train were in collision in fog, the disaster was made worse by the collapse of a bridge onto the wreckage.

4 Tay Bridge, Scotland, 28 Dec 1879   80
As the North British mail train passed over it during a storm, the bridge collapsed killing all 75 passengers and the crew of five. The bridge – the longest in the world at that time – had only been opened on 31 May the previous year, and Queen Victoria had crossed it in a train soon afterwards.

5 Armagh, Northern Ireland, 12 Jun 1889   78
A Sunday school excursion train with 940 passengers stalled on a hill. When 10 carriages were uncoupled, they ran backwards and collided with a passenger train, killing 78 and leaving 250 injured.

6 Hither Green, South London, 5 Nov 1967   49
The Hastings to Charing Cross train was derailed by a broken track. As well as those killed, 78 were injured, 27 of them very seriously.

7 =Bourne End, Hertfordshire, 30 Sep 1945   43
Travelling at about 80 km/h/50 mph, the Perth to Euston express sped through a crossover with a 32 km/h/20 mph speed restriction imposed during engineering works, and was derailed. Its coaches plunged down an embankment.

=Moorgate Station, London, 28 Feb 1975   43
The Drayton Park to Moorgate tube ran into the wall at the end of a tunnel, killing 43 and injuring 74.

9 Castlecary, Scotland, 10 Dec 1937   35
In heavy snow the Edinburgh to Glasgow train ran into a stationary Dundee to Glasgow train and rode over the top of it, leaving 179 injured.

10 =Shipton near Oxford, 24 Dec 1874   34
The Paddington to Birkenhead train plunged over the embankment after a carriage wheel broke, killing 34 and badly injuring 65.

=Clapham Junction, London, 12 Dec 1988   34
The 7.18 Basingstoke to Waterloo train, carrying 906 passengers, stopped at signals outside Clapham Junction; the 6.30 train from Bournemouth ran into its rear, and an empty train from Waterloo hit the wreckage, leaving 33 dead (and one who died later) and 111 injured.

TOP 10 LONGEST RAIL NETWORKS
(Location/total rail length in km/miles)

1 USA, 240,000/149,129 **2** Russia, 154,000/95,691 **3** Canada, 72,963/45,337 **4** China, 64,900/40,327 **5** India, 62,660/38,935 **6** Germany, 43,966/27,319 **7** Australia, 38,563/23,962 **8** Argentina, 37,910/23,556 **9** France, 32,027/19,901 **10** Brazil, 26,895/16,712

THE 10 FIRST UNDERGROUND RAILWAY LINES IN LONDON
(Line/date first section opened)

1 Metropolitan, 10 Jan 1863 **2** District, 24 Dec 1868 **3** Circle, 6 Oct 1884 **4** Waterloo/Bank, 8 Aug 1898 **5** Central, 30 Jul 1900 **6** Bakerloo, 10 Mar 1906 **7** Piccadilly, 15 Dec 1906 **8** Northern, 22 Jun 1907 **9** Victoria, 7 Mar 1969 **10** Jubilee, 1 May 1979

FAST AS A BULLET

The Shinkansen, or Bullet Train, once the world's fastest train, debuted in 1964 and currently covers the 190 km/120 miles between the stations of Hiroshima and Kokura in 44 minutes.

TOP 10 ★
BUSIEST UNDERGROUND RAILWAY NETWORKS

CITY	YEAR OPENED	TRACK LENGTH KM	MILES	STATIONS	PASSENGERS PER ANNUM
1 Moscow	1935	243.6	153	150	3,183,900,000
2 Tokyo	1927	169.1	106	154	2,112,700,000
3 Mexico City	1969	177.7	112	154	1,422,600,000
4 Seoul	1974	133.0	84	112	1,354,000,000
5 Paris	1900	201.4	127	372	1,170,000,000
6 New York	1867	398.0	249	469	1,100,000,000
7 Osaka	1933	105.8	66	99	988,600,000
8 St. Petersburg	1955	91.75	58	50	850,000,000
9 Hong Kong	1979	43.2	27	38	804,000,000
10 London	1863	392.0	247	245	784,000,000

TOP 10 ★
FASTEST RAIL JOURNEYS*

JOURNEY/LOCATION/TRAIN	SPEED KM/H	MPH
1 Hiroshima–Kokura, Japan, *Nozomi 503/508*	261.8	162.7
2 Lille–Roissy, France, *TGV 538/9*	254.3	158.0
3 Madrid–Seville, Spain, *AVE 9616/9617*	209.1	129.9
4 Würzburg–Fulda, Germany, *ICE*	199.7	124.1
5 London–York, UK, *Scottish Pullman*	180.2	112.0
6 Hässleholm–Alvesta, Sweden, *X2000*	168.0	104.4
7 Rome–Florence, Italy, *10 Pendolini*	164.9	102.5
8 Baltimore–Wilmington, USA, *Metroliner 110*	157.3	97.7
9 Salo–Karjaa, Finland, *S220 132*	151.7	94.3
10 Toronto–Dorval, Canada, *Metropolis*	141.0	87.6

* Fastest journey for each country; all those in the Top 10 have other similarly or equally fast services Source: Railway Gazette International

Background image: **KOMSOMOLSKAYA STATION, MOSCOW**

Which is the largest cruise ship in the world?
see p.236 for the answer

A *Grand Princess*
B *Disney Magic*
C *Voyager of the Seas*

235

THE 10 ★
WORST OIL TANKER SPILLS

	TANKER(S)/LOCATION/DATE	APPROX. SPILLAGE TONNES
1	*Atlantic Empress* and *Aegean Captain*, Trinidad, 19 Jul 1979	300,000
2	*Castillio de Bellver*, Cape Town, South Africa, 6 Aug 1983	255,000
3	*Olympic Bravery*, Ushant, France, 24 Jan 1976	250,000
4	*Showa-Maru*, Malacca, Malaya, 7 Jun 1975	237,000
5	*Amoco Cadiz*, Finistère, France, 16 Mar 1978	223,000
6	*Odyssey*, Atlantic, off Canada, 10 Nov 1988	140,000
7	*Torrey Canyon*, Isles of Scilly, UK, 18 Mar 1967	120,000
8	*Sea Star*, Gulf of Oman, 19 Dec 1972	115,000
9	*Irenes Serenada*, Pilos, Greece, 23 Feb 1980	102,000
10	*Urquiola*, Corunna, Spain, 12 May 1976	101,000

In addition to these major slicks, it is estimated that an average of 2 million tonnes is spilled into the world's seas annually. All these accidents were caused by collision, grounding, fire, or explosion.

CARNIVAL DESTINY

The Carnival Destiny, the world's fourth largest cruise ship, is 271 m/892 ft long, and contains a cinema, a library, a gymnasium, and four outdoor pools.

THE 10 ★
WORST PASSENGER FERRY DISASTERS OF THE 20TH CENTURY

	FERRY/LOCATION/DATE	NO. KILLED
1	*Dona Paz*, Philippines, 20 Dec 1987	up to 3,000
2	*Neptune*, Haiti, 17 Feb 1992	1,800
3	*Toya Maru*, Japan, 26 Sep 1954	1,172
4	*Don Juan*, Philippines, 22 Apr 1980	over 1,000
5	*Estonia*, Baltic Sea, 28 Sep 1994	909
6	*Samia*, Bangladesh, 25 May 1986	600
7	*MV Bukoba*, Lake Victoria, Tanzania, 21 May 1996	549
8	*Salem Express*, Egypt, 14 Dec 1991	480
9	*Tampomas II*, Indonesia, 27 Jan 1981	431
10	*Nam Yung Ho*, South Korea, 15 Dec 1970	323

The *Dona Paz* sank in the Tabias Strait, Philippines, after the ferry was struck by the oil tanker *MV Victor*. The loss of life may have been much higher than the official figure (up to 4,386 has been suggested by some authorities).

TOP 10 ★
LARGEST CRUISE SHIPS

	SHIP/YEAR/COUNTRY BUILT	PASSENGER CAPACITY	GROSS TONNAGE
1	*Voyager of the Seas*, 1999, Finland	3,840	142,000
2	*Grand Princess*, 1998, Italy	3,300	108,806
3	*Carnival Triumph*, 1999, Italy	3,300	101,672
4	*Carnival Destiny*, 1996, Italy	3,336	101,353
5	*Disney Magic*, 1998, Italy	2,500	83,338
6	*Rhapsody of the Seas*, 1997, France	2,416	78,491
7	*Vision of the Seas*, 1997, France	2,416	78,340
8 =	*Dawn Princess*, 1997, Italy	1,950	77,441
=	*Sea Princess*, 1998, Italy	2,185	77,441
=	*Sun Princess*, 1995, Italy	2,272	77,441

Source: *Lloyd's Register of Shipping, MIPG/PPMS*

Did You Know? The *Jahre Viking* oil tanker, at 485.45 m/1,504 ft long, is the longest vessel ever built. Its length is equal to more than 20 tennis courts end-to-end.

WORST MARINE DISASTERS
OF THE 20TH CENTURY

LOCATION/DATE/INCIDENT	APPROX. NO. KILLED
1 Off Gdansk, Poland, 30 Jan 1945	up to 7,800

The German liner Wilhelm Gustloff, laden with refugees, was torpedoed by a Soviet submarine S-13. The precise death toll remains uncertain, but is in the range of 5,348 to 7,800.

2 Off Cape Rixhöft (Rozeewie), Poland, 16 Apr 1945	6,800

A German ship Goya carrying evacuees from Gdansk, was torpedoed in the Baltic.

3 Off Yingkow, China, Nov 1947	over 6,000

An unidentified Chinese troop ship carrying Nationalist soldiers from Manchuria.

4 Lübeck, Germany, 3 May 1945	5,000

The German ship Cap Arcona, carrying concentration camp survivors, was bombed and sunk by British aircraft.

5 Off St Nazaire, France, 17 Jun 1940	3,050

The British troop ship Lancastria sank.

6 Off Stolpmünde (Ustka), Poland, 9 Feb 1945	3,000

German war-wounded and refugees were lost when the Steuben was torpedoed by the same Russian submarine that had sunk the Wilhelm Gustloff.

LOCATION/DATE/INCIDENT	APPROX. NO. KILLED
7 Tabias Strait, Philippines, 20 Dec 1987	up to 3,000

The ferry Dona Paz was struck by oil tanker MV Victor.

8 Woosung, China, 3 Dec 1948	over 2,750

The overloaded steamship Kiangya, carrying refugees, struck a Japanese mine.

9 Lübeck, Germany, 3 May 1945	2,750

The refugee ship Thielbeck sank during the British bombardment of Lübeck harbour in the closing weeks of World War II.

10 South Atlantic, 12 Sep 1942	2,279

The British passenger vessel Laconia, carrying Italian prisoners-of-war, was sunk by German U-boat U-156.

Recent re-assessments of the death tolls in some of the World War II marine disasters means that the most famous marine disaster of all no longer ranks in the Top 10. The *Titanic* was a British liner that struck an iceberg in the North Atlantic and sank on 15 April 1912, with the loss of 1,517 lives. The *Titanic* tragedy remains one of the worst ever peacetime disasters.

BUSIEST PORTS

PORT/LOCATION	GOODS HANDLED PER ANNUM (TONNES)
1 Rotterdam, Netherlands	350,000,000
2 Singapore	290,000,000
3 Chiba, Japan	173,700,000
4 Kobe, Japan	171,000,000
5 Hong Kong	147,200,000
6 Houston, USA	142,000,000
7 Shanghai, China	139,600,000
8 Nagoya, Japan	137,300,000
9 Yokohama, Japan	128,300,000
10 Antwerp, Belgium	109,500,000

The only other world port handling more than 100 million tonnes is Kawasaki, Japan (105,100,000 tonnes per annum).

DOCK OF THE BAY

Many docks perform functions other than developing maritime commerce and maintaining cruise terminals, including dredging and public recreational facilities.

THE 10 ★
FIRST PEOPLE TO FLY IN HEAVIER-THAN-AIR AIRCRAFT

PILOT/COUNTRY/AIRCRAFT	DATE
1 Orville Wright, USA, *Wright Flyer I*	17 Dec 1903
2 Wilbur Wright, USA, *Wright Flyer I*	17 Dec 1903
3 Alberto Santos-Dumont, Brazil, *No. 14-bis*	23 Oct 1906
4 Charles Voisin, France, *Voisin-Delagrange I*	30 Mar 1907
5 Henri Farman, UK, later France, *Voisin-Farman I-bis*	7 Oct 1907
6 Léon Delagrange, France, *Voisin-Delagrange I*	5 Nov 1907
7 Robert Esnault-Pelterie, France, *REP No. 1*	16 Nov 1907
8 Charles W. Furnas*, USA, *Wright Flyer III*	14 May 1908
9 Louis Blériot, France, *Blériot VIII*	29 Jun 1908
10 Glenn Hammond Curtiss, USA, *AEA June Bug*	4 Jul 1908

As a passenger in a plane piloted by Wilbur Wright, Furnass was the first aeroplane passenger in the US

THE WRIGHT BROTHERS

Following Orville Wright's first-ever flight at Kitty Hawk, North Carolina, he (right) and his brother Wilbur dominated the air for the next few years.

THE 10 ★
FIRST TRANSATLANTIC FLIGHTS

AIRCRAFT/CREW/COUNTRY	CROSSING	DATE
1 US Navy/Curtiss flying boat *NC-4*, Lt.-Cdr. Albert Cushing Read and crew of five, USA	Trepassy Harbor, Newfoundland, to Lisbon, Portugal	16–27 May 1919*
2 Twin Rolls-Royce-engined converted Vickers Vimy bomber#, Capt. John Alcock and Lt. Arthur Whitten Brown, UK	St John's, Newfoundland, to Galway, Ireland	14–15 Jun 1919
3 British *R-34* **airship**+, Maj. George Herbert Scott and crew of 30, UK	East Fortune, Scotland, to Roosevelt Field, New York	2–6 Jul 1919
4 Fairey IIID seaplane *Santa Cruz*, Adm. Gago Coutinho and Cdr. Sacadura Cabral, Portugal	Lisbon, Portugal, to Recife, Brazil	30 Mar–5 Jun 1922
5 Two Douglas seaplanes, *Chicago* **and** *New Orleans*, Lt. Lowell H. Smith and Leslie P. Arnold/ Erik Nelson and John Harding, USA	Orkneys, Scotland, to Labrador, Canada	2–31 Aug 1924
6 *Los Angeles*, **a renamed German-built** *ZR 3* **airship**, Dr. Hugo Eckener, with 31 passengers and crew, Germany	Friedrichshafen, Germany, to Lakehurst, New Jersey	12–15 Oct 1924
7 *Plus Ultra*, **a Dornier Wal twin-engined flying boat**, Capt. Julio Ruiz and crew, Spain	Huelva, Spain, to Recife, Brazil	22 Jan–10 Feb 1926
8 *Santa Maria*, **a Savoia-Marchetti S.55 flying boat**, Francesco Marquis de Pinedo, Capt. Carlo del Prete, and Lt. Vitale Zacchetti, Italy	Cagliari, Sardinia, to Recife, Brazil	8–24 Feb 1927
9 Dornier Wal flying boat, Sarmento de Beires and Jorge de Castilho, Portugal	Lisbon, Portugal, to Natal, Brazil	16–17 Mar 1927
10 Savoia-Marchetti flying boat, João De Barros and crew, Brazil	Genoa, Italy, to Natal, Brazil	28 Apr–14 May 1927

All dates refer to the actual Atlantic legs of the journeys; some started earlier and ended beyond their first transatlantic landfalls

First non-stop flight

+ *First east–west flight*

THE 10 FIRST FLIGHTS OF MORE THAN ONE HOUR
(Pilot/duration in hrs:mins:secs/date)

1 Orville Wright, 1:2:15, 9 Sep 1908 **2** Orville Wright, 1:5:52, 10 Sep 1908
3 Orville Wright, 1:10:0, 11 Sep 1908 **4** Orville Wright, 1:15:20, 12 Sep 1908
5 Wilbur Wright, 1:31:25, 21 Sep 1908 **6** Wilbur Wright, 1:7:24, 28 Sep 1908
7 Wilbur Wright*, 1:4:26, 6 Oct 1908 **8** Wilbur Wright, 1:9:45, 10 Oct 1908
9 Wilbur Wright, 1:54:53, 18 Dec 1908 **10** Wilbur Wright, 2:20:23, 31 Dec 1908

First ever flight of more than one hour with a passenger (M.A. Fordyce)

Background image: **AN ARTIST'S IMPRESSION OF ONE OF THE WRIGHT BROTHERS' FIRST FLIGHTS**

TOP 10 ★
FASTEST X-15 FLIGHTS

	PILOT/DATE	MACH*	SPEED KM/H	MPH
1	William J. Knight, 3 Oct 1967	6.70	7,274	4,520
2	William J. Knight, 18 Nov 1966	6.33	6,857	4,261
3	Joseph A. Walker, 27 Jun 1962	5.92	6,606	4,105
4	Robert M. White, 9 Nov 1961	6.04	6,589	4,094
5	Robert A. Rushworth, 5 Dec 1963	6.06	6,466	4,018
6	Neil A. Armstrong, 26 Jun 1962	5.74	6,420	3,989
7	John B. McKay, 22 Jun 1965	5.64	6,388	3,938
8	Robert A. Rushworth, 18 Jul 1963	5.63	6,317	3,925
9	Joseph A. Walker, 25 Jun 1963	5.51	6,294	3,911
10	William H. Dana, 4 Oct 1967	5.53	6,293	3,910

* *Mach no. varies with altitude – the list is ranked on actual speed*

THE 10 ★
FIRST ROCKET AND JET AIRCRAFT

	AIRCRAFT/COUNTRY	FIRST FLIGHT
1	Heinkel He 176*, Germany	20 Jun 1939
2	Heinkel He 178, Germany	27 Aug 1939
3	DFS 194*, Germany	Aug 1940#
4	Caproni-Campini N-1, Italy	28 Aug 1940
5	Heinkel He 280V-1, Germany	2 Apr 1941
6	Gloster E.28/39, UK	15 May 1941
7	Messerschmitt Me 163 Komet*, Germany	13 Aug 1941
8	Messerschmitt Me 262V-3, Germany	18 Jul 1942
9	Bell XP-59A Airacomet, USA	1 Oct 1942
10	Gloster Meteor F Mk 1, UK	5 Mar 1943

* *Rocket-powered*
# *Precise date unknown*

GRAF ZEPPELIN II
Sister-ship of the ill-fated Hindenburg, *the equally gigantic Graf Zeppelin II airship flew successfully, but in March 1940, on the orders of Herman Goering, it was dismantled at Frankfurt, Germany, and its aluminium frame used in the construction of Luftwaffe fighter aircraft.*

TOP 10 ★
BIGGEST AIRSHIPS EVER BUILT

	AIRSHIP	COUNTRY	YEAR	VOLUME CU M	CU FT	LENGTH M	FT
1 =	Hindenburg	Germany	1936	200,000	7,062,934	245	804
=	Graf Zeppelin II	Germany	1938	200,000	7,062,934	245	804
3 =	Akron	USA	1931	184,060	6,500,000	239	785
=	Macon	USA	1933	184,060	6,500,000	239	785
5	R101	UK	1930	155,744	5,500,000	237	777
6	Graf Zeppelin	Germany	1928	105,000	3,708,040	237	776
7	L72	Germany	1920	68,500	2,419,055	226	743
8	R100	UK	1929	155,743	5,500,000	216	709
9	R38	UK*	1921	77,136	2,724,000	213	699
10 =	L70	Germany	1918	62,200	2,418,700	212	694
=	L71	Germany	1918	62,200	2,418,700	212	694

* *UK-built, but sold to US Navy*

Although several of the giant airships in this list travelled long distances carrying thousands of passengers, they all ultimately suffered unfortunate fates: six (the *Hindenburg, Akron, Macon, R101, L72,* and *R38*) crashed with the loss of many lives, the *L70* was shot down, and the *L71,* both *Graf Zeppelins,* and the *R100* were broken up for scrap.

Did You Know? The speeds attained by the rocket-powered X-15 and X-15A-2 aircraft are the greatest ever attained by piloted vehicles in the Earth's atmosphere.

239

AIR TRANSPORT

THE 10 ★

WORST AIRSHIP DISASTERS

LOCATION/DATE/INCIDENT	NO. KILLED
1 Off the Atlantic coast, USA, 4 Apr 1933 *US Navy airship Akron crashed into the sea in a storm, leaving only three survivors in the world's worst airship tragedy.*	73
2 Over the Mediterranean, 21 Dec 1923 *French airship Dixmude is assumed to have been struck by lightning, broke up, and crashed into the sea; wreckage, believed to be from the airship, was found off Sicily 10 years later.*	52
3 Near Beauvais, France, 5 Oct 1930 *British airship R101 crashed into a hillside leaving 48 dead, with two dying later, and six survivors.*	50
4 Off the coast near Hull, UK, 24 Aug 1921 *Airship R38, sold by the British Government to the US and renamed USN ZR-2, broke in two on a training and test flight.*	44
5 Lakehurst, New Jersey, USA, 6 May 1937 *German Zeppelin Hindenburg caught fire when mooring.*	36
6 Hampton Roads, Virginia, USA, 21 Feb 1922 *Roma, an Italian airship bought by the US Army, crashed, killing all but 11 men on board.*	34
7 Berlin, Germany, 17 Oct 1913 *German airship LZ18 crashed after engine failure during a test flight at Berlin-Johannisthal.*	28
8 Baltic Sea, 30 Mar 1917 *German airship SL9 was struck by lightning on a flight from Seerappen to Seddin, and crashed into the sea.*	23
9 Mouth of the River Elbe, Germany, 3 Sep 1915 *German airship L10 was struck by lightning and plunged into the sea.*	19
10=Off Heligoland, 9 Sep 1913 *German Navy airship L1 crashed into the sea, leaving six survivors.*	14
=Caldwell, Ohio, USA, 3 Sep 1925 *US dirigible Shenandoah, the first airship built in the US and the first to use safe helium instead of inflammable hydrogen, broke up in a storm, scattering sections over a large area of the Ohio countryside.*	14

TOP 10 AIRLINE-USING COUNTRIES

(Country/passenger km per annum*/passenger miles per annum*)

1 **USA**, 919.816 billion/571.547 billion **2** **UK**, 161.366 billion/100.269 billion **3** **Japan**, 141.812 billion/88.118 billion **4** **France**, 81.594 billion/50.700 billion **5** **Germany**, 77.765 billion/48.321 billion **6** **Australia**, 72.594 billion/45.108 billion **7** **China**, 70.605 billion/43.872 billion **8** **Netherlands**, 62.397 billion/38.772 billion **9** **Canada**, 56.018 billion/34.808 billion **10** **Rep. of Korea**, 55.751 billion/34.642 billion

* *Total distance travelled by scheduled aircraft of national airlines multiplied by number of passengers carried.*
Source: *International Civil Aviation Organization*

THE 10 ★

WORST AIR DISASTERS

LOCATION/DATE/INCIDENT	NO. KILLED
1 Tenerife, Canary Islands, 27 Mar 1977 *Two Boeing 747s (Pan Am and KLM, carrying 364 passengers and 16 crew and 230 passengers and 11 crew respectively) collided and caught fire on the runway of Los Rodeos airport after the pilots received incorrect control-tower instructions.*	583
2 Mt. Ogura, Japan, 12 Aug 1985 *A JAL Boeing 747 on an internal flight from Tokyo to Osaka crashed, killing all but four on board in the worst-ever disaster involving a single aircraft.*	520
3 Charkhi Dadrio, India, 12 Nov 1996 *Soon after taking off from New Delhi's Indira Gandhi International Airport, a Saudi Airways Boeing 747 collided with a Kazakh Airlines Ilyushin IL76 cargo aircraft on its descent and exploded, killing all 312 on the Boeing and 37 on the Ilyushin in the world's worst mid-air crash.*	349
4 Paris, France, 3 Mar 1974 *A Turkish Airlines DC-10 crashed at Ermenonville, north of Paris, immediately after take-off for London, with many English rugby supporters among the dead.*	346
5 Off the Irish coast, 23 Jun 1985 *An Air India Boeing 747 on a flight from Vancouver to Delhi exploded in mid-air, perhaps as a result of a terrorist bomb.*	329
6 Riyadh, Saudi Arabia, 19 Aug 1980 *A Saudia (Saudi Arabian) Airlines Lockheed Tristar caught fire during an emergency landing.*	301
7 Kinshasa, Zaïre, 8 Jan 1996 *A Zaïrean Antonov-32 cargo plane crashed shortly after takeoff, killing shoppers in a city centre market.*	298
8 Off the Iranian coast, 3 Jul 1988 *An Iran Air A300 airbus was shot down in error by a missile fired by the USS Vincennes.*	290
9 Chicago, USA, 25 May 1979 *The worst air disaster in the US occurred when an engine fell off a DC-10 as it took off from Chicago O'Hare airport and the plane plunged out of control, killing all 271 on board and two on the ground.*	273
10 Lockerbie, Scotland, 21 Dec 1988 *Pan Am Flight 103 from London Heathrow to New York exploded in mid-air as a result of a terrorist bomb, killing 243 passengers, 16 crew, and 11 on the ground in the UK's worst-ever air disaster.*	270

TOP 10 COUNTRIES WITH THE MOST AIRPORTS

(Country/airports)

1 **USA**, 14,574 **2** **Brazil**, 3,291 **3** **Russia**, 2,517 **4** **Mexico**, 1,810 **5** **Argentina**, 1,411 **6** **Canada**, 1,393 **7** **Bolivia**, 1,153 **8** **Colombia**, 1,136 **9** **Paraguay**, 948 **10** **South Africa**, 770

Source: *Central Intelligence Agency*

Airports, as defined by the CIA (which monitors them for strategic reasons), range in size from those with paved runways over 3,048 m/10,000 ft in length to those with only short landing strips. Among European countries with the most airports are Germany (613), France (460), and the UK (387).

Which country has the longest rail network?
see p.235 for the answer
A India
B Russia
C USA

AIRSHIP TRAGEDY

US airship Akron was named after the Ohio city known as America's rubber capital. Built in 1931, it crashed into the sea only two years later.

TOP 10 ★
BUSIEST INTERNATIONAL AIRPORTS

AIRPORT/LOCATION	PASSENGERS PER ANNUM
1 **London Heathrow**, London, UK	48,275,000
2 **Frankfurt**, Frankfurt, Germany	30,919,000
3 **Hong Kong**, Hong Kong, China	29,543,000
4 **Charles de Gaulle**, Paris, France	28,665,000
5 **Schiphol**, Amsterdam, Netherlands	27,085,000
6 **Singapore International**, Singapore	23,130,000
7 **New Tokyo International (Narita)**, Tokyo, Japan	22,666,000
8 **London Gatwick**, Gatwick, UK	22,029,000
9 **J.F. Kennedy International**, New York, USA	17,453,000
10 **Bangkok**, Bangkok, Thailand	16,380,000

Source: International Civil Aviation Organization

THE 10 ★
WORST AIR DISASTERS IN THE UK

LOCATION/DATE/INCIDENT	NO. KILLED
1 **Lockerbie**, Scotland, 21 Dec 1988 *(See Worst Air Disasters, No. 10)*	270
2 **Staines**, Middlesex, 18 Jun 1972 *A British European Airways Trident crashed after takeoff.*	118
3 **Siginstone**, Glamorgan, 12 Mar 1950 *An Avro Tudor V carrying Welsh rugby fans from Belfast inexplicably crashed while attempting to land at Llandow; three survived, one dying later. It was the worst air crash in the world up to this date.*	81
4 **Stockport**, Cheshire, 4 Jun 1967 *A British Midland Argonaut airliner carrying holidaymakers returning from Majorca crashed, en route to Manchester Airport, killing all but 12 on board.*	72
5 **Freckelton**, Lancashire, 23 Aug 1944 *A US Air Force B-24 crashed onto a school after being struck by lightning, killing 10 USAAF personnel, 38 children, two teachers, and other civilians on the ground.*	61
6 **Manchester Airport**, 22 Aug 1985 *A British Airtours Boeing 737 caught fire on the ground.*	55
7 **Near Gatwick Airport**, 5 Jan 1969 *An Ariana Afghan Airlines Boeing 727 crash-landed; the deaths include two on the ground.*	50
8 **M1 motorway**, 8 Jan 1989 *A British Midland Boeing 737-400, attempting to land without engine power, crashed on the motorway embankment.*	47
9= **Isle of Wight**, 15 Nov 1957 *Following an engine fire, an Aquila Airlines Solent flying boat struck a cliff.*	45
= **Off Sumburgh**, Shetland Islands, 6 Nov 1986 *A Boeing 234 Chinook helicopter ferrying oil rig workers ditched in the sea, making it the worst-ever civilian helicopter accident.*	45

In addition to disasters within the UK, a number of major air crashes involving British aircraft have occurred overseas, among them a Dan-Air Boeing 727 which crashed into a mountainside at Santa Cruz de Tenerife, Canary Islands, on 25 April 1980, killing all 146 on board.

FLYING BOEING

First flown in 1981, the Boeing 737-300 can accommodate up to 126 passengers and reaches speeds of 801 km/h/495 mph.

SPORTS

OLYMPIC RECORDS

OLYMPIC SPORTS IN WHICH THE US HAVE WON THE MOST MEDALS

	SPORT	GOLD	SILVER	BRONZE	TOTAL
1	Athletics	299	216	177	692
2	Swimming	230	176	137	543
3	Diving	46	40	41	127
4	Wrestling	46	38	25	109
5	Boxing	47	21	34	102
6	Shooting	45	26	21	92
7	Gymnastics	26	23	28	77
8	Rowing	29	28	19	76
9	Yachting	16	19	16	51
10	Speed skating	22	16	10	48

OLYMPIC SPORTS IN WHICH THE UK HAVE WON THE MOST MEDALS

	SPORT	GOLD	SILVER	BRONZE	TOTAL
1	Athletics	47	79	57	183
2	Swimming	18	23	30	71
3 =Cycling		9	21	16	46
=Tennis		16	14	16	46
5	Shooting	13	14	18	45
6	Boxing	12	10	21	43
7	Rowing	19	15	7	41
8	Yachting	14	12	9	35
9	Equestrianism	5	7	9	21
10	Wrestling	3	4	10	17

SUMMER OLYMPICS ATTENDED BY THE MOST COMPETITORS, 1896–1996

	CITY/YEAR	COUNTRIES REPRESENTED	COMPETITORS
1	Atlanta, 1996	197	10,310
2	Barcelona, 1992	172	9,364
3	Seoul, 1988	159	9,101
4	Munich, 1972	122	7,156
5	Los Angeles, 1984	141	7,058
6	Montreal, 1976	92	6,085
7	Mexico City, 1968	112	5,530
8	Rome, 1960	83	5,346
9	Moscow, 1980	81	5,326
10	Tokyo, 1964	93	5,140

The first Games in 1896 were attended by just 311 competitors, all men, representing 13 countries. Women took part for the first time four years later at the Paris Games.

WOMEN'S MOVEMENT

Over 3,500 female competitors took part in the 1996 Atlanta Olympics – 40 per cent more than at the previous games in Barcelona in 1992.

Background image: **OLYMPIC RINGS**

SPECTACULAR ACHIEVEMENT
Larissa Latynina dominated gymnastics for over a decade. In Olympic, World, and European championships she won a total of 44 medals, 24 of them gold.

THE 10 OLYMPIC DECATHLON EVENTS

1 100 metres **2** Long jump **3** Shot put **4** High jump
5 400 metres **6** 110 metres hurdles **7** Discus
8 Pole vault **9** Javelin **10** 1500 metres

TOP 10 ★
LONGEST-STANDING CURRENT OLYMPIC TRACK AND FIELD RECORDS

	EVENT	WINNING DISTANCE, TIME OR SCORE	COMPETITOR/ COUNTRY	DATE SET
1	Men's long jump	8.90 m	Bob Beamon, USA	18 Oct 1968
2	Women's shot	22.41 m	Ilona Slupianek, East Germany	24 Jul 1980
3	Women's 800 metres	1 min 53.43 sec	Nadezhda Olizarenko, USSR	27 Jul 1980
4=	Women's 4 x 100 metres	41.60 sec	East Germany	1 Aug 1980
=	Men's 1500 metres	3 min 32.53 sec	Sebastian Coe, GB	1 Aug 1980
6	Women's marathon	2 hr 24 min 52 sec	Joan Benoit, USA	5 Aug 1984
7	Decathlon	8,847 points	Daley Thompson, GB	9 Aug 1984
8	Men's 5,000 metres	13 min 05.59 sec	Said Aouita, Morocco	11 Aug 1984
9	Men's marathon	2 hr 9 min 21 sec	Carlos Lopes, Portugal	12 Aug 1984
10=	Men's shot	22.47 m	Ulf Timmermann, East Germany	23 Sep 1988
=	Men's 20 km walk	1 hr 19 min 57 sec	Jozef Pribilinec, Czechoslovakia	23 Sep 1988

TOP 10 ★
COUNTRIES WITH THE MOST SUMMER OLYMPICS MEDALS, 1896–1996

	COUNTRY	GOLD	SILVER	BRONZE	TOTAL
1	USA	833	634	548	2,015
2	Soviet Union*	485	395	354	1,234
3	UK	177	233	225	635
4	France	176	181	205	562
5	Germany#	151	181	184	516
6	Sweden	134	152	173	459
7	Italy	166	136	142	444
8	Hungary	142	128	155	425
9	East Germany	153	130	127	410
10	Australia	87	85	122	294

* *Includes Unified Team of 1992; does not include Russia since*

Not including West/East Germany 1968–88

TOP 10 ★
MEDAL WINNERS IN A SUMMER OLYMPICS CAREER

	MEDALLIST	COUNTRY	SPORT	YEARS	GOLD	SILVER	BRONZE	TOTAL
1	Larissa Latynina	USSR	Gymnastics	1956–64	9	5	4	18
2	Nikolay Andrianov	USSR	Gymnastics	1972–80	7	5	3	15
3=	Edoardo Mangiarotti	Italy	Fencing	1936–60	6	5	2	13
=	Takashi Ono	Japan	Gymnastics	1952–64	5	4	4	13
=	Boris Shakhlin	USSR	Gymnastics	1956–64	7	4	2	13
6=	Sawao Kato	Japan	Gymnastics	1968–76	8	3	1	12
=	Paavo Nurmi	Finland	Athletics	1920–28	9	3	0	12
8=	Viktor Chukarin	USSR	Gymnastics	1952–56	7	3	1	11
=	Vera Cáslavská	Czechoslovakia	Gymnastics	1964–68	7	4	0	11
=	Carl Osborn	USA	Shooting	1912–24	5	4	2	11
=	Mark Spitz	USA	Swimming	1968–72	9	1	1	11
=	Matt Biondi	USA	Swimming	1984–92	8	2	1	11

How quick was the fastest knockout in a world title fight?
see p.255 for the answer
A 18 sec
B 19 sec
C 20 sec

SPORTING HEROES

TOP 10 ★
MOST POINTS SCORED BY MICHAEL JORDAN IN A GAME

	TEAM	DATE	POINTS
1	Cleveland Cavaliers	28 Mar 1990	69
2	Orlando Magic	16 Jan 1993	64
3	Boston Celtics	20 Apr 1986	63
4 =	Detroit Pistons	4 Mar 1987	61
=	Atlanta Hawks	16 Apr 1987	61
6	Detroit Pistons	3 Mar 1988	59
7	New Jersey Nets	6 Feb 1987	58
8	Washington Bullets	23 Dec 1992	57
9 =	Philadelphia 76ers	24 Mar 1987	56
=	Miami Heat	29 Apr 1992	56

Source: *NBA*

TOP 10 ★
LONGEST LONG JUMPS BY CARL LEWIS

	STADIUM/LOCATION	DATE	DISTANCE M
1	Tokyo, Japan	30 Aug 1991	8.87
2 =	Indianapolis, USA	19 Jun 1983	8.79
=	New York, USA*	27 Jan 1984	8.79
4 =	Indianapolis, USA	24 Jul 1982	8.76
=	Indianapolis, USA	18 Jul 1888	8.76
6	Indianapolis, USA	16 Aug 1987	8.75
7	Seoul, Korea	26 Sep 1888	8.72
8 =	Westwood, USA	13 May 1984	8.71
=	Los Angeles, USA	19 Jun 1884	8.71
10	Barcelona, Spain	5 Aug 1992	8.68

* Indoor performance

THE MAGIC TOUCH

Nicknamed June Bug as a child, because he was always hopping about on court, Magic Johnson went on to become one of America's best-loved sport stars.

TOP 10 ★
FASTEST 100-METRE RUNS BY LINFORD CHRISTIE

	STADIUM/LOCATION	DATE	TIME SECS
1	Stuttgart, Germany	15 Aug 1993	9.87
2	Victoria, Canada	23 Aug 1994	9.91
3	Tokyo, Japan	25 Aug 1991	9.92
4	Barcelona, Spain	1 Aug 1992	9.96
5 =	Seoul, Korea	24 Sep 1988	9.97
=	Stuttgart, Germany	15 Aug 1993	9.97
=	Johannesburg, SA	23 Sep 1995	9.97
8	Victoria, Canada	23 Aug 1994	9.98
9	Tokyo, Japan	25 Aug 1991	9.99
10 =	Barcelona, Spain	1 Aug 1992	10.00
=	Stuttgart, Germany	14 Aug 1993	10.00

TOP 10 ★
HIGHEST POLE VAULTS BY SERGEI BUBKA

	STADIUM/LOCATION	DATE	HEIGHT M
1	Donetsk, Ukraine*	21 Feb 1993	6.15
2 =	Lievin, France*	13 Feb 1993	6.14
=	Sestriere, Italy	31 Jul 1994	6.14
4 =	Berlin, Germany*	21 Feb 1992	6.13
=	Tokyo, Japan	19 Sep 1992	6.13
6 =	Grenoble, France*	23 Mar 1991	6.12
=	Padua, Italy	30 Aug 1992	6.12
8 =	Donetsk, Ukraine*	19 Mar 1991	6.11
=	Dijon, France	13 Jun 1992	6.11
10 =	San Sebastian, Spain*	15 Mar 1991	6.10
=	Malmo, Sweden	5 Aug 1991	6.10

* Indoor performance

THE 10 ★
LATEST WINNERS OF THE JESSE OWENS INTERNATIONAL TROPHY

YEAR	WINNER/SPORT
1999	Marion Jones, athletics
1998	Haile Gebrselassie, athletics
1997	Michael Johnson, athletics
1996	Michael Johnson, athletics
1995	Johann Olav Koss, speed skating
1994	Wang Junxia, athletics
1993	Vitaly Scherbo, gymnastics
1992	Mike Powell, athletics
1991	Greg Lemond, cycling
1990	Roger Kingdom, athletics

The Jesse Owens International Trophy has been presented by the Amateur Athletic Association since 1981, when it was won by speed skater Eric Heiden, and is named in honour of American Olympic athlete Jesse (James Cleveland) Owens (1913–80). Michael Johnson is the only sportsperson to have won on two occasions, while Marion Jones, the most recent winner, is only the fourth woman to receive the award.

Who is the top male tennis player in the world?
see p.273 for the answer

A Marcelo Rios
B Pete Sampras
C Alex Corretja

THE 10 LATEST WINNERS OF THE *SPORTS ILLUSTRATED* SPORTSMAN OF THE YEAR AWARD

(Year/winner(s)/sport)

1 1998 Mark McGwire and Sammy Sosa, baseball **2** 1997 Dean Smith, basketball coach **3** 1996 Tiger Woods, golf **4** 1995 Cal Ripken Jr., baseball **5** 1994 Johan Olav Koss and Bonnie Blair, ice skating **6** 1993 Don Shula, American football coach **7** 1992 Arthur Ashe, tennis **8** 1991 Michael Jordan, basketball **9** 1990 Joe Montana, American football **10** 1989 Greg LeMond, cycling

First presented in 1954, when it was won by British athlete Roger Bannister, this annual award honours the sportsman or sportswoman who in that year, in the opinion of the editors of *Sports Illustrated*, most "symbolizes in character and performance the ideals of sportsmanship".

THE 10 LATEST WINNERS OF THE BBC SPORTS PERSONALITY OF THE YEAR AWARD

(Year/winner/sport)

1 1998 Michael Owen, football **2** 1997 Greg Rusedski, tennis **3** 1996 Damon Hill, motor racing **4** 1995 Jonathan Edwards, athletics **5** 1994 Damon Hill, motor racing **6** 1993 Linford Christie, athletics **7** 1992 Nigel Mansell, motor racing **8** 1991 Liz McColgan, athletics **9** 1990 Paul Gascoigne, football **10** 1989 Nick Faldo, golf

This annual award is based on a poll of BBC television viewers.

TOP 10 ★
SEASONS BY WAYNE GRETZKY

	SEASON	GOALS	ASSISTS	POINTS
1	1985–86	52	163	215
2	1981–82	92	120	212
3	1984–85	73	135	208
4	1983–84	87	118	205
5	1982–83	71	125	196
6	1986–87	62	121	183
7	1988–89	54	114	168
8	1980–81	55	109	164
9	1990–91	41	122	163
10	1987–88	40	109	149

Wayne Gretzky, who retired in 1999 after 20 seasons in the NHL, is considered the greatest ice hockey player of all time. He gained more records than any player in history, including the most goals, assists, and points in a career. All his best seasons were achieved with his original team, Edmonton, with the exception of 1988–89, which was with Los Angeles. His last three playing seasons were spent with the New York Rangers.

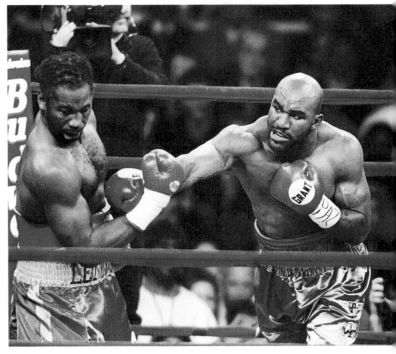

TAKE THAT!

In the 1999 Undisputed World Heavyweight Championship fight at Madison Square Garden, WBC champion Lennox Lewis appeared to dominate IBF/WBA champion Evander Holyfield. The controversial decision by the judges to declare the match a draw led to accusations of bribery and conspiracy, and calls for a rematch.

THE 10 ★
LATEST EVANDER HOLYFIELD WINS BY KNOCKOUT

	OPPONENT	ROUND	LOCATION	DATE
1	Michael Moorer	8	Las Vegas	8 Nov 1997
2	Mike Tyson	11*	Las Vegas	9 Nov 1996
3	Bobby Czyz	5	New York	10 May 1996
4	Riddick Bowe	8*	Las Vegas	4 Nov 1995
5	Bert Cooper	7	Atlanta	23 Nov 1991
6	Buster Douglas	3	Las Vegas	25 Oct 1990
7	Seamus McDonagh	4*	Atlantic City	1 Jun 1990
8	Alex Stewart	8*	Atlantic City	4 Nov 1989
9	Adilson Rodrigues	2	Lake Tahoe	15 Jul 1989
10	Michael Dokes	10*	Las Vegas	11 Mar 1989

* Technical knock out

Born 19 October 1962, boxer Evander Holyfield won his first undisputed heavyweight title in 1990 when he defeated Buster Douglas. His 1993 defeat of Riddick Bowe (when Holyfield won on points) and his 1996 victory over Mike Tyson established him as the only fighter apart from Muhammad Ali to win the heavyweight title on three occasions.

AMERICAN FOOTBALL

LONGEST CAREERS OF CURRENT NFL PLAYERS

	PLAYER	TEAM	YEARS
1	Dave Krieg	Tennessee Titans	19
2 =	Steve DeBerg	Atlanta Falcons	18
=	Wade Wilson	Oakland Raiders	18
4 =	Morten Andersen	Atlanta Falcons	17
=	Gary Anderson	Minnesota Vikings	17
=	Norm Johnson	Pittsburgh Steelers	17
7 =	Henry Ellard	Washington Redskins	16
=	John Elway	Denver Broncos	16
=	Darrell Green	Washington Redskins	16
=	Trey Junkin	Arizona Cardinals	16
=	Dan Marino	Miami Dolphins	16
=	Bruce Matthews	Tennessee Titans	16
=	Reggie Roby	San Francisco 49ers	16
=	Albert Lewis	Oakland Raiders	16

Source: *National Football League*

BIGGEST WINNING MARGINS IN THE SUPER BOWL

	WINNER/YEAR	SCORE	LOSERS/MARGIN
1	San Francisco 49ers, 1990	55–10	Denver, 45
2	Chicago Bears, 1986	46–10	New England, 36
3	Dallas Cowboys, 1993	52–17	Buffalo, 35
4	Washington Redskins, 1988	42–10	Denver, 32
5	Los Angeles Raiders, 1984	38–9	Washington, 29
6	Green Bay Packers, 1967	35–10	Kansas City, 25
7	San Francisco 49ers, 1995	49-26	San Diego, 23
8	San Francisco 49ers, 1985	38–16	Miami, 22
9	Dallas Cowboys, 1972	24–3	Miami, 21
10 =	Green Bay Packers, 1968	33–14	Oakland, 19
=	New York Giants, 1987	39–20	Denver, 19

TOP 10 PLAYERS WITH THE MOST PASSING YARDS IN AN NFL CAREER*
(Player/passing yards)

❶ Dan Marino#, 58,913 ❷ John Elway#, 51,475 ❸ Warren Moon#, 49,097 ❹ Fran Tarkenton, 47,003 ❺ Dan Fouts, 43,040 ❻ Joe Montana, 40,551 ❼ Johnny Unitas ,40,239 ❽ Dave Krieg, 37,946 ❾ Boomer Esiason, 37,920 ❿ Jim Kelly, 35,467

* To end of 1998–99 season
\# Still active 1998–99 season
Source: *National Football League*

ATTACK OF THE QUARTERBACK
During his impressive career, John Elway has taken the Denver Broncos to the Superbowl four times and to the AFC championships three times.

POINTS SCORERS IN AN NFL SEASON

	PLAYER/TEAM/YEAR	GAMES WON
1	Paul Hornung, Green Bay Packers, 1960	176
2	Gary Anderson, Minnesota Vikings, 1998	164
3	Mark Moseley, Washington Redskins,1983	161
4	Gino Cappelletti, Boston Patriots, 1964	155*
5	Emmitt Smith, Dallas Cowboys, 1995	150
6	Chip Lohmiller, Washington Redskins, 1991	149
7	Gino Cappelletti, Boston Patriots, 1961	147
8	Paul Hornung, Green Bay Packers, 1961	146
9 =	Jim Turner, New York Jets, 1968	145
=	John Kasay, Carolina Panthers, 1996	145

* Including a two-point conversion
Source: *National Football League*

LARGEST NFL STADIUMS

	STADIUM/HOME TEAM	CAPACITY
1	Pontiac Silverdrome, Detroit Lions	80,311
2	Jack Cooke Stadium, Washington Redskins	80,116
3	Rich Stadium, Buffalo Bills	80,024
4	Giants Stadium, New York Giants*	79,593
5	Arrowhead Stadium, Kansas City Chiefs	79,409
6	Mile High Stadium, Denver Broncos	76,082
7	Pro Player Stadium, Miami Dolphins	74,916
8	Sun Devil Stadium, Arizona Cardinals	73,273
9	Alltel Stadium, Jacksonville Jaguars	73,000
10	Ericsson Stadium, Carolina Panthers	72,250

* Seating reduced to 77,803 for New York Jets games
Source: *National Football League*

Did You Know? The first professional American football game was played in Pennsylvania in 1895.

TOUCHDOWN!

The ball used in American football is made of pebbled brown leather and has distinctive white lacing.

TOP 10 PLAYERS WITH THE MOST CAREER POINTS

(Player/points)

1 George Blanda, 2,002 **2** Gary Anderson*, 1,845 **3** Morten Andersen*, 1,761 **4** Nick Lowery, 1,711 **5** Jan Stenerud, 1,699 **6** Norm Johnson*, 1,657 **7** Eddie Murray, 1,532 **8** Pat Leahy, 1,470 **9** Jim Turner, 1,439 **10** Matt Bahr, 1,422

* Still active 1998–99 season
Source: *National Football League*

TOP 10 ★ COACHES IN AN NFL CAREER

	COACH	GAMES WON
1	Don Shula	347
2	George Halas	324
3	Tom Landry	270
4	Curly Lambeau	229
5	Chuck Noll	209
6	Chuck Knox	193
7 =	Paul Brown	170
=	Dan Reeves*	170
9	Bud Grant	168
10	Marv Levy	154

* Still active 1999–2000 season
Source: *National Football League*

TOP 10 ★ PLAYERS WITH THE MOST CAREER TOUCHDOWNS

	PLAYER	TOUCHDOWNS
1	Jerry Rice*	175
2	Marcus Allen	145
3	Emmitt Smith*	134
4	Jim Brown	126
5	Walter Payton	125
6	John Riggins	116
7	Lenny Moore	113
8	Don Hutson	105
9	Steve Largent	101
10	Franco Harris	100

* Still active 1998–99 season
Source: *National Football League*

TOP 10 ★ NFL TEAMS*

	TEAM	WINS	LOSSES	PTS
1	Dallas Cowboys	5	3	13
2	San Francisco 49ers	5	0	10
3	Pittsburgh Steelers	4	1	10
4	Washington Redskins	3	2	8
5	Denver Broncos	2	4	8
6 =	Green Bay Packers	3	1	7
=	Oakland/L.A. Raiders	3	1	7
8	Miami Dolphins	2	3	7
9	New York Giants	2	0	4
10 =	Buffalo Bills	0	4	4
=	Minnesota Vikings	0	4	4

* Based on two points for a win, and one for a loss; wins take precedence in determining ranking
Source: *National Football League*

THE WINNING TEAM

In addition to their five World Championship wins, the Dallas Cowboys are also the only team to win three Superbowls in a four-year period.

RUNAROUND

First run in 1970, the original course of the New York Marathon consisted simply of circuits of Central Park. In 1976 the course was redesigned to take in all five boroughs and bridges of New York City.

TOP 10 ★
FASTEST TIMES IN THE LONDON MARATHON

MEN

	RUNNER/COUNTRY	YEAR	TIME
1	**Antonio Pinto**, Portugal	1997	2:07:55
2=	**Abel Anton**, Spain	1998	2:07:57
=	**Abel Kader El Mouaziz**, Morocco	1999	2:07:57
4	**Steve Jones**, UK	1985	2:08:16
5	**Dionicio Ceron**, Mexico	1995	2:08:30
6	**Dionicio Ceron**, Mexico	1994	2:08:53
7	**Douglas Wakiihuri**, Kenya	1989	2:09:03
8	**Yakov Tolstikov**, USSR	1991	2:09:17
9	**Hugh Jones**, UK	1982	2:09:24
10	**Mike Gratton**, UK	1983	2:09:43

WOMEN

	RUNNER/COUNTRY	YEAR	TIME
1	**Ingrid Kristiansen**, Norway	1985	2:21:06
2	**Ingrid Kristiansen**, Norway	1987	2:22:48
3	**Joyce Chepchumba**, Kenya	1999	2:23:22
4	**Ingrid Kristiansen**, Norway	1984	2:24:26
5	**Grete Waitz**, Norway	1986	2:24:54
6	**Grete Waitz**, Norway	1983	2:25:29
7	**Ingrid Kristiansen**, Norway	1988	2:25:41
8	**Veronique Marot**, UK	1989	2:25:56
9	**Rosa Mota**, Portugal	1991	2:26:14
10	**Catherina McKiernan**, Ireland	1998	2:26:25

TOP 10 ★
FASTEST TIMES IN THE NEW YORK MARATHON

MEN

	RUNNER/COUNTRY	YEAR	TIME
1	**Juma Ikangaa**, Tanzania	1989	2.08.01
2	**Alberto Salazar**, USA	1981	2.08.13
3	**Steve Jones**, UK	1988	2.08.20
4	**John Kagwe**, Kenya	1998	2.08.45
5	**Joseph Chebet**, Kenya	1998	2.08.48
6	**Zebedayo Bayo**, Tanzania	1998	2.08.51
7	**Rod Dixon**, New Zealand	1983	2.08.59
8	**Geoff Smith**, UK	1983	2.09.08
9	**Salvador Garcia**, Mexico	1991	2.09.28
10=	**Alberto Salazar**, USA	1982	2.09.29
=	**Willie Mtolo**, South Africa	1992	2.09.29

WOMEN

	RUNNER/COUNTRY	YEAR	TIME
1	**Lisa Ondieki**, Australia	1992	2.24.40
2	**Franca Fiacconi**, Italy	1998	2.25.17
3	**Allison Roe**, New Zealand	1981	2.25.29
4	**Ingrid Kristiansen**, Norway	1989	2.25.30
5	**Grete Waitz**, Norway	1980	2.25.41
6	**Uta Pippig**, Germany	1993	2.26.24
7	**Adriana Fernandez**, Mexico	1998	2.26.33
8	**Olga Markova**, Russia	1992	2.26.38
9	**Grete Waitz**, Norway	1983	2.27.00
10	**Grete Waitz**, Norway	1982	2.27.14

Source: *New York Road Runners Club*

TOP 10 HIGHEST HIGH JUMPS*

(Athlete/country/year/height in metres)

❶ **Javier Sotomayor**, Cuba, 1993, 2.45 ❷ = **Patrik Sjöberg**, Sweden, 1987, 2.42; = **Carlo Thränhardt**#, West Germany, 1988, 2.42 ❹ **Igor Paklin**, USSR, 1985, 2.41 ❺ = **Rudolf Povarnitsyn**, USSR, 1985, 2.40; = **Sorin Matei**, Romania, 1990, 2.40; = **Charles Austin**, USA, 1991, 2.40;; = **Hollis Conway**, USA, 1991, 2.40 ❾ = **Zhu Jianhua**, China, 1984, 2.39; = **Hollis Conway**#, USA, 1989, 2.39; = **Dietmar Mögenburg**#, West Germany, 1985, 2.39; = **Ralph Sonn**#, Germany, 1991, 2.39 *Highest by each athlete only* #*Indoor*

TOP 10 HIGHEST POLE VAULTS*

(Athlete/country/year/height in metres)

❶ **Sergey Bubka**#, Ukraine, 1993, 6.15 ❷ **Okkert Brits**, South Africa, 1995, 6.03 ❸ **Rodion Gataullin**#, USSR, 1989, 6.02 ❹ = **Igor Trandenkov**, Russia, 1996, 6.01; = **Jeff Hartwig**, USA, 1998, 6.01 ❻ = **Dmitri Markov**, Belarus, 1998, 6.00; = **Tim Lobinger**, Germany, 1997, 6.00; = **Maxim Tarasov**, Russia, 1997, 6.00; = **Jeane Galfione**, France, 1999, 6.00 ❿ **Lawrence Johnson**, USA, 1996, 5.98

Highest by each athlete only
#*Indoor*

THE 10 ★
FIRST ATHLETES TO RUN A MILE IN UNDER FOUR MINUTES

	ATHLETE/COUNTRY	LOCATION	MIN:SEC	DATE
1	Roger Bannister, UK	Oxford	3:59.4	6 May 1954
2	John Landy, Australia	Turku, Finland	3:57.9	21 Jun 1954
3	Laszlo Tabori, Hungary	London	3:59.0	28 May 1955
4 =	Chris Chataway, UK	London	3:59.8	28 May 1955
=	Brian Hewson, UK	London	3:59.8	28 May 1955
6	Jim Bailey, Australia	Los Angeles	3:58.6	5 May 1956
7	Gunnar Nielsen, Denmark	Compton, USA	3:59.1	1 Jun 1956
8	Ron Delany, Ireland	Compton, USA	3:59.4	1 Jun 1956
9	Derek Ibbotson, UK	London	3:59.4	6 Aug 1956
10	István Rózsavölgyi, Hungary	Budapest	3:59.0	26 Aug 1956

FASTEST MILE

Within a little over two years of Roger Bannister shattering the four-minute-mile record, nine more athletes achieved this goal.

ON TRACK

Merlene Ottey is the sports-person with the most silver and bronze Olympic medals who has yet to win gold.

TOP 10 ★
FASTEST WOMEN ON EARTH*

	ATHLETE/COUNTRY	YEAR	TIME
1	Florence Griffith-Joyner, USA	1988	10.49
2	Marion Jones, USA	1998	10.65
3	Christine Arron, France	1998	10.73
4	Merlene Ottey, Jamaica	1996	10.74
5	Evelyn Ashford, USA	1984	10.76
6	Irina Privalova, Russia	1994	10.77
7	Dawn Sowell, USA	1989	10.78
7	Marlies Göhr, East Germany	1983	10.81
9 =	Gail Devers, USA	1992	10.82
=	Gwen Torrence, USA	1994	10.82

* Based on fastest time for the 100 metres

TOP 10 ★
FASTEST MEN ON EARTH*

	ATHLETE/COUNTRY	YEAR	TIME
1	Donovan Bailey, Canada	1996	9.84
2	Leroy Burrell, USA	1994	9.85
3 =	Carl Lewis, USA	1991	9.86
=	Frank Fredericks, Namibia	1996	9.86
5	Ato Boldon, Trinidad	1997	9.86
6 =	Linford Christie, UK	1993	9.87
=	Obadele Thompson, Barbados	1997	9.87
8	Bruny Surin, Canada	1996	9.89
9	Maurice Green, USA	1997	9.90
10 =	Dennis Mitchell, USA	1997	9.91

* Based on fastest time for the 100 metres

TOP 10 LONGEST LONG JUMPS*
(Athlete/country/year/distance in metres)

1 Mike Powell, USA, 1991, 8.95 **2** Bob Beamon, USA ,1968, 8.90 **3** Carl Lewis, USA, 1991, 8.87 **4** Robert Emmiyan, USSR, 1987, 8.86 **5** = Larry Myricks, USA, 1988, 8.74; = Eric Walder, USA, 1994, 8.74 **7** Ivan Pedroso, Cuba, 1995, 8.71 **8** Kareem Streete-Thompson, USA, 1994, 8.63 **9** James Beckford, Jamaica, 1997, 8.62 **10** Lutz Dombrowski, East Germany, 1990 8.54

* Longest by each athlete only

Did You Know? The current world record for running a mile is held by Noureddine Morceli, with a time of 3 minutes 44.39 seconds, 15.01 seconds faster than Bannister.

BASKETBALL BESTS

MOST SUCCESSFUL DIVISION 1 NCAA TEAMS

	COLLEGE	DIVISION 1 WINS
1	Kentucky	1,742
2	North Carolina	1,731
3	Kansas	1,684
4 =	St. John's	1,577
=	Duke	1,577
6	Temple	1,515
7	Syracuse	1,496
8	Oregon State	1,475
9	Pennsylvania	1,469
10	Indiana	1,452

Source: *NCAA*

TOP 10 NCAA COACHES
(Coach/wins)

1 Dean Smith, 879   **2** Adolph Rupp, 876
3 Jim Phelan*, 797   **4** Henry Iba, 767
5 Ed Diddle, 759   **6** Phog Allen, 746
7 Bob Knight*, 742   **8** Ray Meyer, 724
9 Norm Stewart*, 731
10 Don Haskins*, 719

* Still active 1998–99 season   Source: *NCAA*

PLAYERS TO HAVE PLAYED MOST GAMES IN THE NBA AND ABA

	PLAYER	GAMES PLAYED
1	Robert Parish	1,611
2	Kareem Abdul-Jabbar	1,560
3	Moses Malone	1,455
4	Artis Gilmore	1,329
5	Buck Williams*	1,307
6	Elvin Hayes	1,303
7	Caldwell Jones	1,299
8	John Havlicek	1,270
9	Paul Silas	1,254
10	Julius Erving	1,243

* Still active at end of 1997–98 season

Source: *NBA*

The ABA (American Basketball Association) was established as a rival to the NBA in 1968 and survived until 1976. Because many of the sport's top players "defected", their figures are still included in this list. During the 1995–96 season Robert Parish moved to the top of this list by playing his 1,561st game on 6 April 1996 at the Gateway Arena in Cleveland, between the Charlotte Hornets and the Cleveland Cavaliers.

TOP POINTS SCORER

Kareem Abdul-Jabbar, the greatest points scorer in NBA history, turned professional in 1970, playing for Milwaukee. His career spanned 20 seasons before he retired at the end of the 1989 season.

POINTS SCORERS IN AN NBA CAREER*

	PLAYER	TOTAL POINTS
1	Kareem Abdul-Jabbar	38,387
2	Wilt Chamberlain	31,419
3	Michael Jordan#	29,277
4	Karl Malone#	27,782
5	Moses Malone	27,409
6	Elvin Hayes	27,313
7	Oscar Robertson	26,710
8	Dominique Wilkins	26,534
9	John Havlicek	26,395
10	Alex English	25,613

* Regular season games only

 # Still active at end of 1998 season

Source: *NBA*

BIGGEST ARENAS IN THE NBA

	ARENA/LOCATION	HOME TEAM	CAPACITY
1	**Georgia Dome**, Atlanta, Georgia	Atlanta Hawks	34,821
2	**The Alamodome**, San Antonio, Texas	San Antonio Spurs	34,215
3	**Charlotte Coliseum**, Charlotte, North Carolina	Charlotte Hornets	24,042
4	**United Center**, Chicago, Illinois	Chicago Bulls	21,711
5	**The Rose Garden**, Portland, Oregon	Portland Trailblazers	21,538
6	**The Palace of Auburn Hills**, Auburn Hills, Michigan	Detroit Pistons	21,454
7	**Gund Arena**, Cleveland, Ohio	Cleveland Cavaliers	20,562
8	**CoreStates Center**, Philadelphia, Pennsylvania	Philadelphia 76ers	20,444
9	**SkyDome**, Toronto	Toronto Raptors	20,125
10	**Byrne Meadowlands Arena**, East Rutherford, New Jersey	New Jersey Nets	20,049

The smallest arena is the 15,200 capacity Miami Arena, home of the Miami Heat. The largest ever NBA stadium was the Louisiana Superdome used by Utah Jazz from 1975 to 1979, which held 47,284 people.

Source: The Sporting News Official NBA Guide

TOP 10 ★
POINTS AVERAGES IN AN NBA SEASON

PLAYER/CLUB	SEASON	AVERAGE
1 Wilt Chamberlain, Philadelphia 76ers	1961–62	50.4
2 Wilt Chamberlain, San Francisco Warriors	1962–63	44.8
3 Wilt Chamberlain, Philadelphia 76ers	1960–61	38.4
4 Elgin Baylor, Los Angeles Lakers	1961–62	38.3
5 Wilt Chamberlain, Philadelphia 76ers	1959–60	37.6
6 Michael Jordan, Chicago Bulls	1986–87	37.1
7 Wilt Chamberlain, San Francisco Warriors	1963–64	36.9
8 Rick Barry, San Francisco Warriors	1966–67	35.6
9 Michael Jordan, Chicago Bulls	1987–88	35.0
10 =Elgin Baylor, Los Angeles Lakers	1960–61	34.8
=Kareem Abdul-Jabbar, Milwaukee Bucks	1971–72	34.8

Source: *NBA*

TOP 10 ★
FREE THROW PERCENTAGES

PLAYER	ATTEMPTS	BASKETS	%
1 Mark Price	2,362	2,135	90.4
2 Rick Barry	4,243	3,818	90.0
3 Calvin Murphy	3,864	3,445	89.2
4 Scott Skiles	1,741	1,548	88.9
5 Larry Bird	4,471	3,960	88.6
6 Bill Sharman	3,559	3,143	88.3
7 Reggie Miller	5,037	4,416	87.7
8 Ricky Pierce	3,871	3,389	87.5
9 Kiki Vandeweghe	3,997	3,484	87.2
10 Jeff Malone	3,383	2,947	87.1

Source: *NBA*

TOP 10 ★
NBA COACHES

COACH	GAMES WON*
1 Lenny Wilkens#	1,120
2 Bill Fitch#	944
3 Red Auerbach	938
4 Dick Motta	935
5 Pat Riley#	914
6 Don Nelson#	867
7 Jack Ramsay	864
8 Cotton Fitzsimmons	832
9 Gene Shue	784
10 John MacLeod	707

* *Regular season games only*
# *Still active 1998–99 season*
Source: *NBA*

Lenny Wilkens reached his 1,000th win on 1 March 1996 when the Atlanta Hawks beat the Cleveland Cavaliers 74–68 at The Omni. Pat Riley acquired the best percentage record with 914 wins from 1,301 games – a 70.2 per cent success rate.

TOP 10 POINTS SCORED IN THE WNBA*
(Game/score)

1 Utah Starzz v Los Angeles Sparks, 102–89 2 Cleveland Rockers v Utah Starzz, 95–68 3 = Sacramento Monarchs v Utah Starzz, 93–78; = Los Angeles Sparks v Sacramento Monarchs, 93–73 5 Los Angeles Sparks v Utah Starzz, 91–69 6 = Cleveland Rockers v Los Angeles Sparks, 89–85; = Houston Comets v Sacramento Monarchs, 89–61 8 Los Angeles Sparks v Sacramento Monarchs, 88–77 9 = Los Angeles Sparks v Cleveland Rockers, 87–84; = Charlotte Sting v New York Liberty, 87–69

* *Ranked by winning score*
Source: *STATS Inc.*

TOP 10 PLAYERS WITH THE MOST CAREER ASSISTS
(Player/assists)

1 John Stockton*, 12,713 2 Magic Johnson, 10,141 3 Oscar Robertson, 9,887 4 Isiah Thomas, 9,061 5 Mark Jackson*, 7,538 6 Maurice Cheeks, 7,392 7 Lenny Wilkens, 7,211 8 Bob Cousy, 6,995 9 Guy Rodgers, 6,917 10 Nate Archibald, 6,476

* *Still active at end of 1997–98 season*
Source: *NBA*

JAZZ MAN
As well as breaking records while playing with his team Utah Jazz, John Stockton was a member of the dream teams that won Gold at the '92 and '96 Olympics.

COMBAT SPORTS

TOP 10 ★ OLYMPIC FENCING COUNTRIES

	COUNTRY	MEN'S MEDALS			WOMEN'S MEDALS			TOTAL
		GOLD	SILVER	BRONZE	GOLD	SILVER	BRONZE	
1	France	34	32	30	4	2	2	104
2	Italy	32	32	20	5	4	4	97
3	Hungary	27	14	20	5	6	6	78
4	Soviet Union*	14	14	15	5	3	3	54
5 =	Poland	4	7	7	0	0	1	19
=	USA	2	6	11	0	0	0	19
7	Germany	4	3	3	2	3	3	18
8	West Germany#	4	6	0	3	2	1	16
9	Belgium	5	3	5	0	0	0	13
10	Romania	1	0	2	1	3	4	11
	Great Britain	0	6	0	1	3	0	10

* *Including United Team of 1992; excludes Russia since then*

\# *Not including West Germany or East Germany 1968–88*

THE 10 LATEST WORLD HEAVYWEIGHT BOXING CHAMPIONS*

(Years/boxer)

1 1997, Evander Holyfield **2** 1996–97, Mike Tyson
3 1995–96, Bruce Seldon **4** 1994–95, George Foreman
5 1994, Michael Moorer **6** 1993–94, Evander Holyfield
7 1992–93, Riddick Bowe **8** 1990–92, Evander Holyfield
9 1990, James Douglas **10** 1989–90, Mike Tyson

* *WBA only*

THE BOXING MINISTER

Thulane Malinga, or Sugarboy as he is usually nicknamed, is a Pentecostal minister from South Africa. In two years, between 1996 and 1998, he won and lost the WBC Super Middleweight title twice. In March 1996 Sugarboy won the title in a fight against Nigel Benn. However, he was dethroned only a few months later, in July 1996, by the Italian Vincenzo Nardiello in a 12-round split decision. In December 1997, the South African boxer regained his title in a fight against Robin Reid, only to see it being snatched away again by Britain's Richie Woodhall just months later in March 1998.

SNAP ★ SHOTS

TOP 10 ★ HEAVIEST BOXING WEIGHT DIVISIONS

	WEIGHT	LIMIT	
		KG	LB
1	Heavyweight	over 86	over 190
2	Cruiserweight	86	190
3	Light-heavyweight	79	175
4	Super-middleweight	76	168
5	Middleweight	73	160
6	Junior-middleweight/Super-welterweight	70	154
7	Welterweight	67	147
8	Junior-welterweight/Super-lightweight	65	140
9	Lightweight	61	135
10	Junior-lightweight/Super-featherweight	59	130

TOP 10 OLYMPIC JUDO COUNTRIES

(Country/medals)

1 Japan, 40 **2** Soviet Union*, 27 **3** France, 26 **4** South Korea, 25 **5** = Cuba, 15; = Great Britain, 15 **7** Netherlands, 10 **8** = Germany#, 9; = East Germany, 9 **10** = USA, 8; = Poland, 8; = West Germany, 8; = Hungary, 8; = Brazil, 8

* *Including United Team of 1992; excludes Russia since then*
\# *Not including West Germany or East Germany 1968–88*

TOP 10 ★ BOXERS WITH THE MOST KNOCKOUTS IN A CAREER

	BOXER*	CAREER	KO'S
1	Archie Moore	1936–63	129
2	Young Stribling	1921–63	126
3	Billy Bird	1920–48	125
4	Sam Langford	1902–26	116
5	George Odwell	1930–45	114
6	Sugar Ray Robinson	1940–65	110
7	Sandy Saddler	1944–65	103
8	Henry Armstrong	1931–45	100
9	Jimmy Wilde	1911–23	99
10	Len Wickwar	1928–47	93

* *All from the US except Jimmy Wilde, who was Welsh*

Did You Know? With 17 weight divisions in boxing, and four major bodies recognizing world champions, there could be 68 world champions at any one time.

THE 10 ★
WRESTLING WEIGHT DIVISIONS

	WEIGHT	KG	LIMIT LB
1	Heavyweight plus	over 100	over 220
2	Heavyweight	100	220
3	Light-heavyweight	90	198
4	Middleweight	82	181
5	Welterweight	74	163
6	Lightweight	68	150
7	Featherweight	62	137
8	Bantamweight	57	126
9	Flyweight	52	115
10	Light-flyweight	48	106

TOP 10 ★
OLYMPIC WRESTLING COUNTRIES/FREESTYLE

	COUNTRY	GOLD	MEDALS SILVER	BRONZE	TOTAL
1	USA	44	33	22	99
2	Soviet Union*	31	17	15	63
3	Turkey	16	11	6	33
4 =	Japan	16	9	7	32
=	Bulgaria	7	16	9	32
6	Sweden	8	10	8	26
7 =	Finland	8	7	10	25
=	Iran	4	9	12	25
9 =	Great Britain	3	4	10	17
=	Hungary	4	7	6	17

* *Including United Team of 1992; excludes Russia since then*

STRANGLEHOLD

Zafar Golyou (Russia) and Hiroshi Kadj (Japan) battle it out at the Men's Greco-Roman prelims in Georgia.

TOP 10 ★
OLYMPIC WRESTLING COUNTRIES/ GRECO-ROMAN

	COUNTRY	GOLD	MEDALS SILVER	BRONZE	TOTAL
1	Soviet Union*	37	19	13	69
2	Finland	19	21	18	58
3	Sweden	19	16	19	54
4	Hungary	15	9	11	35
5	Bulgaria	8	14	7	29
6	Romania	6	8	13	27
7	Germany	4	13	8	25
8	Poland	5	8	6	19
9	Italy	5	4	9	18
10	Turkey	10	4	3	17
	USA	2	5	5	12

* *Including United Team of 1992; excludes Russia since then*

Great Britain, Australia, and Canada have never won a Greco-Roman medal.

TOP 10 ★
FASTEST KNOCKOUTS IN WORLD TITLE FIGHTS

	FIGHT (WINNERS FIRST)	WEIGHT	DATE	SEC*
1	Gerald McClellan v Jay Bell	Middleweight	7 Aug 1993	20
2	James Warring v James Pritchard	Cruiserweight	6 Sep 1991	24
3	Lloyd Honeyghan v Gene Hatcher	Welterweight	30 Aug 1987	45
4	Mark Breland v Lee Seung-soon	Welterweight	4 Feb 1989	54
5	Emile Pladner v Frankie Genaro	Flyweight	2 Mar 1929	58
6 =	Jackie Paterson v Peter Kane	Flyweight	19 Jun 1943	61
=	Bobby Czyz v David Sears	Light-heavyweight	26 Dec 1986	61
8	Michael Dokes v Mike Weaver	Heavyweight	10 Dec 1982	63
9	Tony Canzoneri v Al Singer	Lightweight	14 Nov 1930	66
10	Marvin Hagler v Caveman Lee	Middleweight	7 Mar 1982	67

* *Duration of fight*

Some authorities claim that Al McCoy defeated George Chip in a middleweight contest on 7 April 1914 in 45 seconds. Lightweight world champion Al Singer engaged in only two world title bouts in his career. The first was when he beat Sammy Mandell for the title on 1 July 1930. The fight lasted one minute 46 seconds. He lost the title four months later to Tony Canzoneri in a bout lasting one minute six seconds.

CRICKET TESTS

HIGHEST INDIVIDUAL TEST INNINGS

	BATSMAN	MATCH/VENUE	YEAR	RUNS
1	Brian Lara	West Indies v England, St. John's	1993–94	375
2	Gary Sobers	West Indies v Pakistan, Kingston	1957–58	365*
3	Len Hutton	England v Australia, The Oval	1938	364
4	Sanath Jayasuriya	Sri Lanka v India, Colombo	1997–98	340
5	Hanif Mohammad	Pakistan v West Indies, Bridgetown	1957–58	337
6	Walter Hammond	England v New Zealand, Auckland	1932–33	336*
7	Don Bradman	Australia v England, Leeds	1930	334
8	Graham Gooch	England v India, Lord's	1990	333
9	Andrew Sandham	England v West Indies, Kingston	1929–30	325
10	Bobby Simpson	Australia v England, Manchester	1964	311

* Not out

Sanath Jayasuriya is a new entry not only to this list, but also shares No. 1 status in the list of partnerships in Test cricket, by a 109-run margin over the former record holders.

RUN MAKERS IN A TEST SERIES

	BATSMAN	SERIES/TESTS	YEAR	RUNS
1	Don Bradman	Australia v England, 5	1930	974
2	Walter Hammond	England v Australia, 5	1928–29	905
3	Mark Taylor	Australia v England, 6	1989	839
4	Neil Harvey	Australia v South Africa, 5	1952–53	834
5	Viv Richards	West Indies v England, 4	1976	829
6	Clyde Walcott	West Indies v Australia, 5	1954–55	827
7	Gary Sobers	West Indies v Pakistan, 5	1957–58	824
8	Don Bradman	Australia v England, 5	1936–37	810
9	Don Bradman	Australia v South Africa, 5	1931–32	806
10	Brian Lara	West Indies v England, 5	1993–94	798

Don Bradman's remarkable tally against England in 1930 came only a year after Walter Hammond had become the first man to score 900 runs in a series. Bradman, who was making his debut on English soil, scored his runs in just seven innings at an average of 139. He scored just eight runs in the first innings of the opening Test, but then came the first of his centuries when he went on to score 131 in the second innings.

TOP 10 BATSMEN WITH MOST TEST CENTURIES

(Batsman/country/centuries)

1 Sunil Gavaskar, India, 34 **2** Don Bradman, Australia, 29 **3** Allan Border, Australia, 27 **4** Gary Sobers, West Indies, 26 **5** = Greg Chappell, Australia, 24; = Viv Richards, West Indies, 24 **7** Javed Miandad, Pakistan, 23 **8** = Walter Hammond, England, 22; = Geoff Boycott, England, 22; = Colin Cowdrey, England, 22

LOWEST COMPLETED INNINGS IN TEST CRICKET

	MATCH/VENUE/YEAR	TOTAL
1	New Zealand v England, Auckland, 1954–55	26
2=	South Africa v England, Port Elizabeth, 1895–96	30
=	South Africa v England, Birmingham, 1924	30
4	South Africa v England, Cape Town, 1898–99	35
5=	Australia v England, Birmingham, 1902	36
=	South Africa v Australia, Melbourne, 1931–32	36
7=	Australia v England, Sydney, 1887–88	42
=	New Zealand v Australia, Wellington, 1945–46	42
=	India* v England, Lord's, 1974	42
10	South Africa v England, Cape Town, 1888–89	43

* India batted one man short

England's lowest total is 45, when dismissed by Australia at Sydney in 1886–87. The West Indies' lowest total is 51, in their Test against Australia at Port of Spain in the 1998–99 season.

MOST CAPPED CRICKETERS

	NAME/COUNTRY	CAPS
1	Allan Border, Australia	156
2	Kapil Dev, India	131
3	Sunil Gavaskar, India	125
4	Javed Miandad, Pakistan	124
5	Viv Richards, West Indies	121
6	Graham Gooch, England	118
7	David Gower, England	117
8=	Desmond Haynes, West Indies	116
=	Dilip Vengsarkar, India	116
10	Colin Cowdrey, England	114

TOP 10 RUN MAKERS OF ALL TIME IN TEST CRICKET

(Player/country/years/Tests/runs)

1 **Allan Border**, Australia (1978–94), 156, 11,174 **2** **Sunil Gavaskar**, India (1971–87), 125, 10,122 **3** **Graham Gooch**, England (1975–95), 118, 8,900 **4** **Javed Miandad**, Pakistan (1976–94), 124, 8,832 **5** **Viv Richards**, West Indies (1974–91), 121, 8,540 **6** **David Gower**, England (1978–92), 117, 8,231 **7** **Geoff Boycott**, England (1964–82), 108, 8,114 **8** **Gary Sobers**, West Indies (1954–74), 93, 8,032 **9** **Colin Cowdrey**, England (1954–75), 114, 7,624 **10** **Gordon Greenidge**, West Indies (1974–91), 108, 7,558

TOP 10 ★

HIGHEST INDIVIDUAL INNINGS IN A TEST DEBUT

	PLAYER	MATCH	VENUE	YEAR	SCORE
1	Reginald Foster	England v Australia	Sydney	1903–04	287
2	Lawrence Rowe	West Indies v New Zealand	Kingston	1971–72	214
3	Brendon Kuruppu	Sri Lanka v New Zealand	Colombo	1986–87	201*
4	George Headley	West Indies v England	Bridgetown	1929–30	176
5	Khalid Ibadulla	Pakistan v Australia	Karachi	1964–65	166
6	Charles Bannerman	Australia v England	Melbourne	1876–77	165*
7	Archie Jackson	Australia v England	Adelaide	1928–29	164
8 =	Javed Miandad	Pakistan v New Zealand	Lahore	1976–77	163
=	Andrew Hudson	South Africa v West Indies	Bridgetown	1991–92	163
10	Kepler Wessels	Australia v England	Brisbane	1982–83	162

* Not out

TOP 10 ★

PARTNERSHIPS IN TEST CRICKET

	BATSMEN	MATCH	YEAR	RUNS
1	Sanath Jayasuriya/Roshan Mahanama	Sri Lanka v India	1997–98	576
2	Andrew Jones/Martin Crowe	New Zealand v Sri Lanka	1990–91	467
3 =	Bill Ponsford/Don Bradman	Australia v England	1934	451
=	Mudasser Nazar/Javed Miandad	Pakistan v India	1982–83	451
5	Conrad Hunte/Gary Sobers	West Indies v Pakistan	1957–58	446
6	Vinoo Mankad/Pankaj Roy	India v New Zealand	1955–56	413
7	Peter May/Colin Cowdrey	England v West Indies	1957	411
8	Sidney Barnes/Don Bradman	Australia v England	1946–47	405
9	Gary Sobers/Frank Worrell	West Indies v England	1959–60	399
10	Qasim Omar/Javed Miandad	Pakistan v Sri Lanka	1985–86	397

Gundappa Viswanath, Yashpal Sharma, and Dilip Vengsarkar put on 415 runs for India's third wicket against England at Madras in 1981–82; Vengsarkar retired hurt when the partnership was on 99.

TOP 10 ★

WICKET TAKERS OF ALL TIME IN TEST CRICKET

	PLAYER/COUNTRY/YEARS	TESTS	WICKETS
1	Kapil Dev, India, 1978–94	131	434
2	Richard Hadlee, New Zealand, 1973–90	86	431
3	Courtney Walsh, West Indies, 1984–98	107	404
4	Ian Botham, England, 1977–92	102	383
5	Malcolm Marshall, West Indies, 1978–91	81	376
6	Wasim Akram, Pakistan, 1985–99	86	368
7	Imran Khan, Pakistan, 1971–92	88	362
8 =	Dennis Lillee, Australia, 1971–84	70	355
9 =	Curtley Ambrose, West Indies, 1988–98	85	355
10	Bob Willis, England, 1971–84	90	325

TOP 10 HIGHEST TEAM TOTALS IN TEST CRICKET

(Match/venue/year/score)

1 **Sri Lanka v India**, Colombo (1997–98), 952–6 dec **2** **England v Australia**, The Oval (1938), 903–7 dec **3** **England v West Indies**, Kingston (1929–30), 849 **4** **West Indies v Pakistan**, Kingston (1957–58), 790–3 dec **5** **Australia v West Indies**, Kingston (1954–55), 758–8 dec **6** **Australia v England**, Lord's (1930), 729–6 dec **7** **Pakistan v England**, The Oval (1987), 708 **8** **Australia v England**, The Oval (1934), 701 **9** **Pakistan v India**, Lahore (1989–90), 699–5 dec **10** **Australia v England**, The Oval (1930), 695

Who was the first player to be inducted into the Rugby Union Hall of Fame?
see p.271 for the answer

A Graham Mourie
B Peter Dixon
C Serge Blanco

DOMESTIC FOOTBALL

TOP 10 ⭐

HIGHEST-SCORING FOOTBALL LEAGUE MATCHES

MATCH (WINNERS FIRST)	DIVISION*	SEASON	SCORE	GOALS
1 Tranmere Rovers v Oldham Athletic	3N	1935–36	13–4	17
2 =Aston Villa v Accrington	1	1891–92	12–2	14
=Manchester City v Lincoln City	2	1894–95	11–3	14
=Tottenham Hotspur v Everton	1	1958–59	10–4	14
5 =Stockport County v Halifax Town	3N	1933–34	13–0	13
=Newcastle United v Newport County	2	1946–47	13–0	13
=Barrow v Gateshead	3N	1933–34	12–1	13
=Sheffield United v Cardiff City	1	1925–26	11–2	13
=Oldham Athletic v Chester	3N	1951–52	11–2	13
=Hull City v Wolverhampton Wanderers	2	1919–20	10–3	13
=Middlesbrough v Sheffield United	1	1933–34	10–3	13
=Stoke City v West Bromwich Albion	1	1936–37	10–3	13
=Bristol City v Gillingham	3S	1926–27	9–4	13
=Gillingham v Exeter City	3S	1950–51	9–4	13
=Derby County v Blackburn Rovers	1	1890–91	8–5	13
=Burton Swifts v Walsall Town Swifts	2	1893–94	8–5	13
=Stockport County v Chester	3N	1932–33	8–5	13
=Charlton Athletic v Huddersfield Town	2	1957–58	7–6	13

* 3N/3S refer to Northern and Southern divisions prior to 1958

TOP 10 ⭐

TRANSFER FEES BETWEEN ENGLISH CLUBS

PLAYER	FROM	TO	YEAR	FEE (£)
1 Alan Shearer	Blackburn Rovers	Newcastle United	1995	15,000,000
2 Dwight Yorke	Aston Villa	Manchester United	1998	12,600,000
3 Stan Collymore	Nottingham Forest	Liverpool	1995	8,500,000
4 Kevin Davies	Southampton	Blackburn Rovers	1998	7,500,000
5 Stan Collymore	Liverpool	Aston Villa	1997	7,000,000
6 Andy Cole	Newcastle United	Manchester United	1995	6,250,000
7 =Les Ferdinand	Newcastle United	Tottenham Hotspur	1997	6,000,000
=Les Ferdinand	Queens Park Rangers	Newcastle United	1995	6,000,000
9 Nick Barmby	Middlesbrough	Everton	1996	5,750,000
10 Gary Speed	Everton	Newcastle United	1998	5,500,000

THE 10 ⭐

LATEST FOOTBALLERS OF THE YEAR

YEAR	PLAYER	TEAM
1999	David Ginola	Tottenham Hotspur
1998	Dennis Bergkamp	Arsenal
1997	Gianfranco Zola	Chelsea
1996	Eric Cantona	Manchester United
1995	Jürgen Klinsman	Tottenham Hotspur
1994	Alan Shearer	Blackburn Rovers
1993	Chris Waddle	Sheffield Wednesday
1992	Gary Lineker	Tottenham Hotspur
1991	Gordon Strachan	Leeds United
1990	John Barnes	Liverpool

The Footballer of the Year award is presented by the Football Writers' Association. Players in the English League, irresepective of country of origin, are eligible.

TOP 10 ⭐

OLDEST FOOTBALL LEAGUE CLUBS

CLUB	YEAR FORMED
1 Notts County	1862
2 Stoke City	1863
3 Nottingham Forest	1865
4 Chesterfield	1866
5 Sheffield Wednesday	1867
6 Reading	1871
7 Wrexham	1873
8 =Aston Villa	1874
=Bolton Wanderers	1874
10 =Birmingham City	1875
=Blackburn Rovers	1875

Scotland's oldest club is Queen's Park, formed in 1867. They remain the only amateur team in League soccer in Scotland or England.

Which country has won the most table tennis world championships?
see p.275 for the answer

A China
B Hungary
C Czechoslovakia

TOP 10 ⭐
HIGHEST-SCORING FA CUP FINALS*

MATCH (WINNERS FIRST)	YEAR	SCORES	TOTAL GOALS
1 =Tottenham Hotspur v Sheffield United	1901	2–2, 3–1	8
=Manchester United v Brighton and Hove Albion	1983	2–2, 4–0	8
3 =Blackburn Rovers v Sheffield Wednesday	1890	6–1	7
=Blackpool v Bolton Wanderers	1953	4–3	7
=Chelsea v Leeds United	1970	2–2, 2–1	7
=Tottenham Hotspur v Manchester City	1981	1–1, 3–2	7
=Manchester United v Crystal Palace	1990	3–3, 1–0	7
8 =Bury v Derby County	1903	6–0	6
=Sheffield Wednesday v West Bromwich Albion	1935	4–2	6
=Manchester United v Blackpool	1948	4–2	6

* Including replays

TOP 10 ⭐
TEAMS IN THE ENGLISH PREMIERSHIP, 1999

TEAM	PLAYED	GAMES WON	LOST	DRAWN	GOALS FOR	AGAINST	POINTS
1 Manchester United	38	22	13	3	80	37	79
2 Arsenal	38	22	12	4	59	17	78
3 Chelsea	38	20	15	3	57	30	75
4 Leeds United	38	18	13	7	62	34	67
5 West Ham United	38	16	8	13	46	53	57
6 Aston Villa	38	15	10	13	51	46	55
7 Liverpool	38	15	9	14	68	49	54
8 Derby County	38	13	13	12	40	45	52
9 Middlesbrough	38	12	15	11	48	54	51
10 Leicester City	38	12	13	13	40	46	49

TOP 10 HIGHEST RECORD ATTENDANCES IN THE FOOTBALL LEAGUE*
(Club/year/attendance)

1 Manchester City, 1934, 84,569 **2** Chelsea, 1935, 82,905 **3** Everton, 1948, 78,299 **4** Aston Villa, 1946, 76,588 **5** Sunderland, 1933, 75,118 **6** Tottenham Hotspur, 1938, 75,038 **7** Charlton Athletic, 1938, 75,031 **8** Arsenal, 1935, 73,295 **9** Sheffield Wednesday, 1934, 72,841 **10** Manchester United, 1939, 70,504

Because of drastic reductions in ground capacities over the last 20 years or so as a result of safety precautions, these records are likely to stand for all time. The last club to establish a new record attendance at its ground, other than clubs moving to new grounds, was Crystal Palace, whose record of 51,801 at their Selhurst Park ground was set in a League game against Burnley on 11 May 1979.

TOP 10 ⭐
MOST CAPPED ENGLAND PLAYERS

	PLAYER	YEARS	CAPS
1	Peter Shilton	1970–80	125
2	Bobby Moore	1962–73	108
3	Bobby Charlton	1958–70	106
4	Billy Wright	1946–59	105
5	Bryan Robson	1980–91	90
6	Kenny Sansom	1979–88	86
7	Ray Wilkins	1976–86	84
8	Gary Lineker	1984–92	80
9	John Barnes	1983–95	79
10	Terry Butcher	1980–90	77

Bobby Charlton's 49 goals scored for England in International matches stand as the all-time record, with Gary Lineker's 48 just behind. Jimmy Greaves's 44-goal tally is even more remarkable, since they were achieved in just 57 matches, while Nat Lofthouse's 30 goals produced from 33 games and Tommy Lawton's from 23 only just miss an average of one goal per game.

TOP 10 ⭐
CLUBS WITH THE MOST FA CUP WINS

	CLUB	FIRST WIN	LAST WIN	TOTAL WINS
1	Manchester United	1909	1999	11
2	Tottenham Hotspur	1901	1991	8
3	=Arsenal	1930	1998	7
	=Aston Villa	1887	1957	7
5	=Blackburn Rovers	1884	1928	6
	=Newcastle United	1910	1955	6
7	=Everton	1906	1995	5
	=Liverpool	1965	1992	5
	=The Wanderers	1872	1878	5
	=West Bromwich Albion	1888	1968	5

The first ever FA Cup Final was played in 1872 at the Kennington Oval cricket ground, with a crowd of about 2,000, when the Wanderers beat the Royal Engineers 1–0. Matches have been played at Wembley since 1923, when Bolton Wanderers met West Ham United in front of a record crowd of 126,047.

WORLD CUP WINNERS

Brazil has taken part in all the final phases of the World Cup since its inception in 1930, and have won four times. In the 1998 Championships they lost the final to France, the host nation and first-time winners.

TOP 10 ★
WORLD CUP ATTENDANCES

	MATCH (WINNERS FIRST)	VENUE	YEAR	ATTENDANCE
1	Brazil v Uruguay	Rio de Janeiro*	1950	199,854
2	Brazil v Spain	Rio de Janeiro	1950	152,772
3	Brazil v Yugoslavia	Rio de Janeiro	1950	142,409
4	Brazil v Sweden	Rio de Janeiro	1950	138,886
5	Mexico v Paraguay	Mexico City	1986	114,600
6	Argentina v West Germany	Mexico City*	1986	114,590
7=	Mexico v Bulgaria	Mexico City	1986	114,580
=	Argentina v England	Mexico City	1986	114,580
9	Argentina v Belgium	Mexico City	1986	110,420
10	Mexico v Belgium	Mexico City	1986	110,000

*Final tie

TOP 10 COUNTRIES WITH THE MOST PLAYERS SENT OFF IN THE FINAL STAGES OF THE WORLD CUP

(Country/dismissals)

1 = Brazil, 8; = Argentina, 8 **3** = Uruguay, 6; = Cameroon, 6 **5** = Germany/West Germany, 5; = Hungary, 5 **7** = Czechoslovakia, 4; = Holland, 4; = Italy, 4; = Mexico, 4

A total of 97 players have received their marching orders in the final stages of the World Cup since 1930. The South American nations account for 27 of them. Brazil, Czechoslovakia, Denmark, Hungary, and South Africa have each had three players sent off in a single game – Brazil twice (1938 and 1954).

TOP 10 ★
GOAL SCORERS IN THE FINAL STAGES OF THE WORLD CUP

	PLAYER/COUNTRY	YEARS	GOALS
1	Gerd Müller, West Germany	1970–74	14
2	Just Fontaine, France	1958	13
3	Pelé, Brazil	1958–70	12
4=	Sandor Kocsis, Hungary	1954	11
=	Jürgen Klinsman, Germany	1990–98	11
6=	Helmut Rahn, West Germany	1954–58	10
=	Teófilio Cubillas, Peru	1970–78	10
=	Grzegorz Lato, Poland	1974–82	10
=	Gary Lineker, England	1986–90	10
10=	Leónidas da Silva, Brazil	1934–38	9
=	Ademir Marques de Menezes, Brazil	1950	9
=	Vavà, Brazil	1958–62	9
=	Uwe Seeler, West Germany	1958–70	9
=	Eusébio, Portugal	1966	9
=	Jairzinho, Brazil	1970–74	9
=	Paolo Rossi, Italy	1978–82	9
=	Karl-Heinz Rummenigge, West Germany	1978–86	9
=	Roberto Baggio, Italy	1990–98	9
=	Gabriel Batistuta, Argentina	1994–98	9

TOP 10 ★
TRANSFER FEES

	PLAYER	FROM	TO	YEAR	FEE (£)
1	Christian Vieri	Lazio	Inter Milan	1999	24,000,000
2	Denilson	São Paulo	Real Betis	1998	22,000,000
3=	Christian Vieri	Atletico Madrid	Lazio	1998	17,000,000
=	Rivaldo	Deportivo la Coruna	Barcelona	1997	17,000,000
5	Ronaldo	Barcelona	Inter Milan	1997	16,800,000
6	A. Schevchenko	Dynamo Kiev	AC Milan	1999	15,700,000
7	Vincenzo Montella	Sampdoria	Roma	1999	15,300,000
8	Alan Shearer	Blackburn Rovers	Newcastle Utd.	1995	15,000,000
9	Gianluigi Lentini	Torino	AC Milan	1992	13,000,000
10	Dwight Yorke	Aston Villa	Manchester Utd.	1998	12,600,000

TOP 10 ★
HIGHEST-SCORING WORLD CUP FINALS

	YEAR	GAMES	GOALS	AVERAGE PER GAME
1	1954	26	140	5.38
2	1938	18	84	4.66
3	1934	17	70	4.11
4	1950	22	88	4.00
5	1930	18	70	3.88
6	1958	35	126	3.60
7	1970	32	95	2.96
8	1982	52	146	2.81
9	1998	64	179	2.80
10=	1962	32	89	2.78
=	1966	32	89	2.78

FOUL!

Every player in the World Cup is required to sign a declaration of fair play, underlining FIFA's belief that the world's top teams and players have a responsibility as role models to their young supporters. However, the pressure to succeed often leads to moments of madness. The France98 World Cup saw 256 yellow cards handed out for rule-breaking and foul play. Of the 22 red cards shown, the one with arguably the most disastrous consequence was awarded to England's David Beckham. Many felt that his display of aggression during the game against Argentina prevented England from going on into the final phase.

SNAP SHOTS

FOOTBALL FACTS

FIFA rules state that the weight of a football at the start of the game should be 369–453 g/14–16 oz, and the circumference should measure 68–71 cm/27–28 in.

TOP 10 ★
RICHEST FOOTBALL CLUBS

	CLUB	COUNTRY	INCOME (£)
1	Manchester United	England	87,939,000
2	Barcelona	Spain	58,862,000
3	Real Madrid	Spain	55,659,000
4	Juventus	Italy	53,223,000
5	Bayern Munich	Germany	51,619,000
6	AC Milan	Italy	47,480,000
7	Borussia Dortmund	Germany	42,199,999
8	Newcastle United	England	41,134,000
9	Liverpool	England	39,153,000
10	Inter Milan	Italy	39,071,000

A survey conducted by accountants Deloitte & Touche and football magazine *FourFourTwo* compared incomes of the world's top football clubs during the 1997/8 season. It revealed the extent to which soccer has become a major business enterprise, with many clubs generating considerably more revenue from commercial activities such as the sale of merchandise and income from TV rights than they receive from admissions to matches.

TOP 10 ★
MOST CAPPED INTERNATIONAL PLAYERS

	PLAYER	COUNTRY	CAPS
1	Thomas Ravelli	Sweden	143
2	Majed Abdullah	Saudi Arabia	140
3	Lothar Matthäus*	W. Germany/Germany	135
4	Andoni Zubizarreta	Spain	126
5=	Marcelo Balboa*	USA	125
=	Peter Shilton	England	125
7	Masami Ihara*	Japan	121
8	Pat Jennings	Northern Ireland	119
9	Heinz Hermann	Switzerland	117
10=	Gheorghe Hagi*	Romania	115
=	Björn Nordqvist	Sweden	115

* Still active 1998–99 season

Some sources quote Héctor Chumpitaz of Peru and Brazilian player Rivelino as having appeared in 150 and 120 Internationals respectively, but many of these were won in matches not recognized by FIFA.

TOP 10 ★
EUROPEAN CUP WINNERS

	COUNTRY	YEARS*	WINS
1=	England	1968–99	9
=	Italy	1961–96	9
3	Spain	1956–98	8
4	Holland	1970–95	6
5	Germany	1974–97	5
6	Portugal	1961–87	3
7=	France	1993	1
=	Romania	1986	1
=	Scotland	1967	1
=	Yugoslavia	1991	1

* Of first and last win

The European Cup, now known as the European Champions' League Cup, has been competed for annually since 1956. It was won that year, and the next four, by Real Madrid (who also won it in 1966 and 1998, making a total of seven times).

Did You Know? The lowest-scoring World Cup was Italia '90 which produced 115 goals from 52 matches at an average of 2.21 per game.

ON TWO WHEELS

BIKER BARRY

Barry Sheene's escapades on and off the racetrack, his charisma, and his talent for self-promotion earned him pop idol status, and made him one of the highest-earning sportsmen of his day.

TOP 10 ★
FASTEST WORLD CHAMPIONSHIP RACES OF ALL TIME

	RIDER/COUNTRY	BIKE*	YEAR	AVERAGE SPEED KM/H	MPH
1	**Barry Sheene**, UK	Suzuki	1977	217.37	135.07
2	**John Williams**, UK	Suzuki	1976	214.83	133.49
3	**Phil Read**, UK	MV Agusta	1975	214.40	133.22
4	**Wil Hartog**, Holland	Suzuki	1978	213.88	132.90
5	**Phil Read**, UK	MV Agusta	1974	212.41	131.98
6	**Giacomo Agostini**, Italy	MV Agusta	1973	206.81	128.51
7	**Walter Villa**, Italy	Harley-Davidson	1977	204.43	127.03
8	**Walter Villa**, Italy	Harley-Davidson	1976	202.90	126.08
9	**Giacomo Agostini**, Italy	MV Agusta	1969	202.53	125.85
10	**Kevin Schwartz**, USA	Suzuki	1991	201.72	125.34

* *500cc except for Nos. 7 and 8 which were 250cc*

All races except for No. 10 were during the Belgian Grand Prix at the Spa-Francorchamps circuit. No. 10 was the German Grand Prix at Hockenheim.

TOP 10 WORLD SUPERBIKE RIDERS, 1998
(Rider/country/points)

1 **Carl Fogarty**, UK, 351.5 **2** **Aaron Slight**, New Zealand, 347 **3** **Troy Corser**, Australia, 328.5 **4** **Pierfrancesco Chilli**, Italy, 293.5 **5** **Colin Edwards**, USA, 279.5 **6** **Noriyuki Haga**, Japan, 258 **7** **Akira Yanagawa**, Japan, 210 **8** **Jamie Witham**, UK, 173 **9** **Peter Goddard**, Australia, 155 **10** **Scott Russell**, USA, 130.5

UNBEATEN RECORD HOLDER

The most successful motorcycle racer of all time, Giacomo Agostini won the 500cc World Title for seven consecutive years.

TOP 10 ★
FASTEST WINNING SPEEDS OF THE DAYTONA 200

	RIDER/COUNTRY*	BIKE	YEAR	AVERAGE SPEED KM/H	MPH
1	**Kenny Roberts**	Yamaha	1984	182.09	113.84
2	**Kenny Roberts**	Yamaha	1983	178.52	110.93
3	**Graeme Crosby**, New Zealand	Yamaha	1982	175.58	109.10
4	**Steve Baker**	Yamaha	1977	175.18	108.85
5	**Johnny Cecotto**, Venezuela	Yamaha	1976	175.05	108.77
6	**Dale Singleton**	Yamaha	1981	174.65	108.52
7	**Kenny Roberts**	Yamaha	1978	174.41	108.37
8	**Kevin Schwartz**	Suzuki	1988	173.49	107.80
9	**Dale Singleton**	Yamaha	1979	173.31	107.69
10	**Patrick Pons**, France	Yamaha	1980	173.09	107.55

* *From the US unless otherwise stated*

TOP 10 RIDERS WITH THE MOST GRAND PRIX RACE WINS
(Rider/country/years/race wins)

1 **Giacomo Agostini**, Italy, 1965–76, 122 **2** **Angel Nieto**, Spain, 1969–85, 90 **3** **Mike Hailwood**, UK, 1959–67, 76 **4** **Rolf Biland**, Switzerland, 1975–90, 56 **5** **Mick Doohan**, Australia, 1990–98, 54 **6** **Phil Read**, UK, 1961–75, 52 **7** **Jim Redman**, Southern Rhodesia, 1961–66, 45 **8** **Anton Mang**, West Germany, 1976–88, 42 **9** **Carlo Ubbiali**, Italy, 1950–60, 39 **10** **John Surtees**, UK, 1955–60, 38

All except Biland were solo machine riders. Britain's Barry Sheene won 23 races during his career and is the only man to win Grands Prix at 50 and 500cc.

TOP 10 ⭐
MOTORCYCLISTS WITH THE MOST WORLD TITLES

	RIDER/COUNTRY	YEARS	TITLES
1	Giacomo Agostini, Italy	1966–75	15
2	Angel Nieto, Spain	1969–84	13
3 =	Carlo Ubbiali, Itay	1951–60	9
=	Mike Hailwood, UK	1961–67	9
5 =	John Surtees, UK	1956–60	7
=	Phil Read, UK	1964–74	7
7 =	Geoff Duke, UK	1951–55	6
=	Jim Redman, Southern Rhodesia	1962–65	6
=	Klaus Enders, W. Germany	1967–74	6
10	Anton Mang, W. Germany	1980–87	5

TOP 10 ⭐
OLYMPIC CYCLING COUNTRIES

	COUNTRY	GOLD	SILVER	BRONZE	TOTAL
			MEDALS		
1	France	32	19	22	73
2	Italy	32	15	6	53
3	Great Britain	9	21	16	46
4	USA	11	13	16	40
5	Netherlands	10	14	7	31
6	Germany*	8	9	9	26
7	Australia	6	11	8	25
8	Soviet Union#	11	4	9	24
9	Belgium	6	6	10	22
10	Denmark	6	6	10	21

* Not including West Germany or East Germany 1968–88

 # Including United Team of 1992, exludes Russia since

TOP 10 COUNTRIES WITH MOST TOUR DE FRANCE WINNERS
(Country/winners)

❶ France, 36 ❷ Belgium, 18 ❸ Italy, 9 ❹ Spain, 8
❺ Luxembourg, 4 ❻ USA, 3 ❼ = Switzerland, 2;
= Holland, 2 ❾ = Denmark, 1; = Germany, 1; = Ireland, 1

TOP 10 ⭐
500cc WORLD CHAMPIONSHIP RIDERS, 1998

	RIDER/COUNTRY	POINTS
1	Mick Doohan, Australia	260
2	Max Biaggi, Italy	208
3	Ales Criville, Spain	198
4	Carlos Checa, Spain	139
5	Alex Barros, Brazil	138
6	Norwick Abe, Japan	128
7	Simon Crafer, New Zealand	119
8	Tadayuki Okada, Japan	106
9	Nobauatsu Aoki, Japan	101
10	Regis Laconi, France	86

The motorcycle World Championship, which included the 500cc class, had its inaugural season in 1949, when it was won by British rider Leslie Graham on an AJS. British riders Geoff Duke and John Surtees dominated the event during the 1950s, and Mike Hailwood in the 1960s, when Italian bikes won every Championship, a role consistently overtaken since the mid-1970s by Japanese motorcycles. In the 1980s, the title was won on six occasions by two American riders, Freddie Spencer and Eddie Lawson. The 1998 Championship was won by Mick Doohan on a Honda.

BIG MIG

For five years from 1990 to 1995, Miguel Indurain dominated the Tour de France. His seemingly unbeatable combination of strength, skill, and stamina made him the focus of media attention and public expectation.

TOP 10 ⭐
TOUR DE FRANCE WINNERS

	RIDER/COUNTRY	WINS
1 =	Jacques Anquetil, France	5
=	Eddy Merckx, Belgium	5
=	Bernard Hinault, France	5
=	Miguel Indurain, Spain	5
5 =	Philippe Thys, Belgium	3
=	Louison Bobet, France	3
=	Greg LeMond, USA	3
8 =	Lucien Petit-Breton, France	2
=	Firmin Lambot, Belgium	2
=	Ottavio Bottecchia, Italy	2
=	Nicholas Frantz, Luxembourg	2
=	André Leducq, France	2
=	Antonin Magne, France	2
=	Gino Bartali, Italy	2
=	Sylvere Maës, Belgium	2
=	Fausto Coppi, Italy	2
=	Bernard Thevenet, France	2
=	Laurent Fignon, France	2

Gino Bartali won the race in 1938 and 1948, and is the only man to win both before and after World War II.

MOTOR RACING

FASTEST GRAND PRIX RACES, 1998

	GRAND PRIX	CIRCUIT	WINNER'S SPEED	
			KM/H	MPH
1	Italy	Monza	237.591	147.632
2	Germany	Hockenheim	227.997	141.671
3	Japan	Suzuka	205.228	127.523
4	Austria	Zeltweg	202.777	126.000
5	Australia	Melbourne	201.100	124.958
6	Luxembourg	Nürburgring	198.534	123.363
7	Spain	Barcelona	196.863	122.325
8	San Marino	Imola	194.117	120.619
9	France	Magny-Cours	190.963	118.659
10	Brazil	Iterlagos	190.764	118.535

TOP 10 DRIVERS TO COMPETE IN THE MOST FORMULA ONE GRAND PRIX RACES

(Driver/country/races)

1 Riccardo Patrese, Italy, 256 **2** Gerhard Berger, Austria, 210 **3** Andrea de Cesaris, Italy, 208 **4** Nelson Piquet, Brazil, 204 **5** Alain Prost, France, 199 **6** Michele Alboreto, Italy, 194 **7** Nigel Mansell, UK, 185 **8** Graham Hill, UK, 176 **9** Jacques Laffite, France, 175 **10** Niki Lauda, Italy, 171

TOP 10 ★

DRIVERS WITH THE BEST PERCENTAGE OF WINS IN FORMULA ONE*

	DRIVER/COUNTRY	WINS	RACES	PERCENTAGE
1	Juan Manuel Fangio, Argentina	24	51	47.06
2	Alberto Ascari, Italy	13	32	40.63
3	Jim Clark, UK	25	72	34.72
4	Michael Schumacher, Germany	34	121	28.10
5	Jackie Stewart, UK	27	99	27.27
6	Alain Prost, France	51	199	25.63
7	Ayrton Senna, Brazil	41	161	25.47
8	Stirling Moss, UK	16	66	24.24
9	Damon Hill, UK	21	69	21.63
10	Jacques Villeneuve, Canada	11	52	21.15

* Up to San Marino Grand Prix, Imola, 2 May 1999

TOP 10 CONSTRUCTORS WITH THE MOST FORMULA ONE WORLD TITLES*

(Constructor/country/years/titles)

1 Williams, UK, 1980–97, 9 **2** = Ferrari, Italy, 1961–83, 8; = McLaren, UK, 1974–98, 8 **4** Lotus, UK, 1963–78, 7 **5** = Brabham, UK, 1966–67, 2; = Cooper, UK, 1959–60, 2 **7** = BRM, UK, 1962, 1; = Matra, France, 1969, 1; = Tyrrell, UK, 1971, 1; = Vanwall, UK, 1958, 1; = Benetton, Italy, 1995, 1

* To end of 1998 season

TOP 10 ★

CONSTRUCTORS WITH THE MOST FORMULA ONE GRAND PRIX WINS*

	CONSTRUCTOR/COUNTRY	YEARS	WINS
1	Ferrari, Italy	1951–98	119
2	McLaren, UK	1968–98	116
3	Williams, UK	1979–98	102
4	Lotus, UK	1960–87	79
5	Brabham, UK	1964–85	35
6	Benetton, Italy	1986–97	27
7	Tyrrell, UK	1971–83	23
8	BRM, UK	1959–72	17
9	Cooper, UK	1958–67	16
10	Renault, France	1979–83	15

* To end of 1998 season

TOP 10 ★

DRIVERS WITH THE MOST GRAND PRIX WINS IN A CAREER*

	DRIVER/COUNTRY	YEARS	WINS
1	Alain Prost, France	1981–93	51
2	Ayrton Senna, Brazil	1985–93	41
3	Michael Schumacher, Germany	1992–98	33
4	Nigel Mansell, UK	1985–94	31
5	Jackie Stewart, UK	1965–73	27
6	=Jim Clark, UK	1962–68	25
	=Niki Lauda, Austria	1974–85	25
8	Juan Manuel Fangio, Argentina	1950–57	24
9	Nelson Piquet, Brazil	1980–91	23
10	Damon Hill, UK	1993–98	22

* To end of 1998 season

TOP 10 ⭐
YOUNGEST FORMULA ONE WORLD CHAMPIONS OF ALL TIME

DRIVER/COUNTRY	YEAR	AGE* YRS	MTHS
1 Emerson Fittipaldi, Brazil	1972	25	9
2 Michael Schumacher, Germany	1994	25	10
3 Jacques Villeneuve, Canada	1997	26	5
4 Niki Lauda, Austria	1975	26	7
5 Jim Clark, UK	2963	27	7
6 Jochen Rindt, Austria	1970	28	6
7 Ayrton Senna, Brazil	1988	28	7
8 = James Hunt, UK	1976	29	2
=Nelson Piquet, Brazil	1981	29	2
10 Mike Hawthorn, UK	1958	29	6

If a driver is eligible on more than one occasion, only his youngest age is considered.

TOP 10 DRIVERS WITH THE MOST GRAND PRIX POLE POSITIONS
(Driver/country/years/poles)

❶ Ayrton Senna, Brazil, 1985–94, 65 ❷ = Jim Clark, UK, 1962–68, 33; = Alain Prost, France, 1981–93, 33 ❹ Nigel Mansell, UK, 1984–94, 32 ❺ Juan Manuel Fangio, Argentina, 1950–58, 29 ❻ = Niki Lauda, Austria, 1974–78, 24; = Nelson Piquet, Brazil, 1980–87, 24 ❽ = Damon Hill, UK, 1993–96, 20; = Michael Schumacher, Germany, 1991–98, 20 ❿ = Mario Andretti, USA, 1968–82, 18; = René Arnoux, France, 1979–83, 18

TOP 10 ⭐
DRIVERS WITH THE LONGEST FORMULA ONE CAREERS

DRIVER/COUNTRY	CAREER	LENGTH YRS	MTHS
1 Graham Hill, UK	May 1958–Jan 1975	16	8
2 Riccardo Patrese, Italy	May 1977–Oct 1993	16	5
3 Jack Brabham, Australia	Jul 1955–Oct 1970	15	3
4 Nigel Mansell, UK	Aug 1980–May 1995	14	9
5 Joe Bonnier, Sweden	Jan 1957–Oct 1971	14	8
6 Maurice Trintignant, France	May 1950–Sep 1964	14	4
7 Niki Lauda, Austria	Aug 1971–Nov 1985	14	3
8 Andrea de Cesaris, Italy	Sep 1980–Oct 1994	14	1
9 Mario Andretti, USA	Oct 1968–Sep 1982	13	11
10 Michele Alboreto, Italy	May 1981–Nov 1994	13	6

TOP 10 CARS IN THE LE MANS 24-HOUR RACE
(Car/wins)

❶ Porsche, 15 ❷ Ferrari, 9 ❸ Jaguar, 7 ❹ Bentley, 5 ❺ = Alfa Romeo, 4; = Ford, 4 ❼ Matra-Simca, 3 ❽ = Bugatti, 2; = La Lorraine, 2; = Mercedes-Benz, 2; = Peugeot, 2

TOP 10 ⭐
FASTEST LE MANS 24-HOUR RACES

DRIVER/COUNTRY	CAR	YEAR	AVERAGE SPEED KM/H	MPH
1 Helmut Marko, Austria, Gijs van Lennep, Holland	Porsche	1971	222.304	138.133
2 Jan Lammers, Holland, Johnny Dumfries, Andy Wallace, UK	Jaguar	1988	221.630	137.714
3 Jochen Mass, Manuel Reuter, West Germany, Stanley Dickens, Sweden	Mercedes	1989	219.991	136.696
4 Dan Gurney, A. J. Foyt, USA	Ford	1967	218.033	135.479
5 Geoff Brabham, Australia, Christophe Bouchot, Eric Hélary, France	Peugeot	1993	213.358	132.574
6 Klaus Ludwig, "John Winter", West Germany, Paulo Barilla, Italy	Porsche	1985	212.021	131.744
7 Vern Schuppan, Austria, Hurley Haywood, Al Holbert, USA	Porsche	1983	210.330	130.693
8 Jean-Pierre Jassaud, Didier Pironi, France	Renault Alpine	1978	210.190	130.606
9 Jacky Ickx, Belgium, Jackie Oliver, UK	Ford	1969	208.250	129.401
10 Johnny Herbert, UK, Bertrand Gachot, Belgium, Volker Wendler, Germany	Mazda	1991	206.530	128.332

TOP 10 DRIVERS IN THE LE MANS 24-HOUR RACE
(Driver/country/years/wins)

❶ Jacky Ickx, Belgium, 1969–82, 6 ❷ Derek Bell, UK, 1975–87, 5 ❸ = Olivier Gendebien, Belgium, 1958–62, 4; = Henri Pescarolo, France, 1972–84, 4 ❺ = Woolf Barnato, UK, 1928–30, 3; = Luigi Chinetti, Italy/USA, 1932–49, 3; = Phil Hill, USA, 1958–62, 3; = Klaus Ludwig, West Germany, 1979–85, 3; = Al Holbert, USA, 1983–87, 3; = Yannick Dalmas, France, 1992–95, 3

GOLFING GREATS

TOP 10 PLAYERS TO WIN THE MOST MAJORS IN A CAREER

	PLAYER/COUNTRY*	BRITISH OPEN	US OPEN	MASTERS	PGA	TOTAL
1	Jack Nicklaus	3	4	6	5	18
2	Walter Hagen	4	2	0	5	11
3 =	Ben Hogan	1	4	2	2	9
=	Gary Player, South Africa	3	1	3	2	9
5	Tom Watson	5	1	2	0	8
6 =	Harry Vardon, UK	6	1	0	0	7
=	Gene Sarazen	1	2	1	3	7
=	Bobby Jones	3	4	0	0	7
=	Sam Snead	1	0	3	3	7
=	Arnold Palmer	2	1	4	0	7

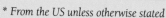

* From the US unless otherwise stated

TOP 10 ★
LOWEST WINNING SCORES IN THE US MASTERS

	PLAYER/COUNTRY*	YEAR	SCORE
1	Tiger Woods	1997	270
2 =	Jack Nicklaus	1965	271
=	Raymond Floyd	1976	271
4 =	Ben Hogan	1953	274
=	Ben Crenshaw	1995	274
6 =	Severiano Ballesteros, Spain	1980	275
=	Fred Couples	1992	275
8 =	Arnold Palmer	1964	276
=	Jack Nicklaus	1975	276
=	Tom Watson	1977	276
=	Nick Faldo, UK	1996	276

* From the US unless otherwise stated

The US Masters is the only major played on the same course each year, at Augusta, Georgia. The course was built on the site of an old nursery, and the abundance of flowers, shrubs, and plants is a reminder of its former days, with each of the holes named after the plants growing adjacent to it.

TOP 10 ★
MONEY-WINNING GOLFERS OF ALL TIME

	PLAYER/COUNTRY*	CAREER WINNINGS ($)#
1	Greg Norman, Australia	12,015,443
2	Fred Couples	10,806,573
3	Mark O'Meara	10,730,943
4	Payne Stewart	10,551,358
5	Davis Love III	10,548,501
6	Tom Kite	10,447,472
7	Nick Price	10,039,234
8	Tom Watson	9,395,292
9	Scott Hoch	9,388,207
10	Mark Calcavecchia	9,120,814

* From the US unless otherwise stated
 # As at March 14, 1999

GOLF'S SHOWMAN

A flamboyant character, Walter Hagen helped raise the status of professional golfers by refusing to accept the limitations imposed by the game's establishment.

TOP 10 ★
MONEY-WINNING GOLFERS, 1998

	PLAYER/COUNTRY*	WINNINGS ($)
1	David Duval	2,680,489
2	Vijay Singh, Fiji	2,398,782
3	Tiger Woods	2,077,197
4	Jim Furyk	2,054,334
5	Lee Westwood, UK	2,022,213
6	Mark O'Meara	2,014,039
7	Hal Sutton	1,838,740
8	Phil Mickelson	1,837,246
9	Davis Love III	1,703,001
10	Colin Montgomerie, UK	1,684,449

* From the US unless otherwise stated

This list is based on winnings on the world's five top tours: US PGA Tour, European PGA Tour, PGA Tour of Japan, Australasian PGA Tour, and FNB Tour of South Africa.

TOP 10 ★
PLAYERS WITH THE MOST CAREER WINS ON THE US TOUR

	PLAYER*	TOUR WINS
1	Sam Snead	81
2	Jack Nicklaus	70
3	Ben Hogan	63
4	Arnold Palmer	60
5	Byron Nelson	52
6	Billy Casper	51
7 =	Walter Hagen	40
=	Cary Midlecoff	40
9	Gene Sarazen	38
10	Lloyd Mangrum	36

* All from the US

For many years Sam Snead's total of wins was held to be 84 but the PGA Tour amended his figure in 1990 after discrepancies had been found in their previous lists. They deducted 11 wins from his total, but added eight others which should have been included, giving a revised total of 81. The highest-placed current member of the regular tour is Tom Watson, in joint 11th place with 32 wins. The highest-placed overseas player is Gary Player (South Africa), with 22 wins. Sam Snead, despite being the most successful golfer on the US Tour, has never managed to win the US Open. After more than 25 attempts, his best finish to date was 2nd on four occasions.

TOP 10 ★
LOWEST FOUR-ROUND TOTALS IN THE BRITISH OPEN

	PLAYER/COUNTRY/VENUE	YEAR	TOTAL
1	Greg Norman, Australia, Sandwich	1993	267
2 =	Tom Watson, USA, Turnberry	1977	268
=	Nick Price, Zimbabwe, Turnberry	1994	268
4 =	Jack Nicklaus, USA, Turnberry	1977	269
=	Nick Faldo, UK, Sandwich	1993	269
=	Jesper Parnevik, Sweden, Turnberry	1994	269
7 =	Nick Faldo, UK, St. Andrews	1990	270
=	Bernhard Langer, Germany, Sandwich	1993	270
9 =	Tom Watson, USA, Muirfield	1980	271
=	Fuzzy Zoeller, USA, Turnberry	1994	271
=	Tom Lehman, USA, Lytham	1996	271

The first time the Open Championship was played over four rounds of 18 holes was at Muirfield in 1892, when amateur Harold H. Hilton won.

TOP 10 ★
LOWEST WINNING TOTALS IN THE US OPEN

	PLAYER/COUNTRY*/VENUE	YEAR	SCORE
1 =	Jack Nicklaus, Baltusrol	1980	272
=	Lee Janzen, Baltusrol	1993	272
3	David Graham, Australia, Merion	1981	273
4 =	Jack Nicklaus, Baltusrol	1967	275
=	Lee Trevino, Oak Hill	1968	275
6 =	Ben Hogan, Riviera	1948	276
=	Fuzzy Zoeller, Winged Foot	1984	276
=	Ernie Els, South Africa, Congressional	1997	276
9 =	Jerry Pate, Atlanta	1976	277
=	Scott Simpson, Olympic Club	1987	277

* From the US unless otherwise stated

Winning the 1980 US Open at Baltusrol, 18 years after his first success in the tournament, Jack Nicklaus did so in record-breaking style: his total of 204 established yet another new record.

TOP 10 ★
WINNERS OF WOMEN'S MAJORS

	PLAYER*	TITLES
1	Patty Berg	16
2 =	Mickey Wright	13
=	Louise Suggs	13
4	Babe Zaharias	12
5	Betsy Rawis	8
6	JoAnne Carner	7
7 =	Kathy Whitworth	6
=	Pat Bradley	6
=	Julie Inkster	6
=	Glenna Collett Vare	6

* All from the US

TIGER ON TOP

Tiger Woods is golf's current phenomenon. Playing since the age of 2, Tiger has had a massive impact on the game, and he looks set for a great future.

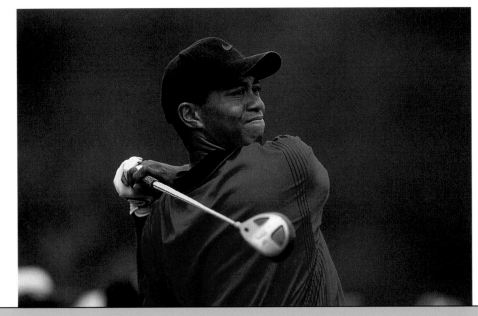

HORSE RACING

TOP 10 ★
FASTEST WINNING TIMES OF THE GRAND NATIONAL

	HORSE	YEAR	TIME MINS	SECS
1	Mr. Frisk	1990	8	47.8
2	Rough Quest	1996	9	00.8
3	Red Rum	1973	9	01.9
4	Royal Athlete	1995	9	04.6
5	Lord Gwyllene	1997	9	05.8
6	Party Politics	1992	9	06.3
7	Grittar	1982	9	12.6
8	Bobbyjo	1999	9	14.0
9	Maori Venture	1987	9	19.3
10	Reynoldstown	1935	9	20.0

TOP 10 ★
JOCKEYS IN THE GRAND NATIONAL

	JOCKEY*	YEARS	WINS
1	George Stevens	1856–70	5
2	Tom Oliver	1838–53	4
3 =	Mr. Tommy Pickernell	1860–75	3
=	Mr. Tommy Beasley	1880–89	3
=	Arthur Nightingall	1890–1901	3
=	Ernie Piggott	1912–19	3
=	Mr. Jack Anthony	1911–20	3
=	Brian Fletcher	1968–74	3
9 =	Mr. Alec Goodman	1852–66	2
=	John Page	1867–72	2
=	Mr. Maunsell Richardson	1873–74	2
=	Mr. Ted Wilson	1884–85	2
=	Percy Woodland	1903–13	2
=	Arthur Thompson	1948–52	2
=	Bryan Marshall	1953–54	2
=	Fred Winter	1957–62	2
=	Richard Dunwoody	1986–94	2
=	Carl Llewellyn	1992–98	2

Amateur riders are traditionally indicated by the prefix "Mr."

TOP 10 ★
JOCKEYS IN THE 2,000 GUINEAS

	JOCKEY	YEARS	WINS
1	Jem Robinson	1825–48	9
2	John Osborne	1857–88	6
3 =	Frank Buckle	1810–27	5
=	Charlie Elliott	1923–49	5
=	Lester Piggott	1957–92	5
6 =	John Day	1826–41	4
=	Fred Archer	1874–85	4
=	Tom Cannon	1878–89	4
=	Herbert Jones	1900–09	4
=	Willie Carson	1972–89	4

TOP 10 ★
JOCKEYS IN THE EPSOM DERBY

	JOCKEY	YEARS	WINS
1	Lester Piggott	1954–83	9
2 =	Jem Robinson	1817–36	6
=	Steve Donoghue	1915–25	6
4	John Arnull	1784–99	5
=	Frank Buckle	1792–1823	5
=	Bill Clift	1793–1819	5
=	Fred Archer	1877–86	5
8 =	Sam Arnull	1780–98	4
=	Tom Goodison	1809–22	4
=	Bill Scott	1832–43	4
=	Jack Watts	1887–96	4
=	Charlie Smirke	1934–58	4
=	Willie Carson	1979–94	4

Lester Piggott has been so dominant in the post-war era that his total of nine Derby winners is five more than Willie Carson's and six more than the next highest post-war winning jockeys, Rae Johnstone, Pat Eddery, and Walter Swinburn, who have each ridden three winners.

THE SPORT OF KINGS
Although horse racing is classified as an equestrian sport, many would argue that it is a huge multinational industry in which betting is the central element.

TOP 10 ★
FASTEST WINNING TIMES OF THE EPSOM DERBY

	HORSE	YEAR	TIME MINS	SECS
1	Lammtarra	1995	2	32.31
2	Mahmoud	1936	2	33.80
3	Kahyasi	1988	2	33.84
4	High-Rise	1998	2	33.88
5	Reference Point	1987	2	33.90
6 =	Hyperion	1933	2	34.00
=	Windsor Lad	1934	2	34.00
=	Generous	1991	2	34.00
9	Erhaab	1994	2	34.16
10	Golden Fleece	1982	2	34.27

TOP 10 ⭐
JOCKEYS IN THE ENGLISH CLASSICS

JOCKEY	YEARS	1,000 GUINEAS	2,000 GUINEAS	DERBY	OAKS	ST. LEGER	WINS
1 Lester Piggott	1954–92	2	5	9	6	8	30
2 Frank Buckle	1792–1827	6	5	5	9	2	27
3 Jem Robinson	1817–48	5	9	6	2	2	24
4 Fred Archer	1874–86	2	4	5	4	6	21
5 =Bill Scott	1821–46	0	3	4	3	9	19
=Jack Watts	1883–97	4	2	4	4	5	19
7 Willie Carson	1972–94	2	4	4	4	3	17
8 =John Day	1826–41	5	4	0	5	2	16
=George Fordham	1859–83	7	3	1	5	0	16
10 Joe Childs	1912–33	2	2	3	4	4	15

TOP 10 ⭐
JOCKEYS IN THE 1,000 GUINEAS

JOCKEY	YEARS	WINS
1 George Fordham	1859–83	7
2 Frank Buckle	1818–27	6
3 =Jem Robinson	1824–44	5
=John Day	1826–40	5
5 =Jack Watts	1886–97	4
=Fred Rickaby Jr	1913–17	4
=Charlie Elliott	1924–44	4
8 =Bill Arnull	1817–32	3
=Nat Flatman	1835–57	3
=Tom Cannon	1866–84	3
=Charlie Wood	1880–87	3
=Dick Perryman	1926–41	3
=Harry Wragg	1934–45	3
=Rae Johnstone	1935–50	3
=Gordon Richards	1942–51	3
=Walter Swinburn	1989–93	3

TOP 10 ⭐
JOCKEYS OF ALL TIME IN THE UK

JOCKEY	CHAMPION JOCKEY TITLES	BEST SEASON TOTAL	CAREER FLAT WINNERS
1 Gordon Richards	26	269	4,870
2 Lester Piggott	11	191	4,513
3 Pat Eddery	11	209	4,000
4 Willie Carson	5	182	3,828
5 Doug Smith	5	173	3,111
6 Joe Mercer	1	164	2,810
7 Fred Archer	13	246	2,748
8 Edward Hide	0	137	2,591
9 George Fordham	14	166	2,587
10 Eph Smith	0	144	2,313

TOP 10 JOCKEYS IN THE PRIX DE L'ARC DE TRIOMPHE

(Jockey/wins)

1 = Jacko Doyasbère, 4; = Pat Eddery, 4; = Freddy Head, 4; = Yves Saint-Martin, 4 **5** = Enrico Camici, 3; = Charlie Elliott, 3; = Olivier Peslier, 3; = Lester Piggot, 3; = Roger Poincelet, 3; = Charles Semblat, 3

The Prix de L'Arc de Triomphe was first run in 1920.

TOP 10 NATIONAL HUNT JOCKEYS WITH THE MOST CAREER WINS

(Jockey/years/wins)

1 Richard Dunwoody, 1983–99, 1,679
2 Peter Scudamore, 1978–95, 1,678
3 John Francome, 1970–85, 1,138
4 Stan Mellor, 1952–72, 1,035
5 Peter Niven, 1984–99, 940
6 Fred Winter, 1939–64, 923
7 Graham McCourt, 1975–96, 921
8 Bob Davies, 1966–82, 911
9 Terry Biddlecombe, 1958–74, 908
10 Jonjo O'Neill, 1972–86, 885

TOP 10 JOCKEYS IN A FLAT RACING SEASON

(Jockey/year/wins)

1 Gordon Richards, 1947, 269
2 Gordon Richards, 1949, 261
3 Gordon Richards, 1933, 259 **4** Fred Archer, 1885, 246 **5** Fred Archer, 1884, 241 **6** Fred Archer, 1883, 232
7 Gordon Richards, 1952, 231 **8** Fred Archer, 1878, 229 **9** Gordon Richards, 1951, 227 **10** Gordon Richards, 1948, 224

Richards rode over 200 winners in a season 12 times, while Archer did so on eight occasions.

Did You Know? The fastest ever racehorse was Big Rocket, who ran at 69.62 km/h/43.26 mph in Mexico City in 1945.

RUGBY RECORDS

TOP 10 ★

HIGHEST WINNING SCORES IN BRITISH RUGBY LEAGUE HISTORY

	MATCH (WINNERS FIRST)	DATE	COMPETITION	SCORE
1	Huddersfield v Blackpool	26 Nov 1994	Regal Trophy	142–4
2	Barrow v Nottingham	27 Nov 1994	Regal Trophy	138–0
3	Huddersfield v Swinton Park Rangers	28 Feb 1914	Challenge Cup	119–2
4	Wigan v Flimby and Fothergill	15 Feb 1925	Challenge Cup	116–0
5	St. Helens v Carlisle	14 Sep 1986	Lancashire Cup	112–0
6 =	St. Helens v Trafford Borough	15 Sep 1991	Lancashire Cup	104–12
=	Keighley v Highfield	23 Apr 1995	Division 2	104–4
8	Leeds v Coventry	12 Apr 1913	League	102–0
9	Hull Kingston Rovers v Nottingham City	19 Aug 1990	Yorkshire Cup	100–6
10	Doncaster v Highfield	20 Mar 1994	Division 2	96–0

TOP 10 ★

POINTS SCORERS OF ALL TIME IN THE SUPER LEAGUE

	CLUB	TOTAL POINTS
1	Wigan Warriors	2,347
2	St. Helens	2,215
3	Bradford Bulls	2,034
4	Halifax Blue Sox	1,849
5	Leeds Rhinos	1,761
6	London Broncos	1,642
7	Sheffield Eagles	1,509
8	Warrington Wolves	1,417
9	Castleford Tigers	1,328
10	Oldham Bears	934

TOP 10 ★

TRY SCORERS IN THE 1998 SUPER LEAGUE

	PLAYER/CLUB	TRIES
1	Anthony Sullivan, St. Helens	20
2	Francis Cummins, Leeds Rhinos	17
3 =	Gary Connolly, Wigan Warriors	15
=	Tony Smith, Wigan Warriors	15
5 =	Keith Senior, Sheffield Eagles	14
=	Paul Newlove, St. Helens	14
7 =	Iestyn Harris, Leeds Rhinos	13
=	Danny Arnold, St. Helens	13
=	Gavin Clinch, Halifax Blue Sox	13
10 =	Bright Sodje, Sheffield Eagles	12
=	Sean Long, St. Helens	12
=	Paul Johnson, Wiggan Warriors	12
=	Henry Paul, Wiggan Warriors	12
=	Tevita Vaikona, Bradford Bulls	12
=	Martin Moana, Halifax Blue Sox	12

TOP 10 TEAMS IN CHALLENGE CUP FINALS*

(Team/points)

1 Wigan, 406 **2** Leeds, 239 **3** St. Helens, 211 **4** Widnes, 158 **5** Huddersfield, 130 **6** Warrington, 129 **7** Hull, 128 **8** Wakefield Trinity, 118 **9** Halifax, 110 **10** Bradford, 113

* Including the two-stage finals during World War II

TOP 10 ★

CLUBS WITH THE MOST LANCE TODD TROPHY WINS

	CLUB	WINS
1	Wigan	13
2	St. Helens	7
3 =	Wakefield Trinity	5
=	Widnes	5
5	Bradford Northern/Bulls	4
6 =	Castleford	3
=	Featherstone Rovers	3
=	Warrington	3
9	Leeds	2
10 =	Barrow	1
=	Halifax	1
=	Huddersfield	1
=	Hull	1
=	Hull Kingston Rovers	1
=	Hunslet	1
=	Leigh	1
=	Sheffield Eagles	1
=	Workington Town	1

The Lance Todd Award is presented to the Man of the Match in the Challenge Cup final at Wembley.

TOP 10 ★

WINNERS OF THE CHALLENGE CUP

	CLUB	YEARS	WINS
1	Wigan	1924–95	16
2	Leeds	1910–99	11
3 =	Widnes	1930–84	7
=	St. Helens	1956–97	7
5	Huddersfield	1913–53	6
6 =	Wakefield Trinity	1909–63	5
=	Warrington	1905–74	5
=	Halifax	1903–87	5
9 =	Bradford Northern	1906–49	4
=	Castleford	1935–86	4

THE 10 FIRST PLAYERS INDUCTED INTO THE RUGBY UNION HALL OF FAME*

1 Serge Blanco 2 Graham Mourie 3 Peter Dixon
4 Gareth Edwards 5 Simon Poidevin 6 Grant Fox
7 Jo Maso 8 Hugo Porta 9 Mike Gibson 10 Andy Irvine

In November 1996 Rugby News magazine launched its own Hall of Fame and each month thereafter nominated a new inductee

TOP 10 ★
BIGGEST WINS IN THE INTERNATIONAL CHAMPIONSHIP*

MATCH (WINNERS FIRST)/VENUE	YEAR	SCORE
1 **England v Wales**, Twickenham	1998	60–26
2 **France v Scotland**, Murrayfield	1998	51–16
3 **Wales v France**, Swansea	1910	49–14
4 **France v Scotland**, Paris	1997	47–20
5 **England v Ireland**, Twickenham	1997	46–6
6 = **France v Ireland**, Paris	1996	45–10
= **France v Ireland**, Paris	1996	45–10
8 **France v Ireland**, Paris	1992	44–12
9 **England v Scotland**, Twickenham	1997	41–13
10 **England v France**, Paris	1914	39–13

Based on the winning teams' scores, not the margin of victory

TOP 10 ★
BIGGEST BRITISH LIONS' TEST WINS

OPPONENTS	VENUE	TEST/YEAR	SCORE
1 Australia	Brisbane	2nd, 1966	31–0
2 South Africa	Pretoria	2nd, 1974	28–9
3 South Africa	Port Elizabeth	3rd, 1974	26–9
4 South Africa	Cape Town	1st, 1997	26–16
5 = Australia	Sydney	2nd, 1950	24–3
= Australia	Sydney	2nd, 1959	24–3
7 South Africa	Johannesburg	1st, 1955	23–22
8 South Africa	Port Elizabeth	3rd, 1938	21–16
9 New Zealand	Wellington	2nd, 1993	20–7
10 = Australia	Brisbane	2nd, 1989	19–12
= Australia	Sydney	3rd, 1989	19–18

This Top 10 is based on the greatest number of points scored by the Lions, not the greatest margin of victory, their record for which is their 31–0 win over Australia in 1966. After this remarkable win, the British Lions continued on an enormously successful unbeaten tour of Australia in which they won seven and drew one match.

TOP 10 RUGBY UNION COUNTRIES*

1 South Africa 2 Australia 3 New Zealand
4 England 5 Scotland 6 France
7 Wales 8 Samoa 9 Ireland 10 Argentina

As at 1 February 1999, as ranked by World Rugby magazine

TOP 10 ★
POINTS SCORERS IN ONE WORLD CUP TOURNAMENT

PLAYER/COUNTRY	YEAR	PTS
1 **Grant Fox**, New Zealand	1987	126
2 **Gavin Hastings**, Scotland	1995	104
3 **Thierry Lacroix**, France	1995	103
4 **Andrew Mehrtens**, New Zealand	1995	84
5 **Michael Lynagh**, Australia	1987	82
6 **Rob Andrew**, England	1995	70
7 **Ralph Keyes**, Ireland	1991	68
8 **Michael Lynagh**, Australia	1991	66
9 **Gavin Hastings**, Scotland	1987	62
10 **Gavin Hastings**, Scotland	1991	61

TOP 10 ★
POINTS SCORERS IN MAJOR INTERNATIONALS*

PLAYER/COUNTRY	YEAR	PTS
1 **Michael Lynagh**, Australia	1984–95	911
2 **Neil Jenkins**, Wales	1991–98	745
3 **Gavin Hastings**, Scotland	1986–95	733
4 **Diego Dominguez**, Italy	1991–98	672
5 **Grant Fox**, New Zealand	1985–93	645
6 **Stefano Bettarello**, Italy	1979–88	483
7 **Rob Andrew**, England	1985–97	396
8 **Thierry Lacroix**, France	1989–97	367
9 **A. Mehrtens**, New Zealand	1995–97	364
10 **Didier Camberabero**, France	1982–93	354

Full International Board countries and British Lions

TOP 10 ★
POINTS SCORERS IN AN INTERNATIONAL CHAMPIONSHIP SEASON

PLAYER/COUNTRY	YEAR	PTS
1 **Jonathan Webb**, England	1992	67
2 **Paul Grayson**, England	1996	64
3 **Simon Hodgkinson**, England	1991	60
4 **Gavin Hastings**, Scotland	1995	56
5 **Jean-Patrick Lescarboura**, France	1984	54
6 **Rob Andrew**, England	1995	53
7 = **Ollie Campbell**, Ireland	1983	52
= **Gavin Hastings**, Scotland	1986	52
= **Paul Thorburn**, Wales	1986	52
= **Paul Grayson**, England	1997	52

Who is the top run maker of all time in test cricket?
see p.257 for the answer

A Allan Border
B Graham Gooch
C Sunil Gavaskar

TENNIS TRIUMPHS

PLAYERS WITH THE MOST US SINGLES TITLES

	PLAYER/COUNTRY*	YEARS	TITLES
1	Molla Mallory	1915–26	8
2 =	Richard Sears	1881–87	7
=	William Larned	1901–11	7
=	Bill Tilden	1920–29	7
=	Helen Wills-Moody	1923–31	7
=	Margaret Court, Australia+	1962–70	7
7	Chris Evert-Lloyd	1975–82	6
8 =	Jimmy Connors	1974–83	5
=	Steffi Graf, Germany	1988–96	5
10 =	Robert Wrenn	1893–97	4
=	Elisabeth Moore	1896–1905	4
=	Hazel Wightman	1909–19	4
=	Helen Jacobs	1932–35	4
=	Alice Marble	1936–40	4
=	Pauline Betz	1942–46	4
=	Maria Bueno, Brazil	1959–66	4
=	Billie Jean King	1967–74	4
=	John McEnroe	1979–84	4
=	Martina Navratilova	1983–87	4
=	Pete Sampras	1990–96	4

* From the US unless otherwise stated

+ Includes two wins in Amateur Championships of 1968 and 1969 which were held alongside the Open Championship

LEFT-HANDED WINNER

Martina Navratilova, a Czech-born tennis player who defected to the United States in 1975, retired in 1994, after winning 167 titles.

TOP 10 FEMALE PLAYERS*

(Player/country)

1. **Lindsay Davenport**, USA 2. **Martina Hingis**, Switzerland 3. **Jana Novotna**, Czech Republic 4. **Arantxa Sanchez-Vicario**, Spain 5. **Venus Williams**, USA 6. **Monica Seles**, USA 7. **Mary Pierce**, France 8. **Conchita Martinez**, Spain 9. **Steffi Graf**, Germany 10. **Nathalie Tauziat**, France

* Based on 1999 WTA rankings

TOP 10 CAREER MONEY-WINNING WOMEN*

(Player/country/winnings in $)

1. **Steffi Graf**, Germany, 20,614,142
2. **Martina Navratilova**, USA, 20,283,727
3. **Arantxa Sanchez-Vicario**, Spain, 14,029,452
4. **Monica Seles**, USA, 10,878,024
5. **Jana Novotna**, Czech Republic, 10,297,692
6. **Chris Evert**, USA, 8,896,195
7. **Gabriela Sabatini**, Argentina, 8,785,850
8. **Martina Hingis**, Switzerland, 8,124,248
9. **Conchita Martinez**, Spain, 7,737,227
10. **Natasha Zvereva**, Belarus, 7,014,631

* To end of 1998

DAVIS CUP WINNING TEAMS

	COUNTRY	WINS
1	United States	31
2	Australia	20
3	France	8
4	Sweden	7
5	Australasia	6
6	British Isles	5
7	Great Britain	4
8	West Germany	2
9 =	Germany	1
=	Czechoslovakia	1
=	Italy	1
=	South Africa	1

The UK was represented by the British Isles from 1900 to 1921, England from 1922 to 1928, and Great Britain since 1929. The combined Australia/New Zealand team took part as Australasia between 1905 and 1922. Australia first entered a separate team in 1923 and New Zealand in 1924. South Africa's sole win was gained when, for political reasons, India refused to meet them in the 1974 final.

MEN WITH THE MOST WIMBLEDON TITLES

	PLAYER/COUNTRY	YEARS	TITLES S	D	M	TOTAL
1	William Renshaw, UK	1880–89	7	7	0	14
2	Lawrence Doherty, UK	1897–1905	5	8	0	13
3	Reginald Doherty, UK	1897–1905	4	8	0	12
4	John Newcombe, Australia	1965–74	3	6	0	9
5 =	Ernest Renshaw, UK	1880–89	1	7	0	8
=	Tony Wilding, New Zealand	1907–14	4	4	0	8
7 =	Wilfred Baddeley, UK	1891–96	3	4	0	7
=	Bob Hewitt, Australia/S. Africa	1962–79	0	5	2	7
=	Rod Laver, Australia	1959–69	4	1	2	7
=	John McEnroe, USA	1979–84	3	4	0	7

S – singles; D – doubles; M – mixed

*Background image: **WIMBLEDON***

TOP 10 ⭐
WINNERS OF WOMEN'S GRAND SLAM SINGLES TITLES

PLAYER/COUNTRY	A	F	TITLES W	US	TOTAL
1 Margaret Court, Australia	11	5	3	5	24
2 Steffi Graf, Germany	4	5	7	5	21
3 Helen Wills-Moody, USA	0	4	8	7	19
4 =Chris Evert-Lloyd, USA	2	7	3	6	18
=Martina Navratilova, Czechoslovakia/USA	3	2	9	4	18
6 Billie Jean King, USA	1	1	6	4	12
7 =Maureen Connolly, USA	1	2	3	3	9
=Monica Seles, Yugoslavia/USA	4	3	0	2	9
9 =Suzanne Lenglen, France	0	2	6	0	8
=Molla Mallory, USA	0	0	0	8	8

A – Australian Open; F – French Open; W – Wimbledon; US – US Open

TOP 10 ⭐
WINNERS OF MEN'S GRAND SLAM SINGLES TITLES

PLAYER/COUNTRY	A	F	TITLES W	US	TOTAL
1 Roy Emerson, Australia	6	2	2	2	12
2 =Björn Borg, Sweden	0	6	5	0	11
=Rod Laver, Australia	3	2	4	2	11
=Pete Sampras, USA	2	0	5	4	11
5 =Jimmy Connors, USA	1	0	2	5	8
=Ivan Lendl, Czechoslovakia	2	3	0	3	8
=Fred Perry, UK	1	1	3	3	8
=Ken Rosewall, Australia	4	2	0	2	8
9 =René Lacoste, France	0	3	2	2	7
=William Larned, USA	0	0	0	7	7
=John McEnroe, USA	0	0	3	4	7
=John Newcombe, Australia	2	0	3	2	7
=William Renshaw, UK	0	0	7	0	7
=Richard Sears, USA	0	0	0	7	7
=Mats Wilander, Sweden	3	3	0	1	7

A – Australian Open; F – French Open; W – Wimbledon; US – US Open

THE 10 ⭐
LATEST WINNERS OF THE US OPEN MEN'S CHAMPIONSHIP

YEAR	WINNER	COUNTRY
1998	Patrick Rafter	Australia
1997	Patrick Rafter	Australia
1996	Pete Sampras	USA
1995	Pete Sampras	USA
1994	Andre Agassi	USA
1993	Pete Sampras	USA
1992	Stefan Edberg	Sweden
1991	Stefan Edberg	Sweden
1990	Pete Sampras	USA
1989	Pete Sampras	USA

TOP 10 ⭐
MALE PLAYERS*

	PLAYER	COUNTRY
1	Pete Sampras	USA
2	Marcelo Rios	Chile
3	Alex Corretja	Spain
4	Patrick Rafter	Australia
5	Carlos Moya	Spain
6	Andre Agassi	USA
7	Tim Henman	UK
8	Karol Kucera	Slovak Republic
9	Greg Rusedski	UK
10	Richard Krajicek	Netherlands

* Based on 1999 WTA rankings

A SWEDISH HERO

The tennis player Björn Borg is such a popular sportsman in Sweden, his home country, that in 1996 a Bjorn Borg Day was organized.

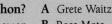

Which woman won the 1998 London Marathon?
see p.250 for the answer

A Grete Waitz
B Rosa Mota
C Joyce Chepchumba

TEAM GAMES

TOP 10 AUSTRALIAN FOOTBALL LEAGUE TEAMS
(Team/grand final wins)

1 Carlton, 16 **2** Essendon, 15
3 Collingwood, 14 **4** Melbourne, 12
5 Richmond, 10 **6** Hawthorn, 9
7 Fitzroy, 8 **8** Geelong, 6
9 = South Melbourne, 3;
= North Melbourne, 3

Australian Rules Football is an 18-a-side game that dates from the mid-19th century. The Australian Football League was formed in 1896.

TOP 10 ★
OLYMPIC SHOOTING COUNTRIES

COUNTRY	GOLD	MEDALS SILVER	BRONZE	TOTAL
1 USA	45	26	21	92
2 Soviet Union	22	17	81	57
3 Sweden	13	23	19	55
4 Great Britain	13	14	18	45
5 France	13	16	13	42
6 Norway	16	9	11	36
7 Switzerland	11	11	12	34
8 Italy	8	5	10	23
9 Greece	5	7	7	19
10 =China	7	5	5	17
=Finland	3	5	9	17

TOP 10 COUNTIES IN THE ALL-IRELAND HURLING CHAMPIONSHIPS
(Country/wins)

1 Cork, 27 **2** Kilkenny, 25
3 Tipperary, 24 **4** Limerick, 7
5 = Dublin, 6; = Wexford, 6
7 = Galway, 4; = Offaly, 4 **9** Clare, 3
10 Waterford, 2

Hurling, one of the world's fastest sports, has a history dating back to prehistoric times.

THE 10 ★
LATEST WINNERS OF THE ROLLER HOCKEY WORLD CHAMPIONSHIP

YEAR	WINNER
1997	Italy
1995	Argentina
1993	Portugal
1991	Portugal
1989	Spain
1988	Spain
1986	Spain
1984	Argentina
1982	Portugal
1980	Spain

Roller hockey, a five-a-side game formerly called rink hockey, has been played for more than 100 years. The first international tournament was held in Paris in 1910, the first European Championships in Britain in 1926, and the men's World Championship biennially since 1936 (odd-numbered years since 1989). Portugal is the overall winner, with 14 titles to its credit; Spain has won 10 times, Italy four, Argentina three, and England twice. The women's World Championship has been held since 1992 and has been won twice by Spain and once by Canada.

HOCKEY HEROES
Controversial and outspoken hockey star Dhanraj Pillay is shown here playing in the men's Olympic qualifying match in 1996. India has accumulated a record number of Olympic Gold medals.

TOP 10 ★
OLYMPIC HOCKEY COUNTRIES

COUNTRY	GOLD	MEDALS SILVER	BRONZE	TOTAL
1 India	8	1	2	11
2 Great Britain*	3	2	5	10
3 Netherlands	2	2	5	9
4 Pakistan	3	3	2	8
5 Australia	2	3	2	7
6 Germany#	1	2	2	5
7 =Spain	1	2	1	4
=West Germany	1	3	–	4
9 =South Korea	–	2	–	2
=USA	–	–	2	2
=Soviet Union	–	–	2	2

* Including England, Ireland, Scotland, and Wales, which competed separately in the 1908 Olympics

\# Not including West Germany or East Germany 1968–88

TOP 10 ★ OLYMPIC ARCHERY COUNTRIES

	COUNTRY	GOLD	MEDALS SILVER	BRONZE	TOTAL
1	USA	13	7	7	27
2	France	6	10	6	22
3	South Korea	10	6	3	19
4	Soviet Union	1	3	5	9
5	Great Britain	2	2	4	8
6	Finland	1	1	2	4
7	=China	0	3	0	3
	=Italy	0	0	3	3
9	=Sweden	0	2	0	2
	=Japan	0	1	1	2
	=Poland	0	1	1	2

Archery was introduced as an Olympic sport at the second Modern Olympics, held in Paris in 1900. The format has changed considerably over succeeding Games, with such events as shooting live birds being discontinued in favour of target shooting. Individual and team events for men and women are now included in the programme.

TOP 10 ★ WINNERS OF THE TABLE TENNIS WORLD CHAMPIONSHIP

	COUNTRY	MEN'S	WOMEN'S	TOTAL
1	China	12	12	24
2	Japan	7	8	15
3	Hungary	12	–	12
4	Czechoslovakia	6	3	9
5	Romania	–	5	5
6	Sweden	4	–	4
7	=England	1	2	3
	=USA	1	2	3
9	Germany	–	2	2
10	=Austria	1	–	1
	=North Korea	–	1	1
	=South Korea	–	1	1
	=USSR	–	1	1

Originally a European event, this was later extended to a world championship. Since 1959, the Championship has been held biennially.

TOP 10 POLO TEAMS WITH THE MOST BRITISH OPEN CHAMPIONSHIP WINS
(Team/wins)

1 = Stowell Park, 5; = Tramontana, 5
3 = Ellerston, 3; = Cowdray Park, 3; = Pimms, 3; = Windsor Park, 3
7 = Casarejo, 2; = Jersey Lillies, 2; = Woolmer's Park, 2; = Falcons, 2; = Southfield, 2

The British Open Championship, which was first held in 1956 (replacing the Champion Cup, which was played at Hurlingham, London, from 1876 to 1939), is played at Cowdray Park, West Sussex. The winning team receives the Veuve Clicquot Gold Cup.

TOP 10 ★ OLYMPIC VOLLEYBALL COUNTRIES

	COUNTRY	GOLD	MEDALS SILVER	BRONZE	TOTAL
1	Soviet Union*	7	5	1	13
2	Japan	3	3	2	8
3	USA	2	1	2	5
4	=Cuba	2	–	1	3
	=Brazil	1	1	1	3
	=China	1	1	1	3
	=Poland	1	–	2	3
8	=Netherlands	1	1	–	2
	=East Germany	–	2	–	2
	=Bulgaria	–	1	1	2
	=Czechoslovakia	–	1	1	2
	=Italy	–	1	1	2

* Includes United Team of 1992; excludes Russia since

This list encompasses men's and women's volleyball in the Olympics of 1964–96, but excludes beach volleyball, first competed in 1996.

OVER THE NET
Originally known as mintonette, volleyball originated in the United States in 1895 when William G. Morgan decided to blend elements of basketball, baseball, tennis, and handball to create a game that would demand less physical contact than basketball.

Who has won the most medals in a summer Olympics career?
see p.245 for the answer
A Nikolay Andrianov
B Edoardo Mangiarotti
C Larissa Latynina

275

WATER SPORTS

TOP 10 ★
OLYMPIC YACHTING COUNTRIES

	COUNTRY	GOLD	SILVER	BRONZE	TOTAL
			MEDALS		
1	USA	16	19	16	51
2	Great Britain	14	12	9	35
3	Sweden	9	12	9	30
4	Norway	16	11	2	29
5	France	12	6	9	27
6	Denmark	10	8	4	22
7	Germany/West Germany	6	5	6	17
8	Netherlands	4	5	6	15
9	New Zealand	6	4	3	13
10	=Australia	3	2	7	12
	=Soviet Union*	4	5	3	12
	=Spain	9	2	1	12

* Includes United Team of 1992; excludes Russia since

TOP 10 POWERBOAT DRIVERS WITH MOST RACE WINS
(Owner/country/wins)

1 Bill Seebold, USA, 912 **2** Jumbo McConnell, USA, 217 **3** Chip Hanuer, USA, 203 **4** Steve Curtis, UK, 183 **5** Mikeal Frode, Sweden, 152 **6** Neil Holmes, UK, 147 **7** Peter Bloomfield, UK, 126 **8** Renato Molinari, Italy, 113 **9** Cees Van der Valden, Netherlands, 98; **10** Bill Muney, USA, 96

Source: Raceboat International

MAKING A SPLASH

The US Women's swimming team show their delight after winning the 4 x 100 metres relay at the 1996 Olympics in Atlanta, Georgia.

TOP 10 ★
OLYMPIC SWIMMING COUNTRIES

	COUNTRY	GOLD	SILVER	BRONZE	TOTAL
			MEDALS		
1	USA	230	176	137	543
2	Australia	41	37	47	125
3	East Germany	40	34	25	99
4	Soviet Union*	24	32	38	94
5	Germany#	19	33	34	86
6	=Great Britain	18	23	30	71
	=Hungary	29	23	19	71
8	Sweden	13	21	21	55
9	Japan	15	18	19	52
10	Canada	11	17	20	48

* Includes United Team of 1992; excludes Russia since
 # Not including West Germany or East Germany 1968–88

TOP 10 FASTEST WINNING TIMES OF THE OXFORD AND CAMBRIDGE BOAT RACE
(Winner/years/time)

1 Cambridge, 1998, 16.19 **2** Cambridge, 1999, 16.41 **3** Oxford, 1984, 16.45 **4** Cambridge, 1996, 16.58 **5** Oxford, 1991, 16.59 **6** Cambridge, 1993, 17.00 **7** Oxford, 1985, 17.11 **8** Oxford, 1990, 17.15 **9** = Oxford, 1974, 17.35; = Oxford, 1988, 17.35

SAIL ON

The USA is consistently outstanding in yachting – one of the most physically demanding Olympic sports.

TOP 10 ★
OLYMPIC CANOEING COUNTRIES

| COUNTRY | MEDALS | | | |
	GOLD	SILVER	BRONZE	TOTAL
1 =Hungary	10	23	20	53
=Soviet Union*	30	13	10	53
3 Germany#	18	15	12	45
4 Romania	9	10	12	31
5 East Germany	14	7	9	30
6 Sweden	14	10	4	28
7 France	2	6	14	22
8 =Bulgaria	4	3	8	15
=USA	5	4	6	15
10 Canada	3	7	4	14

* *Includes United Team of 1992; excludes Russia since*
\# *Not including West or East Germany 1968–88*

TOP 10 ★
WINNERS OF MOST SURFING WORLD CHAMPIONSHIPS

SURFER/COUNTRY	WINS
1 **Kelly Slater**, USA	6
2 **Mark Richards**, Australia	4
3 **Tom Curren**, USA	3
4 =**Tom Carroll**, Australia	2
=**Damien Hardman**, Australia	2
6 =**Wayne Bartholemew**, Australia	1
=**Derek Ho**, USA	1
=**Barton Lynch**, Australia	1
=**Martin Potter**, UK	1
=**Shaun Tomson**, South Africa	1
=**Peter Townend**, Australia	1

TOP 10 ★
OLYMPIC ROWING COUNTRIES

| COUNTRY | MEDALS | | | |
	GOLD	SILVER	BRONZE	TOTAL
1 USA	29	28	19	76
2 East Germany	33	7	8	48
3 Soviet Union*	12	20	11	43
4 Germany#	19	12	11	42
5 Great Britain	19	15	7	41
6 =Italy	12	11	9	32
=Canada	8	12	12	32
8 France	4	14	12	30
9 Romania	12	10	7	29
10 Switzerland	6	7	9	22

* *Includes United Team of 1992; excludes Russia since*
\# *Not including West or East Germany 1968–88*

TOP 10 SURFERS, 1998*
(Surfer/country)

1 **Kelly Slater**, USA 2 **Mick Campbell**, Australia 3 **Danny Wills**, Australia 4 **Shane Beschen**, USA 5 **Shane Dorian**, USA 6 **Sunny Garcia**, USA 7 **Mark Occhilupo**, Australia 8 **Peterson Rosa**, Brazil 9 **Jake Paterson**, Australia 10 **Cory Lopez**, USA

* *Ranked according to the Association of Surfing Professionals*

THE CREST OF A WAVE
Already well-known for his surfing achievements, Kelly Slater became the most famous surfer in the world through his modelling, surfing videos, and regular appearances on the TV show Baywatch.

Who is the highest-earning sportsman in the world?
see p.281 for the answer

A Mike Tyson
B Tiger Woods
C Michael Jordan

WINTER SPORTS

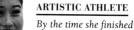

SKATERS WITH THE MOST WORLD TITLES

SKATER/COUNTRY/EVENT	YEARS	TITLES
1 =Ulrich Salchow, Sweden, Men	1901–11	10
=Sonja Henie, Norway, Women	1927–36	10
=Irina Rodnina, USSR, Pairs	1969–78	10
4 =Karl Schäfer, Austria, Men	1930–36	7
=Herma Jaross-Szabo, Austria, Women/Pairs	1922–27	7
6 =Alexandr Zaitsev, USSR, Pairs	1973–78	6
=Lyudmila Pakhomova, USSR, Dance	1970–76	6
=Alexandr Gorshkov, USSR, Dance	1970–76	6
=Carol Heiss, USA, Women	1956–61	6
10 Richard Button, USA, Men	1948–52	5

The British pair of Jean Westwood and Lawrence Demmy won five successive ice dance titles between 1951 and 1955, but the 1951 event is not regarded as an official championship.

FANCY FOOTWORK

Despite being hospitalized four times for injuries caused while performing the hair-raising triple lutz, Kurt Browning's skating exudes showmanship, technical prowess, style, and charisma.

WOMEN'S WORLD AND OLYMPIC FIGURE SKATING TITLES

SKATER/COUNTRY	YEARS	TITLES
1 Sonja Henie, Norway	1927–36	13
2 = Carol Heiss, USA	1956–60	6
=Herma Planck Szabo, Austria	1922–26	6
=Katarina Witt, E. Germany	1984–88	6
5 =Lily Kronberger, Hungary	1908–11	4
=Sjoukje Dijkstra, Holland	1962–64	4
=Peggy Fleming, USA	1966–68	4
8 =Meray Horvath, Hungary	1912–14	3
=Tenley Albright, USA	1953–56	3
=Annett Poetzsch, E. Gemany	1978–80	3
=Beatrix Schuba, Austria	1971–72	3
=Barbara Ann Scott, Canada	1947–48	3
= Kristi Yamaguchi, USA	1991–92	3
=Madge Sayers, UK	1906–08	3

TOP 10 WINTER OLYMPIC MEDAL-WINNING COUNTRIES

(Country/medals)

1 Norway, 239
2 Soviet Union*, 217 **3** USA, 159
4 Austria, 145 **5** Finland, 135
6 Germany#, 116 **7** East Germany, 110
8 Sweden, 102 **9** Switzerland, 92
10 Canada, 79

* Includes United Team of 1992; excludes Russia since # Not including West or East Germany 1968–88

ARTISTIC ATHLETE

By the time she finished competitive skating in 1993, Kristi Yamaguchi's combination of athletic ability and artistic interpretation had made her America's favourite figure skater.

TOP 10 OLYMPIC FIGURE SKATING COUNTRIES

(Country/medals)

1 USA, 39 **2** Soviet Union*, 29
3 Austria, 20 **4** Canada, 18
5 UK, 15 **6** France, 11 **7** = Sweden, 10; = East Germany, 10 **9** Germany#, 9
10 =Norway, 6; = Hungary, 6

* Includes United Team of 1992; excludes Russia since # Not including West or East Germany 1968–88

MEN'S WORLD AND OLYMPIC FIGURE SKATING TITLES

SKATER/COUNTRY	YEARS	TITLES
1 Ulrich Salchow, Sweden	1901–11	11
2 Karl Schäfer, Austria	1930–36	9
3 Richard Button, USA	1948–52	7
4 Gillis Grafstrom, Sweden	1920–29	6
5 =Hayes Jenkins, USA	1953–56	5
=Scott Hamilton, USA	1981–84	5
7 =Willy Bockl, Austria	1925–28	4
=David Jenkins, USA	1957–60	4
=Ondrej Nepela, Czechoslovakia	1971–73	4
=Kurt Browning, Canada	1989–93	4

Did You Know? The Iditarod dog sled race – from Anchorage to Nome, Alaska – commemorates an emergency operation in 1925 to get medical supplies to Nome following a diptheria epidemic.

TOP 10 ★ FASTEST WINNING TIMES OF THE IDITAROD DOG SLED RACE

	WINNER	YEAR	DAY	TIME HR	MIN	SEC
1	Doug Swingley	1995	9	2	42	19
2	Jeff King	1996	9	5	43	19
3	Jeff King	1998	9	5	52	26
4	Martin Buser	1997	9	8	30	45
5	Doug Swingley	1999	9	14	31	7
6	Martin Buser	1994	10	13	2	39
7	Jeff King	1993	10	15	38	15
8	Martin Buser	1992	10	19	17	15
9	Susan Butcher	1990	11	1	5	13
10	Susan Butcher	1987	11	2	53	28

Source: *Iditarod Trail Committee*

TOP 10 OLYMPIC BOBSLEIGHING COUNTRIES

(Country/medals)

1 Switzerland, 26 **2** USA, 14 **3** East Germany, 13 **4** = Germany*, 11; = Italy, 11 **6** West Germany, 6 **7** UK, 4 **8** = Austria, 3; = Soviet Union#, 3 **10** = Canada, 2; = Belgium, 2

* Not including West or East Germany 1968–88
\# Includes United Team of 1992; excludes Russia since then

TOP 10 ★ MEN'S ALPINE SKIING WORLD CUP TITLES

	NAME/COUNTRY	YEARS	TITLES
1	Marc Girardelli, Luxembourg	1985–93	5
2 =	Gustavo Thoeni, Italy	1971–75	4
=	Pirmin Zurbriggen, Switzerland	1984–90	4
4 =	Ingemar Stenmark, Sweden	1976–78	3
=	Phil Mahre, USA	1981–83	3
6 =	Jean Claude Killy, France	1967–68	2
=	Karl Schranz, Austria	1969–70	2
8 =	Piero Gross, Italy	1974	1
=	Peter Lüscher, Switzerland	1979	1
=	Andreas Wenzel, Leichtenstein	1980	1
=	Paul Accola, Switzerland	1992	1
=	Kjetil-Andre Aamodt, Norway	1994	1
=	Alberto Tomba, Italy	1995	1
=	Lasse Kjus, Norway	1996	1
=	Luc Alphand, France	1997	1
=	Hermann Maier, Austria	1998	1

SKI WHIZZ!

Thought by many to be the greatest skier of all time, Marc Girardelli was forced to retire from competitive skiing, on doctor's orders, in 1997.

TOP 10 ★ WOMEN'S ALPINE SKIING WORLD CUP TITLES

	NAME/COUNTRY	YEARS	TITLES
1	Annemarie Moser-Pröll, Austria	1971–79	6
2 =	Vreni Schneider, Switzerland	1989–95	3
=	Petra Kronberger, Austria	1990–92	3
4 =	Nancy Greene, Canada	1967–68	2
=	Hanni Wenzel, Liechtenstein	1978–80	2
=	Erika Hess, Switzerland	1982–84	2
=	Michela Figini, Switzerland	1985–88	2
=	Maria Walliser, Switzerland	1986–87	2
=	Kajta Seizinger, Germany	1996–98	2
10 =	Gertrude Gabl, Austria	1969	1
=	Michèle Jacot, France	1970	1
=	Rosi Mittermeier, West Germany	1976	1
=	Lise-Marie Morerod, Switzerland	1977	1
=	Marie-Thérèse Nadig, Switzerland	1981	1
=	Tamara McKinney, USA	1983	1
=	Anita Wachter, Austria	1993	1
=	Pernilla Wiberg, Sweden	1997	1

SPORTING MISCELLANY

THE IRONMAN CHALLENGE

The Hawaii Ironman Triathlon came into being in 1978, after John Collins, a Navy man stationed in Honolulu, threw a challenge to settle an argument on who the fittest athletes were – runners, swimmers, or cyclists. Fifteen people took part in the first race. At just over 226 km/140 miles, the triathlon includes a swim in the ocean, a long cycle ride, and a marathon, a gruelling combination even without the extreme external factors of scorching sun and strong winds. The Ironman Triathlon has become the benchmark against which all extreme sporting challenges are now measured.

FILM	SPORT
1 *Days of Thunder* (1990)	Stock car racing
2 *Rocky IV* (1985)	Boxing
3 *Rocky III* (1982)	Boxing
4 *Rocky* (1976)	Boxing
5 *A League of Their Own* (1992)	Baseball
6 *Rocky II* (1979)	Boxing
7 *Tin Cup* (1996)	Golf
8 *White Men Can't Jump* (1992)	Basketball
9 *Cool Runnings* (1993)	Bobsleighing
10 *Field of Dreams* (1989)	Baseball

* Based on worldwide box office income

Led by Sylvester Stallone's *Rocky* series, the boxing ring, a natural source of drama and thrills, dominates Hollywood's most successful sports-based epics.

TOP 10 ★

FASTEST WINNING TIMES FOR THE HAWAII IRONMAN

	WINNER/COUNTRY*	YEAR	TIME HRS:MINS:SECS
1	Luc Van Lierde, Belgium	1996	8:04:08
2	Mark Allen	1993	8:07:45
3	Mark Allen	1992	8:09:08
4	Mark Allen	1989	8:09:15
5	Mark Allen	1991	8:18:32
6	Greg Welch, Australia	1994	8:20:27
7	Mark Allen	1995	8:20:34
8	Peter Reid, Canada	1998	8:24:20
9	Mark Allen	1990	8:28:17
10	Dave Scott	1986	8:28:37

* US unless otherwise stated

This is perhaps one of the most gruelling of all sporting contests, in which competitors engage in a 3.9-km/2.4-mile swim, followed by a 180-km/112-mile cycle race, ending with a full marathon. The first Hawaii Ironman was held at Waikiki Beach in 1978, but since 1981 the event's home has been at Kailua-Kona. Dave Scott and Mark Allen have dominated the race, each winning on a total of six occasions.

TOP 10 ★

MOST COMMON SPORTING INJURIES

	COMMON NAME	MEDICAL TERM
1	Bruise	A soft tissue contusion
2	Sprained ankle	Sprain of the lateral ligament
3	Sprained knee	Sprain of the medial collateral ligament
4	Low back strain	Lumbar joint dysfunction
5	Hamstring tear	Muscle tear of the hamstrings
6	Jumper's knee	Patella tendinitis
7	Achilles tendinitis	Tendinitis of the Achilles tendon
8	Shin splints	Medial periostitis of the tibia
9	Tennis elbow	Lateral epicondylitis
10	Shoulder strain	Rotator cuff tendinitis

Many sporting injuries, such as tennis or golfer's elbow, are so closely associated with the repetitive actions of players of these sports that they are named after them. To this catalogue of common injuries may be added less familiar afflictions such as footballer's migraine, which results from heading soccer balls, and turf toe, caused by slipping on an Astroturf surface. Some authorities reckon that as many as 75 per cent of all serious sports injuries involve the knee.

TOP 10 ★

PARTICIPATION SPORTS, GAMES, AND PHYSICAL ACTIVITIES IN THE UK

	ACTIVITY	PERCENTAGE PARTICIPATING*
1	Walking	44.5
2	Swimming	14.8
3	Keep fit/yoga	12.3
4	Cue sports	11.3
5	Cycling	11.0
6	Weight training	5.6
7	Football	4.8
8	Golf	4.7
9	Running, jogging, etc.	4.5
10	Weight lifting	1.3

* In 1996–7, based on the percentage of people over age 16 participating in each activity in the four weeks before the interview

In recent years, walking, keep fit/yoga, cycling, and weight training have become much more popular, while activities such as snooker and darts have declined in popularity.

TOP 10 ★
MOST DANGEROUS AMATEUR SPORTS

	SPORT	RISK FACTOR*
1	Powerboat racing	15
2	Ocean yacht racing	10
3	Cave diving	7
4	Potholing	6
5 =	Drag racing	5
=	Karting	5
7	Microlyte	4
8 =	Hang gliding	3
=	Motor racing	3
=	Mountaineering	3

* Risk factor refers to the premium that insurance companies place on insuring someone for that activity – the higher the risk factor, the higher the premium

Source: General Accident

TOP 10 MOST EFFECTIVE KEEP-FIT ACTIVITIES

1 Swimming 2 Cycling
3 Rowing 4 Gymnastics 5 Judo
6 Dancing 7 Football 8 Jogging
9 Walking (briskly!) 10 Squash

TOP 10 SPECTATOR SPORTS IN THE UK
(Percentage of adults who paid to watch in 1995)

1 Football, 13.1 2 Cricket, 4.5
3 = Horse racing, 3.8; = Rugby Union, 3.8
5 Motor racing, 3.3 6 = Greyhound racing, 2.5; = Stock car racing, 2.5
8 Rugby league, 2.4 9 Motor cycle racing, 2.1 10 Tennis, 1.8

Source: The Sports Council

FERRARI WINNER
Michael Schumacher started his career in Formula 1 in 1991. After only one race with Jordan, he moved to the Benetton team, then in 1996 to Ferrari.

TOP 10 ★
SPORTING EVENTS WITH THE LARGEST TV AUDIENCES IN THE UK

	EVENT	CHANNEL	AUDIENCE (1998)
1	World Cup: Argentina v England	ITV	23,782,000
2	World Cup: Romania v England	ITV	19,480,000
3	World Cup: Colombia v England	BBC 1	19,130,000
4	World Cup: Brazil v France	BBC 1	15,650,000
5	World Cup: France v Croatia	BBC 1	14,620,000
6	World Cup: Brazil v Holland	ITV	14,100,000
7	World Cup: Scotland v Morocco	BBC 1	12,670,000
8	World Cup: Brazil v Scotland	BBC 1	12,090,000
9	World Cup: England v Tunisia	BBC 1	11,430,000
10	The Grand National	BBC 1	11,390,000

In 1997, the Grand National was Britain's most watched sporting event on television, with some 12 million viewers, but in 1998 it found itself relegated to a lowly tenth place as the summer schedule was dominated by World Cup matches. These matches also figure prominently among the UK's all-time highest TV audiences, and the semi-final between West Germany and England in 1990 also resulted in the country's biggest-ever electricity surge, as millions of viewers signalled the end of the game by switching on electric kettles.

TOP 10 ★
HIGHEST-EARNING SPORTSMEN

	NAME	SPORT	TEAM	INCOME ($)
1	Michael Jordan	Basketball	Chicago Bulls	69,000,000
2	Michael Schumacher*	Motor racing	Ferrari	38,000,000
3	Sergei Federov	Ice hockey	Detroit Red Wings	30,000,000
4	Tiger Woods	Golf	–	27,000,000
5	Dale Earnhardt	Stock car racing	–	24,000,000
6	Grant Hill	Basketball	Detroit Pistons	22,000,000
7 =	Oscar De La Hoya	Boxing	–	18,000,000
=	Arnold Palmer	Golf	–	18,000,000
=	Patrick Ewing	Basketball	New York Knicks	18,000,000
10	Gary Sheffield	Baseball	L.A. Dodgers	17,000,000

* From Germany, all others from the US

Source: Forbes magazine

Forbes' most recent analysis of the world's highest-earning athletes lists some 40 with total incomes of $10 million or more. Some have retired from active sport, and many earn the lion's share of their income from endorsements of sporting products. Among those falling just outside the Top 10 are tennis players Andre Agassi ($16 million) and recently retired ice hockey superstar Wayne Gretzky ($15 million). Czech-born tennis player Martina Hingis is the only woman among this elite group with an income of $10 million.

Who is the No. 1 surfer in the world?
see p.277 for the answer
A Mick Campbell
B Kelly Slater
C Danny Wills